The Ministries
of Christian Worship

THE COMPLETE LIBRARY
OF
CHRISTIAN WORSHIP

THE COMPLETE LIBRARY
OF
CHRISTIAN WORSHIP

Volume 7, The Ministries of Christian Worship

ROBERT E. WEBBER, EDITOR

Star Song

PUBLISHING GROUP

Nashville, Tennessee

Unless otherwise indicated, all Scripture quotations taken from the HOLY BIBLE, NEW INTERNATIONAL VERSION. Copyright © 1973, 1978, 1984 by International Bible Society. Used by permission of Zondervan Publishing House.

Scripture quotations marked (KJV) are from the HOLY BIBLE, KING JAMES VERSION.

Scripture quotations marked (NASB) are taken from the NEW AMERICAN STANDARD BIBLE. Copyright © 1960, 1962, 1963, 1968, 1971, 1972, 1973,1975, 1977, the Lockman Foundation. Used by permission.

Scripture quotations marked (RSV) are taken from the REVISED STANDARD VERSION of the Bible. Copyright © 1946, 1952, 1971, 1973, the division of the Christian Education of the National Council of Churches of Christ in the U.S.A. Used by permission.

Scripture quotations marked (NRSV) are taken from THE HOLY BIBLE: NEW REVISED STANDARD VERSION. Copyright © 1989 by Division of the Christian Education of the National Council of Churches of Christ in the United Stated of America. Used by permission.

Scripture quotations marked (TEV) are taken from TODAY's ENGLISH VERSION of the Bible, Third Edition. Copyright © 1966, 1971 American Bible Society. Used by permission.

Produced for Star Song Publishing Group by the Livingstone Corporation. Dr. James C. Galvin and J. Michael Kendrick, project editors.

Typesetting by Red Wing Typesetting, Barrington, Illinois.

Star Song Publishing Group, a division of Jubilee Communications, Inc.
2325 Crestmoor, Nashville, Tennessee 37215.
Printed in the United States of America

ISBN 1-56233-017-9

1 2 3 4 5 6 7 8 9—98 97 96 95 94 93

Library of Congress Cataloging-in-Publication Data

The Ministries of Christian worship / Robert E. Webber. — 1st ed.
    p. cm. — (The complete library of Christian worship; vol. 7)
    Includes bibliographical references and index.
    ISBN 1-56233-017-9; $49.95
    1. Public worship. I. Webber, Robert. II. Series.
    BV10.2.M55 1994
    264—dc20   94-36739
                                              CIP

CONTENTS

Part 2: THE WORSHIPING COMMUNITY

Part 4: WORSHIP AND THE CHURCH'S MISSION TO THE WORLD

List of Illustrations

Additional Contributors

Christopher Beatty
The Upright Foundation, Lindale, Texas

Thomas B. Hoeksema
Calvin College, Grand Rapids, Michigan

Patrick Keifert
*Luther Northwestern Theological Seminary,
St. Paul, Minnesota*

Terry MacArthur
World Council of Churches, Geneva, Switzerland

Donald E. Miller
*Assistant Professor of Sociology of Religion,
University of Southern California, Los Angeles*

Bill Rayborn
TCMR Communications, Grapevine, Texas

Lester Ruth
Notre Dame University, Notre Dame, Indiana

Barbara Schmich Searle
Notre Dame, Indiana

Board of Editorial Consultants

The Board of Editorial Consultants is made up of leaders in worship renewal from major Christian denominations. They have functioned as advisors, often through letter and telephone. Every attempt has been made to include material on worship representing the whole church. For this reason, different viewpoints are presented without any attempt to express a particular point of view or bias. A special word of thanks is due to the executive and consulting editors for their helpful input. Their ideas, suggestions and contributions have strengthened the *Complete Library of Christian Worship*. Omissions and weaknesses in all seven volumes are the sole responsibility of the compiler and editor.

Christine A. Chakoian
Fourth Presbyterian Church, Chicago, Illinois

Bryan Chapell
Covenant Theological Seminary, St. Louis, Missouri

Nancy Chinn
San Francisco, California

John J. Chisum
Integrity Music, Mobile, Alabama

LeRoy Christoffels
Trinity CRC, Artesia, California

William Cieslak
Franciscan School of Theology, Berkeley, California

Donald L. Clapper
Pine Street Presbyterian Church, Harrisburg, Pennsylvania

Linda Clark
Boston University School of Theology

Karen Clarke
Mercy Hospital, Pittsburgh, Pennsylvania

Philip K. Clemens
College Mennonite Church, Goshen, Indiana

Arthur G. Clyde
United Church Board for Homeland Ministries, Cleveland, Ohio

William B. Coker
Ashbury College, Wilmore, Kentucky

Ruth Collenridge
Womens Aglow International, Seattle, Washington

Dori Erwin Collins
Good Shepherd Lutheran Church, Napierville, Illinois

Mary Collins
The Catholic University of America, Washington, D.C.

Patrick Collins
***Modern Liturgy,** San Jose, California*

Philip W. Comfort
Tyndale Press, Carol Stream, Illinois

Bernard Cooke
The Liturgical Press, Collegeville, Minnesota

Gilbert Cope
New Westminster Dictionary of Liturgy and Worship

Robert Copeland
Geneva College, Beaver Falls, Pennsylvania

Judson Cornwall
Fountain Gate Ministries, Plano, Texas

Melva Costen
Interdenominational Center, Atlanta, Georgia

David Cottrill
Wright Air Force Base, Kettering, Ohio.

Harvey Cox
Harvard Divinity School, Boston, Massachusetts

J. D. Crichton
Retired Parish Priest, UK

Daniel A. Csanyi
Little Flower Church, South Bend, Indiana

Robert D. Culver
Grace Theological Seminary, Winona Lake, Indiana

G. J. Cuming
Kings College, London, UK

Joe Cunningham
Trinity Lutheran Church, Davenport, Iowa

Stephen Cushman
Wheaton College, Wheaton, Illinois

Jerald Daffe
Lee College, Cleveland, Tennessee

Harold Daniels
Presbyterian Church USA, Louisville, Kentucky

Randall E. Davey
Fairview Church of the Nazarene, Fairview, Pennsylvania

Robert E. Davis
Temple Bible College, Cincinnati, Ohio.

Pam de Boom
Christ Community Reformed Church, Clifton Park, New York

Sandra DeGidio
Lecturer/Writer, Crystal Lake, Illinois

Carolyn Deitering
Diocese of Tucson, Tucson, Arizona

Cynthia De Jong
Calvin College, Grand Rapids, Michigan

Carla De Sola
The Liturgical Dance Company, New York, New York

Alan F. Detscher
Secretariat for the Liturgy, Washington, D.C.

John Dettoni
Fuller Theological Seminary, Pasadena, California

William De Vries
First Christian Reformed Church, Detroit, Michigan.

Dennis C. Dickerson
Historiographer, African Methodist Episcopal Church, Williamstown, Massachusetts

David J. Diephouse
Calvin College, Grand Rapids, Michigan

Andrew Foster
> _African Methodist Episcopal Zion Church, Red Bank, New Jersey_

Mark R. Francis
> _Catholic Theological Union, Chicago, Illinois_

John Frame
> _Westminster Theological Seminary West, Escondido, California_

Peter Fraser
> _Wisconsin Lutheran College, Milwaukee, Wisconsin_

Dennis Fredrickson
> _First United Church, Elynia, Ohio_

Debra Freeberg
> _Calvin College, Grand Rapids, Michigan_

Eileen E. Freeman
> _Archdiocese of Denver, Denver, Colorado_

Robert A. Freeman
> _Gordon Conwell Theological Seminary, Massachusetts_

Inga Freyer-Nicholas
> _The First Baptist Church of Ottumwa, Ottumwa, Iowa_

Ron Freyer
> _The First Baptist Church of Ottumwa, Ottumwa, Iowa_

Guy B. Funderburk
> _Salem College, Salem, West Virginia_

Virgil Funk
> _National Association of Parish Musicians, Washington, D.C._

Robert Gagne
> _Clinician in Music and Liturgy, Hartford, Connecticut_

John Gallen
> _Editor, **Modern Liturgy**, San Jose, California_

Michael Galvan
> _Roman Catholic Diocese of Oakland, California_

Bryan Gerlach
> _St. Mark's Lutheran Church, Citrus Heights, California_

June Adams Gibble
> _Church of the Brethren, Elgin, Illinois_

Keith Graber-Miller
> _Candler School of Theology, Atlanta, Georgia_

John Grabner
> _First United Methodist Church, Moscow, Idaho_

P. Preston Graham
> _Southern Baptist Church, Mabank, Texas_

George S. Gray
> _St. Nicholas Orthodox Church, Portland, Oregon_

Henry David Gray
> _**The Congregational Journal**, Ventura, California_

Ronald Graybill
> _La Sierra University, Riverside, California_

Philip C. Griffith II
> _Christians in the Arts Networking, Cambridge, Massachusetts_

Thomas H. Groome
> _Boston College, Boston, Massachusetts_

Kenneth Guentert
> _**Modern Liturgy**, San Jose, California_

Thomas Gulbronson
> _First Assembly of God, Alexandria, Virginia_

Gerrit Gustafson
> _Kingdom of Priests Ministries, Mobile, Alabama_

Kevin Hackett
> _Community of Celebration, Aliquippa, Pennsylvania_

Tom Halbrooks
> _Baptist Theological Seminary, Richmond, Virginia_

David Hall
> _Cogi Publishing, Memphis, Tennessee_

Stanley R. Hall
> _Austin Theological Seminary, Austin, Texas_

Donald Hallmark
> _Greenville College, Greenville, Illinois_

John Hamersma
> _Calvin College, Grand Rapids, Michigan_

Susan E. Hames
> _Graduate Theological Union, Berkeley, California._

Jerry Handspicker
> _Andover Newton Theological School, Newton Center, Massachusetts_

Daniel W. Hardy
> _Princeton Theological Seminary, Princeton, New Jersey_

Daniel J. Harrington
> _Weston School of Theology, Cambridge, Massachusetts_

Dirk Hart
> _Christian Reformed Board of Home Missions, Grand Rapids, Michigan_

James Hart
> _St. David's Center for Arts, Jacksonville, Florida_

Darrell A. Harris
> _Star Song, Nashville, Tennessee_

Louis-Charles Harvey
> _Payne Theological Seminary, Wilberforce, Ohio_

John S. Hascall
> _St. Charles Mission, Pryor, Montana_

List of Cooperating Publishers

BOOK PUBLISHERS

Abbott-Martyn Press
2325 Crestmoor Road
Nashville, TN 37215

Abingdon Press
201 8th Avenue South
Nashville, TN 37202

Agape
Hope Publishing
Carol Stream, IL 60187

Alba House
2187 Victory Boulevard
Staten Island, NY 10314

**American Choral
Directors Association**
502 Southwest 38th
Lawton, Oklahoma 73505

**Asian Institute for
Liturgy & Music**
P.O. Box 3167
Manila 1099 Philippines

Augsburg/Fortress Press
426 S. Fifth Street
Box 1209
Minneapolis, MN 55440

Ave Maria Press
Notre Dame, IN 46556

Baker Book House
P.O. Box 6287
Grand Rapids, MI 49516-6287

Beacon Hill Press
Box 419527
Kansas City, MO 64141

Bethany House Publishers
6820 Auto Club Road
Minneapolis, MN 55438

The Brethren Press
1451 Dundee Avenue
Elgin, IL 60120

Bridge Publishing, Inc.
200 Hamilton Blvd.
South Plainfield, NJ 07080

Broadman Press
127 Ninth Avenue, North
Nashville, TN 37234

C.S.S. Publishing Company
628 South Main Street
Lima, OH 45804

Cathedral Music Press
P.O. Box 66
Pacific, MO 63069

**Catholic Book
Publishing Company**
257 W. 17th Street
New York, NY 10011

CBP Press
Box 179
St. Louis, MO 63166

Celebration
P.O. Box 309
Aliquippa, PA 15001

Channing L. Bete Company
South Deerfield, MA 01373

Choristers Guild
2834 W. Kingsley Road
Garland, TX 75041

Christian Literature Crusade
701 Pennsylvania Avenue
Box 1449
Ft. Washington, PA 19034

Christian Publications
3825 Hartzdale Drive
Camp Hill, PA 17011

**The Church
Hymnal Corporation**
800 Second Avenue
New York, NY 10017

The Columba Press
93 Merise
Mount Merrion
Blackrock, Dublin

Concordia Publishing House
3558 S. Jefferson Avenue
St. Louis, MO 63118

Covenant Publications
3200 West Foster Avenue
Chicago, IL 60625

Cowley Publications
980 Memorial Drive
Cambridge, MA 02138

CRC Publications
2850 Kalamazoo SE
Grand Rapids, MI 49560

**Creative Communications
for The Parish**
10300 Watson Road
St. Louis, MO 63127

**Crossroad Publishing
Company**
575 Lexington Avenue
New York, NY 10022

Crossroad/Continuum
370 Lexington Avenue
New York, NY 10017

Dominion Press
7112 Burns Street
Ft. Worth, TX 76118

Duke Univesity Press
Box 6697 College Station
Durham, NC 27708

Faith and Life Press
724 Main Street
Box 347
Newton, KS 67114

The Faith Press, Ltd.
7 Tufton Street
Westminster, S.W. 1
England

Fleming H. Revell Company
184 Central Avenue
Old Tappen, N.J. 07675

Folk Music Ministry
P.O. Box 3443
Annapolis, MD 21403

Franciscan Communications
1229 South Santee Street
Los Angeles, CA 90015

Georgetown University Press
111 Intercultural Center
Washington, D.C. 20057

GIA Publications
7404 S. Mason Avenue
Chicago, IL 60638

Great Commission Publications
7401 Old York Road
Philadelphia, PA 19126

Grove Books
Bramcote Notts
England

Harper & Row Publishers
Icehouse One-401
151 Union Street
San Francisco, CA 94111-1299

Harvard University Press
79 Garden Street
Cambridge, MA 02138

Harvest Publications
Baptist General Conference
2002 S. Arlington Heights Road
Arlington Heights, IL 60005

Hendrickson Publishers, Inc.
P.O. Box 3473
Peabody, MA 01961-3473

Herald Press
616 Walnut Avenue
Scottdale, PA 15683

Hinshaw Music Incorporated
P.O. Box 470
Chapel Hill, NC 27514

Holt, Rinehart & Winston
111 5th Avenue
New York, NY 10175

Hope Publishing Company
Carol Stream, IL 60188

Hymn Society of America
Texas Christian University
P.O. Box 30854
Ft. Worth, TX 76129

Indiana University Press
10th & Morton
Bloomington, IN 47405

Integrity Music
P.O. Box 16813
Mobile, AL 36616

J.S. Paluch Company, Inc.
3825 Willow Road
P.O. Box 2703
Schiller Park, IL 60176

**The Jewish Publication
Society of America**
1930 Chestnut Street
Philadelphia, PA 19103

Judson Press
P.O. Box 851
Valley Forge, PA 19482-0851

**Light and Life Publishing
Company**
P.O. Box 26421
Minneapolis, MN 55426

Liguori Publications
One Liguori Drive
Liguori, MO 63057

Lillenas Publishing Company
Box 419527
Kansas City, MO 64141

The Liturgical Conference
1017 Twelfth Street, N.W.
Washington, D.C. 20005-4091

The Liturgical Press
St. John's Abbey
Collegeville, MN 56321

Liturgy Training Publications
1800 North Heritage Avenue
Chicago, IL 60622-1101

**Macmillan Publishing
Company**
866 Third Avenue
New York, NY 10022

Maranatha! Music
25411 Cabot Road
Suite 203
Laguna Hills, CA 92653

Mel Bay Publications
Pacific, MO 63969-0066

Meriwether Publishing, Ltd.
885 Elkton Drive
Colorado Springs, CO 80907

Michael Glazier, Inc.
1723 Delaware Avenue
Wilmington, Delaware 19806

Morehouse-Barlow
78 Danbury Road
Wilton, CT 06897

Multnomah Press
10209 SE Division Street
Portland, OR 97266

**National Association
of Pastoral Musicians**
25 Sheridan Street, NW
Washington, DC 20011

NavPress
P.O. Box 6000
Colorado Springs, CO 80934

New Skete
Cambridge, NY 12816

**North American
Liturgical Resources**
1802 N. 23rd Avenue
Phoenix, AZ 85029

Oxford University Press
16-00 Pollitt Drive
Fair Lawn, NJ 07410

The Pastoral Press
225 Sheridan Street, NW
Washington, D.C. 20011

Paulist Press
997 McArthur Boulevard
Mahwah, NJ 07430

The Pilgrim Press
132 West 31st Street
New York, NY 10001

Psalmist Resources
9820 E. Watson Road
St. Louis, MO 63126

Pueblo Publishing Company
100 West 32nd Street
New York, NY 1001-3210

Regal Books
A Division of Gospel Light
   Publications
Ventura, CA 93006

Resource Publications, Inc.
160 E. Virginia Street #290
San Jose, CA 95112

The Scarecrow Press
52 Liberty Street
Box 416
Metuchen, NJ 08840

Schocken Books
62 Cooper Square
New York, NY 10003

**Schuyler Institute for
Worship & The Arts**
2757 Melandy Drive, Suite 15
San Carlos, CA 94070

SCM Press Ltd.
c/o Trinity Press International
3725 Chestnut Street
Philadelphia, PA 19104

Servant Publications
P.O. Box 8617
Petersham, MA 01366-0545

The Sharing Company
P.O. Box 2224
Austin, TX 78768-2224

Sheed & Ward
115 E. Armour Boulevard
P.O. Box 414292
Kansas City, MO 64141-0281

Shofar Publications, Inc
P.O. Box 88711
Carol Stream, IL 60188

SPCK
Holy Trinity Church
Marylebone Road
London, N.W. 4D4

St. Anthony Messenger Press
1615 Republic Street
Cincinnati, OH 45210

St. Bede's Publications
P.O. Box 545
Petersham, MA 01366-0545

St. Mary's Press
Terrace Heights
Winona, MN 55987

St. Vladimir Seminary Press
575 Scarsdale Road
Crestwood, NY 10707-1699

Thomas Nelson Publishers
P.O. Box 141000
Nashville, TN 37214

Twenty Third Publications
P.O. Box 180
Mystic, CT 06355

Tyndale House Publishers
351 Executive Drive
Carol Stream, IL 60188

United Church of Christ
Office of Church Life and
   Leadership
700 Prospect
Cleveland, OH 44115

United Church Press
132 West 31st Street
New York, NY 10001

**The United Methodist
Publishing House**
P.O. Box 801
Nashville, TN 37202

**United States
Catholic Conference**
Office of Publishing and
   Promotion Services
1312 Massachusetts Avenue, NW
Washington, DC 20005-4105

University of California Press
1010 Westward Blvd.
Los Angeles, CA 90024

**University of Notre
Dame Press**
Notre Dame, IN 46556

The Upper Room
1908 Grand Avenue
P.O. Box 189
Nashville, TN 37202

Victory House Publishers
P.O. Box 700238
Tulsa, OK 74170

Westminster John Knox Press
100 Witherspoon Street
Louisville, KY 40202-1396

**William B. Eerdmans
Publishing Company**
255 Jefferson S.E.
Grand Rapids, MI 49503

**William C. Brown
Publishing Company**
2460 Kerper Boulevard
P.O. Box 539
Dubuque, IA 52001

William H. Sadlier, Inc.
11 Park Place
New York, NY 10007

Winston Press
P.O. Box 1630
Hagerstown, MD 21741

Word Books
Tower-Williams Square
5221 N. O'Conner Blvd. Suite
   1000
Irving, TX 75039

**World Council of
Churches Publications**
P.O. Box 66
150 Route de Ferney
1211 Geneva 20, Switzerland

**World Library
Publications, Inc.**
3815 N. Willow Road
P.O. Box 2701
Schiller Park, IL 60176

**The World
Publishing Company**
Meridian Books
110 E. 59th Street
New York, NY 10022

Yale University Press
302 Temple Street
New Haven, CN 06510

Zion Fellowship
236 Gorham Street
Canadagina, NY 14424

**Zondervan Publishing
Company**
1415 Lake Drive S.E.
Grand Rapids, MI 49506

PERIODICAL PUBLISHERS

The American Center for Church Music Newsletter
3339 Burbank Drive
Ann Arbor, MI 48105

American Organist
475 Riverside Drive, Suite 1260
New York, NY 10115

ARTS: The Arts in Religious and Theological Studies
United Theological Seminary of the Twin Cities
3000 5th Street, NW
New Brighton, MN 55112

Arts Advocate
The United Church of Christ Fellowship in the Arts
73 S. Palvuse
Walla Walla, WA 99362

The Choral Journal
American Choral Directors Association
P.O. Box 6310
Lawton, OK 73506

Choristers Guild Letters
2834 W. Kingsley Road
Garland, TX 75041

Christians in the Visual Arts
(newsletter)
P.O. Box 10247
Arlington, VA 22210

Church Music Quarterly
Royal School of Church Music
Addington Palace
Croyden, England CR9 5AD

The Church Musician
Southern Baptist Convention
127 9th Avenue N.
Nashville, TN 37234

Contemporary Christian Music
CCM Publications
P.O. Box 6300
Laguna Hills, CA 92654

Diapason
380 E. Northwest Highway
Des Plaines, IL 60016

Doxology
Journal of the Order of St. Luke in the United Methodist Church

1872 Sweet Home Road
Buffalo, NY 14221

Environment and Art Letter
Liturgy Training Publications
1800 N. Hermitage Avenue
Chicago, IL 60622

GIA Quarterly
7404 S. Mason Avenue
Chicago, IL 60638

Grace Notes
Association of Lutheran Church Musicians
4807 Idaho Circle
Ames, IA 50010

The Hymn
Hymn Society of the United States and Canada
P.O. Box 30854
Fort Worth, TX 76129

Journal
Sacred Dance Guild
Joyce Smillie, Resource Director
10 Edge Court
Woodbury, CT 06798

Journal of Ritual Studies
Department of Religious Studies
University of Pittsburgh
Pittsburgh, PA 15260

Let the People Worship
Schuyler Institute for Worship and the Arts
2757 Melendy Drive, Suite 15
San Carlos, CA 94070

Liturgy
The Liturgical Conference
8750 Georgia Avenue, S., Suite 123
Silver Spring, MD 20910

Liturgy 90
Liturgy Training Publications
1800 N. Hermitage Avenue
Chicago, IL 60622

Modern Liturgy
Resource Publications
160 E. Virginia Street, Suite 290
San Jose, CA 95112

Music in Worship
Selah Publishing Company
P.O. Box 103
Accord, NY 12404

Newsnotes
The Fellowship of United Methodists in Worship, Music, and Other Arts
P.O. Box 54367
Atlanta, GA 30308

Pastoral Music
225 Sheridian Street, NW
Washington, D.C. 20011

PRISM
Yale Institute of Sacred Music
409 Prospect Street
New Haven, CT 06510

The Psalmist
9820 E. Watson Road
St. Louis, MO 63124

Reformed Liturgy and Music
Worship and Ministry Unit
100 Witherspoon Street
Louisville, KY 40202

Reformed Music Journal
Brookside Publishing
3911 Mt. Lehman Road
Abbotsford, BC V2S 6A9

Reformed Worship
CRC Publications
2850 Kalamazoo Avenue, SE
Grand Rapids, MI 49560

Rite Reasons
Biblical Horizons
P.O. Box 1096
Niceville, FL 32588

St. Vladimirs Theological Quarterly
757 Scarsdale Road
Crestwood, NY 10707

Studia Liturgica
Department of Theology
University of Notre Dame
Notre Dame, IN 46556

Today's Liturgy
Oregon Catholic Press
5536 NE Hassalo
Portland, OR 97213

Worship
The Liturgical Press
St. John's Abbey
Collegeville, MN 56321

Worship Leader
CCM Communications, Inc.
107 Kenner Avenue
Nashville, TN 37205

Worship Today
600 Rinehard Road
Lake Mary, FL 32746

Preface to Volume 7

When I first envisioned *The Complete Library of Christian Worship,* I did not have in mind this volume, *The Ministries of Christian Worship.* However, as I researched the phenomena of worship renewal, it soon became apparent to me that a volume dealing with the ministries of worship was not an option, but an absolute necessity.

The vision of worship expressed in twentieth-century renewal and espoused by the *Library* is a paradigm that sees the interrelationship of worship with everything the church is and does. The church is the people of Christ's victory over the powers of evil. It is therefore a sign of the kingdom, an expression of the future. The church is no mere aggregate of individuals who gather for the purposes of material and spiritual support. The church is a radical new people of God, the beginning again of creation. Consequently, the vision of the church must be directed toward the world—the re-creation of all things in Jesus Christ, the head of this body.

Worship is where the church comes into being as a new social entity. Here the kingdom in all its newness is signified and anticipated. Here in worship, the church rehearses the living, the dying, and the rising of Christ and the overthrow of the powers of evil. In worship, the church momentarily experiences the shalom of God that rests over the entire created order as it proclaims and enacts the real meaning of life and history rooted in God's saving deed in Jesus Christ. Consequently, the church is called now to become an expression of its ultimate destiny. And it is here in the gathering and assembling of God's people on earth that a foretaste of the eschatological meaning of the church is actually realized.

The Ministries of Worship asks, "Who makes up this new society of God's people?" And it answers: men, women, children, the handicapped, and the multifaceted cultures, peoples, and traditions of the world. Next, this volume asks: "What is happening in worship?" And it answers that in this sign of the future foreshadowed in worship, people are being cared for, made whole, healed, and formed anew into the body of Christ. And this volume asks: "What is the mission of this sign of the kingdom?" And it answers: to be hospitable, to welcome the stranger, to bring people into Christ, and to defend the poor and needy. *The Ministries of Worship* testifies to the healing of the whole creation.

I invite you to enjoy the full range of topics this volume addresses—those within the church, and those matters that move beyond the church that touch the daily lives of the peoples of the world.

Robert Webber, Editor

Introduction

The Complete Library of Christian Worship has been designed to meet a need in the church. Christian leaders and congregations are becoming increasingly interested in the subjects of worship and worship renewal in the local church. Often, however, they lack adequate biblical and historical perspective or the necessary materials and resources to engage in the renewal process.

To fulfill the demand for worship resources, publishing houses, particularly those of specific denominations, have been producing materials for the local church. While these materials may find use within the constituency of a particular denomination, only a few break across denominational barriers and become known throughout the church at large.

The Complete Library of Christian Worship draws from more than one hundred publishing houses and the major Christian denominations of the world in order to bring those resources together in a seven-volume work, making them readily available to all.

The purpose of this introductory material is to acquaint the reader with The Complete Library of Christian Worship and to help him or her to use its information and resources in the local church. First, the reader needs to have some sense of the scope of worship studies and renewal that are addressed by The Complete Library of Christian Worship (see section 101 below). Second, it is important to learn how to use the Library (see section 102). Finally, there is a need to understand the precise content of Volume 7, The Ministries of Christian Worship.

These three introductory entries are a key to the whole concept of the Library, a concept that brings together instruction in worship and vital resources for use in worship. The Library also directs the reader to a vast array of books, audio tapes, videotapes, model services, and resources in music and the arts. It seeks to provide direction and inspiration for everything the church does in worship.

101 • INTRODUCTION TO THE COMPLETE LIBRARY OF CHRISTIAN WORSHIP

The word library implies a collection of resources, together with a system of organization that makes them accessible to the user. Specifically, The Complete Library of Christian Worship is a comprehensive compilation of information pertaining to the worship of the Christian church. It draws from a large pool of scholars and practitioners in the field, and from more than two thousand books and media resources in print.

The purpose of The Complete Library of Christian Worship is to make biblical, historical, and contemporary resources on worship available to pastors, music ministers, worship committees, and the motivated individual worshiper. The Library contains biblical and historical information on all aspects of worship and numerous resource materials, as well as suggested resource books, audio tapes, and video instructional material for every worship act in the local church.

The twentieth century, more than any century in the history of Christianity, has been the century for research and study in the origins, history, theology, and practice of Christian worship. Consequently there are seven broad areas in which worship studies are taking place. These are:

1. the biblical foundations of worship;
2. historical and theological development of worship;
3. resources for worship and preaching;
4. resources for music and the arts in worship;
5. resources for the services of the Christian year;
6. resources for sacraments, ordinances, and other sacred acts; and
7. resources for worship and related ministries.

The Complete Library of Christian Worship is organized around these seven areas of worship renewal. In these seven volumes one will find a wide variety of resources for every worship act in the church, and a select but broad bibliography for additional resources.

102 • How to Use *The Complete Library of Christian Worship*

The Complete Library of Christian Worship differs from an encyclopedia, which is often organized alphabetically, with information about a particular subject scattered throughout the book. The *Library* does not follow this pattern because it is a work designed to educate as well as to provide resources. Consequently, all the material in the *Library* is organized under a particular theme or issue of worship.

The difference between the *Library* and an encyclopedia may be illustrated, for example, by examining the topic of environmental art in worship. Some of the themes essential to environmental art are banners, candles, stained glass windows, lighting, pulpit hangings, table coverings, and Communion ware. In a typical encyclopedia these entries would be scattered in the B, C, S, L, P, and T sections. Although this is not a problem for people who know what environmental art is and what needs to be addressed in environmental art, it is a problem for the person whose knowledge about the subject is limited. For this reason *The Complete Library of Christian Worship* has been organized—like a textbook—into chapters dealing with particular issues. Therefore, all the matters dealing with environmental art can be found in the chapter on environmental art (see Volume 4, *Music and the Arts in Christian Worship*). In this way a reader becomes educated on environmental art while at the same time having the advantage of in-depth information on the various matters pertaining to this aspect of worship.

Therefore, the first unique feature of *The Complete Library of Christian Worship* is that each volume can be read and studied like a book.

The second unique feature of the *Library* is that the materials have been organized to follow the actual *sequence in which worship happens.*

For example, Volume 1, *The Biblical Foundations of Christian Worship*, looks at the roots of Christian worship in the biblical tradition, while Volume 2, *Twenty Centuries of Christian Worship*, presents the development of various historical models of worship along with an examination of the theology of worship. Next, Volumes 3 through 7 provide resources for the various acts of worship: Volume 3, *The Renewal of Sunday Worship*, provides resources for the various parts of wor-

ship; Volume 4, *Music and the Arts in Worship*, presents resources from music and the arts for the different aspects of worship. Volume 5, *The Services of the Christian Year,* branches out to the services of Advent, Christmas, Epiphany, Lent, Holy Week, Easter, and Pentecost, providing resources for those special services that celebrate the saving acts of God in Jesus Christ. Volume 6, *The Sacred Actions of Christian Worship,* deals with Communion, baptism, funerals, weddings, and other special or occasional acts of worship. Finally, Volume 7, *The Ministries of Christian Worship,* deals with evangelism, spirituality, education, social action, children's worship, and other matters impacted by Christian celebration.

Each volume contains an alphabetical index to the material in the book. This index makes desired information readily available for the reader.

The resources in these volumes are intended for use in every denomination and among all groups of Christians: liturgical, traditional Protestant, those using creative styles, and those in the praise-and-worship tradition. Resources from each of these communities may be found in the various volumes.

It is difficult to find material from the free churches (those not following a historic order of worship) and from the charismatic traditions. These communities function with an oral tradition of worship and therefore do not preserve their material through written texts. Nevertheless, a considerable amount of information has been gathered from these oral traditions. Recently, leaders in these communities have been teaching their worship practices through audio tapes and videotapes. Information on the availability of these materials has been included in the appropriate volumes.

The written texts have been the easiest to obtain. Because of this, *The Complete Library of Christian Worship* may give the appearance of favoring liturgical worship. Due to the very nature of written texts, the appearance of a strong liturgical bent is unavoidable. Nevertheless, the goal of the *Library* is not to make free churches liturgical. Rather, it is to expand the perspective of Christians across a wide range of worship traditions. In this way, liturgical resources may serve as guides and sources of inspiration and creativity for free churches, while insights from free traditions may also enrich the practices and understanding of the more liturgical communities.

In sum, the way to use _The Complete Library of Christian Worship_ is as follows:

1. _Read each volume as you would read a book._ Each volume is full of biblical, historical, and theological information—a veritable feast for the curious, and for all worshipers motivated to expand their horizons.

2. _Use the alphabetical index for quick and easy access to a particular aspect of worship._ The index for each volume is as thorough as the listings for an encyclopedia.

3. _For further information and resources, order books and materials listed in the bibliography of resources._ Addresses of publishers may be found in your library's copy of _Books in Print._

4. _Adapt the liturgical materials to the setting and worship style of your congregation._ Many of the worship materials in _The Complete Library of Christian Worship_ have been intentionally published without adaptation. Most pastors, worship ministers, and worship committee members are capable of adapting the material to a style suitable to their congregations with effective results.

103 ✦ INTRODUCTION TO VOLUME 7: _THE MINISTRIES OF CHRISTIAN WORSHIP_

The Ministries of Christian Worship introduces the reader to a number of topics not addressed in the previous volumes. This volume seeks to show the relationship of all that has been presented in volumes 1 through 6 to the immediate practice of worship within the gathered community and in the world to which the community ministers.

In Part 1, Christian groups are given an opportunity to speak for themselves. How do they as denominations or fellowships address the ministries of worship? The readings in this section are quite varied. In the West we are accustomed to treating the various ministries of the church as matters that stand apart from each other. A theology of worship that includes all the ministries of the church requires all Christians, regardless of their particular affiliations, to think creatively in developing a view of worship that ties together the work of the church.

Part 2 focuses on those assembled, particularly those who are sometimes excluded from worshiping communities. Consequently, chapters focus on children, women, and the disabled. A chapter on cultural diversity and liturgical inculturation rounds out the discussion.

Part 3 looks at what happens in worship as the church signifies its meaning as the true eschatological symbol of reality. Hence chapters in this section deal with pastoral care, spiritual formation, initiation, and nurture.

Finally, Part 4 addresses the relation of this eschatological community at worship to the church's outreach by showing the connection of worship to hospitality, evangelism, and social justice.

As you read, I hope you will come to see the great importance worship has in shaping the ministries of the church. The matters treated in this volume concern issues dealing with not only our salvation, but also the world's.

PART ONE

Worship and Related Ministries

✤ ONE ✤

Worship and Related Ministries Among the Churches

Across the panorama of churches and denominations in North America, one encounters great variation in the degree to which the worship life of the local congregation is integrated with other ministries such as evangelism, Christian education, social outreach and witness, spiritual formation of members, pastoral care, women's issues, and children's ministries. Some Christian groups have historically sought to develop the relationship of worship to a wide spectrum of other church concerns; for other groups, this is a fairly recent effort. In some traditions, the worship service itself has been driven primarily by other emphases such as evangelism or education. In others, the worship tradition itself has been dominant in the shaping of local church life, so that all other ministries serve the liturgy. This chapter presents a discussion of worship and related ministries from the standpoint of most of the major Christian traditions and denominations found in North America.

104 ✦ ADVENTIST CHURCHES

In Seventh-day Adventism, the worship service is the center of congregational life. Evangelism, social concern, Christian education, and pastoral care flow from, and are shaped by, worship, which aims at ministering to the whole person.

Worship is the center of activity for the Seventh-day Adventist church. Other activities flow from this center, although this process is not always a conscious one for the majority of worshipers.

Often the worship service, particularly the sermon, is evangelistically oriented because Jesus Christ, the object of worship, has commissioned his followers to spread the Good News of salvation. This sense of mission pervades the Seventh-day Adventist church.

Denominational sources provide materials to both pastors and lay leaders, which relate to various outreach projects both in the local church and in the church's worldwide mission. These materials include suggested sermons, texts, and hymns.

Social concerns also are systematically addressed in these materials. Often these matters of evangelism and social concern are included in announcements at the beginning of the worship hour. They are regularly mentioned in the offering appeals. Pastors generally do not use these materials to frame either the broad outline of worship or the sermon, choosing rather to develop their own church year, or, very rarely, to follow the common lectionary. Thus, the announcements and offering appeals constitute the primary times for relating evangelism and social concerns to worship.

Sabbath schools are by definition the study arm of the church. Sermon and worship texts usually do not correspond to the prescribed curriculum used from nursery through adult classes. Now and then a pastor may choose to preach from the same texts as those for the adult class, and less frequently an adult class may request the pastor's sermon texts for class study.

Home Bible fellowships and other small cell groups are growing among Adventist churches.

Some of these groups deal with weekly worship themes, and a few pastors prepare materials for these groups based on the same texts that will be used for the sermon. Occasionally a specific group is formed for sermon discussion, such as a pastor's breakfast with church leaders.

The worship at the Lakeside, California, Seventh-day Adventist Church is instructive. Here, children are considered an integral part of the worship experience. They might prepare and give a prayer, read Scripture (with careful preparation), help receive the offering, or participate in musical presentations. Readers' theaters (both extemporaneous and rehearsed) for the Scripture lessons often include children. Children are further involved in worship with age-graded bulletins that use the Gospel lesson for the day. Occasionally there will be children's sermons, which tend to be effective for the overall worship experience only if they are related directly to the worship and sermon theme of the day. Such consistency motivates the interest and learning not only of children, but also of the adults. Another common practice is to build the sermon in such a way that the children will find it meaningful.

Pastoral care at the Lakeside Adventist Church is approached in worship primarily in three ways: (1) through palpable expression of openness and care; (2) through opportunity to present specific prayer requests; and (3) through sermons, and other components of worship, that endeavor to meet the needs of parishioners through sensitive and careful interpretation of Scripture.

A curious anomaly exists in the Seventh-day Adventist church: Women are not ordained to the clergy (because of pressures from outside North America); however, they serve as pastors and are given commissioned ministerial credentials. Women are ordained as local church elders and deacons. In common with many other Adventist churches, the Lakeside Church makes a point of using inclusive language and tries to schedule worship leadership equally between women and men.

The Seventh-day Adventist church, in its worship, aims to minister to the whole person, who was created in the image of God and who is redeemed through Jesus Christ and empowered by his Spirit to be a child of God.

Merle J. Whitney

105 ✦ AFRICAN METHODIST EPISCOPAL CHURCHES

When Methodism failed to meet the needs of free blacks in the United States, Richard Allen and others established a new church, the African Methodist Episcopal church. Building on the spiritual legacy of the slavery experience, African Methodist worship has developed its own unique style. Elements of this style include the affirmation of creation and life, emotional responsiveness without sacrifice of intellect, dialogue between the worshiper and God, and expectancy for the future.

When Richard Allen encountered Methodism in the North, he brought with him a heritage that looked at life differently from his white brothers and sisters. He was attracted to Methodism for two major reasons. First, it was a heartfelt religion that stressed the importance of conversion. Second, it was a religion that combined social concern with individual faith. Allen, however, sensed a need to fashion Methodism in a manner that would be helpful to African Americans. Although it provided a good structure and discipline, American Methodism was a segregated church. Allen's experience at Old St. George's Church in Philadelphia led him to believe that the Methodist Episcopal Church could not be the final home for black people. And so he left, but in leaving, he kept in mind the importance of heartfelt religious experience and the necessity for religion to be related to social concerns. This concern is seen in his first act of establishing the Free African Society to address the social, political, and economic needs of the free African American.

While attempting to take care of the physical needs of black people in Philadelphia, Allen was also trying to meet their spiritual needs. This is reflected in his efforts to build a church—efforts that were thwarted at every turn by the officials of the established Methodist body. Not all of them tried to dissuade him; indeed, some well-intentioned Methodists helped raise money for the new building. At one point in the controversy, Allen told the Methodist leaders:

We had no place of worship, and we did not mean to go to St. George's church anymore, as we were so scandalously treated. . . . And if you deny us your name, you cannot seal up the scriptures from us, and deny us a name for all who worship in spirit and truth. And he said, "So you are determined to go on." We told him, "Yes, God being our helper." He then replied, "We will disown you all from the Methodist connection." [We said,] "We believed if we put our trust in the Lord, he would stand by us" (_The Life Experience and Gospel Labors of Richard Allen,_ 27).

Allen, in this passage, demonstrates explicitly the importance he placed on freedom of worship before God. His faith led to the establishment of Mother Bethel Church at Sixth and Lombard Streets in Philadelphia. At this old blacksmith's shop, African Methodists, as a new denomination, began to worship God. What was the nature of that worship? Not much historical evidence exists to uncover the answer to that question. However, it is reasonable to assume that the worship was biblically based and adapted some of the structure and content of Methodist Episcopal worship. Moreover, the worship was based on their experience of being displaced people.

This was not the first occasion of black people—that is Africa's displaced children—worshiping. The first expression had to be when they cried out to the omnipotent God, whom they had known and worshiped in the motherland. When they arrived in America, attempts were made to eradicate that image of God from their minds. But the slave master had forgotten that God is all powerful. In order to worship free from the dictates of the slave master, the slaves worshiped God in the darkness of the forest. Thus the first church for black people was the "steal-away-to-Jesus church," or the so-called invisible church. It was invisible to the slave master, but not to God, who saw the intense worship performed. Some sang, "Steal away to Jesus; I ain't got long to stay here," while others sang, "Deep river, my home is over Jordan." In their ongoing quest for freedom, still others sang, "Walk together, children, don't you get weary; there's a great camp meeting in the Promised Land."

This early worship was filled with the spiritual power of an omnipresent God. Scholars have noted that there was much joyful singing, praying, and preaching. Here, generations of slave preachers were trained to preach a gospel of liberation through the power of the Spirit of God. In fact, one authority has noted that slaves would carry wet blankets along and hang them up on the street in an attempt to muffle the noise of the joyous celebration of praise to the Lord. Thus early

in the lives of our foreparents, worship took on a special significance as preparation to deal with the problems of life. This worship was an empowering worship. Believers often sang, "How do you feel when you come out of the wilderness? Were you leaning on the Lord your God?"

Worship and Life. The chief legacy of this early wilderness church is that worship dealt with life. What one does in the world that reflects goodness and kindness is worship. For the African Methodist, worship is synonymous with the whole of life. This means that we as African Methodists worship God outside of church as well as in church. Part of the African heritage that we build upon is that all of life is sacred. There is no separation between the religious and the secular. Because God is the Lord of everything, God is to be worshiped in every sphere of life.

Worship and Mystery. Another part of this African inheritance is the quality of mystery in worship. Mystery means that we can experience God individually and know something of God's divine mercy, power, and majesty, but we can never comprehend all of God. In worship, we experience God's mystery and meaning. In mystery, there is also miracle. Just as the revelation of God in Jesus is a miracle, the continuing work of the Holy Spirit in the life of the church is a miracle. Samuel Miller has put it well, "The miracle of worship is the sight of God seen through darkness; it is the power of God felt when all other strength fails; it is the eternal manifested in time." Related to the mystery of worship is the miracle of the Incarnation. In each worship service, this miracle is relived as worshipers experience the reality of God's presence in Jesus Christ through the praying, singing, and preaching. The incarnational drama exists where God in Christ through the Holy Spirit comes again into our presence, and we celebrate it.

Worship and Celebration. The third meaning of worship, which is derived from our heritage, is that worship is celebration. We celebrate the fact that the Holy Spirit is with us to give us the strength to feel like going on. This celebration reflects the lifestyle of "persons who live on the existential edge where the creative and the destructive, the wise and the foolish, the sacred and the secular, the agony and the ecstasy, the up and down are different human experiences of existence in the presence of the divine." (William B. McClain, "The Genius of the Black Church," *Christianity and Crisis* (2 and 16 November 1970). In the celebration of worship, under the power of the Holy Spirit, spontaneity and improvisation urge us to turn ourselves loose into the hands of God. Here once again, joy and sorrow are mingled together to witness to the reality of God's work on behalf of God's creation.

Worship and Music. Our fourth inheritance pertaining to worship is that our worship is musical. The rhythm of life itself is seen, heard, and felt through the songs that we sing. We have inherited from Methodism the tradition of singing hymns. But, from a corpus of thousands of hymns, we have formed our own canon. Hymns like "O for a Thousand Tongues to Sing," "We'll Understand It Better By and By," "All Hail the Power of Jesus' Name," "When the Storms of Life Are Raging," "Come Ye Disconsolate," "Guide Me, O Thou Great Jehovah," and many others take on special meaning when they are filtered through the experiences of African Methodists. Although we depend on a number of traditional hymns, we also utilize other forms, such as anthems, Negro spirituals, and gospel music. All of these forms, undergirded by the Holy Spirit's presence, help enlarge our experience through the use of hands, feet, soul, and body.

Worship and Dialogue. The fifth characteristic of worship in African Methodism is that it is dialogical. When we worship, we are in a conscious dialogue, or conversation with God. For us, worship is both revelation and response: God takes the initiative in revelation, and we respond in worship. We have to make a distinction, as Henry H. Mitchell does in *Black Preaching* (Philadelphia: Lippincott, 1970), between *automatic dialogue* and *real dialogue*. Automatic dialogue is the unthinking response to whatever the preacher says, even if it is "collard greens and candied yams." Here the responder is simply reacting without hearing, using stock phrases. Real dialogue, which represents the best of African American worship in the Methodist tradition, occurs characteristically in response to the preacher's reference to something that is vital in the life experience of the respondent—something he or she identifies with. This kind of dialogue is often emotional. Black worship, however, is both an emotional and

an intellectual experience. We want a style of worship, in preaching, singing, and praying, that is balanced and of high caliber—both relevant in content and charismatic in delivery. When all of these elements come together, we have the epitome of African Methodist worship, and black worship in general. The strength of our worship experience is our ability, in Henry Mitchell's words, to combine "fresh impact with impact to feed the people and yet shake them into a recognition that the Spirit of God is always moving, always dynamic."

Worship as Offering to God. The sixth characteristic of worship is that it should be understood as making an offering to God. The purpose of worship is not primarily to receive blessings from God, but to make offerings to God. Both the Old and New Testaments emphasize the importance of giving as an aspect of worship. The Hebrews made an offering in a variety of ways. The psalmist said, "Ascribe to the LORD the glory due his name; bring an offering and come into his courts" (Ps. 96:8). We are to offer our gifts in sincere faith and total obedience, as in the days of Cain and Abel (Heb. 11:4). We must think of giving not only as an offering of money. The true act of giving in worship is the offering of ourselves to God—our intellect, feelings, attitudes, and possessions. Outward gifts are only an expression of our inward dedication. This is the highest expression of giving: the presentation of our bodies "as living sacrifices, holy and pleasing to God" (Rom. 12:1).

Worship and Eschatology. The seventh characteristic of worship in our tradition is that it is eschatological—done with the expectation that God will return. This aspect of our worship sustains our hope that, in the end, we will be with God in eternity, adoring him for what he has done for us.

Several observations regarding worship in the African Methodist tradition have become apparent. African Methodist worship is biblically based, leaning more heavily on the teachings of Jesus than on the Old Testament. It is based in part on our heritage as Methodists, but more fully on the unique contribution of Richard Allen. Finally, worship, as we understand it, is related to our experience as Africa's children in the diaspora—people a long way from home. Although there are these commonalties in the church, there are many different expressions of worship in African Methodism. Each expression is worthy as long as its ultimate end is to give God the glory.

Louis-Charles Harvey

106 ✦ AFRICAN METHODIST EPISCOPAL ZION CHURCHES

The African Methodist Episcopal Zion Church (AME Zion) has been at the forefront of efforts to improve the quality of life for African Americans. Worship services, as well as other church activities, highlight the church's role in social ministries, education, and the recognition of the leadership of women.

The church founded by James Varick and other African Americans in 1796 prides itself on being the church of liberation. Zion Methodism has been in the forefront of involvement in the pressures that negatively influence the wholeness of the communities it serves. This church began as a way to better incorporate the power of the Holy Spirit and the dignity of the human spirit.

We are the church that continues the work of Harriet Tubman, maintaining and enlarging her property in New York state. Zion's Bishop Walters was a part of the Niagara Movement, out of which the NAACP was born. Paul Robeson's father was an AME Zion pastor, while Frederick Douglass was an AME Zion local preacher. Rev. Florence Randolph served as a Zion pastor and was the founder of the Federated Colored Women's Clubs.

Women in Ministry

Zion Methodism has ordained women clergy as deacons and elders since the 1890s. A myriad of women pastors and an increasing number of female presiding elders serve the church. Although the two women candidates for the episcopacy were not elected at the last two General Conferences, the respectable number of votes they received suggests that the effort will be repeated.

Furthermore, the Women's Home and Overseas Missionary Society is the body that promotes mission awareness. Several services, with special bulletins for each, are conducted annually to emphasize this ministry. These include Marie L. Clinton day—Buds of Promise (Children's Missionary Department DWay); Victoria Richardson day—Y's (Teen Missionary Department Day); Agape Sunday with its "second mile luncheon," emphasizing home missions; and Overseas Missions day, focusing on support and expansion of overseas mission work.

Educational and Children's Ministries

The Christian Education department periodically provides material for special services and supplementary activities for special days, such as Children's day. The *Church School Herald* provides general and specific articles for teachers and clergy. The National Christian Youth Conference meets each year in both regional and denomination-wide gatherings, as a forum to address the needs and concerns of youth in the AME Zion church. The Christian Education Convocation every four years involves youth, teens, and young adults.

One local example of a church with an emphasis on saving the children for Christ and from the entrapments of the world is the Shrewsbury Avenue AME Zion Church. This congregation has a children's sermon each Sunday. Each fourth Sunday members of the Buds of Promise, the children's missionary group, make presentations on what they have learned. Instead of children being sent to a nursery or children's church, children and teens sit together in the front eight pews to the pastor's right. They are taught that they are the church of today and tomorrow. Teens, especially high school juniors and seniors, serve as worship leaders each fourth and fifth Sunday. Bulletins and monthly newsletters contain a children's educational activity page. Children are praised in worship for their accomplishments, with a special emphasis on educational excellence.

Graduates day at Shrewsbury Avenue AME Zion Church honors graduates from preschool through graduate school. The church stresses education as the vehicle to help youth to become the movers and shapers of a better tomorrow. Ninety-five percent of the youth in this local church during the past decade have continued their education past high school. Youth and teens participate in the traditional ushering and singing activities. These activities are supplemented by Images/Choices and Challenges programs, which are intended to help young people from ten to eighteen years old to enhance self-esteem and prepare

The Cross Etoile. A cross in the form of a four-pointed star.

ive services to members and to community residents. Assistance with needs is provided by the church, or through referrals to other agencies. Announcements by the pastor during worship include reminders of political and social developments that may impact the families of the congregation.

The pastor of Shrewsbury Avenue AME Zion Church views the African American church as the center for supportive services in its community. Thus, the church must be a seven-day-a-week operation. The church, wherever it is found, must be the means by which the powerless conscience urges and prods the conscienceless power to meet the real needs of the people. The church must be a voice crying out in America's wilderness, demanding the nation to rise up and live out the meaning of the creeds affirmed but not lived out.

Andrew Foster

for living after high school. Our confirmation study is incorporated into these programs. This work is augmented by social and educational group activities organized by leaders of the classes for teens, youth, and children.

Bible study and Sunday school classes for adults at the Shrewsbury Avenue church are geared to the development of a Christian lifestyle conforming to biblical teachings. Denominational and other resource materials are used in these classes. The philosophy behind these classes is that a well-informed Christian is the person best equipped to affect positive change in the world. This educational process begins with oneself.

Social Ministries

The Shrewsbury Avenue AME Zion Church is also active in an AIDS education ministry which serves both the African American and Hispanic communities. The Shrewsbury Avenue congregation is also involved in housing development together with a local United Methodist church. The church in addition serves as a host organization for the SHARE food program. The regional high school's alternative school program and the local NAACP office are housed in its educational wing. Furthermore, the pastor maintains lengthy office hours to provide counseling and other support-

107 ◆ AMERICAN BAPTIST CHURCHES IN THE USA

Although rooted in that wing of the Reformation which made the most radical shift away from highly developed liturgical structure, American Baptist churches are nevertheless undergoing a radical rethinking of the role and shape of worship in congregational life. No longer simply a vehicle for evangelism, worship is emerging as a context for community building and the nurture of believers.

Like other English-speaking Baptists, the American Baptist Churches in the USA (one of more than thirty distinct Baptist denominations in North America) trace their history and heritage to the congregationalist Puritans and separatists from the Church of England. This denomination, as other Baptist groups, is a voluntary association of autonomous local churches organized for mutual aid and the support of common missions and ministries. Thus, there are American Baptist *churches*, but no American Baptist *Church*. In discussing events, trends, and developments among American Baptists, one should always remember that Baptists work together by persuasion, not legislation. One can speak of customs and trends, but not of mandated or uniform principles and practices.

Robin Green says, "When human beings worship, their true self is restored to them individually and socially. Worship is, therefore, an end in itself and by its very nature the most radical critique of every political ideology." In worship people both encounter God and "confront the depth of their own need in the presence of God." Liturgy that cares for people is a meaning-filled, symbol-laden environment encompassing a conceptual and a physical space in which people are sustained, guided, healed, and reconciled to God and to each other. The extent to which liturgy—the worship life—of any congregation fails to mediate care to persons is the extent to which it fails to honor the God who created people or to recognize the _imago Dei_ (the image of God) in which Holy Scripture testifies people are made, even though they are sinful.

Today's Baptists, and the Protestant Reformation's other children, are heirs to a spiritual lifestyle that became almost completely cerebral, which was accompanied by an overly verbal liturgy, a dissolute sacramental life, a fragmented corporate worship for which private devotion in a public place became an accepted substitute, and a highly individualistic gospel. In addition, Baptists have an organizational rather than an organic understanding of church. For some Baptists, Robert's _Rules_ and church by-laws are more significant for the life and work of a congregation than Jesus' words and example: "Having loved his own who were in the world, he now showed them the full extent of his love" (John 13:1); "Love each other as I have loved you" (John 15:12); "I no longer call you servants. Instead, I have called you friends" (John 15:15). How do Baptist churches manage to reconcile the actual work of the churches with the charter Jesus adopted for his earthly ministry (Luke 4:14-21)?

Many American Baptist pastors and congregations have begun to recognize the bankruptcy of the traditional American Protestant worship style, often characterized as preliminaries, sermon, invitation. This style was derived chiefly from Zwingli's reforms in Zurich and was heavily conditioned by the revivalist awakenings of the American frontier. While suited for preaching and for evangelistic outreach, this style is unsuited for the continuing care and feeding of the community of baptized believers gathered in worship and in communion with God and each other. In nearly every major branch of Western Christianity in the post–Vatican II era, worship has taken center stage as an issue of concern, examination, and renewal.

Building upon work done since the mid-1960s by Roman Catholics and by other Protestant mainline denominations, American Baptists in the 1990s adopted a strategy for renewal that encourages congregations to examine worship, evangelism, and service as separate entities, rather than as tools or vehicles for each other. For instance, worship viewed as the act of the redeemed people of God assumes a character different from worship viewed as a delivery vehicle for evangelistic outreach. A similar shift is noted when worship begins to feed and strengthen Christians and ceases to be a launching platform of preachers' causes or social service ministries. Given the significant growth among sibling denominations in their understanding and practice of Christian worship, there is a great expectancy that American Baptists will emerge in the twenty-first century having experienced similar growth.

Baptists, as part of the left wing of the Reformation, along with the Anabaptists and Quakers, are heirs to a reductionist mentality in organization, architecture, liturgy, sacramental life, and view of the place of humankind in God's plan of salvation. Yet some of today's Baptists are reversing the many innovations of those early Baptists who reduced liturgy to an extended Bible study with preaching, who reduced the Eucharist to hurriedly spoken words of institution tacked onto the preaching service, and who purged from their worship the prospect of bodies in motion and visual edification through art and color (other than stained glass).

Many American Baptists have recovered the Christian year, a lectionary, liturgical dance and drama, color, light, and religious art. All of this parallels the recovery of pre-Nicene worship forms and structures, a recovery which sidesteps certain fads and notions of the Reformers and goes back past the sixteenth century to the period when church forms and structures were not far removed from the first generations of Christians. In reclaiming early church forms and structures, American Baptists and other denominations are reclaiming new life from the old. This new life includes a vital concern for the nurture and care of the baptized. This concern is grounded on the recovered understanding that it is the way we as believers characterize ourselves and God in the liturgy that forms and maintains our most fundamental concepts of the eternal and the mortal.

At one time, the revivalistic model flourished in Baptist churches. The preacher's primary interest was targeting, preaching to, and *winning* that one lost soul sitting in the pew (never mind the needs of the rest of the congregation already safely baptized and counted in the annual soul-winning report). Increasingly, American Baptist congregations are understanding that although the need for evangelistic outreach is as pressing as ever, the need of baptized *saved sinners* to meet God in worship and be healed by the encounter is every bit as pressing. Responding to these equally valid but different needs, congregations are adding—rather than dropping—services of worship, giving each service a specialized character. Evangelistic services are intended and structured to introduce God and the gospel to the uninitiated; weekly services of prayer, praise, and the Eucharist (often using second-century forms with modern language) to nurture and encourage today's initiated Christians toward a richer life in the faith; and daily offices to support and uplift those progressing toward or already practicing daily disciplines.

Those pastors and churches growing beyond a one-size-fits-all understanding of Christian worship are beginning to reap the benefits of liturgy that is Spirit-filled, soul-satisfying, God-centered, and in harmony with Scripture and tradition. Their liturgies allow participants to bring before God the anxieties they experience at the boundaries of life and to find comfort from God—and from the assembly. Moreover, such worship helps participants to live among the ambiguities and anxieties of life, not as isolated individuals, but as individuals who are part of something much greater than themselves, part of something and someone who loves them.

R. K. Freyer Nicholas

108 • ANGLICAN/EPISCOPAL CHURCHES

The objective style and biblical structure of worship in the Anglican and Episcopal Book of Common Prayer *allowed its historic forms to endure well into the period when the church became involved in social concerns and ministries. However, revision of the Prayer Book in the latter part of the twentieth century has given renewed liturgical expression to the church's sense of community and social ministry.*

The church's life turns in two directions. First, the community of faith exists for the worship of God. Worship is an activity which in its true form is always directed to the glory of God. Worship is subverted if it is used primarily for other ends—such as instruction, inspiration, or the social good—even though these ends may be valuable. At the same time, the church exists for missions in the world. It is in the world for the sake of the world. It is a community, which does not live for itself, but for those outside it.

———— Worship and Mission ————

It is possible to state the claims of these two things—worship and mission—in such a way as to accord neither of them priority at the expense of the other. Clearly these two directions in which the church turns must relate to one another, for both are rooted in Christ (see J. G. Davies, *Worship and Mission* [London: SCM Press 1966]; P. Dale, *Send Us Out: A Study in Worship and Mission* [Bramcote, Notts.: Grove Books, 1974]). On the one hand, worship for its own sake must arise from, and must inform, a community passionately engaged with the world. Unless it incorporates the experiences of life in the world, worship becomes infected by falseness, theatricality, aestheticism, and irrelevance. On the other hand, a community of service and witness must, for the sake of its service and witness, turn to praise and prayer. Service without worship leads to busy activism and the sense of self-importance that comes from believing that the church is the world's savior.

Anglicanism has not always held these two callings in balance, but certain features of its history have kept it aware of both callings. The Church of England inherited the social structures of medieval Christendom. Thus, for several generations following the Reformation, it held to the ideal that it would be the single church touching, leavening, and judging the society and public structures of the whole nation. The prayers of the church, while they included close-at-hand concerns, were prayers for the commonwealth. The system of geographical parishes meant that everyone was within a unit of the church's life, and the church had pastoral responsibility for what took place in every community. The worst features of individualized, privatized religion and going to "the church of your choice" were avoided.

In time, this ideal for the most part failed. As religious pluralism became a fact of British life, it became clear that the Church of England would be one denomination alongside others—although it held a privileged position for many generations. The growth of cities and industries coincided with a time of pastoral carelessness, and many segments of society were neglected. In the eighteenth century, due to the influence of the philanthropic side of the Wesleyan movement, private societies were founded to care for social needs and for missions to the unchurched, matters from which the official church had largely withdrawn.

In the nineteenth century, the Church of England grew in numbers, and its sense of pastoral ministry was recovered. Some of the Anglo-Catholic clergy, impelled by their doctrine of the Incarnation, went into the slums, where the color and drama of their ritualistic worship, along with their pastoral dedication, made an impact. The Christian Socialist movement, led initially by Charles Kingsley and Frederick Denison Maurice, sought to address systemic inequities from a theological vantage point. (It was Kingsley who first said that the Bible had been used as "an opium-dose for keeping beasts of burden patient while they were being overloaded—a mere book to keep the poor in order," whereas its intent, from beginning to end, is "to keep the rich in order.") As to the practical work of ministering, some large parishes in industrial centers began team ministries to the working class neighborhoods.

In the United States, it had been clear from colonial times that in a religiously pluralistic country the Episcopal church would coexist with other churches. Work for the suffering, the hungry, and the needy was undertaken as American society moved through its westward expansion, the crises of slavery, the Civil War, and industrialization—all exacting terrible human cost. Some important Episcopalian voices, notable among them William Augustus Muhlenberg, spoke for the church's social mission. In the early twentieth century, several pioneering institutional churches developed in urban centers, providing soup kitchens, social services, and related activities.

Through these years, the changes in ministries of outreach—many of them vigorous and effective—had little effect on forms of worship. *The Book of Common Prayer*, with its objective and inclusive style and its biblical, Christological structures, could encompass a great variety of intentions and pastoral concerns without having to undergo much change. Although there were revisions of the Prayer Book in the early twentieth century which included more prayers for the social order and for missions, and although each hymnal revision included more hymns with social concerns, few expressed fundamental restlessness with the church's liturgy. The liturgy seemed to have an order, beauty, and spiritual reality that could be as relevant to situations and events as various congregations required (see B. I. Bell, *The Altar and the World: Social Implications of the Liturgy* [New York: Harpers, 1944]; P. Dearmer, *The Church at Prayer and the World Outside* [London: James Clark, 1923]; P. T. R. Kirk, ed., *Worship: Its Social Significance* [1939]).

Yet the continued twentieth-century use of a sixteenth-century liturgy in time imparted to Anglican worship a considerable remoteness and stiffness. (In this, of course, the Episcopal church was not alone. Until recent decades, most liturgical traditions perpetuated sixteenth-century worship forms with little question.) Apart from special prayers for local, national, and world concerns, it was possible for the liturgical community to exhibit little sense of the passing of time or of the church engaged with society.

In recent decades Anglican churches have recovered a sense of community. The assembly's embodied, social life has been given expression in liturgical rites and concepts. People do not worship as individuals, but as a community of interacting persons—a community that lives in a social context. The sin and redemption of the worshiping community cannot be separated from the sin, redemption, and collective well-being of the social solidarities in which it is set. Such ideas were given important articulation by the English theologian A. G. Hebert in *Liturgy and Society* (London: Faber and Faber, 1945), and in the symposium edited by him, *The Parish Communion* (London: Society for Promoting Christian Knowledge, 1937). The English parish-and-people movement emphasized the social significance of worship (see Peter Jagger, *A History of the Parish and People Movement*). The American counterpart of this movement is "associated parishes" (see M. H. Shepherd, ed., *The Liturgical Renewal of the Church* [New York: Oxford University Press, 1960]; see especially chapter 4, "The Social Implications of the Liturgical Renewal," by A. C. Lichtenburger).

Worship and Community

Concern was expressed (particularly from the 1930s through the 1950s) for the integrity of the worshiping community. It should not be comprised of isolated individuals assembled under one roof, but of persons who in worship give expression to a life they share—a life of mutual faith, support, caring, and forgiveness. (An influential American statement of this was Charles Duell Kean's *The Christian Gospel and the Parish Church* [Greenwich, Conn.: Seabury Press, 1953]). A week seldom goes by without the occurrence of significant events in the congregation. Thanksgiving and intercession of the people should grow from shared joys and sorrow. Such simple devices as exchanging the peace and the weekly shaping of intercessory prayers provide expression for a parish community (see D. B. Stevick, *The Crafting of Liturgy* [1990]; see especially chapter 6, "The Prayers of the People"). Liturgical integrity requires, however, that there be genuine acceptance and caring behind such liturgical gestures.

The community at worship must itself be a witness to the gospel in the church. Since the worshiping community is constituted by baptism, the fundamental sign that forms the redeemed people, no one should be left out or disregarded. Christians at worship should not be cast in silent, passive roles, as though they came merely to be instructed or entertained. (The use of the printed and quite dialogical *Book of Common Prayer* and the frequent significant changes of posture has, over generations, made Episcopalian congregations more vocal and active than most others.) The family service, a marked change in custom beginning in the 1950s, was a response to the recognition that the liturgical community should include the children, who at any time comprise a large portion of the baptized people. If worship emphasizes family participation, it should not ignore those who (by choice or involuntarily) live alone. It should also take into account the elderly.

Out of the worshiping assembly, many people should, according to their gifts, be brought into vocal, visible leadership roles—thereby overturning the clericalism of most worship. In addition to acting as musicians and ushers (roles that have long been open to the laity), lay people should also read the appointed Scriptures, lead (and perhaps prepare) the people's intercessions, bear the bread and wine to the table, and help administer the Communion. If such participation in leadership is based fundamentally on baptism and the gifts of the person, it includes women as fully as men. Since 1974 in the Episcopal church in the United States, women have served as clergy in addition to serving as lay leaders. Other branches of Anglicanism are facing the issue of women leadership at their own pace and out of their own histories.

The fullest form of the assembly of Christians and (by early practice and by the intention of the framers of the modern traditions) the expected form for every Sunday is the gathering for Word and sacrament. The coming together at the Lord's table to share now in the life of Christ once given is both an expression of the community that now is and a call for it to become more fully the community of God's intention.

Worship is particular, but it cannot be true to itself if its agenda is formed out of the local worshipers alone. The local service of the gospel implies participation in the worldwide people of God and their redemptive engagement with today's society. The community which represents humanity transformed must show concern for humanity diminished, deceived, and oppressed. It is frequently noted that the sacramental bread and wine are material things which carry social significance. They stand for life, both human and divine life (see J. A. T. Robinson, *Liturgy Coming to Life* [London: Mowbrays, 1960]; *On Being the Church in the World* [Philadelphia: Westminster Press, 1960]; and the very thoughtful work by Timothy Sedgwick, *Sacramental Ethics* [Philadelphia: Fortress Press, 1987]). Reflecting the prophets' sense of God's care for social justice and that there be enough for all, the prayers of the congregation must be not only for its own needs, but for the well-being of the world. Moreover, the prayers should express the active commitments of the congregation (see L. W. Brown, *Relevant Liturgy* [New York: Oxford University Press, 1965]).

In summary, worship puts the church in touch

with an alternative reality by which the world is judged and redeemed. Out of this alternative vision, the church is impelled into witness and service in the society in which it is set. In society, the church accomplishes some modest things, but it also learns its own helplessness—a recognition which drives it back to the healing and renewing actions of worship.

Daniel B. Stevick

109 • ASSEMBLIES OF GOD CHURCHES

Having originated in the Pentecostal movement of the early twentieth century, the Assemblies of God still exhibit certain worship traits associated with that movement, such as encouraging all to participate visibly and audibly in the service. In other areas, however, the Assemblies have moved toward assimilation into the evangelical mainstream. With assimilation, a larger role for clergy and more attention to musical excellence has emerged in the Assemblies.

From its inception in 1901, the Pentecostal Movement sought to minimize the rigid distinction between clergy and laity typical of most churches. Consistent with their belief that the baptism in the Holy Spirit (Acts 1:8; 2:4), as prophesied by Joel (2:28-29), brings empowerment for Christian witness, leaders have encouraged every believer to seek for this second experience of grace and become active in some form of church work and evangelism. The Spirit provides the enabling power for all Christians to be active in a diversity of ministries (1 Cor. 12) and to carry the gospel to the ends of the earth (Acts 1:8). Through the years and despite the emergence of a trained clergy, church members have made considerable commitment of time, energy, and money to advance the mission of the church.

The Role of Women

For many Pentecostals, the promise of the Spirit's outpouring of power on men and women in "the last days" authorized the right of the laity to lead in worship, preaching, and pastoring (Acts 21:9; Gal. 3:28). Advocates of women in ministry in the nineteenth-century Holiness movement, the precursor to Pentecostalism, also used this line of scriptural reasoning. Their example and biblical exegesis paved the way, perhaps unwittingly, for Pentecostal women who felt called to preach. Not surprisingly, these proponents minimized the contemporary cultural relevance of Paul's admonitions against women speaking in church or being in authority over men (1 Cor. 14:34-35; 1 Tim. 2:11-15).

Unlike some Pentecostals, key leaders in the General Council of the Assemblies of God expressed opposition to, or at least ambivalence about, this unusual privilege. They asserted that Joel's prophecy did not authorize the ordination of women as pastors. Since women were already actively involved in ministries at the denomination's founding in 1914, they shortly afterward received approval as evangelists and missionaries. Nevertheless, women did not receive the right to vote at national meetings until 1920, and had to wait until 1935 to receive ordination as pastors.

Despite the obstacles, an impressive cadre of women has made a major contribution to church growth through evangelism, church planting, teaching, and pioneering missionary endeavors. In spite of all their accomplishments, their number has declined through the years, a trend already observable within a few decades of the denomination's establishment. While church rosters list a considerable number of women as ordained ministers, these statistics do not reflect the level of women's activity in the pulpit. Pastors' wives, who share in many of their responsibilities, occasionally receive ministerial credentials, but do not regularly preach.

Through the years, women have gained only limited access to the decision-making processes of the denomination. Along with their male counterparts, women can vote in district councils, and if ordained, they can also vote at General Council meetings. No woman, however, has ever served on three of the most influential governing boards: the General Presbytery, the Executive Presbytery, and the Foreign Missions Committee (since 1919). This situation reflects quite accurately the secondary status of women.

Many congregations also refuse to allow women to serve on boards of elders. Objections in some quarters to their role in church leadership, leading of worship, preaching, and pastoral ministries have not come exclusively from men. Women themselves are divided on the issue.

Worship and Music

In their zeal to return to the practices of the New Testament church, the Assemblies of God (unlike some Restorationists) have never frowned on the use of vocal and instrumental music. Instead, church members recognize musical compositions and instruments as the fruit of creative gifts given to humankind by God. Furthermore, the music of the Old Testament sets a precedent for using every musical means to praise the Lord (Ps. 150). Thus, choirs and orchestras, vocalists and instrumentalists (playing everything from trombones to drums and guitars) have enriched Pentecostal spirituality.

Worship leaders, whether male or female, have historically encouraged everyone to participate in church services, through congregational singing, clapping of their hands to the music, lifting their hands in praise, praying audibly, giving public testimonies of God's grace and answers to prayer, or ministering to the entire group with a gift of the Spirit (1 Cor. 12; 14). Indeed, many young people, who are offered opportunities to participate in worship, have become skilled musicians. Children's choirs also present special programs, usually at Christmas and Easter, and at other times during the year.

After World War II, many church members moved upward into the middle class. That development increasingly brought more sophistication to the worship of Assemblies of God churches. Bible colleges began offering degrees in sacred music. Churches looked for professionally trained directors of music. Choirs began to wear robes; volunteer orchestras gradually disbanded. Hymnals replaced gospel songbooks. And pastors gradually began to prefer that only persons with commendable voices sing vocal solos. Of course, this development has been more true of larger churches; smaller ones are generally limited by fewer resources.

Spiritual Formation

Sunday services offer an indispensable means of spiritual formation. The sense of community; awareness of the presence and gifts of the Holy Spirit; and the music, prayer, and exposition of the Word all contribute to a deeper Christian life and walk in the Spirit. In addition, Sunday services provide important occasions for leading to Christ any unbelievers who are present. Strongly influenced by nineteenth-century revivalism, Pentecostals have recognized the value of powerful and emotional preaching, gospel songs, and altar calls as means by which the Holy Spirit can draw people to confession and repentance. Some congregations report conversions every Sunday, while for others this is the exception.

In view of its increasing identification with the evangelical mainstream in the United States, the Assemblies of God needs to examine how its acceptance by other groups, the improved social and economic standing of its membership, the *de facto* restrictions on women, and the influence of contemporary culture have impacted their worship.

Gary B. McGee

110 ✦ BAPTIST GENERAL CONFERENCE CHURCHES

Because Baptist churches are congregationally governed, worship practices vary. Thus, general statements about worship are inappropriate. This article describes the relation of worship to other church ministries in a representative member congregation of the Baptist General Conference.

In Baptist polity, each church is autonomous and establishes its worship style independent of any clerical or denominational hierarchy. The following is a description of worship and related ministries in one church associated with the Baptist General Conference, Bethlehem Baptist Church of Minneapolis.

Children and Worship

Some Baptist General Conference churches have a children's church during the worship hour. Bethlehem Baptist has chosen to include children in its regular worship service, so the children can worship with their parents. The church believes that the parents are the best teachers of children on how to worship and of what it means to worship God as a family. It is especially important for boys to see worship modeled by their fathers. Child care is provided during worship for children under age six.

Children participate in leading worship once a quarter through their membership in one of the children's choirs. Special emphasis is given to the role of children on Palm Sunday. Furthermore, children are also involved as liturgical candle lighters during Advent and Lent.

Worship and Evangelism

Worship, not evangelism, is the ultimate goal of the church. Humans were created to glorify God by enjoying God forever. Believers evangelize because the worship of Jesus does not yet exist in the hearts and lives of many of their friends and acquaintances. Therefore, any evangelistic event incorporated into a worship context always seeks to be a God-centered event of worship. Within such visitor-focused evangelistic services, Bethlehem Baptist tries to be sensitive to the way it worships and therefore eliminates any forms that would create unnecessary barriers for those the service is trying to reach.

Such visitor-focused services are typically planned for the Sundays before Christmas and Thanksgiving, and for Easter Sunday. These days were chosen because they seem to be the time when most unchurched people think of going to church. These services begin with a singing prelude which portrays a festive, open mood of people singing songs and hymns as they gather to worship. The song texts are usually printed in the bulletin so visitors do not need to be proficient in using the hymnal. Bethlehem Baptist also tries to incorporate in these services a greater variety of musical styles that will appeal to a wider span of personal tastes. The sermon is geared more toward the entry level person, who is inquiring about Christianity and has no prior knowledge.

Another strategy of worship evangelism is implemented during the summer months. Instead of inviting unchurched people into the building, the congregation takes worship into the public arena. Bethlehem Baptist has adapted Graham Kendrick's concept by planning praise processions down the streets of Minneapolis, with more than a thousand people shouting, clapping, dancing, and singing the praises of the Lord. The same format is used in midweek service in one of the area parks. At these services, about a hundred people gather in a park to worship the Lord with contemporary Christian music. The _Jesus_ film, magicians, storytellers, and free hot dogs also attract the unchurched to these services. The Minneapolis community has responded well to this approach.

Worship and Social Action

One of the most powerful times of worship at Bethlehem Baptist Church occurred on a Martin Luther King, Jr. weekend. The congregation of Bethlehem Baptist is primarily white, with a Scandinavian heritage. On this occasion, however, it invited ten black congregations to join in a multicultural celebration. The issue of racial prejudice was keenly on everyone's mind because of current events throughout the nation. The service, which lasted three hours, included congregational singing of spirituals and gospel songs, greetings from each church, testimonies, impassioned prayers for unity by the pastors, the reading of Dr. King's "I Have a Dream" speech, prayer conducted by prayer huddles within the congregation, a guest speaker (Tom Skinner), and singing by a combined choir. At the conclusion, the entire congregation sang Jester Hairston's "Amen!" Exhausting but joyful experiences such as this one can be used by God to break down the social and ethnic barriers in both church and society.

Worship and Spiritual Formation

Bethlehem Baptist Church believes strongly in the involvement of all its members in a small group for mutual care and accountability. Currently, more than half the congregation is active in small groups. Each September, a worship service is devoted to encouraging people to get involved in this ministry. Usually a sermon explains the biblical foundation for small groups. Hymns and songs focus on what it means to be the body of Christ. Finally, the service sets aside a time for prayer about committing to join one of the groups.

Recently, the congregation has begun to stress the meaning and importance of church membership. This issue is closely related to spiritual formation, since perseverance in the faith is a community project. We are all responsible as church members to hold one another accountable in the faith. Membership in Bethlehem Baptist now involves a Sunday morning rite in which new members publicly vow to uphold the church covenant. Those in this service who already are members are indirectly encouraged to reaffirm their covenant commitments to the Lord and to one another.

Worship and the Role of Women

The Baptist General Conference does not take a position on the ordination of women, allowing each member church to practice its own convictions. At this time, Bethlehem Baptist does not ordain women to the pastoral office or elder's office because of its understanding and interpretation of Ephesians 5:21-33; 1 Corinthians 11:3-16; and 1 Timothy 2:8–3:7.

Some women in the congregation had difficulty with male-oriented language in hymnody. The church tried to be sensitive to the issue by selecting a new hymnal with increased use of inclusive language. However, because of the memories of well-known hymns, some feel that the original wording of historic hymns should have been preserved.

Dean Palermo

111 • BAPTISTS (EVANGELICAL DENOMINATIONS AND INDEPENDENT BAPTIST CHURCHES)

Numerous Baptist groups and independent Baptist congregations exist in North America. The following entry is a general discussion of worship and related ministries in independent and evangelical Baptist churches.

The proliferation of types of Baptist churches and groups indicate that these bodies may differ in various areas of theology and practice, while maintaining Baptist distinctives and essentials. However, within the orbit of evangelical Baptist churches, certain generalities hold true with respect to the role of women, children's ministries, social action, and spiritual formation.

Role of Women

Few women are ordained by independent and evangelical Baptist churches. Because there is no central governing authority at the denominational level, each church is free to establish its own policy on this matter. The majority of Baptist churches take a prohibitive posture on women's ordination for both cultural and theological reasons. The exception to these prohibitive norms is rare indeed, and generally considered suspect or even branded "liberal" by many Baptists. Sometimes the ordination of a woman is approved for an assistant pastor position or for chaplaincy programs, under the supervision of men.

Traditionally, women are not encouraged to join church decision-making boards. They are, how- ever, encouraged to teach Sunday school, especially young children's classes, and to take part in the music ministry as singers or instrumentalists. They are rarely used in ushering, Scripture reading, or preaching.

Children's Ministries

Children become involved in the common worship of the church in several ways. For instance, children enjoy singing in worship, usually the songs they prepared in their Sunday school classes. Furthermore, It is common to have a children's sermon, generally a simple application of the truth given in the sermon for adults. Children are baptized after they make an individual personal commitment to the Lord. Baptists virtually never baptize infants.

Church staffing for the special needs of children and youth typically receives high priority; most churches that exceed one hundred to two hundred members have a pastor whose primary focus is ministry to young people. Baptists widely believe that one of the best ways to attract new adults to the church is first to reach their children through an effective vacation Bible school, and through children's and youth ministries.

Social Action

The sermon, more than the other aspects of worship, is usually the vehicle for motivating persons to make a commitment to social action. The level of the impact of social action by the church often correlates with how concerned the individual pastor is in exploring social issues. Political issues such as homosexual rights, abortion, freedom of speech, freedom from government intervention in education, racial prejudice, and providing food and shelter for the homeless are but a few concerns which may be addressed when calling upon congregations to work toward social change in a community.

Spiritual Formation

For many people, worship is the only arena available for spiritual formation. For that reason, many Baptist church leaders take the opportunity of the worship assembly to exhort parishioners toward spiritual growth. These encouragements most often come through sermons because in small groups, the challenge to build spiritual strength in individuals is often overshadowed by the enjoyment of personal friendships resulting from these groups. Preaching and teaching also focus on the importance of personal fellowship with God. Subsequently, many members of Baptist congregations practice their piety with strong conviction. The sermon may also exhort the individual member to personal evangelism and involvement in the church so that the church may continue to grow.

Larry D. Ellis

112 ✦ BRETHREN (PLYMOUTH) ASSEMBLIES

Among the Plymouth Brethren, the congregation's worship life centers on the "breaking of bread" meeting. This meeting exhibits the Brethren's values of spontaneity and simplicity, although it restricts women's participation. Since this meeting is unplanned, the preaching service which follows more effectively links worship with other aspects of congregational life.

Worship among the Plymouth Brethren has tended to be focused in their weekly "breaking of bread" meeting, in which they "remember the Lord" through reflection, spontaneous hymn singing, prayer, sharing of Scripture, and ultimately in the partaking of the bread and cup. Although other meetings of the assembly occur, such as the preaching service (often called, among the Open Brethren, the "family Bible hour") and Sunday school programs, the breaking of bread meeting is the hub of worship for the Brethren. Even architecture and room seating—with circular patterns preferred and the elements placed in the center—have been used to highlight this fact.

With this background, I will examine Brethren worship and how it radiates out to influence other Brethren practices. Three areas will be singled out: the role of women, general spiritual formation, and other public functions of the assembly.

Women in Worship

The Brethren have traditionally assigned limited roles to women. Since worship and remembrance are connected directly to the weekly breaking of bread meeting, the involvement of women in worship has historically been understood to be silence

during this otherwise participatory meeting. On the basis of the Brethren's interpretation of 1 Corinthians 11 and 14, women are expected to remain silent and to cover their heads with some type of covering (typically, among the Open Brethren, a lace mantilla). Only men are allowed to read spontaneously the Scripture, share a worship thought, lead in prayer, suggest a hymn, or pray over the elements during this central meeting. The women's only verbal participation in this meeting has been to join in the congregational singing of a hymn that may have been suggested by one of the men.

On the other hand, the Brethren for a long time have "commended" women to mission work or other non-preaching ministries. (_Commendation_ is a Brethren parallel to ordination.) Women are excluded only from the final leadership role in a congregation, that of elder, which is understood to be an office restricted to mature males within the congregation. Some of more progressive Brethren assemblies have allowed women a greater leadership role, based on their spiritual gifts, but typically even here there is a reluctance to permit women to preach or teach men (based on 1 Timothy 2:12), or to have them serve as elders (an office limited to men based on 1 Timothy 3 and Titus 1). Normative leadership roles in even the most progressive Brethren assemblies tend to remain hierarchical, rather than egalitarian, because that is how they read the relevant Scripture passages.

Some Brethren assemblies, however, have broken with the tradition of women's silence during breaking of bread worship on the grounds that it cannot be biblically justified. An inconsistency is recognized in requiring a head covering (specified in 1 Corinthians 11:2-16) when a woman prays or prophesies (two forms of public verbalization), while at the same time expecting silence. These more progressive assemblies have come to view 1 Corinthians 14:22-36 as not envisioning absolute silence, but only certain kinds of silence. Therefore, according to this interpretation, this passage does not exclude women from participation in public prayer or prophecy. This new understanding of this passage has caused serious disagreement among some assemblies, since the silence of women is considered by many as a Brethren distinctive clearly derived from the New Testament.

Worship and Spiritual Formation

The relation of Brethren worship to spiritual formation also calls for comment. The centrality and frequency of the breaking of bread meeting places the Brethren concept of worship at the center of life and spirituality. The ability to sit silently and listen to what the Spirit of God is doing in the weekly meeting is understood to be a mark of spiritual maturity. This weekly meeting is given external guidance only when someone is prompted by the Spirit of God to participate in a meaningful way by offering a prayer, suggesting a hymn, or bringing a passage to bear on the theme of worship and remembrance as it is developed for the day. In this way, Brethren expect worship to arise from the corporate and individual life of the Christian community, rather than being produced by following external guidelines or any human leader.

This understanding of worship also develops among the Brethren the twin spiritual values of spontaneity and simplicity. Worshipers are expected to be involved in the Scriptures and prayer on a regular basis, so as to be able, should the Spirit prompt them, to participate in this meeting. But the Brethren do not structure the meeting, or necessarily plan ahead of time to participate in the meeting; this, it is felt, would stifle the movement of the Spirit of God. In the absence of a clergy system, the meeting depends greatly on the participation of mature believers who know the Scriptures and the presence of God.

Further, the ideal of simplicity becomes important to everyone trained in Brethren values of worship. There are certain fundamentals of the faith to which one must return each week, and which call forth worship and praise. Worship should be simple, rather than complex; it should be done "in spirit and truth," rather than through any form of established and learned liturgy. Nothing in the meeting is to be planned, but all is expected to arise in spontaneity from a worshiping heart in tune with the Lord. Children are taught the discipline of sitting still and keeping themselves occupied until they can track the development of the day's worship theme.

At the same time, a tendency exists among some Brethren to limit worship to the confines of the breaking of bread meeting itself. Other meetings of the assembly are for fellowship, evangelism, or instruction, but this one alone is reserved for worship. The entire mood of the congregation often changes from sobriety to a more moderate tone, once the breaking of bread worship time ends and the family Bible hour (the preaching service) begins. Some assemblies have tried to integrate the breaking of bread meeting and the family Bible hour into one continuous time of celebration, proclamation, and worship; this has met with less than enthusiastic response. In this sense, Brethren worship is not always well integrated with the other functions of Christian community.

Among the Brethren, better integration is often found between the preaching of the family Bible hour and other activities of the assembly. Many assemblies, for example, have exchanged the traditional model of a midweek prayer and Bible study session for home groups (sometimes called *home flocks*), in a desire to achieve greater participation. In these groups, prayer, mutual accountability, and Bible study are more effectively brought to a personal level. In some assemblies, the home flocks have been so coordinated by a leader that the study notes used during the week are based on the passage or subject covered by the preacher on the preceding Sunday, reinforcing a continuity of application.

In summary, worship among the Brethren finds its focus in the weekly breaking of bread meeting; all other meetings are secondary to this one. Although severely restrictive in terms of women's participation, the meeting exhibits the values of spontaneity and simplicity. But, since the meeting is not to exhibit the marks of human planning, little is ever done to link the meeting more effectively to the entire corporate life of the assembly apart from the expectation that any male truly in fellowship with the Lord will be present and participate.

Rex Koivisto

113 ◆ CHARISMATIC CHURCHES

Christian education, social outreach, and concern for the development of women in leadership have become increasingly important dimensions in the life of charismatic churches. A growing number of women leaders, social ministries, and educational institutions testify to this vitality.

Charismatic churches are not a denomination, but a series of loosely connected networks of churches which share common traits, such as the belief in the continuity of the apostolic spiritual gifts and an emphasis on a style of flowing praise and worship. They represent a development of certain themes of the Pentecostal revival of the early twentieth century. However, these churches are outside the framework of the Pentecostal denominations.

Women and the Ministry

Through the Pentecostal awakening of the early 1900s and the charismatic renewal of the early 1960s, the roles of women in the ministry have undergone a major shift. Early in the 1900s, for example, Florence L. Crawford became the founder of the Apostolic Faith movement in the Pacific northwest, and Aimee Semple McPherson established the International Church of the Foursquare Gospel. While these women, along with others, became a focal point for change in Christian leadership, the nineteenth century had already set the stage. Phoebe Palmer, Hannah Whitehall Smith, and Jessie Penn-Lewis were key figures in the nineteenth century Holiness movement, which was the precursor to the Pentecostal and charismatic revival. As this awakening spread, women were available for leadership and were often thrust into roles of responsibility and high visibility. Historic changes in the family, creating more free time for women, were partly responsible for making this possible.

Today, virtually every aspect of the ministry in the charismatic community is open to women. Women lead churches as pastors and serve as staff members, worship leaders, teachers, or board members. Several well-known women—such as Marilyn Hickey, Sandy Brown and Artheline Rippy—led their own parachurch ministries, taking the teaching role of women beyond the orbit of women's retreats and conferences, into the larger body of Christ.

In the ministry of the local church, a new phenomenon has developed: the model of the married co-pastorate. Rather than functioning simply as the wife of the minister, many charismatic and Pentecostal pastors' wives have been named co-pastors of their churches, becoming just as involved in the preaching, teaching, organizational, and leadership aspects of the fellowship. Nationally known churches such as Rock Church of Virginia Beach, Virginia (John and Ann Gimenez) and Victory Christian Center of Tulsa, Oklahoma (Billy Joe and Sharon Daugherty) are two examples of highly successful co-pastorate churches.

One reason for this shift in leadership style, which occurred without much opposition, may be the reduction of emphasis upon the liturgical and sacramental aspects of worship. Mainline denominations traditionally viewed men as the symbol of Christ, functioning as his priest in the holy Eucharist. With the rise of congregational Puritanism and evangelicalism in North America, the sacraments received less attention, while the teaching ministry of the Word became dominant. This pulpit-centered emphasis made types and symbols less important, leaving greater opportunity for women in positions of leadership for ministry.

Social Issues

Evangelicals and mainline Protestants have for a long time believed that charismatics are "so heavenly minded they are no earthly good." The charismatics' overemphasis on the Spirit and the gifts of the Spirit, it was thought, left them orbiting in the church, out of touch with the real issues of life. Such is not the case. Charismatic individuals and churches have been at the forefront of many social concerns. They have established ministries and churches in the inner city or have formed outreach teams from suburban churches that minister to the homeless and hungry in the urban scene. Charismatics play an important role in staffing pregnancy counseling centers, and in the witness against abortion. Groups like Youth With a Mission and Teen Mania mobilize thousands of young people each year to give of themselves to others in North America and around the world. Other ministries, such as Feed the Children or the 700 Club's Operation Blessing, are led by charismatics and Pentecostals who are concerned about the world in which they live and have organized various expressions of care for the poor.

Rather than seeing the needs of the world as issues that distract Christians away from the things of the Spirit, contemporary charismatics are seeing these needs as opportunities to flex their spiritual muscles. For instance, one church in Tulsa, Oklahoma, sends teams into the inner city not only to meet the needs of the homeless and poor with food and shelter, but also to proclaim the gospel, to lead people to faith in Jesus Christ, and to offer deliverance from the demonization that often accompanies the lifestyles of the disadvantaged. Through the exercise of spiritual gifts, people have been made whole.

———— Education and Children's ———— Ministries

A significant shift in attitudes about Christian education has taken place within the charismatic movement. Historically, these churches were formed primarily to conduct praise and worship, and were not organized to provide a strong educational program for children. Now these churches offer educational programs for every grade.

For charismatics, one of the problems with graded education had been the development of responsible curricula that could adequately convey biblical values while maintaining Pentecostal and charismatic distinctives. Established denominations such as the Assemblies of God had already been providing such curriculum; independent churches, however, had to use that denomination's materials or settle for other curricula that would either downplay or contradict the values and dimensions of Christian life important to these fellowships. Recently, new curricula have become available to the Christian education ministries of charismatic churches. Organizations such as *Charisma* magazine have established new publishing arms for producing specially designed graded curriculum with a charismatic approach to faith and practice.

Children's ministry has also found a significant place in the charismatic church. Initially, churches provided special presentations such as *Kid's Praise* and *The Music Machine* to minister to children. Children's workers such as Willie George ("Gospel Bill") have produced some of the best quality children's programming on Christian television. All of this fueled a strong emphasis on children's ministry that has continued to expand into the youth departments of these churches.

Another aspect of educational development is the establishment of new colleges, Bible schools, and nontraditional Bible institutes. Historically, Pentecostals and charismatics had shied away from formalized education, which was viewed as antithetical to spirituality. Pentecostal denominations did establish schools, such as the Evangel College of the Assemblies of God, which have offered accredited degrees for many years. More recently, these schools have been joined by independent charismatically oriented institutions such as Oral Roberts University and Pat Robertson's Regent University (formerly CBN University). These institutions now have some outstanding graduate programs as well. Other types of schools provided a more specialized program in ministries and Bible training: Examples are Christ for the Nations Institute and Youth With a Mission's University of the Nations. In recent years, these major and veteran educational institutions have been joined by others schools. Many of these schools are attached to local congregations, which serve regional communities.

Randolph W. Sly

114 ✦ Christian Churches and Churches of Christ

From the movement's beginning, worship in the Christian churches and Churches of Christ has been evangelistic in orientation. In recent years, however, many congregations have begun to adopt a more contemporary style of worship based on worship renewal itself, as well as making the service more attractive to seekers. In this way, worship is being more fully integrated with other ministries of the local church.

Historically, churches of the American restoration movement have focused more on evangelism than on worship. Even today, despite the renewal of interest in worship among many of the independent Christian churches and the Churches of Christ that use instruments, worship is largely seen as a means to an end, and that end is evangelism. So, in reality, much of the so-called worship renewal is a renewal of evangelism methods.

———— Worship and Evangelism ————

Most of the Christian churches have historically used the Sunday morning evangelism model common among nineteenth-century evangelical churches: singing songs of testimony (largely directed toward the unconverted), preaching a rather lengthy evangelistic message, offering a clear invitation to respond at the end, and preparation for baptism. This method has become less effective as the new generation of "baby boomers" has appeared, and churches have realized that new music and new methods must be used. Many are looking to churches such as Willow Creek Community Church in suburban Chicago for a new model, and are developing seeker-sensitive services. These services incorporate more contemporary music, develop a sense of flow to the service, eliminate "dead" time, add drama and other creative arts, and use less pressure in the invitation.

This new style of contemporary worship feels different to the congregation, and has sometimes been controversial. However, it is well received by younger adults. Churches that have adopted it are usually experiencing growth. This shift in style is clearly not due to a fundamental shift in the philosophy about the Sunday service. The goal is the same as always: worship as evangelism. Only the particular methods have been altered to reach a new generation.

At the same time, many among the churches are waking up to the whole concept of worship. Therefore, many of these churches are making similar changes in their worship service for the sake of worship renewal itself, rather than evangelism. In such cases, churches are attempting to make their worship more "visitor-friendly," without significantly diluting their understanding of the assembly as worship.

Because Christian churches are generally conservative, they have traditionally given biblical teaching a higher priority than contemporary issues. Therefore, social action, women's issues, and other matters are largely untouched in the worship assembly.

Women in Worship

Women are rarely given leadership positions in the mixed assembly of men and women. However, among these churches there is lack of uniformity in this matter. Some will not allow a woman to stand behind the pulpit; others have a woman as a full-time ordained music minister, doing everything another minister might do except preaching. The majority of Christian churches fall somewhere between these extremes in their position on women. Almost no women among the churches wear head coverings. They are permitted to sing solos, to give testimonies, to read Scripture, and perhaps even to pray in public, to

direct the choir, and to lead singing on occasion. But most congregations do not feel comfortable with women leading worship regularly or teaching doctrine in the full assembly. Only a few churches ask women to collect the offering or to serve Communion.

Children's and Educational Ministries

Very common among the churches of Christ, also, is the use of children's worship and other alternative opportunities for children during the worship hour. Of those churches that have children present for the service (mostly small and rural churches), the preacher will often give a children's sermon.

Several larger churches with sufficient staff to coordinate such things will integrate the Sunday morning message with the educational/discipleship program of the church. Either discussion questions from the sermon are included in small group activities, or Sunday school classes will discuss subjects related to the sermon. Rarely will the preacher build the sermon around the Sunday school lessons or the lectionary. The weekly sermon is considered the core of congregational instruction and programming.

Bringing About Renewal

The local preacher is the leader and catalyst for change and ministry in the congregation. Thus, the ministry often takes on the personality and agenda of the preacher. The way in which outreach ministries, social action projects, educational opportunities, or opportunities for testimony are spotlighted during the worship assembly will depend on the preacher's style and preferences. Change can occur fairly quickly on the congregational level, especially when the local minister has the enthusiastic support of the elders. However, for change to occur in all of the churches, it must be modeled in a local church, written about in the *Christian Standard*, discussed at the North American Christian Convention, taught in the seminaries and Bible colleges, or passed by word of mouth. In short, sweeping change can only happen at the "grass roots" level.

Such change has been taking place among Christian churches and Churches of Christ over the last decade or more. Small groups are more common; music is more contemporary; women are more active in the assembly; and churches are more aggressively reaching their communities for Christ. The corporate assembly is the rallying point for change in the church. The assembly is still the primary gathering place for worship within the churches.

Ken Read

115 ◆ CHRISTIAN CHURCH (DISCIPLES OF CHRIST)

The Christian Church (Disciples of Christ) has been especially concerned that they understand how worship relates to inclusiveness toward all types of people. In recent years, these churches have been especially concerned to incorporate women and children into full participation in worship.

The words of the preamble to *The Design for the Christian Church (Disciples of Christ)* reveal that worship is at the heart of this group's identity:

As members of the Christian Church,
we confess that Jesus is the Christ,
the Son of the Living God,
and proclaim him Lord and Savior of the world.

In Christ's name and by his grace,
we accept our mission of witness
and service to all people.

We rejoice in God,
maker of heaven and earth,
and in the covenant of love
which binds us to God and one another.

Through baptism into Christ,
we enter into newness of life
and are made one with the whole people of God.

In the communion of the Holy Spirit,
we are joined together in discipleship
and in obedience to Christ.

At the table of the Lord,
we celebrate with thanksgiving
the saving acts and presence of Christ.

Within the universal church,
we receive the gift of ministry
and the light of scripture.

In the bonds of Christian faith,
we yield ourselves to God
that we may serve the One
whose kingdom has no end.

Blessing, glory and honor
be to God forever. *Amen.*

It is worship which inspires the church's mission of "witness and service to all people" and releases "the gift of ministry and the light of scripture." It is worship which celebrates "the communion of the Holy Spirit" as the congregation assembles "at the table of the Lord."

In recent years the Christian Church (Disciples of Christ) has been concerned about the words "all people." How can the church be sure no one is excluded from its message of God's love as revealed through Jesus Christ? How can the church better include those who in the past have been left out? Recent cultural developments have made the church concerned to include women and children in ways they may not always have been included.

The Cross in Glory. A Latin cross behind which is the rising sun, represented by twelve or more rays of light. This form of the cross is often used for Easter decorations or for Easter day vestments. It is always white to represent the festive nature of the Resurrection.

Inclusion of Women

The Christian Church (Disciples of Christ) has been ordaining women since the 1880s, but in the past twenty years the enrollment of women in seminaries has risen from six percent to nearly fifty percent. Forty-five percent of those ordained in the denomination in 1991 were women. More gradually, women are moving into roles as pastors or senior ministers.

In addition to the rising visibility of women in professional ministry, lay leadership in local congregations includes more and more women. The 1985 General Assembly of the Christian Church adopted a resolution commending congregations that have contributed to the dramatic increase in the number of women who serve as deacons and elders.

As more women are seen and heard as leaders, congregations are facing new issues such as the use of inclusive language in worship. Church members are becoming conscious of the bias in the English language that favors men through the use of masculine terms for generic meanings. Because many women feel excluded by such language, issues about language that were unheard of in the past have become topics of conversation and controversy. The New Revised Standard Version of the Bible has been received warmly by people who welcome its use of "brothers and sisters" instead of "brethren," and of "people" instead of "men" to indicate both male and female human beings. Some groups are experimenting with new hymn texts that use more inclusive language.

However, a much more difficult issue to resolve is the use of masculine metaphors for God, especially the name _Father_. Not only hymns, but the Scriptures themselves, are filled with masculine images of God. The formula for the Trinity speaks of the Father and the Son. Some congregations, accustomed to singing the Old Hundredth tune as a doxology, have attempted to substitute other terminology, such as Maker and Savior, at the expense of the personal quality of the traditional words. Baptisms have been "in the name of the Father and of the Son and of the Holy Spirit" (Matthew 28:19). This formula is difficult to replace.

Inclusion of Children

In a different manner, children have not always been included fully as part of the community at worship. The General Assembly of the Christian Church (Disciples of Christ) adopted a resolution in 1989 asking the Division of Homeland Ministries to stress "the evangelistic value of having a well-run, up-to-date church nursery" and to produce more materials to help congregations encourage couples and single parents to bring their children to church.

Many congregations have a "children's church" that begins at the time of the sermon. Children may take part in and observe worship with the congregation as the people gather, sing, pray, and hear the Scriptures. Then, in consideration of their shorter attention span and their different physical needs, they move as a group to another room of the church building, where they hear Bible stories, sing songs suited to their stage of development, and learn to worship in ways they can understand. Although children's sermons have been popular in recent years, many ministers have found the object lessons generally used for this purpose communicate more to adults, who delight in the analogies, than to children. Narrative children's sermons, while probably more effective, are more difficult to prepare.

Another question related to children is when children should begin to take part in the Lord's Supper, which is so central to worship in the Christian Church (Disciples of Christ). It has, until recently, been customary for children to wait until they have been baptized. As many families transfer membership into Disciples congregations from other traditions, where children begin taking communion at an earlier age, some people have questioned whether it is theologically necessary for them to wait. Generally, the answer is left up to a child's parents. Because some children are receiving the bread and cup before they are baptized or confirmed, congregations face this question in a new way today.

These concerns for women and children are but two examples of many other ways members of the Christian Church (Disciples of Christ) seek to include all people in worship, people of all races and cultures, people of all ages, people who are physically able and people who are physically impaired. Generally, while Disciples admit there is a long way to go before the church is fully inclusive, they agree that such inclusiveness is a goal worth pursuing.

Philip V. Miller

116 ♦ CHRISTIAN AND MISSIONARY ALLIANCE CHURCHES

Within the churches of the Alliance, renewal of worship is extending its impact beyond the historic evangelistic *and missionary effort of the Alliance into other minis- tries, especially those of pastoral care and development of congregational community.*

For more than one hundred years, the dual themes of world evangelization and the maturing of the Christian life have been at the heart of the ministry of the Christian and Missionary Alliance. True to the vision of its founder, Dr. A. B. Simpson, the Alliance heralds the message that the person who finds life in Jesus Christ will be compelled to carry the gospel of Christ to the whole world.

Within this context, the Christian and Mission- ary Alliance in the United States is being impacted by a renewal in corporate worship. As people are experiencing freedom and joy in their expression of love for God, they are finding a new level of intimacy with one another, a new desire to share Christ with others, and a heightened expectancy that God will meet believers at the point of their need.

In 1987, the Alliance held its centennial coun- cil. During the service on the closing Sunday, there was a powerful outpouring of evangelistic zeal in the midst of worship. While nearly ten thousand Christians sang "Our God Reigns," hundreds of missionaries from all over the world marched to the platform. As believers worshiped the Lord, a strong fervor for world evangelism was released upon the people. It was a crisis experience for many who attended, and the commitments made that day flowed directly from the worship.

An example of an Alliance church seeking to integrate worship and related ministries is Risen King Community Church in Redding, California. This congregation is discovering that a deepened intimacy with God in worship opens people to new levels of intimacy with each other. In fact, worship renewal and the growth of small group ministries have been complementary priorities. The small groups use the same worship songs that are used in the Sunday celebration service; often new songs are first introduced in the small groups. Discussion questions are prepared each week to facilitate application of the Sunday sermon in the small groups. This method enhances the integra- tion of biblical truth into the life of the believer. The small group worship experience raises the individual believer's level of expectancy that he or she will meet God in the large worship setting.

Each week at this church, hundreds of hurting people come through its doors. There is little opportunity on Sunday for a personal touch from someone on the pastoral staff. However, the wor- ship leaders believe that in the midst of worship God desires to touch people with his Spirit. They invite God to do this in the worship service and encourage those with needs to stand for prayer. Trained ministry team members go to pray with each individual who stands; after inquiring briefly about the need, they lay hands on the individual and ask the Holy Spirit to minister to him or her. Worshipers have witnessed many physical, emo- tional, and spiritual healings. Everything from marriages being restored to people coming to faith in Jesus Christ occur in the midst of worship.

One Sunday morning, one of the pastors re- ceived a word of knowledge concerning a man experiencing severe angina pain. During worship, the pastor spoke the word; a man near the back stood in obvious physical distress. As the minis- try team gathered around him and prayed, he was healed instantly. God loves to work in the midst of the people gathered to praise him.

In a church where the leadership seeks to model intimacy with God, things that often remain hidden begin to come to light. As people begin to sense that God cares and loves them in the midst of their brokenness, this brokenness is revealed and expressed by these people. As a result, the congregation has formed small group ministries for those involved in substance abuse and for adult children of alcoholics. Both of these groups minister to people both inside and outside of the church. In addition, the church has established a food distribution ministry for those in physical need.

Psalm 22:3 declares the following about God: "Yet you are holy, enthroned on the praises of Israel." The image conveyed in this verse is one of God dwelling in the midst of his people as they praise him. When God manifests his presence in worship, everyone and everything is affected. People open themselves to worship renewal, and their lives and ministries are transformed. Wor- ship releases God's presence and power upon all aspects of church life. If worship is cold and life- less, it may be an indicator of the health of that church. When worship is vibrant and alive, no ministry should remain unaffected.

Ron Walborn

117 ✦ CHRISTIAN REFORMED CHURCHES

Originally a denomination consisting largely of people of Dutch origin, the Christian Reformed Church has in recent decades reached out to many cultural groups through a renewal of worship and evangelism. Its traditional strength in education continues to shape worship.

Evangelism and the teaching of Christian doctrine have been priorities of the Christian Reformed Church from the outset. However, the integration of these and other church ministries into the worship life of the local congregation has had a varied history.

Worship and Evangelism

From its beginning in 1857, the Christian Reformed Church has had an interest in missions. One of the first official acts of the church was to declare the first Monday of the month a day of prayer for the expansion of God's kingdom and a day to receive offerings for this purpose. As early as 1888, the denominational synod formulated regulations to guide its mission work (see John Van Schepen, *New Wine and Old Wine Skins* [1989], 18–19). However, the church intentionally separated worship and evangelism. Baptized converts to the Christian faith were placed in chapels or branch churches led by lay evangelists, but the official membership of the converts was in the church which sponsored the chapel. Preaching in the established churches was considered too intellectual and doctrinally advanced for new converts. In most cases, the worship service in these churches was preaching with a few added elements, such as the reading of the Ten Commandments or the Apostles' Creed. In 1957, missiologist Harry Boer published a thorough critique of this paternalistic attitude entitled *That My House May Be Filled*. The practice of organizing chapels, rather than new churches, gradually disappeared, even though some chapels still exist.

In the 1970s and 1980s all this changed. In 1968, the synod received a report from a study committee on worship which gave attention to the Sunday service as more than preaching. The report defined worship as essentially a dialogue between God and the people of God. Partly as a result of this new interest in worship, a standing liturgical committee was appointed. In 1972, a Christian Reformed Church called the Church of the Servant was organized in Grand Rapids, Michigan. From its inception, this congregation was more open to receiving members from different traditions, observed the liturgical year, and celebrated Communion weekly.

In the 1980s, the Board of Home Missions began to pay more attention to organizing churches among the unchurched. These churches were known as "non-nucleus" churches since they did not begin with a group of Christian Reformed people. These congregations were very sensitive to the evangelistic role of the worship service. At the same time, the board published a workshop for the established congregations called *Evangelism and Worship*. The workshop examined everything in the local worship service from the point of view of the visitor, and helped many churches rethink their worship services. Also during the 1980s, the Board of Publications began publication of a quarterly called *Reformed Worship*.

These developments continue to influence the connection between evangelism and worship to this day. More attention is paid to a friendly reception of visitors; sermons are more visitor-friendly; the weekly bulletin is more readable; more contemporary music and songs are used; and a number of churches seek to follow up on visitors to the worship service. Adding incentive to these changes is the realization that biological growth, European immigration growth, and transfer growth have virtually stopped in most congregations.

At the same time, there is considerable debate in the church about the proper connection between evangelism and worship. In March, 1992, both *Reformed Worship* and the denominational weekly, *The Banner*, devoted special issues to this debate. Every year, representatives from a number of Christian Reformed churches attend the semiannual conference at Willow Creek Community Church. This has led to greater "seeker sensitivity" and even to some Saturday services with special attention to the unchurched. Basic to the discussion on evangelism is whether the mission of the church is something added on to the life and worship of the church or whether the church in its entirety—including its worship—is shaped by participation in the mission of God to the world.

Women and Worship

For more than two decades, the most controversial issue in the denomination has been the ordination of women. At first, women were allowed to serve only as deacons. The 1990 synod opened all offices to women, but the 1992 synod did not ratify this decision. The same synod also decided that even though women cannot be ordained as pastors, they can, under the supervision of the elders, who must be men, speak from the pulpit. However, these speeches by women are not considered official preaching. Some congregations have separated from the denomination over this issue, while others have gone ahead and ordained women as elders. These questions will be much debated in the coming years.

Education and Spiritual Formation

The education and spiritual formation of the members has always been a significant part of Reformed worship services. The Christian Reformed *Church Order* specifies that "in the worship services the minister of the Word shall officially explain and apply Holy Scripture." Much attention is paid to careful exegesis in the formation of a biblical message that teaches the truth of God's Word. The *Church Order* also directs that "at one of the services each Lord's day, the minister shall ordinarily preach the Word as summarized in the Heidelberg Catechism, following its sequence." *Catechism preaching,* as this is usually called, is often seen as a teaching tool that helps the congregation to systematically consider the teachings of the Apostles' Creed, the Ten Commandments, and the Lord's Prayer. This practice is not as common as it once was, but the practice is still followed in most congregations.

Other developments in worship include the much appreciated children's sermon and children's worship. The gradual disappearance of the traditional extended family has led to greater attention to small groups in the church. A number of churches are discussing whether the Sunday evening service can on occasion be canceled in order to encourage people to worship in small groups. In the newer churches, this is already a fairly widespread practice.

Worship and Multicultural Outreach

Perhaps the quietest change in the church has been the growing multicultural nature of the de-nomination. For many years the denomination consisted largely of people of Dutch origin. By the 1990s, however, worship services in the United States and Canada were conducted in more than a dozen languages, including a growing number of Korean congregations. In many ways these churches have yet to enter the mainstream of Christian Reformed life, but increasingly their voices are heard. One feature of these multicultural churches is that these churches are committed to numerical growth and, therefore, include the worship service in their strategy to reach as many people in their language groups as they can.

Dirk J. Hart

118 ✦ CHURCH OF THE BRETHREN

Known historically as a pacifist denomination, the Church of the Brethren finds in corporate worship a powerful setting for articulating and advancing the themes of peace and peacemaking.

There will always be a creative tension between a faith response to Jesus Christ and ethical consequences that impact personal lifestyle. Every year books and articles have appeared describing a dialogue between the advocates of personal salvation and the proponents of social action. The New Testament writers give attention to the connection between worship and social relationships.

The Church of the Brethren, one of three historic peace churches (the others being Mennonite and Quaker), has endeavored to relate the concept of God's peace to the many conflicts in the existing culture. Having placed an emphasis on "following Jesus," the Brethren sought to embody Jesus' life and teachings in their encounters with neighbors and representatives of government. Historically, since its origin in Germany in 1708, the church has consistently witnessed to the Brethren conviction that "all war is sin." Accompanying this prophetic judgment and witness, the Church of the Brethren has endeavored to live out corporately the model of a peacemaking community. This Brethren conviction has evoked struggles within the faith community and has accounted for tensions felt by Brethren as they have sought to be faithful to the teachings of Jesus in the face of contradictory demands by governments.

Worship and Peace Concerns

Brethren who have been in tension with the state have found their convictions nurtured through worship. In the worship gathering, they sense themselves accountable to God and to one another in being faithful to the New Testament teachings related to peacemaking. Worship experiences have enabled them to search the Scriptures in a context where the counsel of others within the faith community is assured. Discernment of "the mind of Christ" (a key Brethren motivational goal) has been fostered through church hymnody and preaching. In the worship services, Brethren have examined key biblical texts and retold stories of faithful witnesses who took seriously Jesus' teaching and behavior when Jesus confronted hostile culture. While individual peace with God is a component of Brethren theology, the emphasis in the denomination has always been on corporate experiences of _shalom,_ or peace. Worship has created events where blessing could be experienced and hearts could be strengthened to take up the task of peacemaking in home and community.

Worship has kept the vision focused on those great passages in the Prophets which beautifully describe a people dwelling together in peace, weapons being fashioned into implements of agriculture, and hostility being overcome as fear is replaced with cooperative interaction. As the Brethren have encountered draft boards and hostile neighbors during wartime, the worship hours have brought encouragement and renewal of courage to "keep the faith." Those who labor to change the climate that fosters war-making will often become cynical when the nation continues its mood of anger and seeks to label all dissenters as unpatriotic. Thus, the worship experiences of the Brethren have been intended to create an awareness of the Spirit's power to energize those faithful to Christ and to his teaching of peace. During these encounters with God and with one another, Brethren are guided in moving beyond opposition to war toward the affirmation of God's power to create new communities of faith marked by trust and love. While expressing support for those who have resisted the demands of the state to be drafted as soldiers, church leaders have ensured that worship included a time of celebration and joy for what God did in sending Christ as the Prince of peace. In this way, feelings of powerlessness and despair, often prevalent in a religious minority, have been transformed into spiritual strength and hope.

In the Church of the Brethren, efforts have been made to ensure that people who do not agree with the draft resisters and conscientious objectors to war can remain in relationship with those who support the Brethren's historic peace position. Diversity within the gift of God's unity becomes both proclamation and experience in worship. At one annual conference during the Vietnam War, a respected Brethren sister wearing her prayer veil embraced a draft resister while the congregation sang of being "one in the Lord." Those who enter military service have been able to maintain their membership in this pacifist denomination. During wartime, Brethren have sent gifts and letters both to soldiers and to conscientious objectors.

Worship often serves the function as a catalyst to some prophetic witness for peace and to varied actions of Christian service. It has become common at national youth events for a worship service to be followed immediately by a walk to some industrial facility known to be engaged in fulfilling contracts for the Pentagon. Signing petitions urging a peaceful resolution of an international crisis will on occasion be included in the worship service or be offered as a response in the church's narthex. Persons on the threshold of engaging in some demonstration for peace may be commissioned during worship through the laying on of hands. As an alternative model of international leadership (where nations exchange food and medicine, instead of armaments), the Church of the Brethren initiated and became a strong supporter of the Heifer Project. One church in Ohio laid plastic on the center aisle one Sunday morning as several heifers were led to the chancel and prayers were offered for their safe delivery in Europe.

Finally, worship provides Brethren with a context where reflection, study, and prayer can aid the discernment process. When official statements are issued by the annual conference, the denomination's highest legislative body, they usually include a line to the effect that "this represents our best consensus at the moment on this controversial subject, but we remain open to the further guidance of God's Spirit." Bible stories are retold so as to shed light on contemporary events. During the prelude to the Persian Gulf War, the Biblical account of the Exodus was the subject for a sermon in a Pennsylvanian congregation. Instead of Americans being the children of Israel, the story was told with the American role approximating the part played by the Egyptians. Parallels were drawn between the Egyptian role played in the Exodus story and the role of the United States in mobilizing the coalition against Saddam Hussein.

Worship Components Applied to the Peace Theme

The Church of the Brethren has been characterized as a peace church, possessing a spiritual heritage going back to the days following the intense religious wars in Europe in the early eighteenth century. In their desire to make a strong witness for peace in the contemporary world, Brethren worship planners have utilized every component of the worship hour as a vehicle to promote the peace message. In a given service, several components will relate directly to *shalom* as experienced in home or congregational life, in the community surrounding the church, or in respect to moral issues apparent on the domestic or international scene. Several events in the church calendar, such as Palm Sunday, Peace Sabbath, World Communion Sunday, and World Order Sunday, readily lend themselves to this theme.

Bible Readings. Favorite biblical passages used in the Church of the Brethren are Matthew 5–7, Matthew 18, Luke 14, 2 Corinthians 5, and John 13–17. The great prophetic peace passages from Isaiah and Micah often find their way into Brethren sermons.

Hymns and Musical Interpretations. Brethren worship uses both folk tunes and traditional hymns that focus on peace and justice. The new hymnal published jointly by the Church of the Brethren and two Mennonite denominations in 1992 includes seventy hymns on the theme of peace. Many persons have affirmed the crucial role of hymns and choruses in sustaining the unity of the congregation on the issue of the church's role in wartime.

Prayer. Most Brethren services include a time for the sharing of joys and concerns prior to intercessory prayer. During this time, prophetic voices call for the congregation's witness in social action for peace. Brethren seem to have a sense that their witness is more effective when it honestly reflects personal struggles to discern the will of God. Thus, prayers of repentance are appropriate, followed by prayers for people in areas of conflict, prayers for our nation and its leaders, prayers for enemies, and prayers for members of the congregation.

Sermon. While two Brethren pastors may select the same text, the way they proclaim the Word may differ. Some pastors focus on peace strategy as a method which could work if only it were tried. Others will consider the pragmatic approach inadequate, for to them the necessary factor is faithfulness to Christ and his teaching. More traditional preachers will stress inner peace as a necessary prelude to becoming a peacemaker. Other pastors will take a confrontational stance in the "Christ versus culture" style. A dialogic preaching style seems to be most effective because it recognizes diversity within the congregation on the peace issue, while at the same time proclaiming the biblical message of *shalom* and recognizing the consistent witness of the Church of the Brethren in its official statements as a pacifist denomination. Sermons may include poems, short readings, or eyewitness accounts of wartime events.

Children's Story. Worship in most Brethren churches includes a time for the children to come to the chancel. Stories that children understand are an excellent way to pass on the vision of God's *shalom* as understood by the Brethren. Folk songs, puppets, and dramatic sketches can illustrate ways to deal with conflict that are alternatives to retaliation. Older worshipers find it meaningful to hear the children speak of their hopes and fears during a time of crisis.

Signs and Symbols. Banners, artistic displays on the worship table, bulletin covers, and posters add to an emphasis on peace. An Illinois congregation was being televised on a Chicago station during the Vietnam War. It was not anything spoken or sung that evoked the numerous phone calls of disconcerted viewers to the station, but a depiction of the peace symbol on the worship table.

Silence. With issues of life and death erupting in our consciousness, with young people taking positions that may subject them to harassment and possible imprisonment, with some Brethren withholding war taxes, which could lead to governmental liens against their property, a reality of costly discipleship can hang heavily over a congregation. Thus, it can be extremely important for worship to include quiet moments when the brothers and sisters of faith can drink deeply of the life-giving water that Christ offers. The silence can be a time to "count the cost" or a time to "go to the barricades." The outcome of a crisis such as the 1962 Cuban missile confrontation between the United States and the USSR is often unknown. When such crises have a potential for war and even for nuclear holocaust, silence in worship, during which members of the congregation seek to be still and listen for the voice of God, is imperative.

Commissioning and Benediction. The worship experience provides an occasion to send forth people representing the faith community to some witness for peace or some action of social service to build or strengthen _shalom_. Through the laying on of hands, those making the witness or engaging in the service can sense the prayers and support of those regarded as representatives of Christ's body. Here, the Brethren and others can see the great encouragement of a relationship built on mutual accountability. The one being sent forth is acting out of God's concern for peace. Every person in the Church of the Brethren does not need to duplicate the action, but each can participate vicariously. Thus, everyone feels some involvement in the effort to make the church a model on earth of what God intends in heaven, as the prayer of Jesus envisions.

There are other ways to bring the peace theme into the worship setting. Many traditions exchange a greeting of peace at some point in the liturgy. Litanies and responsive readings can give voice to deep, heartfelt concerns that the gods of war be curbed in their thirst for the blood of young and old alike. Even the time for announcements may include a citing of opportunities to fulfill that beatitude, "Blessed are the peacemakers" (Matt. 5:9). There are times when people leaving worship service can sign a pledge or write a letter of concern that will embody the congregation's commitment to peacemaking activities. Offerings to support those engaged in a peace witness can be another expression of how seriously the congregation makes the connection between personal faith and social action.

There will always be a vital connection between worship and peace. Without the Spirit's enabling action through corporate and private worship, the peace activist can become a frustrated, impatient, and bitter disciple of the Prince of peace. Without Christian brothers and sisters willing to embody a peace concern in their witness and service, the worship of a congregation can become shallow ritual, empty of meaning and devoid of possibilities to become an expression of Christ's peaceable kingdom.

Dean M. Miller

119 • CHURCH OF GOD, ANDERSON, INDIANA

In ascribing worth to God, worshipers find themselves confronting God's presence in the whole of life. In this entry, a representative of the Church of God, Anderson, Indiana, explores the relationships between worship and evangelism, pastoral care, social ministry, and inclusiveness toward all people.

The Westminster Confession states that "the chief end of man is to glorify God and enjoy Him forever." Before the mission of the church can be fully realized, there must be an appreciation and understanding of the importance of worship. The mission of the church flows out of the believers' love for the Lord of the church.

Worship is the believers' positive response to the revelation of God. Worship means _worth-ship,_ or in other words, to give someone the honor or worth that is due that person's name. The Holy Scriptures speak of worship as bowing down: "Come, let us bow down in worship, let us kneel before the LORD, our Maker" (Ps. 95:6). In addition, the Scriptures indicate that worship is a sacrifice of service: "O LORD, truly I am your servant. . . . I will sacrifice a thank offering to you and call on the name of the LORD" (Ps. 116:16-17).

The prophet Isaiah described worship as revelation and response: "I saw the Lord seated on the throne, high and exalted. . . . Holy, holy, holy is the LORD Almighty; the whole earth is full of his glory" (Isa. 6:1, 3). In the context of worship, Isaiah senses the worthiness of God and his own inadequacy. However, in his weakness, Isaiah is made strong by the touch of God's grace. Thus, Isaiah responds with the only appropriate response, "Here am I. Send me!" (Isa. 6:8b)

Worship is complete when the encounter with God issues forth in ministry to and with others. The church meets for divine worship to give praise to God, the Creator of all. However, the gathered church does not represent all of the life of the church. The worshiping community exists credibly only when it remains true to its calling to be the church, not only gathered, but scattered.

Inclusiveness in Worship

Worship involves the recognition that all persons, regardless of race, class, or gender, can experience the grace of God as it is revealed in Jesus Christ. On the day of Pentecost, Peter spoke of a new era in the history of God's revelatory acts: "In the last days, God says, I will pour out my Spirit on all people. Your sons and daughters will prophesy, your young men will see visions, your old men will dream dreams" (Acts 2:17). The apostle Paul speaks of this new wave of grace and ministry when he writes: "There is neither Jew nor Greek, slave nor free, male nor female, for you are all one in Christ Jesus" (Gal. 3:28).

In relation to inclusiveness, scriptural hermeneutics must be approached with caution. One must be cautious not to superimpose culture and circumstances of the first century upon the church of the present century. For example, some of St. Paul's correctives to the church were written within the Jewish culture, which forbade women to learn and take part in the synagogue services. These passages were also written in the Greek culture, which did not protects the rights of women as persons and citizens in their law.

The church in the age of the Spirit must consistently challenge women and men, young and old, to respond positively to the revelation of Christ. Worship demands response, whether that response is to an ordained or non-ordained ministry status. If women have equal access to the grace of God, then women in ministry should not be the exception, but rather the rule. Women with gifts of teaching, preaching, or leading must not be relegated to some secondary status, but be given full participation in church life. Women with the charisma of leadership should serve capably on official boards and committees in a fellowship of leadership. When women meet the criteria for the ordination process, then there seems to be no biblical or rational obstacle to their taking full participation in church leadership.

Worship and Pastoral Care

The church at worship also provides ongoing opportunities for pastoral care. When the Word of God is proclaimed, it often encourages, enlightens, instructs, and sometimes rebukes. One of the ways the church can minister, not only to the corporate needs of the body, but also to the personal needs of members, is through the ministry of the open altar. The open altar gives people opportunity to immediately act on truth that has been revealed to them in the context of worship. Worship should provide people with access to counsel and prayer in the immediacy of the moment. Worship that allows persons to respond in this immediate manner seeks to be relevant to the issues that worshipers bring to the service from week to week. While in-depth counseling does not take place in the service of worship, prayer and counsel at the public altar often open up other opportunities in other contexts to continue the pastoral care of the congregation.

Worship and Evangelism

Evangelism is also a part of the effective worship experience. The proclamation of the gospel of Christ to the unchurched can and should be an integral part of worship. There is a contagious factor about the faith of a community of believers.

While not every worship service is evangelistic in nature, there should be periodic opportunities throughout the year for nonbelievers to respond to what God has done for them in Christ. This response can be facilitated in a number of different ways: by allowing people to pray the sinner's prayer in the privacy of their pew; by inviting people forward to stand at the front of the church as a public testimony of their commitment to Christ; by giving people the opportunity to kneel at a public altar to pray a prayer of repentance; by allowing people to express through uplifted hands a decision for Christ; or by asking people to fill out a commitment card concerning their new decision for Christ, to be followed up at a later date. Christian baptism is also a vital part of public worship as new believers declare their faith in Jesus Christ.

Worship and Social Ministry

Worship that takes place in spirit and truth is worship that offers up the whole of life as a sacrifice of praise. "And do not forget to do good and to share with others, for with such sacrifices God is pleased" (Heb. 13:16). Worship compels some individuals to seek justice and do righteousness. Often a social consciousness is awakened in worship that leads some worshipers to be involved in crossing barriers and becoming involved in social issues.

Social issues are addressed consistently when hearts have been stirred by God. Receptive worshipers provide a linkage between the sanctuary and the streets. For example, some choose to be involved in such social issues as abortion counseling, picketing, and letter writing to create public awareness of theological and moral concerns about abortion. Others are involved in working with handicapped adults by providing a place to meet their particular needs, and then by incorporating them into the worship life of the church at large. Still others respond to worship by seeking to be involved with such groups as Habitat for Humanity in creating decent and affordable housing for the poor. Still others are involved in working with other congregations from the inner city to bring about race reconciliation. These examples are a few of the practical ways that some people choose to respond in worship to the social concerns of the day. In the words of William Temple:

> Worship is the submission of all our nature to God. It is the quickening of conscience by His holiness; the nourishment of mind with His truth; the purifying of imagination by His beauty; the opening of the heart to His love; the surrender of the will to His purpose. And all this is gathered up in adoration, the most selfless emotion of which our nature is capable.

William Hurst

120 ♦ CHURCH OF GOD, CLEVELAND, TENNESSEE

During most of its first century of existence, the Church of God, Cleveland, Tennessee, has concentrated on a free and enthusiastic personal response to the Lord in worship. Other concerns, such as education, social ministry, pastoral care, and gender inclusiveness, have not been related to the worship service as such. In recent decades, however, this pattern has begun to change.

Worship from the heart, evidenced by enthusiastic and often emotional response, is the heritage of the Church of God, Cleveland, Tennessee. Such worship results from an emphasis on two dimensions. First, God is worthy of the congregation's praise. The Bible declares God's glory and holiness, and further, directs the children of God to worship God. Therefore, as obedient and loving children of God, believers offer heartfelt, extroverted worship as their normal action when they gather in the sanctuary. Second, worship is a vital means by which we as believers commune with God and express our adoration, praise, and thanksgiving.

——— Worship and Social Ministry ———

During most of its founding century, the Church of God (Cleveland) has given little consideration to the extended results of worship that should accompany the believer upon leaving the sanctuary. This neglect has been due to a strong emphasis on the divine direction and impact facilitated through the preached Word. How we as believers should live and how we should approach a wide variety of issues were considered the concern of the pulpit, rather than the outcome of the Holy Spirit's impression on us through worship. In summary, the church felt that we speak to God through worship, while God speaks to us through the preached Word and the gifts of the Spirit. This division caused many in the church to view worship as separate from preaching. Scripture reading, prayer, and singing tended to become preliminaries to the more important preaching aspect of the service.

Like other evangelical and Pentecostal denominations, the Church of God (Cleveland) has held to the Matthean commission of Christ for its direction (Matt. 28:19-20). "Winning the lost" and missions outreach have received the greatest emphasis. Social action has been largely absent from the worship and practice of local congregations. One exception has been the care of orphans. In 1920, the Church of God opened a small orphanage in Cleveland, Tennessee. This project has developed into the very modern cottage-style Home for Children located in Sevierville, Tennessee. Within the denomination there are several other homes for children, as well as facilities for troubled youth and unwed mothers. Mother's Day became the Sunday designated for every congregation to receive an offering for the support of the Home for Children.

Within the past decade, a growing social consciousness has emerged within local congregations. Food pantries and benevolence funds for the needy both within and outside the church have been developed. The international denominational leadership also directs funds and needed items to disaster areas. Despite all this, a social consciousness does not seem to find regular expression in worship. This will require both time and education.

Worship and Education

An interesting contradiction on the issue of education, relating to Sunday school and formal education, has been, and at times still is, evident within the worship experience of the denomination. On one hand, from its earliest years, the Church of God (Cleveland) has recognized the role of the Sunday school. Not only does the Sunday school ground children and adults in the Word of God, but it also is used as a tool for church planting. Individuals are encouraged to start a Sunday school in a community as the first step in beginning a new church. In established congregations, Sunday school classes used to be featured in the opening minutes of the worship service by having a class recite their Scripture memory verses and sing their songs. More recently, this practice has been replaced in most congregations with children's choirs and children's church. Thus, children are not as much a part of the worship services as in previous decades.

On the other hand, formal education in areas other than the Bible, music, or basic communication skills was not only frowned upon, but openly preached against. It was viewed as a sure means of destroying spirituality. As a result, the denomination's schools were Bible schools that also included some junior college classes. In turn, the ministers produced by these schools tended to share a limited view of the role of education in the worship of the church. However, the 1960s saw a dramatic change of attitude on this question. Subsequently, all schools related to the Church of God (Cleveland) experienced major advances in enrollment, curriculum, and accreditation.

Women in Worship

The role of women in worship has been much more advanced in the Church of God (Cleveland) than in many other denominations, especially early in the twentieth century. As early as 1909, women became licensed ministries (the second rank of ministry). However, their license did not allow them to officiate at marriage ceremonies or the celebration of Communion, as it did for their male counterparts.

Women were on the cutting edge of evangelism and church planting during both the founding and growing decades of the church. Lay women have regularly served as worship leaders or exercised their spiritual gifts from the pew. Furthermore, women may serve as pastors of local congregations, but cannot be ordained. At the 1992 International General Assembly, women were granted the right to vote on the assembly floor. This action will definitely spur greater discussion on the issue of ordination of women.

Worship and Pastoral Care

The ministry of pastoral care through worship is a relatively new area of consideration within the Church of God (Cleveland). Here too, the emphasis on direction and care through the ministry of the Word and the "seasons of prayer" at the altar has overshadowed the broad impact of worship. The possibility of experiencing the benefits of pastoral care through worship is a dimension only now being explored as part of the increased study of worship that has recently arisen in the denomination. The issue is being discussed in college and seminary classes in pastoral theology and worship.

Cell groups, covenant groups, and other special groups (such as Young Mothers, DADS) exist increasingly in the denomination, more often in larger churches than in smaller ones. A few leaders have experimented with sermon discussion groups, but they have been short-lived due to lack of enthusiasm for this format on the part of both people and pastors.

For a century the hallmark of the Church of God (Cleveland) and its fellow Pentecostal groups has been a vibrant, free style of worship. Allowing individuals to express their inner emotions and expressions through a wide variety of verbal means, gestures, and postures has been the goal of worship services. The challenge is to retain this fresh breath of the Spirit, which so many Christian groups are attempting to regain, while expanding the content of worship to include other areas of concern.

Jerald Daffe

121 • CHURCH OF THE NAZARENE

The spontaneity permitted in Nazarene worship, along with the warm evangelistic thrust of the corporate gathering, has helped to create an openness to the integration of worship with other facets of congregational life such as pastoral care and women's ministries.

On a recent Sunday in a Nazarene church in a midwestern city, a young man home from college sang a solo. Just as he finished and the pastor approached the pulpit to preach, a woman in the choir asked, "Could he sing it again?" So, after the soundtrack was rewound, the song was repeated. About two dozen gathered at the altar for prayer. This was followed by forty-five minutes of testimonies. Dismissal was a half hour later than usual.

Spontaneity has long been accepted in the Nazarene worship format. While an incident like the one described is not routine, neither is it unusual. The essence and spirit of Nazarene worship stems from revivalism and the life of the camp meetings that flourished during the nineteenth century.

Worship, Evangelism, and Mission. One of the most significant features of worship in the Church of the Nazarene is that worship is inseparable from evangelism. That is, the generally evangelistic fervency found in both preaching and singing contributes to spontaneity in the worship style, especially in the use of the altar rail as a place of confession and reconciliation. Churches may also schedule a time of general or specific testimony, during which worshipers may give voice to the operation of God in their lives. Such practices tip the "playing field" of worship in favor of human responses to impressions felt to be from the Lord. That is why pastors, regardless of their personal intuition in a given service, are inclined to remain sensitive to the feelings of parishioners who make suggestions—such as to sing a solo a second time.

Evangelism is practiced during the entire worship service, and especially at the usual invitation to pray after the sermon. The connection between worship and evangelism—personal soul-winning outside the walls of the church—is also visible in the reception of new members by profession of faith during a worship service.

Another feature of Nazarene worship is its historic identification with support for missions as a form of practicing "social concern" both at home and abroad. Every Nazarene church is expected to pay its annual missions budget, which is based on a percentage of the church's annual income. Thus, Nazarenes are familiar with a wide variety of special offerings for world and home missions. The local church is usually directly involved in other mission projects which require offerings above those designated by the denomination. For example, as needed, a church may receive "crisis" offerings for families in emergency situations and "benevolence" offerings for people in need.

A Nazarene church board may have a Spiritual Development Committee with general oversight of worship. Such a committee is a sounding board for worship expectation, assessment, and practice. Ministries related to music, prayer, preaching, and other components of worship are the concern of this committee.

Women and Children in Worship. Since its inception, the Church of the Nazarene has recognized the ministry of women in the official capacity of deaconess and has ordained women since its early days. Women have served as ordained pastors, evangelists, missionaries, and educators. While men have held the preponderance of leadership roles in worship, women have not been excluded from such involvement. They may take part in Scripture reading, praying, and a variety of music activities. They may even address the congregation. Worship leaders of the local church may also remind the congregation of the church's often extensive agenda of women's programs and ministries. Involvement of children in worship may take the form of children's sermons and children's participation in choirs or smaller groups.

Education and Pastoral Care. With respect to the integration of education and worship, some congregations have successfully formed into a number of small groups to study the Sunday morning sermon and its scriptural context in midweek home gatherings. In a few churches, select Sunday school classes are studying the context of the pastor's sermon as a biblical curriculum prior to worship.

Pastoral care concerns are brought into the worship setting through the pastoral prayer and through the attention given to the prayer needs of members of the church family, such as those hospitalized, those confined to their home, and those recently bereaved. Some churches involve lay people in the ministry of pastoral care and may hold a periodic commissioning service for those who have been trained in the listening and counseling skills needed in this work.

James R. Spruce

122 • CHURCHES OF CHRIST (NONINSTRUMENTAL)

A strong renewing movement within the Churches of Christ has made its impact on the integration of worship with other areas of ministry. While worship has historically been evangelistic in emphasis and focused on the preaching of the Word, in many congregations these emphases are shifting to small group ministry and the renewal of corporate praise to God in the worship assembly.

God is the focus of worship. Worship is a divine activity because of the involvement of the Father, the Son, and the Holy Spirit. At the same time, worship is a human activity. We cannot discuss worship without considering its relationship to individuals, groups, and various ministries of the church. What is the relationship of worship in the Churches of Christ to contemporary issues such as social action or the role of women in the church?

The Role of Women

Until recently, the question of women's role in worship was seldom raised in Churches of Christ. Based on the church's interpretation of passages such as 1 Timothy 3:1-13 and Titus 1:6-9, women did not meet the qualifications for serving as elders or deacons in the church. According to the church's interpretation of other New Testament passages, there are no public leadership roles women can fill in the worship assembly. If women must remain silent in the church (1 Cor. 14:34-35), and if they must not teach men or have authority over them in the assembly (1 Tim. 2:11-12), then they are prohibited from key worship leadership roles such as preaching, reading Scripture, and leading prayers. Women often fill many other positions of leadership in the congregation, such as leaders of Bible school and benevolence ministries. However, in the public worship assembly of the Churches of Christ, women are led—they do not lead.

These convictions concerning women's roles in worship leadership still largely characterize Churches of Christ, even among the majority of those engaged in worship renewal. There are some rare exceptions to this position. A few congregations (primarily those who sing a lot of praise music) may use a mixed worship team to lead singing. A few congregations use mixed groups of men and women to usher and to serve the Lord's Supper.

The issue of the women's role in worship leadership has not been a burning question in Churches of Christ—at least not yet. With few exceptions, the issue is largely ignored. However, as women continue to assume increasingly more responsible leadership positions in the marketplace, this issue is likely to become a greater concern to the church.

Worship and Social Action

One area that is beginning to see some change in many renewing Churches of Christ is the way worship relates to social action. The growing popularity of expository preaching has enabled worshipers to see the practical applications of Scripture to daily living. The Bible announces God's concern for the poor, the fatherless, the widow, and the homeless. God wants the people of God to be individuals of integrity, compassion, mercy, and justice.

An example of a Church of Christ responding in social involvement is the Madison Church of Christ in Nashville, Tennessee. For more than thirty years, this congregation has heard sermons which have encouraged its members to get involved in the lives of needy and hurting people. The church has built an extensive benevolence ministry, which helps thousands each year with such services as food, furniture, clothing, foster homes for children, domestic violence counseling for abused women and children, a meals-on-wheels program for shut-ins, and a "room-in-the-inn" program, which provides hot meals and temporary housing for the homeless. Yet social concerns are not viewed as the focus of worship; worship belongs to the Lord alone. However, many congregations view social action as a natural outgrowth of worship.

Spiritual Formation in Small Groups

Another resource helping to bring about renewal in worship in the Churches of Christ is the small group ministry. These groups take a variety of forms. Some are Bible studies that follow a carefully prepared curriculum. Other groups meet just to praise the Lord in song, read the Bible, and pray. Some meet on the church campus, while others meet in homes. Some meet early in the morning, while others meet at night. No standard pattern exists concerning the formation of these groups. Some groups are formed within Bible school classes; others are formed by random selection; and still others are formed by assignment. All of these groups are formed on a voluntary basis—people choose whether or not they want to be in a group.

A number of congregations are following a small group format that looks something like the following. On the second Sunday evening of each month, each small group meets in a home, rather than assembling at the church building. The meeting includes a time of informal fellowship (refreshments are optional). Next, the group joins in a period of prayer and praise. During these sessions, many people learn some of the new praise songs that are being used so effectively in worship renewal. The group leader then shows a brief video clip, which serves as the basis for discussion. The session concludes with more praise and a time for prayer requests. The entire period may last an hour and a half. Almost without exception, congregations that have adopted this format have found the combined attendance at all the small groups greater than the attendance at the assembly at the church building.

Some congregations coordinate Bible school curriculum with the themes of worship services. For example, the Madison Church of Christ studied the topic of worship for thirteen weeks in its adult Bible school classes. During this quarter-long study, the preacher delivered lessons that paralleled the Bible school emphasis on worship. Each service was carefully planned to help people learn how to both worship God appropriately and experience the joy of true worship. This dual approach made an impact on the congregation that would have been impossible if only the Bible school or the sermon alone had been used to communicate the worship theme.

Worship and Evangelism

Worship also has a relation to evangelism in the Churches of Christ. Most sermons conclude with an invitation to the audience to make a public response to the call of God. Throughout most of this century, sermons were highly evangelistic. Lessons were carefully prepared and earnestly delivered to convert those who were not Christians. This evangelistic emphasis probably grew out of the American frontier tradition.

Congregations interested in worship renewal are also interested in converting lost sinners. However, they question the highly pragmatic approach that makes conversion of the lost the primary focus of worship services. Worship leaders in worship renewal churches insist that God is the focus of worship, and that our primary motivation for assembling on the Lord's day is not to convert sinners (although that is extremely important), but to adore the Father. They believe that when God's people worship God as he deserves to be praised, unbelievers will become conscious of their sin and will also fall down and worship him (1 Cor. 14:24-25).

Dan Dozier

123 ✦ CONGREGATIONAL CHURCHES

In Congregational churches, the relationship between worship and other ministries becomes apparent when the church covenant is seen as the link between the formal worship of the gathered church and the other activities of service and witness which make up the life of the church.

Congregational churches are gathered around the church _covenant,_ in which the members pledge their loyalty to God and to one another in their common pursuit of the Christian life. An example is the covenant of the church established in Salem, Massachusetts, in 1629, the first Congregational church to be founded in what is now the United States. (The church of the pilgrims at Plymouth had been founded in Holland.) The Salem covenant reads, in modernized spelling:

> We covenant with the Lord and one with another and do bind ourselves in the presence of God, to walk together in all his ways, according as he is pleased to reveal himself unto us in his blessed Word of truth.

Whenever a new Congregational church is established, a suitable covenant is drawn up and adopted. New members joining the church thereafter "own the covenant" as theirs.

Congregationalism, according to its most thoughtful interpreters, is not simply democracy or independence in church government. Indeed, church government is regarded as Christocentric; the Spirit of Christ is the final authority. For this reason, most Congregational churches acknowledge no creed or statement of faith except the Holy Scriptures. There is no centralized denominational authority; denominational agencies exist to serve the local churches. On the other hand, cooperation and fellowship among churches of like mind are highly valued in the Congregational tradition.

Because of decentralization, the worship format of each Congregational church is the responsibility of its congregation and pastoral leadership, according to their understanding of Scriptural principles. For this reason, the order of worship in a Congregational church may not differ greatly from that of other churches in the community. Nevertheless, there is a sense in which the church's *covenant* provides the underlying structure for its worship. The covenant may be recited as a regular act during the worship service, similar to the way creeds are used in sacramentally oriented churches. This covenant basis for worship is what links the formal worship of Congregational churches with related ministries, such as education, evangelism, pastoral care, or church administration.

Worship and Administration

The decision-making function in Congregational churches is vested in the congregational meeting. The minister and all officers and committees are responsible to the congregational meeting, and serve at its discretion. Because, ideally, a congregational meeting is called for the purpose of discovering the mind of Christ and applying his purposes to the business of the local church, an integral connection exists between worship and church administration.

Worship is the affirmation that "Jesus is Lord." Where this simple New Testament creed and covenant declaration is the conscious basis for the decision-making process, church meetings—not only the congregational meeting, but those of other groups and committees—flow naturally into the worship mode. Specific acts of worship during such meetings—hymns, prayers, and the reading and brief exposition of the Word—serve to remind all participants of what must be the true aim of their gathering, the exaltation of the name of Jesus.

Worship and Outreach

Evangelism, the sending and supporting of missionaries, and the ministries of social concern and witness are motivated by the desire to extend the Lord's offer of the covenant to members of the human family who have yet to respond to the gospel or to accept its benefits. To acknowledge the authority of Christ the King is to place oneself under that divine order which alone brings meaning, wholeness, and dignity to the human enterprise. The imperative of evangelism is an imperative of worship: "that at the name of Jesus every knee should bow . . . and every tongue confess that Jesus Christ is Lord, to the glory of God the Father" (Phil. 2:10-11).

As Christ emptied himself that this worship might become a reality (Phil. 2:7), so the church empties itself in ministries of benevolence and social involvement. By emptying itself in this manner, the church points beyond its own prerogatives to the greater sovereignty of the living God, who graciously offers to all who receive it that bond of mutual responsibility: "I will be their God, and they will be my people" (Jer. 31:33). In this bond, God comforts those who are sorrowful; wipes their tears away; and restores the errant and disadvantaged to that relationship of worship and community for which their Maker has designed them (Rev. 21:3-4).

Worship and Church Fellowship

The covenant of the local Congregational church involves an incipient covenant with all Christians and Christian bodies united in the same end, the true service of the Lord of lords. Congregationalists have manifested an historic openness to fellowship with other churches in the community in acts of cooperative witness to the sovereignty of Christ. These acts may take the form of united worship at particular seasons, such as Lent or Thanksgiving, or special times of prayer and intercession for the nation and community.

In conducting its affairs as a Congregational church, the local body often has occasion to participate with other Congregational churches in ecclesiastical councils, usually for the purpose of examining candidates for ordination to the ministry. Such events, far from being mere procedural exercises, are often times of reverent and intense inquiry into the expression of Christian truth. The ordination or installation of a new pastoral leader brings churches together for celebration, as do regional or national assemblies convened to transact denominational business and further the churches' corporate witness. Such events are often occasions of worship and ceremony, made possible by the covenanted relationship of sister churches.

Worship and Educational Ministries

The educational ministries of the church serve to advance the understanding of the covenant and its implications in ways appropriate to the learning level and spiritual maturity of each group involved. At the heart of the covenant, in most Congregational churches, is the promise to abide by the principles of the Word of God. The Scriptures, therefore, are the content of the covenant and the foundational subject matter for all educational ministries, whatever their specific or momentary focus. At its best, the educational program of a Congregational church is an extension of the service of the Word, the historic counterpart to the service of the Lord's Table in Christian liturgy.

The training of younger members of the church family is an activity of Christian nurture in fulfillment of the vow made by parents and the congregation in the solemn ceremony of baptism or dedication of these children. In this way, children and young people are guided in preparing for the worship act of covenanting or confirmation, which will symbolize their entrance into the adult responsibilities of Christian discipleship.

Christian education—whether of children, youth, or adults—is undertaken in the conviction that the Scriptures are inspired and "useful for teaching, rebuking, correcting and training in righteousness, so that the man [or woman] of God may be thoroughly equipped for every good work" (2 Tim. 3:16-17). Through educational ministries, Christians are prepared for genuine worship, not only for "worship in spirit" through visible manifestation of commitment, but also for "worship in

The Cross of Four Pheons. *This cross is made up of four dart heads whose points touch. It symbolizes the "fiery darts of the wicked" and the duty of the Christian to resist them through the power of the cross.*

truth," according to the principles of God's Word and in fulfillment of the biblical vow to offer a tribute of praise.

Worship and Pastoral Care

The covenanted people of God are "the people of his pasture, the flock under his care" (Ps. 95:7). The work of the pastor is undertaken in response to Jesus' mandate to Peter and the other apostles, "Take care of my sheep" (John 21:17). In counseling, the pastor-shepherd seeks to guide those bound in dysfunctional behavior patterns toward amendment of life through application of the principles of God's covenant with its promise of blessing as the reward for obedience. The troubled and depressed may be led toward healing through the nurture of the church community. This community finds its expression in Christian worship, as articulated by Paul, "Is not the bread that we break a participation in the body of Christ?" (1 Cor. 10:16). The goal of pastoral care will be to help the hurting to "own the covenant" in every way and to make the life-giving confession that Jesus is Lord.

The pastoral approach to both marital and premarital counseling involves the recognition that the covenant of marriage between Christian believers is a reflection of the greater covenant between Christ and his bride, the church (Eph. 5:25-33; Rev. 21:2). At another stage in life's continuum, the pastor-shepherd proclaims the Lord's faithfulness when standing with those passing through the sorrow of bereavement. Whether celebrating the witness of departed saints or interpreting the life-opportunities in response to the gospel for those who remain, the shepherd communicates the value of the covenant bond and calls attention to its imperative to worship and acknowledge the sovereignty of an all-wise God.

While much that has been said applies to all Christian churches, the covenant of Congregational churches gives special verbal expression to that relationship of corporate life in which the links between worship and related ministries and activities may be forged.

Richard C. Leonard

124 ◆ Eastern Orthodox Churches

The Divine Liturgy of the Eucharist has been the historic center of life in Eastern Orthodox churches. The liturgy is the means of spiritual formation. All other ministries of the church--such as education, evangelism, or pastoral care—serve to relate people to the liturgy as the locus for experiencing the presence and power of God.

For the Eastern Orthodox church, the eucharistic liturgy is the central constituting experience of the church. In the Eucharist, the church both expresses what it is—the body of Christ—and is made into what it is by partaking of the body of Christ. Worship is the center and the reason for the church's existence. Every other aspect of the church's life flows from participation in this sacrament. In the Eucharist, the fullness of communion with God is found. Salvation, for the Orthodox Christian, is to be transformed, both individually and corporately, into the fullness of the image and likeness of God. We, Orthodox Christians, exist for God and exist to commune with God.

Spiritual Formation through the Liturgy

Worship and liturgy therefore are central in the Orthodox church's practice and understanding of spiritual formation. Orthodoxy understands the goal of the Christian life to be the transformation of the human person into the fullness of the likeness of Christ, a process called *theosis* or deification by the Fathers of the church. For Orthodox Christians, spiritual formation is more than a change in behavior patterns or a growth in knowledge of scriptural truth. It is the progressive participation in the energies of God, a communion with God that transforms Orthodox Christians "from glory to glory," into the fullness of the likeness of God. The eucharistic liturgy, above all others, is the place where we, Orthodox Christians, "taste the powers of the age to come." Thus, in the Eucharist, we are formed and changed spiritually.

This transformation is accomplished in several ways. First, the preparation for partaking of Communion is itself spiritually forming for Orthodox Christians. Orthodox worshipers are conscious that the Eucharist, the body and blood of Christ, is holy and is approached only in a worthy manner. "Holy things are for the Holy!" the priest declares in the liturgy. The people respond, "One is Holy; One is the Lord Jesus Christ, to the glory of God the Father. *Amen*." Prayers, confession, and fasting are used as means of preparing for participation in Communion. These actions are not viewed as works of law, able to make the participants worthy in themselves of communion with God, but as means by which their hearts can be made soft and ready to receive the grace, forgiveness, and mercy that God wants to give them. "With the fear of God, with faith, and with love, draw near."

Particularly important is the sacrament of confession. In it, the Orthodox Christian is able to receive spiritual counsel and enter into prayers focused on the individual's pilgrimage toward spiritual maturity. Fasting reminds the individual that "man does not live on bread alone" (Matt. 4:4), and begins to take the heart from the things of this world to the things of heaven. Prayer, of course, is the essence of an individual's personal communion with God.

The liturgy itself shapes the spiritual understanding of the Orthodox Christian. The first section of the Liturgy of St. John Chrysostom (the service ordinarily used in the Orthodox church) is called the liturgy of the Word. During this time, psalms, the Beatitudes, and special hymns (called *troparia* and *kontakia*) that focus upon the theme of the day are sung. This liturgy calls Orthodox Christians to meditate upon various aspects of what Christ has done for them, the meaning of his resurrection, and his teachings regarding their manner of life. Further, there are readings from the Scriptures, at least one reading from the Epistles and one from the Gospels. In the Orthodox church, the readings follow an annual pattern correlated to the celebrations of events in the life of Christ or of the saints. The sermon usually follows the Gospel reading, and generally explicates the themes of the Scripture readings.

Following the sermon, prayers are said for all in need. Then begins the procession to the "holy of holies," where the Orthodox worshiper will taste the body and blood of Christ. In a beautiful procession, the paten and the chalice with the bread and the wine are brought to the altar from the table of preparation. The kiss of peace is exchanged, calling the faithful to be in unity with one another. Prayers of thanksgiving for the greatness of God's saving work are offered to God. Then the celebrant asks God to "Send down your Holy Spirit on us and on these gifts, making this bread the body of Your Christ, and that which is in this cup, the precious blood of Your Christ, changing them by Your Holy Spirit." Finally, the people of God approach the chalice, where they partake in the mystery of him who is the Bread of Life. Having partaken of this mystery, the worshiper, changed and renewed by the grace of the sacrament, returns to the world.

For the Orthodox Christian, all spiritual formation comes from communion with God. Prayer, fasting, almsgiving, reading the Scriptures, reading the writings of holy persons, and participating in the sacrament of confession are all means by which we as Orthodox Christians are changed into his likeness. But the chief instrument in forming that image in us is the Eucharist.

Orthodoxy does not view the Eucharist as a mere symbol, if by that word one means something that is a sign of some other reality that is not present in that thing. We, as Orthodox Christians, may not be able, nor willing, to explain how Christ is present in the bread and wine or how these elements can be proclaimed the body and blood of Christ. But we confess that these statements about the bread and wine are true because the Holy Spirit has the power to perform these tasks. Worship services are not primarily designed to inform us of spiritual truths; they are means by which we actually commune with and encounter the living God.

Liturgy and Evangelism

Evangelism, education, and pastoral care in the Orthodox church are designed to bring people to the fullest experience of God in the Eucharist.

Evangelism is not the primary goal of an Orthodox Christian service. Worship is the primary goal. There is a significant difference between what happens in a typical Protestant church and what occurs in Orthodox services. Evangelism takes place through instructional classes, Bible studies, personal conversations, seminars, programs, literature distribution, preaching, and so on. When a person has come to faith, that person, then, is brought systematically into the full experience of life in the church, generally through completing a course of catechetical instruction. Orthodox meetings rarely have "altar calls," in which those present are asked to come forward and commit their lives to Christ. Conversion is seen as a process. It may begin in a moment, but the transformation of necessity will take time. The "altar call" for Orthodox Christians is a call to participation in the full sacramental life of the church, and is fulfilled only in partaking of the Eucharist. For those who are converts, the partaking of the Eucharist comes at the end of the process of catechesis.

Because the Orthodox church for many centuries primarily has existed in societies in which the overwhelming majority of the people were already Orthodox Christians, the concept of evangelism and missions has only in recent times been revived. Efforts are currently under way to provide literature and liturgy in the languages of peoples who traditionally are not Orthodox and to aggressively renew the proclamation of the Good News of the Orthodox faith in North America, Africa, Asia, and other parts of the world.

Liturgy as a living demonstration of the encounter with God is a part of the evangelistic effort of Orthodoxy. Liturgy's end is not evangelism or education; its goal is the worship of God. But the worship of God is not ineffective for evangelism, for it is the Spirit of God who draws all people to God.

Liturgy and Education

The liturgical life of the church is also crucial in Christian education for the Orthodox Christian.

In societies such as the former Soviet Union and other communist countries, or in the Islamic world, the Orthodox church has not been allowed to carry on an active program of Christian education. In these circumstances, the richness of the scriptural and theological content of the liturgy has nurtured the understanding of the faithful. The Orthodox liturgy is literally filled with references to the Holy Scriptures. One of the most valuable resources is the liturgical calendar. At different times of the year, the various aspects of God's work for human salvation are emphasized. At Christmas, for example, the emphasis is upon the incarnation of the Word of God, and its meaning for the salvation of human nature. The hymn for Christmas morning declares the incarnational truth, "God is with us!"

One of the most important times of the year for Orthodox Christians is the preparation for Pascha (Easter), the holiest of holy days. Orthodox worshipers observe a forty-day period of prayer and fasting, coupled with repentance, in preparation for the celebration of the resurrection of Christ. During this time, they abstain from eating meat or meat products and participate in special services, including the Liturgy of the Presanctified Gifts.

During Holy Week, the week beginning with Lazarus Saturday and Palm Sunday and ending with Pascha, services are held commemorating the events of the passion of Christ. The gospel accounts are read; hymns are sung; and the church reenacts the solemn events. On Palm Sunday, the faithful receive palm branches and display them in procession around the church, showing their commitment to Christ as King. On Holy Thursday, the institution of the Lord's Supper is commemorated with a Communion service. On that evening, all of the Gospel accounts of the passion of Christ are read. The icon of Christ and his cross are carried around the church and set in the middle of the congregation. On Holy Friday, the faithful gather around the tomb of Christ to lament the death of the Creator and Giver of life and to look forward to the raising of Christ from the dead. Finally, in the darkness of Sunday morning, light comes into the church. The people process around the church by candlelight, coming with the myrrh-bearing women to the tomb, and enter the church with great joy to discover and affirm that "Christ is risen from the dead, trampling down death by death, and upon those in the tombs bestowing life."

These kinds of celebrations instruct the faithful in the truths of the gospel. Increasingly, Orthodox churches are instructing in other kinds of ways as well. Many parishes are using Sunday school programs, usually after the Divine Liturgy, for instruction. As an example, in Holy Resurrection parish in Hobart, Indiana, there are classes for all ages including adults. Bible study groups are held both in homes and in the churches. Often, during the Lenten season in particular, retreats and seminars, focusing on spirituality, prayer, and repentance, are popular. In most Orthodox parishes, the curriculum is designed to reflect the seasons and emphases of the church year. Special needs are met through special speakers, catechism classes, books and literature, and periodic seminars. Vacation church schools and summer youth camp programs, both of which have been used successfully by other Christian churches for many years, are being developed in many Orthodox churches and dioceses.

Small Group Ministries and the Liturgy

One new emphasis for Orthodox congregations is the development of small group structures for encouragement, ministry, fellowship, prayer, study, and pastoral care in the local parish. A number of churches are trying to develop networks of small groups to address certain needs in education and spiritual formation. These small groups then gather together as one community for worship.

Worship is the center of life in the Orthodox church. The goal of all programs of education and evangelism is to bring as many people as possible to participation in the worship of the triune God. Worship is not so much the means of accomplishing these things as it is the end. It is the center of spiritual formation because it is the center of communion with God, who forms Christians by the Holy Spirit.

Frederick Gregory Rogers

125 • Evangelical Covenant Churches

Though heir to the liturgical tradition of pietistic Lutheranism, the Evangelical Covenant Church adapted to a revivalist milieu in America with its focus on Scandinavian immigrants as the target group for evangelistic and pastoral outreach. A new sense of mission, however, pervades the denomination, creating expanded horizons both for worship and for ministry to the unchurched.

With its roots in the Lutheran state church of Sweden and the pietistic renewal in the mid-nineteenth century, the nascent Scandinavian immigrant church, which is today called the Evangelical Covenant Church, took on a character that retained the church's historic identity while adapting to the influences of American revivalism. The theological-historical nature of the Evangelical Covenant Church, coupled with its immigrant sociology, gave clear definition to its worship forms and to the influence of worship on related church ministries.

The Original Ethnic Focus

From its Lutheran roots, Covenant worship emphasized both Word and sacrament. American revivalism intensified the former and muted the latter. Pietism buttressed both of these aspects of worship and added the dimensions of personal and corporate prayer to worship. The development of all three emphases was focused on the needs of a particular ethnic group of immigrants to the New World, the Scandinavians. These liturgical, theological, and sociological characteristics gave both intensity and limitations to ministries of outreach, and were foundational for ministries of nurture and care.

Early Covenant worship was expressed in at least four forms. (1) On Sunday morning, a formal liturgy (_högmässan_, the "high mass") reduplicated Lutheran antecedents, without weekly Eucharist, but with an emphasis on the reading and preaching of the Word. Such worship was characterized by reverence, festivity, and dignified beauty. (2) Sunday evening worship was more informal. Serving both evangelistic and socialization functions, the emphasis in these services was on renewal, rebirth, the young, and those in the immigrant community who needed to "come home" to Jesus. (3) Usually, Wednesday evening prayer meetings reemphasized pietistic motifs of corporate prayer, Bible study, and the sharing of an individual's pilgrimage with the group. (4) Seasonal "mission meetings" in larger geographic

collectives underscored the immigrant church's primary values, which were the preaching and hearing of the Word and fellowship.

Ministries of outreach in the Covenant church have been, and continue to be, focused by revivalism, fueled by pietism, and shaped by Lutheranism both theologically and liturgically. Outreach in evangelism is a primary focus of the church. Evangelism occurs in the gathered community through the proclamation of the Word. Its public and verbal character is reproduced in camp meetings, revival services, and children's church. Even when conversion is a private act, its validity rests on public acknowledgment.

The pietistic concern that faith not only be believed, but lived, has produced outreach ministries that focus on the destitute in the community. The immigrant experience of church members contributes to their defining the recipients of care as those separated or distanced from community: the orphaned, the aged, the ill, or the wayfaring. Thus, the Covenant church in its outreach ministries established children's homes, hospitals, retirement homes, and seaman's missions. Such extensions of care were periodically tied to worship by special offerings in which those who were "safe" gave generously to ministries to the insecure.

Social Ministry and Pastoral Care

Several factors combined to constrain the Covenant church from any significant manifestation of outreach ministry as social action. These factors were a heritage of Lutheran two-kingdom theology, which imaged the church as a hospital, rather than an agency of change; a lack of a structural understanding of sin; and a political conservatism built on both revivalism and a "no-offense" attitude of a minority immigrant group. Social action is not in the liturgy or in the life of the church, except for isolated individuals, a few congregations in particular environments, and more recently in such new Covenant ethnic congregations as the African Americans.

Covenant worship has been much more intimately tied with related ministries of nurture and care. The primacy of the Word as read and preached has been a regular source of both instruction and comfort, or pastoral care, to its hearers. Though secondary to proclamation, the sacraments in the

Covenant churches have been and remain strong symbols and occasions of fellowship, care, healing, and spiritual renewal. This contribution from the Evangelical Covenant Church's Lutheran heritage has always been a matter both of contention from the revivalistic side and of sustaining comfort for those who have discovered, as the poet Auden said, that "only in rites are we fully entired."

Thus, more recently, spiritual formation through both Word and sacrament has become a motif in some Covenant churches. It is likely, as well, that in such churches the liturgical act of confirmation remains significant. This educational process and heritage of Lutheranism has been varyingly received and understood in Covenant churches. Even though in some churches confirmation is one of the central educational rites-of-passage for young persons, it has increasingly fallen out of favor because of the revivalist heritage, which views Christian nurture in a plateau model.

––––––––– **Renewed Sense of Mission** –––––––––

In the last two decades (beginning about 1972), pressures in American denominations affecting the maintenance of the church's organization in relation to its mission have likewise influenced the Covenant church. Departments of home mission have become departments of church growth and evangelism. There is a renewed emphasis on conversions, prayer, growth, and extension. Such phenomena have several liturgical consequences: (1) production of a hymnal supplement which includes many contemporary choruses and songs; (2) creation of a committee to completely revise the *Covenant Hymnal* and *Book of Worship;* and (3) divestiture of much of the liturgical heritage of the church for the sake of effective new church development or for the sake of reaching an unchurched population. This last concern is exemplified by some Covenant churches (that typically assume the name *community church*) which divest worship of any symbols such as pulpit, table, font, hymnal, vestment, ordered liturgy, office, or offering in order to make access to God "seeker-friendly" and nonthreatening to the religiously uninitiated. This evangelistically motivated, liturgically disparaging emphasis in several newer churches is balanced by churches who are committed to the liturgical tradition. Furthermore, this new emphasis is muted as well by generic evangelical expressions that hold on to worship patterns that may be dated, but are still comfortable.

At issue for the Evangelical Covenant Church and its future in liturgy, mission, and ministry is the effect that its growing number of non-Scandinavian ethnic congregations will have, particularly African American, Hispanic, and Korean congregations. New immigrants bring similar problems but new patterns. They name and frame their realities in fresh ways, rhythms, sights, and sounds. How these new groups will affect the Covenant heritage in its liturgical expressions in the church and the world is both an anxiety and adventure to the host heritage.

Richard W. Carlson

126 • EVANGELICAL FREE CHURCH OF AMERICA

The pattern of local church autonomy in the Evangelical Free Church of America results in great variety among the local churches in worship and in the impact of worship on other ministries. This entry selects one local region and congregation as a representative of what may be characteristic throughout the denomination of the relationship of worship to evangelism, education, social action, spiritual formation, and the role of women.

Churches affiliated with the Evangelical Free Church of America enjoy autonomy and broad freedom within the denomination. The confession of faith of the denomination's Ministerial Association declares "that Jesus Christ is the Lord and Head of the Church, and that every local church has the right under Christ to decide and govern its own affairs." Therefore, one cannot make sweeping generalizations about worship practices throughout the Evangelical Free Church of America. In discussing the ways in which worship relates to and informs the various ministries of Evangelical Free churches, I will limit the scope of this article to one representative area, the Great Lakes District, and particularly to one congregation, the Evangelical Free Church of Naperville, Illinois.

Worship and the Arts. Recently, a number of ministers of music and worship in the Great Lakes District formed a committee for worship and the arts. The purpose of this group is to help local churches to fulfill their purpose in worship. This group seeks to fulfill this purpose by (1) cultivating a scriptural understanding of worship as the church's highest priority; (2) providing resources and ideas for pastors and leaders, through a variety of forums; (3) encouraging musicians and artists in the local church; (4) promoting the development of interest in the arts in the local church, and (5) developing a network for communication among worship leaders in the district. To facilitate these purposes, ministers of music and worship from the Great Lakes District meet once a month to share ideas and resources and to pray for and encourage one another.

Worship and Evangelism. The Evangelical Free Church of Naperville, Illinois, a thirty-five-year-old congregation of about a thousand worshipers, serves as an example of a Free church dealing with the relationships between worship and other church ministries. The church has articulated as its task the fulfillment of Christ's great commission to make disciples and followers of all people (Matt. 28:19-20), and has sought to relate all ministries of the church, including worship, to this task.

Each worship service is viewed as an opportunity, not only for participation in the expressions of praise and worship to the Lord, but also for evangelism. Visitors often attend worship, and the church aims to be "visitor-friendly" and sensitive to those who are seeking a relationship with God. Wherever possible, archaisms and religious clichés are avoided in hymns and Scripture lessons. When teaching from the Scriptures, illustrations relevant to contemporary society are used. Often, people are invited to respond to the gospel in ways that demonstrate the Holy Spirit's prompting.

The congregation reaches out to the community through music/drama groups and concerts by guest artists. Evangelism Explosion teams visit those who attend worship services, welcoming them with a personal call.

Worship and Educational and Children's Ministries. The Evangelical Free Church of Naperville provides classes for the time of each of the three worship services. Worship services are not generally integrated with the education program, except during a week of special emphasis, such as missions. Usually worship services are targeted to an adult audience, although occasionally a children's message will be given in a morning worship service. A separate worship service is provided for children through the fourth grade. Currently the church is experimenting with a kids' bulletin to make the services more meaningful for children.

Sunday evening services focus on the family unit, with more attention given to the needs of junior and senior high school students. The service includes a fifteen- to twenty-minute period of upbeat contemporary praise led by a variety of worship teams with the piano and other instruments. Young people are also involved regularly in singing special music, playing accompanying instruments, reading the Scripture, or leading in prayer. Other features of this service include opportunities for spontaneous testimonies, the sharing of concerns, and prayer. Younger children take part in separate choir rehearsals and separate times of praise during the time of this service.

Worship is a key theme for the annual Great Lakes District youth festival, held each year at the denomination's Trinity College. Here, the young people from Naperville meet with those from other Evangelical Free churches in order to fellowship and to share their gifts in music, art, drama, writing, multimedia presentations, and public speaking. Those who demonstrate superior ability are encouraged to attend the denominations' biennial national youth conference, where they are further challenged to commit their lives and talents to Christ. The youth festival has a noticeable effect on worship in the local churches that participate.

Worship and Social Action. Social concern is a by-product of the worship experience. As the church worships, God awakens within each worshiper the desire to respond to the needs of the community and nation. At the Evangelical Free Church of Naperville, worshipers are challenged to vote and to exercise Christian citizenship. They are encouraged to participate as God directs in a variety of programs involving inner-city missions, right-to-life concerns, addictions, financial difficulties, needs of the homeless, marital and family counseling, job placement, and other areas of critical human need.

Women and Worship. "Does the Word of God permit a woman to appear as a preacher, to take part in the general Christian work, and have a voting right in the urgent matters before a congregation?" This question was addressed as early as 1888 in a conference held by delegates of the Swedish Evangelical Free Church. Shortly after this conference, four women were sent as missionaries.

In 1896 Fredrik Franson, who was a powerful and articulate force in the formative years of the Evangelical Free church, wrote a pamphlet entitled *The Prophesying Daughters.* This pamphlet provided biblical support for the conviction that the great commission was not for men only. In the Norwegian-Danish Association, an early constituent of the Evangelical Free church, Catherine Juell was listed as just one of many women evangelists and teachers before the turn of the century.

Today in the Evangelical Free church, women minister in most areas of service. They direct missions and other programs. They teach and lead Bible studies. In worship services, they lead in prayer, in readings, and in drama. They direct or accompany choirs and congregational singing.

Although there are no ordained women pastors or elders in the Evangelical Free church, women are licensed as full-time pastors serving in areas such as the military chaplaincy, children's ministries, or Christian education. Free churches consider these leadership roles for women as biblical since most Free church pastors are limited in their authority over congregations. Instead, authority rests rather in the elders, who represent the people of the church.

Worship and Spiritual Formation. Accountability groups, discipleship groups, and other Bible study and prayer groups are all vital ministries in the Evangelical Free Church of Naperville. They aid in spiritual formation because they bring people together at times other than the formal worship services. The church also has approximately thirty "flock groups," which meet regularly for worship, Bible study, prayer, and social activities. This network of groups assists people in identifying their gifts and finding their service niche in the body. Choir, instrumental groups, and drama groups integrate times of worship, biblical teaching, and prayer with their artistic preparation for services.

In this local congregation as in many Free churches, each ministry is equally important and complements all others. At the same time, each ministry is dependent upon worship in which Almighty God is the primary focus. As we as a congregation adore God, he inhabits the praise of the people of God (Ps. 22:3). As the Holy Spirit links with our spirits in a life-changing way (John 4:23-24), worship becomes the catalyst for the growth of other ministries in the church and the hub from which all the spokes in the wheel of church ministry radiate.

Tim Allen

127 ◆ EVANGELICAL LUTHERAN CHURCH IN AMERICA

Ministries of social justice, pastoral care, and evangelism are all advanced by the liturgy itself in most Evangelical Lutheran Church in America congregations. When conducted with authenticity, the liturgy provides for the proclamation of the gospel, for the comforting of the sorrowing, and for the addressing of social issues in light of God's Word. Full participation of women and the inclusion of children also signify that the liturgy itself is a symbol of the coming kingdom of God.

As a liturgically and sacramentally oriented church, the Evangelical Lutheran Church in America (ELCA) has given considerable attention to the ways in which worship finds integration with other ministries of the church. Women's issues, outreach, social concerns, spiritual formation, education, children's ministries, and pastoral care are all areas which Lutheran worship has attempted to address in some way.

Women's Issues and Worship

Full participation of women in worship and ministry in the Evangelical Lutheran Church in America is ensured by the fact that the church ordains women to the ministry of Word and sacrament. Official ELCA policy mandates the inclusion of women in every aspect of church life. A Commission on Women promotes and monitors this inclusion throughout the denomination.

This commitment means that this church has chosen to express in its mission the eschatological ideal articulated by St. Paul in Galatians 3:28, rather than the culture-bound instructions he gives in 1 Corinthians 14:33b-35 (and which seem to contradict the assumption in 1 Corinthians 11 that women may pray and prophesy in public worship). Accordingly, women in the ELCA routinely serve in every liturgical role. Even traditional male roles, such as ushering, can include women; while traditional women's roles, such as the altar guild ministry, can include men.

Nevertheless, the feminist critique has raised questions related to the content of worship itself, especially concerning the language used in public worship. When the _Lutheran Book of Worship_ was published in 1978, there was already concern to avoid language which suggested that the male is the representative of the species and that the female is subordinate. Feminists would claim that this book did not go far enough. In addition to sins of commission, such as the predominance of masculine images and references, sins of omission, such as the paucity of references to female saints in prayers or of stories about women in the lectionary selections, also exist. Since no biblical translation was mandated by the _Lutheran Book of Worship_, ELCA congregations were free to experiment with such resources as the _Inclusive Language Lectionary_ (National Council of Churches of Christ) and the _Lectionary for the Christian People_ (Yukon, Oklahoma: Pueblo Publishing House, 1986) prepared by Lutheran scholars Gordon Lathrop and Gail Ramshaw. The advent of the New Revised Standard Bible has provided a mediating translation that is finding widespread use in ELCA congregations, especially through bulletin lectionary inserts published by the denomination's publishing house.

More problematic has been language about God used in worship. While Lutheran ministers can be routinely heard to refer in modalistic terms to God the Creator, Redeemer, and Sanctifier, the bishops of the ELCA, in an exercise of teaching authority, have mandated that baptisms should be performed only in the name of the Father, and of the Son, and of the Holy Spirit. If the name of God revealed by Jesus can be protected, people may be open to have their understanding of God enlarged through edifying use of other titles and images found in Scripture and tradition. However, no matter how expansive the use of various titles and images of God, orthodox Christian prayer will continue to be addressed to God the Father, through Jesus Christ his Son, our Lord, in the Holy Spirit.

———— Worship and Evangelism ————

Typical Lutheran worship has been regarded as an obstacle to evangelism, if by evangelism one means an outreach to unchurched people with the gospel. Lutheran worship requires a knowledgeable use of a sophisticated worship book. The liturgy is typically sung throughout, which requires familiarity with liturgical chants and classical hymns. This corpus of liturgical and hymnological material, however, enshrines a witness to the catholic and apostolic faith. It is evangelistic in the sense of being an authentic proclamation of the gospel. Lutherans are aware of the fact that in some periods of church history, such as the age of the Enlightenment, liturgy alone proclaimed the gospel while preaching degenerated into rationalism and moralism. The loss of the historic liturgy, therefore, would be risky in terms of the mission of the gospel.

Interest in the church growth movement poses just such a risk. The bedrock principle of this movement is that the Sunday morning worship experience should be tailored to the unchurched. In its extreme form, this has meant celebrational events—lacking Scripture readings, creeds, or even the Lord's Prayer—in which musical groups and drama capture people's attention and an upbeat message is given. In this format, requirements of overt participation are minimal. Those who show an interest in church membership are moved by stages into a liturgy of the faithful on some other evening. Relatively few ELCA congregations have opted for this approach.

The positive effect of the church growth movement has been to raise the consciousness of congregations about their practices of hospitality to guests and strangers. Within the ELCA, literature designed to help congregations assess their practices of hospitality is being developed (see especially Gerald J. Hoffman, _How Your Congregation Can Become a More Hospitable Community_ [1990]; Patrick Keifert, _Welcoming the Stranger: A Public Theology of Worship and Evangelism_ [Minneapolis: Fortress Press, 1991]).

The other approach to moving the unchurched into the liturgy of the faithful by careful stages is through the catechumenal process embodied in the Christian initiation of adults. The Roman Catholic Rite of Christian Initiation of Adults is a ritual process which is only beginning to make an impact on Roman Catholic and non–Roman Catholic Churches alike. The ELCA has cooperated with the Evangelism Office of the Episcopal Church in the USA on an adaptation of the Roman Catholic rite called The Catechumenal Process. Professor Walter Huffman (Trinity Seminary, Columbus, Ohio) has been preparing catechumenal rites for the Evangelical Lutheran Church in Canada. Several joint Lutheran-Episcopal training sessions for catechists have taken place. (See also *The Catechumenal Process: Adult Initiation and Formation for Christian Life and Ministry,* ed. by E. P. McElligott [1990]; and Frank C. Senn, *The Witness of the Worshipping Community* [New York: Paulist Press, 1993].)

The advantage of this catechumenal process for Lutherans is that it includes the preparation of adults for holy baptism, the preparation of baptized persons for the affirmation of baptism (restoration to membership), and the preparation of parents for the baptism of infants and young children, all during the initiatory seasons of Lent and Easter. This practices takes into account the pastoral reality of the actual candidates for Christian initiation in Lutheran parishes.

Other Issues

Worship and Social Concern. Social concern is expressed in three elements of Lutheran worship: in hymns, in sermons, and in prayers. In hymns, social concern is expressed by the singing of the "church and society" hymns. More of these hymns are in the *Lutheran Book of Worship* than in previous Lutheran hymnals. Sermons are an opportunity for preachers to explore the social consequences of Christian life and witness, as this unfolds in the lectionary readings. The prayers of the church (intercessions) routinely include petitions for "the whole church, the nations, those in need, the parish, and special concerns." Synodical committees and churchwide departments occasionally send to parishes suggested prayer concerns and to pastors homiletical ideas concerning social issues. Rarely, however, would the regular liturgy of Word and sacrament be replaced by a "creative liturgy" which develops a "theme" and manipulates a "response."

Worship and Spiritual Formation. The liturgy itself is a school of spirituality. Much spiritual teaching on the parish level is geared toward a greater appreciation and understanding of the liturgy. Home devotions, especially during Advent and Lent, are related to these seasons of the church year. The church year is viewed as a way of reflecting on the life of Christ and life under God's reign. From time to time, attempts have been made to encourage a regular use of the morning and evening prayer offices (matins, vespers, compline) in parishes, retreat settings, and family devotions. The two-year lectionary and table of psalms in the *Lutheran Book of Worship* provides the propers for the prayer offices.

Worship and Education. The historic liturgy itself has a certain educational value in the ways in which it uses Scripture and conveys Christian doctrine. At the same time, parish education in Lutheran congregations often relates to the liturgy, especially the church year calendar and lectionary. Church school curricula take into account the major festivals of Christmas, Easter, Pentecost, and the preparatory seasons of Advent and Lent. Some pastors use the Sunday pericopes (Scripture readings) as the texts for adult Bible study groups. In many locations, pastors gather in ecumenical groups to study the readings in the Common Lectionary. This is a practice that might be extended to ecumenical lay groups (see the Liturgical Conference's *Passage to the Paschal Feast, Weeks of Lent: Year C* [Washington, D.C., 1992]).

Children and Worship. The trend in recent years in Lutheran congregations has been to integrate children into the liturgy, rather than to segregate them into a Sunday school or a children's church during the service. Children's homilies have been one approach (usually appreciated by the adults as well because they understand the point and find these homilies entertaining). One would expect Lutheran pastors to avoid moralism in children's homilies as much as in their sermons (that is, directives on "what we should do"). The most effective children's homilies are those that provide the children with instruction on the Scripture readings, the day's observance, the parts of the liturgy, symbols, or ritual actions.

Children and youth also participate in worship by exercising liturgical roles as acolytes, members of children's or youth choirs, ushers, and offering bearers. Confirmed youth might also serve as assisting ministers to read lessons, lead intercessions, and administer Communion.

Worship and Pastoral Care. The needs of worshipers are knowingly and unknowingly addressed by the reading and preaching of the Word of God and the administration of the sacraments. Some parishes make provision for personal needs to be explicitly included in the intercessions. One approach is to have a page in the narthex on which worshipers may write their prayer requests as they enter the sanctuary. In some smaller congregations, worshipers are invited to offer their own petitions and thanksgivings at the appropriate time in the prayers. Pastors may handle sensitive issues such as divorce in public announcements before the prayers. Pastoral counseling can lead to the use of the rite for "individual confession and forgiveness" in the _Lutheran Book of Worship_. Additional resources—such as rites for baptism in emergency, blessing of a civil marriage, celebration or distribution of Communion with people in special circumstances, laying on of hands and anointing of the sick, and commendation of the dying—are found in _Occasional Services: A Companion to The Lutheran Book of Worship_ [1982].

Frank C. Senn

128 ✦ FRIENDS (QUAKERS)

The conviction of Quakers, or the Society of Friends, is that genuine worship results in a change of attitude that has implications for all of life, especially areas of personal integrity and sensitivity to suffering and injustice. Therefore, Quakers have developed specific personal and corporate disciplines which help the worshiper to live out his or her faith.

In a publication called _Friends Worship in a Pastoral Meeting,_ one Quaker expressed his group's vision for worship as follows:

> True worship is as leaven in life. It permeates the soul or spirit and becomes the chief factor in determining the attitudes of life. . . . Participating in real worship, meeting God in worship, results in profound changes in our attitudes. Since attitudes determine our actions, worship can leaven all of life.

The impact of worship on Quaker life and ministry is rooted in two fundamental beliefs. The first is the belief that the ultimate purpose of worship is to conform human beings to God's image and that "no part of our lives can remain untouched . . . [because] religion and life are of one stuff" (Punshon, _Encounter with Silence_ [Richmond, Ind.: Friends

United Press, 1987]). True worship helps mold Christian values and attitudes toward injustice and suffering, making the worshiper aware of and sensitive to these aspects of life. Second, Quakers believe that all people are equal—regardless of gender, race, social status, or any other human distinction, including religious office—and that all people possess the potential for good. These beliefs have been augmented by the Friends' commitment to a high level of personal piety and biblical literacy.

A survey of Quaker life and ministry reveals that the worship experience of Quakers has led them to practice family Bible reading and devotions, to treat women as equals, to maintain a commitment to social reform, to oppose slavery, to link worship and justice, to establish "first-day" schools for religious education, and to spread the gospel through world missions.

The life and ministry of Quakers, like their worship, have taken unique forms. Liturgical scholar James F. White describes the Friends' lifestyle as a kind of "worldly asceticism. But unlike most ascetics, they have lived married lives within the world" (_Protestant Worship: Traditions in Transition_ [Louisville: Westminster/John Knox Press, 1989]). In their attempt to live out their worship, the Friends developed unique forms and a vocabulary that includes words such as _queries, concerns, testimonies,_ the _manner of Friends_ and other terms.

The _Book of Discipline_ or _Faith and Practice_ of each of the regional Quaker bodies—called _yearly meetings_—contains a series of questions or _queries._ The queries are formulated to help each member determine through self-examination whether he or she is living a consistent Christian life. They are arranged topically and focus on issues such as spiritual growth, meetings for worship and business, Christian fellowship, home and family, youth and the church, standards of life, business responsibility, missions, peace, race relations, and social conscience. Quakers are encouraged to read the queries regularly in private devotions as well as at public meetings.

Quakers have always been sensitive to human needs. Under a sense of _concern,_ an inner prompting of the Spirit that calls for obedience and sense of urgency, Friends have developed education and evangelism programs, carried out service projects, and initiated other kinds of spiritual and humanitarian actions.

The Quaker testimonies, or public Christian witness, have been displayed historically in their simple lifestyle, their integrity in personal and business relations, and often their controversial stands on public issues. The testimonies have included opposition to war, slavery, and racial inequality. The *Quaker way* or *the manner of Friends* describes the way in which Friends try consciously to put their beliefs into practice in ministry and service to others. They identify and work with people in need and respond nonviolently when wronged.

Today, commitment to the Good News of the gospel and its implications for all of life motivates evangelical Friends to witness for Christ through missions and evangelism. Many Quaker churches have strong outreach programs, and Bible study and accountability groups. In addition, Quakers continue to work for the spiritual and general welfare of ethnic groups and indigenous peoples throughout the world through both Quaker and other mission and relief organizations.

Warren Ediger

129 • INDEPENDENT FUNDAMENTALIST AND EVANGELICAL CHURCHES

Worship is the adoration of God. Worship can also be an important vehicle for spiritual formation, and for the education and the influencing of children. But since these churches believe that only believers can truly worship, evangelism and worship are maintained as separate functions.

The impact of worship on the life of a healthy congregation goes far beyond what happens in a service. Worship has an impact in many areas of parish ministry, including spiritual formation, education, and evangelism. It also influences children who attend worship.

—— Worship and Spiritual Formation ——

Spiritual formation is related to events, activities, or ideas that help shape the concept of the Christian life and how it is lived. How are people's spiritual lives and thoughts molded or guided? What are some ways this is done? One popular method is the organizing of small cell groups,

covenant groups, or accountability groups. This unit meets regularly, usually for Bible study, prayer, and sharing of personal concerns and needs. Most groups are composed of six to eight people.

Worship can assist these groups, as well as the individuals in them, by: (1) offering a truer perspective on the individuals' selves, thus making the group more effective; (2) cleansing the inner life, resulting in greater honesty, transparency, and holiness; (3) bringing unity to the group in the shared activity of worship; and (4) providing insight into one another through observing each other in worship.

These groups may begin their meetings with a time of worship, which includes the singing of hymns or Scripture songs and the reading of Psalms or other portions of Scripture. Often in these first minutes together, the group is drawn together in spirit as the focus shifts from various concerns to worshiping the Lord. As God is worshiped, individuals become aware of who God is and who they are in relation to God and to each other. This gaining of perspective on one's life is one of the most essential elements of small group dynamics.

Worship brings cleansing. As a result, love, accountability, openness, transparency, and honesty have a better chance of being realized in the group when people attain a clear perspective on who they are. Worshiping together is the most powerful way to bring a personal life into focus. Authentic worship always brings truth to bear on the individual's life. There is often greater courage and honesty in sharing after a group has worshiped together.

Worship also helps to give insight into other members of the small group, as we, the members of the group, observe each other in worship. In worship, we voice our common beliefs. We have opportunity to see, be it ever so dimly, into the soul of the individual as he or she worships. We hear one another pray and lift our voices in singing. We may hold each other's hands in prayer. We break bread and share the cup together. We rejoice together and weep together. Together, we experience intimate communion with the Father.

Of course, at the heart of worship, as our attention is focused on God, is all that we learn of God's thoughts, God's love, and God's counsel. Our spiritual lives are enlarged, reshaped, pruned, and transformed as we encounter our Lord.

Though activities and disciplines assist us, these can not replace worship.

Worship and Education

How do worship and education relate? In Deuteronomy 6:20, Moses writes, "When your children ask you in time to come, 'What is the meaning of the decrees and the statutes and the ordinances that the Lord our God has commanded you?' then you shall say to your children . . ." (NRSV). The Scriptures clearly teach that worship of God is something to be discussed at length at home. It is to be a part of the everyday life of a family.

Worship is the laboratory experience that provides the grist for Christian education in its best and truest sense. In worship, we as believers learn of the Father and his love, mercy, patience, justice, and faithfulness. We learn of God's character, identity, and worth.

In one congregation, the minister of music and worship wrote each week a three-paragraph summary of the worship service for that day. He wrote of the importance of preparing for worship and included in the bulletin a brief thought from one of the great devotional writers. He commented on the significance of each piece of music, touching on its purpose for inclusion in that particular day. He commented on creeds, responsive readings, and hymns. He explained, where appropriate, how the entire service was woven together in support of the pastor's sermon topic. In short, these "notes on worship" were intended to guide and to teach.

At other times, topics such as the relationship between "heart and mind" would be addressed as they related to the service that Sunday. This particular pastor planned out two years of weekly topics to be covered in an effort to educate his congregation in the whole area of worship and to raise the congregation's expectations whenever they gathered. Over a period of years, the congregation became much more aware of some of the continuity and flow, as well as the theology, of worship.

The wise pastor takes every opportunity to speak on worship to Sunday school classes from children through adults. One pastor taught the book of Hebrews to an adult Sunday school class solely from the perspective of developing the individual's worship life. The class lasted a whole year, and each week some of the elements of the lesson were related to the service that followed.

Another natural place for education on worship to occur is in the choir loft. Each week, a group of worship leaders come together to prepare and to worship. This is a natural laboratory experience to teach what is happening and what can occur as God's people gather for worship.

A well-worded introduction to the Scripture reading, hymn, or choir anthem is yet another low-profile kind of education. The pastor has only a short time with the people each week. Subsequently, every word must be thoughtfully prepared. Worship must become a major contributing factor to Christian education in the broadest sense.

Worship and Evangelism

Much has been written toward the end of the twentieth century regarding evangelism and worship. In vogue are the *seekers' services,* a contemporary version of the old camp meetings at the turn of the twentieth century. The point of this service is to aim at the lowest common denominator of theological understanding or interest. The music idiom is popular contemporary music. The congregation is truly a passive audience. Many who are involved in seekers' services do not call what they do worship; it is, rather, evangelism. The service is an event that provides the opportunity for people mildly interested in religion to come, to hear, and to think about their own relationship to God.

Some congregations have sought to combine worship and this kind of evangelism in the same service, even though the aims, purposes, and focuses of these two activities are entirely different. The aim of the latter is to encourage a person to have a relationship to God. The purpose of the former is to provide an opportunity for those who are already in a relationship to God to express that intimate relationship. Scripture is clear in teaching that only believers can worship.

The apostle Paul does, however, acknowledge a relationship between worship and evangelism in his first letter to the Corinthians. He comments that if unbelievers are present when authentic worship by Christians takes place, they will declare that "God is really among you." All too often those unbelievers present in worship see lethargic, passionless believers going through the motions of worship. The singing is insensitive; the prayers are repetitions of old tired phrases; the sense of awe and wonder exists nowhere in the service. Paul strongly suggests that this ought not to be! The majesty, awe, and reverence of real worship will have an impact on those gathered as the Holy Spirit moves in the congregation.

It is imperative that worship planners think through their purpose in a service. Worship and evangelism are not interchangeable concepts. When the purpose of a service is evangelism or reaching unbelievers, the entire meeting will have one shape. When the reason for gathering is the worship of God by believers, then the focus of the service will be different. This is not to say that people are never confronted with the gospel and their need of a Savior in a worship service. However, this purpose is not the point of the gathering. Worship is an indirect form of evangelism. People may be converted through a worship service, but the primary focus of worship is the adoration of God.

Children in Worship

The church at worship has an impact on children. This impact is either positive and constructive, or it is neutral, negative, and destructive. All too often children occupy the neutral role of observers in a worship service. If we as believing parents are not careful, we will teach our children that worship is boring and incomprehensible. For our children, the worship service becomes a place where they go to sit still and draw until they are permitted to leave.

There is no reason children cannot be involved in helping to lead worship on occasion. Older elementary children can certainly read Scripture, sometimes along with adults. For example, children and their grandparents might read passages particularly appropriate to different generations, such as Psalms 100 and 103 or 1 Samuel 3. Children can lead in prayer at appropriate times or help with the receiving of the offering. Certainly any age group can sing. On occasion, children can participate in simple dramatic sketches illustrating a point or principle, perhaps as the opening illustration of a sermon. Or the "children's sermon" could provide an illustration that families can use for a discussion following the worship service.

If times of worship are conceived as authentic expressions of love for God, then both children and mature believers should grow through worship in their understanding of God and their faith in God. In real worship, the Holy Spirit is at work. Worship is the most dynamic work a church can do, and affects small groups, evangelism, education, the influencing of children, or other related areas of church life. Through worship that is in spirit and in truth, the power of God is released to accomplish its creating and transforming work.

Daniel Sharp

130 • International Church of the Foursquare Gospel

Jesus' imperative of making disciples of all nations implies an inclusive ministry. Women, children, and physically challenged persons all find an important place in Foursquare churches. Worship is important for modeling inclusivity as a characteristic of the whole Christian life.

The *real* call to worship is often not heard by Christians. Culture, ethnic exposure, and ignorance keep Christian from worshiping the way God intended. Rather than being only music and physical gestures toward God, worship encompasses all that believers do in their relationship with God and how they live out their daily lives. In Matthew 28:19, Jesus declares that worship should involve a concern for the world and everyone in it. The goal of Christ for the church was for it to possess an inclusive ministry, rather than an exclusive one.

How easy it is to verbally proclaim a commitment to the world, but devote little discipling time to those whom God has called the church to touch. When most ministries establish their worship agenda, three categories of people are often overlooked: women, children, and the physically impaired. Moreover, the worship of the church must be part of an overall, deliberate plan of pastoral care that releases the members of the congregation to live victoriously and minister effectively to those about them, outside the walls of the sanctuary.

Women in Worship

Through the centuries, women have borne the

The Cross of the Four Ermine Spots. A beautiful form of the cross frequently used in church embroidery and printing.

should strongly affect one's philosophy toward worship. In many cases, worship services are not designed to meet the needs of children. The young are expected to adapt to a service geared for adults, without being given a time when they can, on their own level, express their love for God. The church must strive to present God's principles to every generation represented in the congregation.

To respond to such a need, Foursquare churches usually select one of two options. Many have set aside specially designed facilities and have trained personnel to lead children's church. In most cases, this service is conducted simultaneously with the adult worship time. Music and teaching are provided at this service to fit the understanding and needs of the respective age groups.

The alternative to this arrangement is to allow the children to participate in the adult worship services. At the adult service, they are able to take part in cross-generational worship. One recent innovation has been to allocate time within the adult worship period to allow for the expression of children.

Worship and the Physically Challenged

When a person is stricken with some major physical limitation, it seems as if the church brands that person as "unevangelizeable." When a person uses the term *evangelism,* that person is usually focusing the evangelism effort on those who are mobile, rather than on the bedridden, blind, or on those who cannot join in the forms that the church accepts as norms of worship.

Congregations must not only get the physically impaired into the sanctuary and provide suitable seating arrangement. They must also provide these people with appropriate opportunities for the expression of worship. This continues to be a challenge for the Foursquare Church, as well as for every other fellowship of believers. New and creative ways must be found to touch those who cannot see, who cannot hear, and who cannot come.

One fruitful entrance into the homes and rooms of many has been that of media ministry. In 1924, Angelus Temple, the headquarters church for the Foursquare denomination, founded radio station KFSG as one of the first Christian radio broadcasting stations in North America. Since that

children and taken responsibility for their care. Yet they have carried the stigma of being viewed by some as a secondary part of God's agenda. Thus, women have exerted little influence within the worship structure of many congregations. They have been viewed as having only a supporting role, with no potential for leadership.

The International Church of the Foursquare Gospel places high value on the grace God has given to the church through its women because it was founded by a woman and because it has the conviction that in the last days God's Spirit would be poured out on sons and *daughters* anointed to prophesy (Joel 2:28). Thus, women hold leadership and pastoral positions in the denomination and are active in leading worship in local congregations. Through conferences, seminars, and special worship opportunities, women come together to give God praise and to discuss those matters most relevant to their interests and needs.

Worship and Children's Ministries

When Jesus commanded, "Let the little children come to me" (Matt. 19:14), he voiced a truth that time, many Foursquare congregations have expanded their outreach by supporting local television and radio stations or programs for these media.

———— Worship and Pastoral Care ————

Pastoral care is the key to the development of worship within a congregation. It is at this level that the boundaries and philosophy of, and overall attitude toward, worship are determined. It is crucial for leaders to be examples in word, spirit, conduct, and leadership. The Word of God must be taught by people of credibility of character and professional excellence, so that believers will worship God in spirit and in truth.

For many years, through its Bible colleges, the Foursquare Church trained most of its future ministers in pastoral theology—including the art of shepherding the congregation from the pulpit—and in related subjects. Today, however, due to an unusual increase in the number of pastors without formal Bible college training (many have equivalent college education), the need has arisen for enlightenment of those who are already serving in leadership. On the national level a new program, entitled "Leadership Enrichment and Development" (LEAD), has been inaugurated, wherein study of the subjects taught in Bible colleges will continue to produce positive, strong spiritual leaders.

Locally, many Foursquare churches are encouraging small-group accountability opportunities as a follow-through for the corporate worship and teaching experience. One outstanding example is Windward Hope Chapel on the island of Oahu, Hawaii. Meeting throughout the week in the homes of trained leaders, members discuss the previous Sunday's message and make personal application to their situations.

———— Related Concerns to Worship ————

A church's worship is influenced by four related concerns: societal needs and the influence of society, the facilities of worship, daily Christian life, and the various styles of worship.

First, a balance must be maintained between upholding spiritual values in worship and responding to social needs. While recognizing that events within society have a direct impact on events in the church, the church understands that its mode of worship should be defined by Scripture and not by external societal influences. However, when the church loses sight of the social needs around it, it becomes like those in Jesus' Good Samaritan parable who passed by the sufferer. On the other hand, if the church expends its time and resources attending to physical needs, what will happen to people when they face the eternal God? Thus, the church needs to maintain a balance between these two elements.

Second, worship should always be focused on the Father, and not on the magnificent facilities. At times, the church's worship focus can be consumed by a prolonged fascination with facilities. For some, rather than serving the needs of a congregation, the facility itself becomes a symbol of pride and accomplishment. The object of worship, unfortunately, shifts from God to that which houses God's people.

Third, the church must train its people to enjoy the emotional bliss of worship experiences and to retain, in addition, a song in their heart when surrounded by the darkness and trials in everyday life. God has determined times of worship which are filled with spiritual excitement and joy to provide refreshing and renewal. Yet such moments are never designed to create emotional dependence. When a worshiper comes to rely on a spiritual "high" in the worship experience, the daily reality of living one's faith can result in discouragement and dismay. Churches must counteract this tendency in their people.

Finally, believers must accept other Christians' worship styles along with their own. Everyone's life is influenced by the opinions of others. Some of these influences are good; others are absolutely deadly. Many church leaders and congregations have admired other ministries or fellowships so much that they have lost their ability to prayerfully discern for themselves the direction of worship God wants them to take. Though gifted people encourage believers to dream beyond themselves, God never intended peer pressure from these gifted people to dictate the flavor of believers' worship or their sense of acceptance in the body of Christ. Believers may accept the distinct "flavor" of their worship and their special gifts, without rejecting the abilities and tastes of other Christians who offer worship in and through "the same Spirit" (1 Cor. 12:4).

Ricky Temple

131 ♦ LUTHERAN CHURCH–MISSOURI SYNOD

In the Missouri Synod, the public liturgy is viewed as the life of the church of Jesus Christ. Consequently, the liturgy is the proclamation of the gospel and the mission of the church. The liturgy is also an important means for pastoral care, and is a lifelong vehicle for Christian formation through the Word of God.

A contemporary portrait of liturgical life in the Lutheran Church–Missouri Synod must be painted in a kaleidoscope of colors. Having survived an intense theological struggle over the authority of the Scriptures in the 1960s and 1970s, the Missouri Synod retains its strong commitment to doctrinal unity. Yet, from its founding in 1847, this commitment has been coupled with freedom in matters of practice. Consequently, while the visitor to Missouri Synod churches finds uniformity in doctrine from one congregation to another, the visitor also encounters a wide diversity in the way public worship is conducted.

This diversity has become increasingly noticeable in recent decades. According to a 1991 survey, _The Lutheran Hymnal_ (1941) is used in about 32 percent of Missouri Synod churches. The _Lutheran Book of Worship_ (1978) is used by 8 percent, and _Lutheran Worship_ (1982) is used by approximately 49 percent. The remaining 11 percent of congregations use a variety of worship resources. Desktop publishing technology has given parishes the possibility of producing their own worship materials. The use of computers in the church has accelerated a movement away from traditional Lutheran liturgies toward more of an entertainment orientation in Sunday morning worship.

Despite the diversity of worship practice in the Missouri Synod, it is still possible to outline a general framework in which liturgical practice defines and shapes Christian life in Missouri Synod parishes.

Liturgy as Life

Lutheran liturgical piety understands public worship as _Gottesdienst_ (German for divine service). That is, public worship is essentially God's activity. Martin Luther's _Small Catechism_ defines the church as God's own creation:

> I believe that I cannot by my own reason or strength believe in Jesus Christ, my Lord, or come to Him; but the Holy Spirit has called me by the Gospel, enlightened me with his gifts, sanctified and kept me in the truth faith.

Lutherans therefore understand their worship life not as the coming together of like-minded people who wish to create a "worship experience" for one another. Instead, they understand it as the calling together of people by God's own action in Word and sacrament to stand in God's presence and receive the good gifts—the means of grace—God dispenses in that same Word and sacrament.

In the liturgy, the Holy Trinity comes to meet the people of God through the means of grace and to serve them with the forgiveness of sins earned by Jesus Christ, the Lord of all life. As it was in the beginning, so it is now. As God first breathed into Adam the breath of life, so God now breathes into the church the breath of the life-giving Spirit of God. Liturgy, in Lutheran thinking, begins in a receptive posture. The Christian first prays, "O Lord, open thou my lips," and only afterwards, "my mouth shall show forth they praise" (Ps. 51:15).

In the liturgy, the church receives its life and gives this life back again. Liturgy is both the source and the shape of the life of the church. In the liturgy, the church inhales; the church receives forgiveness of sins, life, and salvation through the means of grace. But in the liturgy the church also exhales; the church offers its sacrifice of worship _to_ the Father, _through_ the Son, and _in_ the Spirit.

Liturgy as Proclamation

Lutherans have always understood the office of the public ministry in terms of the means of grace, as expressed in the Augsburg Confession of 1530:

> To obtain such [saving] faith, God instituted the office of the ministry, that is, provided the Gospel and the sacraments. Through these, as through means, He gives the Holy spirit, who works faith, when and where he pleases, in those who hear the Gospel (art. 5).

The Lutheran Church–Missouri Synod has no female pastors. It addresses the question of women's ordination theologically rather than sociologically. The church understands apostolic prohibitions against the ministry of women to be divine directives, not first-century cultural prejudices. Though a wide variety of public offices are open to women (teacher, parish worker, director of Christian education, deaconess), the Missouri

Synod does not ordain women to the pastoral office.

The restriction of the public ministry in the Lutheran Church–Missouri Synod to male candidates stems from the church's commitment to the Holy Scriptures and the church's perception of God's servant in the public liturgy. He is a steward of the sacred mysteries (Word and sacrament) by which Christ, the heavenly Bridegroom, comes to his bride, the church.

In the arena of public worship, the living Lord himself comes through the proclamation of his gospel and in the partaking of his holy Supper. These two focal points of the public liturgy are both the proclamation of Jesus Christ. In the sermon, his Word is spoken. And in the sacrament of his body and blood, public testimony is given: "For whenever you eat this bread and drink this cup, you proclaim the Lord's death until he comes" (1 Cor. 11:26).

Liturgy as Mission

Among the pioneers in Christian radio (*The Lutheran Hour,* established in 1930) and Christian television (*This Is the Life,* established in 1951), the Lutheran Church–Missouri Synod and its auxiliary, the Lutheran Laymen's League, have consistently demonstrated an innovative approach to winning the lost. While eager to utilize the latest technology and strategy, the Missouri Synod views the public worship of the church as the heart and center of its mission. This mission is considered to be a corporate, rather than an individual, mission; winning the lost is not a solo operation. Rather, this evangelistic mission continues in the context of the public ministry of God's Word and sacrament. That is, the goal of evangelism is incorporating men and women into the church, where God is at work. First, God gives the unbeliever a new birth, adopting him or her as a child of God. Then God raises Christians to maturity in the nourishment God provides in the Word and sacrament.

In other words, the mission of the church originates in the mission of God. The Father sent the Son, who sends the church in the power of his Spirit. "As the Father has sent me, I am sending you" (John 20:21). There is no ministry apart from this mission of Christ. Neither is there any mission today, apart from the ongoing ministry of Christ's own Word and sacrament in and through

his church. The goal of evangelistic activity in the Lutheran Church–Missouri Synod is always catechetical instruction, initiation into the congregation, and continual communing membership. Central to membership is participation in the public worship of the congregation.

Liturgy as Pastoral Care

Historically, the Lutheran Church–Missouri Synod has had the largest network of parochial elementary schools of any Protestant church in America. Recent additions to parish life in Missouri Synod congregations include counseling services, social ministries, and programs of evangelism and Christian education. Whether in the time-honored office of the Lutheran school teacher or in more recent innovations in staffing such as the parish nurse or assimilation director, Missouri Synod churches continue to demonstrate a sensitivity to the needs of their parishioners.

Yet the heart of pastoral care in the Missouri Synod still revolves around the means of grace. According to Luther's *Small Catechism,* "In this Christian Church he [the Holy Spirit] forgives all sins to me and all believers." The justification of sinners by grace, for Christ's sake, through faith, remains the chief article of faith for Lutheran Christians. Therefore Lutherans understand the forgiveness of sins as the heart of every Christian's life.

While counseling and instruction on the "how to's" of Christian living have their place in today's church, Missouri Synod Lutherans consider these to be external aids only. Genuine healing and real nourishment for the Christian life are to be found in the historic tools for pastoral care found in the public liturgy: preaching, absolution, and the sacraments. Each of these time-honored components of the liturgy contain but one life-giving ingredient, the Word of God.

Harold L. Senkbeil

132 • MENNONITE CHURCHES

With its roots in the radical wing of the Protestant Reformation, the Mennonite church has historically emphasized Christian discipleship and has understood worship as continuous with daily living. In recent years, however, as a result of growing awareness of the multifac-

eted nature of worship, much more attention is being given to the integration of worship with other ministries in the congregation.

Worship in North American Mennonite churches has been changing rapidly since 1960. In the past, churchgoers could reasonably expect to find similar patterns of worship in Virginia, Kansas, Oregon, Ontario, or anywhere between. Today Mennonite worship is characterized by creative ferment. Increased participation of many kinds of people, expressions of varied streams of spirituality, changing styles of music and language, greater attention to the Christian year, and hunger for the reality of God's presence have all contributed to renewal in worship.

Perhaps one of the most significant developments in Mennonite worship renewal is a fresh vision of the intimate relationship between worship and other dimensions of congregational life. Worship is indeed a vertical experience—an encounter with the living God. But it is also a horizontal experience—communion within the body of Christ. Further, worship is the energizing source of the congregation's daily life and ministry in the world.

Worship as Encounter with God

Mennonite worship has always included singing, prayer, and preaching. More recently, attention is being given to a wider range of acts of worship that encourage people to become aware of God's presence, hear God's Word, and respond in faith and obedience. An example of this focus can be found in the new _Hymnal: A Worship Book_ (1992). Instead of organizing the new hymnal in doctrinal or topical sequence, the Hymnal Council chose to organize music and worship resources according to the acts of worship in a typical Sunday morning service. The acts of gathering, praising, confessing, reconciling, offering, hearing God's Word, affirming the faith, responding in prayer, and sending can all help worshipers to focus their attention on the God whom they have come to meet.

Without a doubt, singing (often _a cappella_) is the single most important element of Mennonite worship. It provides ample support for the vertical dimensions of worship, as well as providing a vehicle for building community. Although only a handful of churches employ staff persons in mu-

sic ministry, considerable effort, both denominationally and locally, goes into training song leaders. A wider range of songs, hymns, instruments, and musical styles has broadened the possibilities for meeting God in worship.

Although the Mennonite heritage belongs to the didactic, iconoclastic wing of the radical Reformation, many churches today are rediscovering the power of the fine arts (in addition to music) to mediate God's presence and grace. The use of sculpture, banners, liturgical movement, drama, color, texture, gesture, and ritual has contributed to more vital experiences of God's presence.

Some churches plan a worship center which visually highlights the focus of a particular service. Others have introduced simple hand or body movements to express praise, confession, or supplication. Some churches train Scripture readers to proclaim the Word with passion and skill. An emphasis on narrative theology, storytelling, greater use of images and metaphors, and more effective communication skills has made the sermon "an event in time" rather than simply teaching. Preaching is no longer just proclamation; it is also a manifestation of God's presence and power. All these possibilities invite members with artistic talent to bring their gifts as an offering to common worship.

The spiritual formation aspects of worship are being undergirded in several ways. These ways include increased emphasis on the Christian story via the church year calendar; intentional teaching about modes of prayer, both personal and corporate; more frequent celebration of the Lord's Supper (formerly observed only twice a year in most congregations); and encouragement of personal or small group meditation on lectionary texts during the week. Denominational publishers and education leaders have worked to develop integrated models for Sunday morning in which both the worship hour and education hour have the same focus. In some congregations, the pastor may meet with Sunday school teachers during the week to coordinate the preaching and the teaching focus.

Worship as Engagement of the Community

The emerging vision for worship renewal among Mennonites in North America includes an awareness that the horizontal dimensions of worship must continue to be fortified. Because of strong ethnic ties, Mennonites have traditionally experienced worship as a community-building event. Today the breakdown of the community and the increasing cultural diversity of the church have called for renewed attention to relationships. Worship is understood to be a corporate spiritual discipline. It involves the entire body of believers—all ages, races, sexes, and economic groups. Mennonites believe true worship demands the active participation of all the people of God.

The desire to be more inclusive in worship affects the structures for worship planning, worship styles, the use of language, and the involvement of all generations (children, for example, typically remain with their parents during worship). In contrast to clergy-dominated patterns of worship leadership, today's worship is often planned and led by lay people, often including women, although elders or deacons may establish worship themes and guidelines. In some churches, the pastor (or preacher) meets early in the week with the worship and music leaders. Together they plan the order of service using the Scripture focus for the week as the organizing framework. What may be lost in expertise is gained in wider participation in and ownership of worship concerns.

Worship styles are also more participatory, partly in response to the increased presence of women in leadership and their sensitivity to including people in more dynamic ways. The congregation may be involved in calls to worship, responsive Scripture readings, litanies, spontaneous prayer, and sharing of joys and concerns. People may rise to sing or to hear the reading of the Scriptures. In the act of reconciliation, they may turn to each other, shake hands, and offer assurances of God's forgiveness.

Sunday evening services in the past were often more informal and participatory than Sunday morning services. Because many churches no longer hold Sunday evening services, those less formal elements of these services have tended to become incorporated into Sunday morning worship. For example, the Sunday evening children's meeting is now often replaced by a children's story or experience on Sunday morning.

Testimonies of personal spiritual experiences were formerly included in Sunday evening services, while requests for prayer were usually part of the traditional Wednesday evening prayer meet-

ing. With the disappearance of both these settings has come the desire to introduce some elements of community sharing on Sunday morning. The sharing time in the service often follows the sermon and includes personal testimonies, affirmations, and concerns about health, work, or relationships. Usually this time concludes with a pastoral prayer; sometimes members gather to pray with the individuals who have requested prayer.

Another way worship is becoming more participatory is through increased sensitivity to language that includes all people. The words of worship must welcome the disabled, the poor, women, and racial minority groups. Even the language used to describe God is being reexamined for exclusiveness. Although congregations are still struggling with language issues, the issue of greater sensitivity in the use of language has clearly become an issue of justice.

Pastoral care rituals in worship have expanded in importance. Child blessings, commissionings of church workers, and even, in some places, regular prayers for healing are familiar elements of worship.

One consequence of these additions to worship is that more time is needed for the Sunday morning service. Whereas an hour used to be a standard length, many congregations now meet for up to an hour and a half, and in some cases, even longer.

Worship as Empowerment for Mission

Because of a theological emphasis on discipleship, worship among Mennonites has always been seen as continuous with daily living. In recent years, however, the church's ministries of evangelism, peacemaking, and service have been more explicitly connected with worship.

People who have returned from service assignments abroad have brought back with them a broader social consciousness and awareness of injustice. Because of their influence, calls to action in peacemaking, stewardship, or community service have become more frequent. Intercessory prayer may include prayers for peace in the world, as well as laments of the tragedy and pain in the world.

Some churches take their worship to the streets as a form of witness. On Palm Sunday, these churches may march around the block singing songs of praise to God. On Good Friday, they may carry a wooden cross through the city as part of their worship. Marchers for peace may gather in public places to pray for the end to war.

The relationship between evangelism and worship has also been strengthened. Congregations are learning to become more hospitable to visitors; care is taken to avoid exclusive words or the use of terminology in worship that is unclear to visitors or new Christians. Styles of music have expanded to include contemporary song, as well as familiar and traditional music. Although altar calls are not longer a common practice, a variety of opportunities are given in a service for calling people to faith. Sometimes churches host a weekly potluck for visitors and newcomers as a way of extending friendship and integrating them into the community of faith. Finally, churches provide news releases to the local press regarding church services and special activities.

The growing number of racial and cultural groups which make up the Mennonite church today have caused the church to be more keenly aware of its identification as a global church. Leaders are attempting to reflect this new reality as they choose worship styles and resources. The new hymnal, for example, includes a greatly expanded repertoire of music from non-Western sources.

In a time of much ferment and change, it is easy for worshipers to lose sight of the focus of worship, meeting the living Christ. It is also easy for conflicts to develop over various expectations and preferences. Education in worship and additional training for worship leaders are sorely needed in Mennonite congregations. To strengthen worship in all its dimensions calls for the Spirit's guidance and power.

Marlene Kropf

133 ✦ MESSIANIC SYNAGOGUE

Messianic Jews occupy an uncomfortable position between a Christian church that sometimes fails to appreciate their distinctives and a Jewish community that often rejects them as intruders. In living out their faith in Jesus as Savior in the framework of Jewish identity and tradition, Messianic Jews experience their "in-between" status as a major factor in their own spiritual formation.

Rabbi Hayim Halevy Donin has called the Jewish community "a family, an expanded family to be sure and ofttimes a far-flung family, but a family nevertheless" (_To Be a Jew_ [New York: Basic Books, 1972], 8). Messianic Jews consider themselves to be an integral part of that family and reflect Jewish cultural and religious forms in their worship and throughout their lives. Nevertheless, there is a distinctive of Messianism, as understood by Messianic Jews, which is fiercely disputed by most, if not all, of the balance of the Jewish "family." For Messianic Jews believe that Yeshua ben Yosef—Jesus—is the Messiah of Israel (Matt. 1:16; Luke 4:23).

Despite this serious controversy within the greater Jewish community over their beliefs and, indeed, over their status within Judaism, Messianic Jews equally strongly identify themselves as Jews. In fact, within _halakha_ (Jewish law and tradition) itself, Messianic Judaism finds support for its argument that no matter how non-normative their beliefs, they remain Jews.

Theology, as done in a Messianic Jewish setting, in some ways resembles evangelical Christian theology. Inevitably, however, issues emerge that are of concern only to Jews. Imbedded in Jewish religious thought are the concepts of _torah_, covenant, and _mitzvah_ (commandment), which are important to the religious self-identification of most Messianic Jews as well. Indeed, the importance of _halakha_ is a matter of survival itself, as at least a few Messianic leaders are beginning to realize and deal with seriously.

Circumcision is the rite of initiation for a Messianic Jew, as it is also the rite of initiation into the community of Israel. Although many Messianic congregations practice the _mikvah-brit_, a form of baptism as seen through Jewish religious rites and history, the primary rite (both chronologically and in terms of fundamental scope) is the _brit milah_ or circumcision—that is, incorporation into the covenant of Abraham. This covenant of Abraham makes a person a Jew.

One of the essential elements of the covenant has always been the land, _eretz Yisrael_, which is now being manifested once again in the nation of Israel. Therefore, Zionism is an important ingredient in Messianic Judaism, especially in the relationship of the individual members of Messianic synagogues and the larger community, for whom Zionism often means "a vague, though by no means insincere, friendliness to the State of Israel" (Will Herberg, *Protestant, Catholic, Jew* [Garden City, N.Y.: Anchor Books, 1960], 190).

Tradition, yet another identifying feature of Messianic Judaism, is viewed in a manner similar to that of reformed Judaism. *Torah* also is an identifying feature of Messianic Judaism, as it is for all forms of Judaism. In most Messianic synagogues, the reading of the Torah is an integral, if not the central, element of the worship service. Sermons, as one would expect, draw heavily upon the Hebrew Bible, and Bible studies frequently use it.

Being Jewish involves at least some kind of incorporation within the Jewish community. Subsequently, this community is an inherent ingredient in the spiritual formation of every Jew, except for the most isolated Jew from the community life. Participation in the living community, *am Yisrael* or the "people of Israel," is so important that without this participation Jewish people would wither away.

Messianic Jews are an "in-between" people. They are caught between a Christian church which often lacks understanding of or appreciation for their ambivalent situation and the Jewish community which is often hostile to and even less understanding of their desire to remain who they are—Jews—and simultaneously to live as believers in Yeshua, their Messiah and Savior. Messianic Jews are sometimes criticized by the church for holding on to their rituals and almost always rejected by Jewish community institutions as fraudulent intruders from the outside, rather than as an indigenous Jewish movement. Their uncomfortable position between two religious systems incorporates itself into the identity of Messianic Jews. The Messianic community is, in a real sense, a persecuted people, and this persecution influences their self-understanding both as believers in Yeshua and as Jews.

However, Messianic Jews are more than just another movement within the Jewish community. They are a people who have acknowledged that they have been redeemed by the sacrifice that Jesus, Yeshua, made once for all on the cross at Calvary. This fact inevitably shapes the spirituality of Messianic Jews, both as individuals and as worshiping people. They are evangelical in their theology, for they have—often under extremely harsh circumstances—appropriated an individual and personal faith in Jesus' substitutionary atonement. This concept is a powerful one for Jews who come to faith in the Messiah.

But Messianic Judaism is still a young movement. This should dissuade the observer from making projections or trying to generalize. As a young movement, Messianic Judaism is characterized by excitement and fervor. Messianic Jews are seriously attempting to discover what it means to be a Jewish people who try to appropriate the tradition of the Jewish community while simultaneously taking a radical stand that often results in rejection from that community.

Kenneth Warren Rick

134 • THE NATIONAL BAPTIST CONVENTION OF AMERICA, INC.

Worship in the National Baptist Convention of America is respect for the "worthship" or worthiness of God. Worship, private or public, which praises God and proclaims the gospel encompasses all the ministries of Christ's church in which Christians are all called to serve.

Worship is our response to the "worthship" or worthiness of God. This means that corporate worship, private worship, or any other environment in which God is praised and the gospel proclaimed cannot remain within the confines of specific worship settings. Given the nature of our world and the myriad problems which impact spiritual commitment and growth, the worship experience must have a ripple effect beyond the sanctuary walls to the people engaged in specific church ministries.

For a long time, member churches of the National Baptist Convention of America, Inc., held to a worship style focusing on the pastor/preacher, who directed the worship and proclaimed the gospel of Jesus Christ to a waiting congregation. But now these churches have become acutely aware that preaching, singing, praying, and Bible reading alone in the public worship service do not provide the comprehensive ministry about which our Lord Jesus Christ spoke and which he enacted while he sojourned on this planet.

Worship in National Baptist churches has always

been related to a number of other concerns. First of all, worship in National Baptist churches has always tried to relate to the spiritual development of children and has always provided a significant niche for the participation of women. This is not to say that member churches have always developed specific ministries for children or have always confronted the challenges of women's issues. What has been described as spiritual formation has always been active and present in the member churches through church auxiliaries which function primarily for fellowship and growth. Evangelism, social action, education, and pastoral care are ministries which also have always received impetus from corporate worship.

Women in Worship and Ministry

Most Baptists have always looked with disfavor on ordained women serving in pastoral ministry. The National Baptist Convention of America has published no official stance relating to the ordination of women for pastoral ministry; however, it is tacitly understood that the Convention has not endorsed women for this form of ministry. On the other hand, because of the number of women members of the Convention who are pursuing full-time Christian vocations in accredited seminaries and divinity schools, there is constant pressure to reassess this position. More importantly, the Convention has endorsed female commissioned chaplains in the armed forces of the United States, some of whom have indicated that their long-term goal is the pastoral ministry.

Women have always contributed to worship as Christian education directors, mission leaders, ushers, choir members, trustees, and children's department leaders. With participation in worship as a springboard, they have engaged in a broad outreach ministry to the physically ill, to homeless and displaced persons, to those needing family counseling, and to those affected by substance abuse. They have served as hospital volunteers and in other significant voluntary capacities in social and community agencies. Women members are also cognizant of their responsibility in matters of family life, pregnancy and abortion, discrimination in the workplace, sexual harassment, and other issues of public policy. Their thinking and actions have been shaped through in-service courses and institutes in the local churches, which have helped them to come to grips as Christians with these vital women's issues. Their outreach ministry and continued study have been impacted by their experience in worship of the God who inspires them to demonstrate practically and apply their faith.

Worship and Evangelism

Worship in the National Baptist tradition is the expression of gratitude to God through adoration and praise. The proclamation of the gospel is a central component of this worship. Thus, evangelism is closely aligned to worship. The proclamation of the Word challenges worshipers to accept the saving grace of God through the redemptive act of Christ. The National Baptist Convention of America is deeply committed to evangelism; its constitution and by-laws incorporate a functioning Evangelical Board with the overall responsibility for promoting the ministry of evangelism throughout the Convention and thereby implementing the Great Commission of our Lord (Matt. 28:19-20).

The National Baptist Convention of America, Inc., meets three times annually. Each session includes evangelistic services. In addition, the Evangelical Board conducts an annual winter evangelism conference which focuses on methodology for Christian witness; courses are offered in such areas as reclamation of inactive members, evangelism and the incarcerated, street evangelism, and evangelism and the Bible. The Evangelical Board also conducts a tent revival in April. The goal of this revival is to reach those persons who have not accepted Jesus Christ as their personal Savior, intensely counsel them upon their acceptance, and teach them what their decision requires.

Worship and Social Action

For National Baptists, the focus on social concerns emerged in the early 1960s. National Baptists testify that the late Dr. Martin Luther King, Jr., pricked their spiritual consciences and caused them to embark upon social concerns and actions as an outcome of the worship experience. Dr. King was immersed in the Baptist worship tradition, a tradition which influenced the formation of his philosophy of nonviolence.

As a result of King's impact, the National Baptist Convention of America established a Commission on Social Justice with the responsibility "to plan and promote such programs as will provide Christian concern for the welfare of oppressed peoples." The Convention's mission statement includes a clause that affirms "safeguarding the principles of religious liberty, social justice, and the equality of humankind as children of God."

The movement for social justice in National Baptist churches was an outgrowth of worship stimulated by the proclamation of a gospel, that included within its scope both local community needs and global concerns. National Baptists have accepted the responsibility implicit in the gospel to address the critical social and ethical issues of contemporary society. Because of this commitment, some member churches have been accused of preaching a *social gospel.* They have responded by asking, "How can the gospel of Jesus Christ, except for its divine dimension, be other than social?"

Worship has moved from the pew and the sanctuary into the crucible of human experience. It has created through the proclamation of the Word a spiritual challenge to the social conscience. It has motivated worshipers to become concerned and involved in issues of racism, black economic strategies, problems of drug and alcohol abuse, unemployment, black-on-black crime, and other matters affecting the African-American community. Through worship, that Word is proclaimed; its purpose is, in the words of Christ himself, "to preach good news to the poor, . . . to proclaim freedom for the prisoners, . . . to release the oppressed" (Luke 4:11).

However, the social action concerns of National Baptist churches are not limited to issues within the African-American community, even though the Convention is predominantly black. Low-income and senior citizens' housing, soup kitchens and "meals on wheels," job training, literacy programs, teen-age pregnancy counseling, drug prevention seminars, and family counseling centers are concerns and focuses of the National Baptist Convention of America, which touch the lives of people of all backgrounds.

Worship and Education

Because the proclamation of the gospel has always been instructional, worship and education have always been integrated in National Baptist churches. While the image of black Baptists as emotional is a stereotype, they do react demonstrably to the work and direction of the Holy Spirit. To undergird this enthusiasm, National Baptists establish the proclamation of the Word in worship as an integral part of the teaching ministry of the churches. Two denominational agencies, the Educational Board and the Christian Education Board, assist education in the denomination. The Educational Board identifies young people in member churches whose goal is to pursue a college degree or graduate theological training in order to be able to serve in full-time Christian ministries. The Christian Education Board has the responsibility for developing curriculum materials and publications, used in every aspect of the church's teaching ministry, from mission studies to men's groups. In 1992, the first set of church study materials was published on the theme of "reclaiming the black family."

The integration of worship and education is clearly demonstrated in the Convention's annual session. In a study program implemented through the National Baptist Congress of Christian Workers, the Convention meets in plenary sessions for worship. Devotional messages, Bible studies, symposia, and lectures addressing contemporary issues relevant to the body of Christ are interspersed. Curricular offerings cross a broad range of topics which include teaching methodologies, biblical and doctrinal studies, marriage and family counseling, evangelism, spiritual discipline, and pastoral studies.

Church school instruction at the local church level utilizes a curriculum designed specifically to apply to the needs of African Americans as a cultural group. A worship format is included in these materials as a prelude to actual study sessions. Many local churches offer discipleship training institutes set within a worship format. With the development of multiple-staff ministries, National Baptist churches have established children's churches. Their worship format follows that of adult worship, but the services are conducted at the children's level of comprehension. The inquiring minds of children require special preparation for the pastor who gives the message and for the children's church staff who must explore that message further and follow it up.

Richard A. Rollins

135 ❖ PRESBYTERIAN CHURCH IN AMERICA

Discussion of worship issues within the Presbyterian Church in America centers on interpretation of the regulative principle embodied in the Westminster Confession. More than all other ministries related to worship, concern for evangelism drives worship renewal in this church.

The hallmarks of the Presbyterian Church in America are, first, Reformed orthodoxy and then second, evangelism. Not surprisingly, most discussions of worship in this Presbyterian body arise out of one or both of these contexts.

The Regulative Principle of Worship

Theological consideration of worship within Reformed orthodoxy focuses on the regulative principle of worship. That principle is set forth in the Westminster Confession, which forbids worship "not prescribed in the holy Scripture" (XXI, 1). On this principle, "whatever Scripture does not prescribe is forbidden," as opposed to Roman Catholic, Eastern Orthodox, Lutheran and Anglican worship, which assumes that whatever Scripture does not forbid is permitted. The regulative principle, however, is subject to a qualification since the Westminster Confession indicates that some circumstances of worship and church government are to be determined by "the light of nature and Christian prudence, according to the general rules of the Word" (I, 6). Some in the Presbyterian Church in America would also claim that other qualifications of the regulative principle are implicit in the Confession's system of doctrine. Proponents of the regulative principle defend it by appealing to Scripture's concern for purity in worship, its disapproval of worship "according to the imaginations of [peoples'] own hearts," and its condemnation of those who would add to the Word of God.

All officers in the Presbyterian Church in America subscribe to the regulative principle as part of the Westminster Confession. However, there are those who minimize and those who maximize the qualifications of this principle. Those who minimize the qualifications and press its literal meaning as stated in the Confession tend toward a very plain and even austere form of worship: no choirs or soloists, no symbolic decorations (not even the cross), no lay leadership in worship, no testimonies, no altar calls, and traditional music only, with special emphasis on the Psalms. This type of worship is most easily described in negative terms, since few things are literally _commanded_ in Scripture for Christian worship. Some in the Reformed tradition have argued that the regulative principle requires use of the Psalms exclusively for Christian hymns and forbids the use of musical instruments. Only some congregations of the Presbyterian Church in America take this extreme position, though this position is mandated in some Reformed congregations and denominations.

Even in churches whose adherence to the regulative principle is relatively unqualified, it is possible to increase congregational participation through such liturgical elements as unison prayers or antiphonal responses. Some churches will use features of worship found in the original Reformed liturgies of Geneva, Strasbourg, and elsewhere. Even relatively nonliturgical churches will sometimes include the regular sequence of the service: reading of the law, prayer of confession, and assurance of pardon.

Evangelism and Worship

Others in the Presbyterian Church in America press the qualifications of the regulative principle and therein find more areas of freedom in worship. Most who defend such freedom argue that it should be employed in the service of evangelism; thus, the second hallmark of the Presbyterian Church in America enters our consideration. Currently, a denominational study committee is dealing with matters of worship. Significantly, however, that committee exists not by direct mandate of the General Assembly nor of a presbytery, but by the order of Mission to North America, the committee responsible for domestic church planting. Seeking to establish guidelines for church planters, the committee is asking, "What sort of worship shall we have in the new churches?" Thus, the discussion of worship falls into the context of evangelism.

As an example, there is considerable discussion in the Presbyterian Church in America about the worship practices of the nondenominational Willow Creek Community Church in suburban Chicago. Some Presbyterian Church in America church planters have sought to emulate the worship style of the Willow Creek seekers' service by incorporating drama, contemporary music, and multimedia presentations in the Sunday service while reserving the sacraments for more traditional midweek services. Apart from questions about the view of the Sabbath underlying this approach, the main question is: "To what extent should we use our freedom in worship to speak the unbeliever's language, to meet the unbeliever on his or her own terms?"

Other Presbyterian Church in America churches view the Sunday worship not primarily as evangelism, but as a meeting of the body of Christ to worship God. These churches, nevertheless, seek to make worship intelligible to any unbelievers who may be present (1 Cor. 14:24-25) through friendliness and informality and through contemporary music and language. These churches sometimes describe themselves, in the context of the Willow Creek discussion, as "seeker-sensitive, but not seeker driven."

Other churches in the Presbyterian Church in America seek to evangelize by *contextualization*, by adapting the Presbyterian worship style to ethnic and socioeconomic groups other than the upper middle-class whites who dominate American Presbyterianism. The New City Fellowship of Chattanooga, Tennessee, has a black pastor and a white worship leader (recording artist James Ward). The church's music is influenced by many traditions, including black gospel. Many Presbyterian Church in America leaders see that church as a model of contextualization in worship.

John Frame

136 • PRESBYTERIAN CHURCH (USA)

Presbyterians are convinced that worship, work, and witness are inseparable within the one life of the church. Through worship and the proclamation of the Word, faith matures into a commitment that touches other lives with the Good News of Christ.

Presbyterians believe that every person called into the community of faith is gifted by the Holy Spirit for worship and for work. However, they often find it a challenge to live up to their theology about equal privilege and responsibility.

In the decades since the churches which now make up the Presbyterian Church (USA) opened ordination to women, the denomination has made noticeable progress toward realizing the priesthood of believers in public worship. For example, people gathered for a recent ordination service were called to worship by a poised six-year-old reciting the Psalm for the day, while the charge to the congregation was given by an eighty-six-year old. An African-American woman pastor gave the invocation; a Korean elder led the recitation of the creed; and an unemployed young man read the Gospel lesson. The entire celebration was a glad microcosm of the church universal, reflecting the denomination's creative and visible inclusion of those who join in worship.

In principle, every believer—each child, each woman, each man—participates in worship as an act of service and in work as an act of worship. Worship pervades and unifies all facets of Presbyterian life. The constitutional *Directory for Worship* supports this understanding by devoting two full chapters to the relationship between worship and service. One chapter deals with the Christian's mutual ministries to one another within the church: Christian nurture and pastoral care. The other chapter addresses the church's ministries in the world: evangelism, compassion, reconciliation, and stewardship. I will explore here how these ministries interact in the common life of the Presbyterian Church (USA).

Worship and Christian Nurture

Christian nurture begins in baptism, the act of worship in which the entire congregation makes a commitment to the spiritual formation of the child or the new believer. The Lord's Day service is the primary center for Christian nurture. There, faith is brought to maturity through the regular hearing of the proclamation of the Word, through coming to the Lord's Table with an age-appropriate understanding, and through sharing in the worship life of God's people in the community.

Most Presbyterian congregations have been creative in designing services to involve children and the unique gifts they bring to worship. From offering an alternative informal family-oriented service each Lord's Day to providing special bulletins for children, local churches employ a broad spectrum of incentives for children who participate in public worship. Some congregations use church school classes to help children to learn hymns, prayers, and creeds; others incorporate contemporary music into the service; still others encourage adult friends to extend special invitations to a child ("Come sit with me during worship today").

When children's sermons are a regular feature of public worship, most congregations request the children to remain for the entire service, just as they do when the children's choir sings. The concerns about children in worship include: "If we dismiss them, aren't we sending them the message that the 'real' worship service isn't for them? Won't they feel we don't want them unless they're performing?"

Worship and Pastoral Care

Pastoral care in times of crisis and transition has always drawn upon worship resources. Prayer, shared Scriptures, or a beloved hymn come alive to comfort and support people. And offering Communion to those who are hospitalized, imprisoned, or confined to the home celebrates the presence of Christ beyond the sanctuary.

One suburban congregation has discovered that when two or three lay persons visit a local nursing home, singing the doxology or reciting the Lord's Prayer not only touches chords of personal spirituality, but also makes people feel more a part of their home congregation again. Similarly, people in the worshiping community experience a sense of oneness with absent loved ones when the concerns of the people or prayers of intercession bring those names into corporate worship.

Worship and Evangelism

Evangelism also happens most naturally and most effectively in the context of weekly worship. Where else will people hear the gospel faithfully and consistently proclaimed? Where else are they likely to see and experience the loving interactions of people being transformed by God's love? Where else will they hear a clear call to commitment and discover the promises of God? It is natural and effective for Christians to invite those they meet in their daily lives to come to worship with them.

Renewed interest in challenging people to discipleship has prompted an increasing number of congregations to incorporate a call to commitment into the Lord's Day service. "Worship should always offer opportunities to respond to Christ's call," affirms the _Directory for Worship_. Fre-

quently, the call to discipleship also provides an opportunity for people to renew commitment or to offer themselves in service and in mission.

Worship and Social Ministry

Works of compassion, reconciliation, social concern, and stewardship, when done as acts of Christian service, most often arise out of worship which calls Christians to these acts and equips and strengthens Christians for these acts. Hearing God speak through Scripture, being touched by the reality of intercessory prayer, recognizing the spiritual connection between all believers, all these experiences in worship move people into the world in service to Christ.

Following the perceptive example of African Americans, Presbyterians bracket their actions for social justice or for peace with prayer. They have learned the need for confession and empowering if their social witness is to be heard.

In seeking to intercede as if they were fellow suffers with those for whom they pray, Christians find themselves drawn to new worship disciplines. Some Presbyterian congregations now use the daily news as a prayer resource along with _The Mission Yearbook_. Others encourage members to develop simpler lifestyles for the sake of both economic justice and the exercise of the discipline of stewardship of the earth and earth's goods. Members of one congregation are challenged to retire early in order to offer years of freely given ministries of compassion or encouragement.

How do Presbyterians pull all these diverse ministries together? One elder used this image: "Worship is the glue that holds our life together. When we are all going our separate ways in the weekday world, what we do isn't fragmented, because we will all come back to this same place at the same time and bow our heads together in the same motion before the same Almighty God."

Mellicent Honeycutt-Vergeer

137 ✦ PROGRESSIVE NATIONAL BAPTIST CONVENTION

The congregations which make up the Progressive National Baptist Convention are not bound by denominational directives. Nevertheless, across the denomination there is a discernible trend toward inclusiveness in wor-

ship. Also integral to worship is a tradition of social witness, particularly in issues that affect the African-American community.

The churches which make up the Progressive National Baptist Convention, Inc., are involved in several efforts to integrate the worship life of the congregation with the overall ministry of each local church.

Inclusiveness in Worship

The Progressive National Baptist Convention has no stated policy on women in the ordained ministry. Women pastors are active in the national, regional, state, and district associations in which Progressive Baptist churches convene. The fact that the local Baptist church is autonomous prevents the structures of the denomination from dictating the policy and practices of the local church, as is the case with churches governed by episcopal or synodical systems of church administration.

Nevertheless, many local churches with a fundamentalist hermeneutical style argue that since the twelve apostles were males, it is heretical for churches to ordain women. Some churches will accept women ministers for staff positions other than senior pastor. However, the majority of churches whose pastors are college- and seminary-trained do not reject the ordination of women who are themselves theologically trained. It is also true that attitudes toward women are shaped by tradition and culture much more than by theological perspective. Women ministers are in need of basic support from the women in the membership of the local churches. Efforts are being made to raise consciousness in these areas.

The church is also attempting to encourage people who sing, read Scripture, pray, and preach to use nonsexist language. The challenge to use inclusive language is a new frontier for Progressive National Baptists. Although theological schools are on the cutting edge of change on this issue, the diffusion of new ideas from trained clergy to laity is often painfully slow. The increase in the pace of transmission of these new concepts and of transformation of attitudes depends largely upon the proactive leadership of women who will tirelessly push for such change.

For children, a special worship service takes place concurrently with the adult worship service

time. The children's church uses the imagery of the children's world of reality. However, during the observances of the ordinances of baptism and the Lord's Supper and at special observances such as Christmas, Easter, Mother's day, Father's day, and Children's day, the children and adults worship together as an inclusive community.

Social Ministry in Worship

The relation of social involvement and worship varies with the individual Progressive National Baptist congregation. An example of a church involved in social ministry is Allen Temple Baptist Church of Oakland, California. Here, the Hispanic community worships in a separate Spanish-language service. At least three times a year, the Hispanic and English-speaking members worship together. A highlight of joint celebration is the observance of Cinco de Mayo.

At Allen Temple, a special service is held semi-monthly for senior adults in the housing projects sponsored by Progressive National Baptist churches. A minister is assigned to work with these adults. Although the seniors have their own choir, the church's children's choir and youth choir are invited guests so as not to isolate senior adults from the larger church community.

Progressive National Baptist churches are rich in liberation theology. Hence, the concerns of the social context of the church are an inescapable part of the worship experience. Voter registration, poverty, civil rights, apartheid, policy brutality, law enforcement, and public safety are some thematic emphases of worship gatherings in Progressive National Baptist churches.

In his Lyman Beecher lectures, later published as *Social Crisis Preaching*, Kelly Miller Smith, a Progressive National Baptist pastor and as assistant dean and professor of Vanderbilt Divinity School, declared,"Black existence in America has been one of continuous social crisis. Virtually all of the preaching that blacks do is social crisis preaching, although some preaching is cleverly disguised" ([Macon, Ga.: Mercer University Press, 1984], 50). Such preaching interweaves the music and litany of worship with the sacred prophetic Scriptures and the life challenges of the community assembled for worship. L. T. Daye points out, "There are many whose strength to overcome the struggles and hardships of the week is gained by the awareness that it is necessary to make it to the preaching event on Sunday morning" (_The Pastoral Crises_ [1989], 58).

─────── **Worship as Celebration** ───────

The emphasis of the order of worship is clearly expressed in the sermon content and in the music of the service. Nevertheless, members of the congregation are not spectators attending a performance by choirs, worship leaders, and the preacher. Worship in Progressive National Baptist churches has a free and expressive participatory style. There exists in these worship services a communal expression in which prayers, music, and preaching together produce a sacrifice of praise to the living God. As James L. Christensen has said, "Worship is not the funeral of a dead God; rather it is celebrating the exciting, exhilarating, assurance of a living Lord who has vindicated love, righteousness, and hope" (_New Ways to Worship_ [1973], 15). Celebration, therefore, is the characteristic of worship in the Progressive National Baptist tradition.

Worship in Progressive National Baptist churches in the future will continue to express celebration through changing forms. More and more churches are using contemporary music, orchestras, heavy percussion, liturgical dance, and even sermons adapted to the genre of secular rappers who now influence the youth and young adult population. Visual aids and sermons delivered with the assistance of actors who dramatize the preacher's words will become more common. In urban areas, street-corner worship services will increase.

J. Alfred Smith, Sr.

138 • REFORMED CHURCH IN AMERICA

Congregations of the Reformed Church in America strive to make their worship both orderly and informal in the effort to reach out to visitors and others seeking a church relationship. Other church ministries, such as social witness, education, and pastoral care, find expression through the church's worship life.

The Reformed Church in America is one of the oldest denominations in North America, tracing its roots to the Dutch Reformed church that established a congregation on Manhattan Island in 1628. The Reformed church presently has about 330,000 members in almost 1,000 congregations in the United States and Canada. The denomination has a presbyterian form of government in which lay people are elected as elders, to care for the spiritual concerns of a congregation, and as deacons, to care for the needy. Elders, deacons, and the minister make up the consistory, which is responsible for the worship and ministry in a local congregation.

Worship in Reformed congregations may be described as semi-liturgical. This means that the orders for the sacraments (baptism and the Lord's Supper) are determined, but the format of weekly worship is left to the discretion of the consistory.

Women in Worship. Women have been ordained in the Reformed church since the late 1970s. Although women represent more than 25 percent of the present seminary population, they continue to find it difficult to be called into pastoral ministries. The slow but sure process of integration of women into the ranks of the ordained is expected to take at least a generation. The issue of language in worship is as important in the Reformed church as in other mainline denominations. Although liturgical language regarding people has become far more inclusive, images regarding God remain dominantly masculine.

Worship and Social Ministry. Reformed congregations are often deeply involved in the concerns of their local communities. It is not unusual to find day-care centers, food pantries, counseling services, and recreational programs housed in local churches. Because of the denomination's deep and historic commitment to world and local missions, international and neighborhood concerns play an important role in the sermons, prayers, and programs of the church. For example, the crisis in South Africa, because of its connection with the white Dutch Reformed church in that country, has been a major focus for the denomination and local churches for the past decades, in both the church's worship and witness life. Services may include intercessions, sermon allusions, and an offering of letters on behalf of those who suffer the pain of apartheid.

In the denominational program offices, both social witness and worship are the responsibility of the same staff person. This combination of worship and witness illustrates the support each give to the other.

Worship and Education. The integration of children into worship took a new turn in the 1980s when the General Synod approved the right of each board of elders to admit children to the Lord's Supper. Although many churches have children's sermons or have developed a ministry entitled "Children and Worship" which often runs concurrently with the adult service, the move to allow children to participate in the sacramental meal may mean that local worship will become more accessible to the church's youngest members. As the Reformed churches in general embrace the liturgical year as one of the guiding principles of their worship, educational curricula utilized by Reformed Church in America congregations, developed in cooperation with other Reformed bodies, have grown far more conscious of the church year and the Common Lectionary in their lessons.

Worship and Pastoral Care. Pastoral care enters the worship service when those who are in the hospital or in need are mentioned by name in the intercessions of the church. The pastoral care of members and friends of the local congregation is a high priority and is exercised through public worship, pastoral calls, and the private sharing of the sacrament with the homebound. In the mid-1980s, the denomination published a service for healing in a collection of optional liturgies. This service, which can be integrated into morning worship or stand by itself, has been utilized by a broad spectrum of churches. Congregations which would describe themselves as deeply evangelical and pietistic, as well as those that would claim the adjective *liturgical*, have discovered it to be an important aid in healing. The service includes prayers for the sick and the option of anointing with oil those who seek healing.

Worship and Evangelism. Evangelism is also a high priority to many Reformed congregations. The last decade has witnessed a growth in intentional programs designed to encourage the inviting of friends and neighbors to worship services and congregational gatherings. In addition, local congregations have tried to make worship more friendly to visitors by being conscious of hospitality and by making the Sunday bulletin and service more accessible to someone who is not familiar with church language and traditions.

The Reformed Church in America published its own hymn book, *Rejoice in the Lord*, in 1985. It has been received with considerable approval both within the denomination and beyond. Because the denomination has no required hymn book, however, there is wide divergence in the use of hymns in local congregations. A survey of worship life conducted in 1987 revealed that the most popular hymn books were *The Hymnbook*, *Worship and Service*, and *Rejoice in the Lord*. Almost half the congregations reported the use of other hymn books. The freedom of local congregations to create their own worship styles is probably seen most clearly in the great variety of hymns sung across the denomination.

Although the Reformed Church in America was dominantly a Dutch church in the early centuries, it has always welcomed a variety of immigrants into its life. There presently are four councils which represent the concerns and gifts of the African American, Native American, Hispanic, and Pacific Asian members of the Reformed church. The presence of a multitude of cultures and language groups has been an important ingredient in moving the denomination to look beyond its predominantly white, middle-class membership.

Worship remains for the Reformed Church in America the central activity of the local church. Congregations pride themselves in worship that is both orderly and informal and in preaching that is both biblical and relevant. In addition, a regular and sensitive experience of the sacraments, music that brings joy to worship, the emphasis on pastoral care of its community, and a socially involved congregation have become the hallmarks of worship in the Reformed church.

Greg Mast

139 ✦ REFORMED EPISCOPAL CHURCH

The Reformed Episcopal Church reveals its evangelical and liturgical heritage in worship which proclaims the gospel through traditional forms, while reaching out to others and emphasizing ministry to families.

Worship has an important relationship to all forms of ministry in the Reformed Episcopal Church. As an evangelical church, it is committed not to divorce worship from true faith. As a liturgical church, it seeks to avoid conducting evangelism in a vacuum. The proclamation of the gospel is for a specific doxological end.

This dual emphasis on evangelical faith and worship grows out of the Reformed Episcopal Church's foundation in Holy Scripture. St. Paul, in particular, weaves the two together in his letter to the Romans:

> For it is with your heart that you believe and are justified, and it is with your mouth that you confess and are saved. As the Scripture says, "Everyone who trusts in him will never be put to shame." For there is no difference between Jew and Gentile—the same Lord is Lord of all and richly blesses all who call upon him, for "Everyone who calls on the name of the Lord will be saved" (Rom. 10:10-14).

The phrase, "call upon the name of the Lord," highlights the connection between true faith and worship. This expression has its origin in the Old Testament, as the predominantly Jewish believers of the first century would have recognized. In fact, the phrase is a direct quote from the Book of Genesis in a context that has everything to do with worship. When the Lord appeared and called Abram to the land of Canaan, God promised the patriarch, "To your offspring I will give this land" (Gen. 12:7). Abram's faithful response to the Word of God is significant: "He built an altar to the Lord and called on the name of the Lord" (Gen. 12:8). In other words, Abram's first act of faith was to worship God—a pattern which is repeated several times in Genesis (cf. 13:4, 33). When one reads St. Paul's comments to the Romans with the Old Testament background in mind, one understands that evangelical faith and worship are vitally linked. The apostle was not making faith the end of worship, but a means to worship. He wanted the Romans to associate living faith in the Lord Jesus Christ with Christ's altar of worship. He called for faith that worships and faithful worship that acts.

Influenced by the association of these great evangelical and liturgical truths, the Reformed Episcopal Church has developed worship and related ministries in several areas.

Evangelism and Worship

First, evangelism has been directly related to worship in the denomination. The Prayer Book of the Reformed Episcopal Church essentially follows that one produced by Thomas Cranmer, the sixteenth-century Archbishop of Canterbury, who was martyred for his convictions. It reflects the leading evangelical emphasis of the Reformation: justification by faith. Henry James Burgess points out that the Prayer Book services are the "best liturgical expression of justification by faith" (*Prayer Book Spirituality* [1987], 15). The pattern of this form of worship is the acknowledgment of sin, the proclamation of grace, and the response of faith. In other words, the worship service moves through a basic statement of the gospel. In particular, the liturgies (the Daily Office and Communion) move through this pattern three times each service. The effect is that a person is evangelized through the liturgy itself.

Many parishes of the Reformed Episcopal Church have applied the evangelical character of the Prayer Book to specific evangelistic efforts. One example is the concept of St. Andrew's days. The apostle Andrew is the prototype of evangelism, for he was the first disciple to bring someone to Jesus. Specific Sundays are designated St. Andrew's days in order to encourage the inviting of friends and even non-Christians to church. Usually a Morning Prayer service is conducted on this day because it does not include the Eucharist. Sometimes these days coincide with a Sunday when a baptism is performed because of the particular evangelical opportunity and message of this sacrament. St. Andrew's days have become quite effective in church development and revitalization; both new and established churches have utilized the concept. The approach can be combined with other appropriate outreach methods, such as calling people who have not attended church for some time to invite them to come. St. Andrew's days are a primary example of the relationship between worship and other ministries in the congregation.

Worship and Family Ministry

One other area of ministry related to worship involves work with families, especially children. Again, evangelical commitment has opened up new ways to reach families through the worship of God. The Reformed Episcopal Church has always focused on the need to believe in Christ, not just as individuals, but as a family. The practice of infant baptism is a reminder that entire households can "call on the name of the Lord." Since families can come to Christ and be part of his kingdom, they can also be part of the worship service. Mothers and fathers are encouraged to participate in Scripture reading and prayer as lay readers. Children light candles, sing in choirs, and join in special children's moments when the minister or some other person offers a Bible story geared to the child's level. In some parishes, families bake the bread for Communion and present it as a family when the offering is received just before the Eucharist. In all of these ways, families actively participate in the worship of God. Jesus' comment about children, "The kingdom of God belongs to such as these" (Luke 18:16), has become a real and tangible part of Reformed Episcopal worship.

Worship is not isolated from the rest of life. It is at the center of life, similar to the hub of a wheel. Yet, if the analogy can be extended, there are spokes which radiate from the hub. These spokes are the related ministries. Just as the hub turns the spokes, so worship guides the ministries. But just as a hub cannot provide movement by itself, neither can worship remain in a vacuum. Worship can and must produce life, the real life of ministry inside and outside the living community of the body of Christ.

Ray Sutton

140 • ROMAN CATHOLIC CHURCHES

For Roman Catholics, the liturgy is the foundation for living the Christian life in the exercise of all ministries of the church. Worship has an integral relationship to spiritual formation, education, social justice, and other areas of Christian witness.

The worship of the Roman Catholic church, referred to as the liturgy, is ideally seen as the summit of all the various activities of Christian living and ministry and as the source or inspiration for these activities and beliefs. It is described as such in the foundational document on liturgy from the Second Vatican Council, *Sacrosanctum Concilium* 10: "The liturgy is the summit toward which the activity of the Church is directed; it is also the font from which all her power flows." The most prominent issues in contemporary discussions on the relationship between liturgy and the Christian life could be grouped into the following areas: spirituality, catechesis, and social justice.

Worship and Spirituality

Christian spirituality, or the living out of the relationship between a Christian and God, mediated through Jesus Christ, is the personal foundation upon which liturgy is built. Having received the gift of faith from God, having sought understanding of that faith through theology, a Christian then brings that faith to the corporate worship or liturgy of the church because it is through the community that the faith is interpreted and that the reality of the kingdom of God on earth is recognized.

Conversely, how is liturgy the source of one's spirituality or spiritual formation? Worship is primarily praise of God by believers, not catechesis of nonbelievers. Therefore, proclamation of the Word and particularly preaching facilitates the community of believers, gathered to celebrate the liturgy, to celebrate the liturgy more deeply and faithfully. In this manner, believers are formed for effective Christian witness. On the other hand, believers bring to worship their experience of living a Christian life. In the liturgy, they are nourished and strengthened through praise and proclamation and then sent forth to witness by example to the saving power of God. The liturgy also serves as a reminder to individual Christians that their individuality is not the beginning nor the end of the story. The communal, corporate dimension of the body of Christ, the church, is made concrete in the liturgy and serves as an inspiration for works of social justice.

Worship and Instruction

Catechesis, the oral instruction or verbal passing on of interpretations of faith, also has a reciprocal relationship to worship. Thus catechesis both leads to worship and draws from it. The gift of faith draws people to a place where that faith can be interpreted and explained. Catechesis, either of adults or children, is instruction in the meaning of faith and in the tradition of the church. In very practical ways, this is intimately connected to the liturgy. Since 1988, the Rite of Christian Initiation of Adults has been the only way adults may enter the Roman Catholic church in the dioceses of the United States. This rite is a process which involves public ceremonies that mark the catechumens' movement from one part of the process to another, particularly as they approach their initiation at Easter. The liturgy is part of the catechesis, not in a didactic manner, but in the action of ritual gesture, in the prayers, and in the presence of the larger church community which supports the catechumens. In addition, the process of catechesis has proven to have a renewing impact on church life. One of the most fruitful dimensions of the Rite of Christian Initiation of Adults is the effect it is having on other members of the community who have been baptized as infants. It reminds them of the importance of being a member of the body of Christ.

Partially because of the influence of this rite, many catechetical programs for children have been reintegrated with the liturgy through Sunday school (in the Roman Catholic church, the Confraternity of Christian Doctrine) classes based on the lectionary. In other words, the readings around which each lesson is built are the same readings used in the Sunday liturgy. This parallel sequence allows for continuity between all age levels of a parish and introduces children at a young age to the major readings and movements of the liturgical year.

———— Worship and Social Justice ————

Social justice is really not a distinct area in Christian life and liturgy, but a way of acting and being which permeates all Christian life and practice. Justice is the fruit of peace and recognition of the dignity of each human being. A liturgy which begins and ends with an exchange of the peace of Christ does so in order to stress the continuity between the way one worships and the way one lives one's life.

An example of the interaction of social justice and liturgy can be found in the Eucharist, the primary liturgical celebration in the Roman Catholic church. At the Table of the Lord, spiritual hunger and thirst are met. However, the reception of the body and blood of Christ is not solely a relationship between God and each individual human being. It is also a communion of Christians with each other and a representation of their responsibility to the world. In other words, one cannot eat at the Lord's Table and not, in turn, feed the hungry. By becoming what we as Christians eat, the body of Christ, we must in turn be the body of Christ to the world, caring for all people as ex-

emplified in the actions of Jesus of Nazareth.

Liturgy also addresses human equality, as the Bishops' Committee on the Liturgy states:

> Liturgy requires the faith community to set aside all distinctions and divisions and classifications. By doing this the liturgy celebrates the reign of God, and as such maintains the tension between what is and what must be [the completeness of the kingdom] (*Environment and Art in Catholic Worship*, 32).

In liturgy, the church calls for an end to racism, sexism, and classism as reflected in the belief in the basic dignity of each human being, which is the foundation of peace.

One of the most controversial, and therefore prominent, dimensions of this discussion in the Roman Catholic church is the issue of equality for women. To date, women are not ordained in the Catholic church to the rank of either deacon or presbyter. While this remains a rule, women are increasingly fulfilling roles of ministry once restricted to the domain of the clergy. Since the Second Vatican Council, the theology of the priesthood of all believers has found fruition in a multitude of ways, particularly in the involvement of lay people in liturgical ministries such as lector, eucharistic minister, acolyte, preacher, non-eucharistic presider, cantor, and minister of hospitality. In addition, women and men are fulfilling ministerial roles in pastoral care of the sick, including taking Communion to them. The experience of fulfilling these ministries, together with the rise of an increasingly well-educated laity, has led many in the church to question the denial of the priesthood to women, a restriction perceived as a denial of full equality within the church.

This issue of social justice and liturgy, like all of the categories mentioned above, challenges the connection between belief and prayer. It also reminds Christians that the work of integrating liturgy into all facets of Christian life and praxis is not yet complete.

Theresa Koernke

141 ✦ SALVATION ARMY

Within the Salvation Army, recognition is growing that the dual priorities of evangelism and social action can find effective expression through worship.

One of the most important debates of the twentieth century involves the relationship of evangelism and social action. Are they of equal importance or does one take precedence over the other? When the Salvation Army debated this subject in its Second Century Advance Task Force, the phrase *balanced ministry* became the byword. Further expression of this concept was given in the Army's recently completed International Mission Statement:

> The Salvation Army, an international movement, is an evangelical part of the universal Christian Church. Its message is based on the Bible. Its ministry is motivated by the love of God. Its mission is to preach the gospel of Jesus Christ and to meet human needs in His name without discrimination.

The statement is clear in describing a dual mission, one that is both social and spiritual. The Salvation Army is concerned with God's plan for individual and social salvation. In sorting out the evangelical and social mandates, some call for prioritization and some call for partnership. This is true not only of the Salvation Army, but of many groups within the church at large.

George Hunter, in a succinct statement affirming the principle of priority, asserted:

> Whenever the Christian mission has neglected disciple-making and concentrated on the other facets of Christ's work, we have not made many disciples or planted many churches and have not had much social influence either (*Church Growth Bulletin,* March 1977).

Ron Sider, on the other hand, has argued for partnership:

> The time has come for all biblical Christians to refuse to say, "The primary mission of the Church is . . ." I do not care whether you complete the sentence with "evangelism" or "social concern." Either way is not biblical and misleading. Evangelism, social concern, fellowship, teaching, worship—all these are fundamental parts of the mission of the Church. They must not be confused with one another, although they are inextricably interrelated. Scripture shows that the church has many tasks, and it does not give a choice of which to obey (*Christianity Today,* October 8, 1976).

By 1988, the Salvation Army had completed several documents to assist congregations in creating a partnership between the fundamental areas to which Sider referred. A symposium on "The Theology of Social Services" at Catherine Booth Bible College combined excerpts from selected papers into a booklet, "Creed and Deed." The same year, the Social Services Commission produced additional documents. The "fundamental parts" of evangelism, social concern, fellowship, teaching and worship were very much in evidence in these writings. Upon reflection, more could have been said about the relationship of *worship* to evangelism and social services. This is the case because what we as Christians believe and how we behave are often determined by the worship experience and its content. For evangelism and social concern to be practiced, they need to be emphasized in worship.

Four basic postures that undergird worship are adoration, confession, thanksgiving, and supplication (forming the acrostic, ACTS). Worship is generally agreed to involve both revelation and response, or Scripture and prayer. Incorporating these elements with the elements of the acrostic provides an outline for a worship experience that encourages evangelism and social concern.

As an example, the words of Isaiah—which Jesus quoted in describing his prophetic anointing—may call forth from us a response of confession:

> *Scripture:* The Spirit of the Sovereign Lord is on me, because the Lord has anointed me to preach the good news to the poor, . . . the prisoners, . . . all who mourn . . . (Isa. 61:1-3).

> *Prayer:* O Lord, we must confess that sometimes in our eagerness to witness we care more about the soul of man than the whole of man. Help us to realize your Son had no reservation about coupling evangelism and service, and let us imitate Christ.

Again, Paul's statement of the gospel's inclusiveness evokes a response of thanksgiving:

> *Scripture:* There is neither Jew nor Greek, there is neither slave nor free, there is neither male nor female, for you are all one in Christ Jesus (Gal. 3:28).

> *Prayer:* O Lord, we are truly thankful that your gospel is for everyone; that in you all barriers come down. Not only do we thus understand that the gospel is to be shared with everyone, but we also receive it as a powerful unifying force, making us one in a way no other power can. Thank you, Lord.

Scripture and prayer are but two worship elements that can and do illustrate the relationship between evangelism and social action. Other elements, such as the music, the sermon, or testimonies, can further illustrate the relationship. When the dual mission is proclaimed and practiced, life-transforming, God-honoring change occurs in redeemed lives.

Raymond L. Peacock

142 ✦ SOUTHERN BAPTIST CONVENTION CHURCHES

Like Baptist groups in general, the Southern Baptist Convention is an association of congregations which function autonomously at the local level. Thus, it is difficult to speak in generalities about worship and related ministries in the member churches. This entry discusses a representative congregation.

Crescent Hill Baptist Church in Louisville, Kentucky, is a Southern Baptist church seeking to integrate its worship life with the other ministries of the local congregation. Evangelism, education, pastoral care, the role of women, and other aspects of church life are all affected by worship and receive attention within the sphere of worship.

Women, Ordination, and Worship. Since in Baptist polity each congregation is autonomous and thereby free to interpret Scripture for its faith and practice, some congregations ordain women to the diaconate and to preaching and pastoral ministries, while others staunchly oppose women's ordination. Currently approximately eight hundred women are ordained to the ministry by Southern Baptist churches, serving in a variety of roles; but only twenty serve as a pastor of a congregation. The Center for Women in Ministry, which houses the national office of Southern Baptist Women in Ministry, is located at Crescent Hill Baptist Church.

This congregation practices the laying on of hands at baptism, believing that it ordains all believers—both men and women—to the ministry of Christ. Following a theology of the Pentecost, which understands the Spirit being poured on all the believers—both male and female—as normative for the church, Crescent Hill believes that both women and men should be ordained as representative ministers of the whole body, called and empowered to ministry. In the conviction that women's voices, bodies, and experiences should be a part of worship, the church also uses both lay and ordained women each week as worship leaders. Other congregations are also trying to break down the traditional male dominance in worship leadership.

Worship and Evangelism. Following every sermon, most Southern Baptist churches offer an "invitation," an evangelistic call to response. Special evangelistic services are normally held once a year in many churches. Some churches, like Crescent Hill Baptist, use the performing, dramatic, and visual arts to share the gospel of Christ with the community. This use of the arts is proving effective with those people who are resistant to more direct approaches of evangelism.

Children and Worship. Crescent Hill Baptist Church provides children's bulletins each week, containing visual aids and games related to acts of worship, seasonal themes, texts, and the sermon. A child dedication service is held approximately fifteen Sunday mornings a year. Parents and congregation affirm at this service their covenantal vows to raise the child in the Lord, and the child is welcomed into the congregation's life.

Children's sermons are growing in popularity among Southern Baptist churches. Some churches offer one every Sunday, while others use them occasionally. Although children's sermons vary greatly in quality and purpose, they, when properly used, are designed for the edification of the children and not the entertainment of the congregation. Their main value lies in helping children to experience a special place in worship and a personal contact with the pastor. Crescent Hill Baptist Church uses children throughout the year in acts of worship leadership, including performance of choral and instrumental music, praying, and Scripture reading.

Worship and Education. Every important educational objective in the church needs some embodiment in worship. At Crescent Hill Baptist Church, the Sunday school and worship hour occasionally build on the same texts. The Christian year, with its themes and Scripture readings, is often reflected in the Sunday school lessons and the worship service theme for a given season.

In addition, this congregation has created a number of spiritual formation groups. Some of them, like the "feminine spirituality" group, occasionally create and conduct worship for the congregation. Members of the congregation contribute to daily devotional guides for Advent and Lent and form special prayer and study groups.

A service devoted solely to intercessory prayer takes place the first Sunday evening of each month. This service enhances the total prayer life of the congregation. Furthermore on Sunday morning, the congregation is occasionally invited to enter into spontaneous open prayer. The Sunday evening prayer service has helped to free people to participate in such avenues of public prayer.

Ministry to the Aged and Physically Challenged. Many churches are renovating their worship and educational spaces to make them accessible to those who are physically impaired. At Crescent Hill Baptist Church, Communion is taken four times a year to those confined to the home and to members in nursing homes.

The church affirms that the kingdom of God does not exclude the infirm, the sick, the impaired, and those on their way toward healing. To welcome these persons is to welcome Christ.

Worship and Social Action. Through worship, people reflect on the social dimension of the gospel. At Crescent Hill Baptist Church, important social, moral, and political issues are addressed in the worship service. However, since Baptists believe in the separation of religion and government, the church avoids any advocacy of partisan political activity.

Crescent Hill Baptist Church also sponsors workshops on peacemaking, AIDS, family life, recovery from divorce, and the church and ecological concerns. Church leaders urge a thoughtful, compassionate response to these issues on the part of the membership.

Worship and Pastoral Care. The "care of souls" takes place each week through the rhythm of worship: praise, confession, thanksgiving, intercession, the offering of self, the hearing of God's Word, and the response. The congregation's needs in pastoral care are voiced in the gatherings on Sunday morning, in the Wednesday night prayer meetings, and in the Sunday evening in-

tercessory prayer services. On the Sunday evening before Christmas, worshipers leave the sanctuary to go caroling to homebound members. On Easter Sunday, some worshipers take the flowers that have adorned the sanctuary to members who are homebound or ill. At the close of every Communion service, the church receives an offering for benevolence ministries in the community. Special worship services are held with a specific purpose relating to pastoral care. These services have included an annual "community bereavement service" on the Sunday before Christmas; a service that ministers to those suffering great sorrow during the holiday season; a service of healing for Vietnam veterans and others affected by the war; and a healing service for those affected by AIDS.

H. Stephen Shoemaker

143 ✦ United Church of Christ

The United Church of Christ has encouraged member congregations toward greater inclusiveness in worship and related ministries, toward expanded social concern, and toward openness to visitors and new worshipers. The following entry describes how one local church has tried to realize these goals in relation to its worship service.

The worship life of any local congregation reveals far more about that fellowship than one might surmise at first glance. Embedded in the various elements of a standard Sunday morning hour of worship are not only the obvious current approaches to music, prayer, and Scripture, but also the elements which reflect the history, theology, and wide range of expressions of the ministry of that local church and that denomination.

Euclid Avenue Congregational Church in Cleveland, Ohio, serves as a representative example in the United Church of Christ because its long history shapes its present in so many ways and because the diversity of its membership reflects the membership in the denomination as a whole. The congregation was founded in 1843 and is currently housed in a building constructed in 1887. The congregation once numbered more than a thousand, but with the decline of the urban community it dwindled into the two hundreds. It now has 246 members and is even growing in the following ways. It has a solid financial base, a large staff, strong programming, and an active mission life. The building houses a number of outside programs in addition to the church's own day-care program. The congregation is active in denominational, ecumenical, and interfaith life. Of special note is the fact that this congregation has an exact balance between white and black members. This racial diversity is celebrated every Sunday morning when the congregation assembles for worship.

The worship service has a format that remains tied to the church's congregational heritage, but also reflects its thirty-four years with the United Church of Christ. A narrative of the Sunday worship, with commentary, is instructive for explaining the dynamic interplay between the past and present, between tradition and the changes brought about through diversity, and between worship and the larger context of parish life.

Worship begins with the ringing of the steeple bell, followed by organ prelude. The beauty of the sanctuary sets a formal tone, but greeters offer everyone a friendly welcome and provide name tags for everyone. The church makes a special effort to make everyone feel welcome. Guests are invited to fill out a visitor card and to join the congregation for the coffee hour after worship.

Visitors receive a letter and often a follow-up visit. The bulletin periodically includes an invitation to join the church; for those who express the desire to join, there is a new member's class. Each United Church of Christ congregation determines its own curriculum for new members; Euclid Avenue Congregational Church offers a brief class coupled with the invitation to join the congregation in what should be seen as a life-long educational journey.

As the service begins, the worship leader (usually the senior minister, but at times the associate minister or a lay person) leads a responsive call to worship, based on the lectionary texts and inclusive in its language—a recent intentional change in response to women's concerns within the denomination and congregation. A hymn follows, and then a unison prayer, silent prayer (preceded by pastoral concerns of the congregation), and the Lord's Prayer.

By this time most latecomers have arrived (a reality in a diverse, urban church with a large radius of membership). Words of welcome and announcements provide further opportunity to share pastoral concerns and to present a wide range of program options and local mission opportunities. After this informal break, the formal service resumes with an anthem, usually by the traditional choir, but once a month by the volunteer gospel choir. This combination of choirs reflects the diversity of the church's membership in terms of both race and theology.

Children are present for all of the above portions of the service (and on other occasions, for the rites of baptism and reception of new members). Children are then invited forward for the word to young worshipers, which relates to the texts and theme for the day. This word is given by the associate minister or by a lay person. Children and students through high school age usually leave for church school, unless they are assisting as ushers, lay readers, or junior choir singers. The

The Anchored Cross. This form of the cross, which combines the cross with an anchor (a symbol of hope), is found in the catacombs of the primitive church.

church school curriculum is not tied to the lectionary texts, although the United Church of Christ is developing such a curriculum.

At this point, the congregation shares in a "mission moment," which may reflect a variety of concerns, local or international. This portion of the worship service reflects the active social involvement of the United Church of Christ and of this congregation. The focus of the United Church of Christ mission is on the partnership with local people in the sharing of faith and the development of human and material resources. Euclid Avenue Congregational Church's local mission reflects that same focus and especially stresses work in the inner city through food distribution, tutoring, and youth programs.

The next portion of the worship service is the reading of Scripture with explanatory remarks. Usually two lectionary texts are read from the New Revised Standard Bible. The sermon which follows is about fifteen minutes in length. In this congregation, the sermons reflect the liberal side of the United Church of Christ's theological tradition and are directed as well to goals of social concern and spiritual formation. The sermon hymn is chosen by the preacher to relate to the sermon theme; it is followed by a pastoral prayer and at times by a denominational statement of faith or responsive Psalm reading.

The service then moves toward closure with the offertory and doxology (in inclusive language), a prayer of dedication, a hymn (chosen by the music director), and a responsive commission and blessing. Usually the choir sings a choral amen; the congregation remains seated and silent during the meditative music at the end of the service.

The entire service lasts about an hour and a quarter. It is followed by a time for greeting people in the front of the sanctuary or in the parlor where the coffee hour is held. This time is a prime opportunity for further sharing of pastoral concerns with the church staff. Sometimes further educational opportunities follow, usually preceded by lunch. Such educational times enhance community life, and the educational focus often relates back to the content of worship. The mealtime is intergenerational, and child care is provided during the study time. Other churches in the United Church of Christ tend to offer more regular adult Bible studies, studies on current issues, and ser-

mon "talk backs"; in addition, other churches sometimes offer more curricula options or form accountability groups. The smaller size and geographical spread of Euclid Avenue Congregational Church make it difficult to do these things on a regular basis.

Euclid Avenue Congregational Church attempts to make both its worship and its fellowship as inclusive as possible, reflecting the diversity and complexity of God's creation. The building is ramped and equipped with chairlifts; a church van transports people who would otherwise have difficulty getting to the church. During worship, a sound system includes individual units for the hearing impaired, and large-print bulletins are provided for the visually impaired. The United Church of Christ has been helpful in encouraging greater inclusiveness, for the denomination advocates ministries to the elderly, the infirm, the mentally impaired, and the physically challenged.

Randall L. Hyvonen

144 ✦ United Methodist Churches

Social concern, evangelism, and Christian education have all been important aspects of the Methodist movement since the era of John Wesley. United Methodist churches have traditionally sought to integrate these concerns into the worship service, especially through special program emphases promoted by various denominational boards and agencies.

The historical roots of the United Methodist Church include a concern for social piety and worship. John Wesley's General Rules required Methodists to give "evidence of their desire of salvation" by "doing no harm," which meant avoiding such evils as slaveholding, buying or selling liquors, and usury. The rules required Methodist to do good "by giving food to the hungry, by clothing the naked, by visiting or helping them that are sick or in prison." The rules instructed Methodists further to "attend upon all the ordinances of God," which included worship, the Lord's Supper, and the expounding of the Word. Thus, from the beginning, Methodists connected commitment to social concerns with public worship as marks of the Christian life.

Though the United Methodist Church in the late

twentieth century encompasses a wide range of theological trends from liberal to evangelical, a general consensus exists in the church that the life of faith involves engagement in social ministries and a commitment to social justice. Moreover, these concerns continue to find expression in the worship of the church, both in liturgy and in preaching.

Likewise, United Methodists have been committed to evangelism and education, and these also have exerted strong influence on the worship of the church. From the standpoint of evangelism, the most important influence on worship has been nineteenth-century revivalism, with its use of gospel music and altar calls. From the standpoint of education, the most important influence has been the Sunday school, with its emphases on lay leadership, special days such as World Communion Sunday, and the didactic use of worship materials.

The main worship resources for the United Methodist Church are the _Hymnal_ (1988) and the _Book of Worship_ (1992). These books have official status in the church due to their authorization by the General Conference. However, other bodies within the church, such as the General Board of Discipleship, regularly publish worship resources which are widely used. Furthermore, local pastors and congregations have tremendous freedom to adapt the order of worship and incorporate resources as they see fit. The result of this freedom is that the chief characteristic of United Methodist worship is its diversity of order, style, and content. However, the concern for social justice, evangelism, and education appears at every level.

——— Worship and Social Justice ———

The concern for social justice is found in the ritual of the church, as published in the _Hymnal_. Several examples may be cited. The confession in "A Service of Word and Table" (I and II) acknowledges that "we have not loved our neighbors, and we have not heard the cry of the needy." The Great Thanksgiving quotes Luke 4:18, which praises God for sending Jesus "to preach good news to the poor . . ." and later asks God to unify the congregation "in ministry to all the world." The orders for baptism ask the candidates or their sponsors "to resist evil, injustice, and oppression in whatever forms they present themselves." The _Hymnal_ also includes prayers for justice and a section

of hymns with the theme of "social holiness."

United Methodists celebrate six special Sundays in their church year, five of which focus on social issues or concerns. These five Sundays are Human Relations Day, observed in connection with the birthday of Martin Luther King, Jr.; One Great Hour of Sharing, observed on the fourth Sunday of Lent, which focuses on the United Methodist Committee on Relief; World Communion Sunday, observed on the first Sunday of October; Peace with Justice Sunday, observed on the second Sunday after Pentecost; and Native American Awareness Sunday, observed on a date set by the General Council on Ministries. Worship resources for these special days developed by the General Board of Discipleship are distributed to every local congregation. Additional resources usually appear in such denominational publications as _Interpreter_ magazine. These worship resources typically include calls to worship, confessions, responsive readings, and prayers based on the theme of the day.

——— Worship and Inclusiveness ———

Racial justice and human equality have been important, if occasionally controversial, issues within the church. The _Hymnal_ (1988) includes hymns from the Hispanic, Asian-American, African-American, and Native American traditions. United Methodists have produced additional hymnals and other liturgical materials for use within ethnic-minority congregations. Examples include _Songs of Zion_ (1981) for African-American congregations and _Songs from the Four Winds_ (1983) for Asian-American congregations. The _Book of Worship_ (1992) demonstrates the United Methodist commitment to ethnic diversity in its inclusion of worship resources that originated within ethnic-minority congregations.

Feminism has greatly influenced United Methodist worship practices. The number of ordained women in the United Methodist Church has increased greatly during recent decades. Women clergy have generally been well-accepted as pastors, preachers, and worship leaders. More problematic is the use of gender-inclusive language in worship, especially as this involves the altering of hymn texts and prayers. All official publications of the United Methodist Church attempt to use gender-inclusive language for people. This is evident in the _Hymnal_ and the _Book of Worship_. For example, the *Hymnal* suggests the substitution of "Ye Saints" for "O Men" in the hymn "Rise Up, O Men of God." More controversial is the altering of traditionally male terms applicable to deity. Some congregations have experimented with substituting terms that are not gender-specific for terms for the deity that are masculine (for example, substituting "Creator, Redeemer, and Sanctifying Spirit" for "Father, Son, and Holy Spirit"). Other congregations have experimented with including female terms along with male terms when addressing God (for example, "Our Father and Mother in heaven . . ."). However, none of these solutions has received wide approval. The issue promises to remain problematic for some time to come.

Worship, Education, and Evangelism

The use of the lectionary, while not required, has become widespread in the United Methodist Church. Many church education programs find it beneficial to employ the lectionary in youth and adult study groups as a means of coordinating education with worship. The use of children's sermons has also become widespread, though their place varies in the order of worship. Some churches put these sermons near the beginning of the service; other congregations find it more useful to place these sermons immediately before the adult sermon in order to consolidate the proclamation of the Word. Typically, children are called forward to sit with the pastor in the chancel area during this part of the service.

The influence of the revival pattern of evangelistic services remains strong in some areas, particularly the southern United States. Many pastors continue to have an "invitation to Christian discipleship" following the sermon, a form of which appeared in the order of worship in the 1964 *Methodist Hymnal*. The 1988 *Hymnal* suggests a variety of responses to God's Word, such as "acts of commitment and faith with offering of concerns, prayers, gifts, and service for the world and for one another." Furthermore, the *Hymnal* includes a rite for the "Reaffirmation of the Baptismal Covenant," to be used by individuals who wish to reaffirm their faith or by a whole congregation at particular times during the year such as Easter and Pentecost.

There is a movement in the United Methodist Church toward more frequent celebrations of Holy Communion. This movement has been encouraged by educational materials from denominational headquarters and has found much support in renewal movements within the denomination. Some larger congregations have found it useful to offer a weekly Eucharist at an early service on Sunday, in addition to monthly celebrations at a later service. This trend signals a return to Wesleyan roots. John Wesley himself encouraged "frequent communion" (at least weekly) for the early Methodists as a means of spiritual formation (i.e., sanctification) and as a "converting ordinance" for those who had yet to experience the new birth.

L. Edward Phillips

145 ✦ VINEYARD

The relationship of people with God, expressed through worship, is the central focus of the Vineyard churches. Viewed in this relational perspective, worship clearly enhances and interacts with all other areas of ministry in the church.

The priority of each Vineyard gathering (including staff and other business meetings) is to express the worship of the Lord. Among other things, this worship helps to soften the ground of people's hearts to other ministries. What follows are a few comments with respect to the relationship of worship to evangelism, social action, intercession, and the roles of women and children in the church.

The Role of Women. The place of women in worship has not been a major issue in Vineyard churches. Several factors may account for this. Many women are involved in the various visible functions of worship as leaders, musicians, vocalists, and dancers. It is the conviction of Vineyard leaders that a person's function in the church should be based on that person's calling, character, and gifts, rather than on gender. Roles performed by women vary across the Vineyard movement, but all forms of ministry are open to them. Furthermore, it is perhaps because of the emotional openness of many women that the intimacy of Vineyard worship is especially satisfying to them, both musically and lyrically.

Worship and Social Action. Worship in Vineyard churches also relates strongly to the areas of social action and ministry to the disadvantaged. In times of worship, participants are able to recognize the heart of God for the poor and fatherless. Indeed, worshipers come to understand themselves as the poor and fatherless, standing in awe of the favor and compassion shown to them by the Lord. Worship is a time to invite God's compassion to fill us as believers, so we may go forth to love as we have been loved. This thought is expressed in prayer, in teaching, and in song. The "Lord of the Poor" by Brian Doerksen is an example:

> You have chosen the poor to be rich in the faith.
> You have chosen the weak to shame the strong.
> So pour out your mercy on the ones who know their need;
> Pour out your Father's love on the fatherless children.
>
> Lord of the poor, God of the weak and helpless ones,
> Stretch out your arm,
> And be a safe refuge for the ones who have no hope at all.
> Arise, O Lord, and have compassion on the poor and needy ones.
>
> You hear every cry of all the lonely ones.
> You reach out your hand to care for the children.

Worshipers are encouraged to incorporate acts of kindness for the disadvantaged into their Christian lifestyles. Many congregations sponsor annual banquets for the needy.

Evangelistic Worship. At this point in the Vineyard movement, evangelistic worship is a major concern. It is the conviction of Vineyard leaders that worship encourages evangelism, for in evangelism we are calling people to worship—that is, to a relationship with God. More and more, congregations are discovering that worship is evangelistic in and of itself. When a person witnesses another person involved in true worship, something in his or her spirit says, "That is what I was made for!" It is not unusual for people to be converted to Christ during worship, even if nothing expressly evangelistic is emphasized.

Vineyard leaders are looking for ways to take worship beyond the walls of the church to the watching and waiting world. People have a deep hunger for stability, intimacy, and unconditional love. All these desires are found in worship. Responding to these needs, some Vineyard churches have set worship bands in public areas and played worship songs, both to lift up Jesus in that place and to ask his Spirit to draw people to himself. Ministry team members, scattered throughout the crowd that gathers, are prepared to share Christ and to pray with those touched by the Spirit of God. In addition, public praise in the form of "marches of Jesus" (pioneered by Graham Kendrick in England) is taking worship to the streets and making a global impact. The Vineyard organized Vancouver's first "march for Jesus" in 1992 as part of a worship festival; in this event, approximately ten thousand people took to the streets proclaiming Jesus as Lord in a powerful demonstration of Christian unity.

Worship and Intercession. More and more, the ministries of worship and intercession are being placed together; these two ministries seem to empower one another. Worship without intercession can eventually lead to losing touch with the needs of others, while intercession without worship can lead to human-centered prayers and to humanitarianism, or even to depression. Some of the most powerful experiences of intercession, both in praying the prayers of Scripture and in extemporaneous prayer, have occurred in the context of worship. One way this has been facilitated is through "worship intercession," an informal gathering on Saturday evening in which these two actions are combined.

Children in Worship. In a typical Vineyard church, families remain together expressing their worship. Then, after a break, children are divided into different age groups, in which they may also worship together using songs appropriate for each age level. The purpose of these times with children is to nurture their relationship with God and to train them in doing the work of God's kingdom. The Vineyard also publishes worship music and worship training resources for children.

In conclusion, members of the Vineyard believe that worship is to permeate every part of the life of the church. As we worship, the presence of God comes with healing, empowering us to serve and to be the body of Christ in this world.

Brian Doerksen

146 ✦ WESLEYAN CHURCHES

The Wesleyan Church, throughout its history, has emphasized social concern, evangelism, and personal holiness. Thus, the Wesleyan Church finds it natural to express these aspects of the Christian life, along with other church ministries, in corporate worship.

Worship in Wesleyan Churches is shaped by its history, traditions, convictions, and ministries. Each of these dimensions informs the congregational worship experience and worship's related concerns.

Women and Worship. Wesleyans have been ordaining women for most of their 150-year history. When Congregationalist Antoinette Brown became in 1853 the first fully ordained woman in a recognized American denomination and possibly the first in Christian history, her ordination sermon was preached by Luther Lee, a Wesleyan. The first women's rights convention in America was held in a Wesleyan chapel in Seneca Falls, New York, in 1848.

Women currently serve the Wesleyan Church as pastors, as co-pastors with their spouses, and as staff ministers, although not in significant numbers. The trend is toward more women in college and seminary pastoral preparation tracks. Subsequently, the placement of women in ministry positions seems certain to rise. That will mean, among other things, more women in worship leadership. In addition, the number of lay women in worship leadership is on the rise. There is greater sensitivity to the need for inclusive language in worship, where it does not conflict with biblical revelation, as in the names and pronouns for God in Scripture.

Children and Worship. In general, children's sermons have been replaced by creative worship experiences for children. Children's church has been around for a generation or more, but today's version is more hands-on and more worship intensive than its predecessors. Some churches begin the worship service with the family together, dismissing the children to their worship center during a hymn in the middle of the service. More liturgically oriented congregations use children as acolytes or in other worship roles, such as bearing branches in a Palm Sunday processional. Children's choirs are common across the denomination.

Evangelism and Worship. The Wesleyan Church comes out of the revivalistic tradition, and the altar call has a long and honored history. The invitation-response model, dating back to Charles Finney's "anxious bench" (or, in holiness history, the "mourner's bench"), typifies Wesleyan worship evangelism. Still, the Lord's Supper is offered "evangelistically" in the Wesleyan Church, and Wesleyans certainly affirm the evangelistic power of the gospel in elements of worship apart from the sermon and the invitation.

Social Concerns and Worship. The first Wesleyans were abolitionists, separating from the Methodist Episcopal Church long before the Civil War over the issue of slavery and over what they considered a heavy-handed episcopacy that tried to silence their crusade. Not surprisingly, the sermons and the liturgy of that era were saturated with social concerns. Today's church also has a social agenda, and it too often finds expression in worship—in sermons, but also in the principal prayers, in the litanies for issue-oriented special days, and in lay witness and testimonies.

Spiritual Formation and Worship. In recent years, spiritual formation has become a denominational priority. Growing Wesleyan churches almost always make profitable use of small groups, often patterned after Wesley's classes and bands, and stressing spiritual accountability. One congregation's well-publicized experiment in the 1960s with house churches that replaced the corporate worship assembly was not successful; however, cell groups still abound from "caring-sharing" Sunday School classes to support groups meeting a variety of needs. Worship in Wesleyan churches both shapes the context of these groups and reflects their ministries.

Pastoral Care and Worship. One of the strengths of the Wesleyan Church is its healthy sense of congregational community. Worship meets personal needs—a primary goal of pastoral care—by fostering that atmosphere of inclusiveness in a regular, structured format. Pastoral sermons (as opposed to evangelistic, doctrinal, or moral and ethical sermons) appear to be increasingly popular in Wesleyan pulpits. Both weddings and funerals, important occasions for pastoral care, are more often *worship services* than they were in the past—another welcome trend in church life.

As worship renewal continues its course and as more of these denominational emphases make the transition from the narthex into the sanctuary, Wesleyan worship will become not a copy of some other church, but more fully Wesleyan and more fully Christian.

Bob Black

147 ◆ WISCONSIN EVANGELICAL LUTHERAN SYNOD

The life of Wisconsin Synod congregations centers around worship in Word and sacrament. Evangelistic and educational ministries are oriented around the liturgy, and the role of other ministries within the denomination is shaped by the degree to which they are integrated into congregational worship life.

Members of the twelve hundred congregations affiliated with the Wisconsin Evangelical Lutheran Synod are generally agreed that public worship is the most important activity of a Christian congregation. A higher percentage of the Synod's members, by far, attend Sunday services than participate in organized or informal Bible study. Most pastors spend more time planning and preparing for worship, along with the Sunday sermon, than they do for other congregational activities. With few exceptions, new congregations build churches before they erect schools, educational buildings, or fellowship buildings.

Probably, few lay people could articulate a rationale for this attitude toward public worship. This attitude flows naturally, however, from the truths that the church body and its members firmly confess.

Members of the Wisconsin Synod believe that Christian faith, which includes both trust in God's promises and a determination to live according to God's will, is lived out only through the power of the Holy Spirit. They also believe that the Holy Spirit creates and strengthens faith only through the gospel contained in the Word of God and the sacraments. With Martin Luther, they confess:

> I believe that I cannot by my own thinking or choosing believe in Jesus Christ, my Lord, or come to him. But the Holy Ghost has called me by the gospel, enlightened me with his gifts, sanctified and kept me in the true faith (*Small Catechism*).

Wisconsin Synod Lutherans believe that the primary objective of public worship is to give glory to the Triune God by proclaiming the gospel in Word and sacrament and by presenting to God the church's confession, prayer, and praise. They believe that the church's public praise not only summarizes, but also sets the pattern for each individual believer's life of daily thanksgiving. Since Wisconsin Synod Lutherans hold to these truths and since more of them gather around the gospel and respond with their praise at public worship than at any other time and place, it becomes understandable why members of this Synod believe that public worship is the most important activity of a Christian congregation.

Worship and Education

Most Wisconsin Synod congregations worship according to a relatively complete version of the historic Lutheran liturgy. The corpus of familiar hymns has tended to include many of the Lutheran chorales, although the church's 1993 hymnal, *Christian Worship: A Lutheran Hymnal*, includes hymns from a wide range of Christian traditions.

Long-term use has made the liturgy familiar, and a strong commitment to religious education has helped to make the liturgy understandable. The Synod's extensive kindergarten-through-high-school parochial educational system includes training in liturgical forms and hymnology. Although there is not an explicit connection between the church year emphases of the liturgy and the religious curriculum of the parish and Sunday schools, even young children are easily able to participate in public worship. Some pastors preach a short children's sermon before the regular Sunday sermon. However, congregations are discovering that smaller children and their parents receive greater benefit from a staffed nursery than from artificial attempts to include the participation of children in the service.

Evangelistic Aspects of Worship

Generally, the Synod's traditional liturgies and hymns serve its members better than they do visitors and the unchurched. However, many congregations have found that the interest visitors and the unchurched have in gospel preaching offsets any intimidating effect of a sophisticated liturgy with unfamiliar hymns. This is especially true in congregations where the liturgy is used wisely and enthusiastically by worship leaders and worshipers.

The denomination's Commission on Evangelism has encouraged pastors and congregations to remove unnecessary barriers to the unchurched wherever they may exist. Some congregations print the entire liturgy, including hymns, in a bulletin for each main service. Many congregations post greeters at the narthex door and place directions to rest rooms and nursery facilities on the narthex walls. Some churches have occasionally attempted to simplify the liturgy for the sake of visitors, but even in congregations with a strong evangelistic emphasis there seems to be little interest in a wholesale repudiation of the Lutheran liturgical heritage.

A number of Wisconsin Synod congregations use radio and television to broadcast services as an evangelistic outreach; some have achieved notable success through these media. The Synod's Commission on Evangelism has produced several radio and television broadcasts for national syndication.

The broadcast media have also been used for ministry to homebound and physically impaired members. A growing number of congregations offer signed worship for the hearing impaired; many have installed hearing aid systems in the pews. Large print and Braille versions of the hymnal are available from the denominational publishing house and are used widely. Lay people have tended to be more sensitive in recent years about including in church designs easy access for the physically challenged.

Social Concerns in Worship

The synod's commitment to the gospel and its liturgical worship style leave few opportunities to accentuate social concerns. The Christian's personal obligation to his or her fellow human beings often finds its way into sermon applications and is included in many hymns. Occasionally, congregations depart from the liturgical church calendar to focus especially on social concerns. The Synod's Commission on Relief, which oversees the gathering and distribution of individual gifts for disaster aid, often invites gifts near Thanksgiving Day. In recent years, some congregations have designated a Sunday in January for an emphasis on life issues.

Role of Women

Although lay men are occasionally called upon to assist with the distribution of the sacrament, the church body has no tradition of using lay readers or deacons at public worship. Women are not ordained and do not serve in the pastoral ministry. Many women serve as organists, choir directors, ushers, greeters, and altar guild members.

James P. Tiefel

148 ✦ WOMEN'S AGLOW INTERNATIONAL

Women's Aglow, an international organization of women, experiences an intimate connection between worship and its major emphases of intercession and evangelism.

Women's Aglow International is an all-women's ministry. Its members are conscious of the call of God upon the organization to reach women of all ages, races, and cultures with the gospel. According to its mission statement, the goal of Women's Aglow is "to lead women to Jesus Christ and provide opportunity for Christian women to grow in their faith and minister to others."

Women's Aglow seeks to fulfill its mission through the dual thrust of prayer and evangelism. The members of Women's Aglow believe that all their efforts to evangelize the women of the world must be preceded by prayer. The members form a network of prayer that covers the face of the earth. It is estimated that nearly a million Aglow women pray and intercede daily that the Lord's will might be accomplished in human affairs.

During its international conferences and on other occasions, members of Women's Aglow may spend time worshiping and interceding for the work of God, and especially for the needs of women in different parts of the world. These times may involve extended periods of singing and playing instruments in the Spirit. A year after praying for the women of Cuba, Women's Aglow established a ministry for the evangelism of women in that nation. Following a meeting in Moscow with strategic prayer for the freedom of women in the states of the former Soviet Union, several Women's Aglow fellowships were established in those countries.

Along with a continual stress on the importance

of intercession and evangelism, Women's Aglow also recognizes the need to teach women to become worshipers as well. Worship plays a key role both in both developing and in maintaining a living and vital relationship with the Lord. Our emphasis on worship is evident in instruction, in worship methods, as well as in the process of entering into the experience of worship. Praise-and-worship leaders are trained through seminars and workshops taught by the more experienced worship leaders in Women's Aglow. Often pastors and other church leaders attend these training sessions. Training materials for worship are also available from the organization.

Because women are by nature highly relational and intuitional, most find it relatively easy to move into both the attitude and practice of worship. In the story of Mary and Martha (Luke 10:38-42), one sees Mary demonstrating the attitude of worship. Although she could have kept busy performing tasks like her sister, she instead followed the desire of her heart and sat at the feet of Jesus, enjoying his presence and listening to his words which brought life and joy to her soul. Often women, too, are faced with that same choice in their daily lives: to spend time with Jesus or to be drawn aside by the endless tasks that face them.

All women long for intimacy with those they love. Women's Aglow finds that as intimacy is attained through a relationship with the Lord, the resultant outflow is evangelism. Leading others to Jesus occurs quite naturally as women share with one another the blessings of the relationship they have with the Lord Jesus Christ, who loves them perfectly and completely.

Many times during praise and worship at Women's Aglow meetings or retreats, the presence of God is so evident that nonbelievers in the room realize their need for a Savior. Unbelievers have also been touched by a prophetic word during the praise-and-worship time, a word which has convinced them of their need for a personal relationship with God. Opportunity is always given for such people to receive Jesus, either before the close of the meeting or through individual prayer and counseling afterwards.

The strong thrust of evangelism in Women's Aglow is also reflected in some of the music worshipers sing, as well as in the exhortations given to worshipers. Exodus 3 is God's mandate sending us forth to "go and tell":

Tell them that I AM sent you,
Tell them Jehovah has heard.
Tell them I've seen their deep sorrows—
Yahweh the hope of the world.

Lift up the weary, restore the oppressed,
Care for the faint and rejected.
Brighten the dreary, bind guilt and fear,
Taking the shame from their face.

(Ruth Collingridge, "Tell Them," Copyright © 1991, SpiritSong Celebration)

Women's Aglow's commission is to "go and tell" people that Christ is salvation, healing, life, and love, and that in his name there is hope. In a world filled with darkness and despair, people need to hear of the great hope available through Jesus. Christians have the privilege of responding to many opportunities to share the life of Christ with those around them. Women's Aglow International seeks to be faithful in presenting the gospel message clearly to all who will listen.

Ruth Collingridge and Lorene Carlson

149 • ALTERNATIVE WORSHIP IN THE LITURGICAL TRADITION

Liturgical traditions can still offer great flexibility for integrating into worship a broad spectrum of church ministries. This entry describes a congregation in which this flexibility is demonstrated.

Worship at St. Gregory Nyssen Episcopal Church in San Francisco encourages participation from everyone. Such worship has an evangelical emphasis, since it helps to spread the gospel because it shows the gospel. Participatory worship embodies Jesus' distinctive teaching that God's presence now comes to all and calls for an active response from each of us. Rather than trim its liturgical sails in order to appeal to contemporary secular culture, the church instead encourages its worshipers to participate in popular worship from diverse traditions, to an extent that many had thought they could not.

St. Gregory's makes lay ministries accessible to all, including the elderly, the youth, the physically impaired, and people entering the church for the first time. For example, lay people read all the public readings, including the Gospels. The deacon may even invite newcomers to read; many enjoy this way of contributing before committing themselves to the church. After the sermon and two minutes of silence, the church invites all to share their own experiences as they come to mind and to offer their own petitions and thanks during the prayers that follow. Regular churchgoers set an example, and visitors regularly join in.

Every musical skill level has an active place in worship at St. Gregory's. People entering the church receive a personal welcome and a sheet of printed music that will be sung, with a short pamphlet explaining worship and church life. In addition, cantors introduce the music in a quick rehearsal each Sunday. Deacons announce each event throughout the service, giving simple directions so that visitors can participate fully with the rest of the worshipers. The wide repertoire of congregational music ranges from simple chants and authentic folk music to classic hymns in four-part harmony, which are mostly sung unaccompanied in the resonant worship space. The congregation dances twice, before and after the eucharistic feast. While drums and rhythm instruments support the dance and the accompanying hymns, the congregation circles around the altar table, using simple Greek steps. These steps are quickly explained each time and used again for weeks in a row. Subsequently, newcomers can follow along in the dance at once and within two Sundays are experts. In addition, singers, who have practiced previously, perform choral works from the Renaissance to modern times. Composers in the congregation, under the leadership of the music director, write new pieces for both the congregation and the choir.

A dancing church attracts some types of worshipers more than other types; however, the experience of St. Gregory's shows that the choice of attending a dancing church does not necessarily depend on the worshiper's physical ability alone. Most elderly or disabled people dance the first and simpler dance, and some join the second dance as well. A seminarian in an electric wheelchair led the line each Sunday during her intern year. Moveable chairs nearby serve any who wish to sit out a dance, hymn, or prayer. The church facilities are fully accessible to worshipers in wheelchairs.

Women's Concerns in Worship

At St. Gregory's, women and men share all li-turgical ministries: welcoming newcomers, reading Scripture, singing, dancing, praying aloud, presiding, serving as deacons, preaching, teaching, and consecrating and distributing the Eucharist. The church uses Scripture translations and liturgical texts edited to make gender-specific language general where possible. Several standards of inclusiveness are applied in this editorial process in order to take into account modern biblical scholarship, classical doctrine, and good aesthetics. *A New Zealand Prayer Book* (1989) of the Anglican Church in New Zealand provides psalmody and prayers free of divisive nationalistic speech as well as gratuitous gender distinctions. In alternate years, the church follows the Church of England's modular *Lectionary 2,* which offers biblical readings about women to balance readings about men for part of the church year. Slowly the church is collecting or writing new prayers and songs that use feminine imagery to enrich the language of prayer. A long-standing women's group is growing under female clergy leadership and meets for mutual support, spiritual discussions, and retreats.

Children's Ministries and Worship

At St. Gregory's, children gather in Sunday school during the liturgy of the Word. At Sunday school, they enjoy a simple service that parallels the adults' worship—including the distinctive use of silence, bells, singing, praying, and dancing—and an education program that parallels the lectionary readings. What they learn in Sunday school, they can share with their parents after church, as the whole family talk about the day's Scripture and discussion. Children join the adults for the liturgy of the Table and often bring gifts of their own to lay on the altar. These gifts may include art work responding to the Scriptures or perhaps fresh bread they have baked for the Eucharist. At least quarterly, the congregation prays eucharistic prayers improvised in language and imagery suiting children's understanding. At every celebration, the children share the consecrated bread and wine along with adults. Then under the deacon's guidance, children gather alms from the congregation following the Communion and bring these to the Table along with food for the hungry and homeless. At the end, they join hands with everyone in the dance. On occasional weeknights, the church celebrates the Eucharist as the early Christians did, as a community supper, following the second-century *Didache* rite. At this occasion, children may dine with their families. Sometimes they dine at their own table in order to enjoy a special educational program matching the adults' discussion.

Social Ministry and Worship

In keeping with its focus on worship participation, St. Gregory's approach to service work stresses everyone's ability to help. An annual canvass of the membership identifies what people value and want to accomplish in the church and uncovers gifts and opportunities for service. Lay people respond to pressing needs in the city by donating time and money to projects outside the parish. During Sunday liturgy, lay people enlist fellow church members' prayers and participation, often drawing collaboration from people of diverse politics. Members have likewise cared for AIDS patients and others among the congregation enduring long hospitalization. Some members have volunteered in such activities as suicides' and battered women's hotlines and homeless family programs.

Every two months, the congregation collects donations for projects outside the parish that are nominated and presented by members. These projects also represent a wide range of social service models and draw broad financial support. The people mix their love for dancing and giving at the annual diocesan ball benefiting Episcopal Charities. Two members have opened a college scholarship fund for the Sunday child-care worker. Another member has adopted a single-parent family in a nearby housing project and has started a food and clothing cupboard at St. Gregory's. Furthermore, the whole congregation gave generously to help parishioners who lost their homes in a recent Oakland hills wildfire disaster. The liturgical assembly forms the heart of this work and generosity, as worshipers pray together for the needy and for God's help in assisting them.

Demographics of Worshipers

The roughly one hundred regular worshipers at St. Gregory's show demographic similarities. On the average, they are twenty years younger (thirty-five to forty) than Episcopal parishioners nationally, college educated, and open to new life

experience. Most worshipers move or change jobs within six months before or after joining the congregation. Members are predominately Caucasian, with a few African-Americans and Asian-Americans. On the other hand, St. Gregory's incorporates members with diverse lifestyles and an unusually wide range of political opinion, from radical left environmentalists to neoconservative entrepreneurs. Public intercessions serve both creative reconciling dialogue and mutual personal support between the members of St. Gregory's.

The rich use of music and dance has not attracted professional musicians; instead it has chiefly attracted people who like music and welcome the chance to get involved. In addition, aspiring part-time writers have also been drawn into the church. Subsequently, St. Gregory's sponsors twice a year weekend working retreats for writers and composers, including people outside the parish and many currently not related to any church.

Educational Ministries and Worship

During the week, clergy and trained lay leaders pursue counseling and adult education within the parish and beyond. Courses in Scripture, tradition, and issues in daily living feature up-to-date scholarship, modern research into human behavior, and reflection on personal experience. One presbyter, a founding board member of Spiritual Directors International, supervises an extensive ministry and leads prayer courses. A lay member teaches group spiritual life to diaconal students from four dioceses. Furthermore, several church members supply professional counseling services. In addition, a lay spiritual direction group meets monthly. Another presbyter of the church teaches the New Testament and liturgy to parish classes and diaconal students and convenes the North American Academy of Liturgy work group on early liturgical history.

St. Gregory's often receives visits from students and scholars who come to experience its worship in person, and these people also encourage their friends to visit. The church has also desktop published music and pamphlets that share the church's work with the church at large. Visitors periodically write from around the United States and Canada, relating how they have appropriated some insight or usage they observed at St.

Gregory's and offering discoveries and suggestions the church might try out in turn. This dialogue greatly enriches worship and church life.

Richard Fabian

150 ♦ ALTERNATIVE WORSHIP IN THE FREE-CHURCH TRADITION

Because worship motivates believers to care for a broken creation and instills in them a vision of God's new creation, it lies at the heart of a congregation's outreach into other ministries. The following is a description of a church in the free evangelical tradition that is breaking new ground in the integration of worship and related areas of service.

Worship is the great corrective to the voices that insistently tell us that *we* are in charge of our lives. In worship, God looks us in the eye and graciously tells us that we are not, as we supposed, the center of the universe, but that God is. Finite and feeble creatures that we are, we are released from the burden of having to accomplish eternal things in our lives and in our world because these eternal things have always been God's business. Worship offers to us the gift of a new perspective. This new perspective allows us to see the world not as we experience it, but as it really is: God-centered, God-loved, God-owned.

At Grace Fellowship Community Church in San Francisco, the congregation views the weekly gathering of God's people in worship as central to all they are and all they do. Celebrating the life, death, and resurrection of Jesus Christ in the sanctuary makes Christians alive to his call to participate in his life, death, and resurrection as they live their lives. Worship is not an escape from the world outside; it is not a kind of drug which makes people forget where they have come from. Rather, worship is what drives believers to care for a broken creation because it nurtures them in the vision of a "new heaven and a new earth" and of the God who has promised to bring this about.

The leadership of Grace Fellowship tries to bring this perspective to the planning of worship each week. Every service, not just those with a "missions" emphasis, must open worshipers up to the life-changing, world-changing mission of Christ and the revolutionary work of his Kingdom. The songs, prayers, affirmations, and sermon must be "big" enough to include a needy world, not just a chosen people. This occurs most specifically for Grace Fellowship in the sermon. This "truth-telling" in the sermon leads us at Grace Fellowship to see that the gospel has a far larger goal than our personal transformation. The sermon takes the eternal truths of Scripture and the constantly shifting issues of contemporary society and helps us to see where these two intersect. Our society is more informed than ever, but our society is also more confused. The people of our society need a clear word, a Word from God, which will not only call them to the light but which also interprets their darkness.

We at Grace Fellowship have had occasions in worship when the events of the week have made us especially sensitive to our need for the Deliverer. When San Francisco experienced the devastating earthquake in 1989, when America and Iraq went to war, when the 1992 riots occurred and south central Los Angeles literally went up in flames—when all the images filling our minds were pictures of destruction, death, and confusion, we needed to worship. Through worship, we needed to see an active and purposeful God still in charge of God's creation and grieving with us. Never before has praying "thy Kingdom come" filled us with more longing and hope.

Once, in a Christmas Eve service, the congregation used a litany composed from the news headlines of that year's tragic events. These headlines were about war, poverty, injustice, and division. They made us realize the power of sin over God's beloved creation. In response to this, we included the awesome words from Isaiah 9 as a reminder that the Messiah comes with one intention, total deliverance of a world bent on destroying itself. The Good News sounded truly good; that is how worship works. Worship in a vacuum is meaningless, an offense to God. The prophet Amos says, "I hate, I despise your religious feasts; I cannot stand your assemblies. . . . Away with the noise of your songs! I will not listen to the music of your harps. But let justice roll on like a river, righteousness like a never-failing stream!" (Amos 5:21, 23-24). True worship prevents us from serving out of panic, anger, or guilt because in worship we find that God cares more than we do. True worship encourages us to love justice because God does.

Each service concludes with a sending. Hymns are used that call us to let our worship be a prophetic witness to the world. After this, the pastor gives a charge that reminds us of the enabling power of Jesus who alone fits us to be his servants. The purpose of this sending is to reinforce the idea that worship is meaningful only when it translates into ministry.

Grace Fellowship is in agreement with the organization known as Bread for the World and with its views on the interrelatedness of worship and justice. Bread for the World, headquartered in Washington, D.C., lobbies on behalf of the world's hungry in the name of Christ. Grace Fellowship appreciates this organization because it has a desire for justice that flows not out of merely humanitarian concerns or a narrow political ethic, but out of God's generous and holy heart. Its prayers, affirmations, and songs, used often in services at Grace Fellowship, address the healthy tension of living justly and compassionately in a sinful, needy world. Grace Fellowship is also grateful to find that many of the new hymn writers such as Jane Parker Huber, Timothy Dudley-Smith, and Margaret Clarkson are giving expression to this eschatological tension in their music.

If God is to fashion a people out of us, we must work hard at listening to God. So, in Grace Fellowship, adult education and small group times are spent trying to work out the implications of the call heard in the sermon. What does it mean for us to be the people of God in these times and in the context of San Francisco? What does it mean for us to sit under the authority of God's Word? How do we become accountable and serve? These gatherings are occasions to _respond_ to God's Word, not just to discuss it. The difference is crucial. A discussion puts _us_ in charge. We can either agree or disagree with the points we've heard. Instead, a response says, "God has a claim on my life; how can I follow him?" In this way, the perspective of worship is the context for discipleship.

How does worship form us? By telling us who we are. We are not primarily wage earners, consumers, parents, or homeowners. We are God's. We belong to God. The rituals of worship—coming to confession, to God's Word, to God's world, to the Creator—are the holy habits that can shape the whole of our lives. Worship can form in us a

truly Christian identity that goes far beyond the definitions we have for ourselves. In worship, we are named as children of God, as sinners, as participants in truth, and as servants in the world. In the mystery of God's grace, God gives us a destiny that is as big as God is. Bernard of Clairvaux said, "What we love, we will become." In worship, it is not what we love, but _whom_ we love. To love God and become like God is our highest calling.

Sharon Huey

151 • Alternative Worship in the Pentecostal-Charismatic Tradition

Within the Pentecostal-charismatic community, worship renewal may take the form of a reappropriation of more traditional liturgical elements, such as the use of a lectionary and a consistent emphasis on the sacraments. In churches where this is occurring, members are finding a relationshipo between many areas of Christian ministry and worship. This entry discusses the experience of one such congregation.

Pentecostals and charismatics center their spiritual lives around the worship experience and evangelism. They are often weak in areas that motivate other communities of Christians, such as development of the inner life, study of the Scripture, or the application of Christians values to culture. In worship and evangelism, however, they excel.

The term _worship experience_ has been carefully chosen because as anyone who has been raised in a Pentecostal environment knows, worship experience is not always the same as worship. Sometimes Pentecostals and charismatics worship the experience itself. Still when their worship is genuinely directed toward God, there are few experiences in life that are as powerful as sensing the glory of God in one of their services. The worship experience is the central element that draws millions of Christians around the world to Pentecostal and charismatic churches and fellowships.

The Pentecostal worship service is almost always directed toward motivating the worshipers to win others to Christ. Pentecostals and charismatics are sometimes faulted for not teaching the Word and the heritage of the church as they should, for not emphasizing ethics, and sometimes for spiritual arrogance; however, everyone agrees that they are evangelists. Their evangelism grows out of their highly charged worship service.

Christ Church in Nashville, Tennessee, is an assembly with Pentecostal roots that is involved in liturgical renewal. For several years, it has been incorporating features of historic Christianity in the life of the Christ Church. The ministers preach from the lectionary, observe the church year, and have adopted a sacramental theology. Still, many of the best features of their Pentecostal heritage remain. They pray for the sick expecting them to be healed; they worship freely and powerfully; and they are evangelistic.

Christ Church has been greatly influenced by the ministry of Loren Cunningham and his organization, Youth With a Mission. Cunningham preached a series of missionary services at the church and highly motivated the business and music community within the church. Now, a constant stream of members go out to all parts of the world to do everything from preaching and building churches to giving business advice to leaders of emerging nations. With the church's blessing, many have formed single-purpose parachurch organizations that network members of the church with ministries abroad. Members often take vacation time to work at their own expense in a place of need.

The Sunday worship service acknowledges the activities of its associated parachurch ministries in the laying on of hands and in the anointing of those who will serve in such ministries. The congregation is made aware of the nature of the mission and is encouraged to remember the participants in prayer. Intercessory prayer groups throughout the church pray for church members while they are away. On most Sundays, a victory resulting from the efforts of the church's members is reported; the congregation responds by celebrating and praising God in its typical Pentecostal/charismatic fashion.

Motivated by its Sunday worship service, the church has become highly mobilized. A few months after the failed Soviet coup of 1991, the church established a daughter assembly in St. Petersburg (formerly Leningrad). Within a year, that church grew to a Sunday morning attendance of fifteen hundred. Recently another group was started in Kiev, in the Ukraine. Business leaders in the congregation are now involved in the rebuilding of the health infrastructure of the former Soviet republics. All these efforts are intimately tied to the Sunday worship service of Christ Church.

Christ Church believes passionately in the priesthood of all believers. The church is convinced that every member has a spiritual gift for the edification of the body. More than two hundred people have been trained and consecrated to the work of pastoral care. These people assist in the administration of the sacraments, in counseling, and in the general caring of the spiritual and social needs of the congregation. They are fairly visible during the Sunday worship service, and are thus approachable by the congregation.

One of the church's associated parachurch ministries is dedicated to the care of single expectant mothers. The senior pastor believes it is unreasonable to take a stand on the abortion issue without providing an economic support system for those about to give birth. A member of the church who had been a state social worker took the lead in establishing Mercy Ministries in response to that need. Expectant mothers are cared for both during and after pregnancy with physical, spiritual, and emotional help. If they make the choice to offer the child for adoption, families within the congregation often take the child. The dedication of these babies is a celebration in which the congregation joyfully participates. In this way, this associated parachurch ministry is related to the Sunday morning worship service.

The church works at keeping the service directed toward God rather than toward promotional goals. Prayer, praise, and sacramental rites remind the people that they are, in the words of the Abrahamic covenant, "blessed to be a blessing."

Christ Church is only one example of the adoption of the idea that worship prepares the worshipers for service. Many other Pentecostal and charismatic congregations are beginning to adopt the concept. Elton Trueblood said that worship is a matter of the camp and the field. When worshipers come to the sanctuary they are returning to the "camp" to receive instruction, to worship their God, and to be empowered by the Holy Spirit to do the ministry that God has created them to do. Then these worshipers go into the "field," to proclaim the kingdom of God by their words and deeds. Going into the "field" is also worship.

Dan Scott

152 • Alternative Worship in Seekers' Service/Believers' Worship

Churches that have adopted the format of a broad-based seekers' service (accompanied by a separate, more intense worship service for committed believers) are breaking new ground in the integration of worship with other aspects of Christian ministry.

The dual worship format of a Sunday worship service geared to the needs of people seeking a Christian identity, together with a midweek experience of deeper worship for those who have committed themselves to Christ and to Christian growth, has been pioneered on a large scale by Willow Creek Community Church in Chicago's northwest suburbs. A growing number of churches in North America have begun to adopt this format in one variation or another.

Willow Creek's uniqueness gives it high visibility among American and, to an extent, international churches and communities. The church has responded in several ways to requests from other churches for information and guidance on how they may use their resources in their own communities to increase cohesion and purpose among their members and seekers.

Willow Creek offers several avenues of ministry resources, including Network, New Community Institute, and the Willow Creek Association. All reflect the basic philosophy of ministry at Willow Creek Community Church, which teaches that believers must follow and use their passions and gifts in ways that God directs. While no human organization is perfect, Willow Creek's approach has been highly effective in changing worship communities in the Chicago area and, through the Association, around the world.

Willow Creek is known as a seeker-driven church, but those who faithfully attend the church know it also as a place where there is plenty of room to be involved in meaningful ways. With so many people moving into the area, or simply visiting, church leaders are challenged to harness and focus this human potential.

The Network ministry is the first step for anyone who wants to pitch in. One night a week, for one month, interested believers attend well-organized seminars on how to use the gifts that God has given to every Christian. Several low-level personality tests are given to help focus one's self-evaluation and match it with opportunities within the church body. From these tests and seminars, along with interviews administered by Network counselors, specific directions for each individual naturally emerge. The believer is both educated in the gifts that God grants and is shown how to apply them in the church.

There are more than ninety ministries at Willow Creek, ranging from car repair to a food pantry ministry, from drama to career fellowships. The church has always emphasized helping and working with other people. Though there are almost three hundred full-time staff members, the vast majority of the work is done by volunteers who have all passed through the Network program.

Direction and supervision for these groups comes ultimately from the appropriate ministry staff person, who in turn receives guidance and counsel for ministry development from the management team and other leaders in the church. The goal of these programs is to bring more believers into a committed life with God and to a public confession of this commitment, by open association with the church.

A new teaching ministry offered to those attending the weeknight services is the New Community Institute. The Institute runs for a period of four consecutive weeks, with different options on either Wednesday or Thursday evenings. In a manner similar to traditional Sunday school classes, people choose seminars and workshops from a wide variety of topics, including small group management, current issues, and doctrinal and Bible studies. After a time of worship and praise, people move to the many rooms scattered around the 250,000 square-foot facility for their classes. The purpose of these efforts is to deepen the spiritual understanding and knowledge of believers by challenging them to think further. Members of the teaching staff or other department heads lead each class, and the subjects change every other month.

Another important ministry, which grew out of Willow Creek's vision for the church today and is now a separate organization, is the Willow Creek

Association. This is a growing network of both national and international churches that are catching a renewed vision for reaching the unchurched. Before the formation of the Association, special leadership teams from Willow Creek Church would volunteer their time and talents to travel to other churches around the world and assist them in forming their own seeker-driven ministries. Members of the teaching, programming, music, and drama teams would conduct workshops and lectures to demonstrate Willow Creek's approach.

The Association began officially in early 1992 and quickly added members from the hundreds of ministers and other church leaders who have attended various Willow Creek conferences over the years. It is a nonprofit, nondenominational organization governed by a board of directors independent of the church. The Association states its purpose this way: "Our mission is to assist churches in re-establishing the priority and practice of reaching lost people for Christ through church ministries targeted to seekers." The Association promises to become one of the country's largest nondenominational networking groups, with information exchange flowing easily among the membership. The Association is developing its own literature, material, and programs in conjunction with a Christian publishing house.

Willow Creek Community Church pointedly avoids getting involved in local or national partisan politics and refuses to endorse any candidate. It does, however, conduct community outreaches in the Chicago area through food pantries and crisis counseling and has sponsored building and teaching projects in Mexico and Jamaica.

The newest program changing the face of Willow Creek Church is the small-groups ministry. As the church gets larger, it also gets smaller. Interlacing networks of leaders, apprentices, and coaches bind groups of no more than ten committed believers through ties of accountability, service, and community. With such a structure, Willow Creek wants to connect members more effectively to the life of the church and to bring the uncommitted Christian into the kind of worship and church life that promotes the greatest spiritual growth.

Steve Burdan

PART TWO

The Worshiping Community

The worshiping community is the body of Christ, those redeemed in Christ and called to be a witness to the world. The body of Christ consists of persons of every type: men and women, young and old, red, yellow, black, and white. When the church gathers for worship, the contribution of each person is important and valued. Without the full contribution of each member of the church, worship is impoverished and the church fails to realize its calling to be the body of Christ. This section outlines ways in which the church can acknowledge the importance of and encourage the full participation of each worshiper. When pursued thoughtfully and sensitively, the goals suggested in this section provide an important outline of both the church's ministry of worship and its ministry of pastoral care.

❧ TWO ❧

Children in the Worshiping Community

Jesus' call to let the children come to him provides Christians with the joyful task of training and forming children in the Christian faith and encouraging them to offer whole-hearted worship. In so doing, children take their place as an essential part of the body of Christ, with as much to teach others as to learn themselves. The church that neglects children in planning and leading worship certainly deprives both its children of the opportunity for meaningful corporate worship and the church of their joyful and profound faith. This chapter outlines ways in which the church can take greater responsibility for the spiritual formation of children and can encourage them to participate more fully in worship.

---

153 • BIBLICAL PERSPECTIVES ON CHILDREN IN THE WORSHIPING COMMUNITY

The Bible presents to us as Christians a multifaceted view of children that helps us understand our relationship with God and challenges many common assumptions about the role of children in the community of faith. Children are a gracious gift from God, images of trusting faith and witnesses to God's love and hospitality in Christ. Patterning our view of children after these images helps the church become the body of Christ.

The role of children in Scripture is a theme that has all the richness and variety of an oriental tapestry with its contrasting colors, moods, and patterns. If this variety of perspective is not taken into account, the result could easily be a modest essay on the virtue of childlikeness. But the Word of God is far richer than this single perspective. The biblical vision of children carries us into the mystery of the human condition itself—its tensions, its beauty, and its paradox.

In essence, the biblical evidence tells us that the experience of being a child is both a gift and a challenge. On the one hand, children are the privileged ones of God. Their simplicity and spirit of trust are to be imitated as the model of our

relationship with God. On the other hand, to be a child is to be unfinished, immature, and in need of formation. It is precisely this creative tension between the child as a faith model and the child in need of growth that lies at the heart of the biblical perspective.

The primordial instance of this tension is found in the relationship between Israel and Yahweh. The Hebrew Bible frequently describes God's care for Israel in terms of a parent-child relationship. Israel is God's favored one; the "first-born son" (Exod. 4:22). The Lord chooses this people above all other nations of the earth (Deut. 7:7-8), and brings them into birth as a true community in the Exodus event. The long journey through the desert becomes Israel's education. "Remember how Yahweh your God led you for forty years in the wilderness," writes the author of Deuteronomy, "to humble you, to test you and know your inmost heart . . . Learn from this that Yahweh your God was training you as a man trains his child" (Deut. 8:2-5).

Because of God's creative act and seeking love, we can see all the positive qualities of a child in the people of Israel. They are dependent on the Lord and secure in God's care. They are filled with childlike wonder at his love. But there are the unfinished, immature qualities of the child in Israel as well. In a striking passage, Hosea puts these words on the lips of Yahweh:

When Israel was a child I loved him,
    and I called my son out of Egypt.
But the more I called to them,
    the further they went from me;
They have offered sacrifices to the Baals
    and set their offerings smoking
        before the idols.
I myself taught Ephraim to walk;
I took them in my arms;
yet they have not understood that I was
    the one looking after them.
I led them with the reins of kindness,
    with leading-strings of love.
I was like someone who lifts an infant
    close against his cheek;
stooping down to him I gave him his food.
    (Hos. 11:1-14)

This tension between healthy childlike qualities and the need to grow toward maturity is found elsewhere in Scripture. In a sense, it is simply a description of the human condition. The child is a paradigm of human growth. In our adult lives, we continue to confront this ambiguity and tension.

On the one hand, we experience our lives and ourselves as gifts. We know moments of surprise and wonder. We break through the routine of our lives to encounter spontaneity and joy. We see things simply and feel nurtured by life. On the other hand, we confront in ourselves the recurring problems of jealousy, inconsistency, and the dark feelings of resentment. We are erratic in our behavior. We pout in the face of failure. We complain at times of adversity. We give up easily or sell out.

The body of this article will be devoted to exploring the creative tension between gift and growth as an underlying biblical theme related to children.

The Child as Gift

The early Hebrews did not have a developed concept of eternal life. Their focus was on this life with its blessings and burdens. In choosing to follow the way of Yahweh rather than the way of wickedness, they trusted in the nearness of God to their lives and the earthy blessings of a prosperous life. One of the most significant of these blessings was the gift of children:

Happy, all those who fear Yahweh
    and follow in his paths.
You will eat what your hands
    have worked for,
happiness and prosperity will be yours.
Your wife; a fruitful vine
    on the inner walls of your house.
Your sons: round your table
    like shoots round an olive tree. (Ps. 128:1-3)

The underlying theme of this Psalm is clear: children are a sign of fruitfulness, a blessing of life. Just as the earth brings forth its abundance in the harvest, so human love finds its abundance in the gift of children. Children are "the crown of old men," says the book of Proverbs (17:6). They are the promise of immortality; the assurance that one's name will be remembered forever.

In the gift of children, the Hebrews heard echoes of the promise God made to Abraham: "Look up to heaven and count the stars if you can. Such will be your descendants" (Gen. 15:5). Children were a living sign that God keeps the promises of God and that God's name would continue to be praised from generation to generation.

The Child as a Privileged One of God

Because of their fragility and helplessness, children become a symbol of the "little ones" of the earth—those whom God chooses to protect and to use as instruments in the plan of salvation. So true is this that Yahweh reserves the right of intervening directly to care for those who are without the usual safeguards of society. "You must not be harsh with the widow or the orphan," God tells the people, "if you are harsh with them, they will surely cry out to me, and be sure that I will hear their cry" (Exod. 22:21, 23). This same theme is echoed in Psalm 68 where Yahweh is described as "father of orphans and defender of widows" (68:5).

In a society in which the adult male is the predominant religious figure, it is unusual that provision would be made for the participation of children. Yet this is, in fact, the case in Israel. The child is granted the privilege of participation in several aspects of Jewish worship. They share in the nation's call to prayer and fasting (cf. Joel 2:16). Their song of praise is understood as especially pleasing to the Lord (cf. Ps. 8:2; Matt. 21:15).

In Isaiah's vision of the return from the Exile, the people are pictured as the privileged ones of

God. They are described as an infant, who will be suckled and cared for by Jerusalem. What is all the more remarkable about this passage is that Yahweh is cast in a maternal role toward the chosen people: "Like a son comforted by your mother will I comfort you" (Isa. 66:13).

If children fall under the special care of God, it is not surprising that they often play a privileged role in the history of salvation. In Scripture, God frequently chooses children as the first beneficiaries and messengers of salvation. Thus, young Samuel is chosen to be God's instrument (1 Sam. 1–3); the youthful David is singled out in preference to his older brothers (1 Sam. 16:1-13); and Daniel shows that he is wiser than the elders of Israel in saving Susanna (Sus. 44–51). When Isaiah announces the messianic kingdom, he does not speak of it in terms of a warrior prince, but in terms of a coming of a child:

> For there is a child born for us,
> a son given to us
> and dominion is laid on his shoulders;
> and this is the name they give him:
> Wonderful Counselor, Mighty God
> Eternal Father, Prince of Peace. (Isa. 9:6)

Childlikeness

What is the inner quality of children that most attracts us to them? Is it their need to be cared for and our need to reach out? Is it the innate dependency of their lives on ours? Certainly these are some of the reasons that make children lovable to God and ourselves. But there is another dimension of a child's experience that becomes a model of faith and human growth: the quality of _childlikeness_. This quality encompasses a spirit of openness and wonder before life. It speaks of trust as the precondition of all faith. It involves simplicity and the capacity of being spontaneous.

When the psalmist seeks for an image of serenity and inner peace, he turns to that of an infant:

> Enough for me to keep my soul
> tranquil and quiet
> like a child in its mother's arms,
> as content as a child
> that has been weaned. (Ps. 131:2)

To be childlike is not the same as being childish. The simplicity that Scripture praises is not a form of infantilism or immaturity. On the contrary, it implies a strong integrity and a spirit of uprightness. Yahweh points to this quality in Job. "Did you notice my servant Job?" God says to Satan, "there is no one like him on earth—a sound and honest man who fears God and shuns evil" (Job 1:8). It is this same simplicity of heart that Paul urges the Christians at Philippi to choose as their inner attitude of faith: "Do all that has to be done without complaining or arguing, and then you will be innocent and genuine perfect children of God among a deceitful and underhand brood, and you will shine in the world like bright stars because you are offering it the word of life" (Phil. 2:14-16).

In the gospel account, Jesus points to himself as a model of childlikeness. In the context of blessing his Father for the "little ones," Jesus says, "Come to me, all you who labor and are overburdened, and I will give you rest. Shoulder my yoke and learn from me, for I am gentle and humble in heart, and you will find rest for your souls" (Matt. 11:28-29).

The Child as Unfinished

Scripture praises the qualities of simplicity and trust in children, but it also looks realistically at the limiting dimensions of childhood. It sees the child as essentially unfinished. Children are in the process of struggling toward adulthood. They are still immature in their ability to accept responsibility—thus their behavior is often inconsistent; their moods and demands often change.

"Innate in the heart of a child is folly," writes the author of Proverbs (22:15). In a similar vein, Jesus quotes a familiar saying to describe the fickle response of the crowds. "What description can I find for this generation? It is like children shouting to each other as they sit in the market place: 'we played the pipes for you, and you wouldn't dance, we sang dirges, and you wouldn't be mourners'" (Matt. 11:16-17).

Of all the scriptural writers, it is Paul who emphasizes the unfinished, imperfect dimensions of childhood most strongly. He compares the dissension and bickering in the Corinthian community to a childish response to life. "I myself was unable to speak to you as a people of the Spirit," he tells them. "I treated you as sensual men, still infants in Christ. What I fed you with was milk, not solid food, for you were not ready for it; and indeed you still are not ready for it. . . ." (1 Cor. 3:1-2). Paul tells the same community that they must move beyond their childish ways, just as he has had to do in his life. "When I was a child, I used to talk like a child and think like a child and argue like a child, but now that I am a man, all childish ways are put behind me" (1 Cor. 13:11).

Because children lack the wisdom that comes from experience and maturity, they are not stable in their vision and commitment. Paul contrasts the mature faith of those who have "grown up in Christ" with the tendency of children to be capricious and inconsistent. When our vision has deepened and taken root, we will live a more stable life of faith: "Then we shall not be children any longer, or tossed one way and another and carried along by every wind of doctrine" (Eph. 4:14).

The mystery of the Incarnation is rooted in the self-emptying of the eternal Word. In Jesus, the transcendent God becomes Emmanuel—God with us. John develops the meaning of the Incarnation in sweeping theological language that speaks of the Word in eternity becoming flesh in time. Paul turns to the cosmic Lord, the Incarnation, in order to explore the meaning of his kingship over the entire universe. When Luke writes of the Incarnation, however, it is not through theological language or a cosmic vision. Luke simply gives us Jesus as a child. He captures the wonder and mystery of salvation in simple images of Jesus: the child in the manger, the child presented in the temple, and the young man growing up quietly in Nazareth.

In his youthful experience, Jesus summarizes the theme of children in Scripture. This is especially true of the scene in the temple, where Luke pictures Jesus talking with the doctors of the Law. In this setting, Jesus experiences the tension between his desire to do the work of his Father and the realistic necessity of returning home to Nazareth with his parents (cf. Luke 2:43-51). On the one hand, he is reaching out toward the independence and maturity of adult life. On the other, he finds himself still called to be obedient to his parents.

It is this tension between the desire for responsibility and the need for security that describes the experience of growing up. At a still deeper level, this tension characterizes all of human life. A child is a person in pilgrimage. But then, so are all of us as adults in pilgrimage. The tension between independence and dependence does not end when we achieve physical maturity. It is an integral part of the human condition for the rest of our lives.

Jesus and Children

Jesus began his public ministry by taking up the preaching of John the Baptist. At first hearing, the words of Jesus appear to be a simple extension of the Baptist's call to conversion and preparation. But there is a radical difference. Jesus does indeed call for conversion, but he does so on grounds that the kingdom is here. It is no longer a question of preparation, but of realization.

The most dramatic sign that God's kingdom has burst into human life is seen in the new relationship which Jesus has with the Father. Jesus speaks of God as *Abba*—a term of endearment from everyday Jewish life. It was the name that children used to address their fathers. It can best be translated as *dearest father,* or more commonly as *daddy.* Scholars have pointed out that Jesus' use of *Abba* is unprecedented in Jewish religious history, or, for that matter, in the history of world religions. It implies a closeness to the divine that was unknown up to this time. Thus, the relationship that Jesus has with his Father becomes a *sacrament* of the kingdom. It implies a radical intimacy with the divine—a relationship not based on God as Creator or King, but as loving Father.

If God is Father, then the disciples are God's children. According to Joachim Jeremias, being a child is *the* characteristic of the kingdom of God (*New Testament Theology* [New York: Charles Scribner's Sons, 1971], 178ff). The expression *child of God* occurs only three times in the synoptic Gospels (Matt. 5:9; Luke 6:35; 20:36). In all three instances, the term has eschatological significance. In other words, being a child of God is not a consequence of Creation, but represents an eschatological gift of salvation. Only one who recognizes and accepts the kingdom may call God *Abba.*

It is not surprising, given the context that we have just discussed, that Jesus would hold up the child as a model of discipleship. "I tell you solemnly," Jesus says to his followers, "anyone who does not welcome the kingdom of God like a little child will never enter it" (Mark 10:15). In John's Gospel, Jesus describes entrance into the kingdom as the willingness to be reborn as a child of the Spirit (John 3:5).

The true disciples therefore are the "little ones" to whom God reveals the secrets of God (Matt 11:25ff). So insistent is Jesus on this that in the synoptic Gospels the terms _little_ and _disciple_ seem at times to be equivalent (Matt. 10:42; Mark 9:41).

Jeremias points out three experiences which characterize what it means to be a child in the teaching of Jesus:

(1) Being a child brings the certainty of _a share in future salvation._ From the outside, it appears that the little ones are dispossessed and without power. But they are not to fear. The Father has promised them the kingdom. In the teaching and vision of Jesus, none of these little ones will be lost (Matt. 18:10, 14).

(2) Being a child brings _everyday security._ In his providence, the Father carries us like children. He knows what we need (Matt. 6:8; Luke 12:30), and his care for us is boundless (Matt. 5:4ff). In Matthew's Gospel, Jesus uses a striking metaphor to illustrate the kind of security that the children of God enjoy. He says, in effect, that nothing is too small for God (Matt. 18:5-14). Many of the Pharisees had explicitly prohibited prayers that asked God to extend his mercy "even to a bird's nest." They thought it was disrespectful to associate God with something as small as a tiny bird. In contrast, Jesus points out that God's care embraces even sparrows, even though two of them can be bought for a tiny worthless copper coin (Matt. 10:29ff). The message is clear. God extends God's special love to the smallest of creatures. If God does so for the smallest sparrow, how much more will God do it for the disciples of God. "Do not be afraid, you are worth more than hundreds of sparrows" (Matt. 10:31).

In the heavenly world, which the ancient world saw as constructed in circles around God's throne, the guardian angels of the _microi_—the throne, the little ones, stand in the innermost circle, immediately before the throne of God (cf. Matt. 18:10).

(3) Being a child gives the disciples _the courage to submit to what is unpredictable in the divine will._ Following the Lord does not remove the riddles of life; there will still be suffering and pain. But the disciple has the confidence of knowing that in the end nothing can destroy him or her. Suffering for Jesus' sake becomes an occasion of joy, because it serves to glorify God and is there-fore rewarded by God (Matt. 5:11ff; Luke 6:23).

Pablo Picasso was once quoted as saying that "it takes a long time to become young." His words may be taken as a succinct summary of the biblical perspective on childhood. The Word of God, as we have seen, views the experience of childhood as both a gift and a challenge. Children are models of simplicity and invitations to growth. They are the privileged ones of God, who nevertheless stand in need of maturation.

The scriptural evidence seems to point to three levels of growth in "becoming young." The first level is the childlike qualities of trust and dependence that so tenderly characterize an infant. The second level is the transition of a child toward adult responsibility. Jesus praises the quality of childlikeness, but he doesn't want his disciples to remain infants. This second stage is often marked with the turbulence and confusion of growing up. The final stage of "becoming young" is the rewinning of childlike trust and adult decisions to Christian love. In the growth from childlike faith to mature commitment, we are challenged to take charge of our lives and to clarify our values. But the paradox of the gospel is that the highest form of freedom is self-surrender. The highest form of responsibility is to become totally open to the Father. It is to return to the vulnerability of a child through the mature freedom of an adult.

John Heagle[1]

154 ✦ FORMING THE SPIRITUALITY OF CHILDREN

As children grow and develop, it is the privilege of both parents and the church to foster their spiritual sensitivity. This article describes how both the life of the home and public worship are vitally important in this process. This article is written from a formal liturgical perspective, but can easily be applied in every worship tradition.

A Religious Home

Our first task is to learn how to maintain religious homes, homes which cherish and nurture the religious dimension of life, instead of denying or ignoring it. By religious, I mean that answer to the human need to concur on a set of symbols and rituals which create order, give identity, and provide motivation. More and more people are being raised to ignore this dimension of their lives, to deny the need for symbol, and to survive somehow without order, identity, and motivation. Thus in the first place, the home must be a religious place. Are meals shared in common? Are there rituals particular to the needs and strengths of the family? Is that which is beyond human comprehension given its respectful place? Is nature reverenced? Do we as parents teach our children to stand humbly before great works of art? Are we able to stand before one another and, weepingly, say good-bye? How do parents help their children deal with the monsters of the night? (Telling the children that there are no monsters does, I am convinced, no good; the monsters seem to return as soon as the adults leave the bedroom.) How is death explained? Do the children attend funerals and visit grave sites? We can learn from fine children's books, like those by Maurice Sendak, in which monsters are faced and dreams are relived, in which the rhythm of the text and the magnificent illustrations allow the children a religious response to these forbidden fears of life. One of my criticisms of the Roman eucharistic prayers for masses with children is that they are in the first place poor religion. They trivialize children's experience. The prayers depict children as happy-go-lucky and innocent; they describe the world as a wondrous place of sunshine; they offer prosaic explanations, instead of vivid images; the language of the prayers is not in any way incantatory; and the prayers have no illustrations! The children I know are more deeply aware of the religious dimension of life than these prayers would suggest.

One further opportunity for the religious home is to use those very early years to talk about God as one far other than a big daddy in the sky. Small children have not yet seen the history of Western art, which gives us all the indelible mental image of God as an old bearded man on a mountain. Especially in those early years, we can speak of the mysteries of God: God, our treasure, our rock, our cup, our river, our bread, and our fortress. Before the onset of logical and discursive thought, children are able to talk of God in the same creative ways that the Psalms do. Our respect for the mystery of God demands that we use this stage to its religious advantage.

A Sanctified Home

Our second task is to sanctify the religious home with the Christian faith. In such a home. all the religious longings and the human terrors are turned to the Cross. It is not that there are no monsters—for there are—but God is bigger than the monsters. The primary manner in which the home is sanctified by faith is by responding to the call to praise; that is, by participating in the life of Christian worship. Do Christian families visit churches before moving so that the location of the parish will help them decide where to live? Are family activities and commitments based around the centrality of the Sunday worship experience? It is my firm resolution that children belong in the Sunday Eucharist from baptism on. Yes, this requires dedication on the parents' part and no small understanding of the liturgy themselves, as they play the role of sportscaster for their young ones—"Look here, see this, there's the important thing." We can share with one another ideas for helping small and growing children understand and participate in the liturgy. For, granting children's ability to take in complex stimuli, to tune in and out at their own attention level, to sense the meaning of symbol, and to flow with the movement of ritual, children are readily able to worship with the parish long before they can verbally demonstrate this ability. Children enjoy the mingling of images that is in the liturgy, and even a very small child can learn to say, "Lord, have mercy."

Beside worship in church, there is worship in the home. I resist the despair which groans that contemporary homes cannot sustain a devotional life. Patterns formed when the children are still infants, a good night prayer at the crib, can be maintained. Good Bible story books (a trick to find, among all the poor ones on the market) can be read. Perhaps the parish can give such books as baptismal gifts. Sacred songs can be sung. The historic responses of the faithful—"O God, come to our assistance, O Lord, make haste to help me"—can be incorporated into meal times. Times of family significance, trips, reunions, parties, and mournings, all can be offered to God on the family altar.

This essential task, the sanctification of the religious home by the Christian faith, has a parental focus. The issue is not so much the education of the children of believing parents, as the education of parents of believing children. If the faith is experienced as integral also to adult life, if the parents continue to grow also in their spiritual life, the children will see this faith as part of a healthy human experience. The parents ought not merely to recite kiddie prayers with their children, but use devotional times to offer their own prayers also, so that children see their parents pray. Do the parents discuss the homily? Do they debate moral issues? Do they sing the sacred songs? Do they recall the saints' days? All too often, we encourage children in religious education until they are pre-teen age, but then ignore any further development. This only suggests to children that religious training, like Saturday morning television, is kids' stuff. The faith must be lived by the parents as something that remains significant for maturing human life. How does Deuteronomy 11:19 suggest we teach our children? "And you shall teach them to your children, talking of them when you are sitting at your house and when you are walking by the way, and when you lie down, and when you rise."

Children and Liturgy

Our third task is to incorporate the children into the liturgical life of the parish. In the first place, we must make the liturgy and the children more amenable to another. This suggests a host of considerations, from training children to be lectors to giving toddlers their own service orders, to redesigning our seating arrangements. But it also implies several more significant changes in our practice, the most important being the age of first Communion. The time has come to end the church's seven hundred year old separation of baptism from first Communion. It was not until the twelfth century that, because of an over scrupulous concern that the body and blood of Christ might be dropped or spilled, nursing infants were first deprived the bread, and later all the laity deprived of the wine. Small children were then left not communing at all. Subsequently, we drew up logical reasons to explain the situation we had inherited. As the culture becomes increasingly pagan, our parish life must be more inclusive for all its baptized members—and we become members at baptism. All baptized members should be encouraged to eat and drink at the Table of the Lord. My four year old daughter said, "We drink God in the wine," and I could not have said it better. The wine is not like the liquor of a cocktail party, but like milk for all who are nursed by God's Word.

Another major concern is the American practice of confirmation in early preteen years. We have not been true to the intent of the rite in our language and practice. If we say that confirmation is the adult renewing a promise made during infancy, then we are fooling ourselves to give such a decision to children. We are in fact encouraging perjury. If we say that confirmation is a puberty rite, we can design one more appropriate to our culture without suggesting that an adult has more of the Holy Spirit than a child. If confirmation is, really, a kind of graduation from the parish's formal religious education, we do the maturing life of faith an enormous disservice. Confirmation was historically the bishop's prayer over the baptized child. Indeed, we need much more study on how history and present practice can help us shape the ritual into one which enlivens both the children and the church with the Spirit. Perhaps periodic public reaffirmations of faith at times of life passage might be shaped liturgically as parish celebrations. Meanwhile, the bishop's prayer might be restored to its original place, baptism.

In conclusion in my experience, the people who sit with toddlers in church, the parents who have prayed their children through childhood, can tell story after story—some almost incredible—that point to the religious nature of small children, to their ability to catch images as they fly by, and to their delight in participating in liturgical action. These stories testify only to what we adults observe: surely much is going on that we do not see.

Alexander Schmemann has written of his despair that some Orthodox Christians in the United States have adopted the pattern of conducting Sunday school during church. He rails against the incongruity of rearing children in the faith by keeping them out of the divine liturgy. For to be a Christian is to be called to worship God. That call comes to all of us who are baptized, at whatever age we are.

When we baptize our children, we are accepting the responsibility of training them in the practice of the faith. Such formation is not easy, but neither is it nigh to impossible. Such formation is a way of life, the way of life of the Spirit.

Gail Ramshaw Schmidt[2]

155 ✦ THE PLACE OF THE INFANT IN THE WORSHIPING COMMUNITY

Even the youngest children have an important role in the Christian community. Both parents and the church must be conscious of how important their actions are for encouraging the faith and the participation of infants.

Premises About the Role of Infants in the Faith Community

(1) **The infant has full membership in a covenanting community.** At birth the infant becomes a member of the family in which he or she is born. Likewise, baptism is the sign that the infant is born into full membership of the covenanting church community in which his or her parents are members.

In the covenanting community, all members of every generation covenant to care and support one another. The infant not only receives this promise, but, as appropriate to his or her development, cares for and supports the other members of the community. All adult members of the covenanting community accept an active role in the nurture and care for the new member and the member's family. The infant, in turn, develops a supporting relationship with older members of the community through the loving, trusting, interacting experiences that occur in the activities of the community. The infant is an equal member among members, who give and receive within the membership.

(2) **The infant develops faith through participation in the life of the covenanting community.** All members of the covenanting community are, in a sense, catechumens. They are learning about their heritage and God's teaching through the gospel, through their involvement in the rituals, in socialization, and in responsibilities undertaken by the covenanting community. Although there may be opportunities for education through specific instruction in a Bible study or in an organized church school class, understanding the faith is developed through intentional catechesis in ritual, social gatherings, meetings, and worship. Understanding the Christian life and faith is gained largely through participation and action.

The infant, too, is a catechumen, who learns of faith by experiencing relationships in the community, by actively participating in ritual, by experiencing the objects of ritual, and by playing alongside others in a loving setting. Although young infants cannot speak, they initiate and react to a variety of experiences, each time expanding their understanding of the meaning of faith.

(3) **The infant is a minister and is ministered to in the multigenerational enculturation of the covenanting community.** The covenant community is composed of a collection of individual members, who minister to one another in the development of the faith. Through enculturation, a process whereby level of membership is equal for all as lines between adult and child or student and teacher are erased, all members learn and teach. In a congregation that spans several generations, education includes events wherein all are gathered together to exchange information and provide support for those who need it, and all grow in the faith from the contributions made by members of every age.

When age groups and generations are not separated, members of the community develop closer relationships as they minister to one another. The joyful presence of the infant ministers to those around. Because the infant is open and trusting, she or he brings a gift of freshness to other members. Likewise, when the infant is tired, uncomfortable, or restless, she or he is ministered to by caring others in the church family.

(4) **The infant learns through direct experiences.** The newborn infant is in what Piaget calls the sensorimotor period of development; that is, it learns through its senses and physical actions. The infant learns less by watching than by experiencing. The infant learns more from initiating activity than by being "taught." Until eighteen months of age, the infant learns by using the senses and physical abilities to "try out" the world. Piaget teaches that through the process of assimilation and accommodation the child expands his or her knowledge with each experience.

At church, the infant learns by exploring, hearing, seeing, touching, and smelling the real things around. At first, the infant can associate meaning only with actual objects such as kittens, flowers, the sanctuary, and the organ. Later, the toddler can come to understand that visual symbols represent the objects themselves.

The infant learns about worship by attending worship and trying to sing hymns, putting coins in the collection plate, and absorbing the atmosphere in the sanctuary.

In Hebrew families, during the years of tribal wandering, infants took part in family rituals. Priests instructed fathers that they were to talk to their infants and explain the observances that were being celebrated. In the home as well as in corporate worship today, the infant should be included in the celebration of ritual. Parents and other adults should talk with young children about the elements in ritual and their meaning. In intergenerational settings, the infant can be assisted by older members to observe the Christian holy days. Infants and toddlers should have a role in events at Christmas, Easter, and other significant occasions celebrated by the church family. Over a period of time continued participation will lead to the development of deeper meaning for the growing child.

(5) The role of the infant in the covenanting community is inextricably bound to the relationship of the parents and family within the community. Young families in the church live daily with the problems of the world in which they live and work. Faced with the realities of contemporary living, which may include both parents' working, a one-parent family, parents living and working in different communities, and more recent financial worries caused by inflation, parents of infants need the support of the covenanting community.

Because today's parents may move frequently and often are separated from their extended family, the church has an opportunity to extend security to its members through activities formerly provided by a family relationship.

Families with infants need help with parenting. Beginning when the parents know a new family member is expected, they can join a parenting program for study, for support from other parents and parenting leaders, and for socialization with other members in the parenting group.

When the baby arrives, parenting enters a different phase. Involvement in the parenting program continues, with additional services needed. Hopefully, more churches will establish day-care centers for members of the church community, as well as for the larger community as a means of outreach. Because good day-care programs are desperately needed in the United States, churches should seriously consider using existing facilities to serve their own families and the community with day care. Parent-support activities can be part of the day-care program, providing the infant and family with an extended, comprehensive support base.

The family may participate in the church school program for the infant. The church school class is an intergenerational community class where an older sibling, parent, church member, or minister participates with one or two infants in the class. A class leader explains the activities of the session, as well as their purposes for the infant. The concepts of catechesis and enculturation are involved as infants and their facilitators learn from each other. The infant is well acquainted with the facilitator. Take-home materials are sent home with the infant frequently to keep the family informed about the church school program.

Parent-Infant Curricula

The Curriculum of Christian Heritage. Infants learn about their Christian heritage through involvement in worship and intergenerational observances of Christian celebrations at the church and in the family. Parenting programs can provide information for parents as to how they can help their infant participate in home activities such as reading the Bible, telling stories about the Bible, and discussing child-raising practices and family traditions.

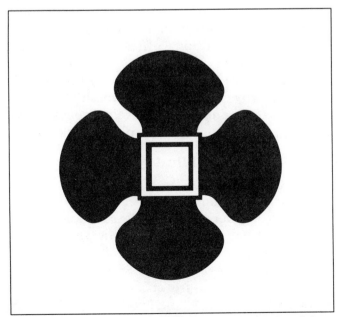

The Canterbury Cross. This cross is made of four hammer-like arms that spring from a square.

The church school curriculum also includes activities related to the Christian heritage. Stories of the Bible are told. The child learns about the Christian heritage through hearing the music of the church and singing simple songs.

God's world is part of the heritage of the infant. In the home, at the day-care program, and in the church school, the infant should learn about the gifts of God in the world through experience with such things as animals, plants, and the phenomena of seasonal changes and growth.

The Curriculum of Ritual. The infant and family learn about ritual through participation in worship and rites such as baptism and through involvement in intergenerational events in which the rituals of the church are discussed and explored.

The infant and family also grow in understanding of ritual through family observances in the home. Prayers, celebration of holidays, remembering baptism and confirmation, and other home observances should provide an active role for the infant.

In the church school program, experiences are provided to help the infant expand the understanding of ritual. The infant is taken for example to the sanctuary to touch the water in the baptismal font, play on the organ, and touch the minister's Bible. The infant is told about the purpose and meaning of the paraphernalia of ritual, as well as the functions of the sanctuary. Thus, the child grows in understanding and desire to participate as a natural result of a process begun even before birth, and continued through participation in a holistic experience of the Christian life.

Sue Wortham[3]

156 • WHY CHILDREN SHOULD WORSHIP

Children are uniquely equipped to enter into the mystery of worship. Yet the Christian church has often considered children to be less than essential to the worshiping community. The following article explains why and how children can be included as full participants in the worshiping community.

My family attended the worship service at Duke University Chapel one Sunday. Although we were looking forward to being away from our regular worship responsibilities and being part of worship at Duke Chapel, we were a little apprehensive about how our seven-year-old daughter would respond to this new worship environment with its Gothic architecture, different ministers, and unfamiliar order of worship. As we entered the chapel, we were given two orders of worship, one for adults and one for children. The children's worship guide, "Elementary Worship," was informally prepared with pictures, explanations, space for responses by the child in words and drawings, words to responses and creeds known by the congregation, and general instructions for making worship more understandable for children. My daughter's response was positive. This carefully prepared worship guide had succeeded in making worship more meaningful to her.

Upon leaving, I realized how our church needed to rethink its approach toward children and their role in worship. It was readily apparent to me that my daughter's response to worship at our church was much less enthusiastic, except during special seasons or when the children's choirs were participating. This realization caused me to reconsider the role of children in the worship experience.

Worship is one of the most selfless acts of Christians. It is not for us, Christians, but is our service directed *to* God and *for* God in words and deeds of praise, adoration, confession, and commitment. For our children to grow in their ability to relate to God through worship, we as adults must make an intentional effort to sensitize them to all of its facets.

The purpose of this article is to lay a brief foundation for why children should worship. Material will be drawn from biblical, developmental, theological, and spiritual formation authorities.

—— A Short Biblical Perspective ——

The Old Testament stresses a covenantal perspective in relation to children in the life of Israel. Children were a part of all that took place in the saga of Israel: the times of joy, the times of sorrow, the times of hunger, the times of captivity, and the times of worship. Scattered throughout the Pentateuch are descriptions of Israel's worship (e.g., Exod. 33:10; Exod. 35:1; Num. 10:3, etc.) In Deuteronomy 31:12-30, as they approached the Promised Land, Moses called together all of the people specifically including the children, so that they might learn a song of great significance to the future of Israel. Thus, one of the contributions of the Old Testament to the role of children in the religious community is that of involving the entire family in sharing the responsibilities and rewards of the covenantal relationship.

Later in the Old Testament, the prophets used children metaphorically to describe the relationship between the Israelites and the God of Israel. Isaiah especially is fond of the image of child or son (Isa. 7:14; 9:6). The most poignant example is found in Isaiah 11:6, " . . . and a little child shall lead them."

The continuity between the Old Testament metaphors concerning children and Jesus' teaching is remarkable. In Luke, Mary's song (Magnificat), the Angels' song (Gloria in excelsis Deo), and Simeon's song (Nunc Dimittis), all revolve around Jesus Christ as a baby, and not as an adult political or military ruler. Jesus quickly told the disciples, who attempted to keep children from him, that his kingdom had a place for children (Matt. 19:13-15; Mark 10:13-14; Luke 18:15-17). In addition, the services of a child were used by Jesus to feed the multitudes (John 6:9).

The metaphorical use of children in Jesus' teaching is also quite strong. Children were a symbol for humility (Matt. 18:2-6; Mark 9:36; Luke 9:47-48) and a symbol for the greater masses of the poor and powerless (Matt. 18:5; Matt. 25:40). It is difficult for congregations to appreciate the power of these metaphors and for children to realize the potential they have as children for the kingdom of God unless they become a meaningful part of the worship experience. Often worship tends to insulate children from the rest of the world, rather than open it to them. As Jesus stressed, "if you have given to the least of these, you have given to me" (Matt. 25:40). It might be said that those churches which do not provide a meaningful role for children in worship probably do not include diverse ethnic groups and/ or people from a broad range of socioeconomic situations. Attitudes toward children in worship may be indicative of a more pervasive narrow-mindedness in other areas. Dealing with children in worship may be the first step toward dealing with the larger problem of exclusiveness in worship.

We need to regain Israel's concern for the whole family's involvement in the covenant and for passing on our worship traditions to children in an intentional manner. Additionally, we need our children among us in worship so that we might experience first hand the power of Jesus' teaching on humility and the nature of the Christian life and worship as inclusive (of children, the poor, and the powerless).

Developmental Priorities and Worship

Child development models teach us many things. I will look briefly at just a few models that have great importance for incorporating children into the community.

(1) Children must have the opportunity to learn to worship, just as they learn other skills. This is a lifetime process. The context of the Lord's Prayer comes from a question to Jesus by the disciples to *teach* them to pray. Our children need to be taught the "stuff" of worship. They need to be taught to pray, to praise, to share, to listen, to confess, and to respond to the message of Christ in word and witness.

Developmental psychologists tell us that our learning takes place through the building of and gradual internalization of patterns of behavior. The actions of worship (ceremony) and the words of worship (ritual) gradually become a part of our intellectual processes simply by doing and saying them at the earlier stages of life. Meaning is added later through experience and relationships. This developmental model shows us that children learn best by actively participating in worship, rather than by watching.

(2) We also know that children learn best when they start at a young age. The sounds of the organ, the lighting of candles, the procession of the choir, the use of colorful banners, the full-voiced singing of hymns by the congregation, the hearing of the Word retold in the engaging manner of a storyteller, and the meeting and greeting of the congregation can have a tremendous emotional impact upon children (even at four or five years old), if they are encouraged to understand and participate. The more worship appeals to all of the senses, the more effective the impression will be on the children. Where feelings are strong, the desire for information often follows. Even as adults, we can recall the feelings of a

situation long after we have forgotten the specific circumstances surrounding it. Adults often say, "The children can't participate because they don't understand." Understanding starts at the level of impression and awareness. If interest is created on the basic level, then understanding will follow.

(3) Developmental psychologists also tell us that children use words before they fully comprehend them. They are motivated by language at the level just above where they are. For example, the elementary-aged child might respond better to language geared for the junior high student. The implications here are many; but the most obvious implication is that worship designed for involving children should not be condescending, but challenging.

Developmental research offers many other insights into the way children learn, but let me summarize. A child learning the skills of worship demands an *active* and *participatory* approach. The child should be exposed to the sights, sounds, and general impressions of worship at a young age and in a challenging manner.

Faith, Development, and Worship

When planning for worship, we need to be aware that those who worship together reflect various stages of faith. John Westerhoff III provides an easily understandable model for understanding how faith is perceived at various stages of faith. The stages are as follows:

(1) **Affiliative Faith.** This is usually the faith of the child based on the models of parents and other influential adults. The child starts the journey of faith by learning those rituals and patterns of the worshiping community of which he or she is a part. The priorities of this stage of faith are based upon the priorities and expectations of those whom the child knows and trusts.

(2) **Searching Faith.** Often during adolescence, the growing person starts to react to those values that were accepted without question during earlier years. Based upon the experiences of growth and development, the adolescent starts to look for new rituals, patterns, and means of expression in all areas of life, including the areas of faith and worship. This is a natural process. By questioning the inherited values of the community, the person develops a sense of ownership of those values that seem most relevant to life as that person has experienced it. It is a time of experimentation with new forms, styles and modes of expression in worship.

(3) **Mature Faith.** This stage of faith integrates the experience of the earlier stages. It reflects flexibility, openness, and personal relationship with God that results from freedom rather than authority. Persons at this stage of faith can share from their broader perspective with those in the affiliative and searching stages.

All of these stages need to be part of our worship awareness and preparation. Unless the child has been raised with a strong sense of affiliative faith (notice the covenantal overtones), the adolescent will not have a spiritual foundation from which to test life's obstacles. A strong worship tradition is important for a healthy affiliative faith. If the adolescent cannot search within the confines of the church for answers, then he will search elsewhere. Adults with maturing faith are needed as models for children acquiring an affiliative expression of faith and as friends for adolescents searching for answers to faith. A growing faith is a vital faith.

Worship is the ideal arena for all stages of faith. Adults can easily slip into a complacency about worship that values aestheticism over spirituality or structure over vitality. Worship, then, becomes a "museum" experience where the songs, sermons, and liturgy are idolized over the God they are to praise. This complacency will not likely happen in worship that encompasses all stages of faith. The children will keep worship structured and participatory because those are the traits that help them best learn. The adolescents will keep worship relevant and responsive to the issues in the world around us, awakening us with their insights and innovations. Finally, the adults should bring a sense of purpose, continuity, and challenge to all who participate.

Biblically, we must take the needs of children seriously. They are a part of our covenantal inheritance and a constant reminder that a childlike faith of humility and inclusiveness is at the heart of Jesus' Good News.

Developmentally, we learn the need to teach children the vocabulary of worship at a young age and to challenge them in the process of worship education and understanding, rather than to condescend to their apparent level.

Faith development teaches us that there is a process of faith development. Worship is one of the most important arenas for experiencing growth in the faith process. Those in each stage of the faith process contribute to the overall health and vitality of the worshiping community.

Where to go from here? The second part of this series is designed to offer specific ideas about curriculum content and practical suggestions for making worship more dynamic for children.

C. Michael Hawn[4]

157 ✦ Practical Suggestions for Children in Worship

This article presents dozens of practical suggestions for encouraging and teaching children to worship and for including children in regular worship life of the community. These suggestions pertain to every aspect of the worship experience, including the worship environment, music, prayers, and gestures.

General Areas of Concern

Any program of worship education will need to have several areas of focus. The content of worship can be taught to children in some manner regardless of age. The preschooler experiencing the season of Advent for the first time can feel the sense of expectation, sing some of the songs, and learn the names of the major characters in the Advent drama. Each time Advent is approached thereafter, new layers of understanding and participation can be added. We as Christians never outgrow our potential for perceiving new meaning during the Advent/Christmas season. The same is true for other worship concepts. First, let us look at some of the content areas of worship education, and then let us suggest some organizational ideas for implementation.

A Special Sense of Time. In order to appreciate the life and ministry of Jesus Christ, it is very helpful for the child (indeed, for all of us) to relive that life and ministry in a systematic fashion. The Christian year is such a tool. One of the important aspects of a child developing cognitive skills is that of a sense of time. Understanding and reliving the Christian year, each year offers the child an organization and experimental basis for relating to Jesus Christ as a person and friend. Without the Christian year, the events and teachings of Christ become a series of episodic activities that lack cohesive structure and intent. We weaken the message of Jesus Christ by not leading the child to an understanding of this special sense of time.

A Special Sense of Place. Children identify worship and their understanding of God with the church building, especially in the preschool and early elementary years. While adults can conceptualize worship at any time and at any place, children live in a concrete world, where such abstract ideas do not have any relevance or significance. Church buildings exist to promote a variety of ideas and feelings, including a historical tradition, fellowship, ministry to the community, and worship. Naming the parts of the sanctuary and explaining their function should be a part of the worship education. Developmentally, the child will be much more at home if he understands the place of worship. There will be time later to expand the child's concept of where God is and where we might worship God.

A Special Sense of Order. Children need to learn why things are done the way they are in worship. How is a service organized? Where can the child participate in the service? What are the different moods expressed in the service? Why are certain words said (rites) and certain actions done (rituals)? The words, actions, and symbols of a worshiping congregation are unlike those of other gatherings and need to be explained.

A Special Sense of Community. The worshiping community gathers to praise God, to confess, to hear God's Word, and to go from that time of worship to share what it has experienced. These are different reasons from any other grouping of people that are a part of the child's life. Children need to understand worship so that they may more fully appreciate this special community of which they are a part.

These are some broad ideas for worship curriculum for children. There are many specifics to be answered, but it is important that these areas, at least, be covered.

Specific Suggestions for the Child in Worship

PREPARING CHILDREN FOR WORSHIP

(1) Make arrangements to acquaint the children personally with ministers and worship leaders.

(2) Give the children a tour of the sanctuary, including the chancel area, nave, narthex, and the furniture used in worship, including the pulpit, lectern, communion table, baptistry or baptismal font, organ, etc.

(3) Teach the children to use the hymnbook, including how to find hymns, read stanzas from the hymnbook, read responsive readings, etc.

(4) Learn the basic hymns used in the church's worship.

(5) Learn songs and responses that are usually memorized by the congregation, e.g., Doxology, Lord's Prayer, Apostles' Creed, etc.

(6) Learn key terms associated with worship.
- Musical terms: prelude, introit, anthem, offertory, hymn postlude, choral response, gradual, antiphon, psalmody, voluntary, etc.
- Types of prayers: invocation, morning prayer, prayer of confession, prayer of adoration, prayer for illumination, offertory prayer, benediction, collect, etc.
- Other liturgical acts and terms: passing the peace, Lord's Supper, Communion, Eucharist, baptismal call to worship, Old Testament and New Testament Lessons, etc.

(7) Encourage the children to write prayers of various kinds, e.g., prayers of praise, thanksgiving, confession, dedication, etc.

(8) Introduce the children to the meaning of Christian symbols.

(9) Introduce the children to the Christian year by preparing banners, singing hymns, and using other worship aids that reflect the character of each session.

(10) Prepare the parents for involving their children in worship through special seminars or classes. Topics might include the following:
- How to help your child during worship;
- Introduce your child to those around him in worship;
- Singing hymns and responses at home;
- Praying with the child at home;
- Involving the children in home worship that reflects the various seasons of the church year, e.g., a home Advent wreath;
- Learning a hymn-of-the-month at home;
- Reflecting on the worship service at home with the child after each service;
- Looking over the order with your child before the service, anticipating what is to happen.

Encourage parents to sing and respond actively as a model for the child; e.g., sit closer to the front of the sanctuary.

THE CHILD AS CONGREGATIONAL PARTICIPANT

(1) Involve people that the children know in worship leadership, including church school teachers, choir leaders, parents, children's ministers, etc.

(2) Involve family units as liturgists in worship.

(3) Use more stories or a more narrative approach to the presentation of Scripture and biblical events, as well as in sermons. These stories can be sung, as well as spoken. Many hymns stress a narrative approach to the life of Christ or other biblical characters.

(4) Use sermon illustrations that cite children as examples.

(5) Use illustrations from children's literature during sermons. C. S. Lewis' *Chronicles of Narnia* are good examples.

(6) Look for ways to allow children to participate in the sacraments. While this is not the place to argue for a particular approach to children and the sacraments, each tradition can decide what points allow for more participation. One possible substitute for the sacraments that is more inclusive of children is to develop the idea of the *agape* or love feast, which is a family meal used by the early church and carried on in traditions such as the Moravians. The Presbyterian hymnal, *The Worshipbook*, has a suggested order for a love feast.

(7) The use of simple dramatizations of biblical/historical figures in costume doing monologues can add to the child's experience in worship.

(8) Use litanies and responsive readings that single out children as a participating group.

(9) Include the concerns of children in prayers, as well as the concerns of adults.

(10) Developing worship guides for children can play a major role in improving the child's involvement in and comprehension of the worship experience. The following is a list of options to

choose from in preparing worship guides for children:

(a) Pre-worship checklist of things to look for in the up-coming service, e.g., worship leaders, themes, hymns needed, symbols used, Scripture lessons needed, etc.

(b) Hymn bookmarkers for hymns to be used.

(c) Bible bookmarkers for Scripture to be read.

(d) Inclusion of texts that the congregation usually knows by memory, e.g., Lord's Prayer, Doxology, Gloria Patri, Apostles' Creed, etc.

(e) Litanies and responsive readings.

(f) Space for writing prayers.

(g) Puzzles and games that reflect on the content of the sermon and Scripture lesson, or the nature of the particular season of the Christian year.

(h) Space for guided drawing that reflects the theme of the service.

(i) Meanings of words used in worship that may be difficult to understand.

(j) Texts of choral or solo music.

(k) Graphics and pictures that illustrate a particular section of the service or use various Christian symbols.

(l) Background on the worship leaders that might be of interest to children.

(m) Information on hymn writers or background on how certain hymns were written.

(n) Elements that personalize worship for the child, e.g., "What can you offer to God?" or "The body of Christ broken for _____ [child's name]."

CHILDREN AS WORSHIP LEADERS

(1) Use children or family units for greeting and for preparing the sanctuary for worship, e.g., helping with envelopes, pencils, bulletins, inserts, flowers, banners, etc.

(2) Have children sing for those events that they cannot participate in directly, e.g., Communion, baptism, parent-child dedication, ordination, dedication of teachers and other church leaders, etc.

(3) Use children to read Scripture lessons or involve children in a reader's theater presentation of Scripture.

(4) Use children to teach the congregation a new hymn.

(5) When using children to sing anthems, always stress the function of what they are to do, rather than the performance aspect of their involvement.

(6) Have children write and lead prayers and litanies suitable for worship.

(7) Place special children's musical presentations in a worship service, rather than a performance context.

CHILDREN AND THE APPLICATION OF WORSHIP (WORSHIP IN PRACTICE)

(1) Bringing food, clothing, toys, etc., as a part of the child's offering to God.

(2) Visiting shut-ins, hospitals, nursing homes with music and Scripture for those who are ill or unable to attend worship.

(3) Participate in the sharing of the gospel in Scripture and in song in malls, in shopping centers, and in areas that demonstrate differing cultural and socio-economic situations.

(4) Participation in cleaning, decorating, and beautification projects around the church and for those who are unable to do these for themselves.

(5) Sending cards, letters, pictures, etc., to those who are unable to attend worship or for those who represent the church or denomination in mission positions.

—— A Program of Worship Education ——

Any program of worship education needs a philosophy of implementation. This philosophy of implementation needs to be consonant with the content you wish to teach and the nature of worship you wish to communicate. For example, if you wish to teach that worship is an inclusive activity involving the whole family, it is best not to use an approach that takes children out of worship every Sunday. A more consistent approach would be to develop a format that allows children to participate actively in worship at least part of the time. The following are some general suggestions for enacting a program of worship education.

(1) Invite other church programs to share in the responsibility for teaching some of the tasks of worship. For example, the children's choir program might teach specific hymns as well as the use of the hymnal. The church school program might sing one or more of the hymns to be used later in the worship service.

(2) A modified children's church program

might be used for a part of the year that allows children to learn the vocabulary of worship, practice some parts of the worship service, and, most importantly, create worship experiences for themselves. Then the children could be brought back into the worship service during special seasons of celebration, participating more fully and with greater understanding. When the children are involved in worship, those adults whom the children trust and know should be used as worship leaders as well.

(3) Form a committee for coordinating children's worship education among various church organizations and for drawing up children's worship guides with the help of the ministers.

(4) Provide activities and materials that will aid parents in the task of worship. These might be included on a weekly basis in the children's worship guide. Suggestions for family worship might also be a part of family Advent and Lenten devotional guides meant to be used at home. Special family services could be a part of the church tradition that involve children in special and more active ways, e.g., Thanksgiving. These may be held in other areas of the church to allow for greater flexibility. Worship education at the church will never have the impact it should, unless the family practices some kind of worship preparation and experiences worship at home.

Involving children in the worship life of the church should be an adventure. Most adults will appreciate the freshness and vitality that children can bring to the occasion. Some will find the children's involvement distracting and perhaps offensive. No prophetic activity will meet with unanimous support, but the ground work can be laid in a careful manner to help to ensure as broad a base of support and involvement as possible. You will only learn by experimenting and worshiping together.

C. Michael Hawn[5]

158 ◆ Teaching Children the Four Acts of Worship: The Children's Worship Center

The following article describes an effective method for teaching children the meaning of each act of worship. Children gather in worship centers, where they lead through stories, prayers, songs, and gestures that introduce them to the mystery of Christian worship.

Our experience with young children convinces us that they know, love, and worship God. But corporate worship is structured and full of words and symbols based on stories and memories children do not yet have. For children to participate meaningfully in corporate worship, they must first experience the essential parts and stories of worship through sensorimotor means. Our children's worship centers permit this. In the worship centers, the flow of activity corresponds to the order of congregational worship, instead of the traditional sequencing of nursery schools.

In Christian worship, the scattered people of God come together to praise, listen, and respond to God by celebrating the creative and redemptive acts of God, particularly the resurrection of Christ. The order of the service helps us do this. Christian worship has a fourfold structure, regardless of denomination or tradition. Your service may be highly liturgical or informal, even spontaneous, but the fourfold order is there. This order reflects the ordinary social activities of family celebrations: gathering, listening, thanking, and going. Expressed in the language of worship, this weekly celebration of the family of families uses terms, such as the following examples to order the time together: "Assemble in God's name," "Proclaim God's Word," "Give thanks to God" (Eucharist), and "Go in God's name."

The first and fourth parts of the order are preparatory in the sense that the first helps us get ready to be with God in the Word and sacrament, while the fourth helps us get ready to reenter the ordinary world to do Christ's ministry and mission. The two middle parts are sometimes called the liturgy (or service) of the Word and the liturgy (or service) of the Lord's Supper, respectively. Sometimes the terms are different. You might call these four: "The approach to God," "The Word of God in proclamation," "The Word of God in sacrament," and "The response to God." Substitute your names, if you wish. We have used the Presbyterian order here.

To work with young children, we focused on the foundational and essential components of worship and on the biblical stories that give content to the images, symbols, and actions of worship. We took each part of the order of worship, selected the most essential parts for young children and developed our approach around these parts. What follows is a description of the four parts of the order of worship, and what we chose to do with our young children for each part.

———— (1) Assemble in God's Name ————

Each Sunday as we gather around the Lord's Table (altar), the first part of the order of worship helps us move from the world of ordinary time and place to the holy.

Call to Worship
Hymn of Praise
Confession
Declaration of Pardon
Response of Praise

As we gather we need a way to get ready to be with God. We need to move our attention from ourselves and our world to God. So our approach to God, our gathering in God's name, is a time for preparing ourselves to listen to God. While getting ready comes from within, the liturgy helps us refocus and center in God as it shifts our everyday language to religious or biblical language, images, symbols, and signs of God. We greet one another in the name of the Lord. We sing and speak our praise to God. We confess our sins so that our relationship with God is restored and nothing stands in our way of being ready to listen to God.

Two things are essential in the first part of the order for worship: our awareness of the presence of God and our ability to get ready to be with God.

Just as pastors and elders meet before the worship service for preparation and prayer, so the children's worship leader and the greeter (or greeters) arrive early. While the greeter prepares the "feast," the worship leader sits on the circle on the floor, praying and becoming centered in God in order to be ready when the first child arrives. The greeter moves to the door to meet the children. While still outside the room, each child begins to prepare to enter this special place to be with God.

The leader greets each child as he or she sits down on the circle. New children are introduced and conversation continues until all have arrived. Then the leader helps transform this ordinary time and place into a special time and place to be with God.

The Call to Worship. "This is a very special place," the leader says. "It is very special because God is here. In this place, we have all the time we need. So we don't have to hurry We can walk more slowly. And we can talk more softly, because someone might be talking with God and we don't want to disturb them. This is a special place to be with God, to talk with God, to listen to God, and to hear the stories of God. So we need a way to get ready to be in such a special place with God. You can get ready all by yourself. You don't need me to tell you to get ready. Quietness comes from inside you, not from someone telling you to be quiet. You can get quiet all by yourself."

The Greeting. When the children are ready, a formal liturgical greeting in the name of the Lord is exchanged. We use greetings that coincide with the seasons of the church year. But for the youngest children, perhaps two are enough. From September to Easter we say, "The Lord be with you," and the children reply, "And also with you." This greeting is used in various places in the liturgy and is the first part of the greeting exchanged at the beginning of the Great Prayer of Thanksgiving. From Easter to September, we exchange the great Resurrection affirmation. The leader says, "Christ is risen," and the children reply, "The Lord is risen indeed."

Songs of Praise. We sing one or two songs of praise, such as "O God, We Adore You" or "Praise God from Whom All Blessings Flow." We end by singing, "Be Still and Know That I Am God," as a way to get ready to hear a story of God and to mark our transition to the second part of the order of worship. Your church organist or music director can help you find music.

———— (2) Proclaim God's Word ————

The second part of worship involves hearing and responding to the Word of God. It looks something like this.

Hearing the Word of God
Prayer of Illumination of the Holy Spirit
Old Testament Lesson
Psalm
New Testament Lesson
Sermon

Responding to the Word of God
Hymn or Creed

Baptism, Commissioning or Confirmation, Reception of Members
Prayers of Intercession
Offering

When we are ready to listen to God's Word proclaimed through Scripture and sermon, we want to receive it as God intends, so we ask the Holy Spirit to guide us as we hear and respond. After Scripture is read, a sermon provides an interpretation of and witness to God's Word today. But just listening to God's Word is not enough; the Word of God invites response. We respond to the Word in a variety of ways: with a hymn, a confession of faith, baptism, prayers, and offerings.

The actions of receiving and responding to God's Word are the heart of worship in the children's center. For young children, one biblical or liturgical story each session is enough; and it needs to be told and responded to in ways appropriate to young children. As we have said, this requires a sensorimotor approach that uses materials children can work with after the story is presented and that fosters an environment of appropriate freedom in which they can repeat the story and incorporate it into their lives.

The parable of the good shepherd and the lost sheep illustrates our procedure. The storytelling and the response time are so important, they are discussed in separate sections. For now, we will say that after the singing of "Be Still and Know That I Am God," the story begins as the leader walks to the shelf where the parable or story is kept. The materials are visual translations of the Bible and are treated as such. The leader returns to the circle and places the materials on the floor. In good biblical fashion, the story is told using as few words and materials as possible.

The response time follows the story and takes two forms: a time of wondering and reflecting together on the story and a time for personally responding and continued working with the story and art materials. After the wondering, each child personally decides what "work" he or she will do. Since the orientation sessions have shown the children how to select a place to work and how to get their materials and put them away, they are now free to move about the room "all by themselves." In this way, they can interact with the materials as the Spirit moves them.

To give closure to the response time, the children return to the circle, where the story or parable of the day is read from the Bible. Having seen the story presented and having personally worked with it, they can now picture the story and bring memories to it as they hear it read, a skill they will carry into corporate worship. Their offerings are presented, and the transition to the third part of the order of worship occurs.

_____ (3) Give Thanks to God _____ (Eucharist)

Each Sunday is a feast day celebrating the Resurrection of Jesus Christ; therefore, we gather around Christ's table to be fed by him.

Preparation of the Lord's Table
Great Prayer of Thanksgiving
The Lord's Prayer
Words of Institution
Breaking of Bread, Pouring of Wine
The Communion

At this solemn but joyful feast, we offer our thanksgiving to God through the Great Prayer of Thanksgiving (the eucharistic prayer), which summarizes God's mighty acts from Creation to the promise of Christ's return. We thank God for Creation, for the covenant, for the Law and the Prophets, and for Jesus Christ and the promise of Christ's return. Together, we pray the Lord's Prayer. Then, we listen to the words of institution and witness the taking, blessing, breaking, and giving of the bread and wine. United in one body, we commune together.

In most Protestant congregations, the Lord's Supper is not celebrated weekly, but the Great Prayer of Thanksgiving and the Lord's Prayer are offered. Of course, the Lord's Supper is not celebrated in the children's worship centers. But indirect preparation for the Eucharist is. The atmosphere is one of joy, warmth, thanksgiving, and fellowship. The children offer their own prayers of thanksgiving, in place of the Great Prayer of Thanksgiving, by saying the last two lines of the exchange. The leader says, "Let us give thanks to the Lord our God," and the children reply, "It is right to give thanks and praise." (Later in the year, when the children have learned these words, we add the following two preceding lines of the exchange: The leader says, "Lift up your hearts," and the children reply, "We lift them up unto the Lord." Then, the children continue with the two lines they already know.)

The Cross Bezant. This ancient cross was made from five golden discs.

render no one evil for evil, to love and serve the Lord. Finally, we receive the benediction as a sign of God's presence, the presence of the Holy Spirit empowering us for ministry and mission.

In the children's worship center, we sing until the parents arrive. The greeter tells each child when his or her parent comes. Then, the child goes to the leader, is hugged or touched, and receives a good word said quietly, so no one else can hear. This word names a gift for ministry observed that day, such as "Your smile made me feel so good today" or "Thank you for helping serve the feast" or "The storybook you made for Jim will help him while he has to stay in the hospital." Then, a benediction is given, ending with "Go in peace."

Sonja M. Stewart and
Jerome W. Berryman[6]

A "feast" follows. The children prepare "tables" with their white napkins. Fruit, cheese, bread, and juice are served. This is a pleasant time of talking and sharing. Sometimes, we talk about food and the great feasts Jesus gave, such as the feeding of the five thousand, or about Messianic banquets.

————— **(4) Go in God's Name** —————

When the feast is over and the cups and napkins collected, we move to the fourth part of the order of worship.

Hymn
Charge
Blessing
Going Into the World as Christ's Ministers

Just as the first part of the service is a time for getting ready to be with God, so the fourth part is a time for getting ready to go into the world as the body of Christ, living as Christ's ministers and missionaries. Having experienced God and being renewed by God's grace, we know that the God who is present in this special time and place can be present with us in every time and every place. We sing a hymn of praise and are commissioned to be a source of God's healing in the world. We are then told to go out into the world in peace, to

159 • TEACHING CHILDREN TO WORSHIP WITH ADULTS

In many worship traditions, children are encouraged or expected to participate in corporate worship with adults. This article suggests ways in which children can be taught the meaning, structure, and significance of worship.

"Let's sit here so I can see."
"I like to sing this song."
"Am I a 'child of the covenant'?"

Children are heard more frequently now during corporate worship on Sunday. Catholic and Protestant churches alike are enjoying greater participation in worship by children under twelve years old. More of them are coming to worship and staying for much or all of the service. The presence of children in worship indicates adult interest and acceptance; our Christian churches may be moving toward genuinely intergenerational worshiping communities.

Along with the blessings that come with the joyful inclusion of children in worship has also come some confusion of practice. Adults worry that children, many of them preschool age, are not able to follow the flow of worship or understand the significance of its actions. Worship leaders worry that they do not communicate with children nor know how to accommodate to their levels of interest and knowledge. Parents are concerned about their children's behavior during services that seem beyond their attention span and designed more for adults than for children. And many adults quite frankly do not wish children to be present to interrupt and distract sacred and solemn worship.

Is it appropriate to include children in the congregation's corporate worship? If so, how can this be done so that the integrity of worship is not violated, and the interests of children honored?

Starting with Theology

Any consideration of how worship is done must start with theological understandings. To start anywhere else is to risk serious diminution of the integrity of worship. The theses listed below attempt to state some of the theological principles that inform our worship practice.

- God is the primary and central focus of worship.
- Worship is receiving God's grace.
- Worship is giving thanks to God.
- Worship is the service of the people rendered to God.
- Worship involves participation by all the people.
- Children are a part of God's people.
- Worship includes all the people of God, including children.
- Children need worship.
- All the people of God, including children, are nurtured by worship.

These statements suggest three general areas of theological concern: the church, worship, and ministry.

The church is the *koinonia*, the fellowship or community of faith, called into being by Jesus Christ. This community is inclusive. Its membership is not self-determined, but established by Christ. Christ called all kinds of persons into his *koinonia*. To fulfill the *koinonia,* we need to include children. While at worship, the *koinonia* falls short of its nature and identity if it excludes children. Children belong.

But worship is participatory. All the people, and not just those appointed to be liturgists, join in the offering of praise and thanks, in the expression of repentance and of need, and in the dedication of life and work to the glory of God. Participation goes far beyond intellectual assent to include the heart and the will. A worshiper's whole body—whole person—is involved. In a congregation, the persons who may be the most whole participants are the children. When children say, "Thank you, God," they *say* it freely and fully. The vital participation of children in the community's worship helps all who are present to participate freely and fully.

The ministry is shared. Not only do adults minister to children by caring for, nurturing, and teaching them; children also minister to adults. A telling example of the ministry of children is provided in the several stories of Jesus and children. Jesus reminded adults that their faith must be like that of a child's—received as a gift from God and responded to in direct, simple trust. A child's faith is a gift, not earned through knowledge or good works. A child's response is not very sophisticated; it is simple, trusting, and sincere. Children witness to these truths and exemplify for the whole church the nature and quality of faith. This type of witness is needed in the worshiping community.

Developmental Understandings

Basic knowledge of how human beings develop mentally and socially indicates that children are not at the same developmental stage as are adults. Adults can deal with abstractions, symbols, and historical references. Adults can sit and listen for fairly long lengths of time. Adults, even when they feel one way, can express themselves in another, more socially acceptable way. On the other hand, children think concretely. Preschool children think one idea at a time and are not prone to fashion whole sequences or to see more than one meaning in a given object, action, or idea. They see an object for what it is on the surface, and not for its implied, symbolic meanings. A butterfly, for example, will remind a child of the Resurrection not because it symbolizes metamorphosis, but because the child has been told this meaning by a person whom he or she trusts. We all know that young children need to stand up or move about after every few minutes of sitting still.

Older children begin to take individual ideas and actions and relate them into meaningful wholes. They understand how one activity follows another, and why. The fact that certain people lived and did important things can be understood in terms of historical sequence. Younger children ask about the what; older children understand the why. A liturgy makes sense to older children.

Those who plan and conduct worship need to keep it concrete, tangible and orderly, so that children can participate with some sense of understanding and security. The pace, movement, and drama of the liturgy should be expressed, so that children can be involved. If not during worship, then whenever children gather, there need to be explanations of the liturgy. Objects need to be given names; actions need to be demonstrated and explained; and ways of participating need to be practiced.

Given the richness and mystery of the liturgy, children will engage in it according to their abilities. While no child—or adults, for that matter—will participate as one who fully understands the meaning and power of the liturgy, each child who is a part of the worshiping community can derive many meanings and personal benefits. Each child can contribute to the community's ability to worship.

On the one hand, we should be sensitive to the abilities of children and conduct worship so that they have a chance to participate meaningfully. On the other hand, we are confident that worship is not age-specific. Persons of all ages need worship and can benefit from and contribute to worship. The liturgy nurtures us all. We all need opportunities to praise God, to seek forgiveness and be assured of pardon, to hear God's Word, and to respond to God by the giving of ourselves in total commitment. In all these activities, children, as well as adults, can function with meaning and integrity. The grace given through the sacraments, especially through the Eucharist, is for all of God's children, young and old alike. Old and young are together, the community of faith.

How Children Participate

Once it is agreed that children can participate in worship, there remains the practical question, "How?" In many congregations, particularly in churches with much liturgical freedom, children are encouraged to participate at the point of the preaching of the Word. Thus, many churches practice what is called a _children's sermon_. This activity usually comes just before the Scriptures are read and the homily or sermon is preached. The children's sermon, usually a story or simple lesson, sometimes takes on moral force, when the preacher says, "The point of this story is . . ." or something along these lines. The sincerity of children's sermons may be appreciated, but the practice must be questioned. There is no encouragement for such a practice in Scripture or tradition. It is doubtful if children can comprehend symbols or objects used to illustrate a point. Indeed, they are often confused when asked to think of a theological truth in terms of objects, such as a jar full of jellybeans or a flock of sheep. The gravest concern, however, is for the children's sermons that offer moralisms, rather than the gospel. A children's sermon does _not,_ in fact, include children in the corporate worship, but subtly isolates them by giving them two or three minutes of special time during an otherwise adult-oriented service.

It is helpful for congregations to listen to their best educators in order to identify appropriate ways for children to participate as much as possible in every act of worship. Reading Scripture need not be limited to one form. Dramatic readings, simple retellings of the story, body movements or pantomime to illustrate the readings, and similar dramatizations are possible. Even when the homily is short, it is not heard by every worshiper in its entirety. If this is recognized and admitted by preachers, they can then relax a bit and not feel the that the homily must be heard in its entirety by each child. It is sufficient if even one illustration, image, or idea makes its impression on a young person. Any sermon, however sophisticated, can have some material that a child can appreciate. The entire congregation will respond to the preacher, who makes it a custom to introduce the sermon with examples from the lives and experience of children.

There are many ways that children can participate in worship. Examples include the reciting traditional material such as the Our Father and the creed, coming forward to surround a child being baptized, providing music by singing or with simple instruments, serving as greeters and ushers, singing hymns, putting money in the offering plate, and standing, sitting, and kneeling at appropriate times. Children can take part in the acts of worship that are well within the bounds of tradition. Where a congregation engages in forms and styles beyond tradition, there are numerous ways children can take part and contribute, with banners, processions, pantomimes, movements, handclasps, and hugs.

Helping Children Worship

The modern church can learn about teaching religion and worship to children by consulting its ancestors. In the centuries before Christ, the people of God practiced a naturally religious life. From the time of birth—when a child's identity was reinforced by such marks as circumcision or the planting of a tree—to the daily observances of prayers of gratitude and supplication, to the celebrations of the festivals, a child was exposed to worship. Particularly instructive to us is the pattern of the seder in which the young child asks questions—"Why is this night different from all nights?"—and the parent answers with explanations.

An apprentice model was used to teach children who they were and how they could express their faith. A questioning child participated in religious activities in the company of a knowledgeable adult. Learning was by doing, with patient guidance. Specific acts were learned in the context of a worshiping family and a worshiping community.

One contemporary congregation recognizes children as full participants in worship as soon as they reach school age. In a ceremony that invites the children to become responsible worshipers, the church gives them a gift, a hymnal—not a Bible which they cannot read yet, but the tool that they need as worshipers. The children are then incorporated into the children's choir, where they receive careful instruction about worship in ways that are enjoyable and understandable for six-year-olds. Their parents attend an orientation session that prepares them to teach their children how to pray and worship at home and how to encourage their children during corporate worship. Children and parents engage in a "trip through the church," in which, with small suitcase in hand, they follow the instructions on their "ticket" to go to various places in the church. A portion of the ticket (it is a long ticket) leads the family to a pew, where they all sit while an older member explains what a pew is. Another portion of the ticket may lead to the choir loft, or to the baptismal font, or the lectern, or to some symbols that are to be explained. At each destination, handouts are distributed for use at home to continue the learning about worship.

Two general areas of education about worship can be considered. First, children need to learn specifically how to worship. Much of this takes place outside of worship in the classes and other gatherings of children in the church. Such teaching can be designed to meet the exact developmental stages of the several ages of the children of the church. The other area might be called a "climate for worship" and would include the need to teach adults, as well as children. The whole congregation can be shown the validity and value of having children in corporate worship. Parents can be given specific methods and resources for helping their children in worship. Parents, teaching their children how to worship in the pews, need to be freed from the usual anxieties and nervousness that parents feel when they sit with their children in the pews. Adults can be shown that children participate with meaning and enthusiasm in worship and contribute to the welfare of the whole congregation. Worship planners and leaders—pastors included—can be apprised of good examples and useful resources. To know that children's participation in worship is possible and that pastors can facilitate this participation without embarrassment or threat to themselves or to the liturgy is most encouraging to otherwise reluctant pastors.

Nurturing and Caring

Children, who are a part of the worshiping community, gain not only in terms of becoming worshipers. Worship also becomes a means of nurture and pastoral care for participants. Through experience, parents and children alike learn again and again of the gracious love that God has for them. Sincere worship leads to deeper relationships with God and to greater concern for the people of the world. Children, as well as adults, go to worship to praise God, and find that they depart from worship with a sense of faithfulness and mission.

Pastors and church leaders can support young worshipers and their parents with pastoral care. Listening for questions about worship may lead to hearing statements of concern. Pastors may find occasions to help parishioners with matters of a relationship with God, which are brought to surface through experiences of worship. Children become involved in the realization of sinfulness, of God's reaching out to them, of the support of the community, of God's call to them, and of their need to respond to the call. These are worthy matters for pastoral conversations and visits. It is entirely possible that when children become worshipers, they also become participants in the pastoral ministries of the church.

For too long adult Christians have considered children either as nuisances to be set aside or as immature humans in great need of adult teaching. Now, we realize what Jesus may have meant when he said, "Let the children come to me, do not hinder them; for to such belongs the kingdom of God." (Matt. 19:14). Children are God's messengers to us. They help us to be the church. They help us to worship. They minister to us. With their help as fellow worshipers, we may renew our worship and our church life. Thank God for children!

David Ng[7]

160 ◆ A HISTORY OF CHILDREN'S HYMNODY

One meaningful way in which children participate in worship is through song, especially through songs written for their unique abilities and interests. Children's hymns have been written for many centuries; studying this history gives us important perspectives for how Christians can include children in worship today.

Give me the making of ballads and I care not who makes the laws.
—Archibald Alexander, _A Selection of Hymns Adapted to Devotions of the Closet_ (Family and Social Circle, 1931).

Let me write the hymns and I care not who writes the theology.
—R. W. Dale, _The English Hymn Book_ (1874), preface.

These two quotes ascribe considerable power to the sung word. Unless hymn singing can really make a difference in Christian education and the values that influence behavior, then this article need not be written. With the hope of strengthening this fundamental premise, I will share a story.

A medical mission team was sent to Cambodia following the downfall of the Pol Pot regime during the Southeast Asia conflict. Many Cambodian villages were on the verge of starvation because of the ravages of the war and the disruption of the life of the villagers. The cycle of food production had been broken by years of war and political oppression. The will to live was fading, and people were starving. Among those participating on the team was a Catholic sister, who had been involved in many other such ventures including famines in Africa and Biafra.

Almost from the beginning, Sister Miriam Therese Winter felt that there was something different about the children of the village, where the medical mission team was concentrating its efforts, but she had a difficult time articulating what the difference was. She knew from first-hand experience the familiar cycle of providing nutrition to famine and war-torn people—the listlessness of the people, the setting up facilities for medical attention and nutrition, the reestablishing of daily routines that were so necessary for the preservation of life, and finally seeing the spirit of the people return. But somehow, this village was different. Food and medical attention were being provided. The people were becoming physically stronger, but the spirit of the people did not seem to be returning even in the children, who were usually the first to show signs of a renewal of spirit. It finally dawned on her that these children never sang.

Most people would not find such a fact to be of importance. After all, the children were starving; one could hardly expect them to break forth into song. But Sister Miriam Therese knew from other experiences that after just a few days of proper nutrition, the sound of children singing returned to even the most impoverished villages. After a couple of weeks, she became even more concerned; although the people's physical needs were being met, the absence of song among the children seemed to indicate a lack of hope. She began to accompany her daily task by singing the familiar folk song, "Kumbaya" ("Come by Here, Lord"), a seemingly universal tune. The people listened, but no one sang. The sister knew that they heard her sing because the children started to call her the Kumbaya woman. Although she continued to sing her song for days, no one sang.

Then one night, she heard at the other end of the village the sweet voice of a child singing what sounded to her like a folk tune. She grabbed her tape recorder and ran to the source of the sound and recorded the child's song. The next morning, Sister Miriam Therese played the recording for one of the elders of the village and asked him what it was about. He seemed embarrassed and very hesitant to discuss the song of the child. What could be the problem with a child's song? Finally, he told her that the child had sung a political propaganda song of the Pol Pot regime. This song extolled the virtues of this oppressive and cruel communist government. Why would a child sing such a song? Were there no other songs for a child to sing? It was explained to her that under the regime, all former songs had been banned and only two political songs were allowed. These songs were taught to the people in the Khmer Rouge camp, and the children had grown up knowing no other songs. By restricting the songs of the children, the Khmer Rouge had raised a generation that knew only the ideals of their regime. By allowing only two political songs to be sung, the oppressive regime was able to practice a very powerful form of mind control.(This story appeared originally in the following article by the author, "Children's Choirs: A Means or an End?" *Creator* 10:7 [October/November 1988]: 5–8.)

From this story, we can deduce several things about the importance of hymn singing for the church. First, it is natural to sing one's faith. Singing is a holistic human activity that joins both rational discourse (left brain) and emotional sensibility (right brain) into a unified expression. If children are taught to sing during the preschool years, musical expression becomes as natural as talking.

Second, the fostering of religious values is strengthened through hymn singing. Hymn singing has been at the core of the Judeo-Christian experience, as a means of communicating the important precepts of faith. Paul indicates in Ephesians 5:18-19 that singing is a sign of being "filled with the Spirit." A brief historical overview of the role of hymnody in the education of children will follow in the next section.

Finally, hymn singing is a major factor in the building of community throughout the history of Christendom. There was a void in the community spirit of the Cambodian village without singing. One of the primary examples of the use of singing to build community was the role of singing during the great revivals of the nineteenth and twentieth centuries. Evangelists were aware of the power of hymn singing to solidify diverse groups of people and, in doing so, creating a friendly atmosphere even among strangers. The singing of

hymns "prepared the hearts of the people" to receive the spoken Word. John Wesley, more than perhaps any other evangelist, realized the power of hymn singing for all of the purposes mentioned above—as a natural, educational, community building experience—through the use of his brother Charles' excellent hymns.

A Brief History of Children's Hymnody

While the hymnbook has educational potential for all ages, the focus of this article will be upon the hymnal as a resource in the Christian education of children. A brief survey of the history of children's hymnody will allow us to see how children were viewed through hymnody in earlier days and then to suggest guidelines for the use of hymnody in children's Christian education today. (Portions of the following section appeared in an article by the author, "Hymnody for Children," *The Hymn* 36:1 [January 1985]: 19–26.)

Isaac Watts: Divine and Moral Songs. Although there were sporadic efforts in children's hymnody by people such as the Reformer Martin Luther ("From Heaven on High") and the school master Thomas Ken ("Awake, My Soul, and With the Sun" and "All Praise to Thee My God This Night"), the first significant writer of children's hymnody was the famous Isaac Watts. His *Divine Songs, attempted in easy Language, for the use of Children* (1715) was influential for at least two hundred years after its publication. Written at the request of a friend, who wished an additional pedagogical tool for catechesis, *Divine Songs* ran through an astonishing six hundred editions and seven million copies between 1715 and 1900. As a result of this collection, hymn writing for children became acceptable and even to some degree popular in England during the eighteenth and nineteenth century, although the quality varied greatly.

A critique of Watt's hymns in this genre centers primarily around two problems. The first critique has to do with his pessimistic view of human nature which was a result of John Calvin's doctrines of original sin and election on the one hand and the belief in the uncertain state of humanity before a righteous God on the other. The poetic result was often a moralistic verse, which attempted to nip the problem of original sin in children in the proverbial bud. One example of Watt's verse for children was a stanza designed to quell sibling rivalries.

> Whatever brawls disturb the street,
> There should be peace at home;
> Where sisters dwell and brothers meet,
> Quarrels should never come.

(Isaac Watts, *Horae Lyricae and Divine Songs* [Boston: Little, Brown, and Company, 1854], 317)

Watts was not above striking terror into the heart of a child, whose sinful condition demanded the judgment of God.

> Just as a tree cut down, that fell
> To North or Southward, there it lies,
> So soon man departs to heaven or hell,
> Fix'd in the state wherein he dies.

(Isaac Watts, *Works of the Reverend and learned Isaac Watts, D.D.*, 6 vols., ed. George Burder [London: J. Barfield, 1810], xix)

The second area for critique is described by Lionel Adey as Watt's celebrated principle of kenosis or lowering of himself in his approach to children (Lionel Adey, *Class and Idol in the English Hymn* [Vancouver: University of British Columbia Press, 1988], 94). This is clearly stated in the complete title of the collection, . . . *attempted in easy Language, for the use of Children.* Such condescension toward children would not be acceptable by developmental psychologists today, although many teachers continue to approach children in this manner. Erik Routley stated that Watt's emphasis on kenosis led to the Victorian view of children as little and feeble, inviting adolescents to "grow out of" such religion (Erik Routley, *A Panorama of Christian Hymnody* [Collegeville: Liturgical Press, 1979], 124). According to Watts, children should be taught while they are young in the same manner as one would train "the Jews and heathens" in ancient civilizations (Watts, *Horae Lyricae*, 295).

For Isaac Watts a child was homunculus or a miniature adult. Children were not viewed for what they might offer as young people to God's world, but as small people that could become of value only after they reached adulthood. While the fallacy in this approach would seem apparent, David Elkind has identified the same tendencies among adults today (David Elkind, *The Hurried Child: Growing Up Too Fast Too Soon* [Reading, Mass.: Addison-Wesley Publishing Co., 1981]). He suggests that parents, teachers, and the media encourage children to take on the responsibilities and pressures of adults, before they are developmentally ready.

Why was Watts so successful? I would propose several reasons. First, his view of children fit the extremely class-conscious British mentality of his day. As Adey has pointed out, everyone in society had to find their place in the hierarchy of British life (Adey 5). Children were simply a subset of the particular class to which their parents were born. Watts' hymns helped to keep children in their place within the structure of society. Another reason for his popularity as a writer of children's verse was his use of concrete images associated with the everyday lives of children. Birds, bees, dogs, and trees filled the stanzas of Watts' hymns. He could also become very specific and concrete in his images of hell, though less so about heaven.

> There is beyond the sky
> A heav'n of Joy and love;
> And holy children, when they die,
> Go to that world above.

> There is a dreadful Hell.
> And everlasting pains;
> There sinners must with devils dwell
> In darkness, fire and chains.

(quoted in Adey, 101)

Because Watts wrote hymns for children in such quantity, quality and variety, the children's hymn movement gained in popularity.

John Wesley: Hymns for Children. John Wesley's *Hymns for Children and Others of Riper Years* (1763), while continuing the tradition of children's hymnody established by Watts, was not nearly as popular outside Methodist circles. While Watts' views toward children might not stand up to the rigors of modern child psychology, he understood children better than did the Wesleys. Rather than assuming Watts' kenosis posture toward children, John Wesley attempted to raise children to loftier heights through his hymnody:

There are two ways in writing or speaking to children: the one is to lower ourselves down to them; the other is to lift them up to us. Dr. Watts wrote [sic] in the former way and succeeded admirably well, speaking to children as children and leaving them as he found them. The following hymns are written on the other plan; they contain a strong and manly sense, yet expressed in such plain and easy language, as even children may understand. But when they do understand them, they will be children no longer, only in years and stature (John Julian, *Dictionary of Hymnology,* 2 vols., 2nd ed. [1907; reprint, New York: Dover Publications, 1957], 221).

While Wesley's verse may have been more appealing to adults, it was by no means as popular as Watts' *Divine Songs*.

Much of the dreary descriptions of hell and the negative theology found in Watt's verse is also present in Wesley's hymns.

> Dark and Bottomless the pit
> Which on them its mouth shall close;
> Never shall they 'scape from it;
> There they shall in endless woes
> Weep and wail and gnash their teach,
> Die an everlasting death.

(Frederick John Gilman, *The Evolution of the English Hymn* [New York: Macmillan Co., 1927], 268)

Charles Wesley's "Gentle Jesus, Meek and Mild" is the only children's hymn by the Wesleys that has gained lasting and popular appeal. Even this hymn is now rarely found in hymnals. In it, children are characterized by terms such as *little* and phrases such as "pity my simplicity." This language became more predominant in children's hymns of the Victorian era.

The Sunday School Movement in England and America. The Sunday school movement in England made use of children's hymns with strong Calvinistic leanings in the tradition of Watts. Death and judgment continued to be major emphases. In spite of Watts' influence, the nature of the Sunday school demanded new literature and more attention be given to not only the earlier catechistic tradition, but also to the spiritual nurture of the child. Fifteen years before Robert Raikes began the first Sunday school, John Newton started a special midweek lecture service in Olney, England (1764) and also made special provisions for the children of Olney to engage in biblical education and hymn singing (John Pollock, *Amazing Grace: John Newton's Story* (San Francisco: Harper and Row Publishers, 1981], 154). Further-

more, Rowland Hill was quite successful with several texts including *Divine Hymns, attempted in easy Language, for Children* (1790; with revisions by William Cowper).

The Taylor sisters, Ann and Jane, published their *Hymns for Infant Minds* in 1809. This collection was considered innovative because of the Taylors' ability to view topics from a child's perspective. Jane's practice was to address hymns to an imaginary child listener. The verse of the Taylor sisters could also take a strong judgmental approach as indicated in this stanza:

> Down to this sad world he flew,
> For such little ones as you!
> You were wretched, weak and vile,
> You deserved his holy frown;
> But he saw you with a smile,
> And to save you hastened down.

(Ann and Jane Taylor, *Hymns for Infant Minds,* 37th ed.[London: 1846], hymn no. 34)

While the Taylor sisters did not have the poetic abilities of Isaac Watts, they appreciated more the perspective of children, the beauty of nature, family love, and friendship in their verse. The descriptive words used for Christ were most often feminine, which contributed to the concept of a submissive Victorian womanhood for the girls (Adey 104).

Many collections aimed toward the purposes of the Sunday school movement were intended primarily for those of lesser rank and privilege. The Sunday schools were founded in order to enable the poor to read the Bible. Watts and Wesley were included in popular collections by Joseph Benson (*Collection of Hymns for the Use of Methodist Sunday Schools* [1808]) and Independent Rowland Hill (*Hymns for Children, Principally [of a] Sunday School* [1819]). The theology of these collections tended, however, to be more Calvinist than Wesleyan. Watts' *kenosis,* or lowering of one's self to the child, was preferred over the Wesleyan principle of "manly sense," intended to raise a child's understanding to that of adults.

In America, the emphasis was upon conversion with the more easily sung melodies of the gospel song tradition. Vestiges of Calvinistic theology still remained, but the texts were less artistic and more repetitive. Nineteenth-century sentimentality, interest in nature, and fascination with exotic lands (due in part to the development of missions), all influenced the writers of hymn texts. The pietistic emphasis upon the individual and a personal faith found fertile ground in children's hymns for Sunday school. George F. Root, William B. Bradbury and Robert Lowery, all wrote children's hymns for evangelistic occasions.

The Sunday school movement made several contributions to the development of children's hymnody. Children were given an increasingly special place in evangelistic traditions. The motivation of conversion provided the impetus for a great outpouring of literature. Among the benefits was less denominationally-oriented literature and an increasing awareness of the abilities and interests of the child. Hymn tunes took on the flavor of popular and folk melodies with the advent of the gospel song. The repetitive nature of the gospel song, with its refrains and repeated phrases, made the hymns more easy to learn, but sacrificed some of the text's content and development of thought.

The Oxford Movement. The more classical style of children's hymns continued in mainstream religious life. John Mason Neale published a series of _Hymns for Children_ beginning in 1838 and translated many others appropriate for the child. The quality of translations, such as the ninth-century "Gloria, laus et honor" ("All Glory, Laud and Honor"), provides a rich resource for children. Many of Neale's hymns became very popular in both England and America, offering the child theological depth and a well-written text.

With Cecil Frances Alexander's _Hymns for Little Children_ (1845), came the best blend of textual quality, theological foundation, and child awareness experienced thus far. Julian states it well:

> Charmingly simple and tender, clear in dogma, and of poetic beauty, combining the plainness of Watts with the feeling for and with the childhood of the Taylor sisters, and uniting with both the liturgical associations of the English Prayer Book, they remain unequaled and unapproachable. (Julian 222)

Mrs. Alexander's hymns were built around a consistent theological framework and textual quality. The forty hymns of her hymnal were based on the Apostles' Creed, the Ten Commandments, and the Lord's Prayer. Of her hymns still in use today, some of the more famous ones written for children include "All Things Bright and Beautiful," "There Is a Green Hill Far Away," and "Once in Royal David's City." Notice the use of concrete detail in the less familiar stanzas below.

> On the dark hill's western side
> The last purpose gleam has died,
> Twilight to one solemn hue
> Changes all, both green and blue.
> In the fold and in the nest,
> Birds and lambs are gone to rest,
> Labour's weary task is o'er,
> Closely shut the cottage door . . .
>
> 'Twas a starry night of old
> When rejoicing angels told
> The poor shepherds of Thy birth,
> God became a child on earth.
> Soft and quiet is the bed,
> Where I lay my little head;
> Thou has but a manger bare;
> Rugged straw for pillow fair.

(Gilman 277)

Lionel Adey praises Mrs. Alexander as "the most successful Victorian hymnographer for children," but also points out that, as a lady of the upper class, she was "unavoidably patronizing [to] the poor whom she served with such devotion" (Adey 143).

Historical Analysis

This has no means been a complete history of children's hymnody. It is of sufficient detail, however, for us to stop and draw some conclusions and look at ideas and resources for the use of hymnody in the Christian education of children today.

Problems of the Past.

(1) Children's hymnody suffered in varying degrees when an adult-oriented posture has been assumed by the hymn writer. The hymns of Watts and the Wesleys, in spite of textual quality, were less effective because of this attitude.

(2) The use of negative patterns of theological reinforcement are not productive as a learning approach with children. The harsh Calvinistic influence in much of hymnody for children hindered the continuing relevance of these hymns.

(3) The patronizing style prevalent in many nineteenth-century hymns is not appealing to the young child, who values authentic and genuine relationships with adults.

(4) An approach that is too direct and moralis-

tic has not proven to be successful with children. Children appreciate quality and depth in their hymns. How a point is made is as significant as what point is made.

(5) Much of the hymnody for children during the growing Sunday school movement in England combined immediacy of textual content with singable, enjoyable tunes. While these hymns appealed to the child initially, they did not offer content to foster growth and music of lasting value. Many of the best hymns for children are hymns that they can sing throughout life.

(6) Finally, many of the hymns used with children lacked language that appealed to the child's imagination or images that were within the child's experience. The Wesleys' hymns have been noted for having this deficiency.

Positive Contributions. Hymn writers throughout history have offered us positive examples of children's hymns. Let us take a moment to examine some of these.

(1) Children's hymnody seems to have been more effective when taught within a theological framework. The best hymns of Watts and the catechistic hymns of Mrs. Alexander are good examples of this.

(2) There are many hymns throughout the history of hymnody that combine appropriate imagery with depth of theology. These hymns have been able to withstand the changing vocabulary of the years and remain meaningful to children today because of what they have to say. Consider the translations of John Mason Neale; the hymns of Martin Luther; some hymns of Isaac Watts and Cecil Frances Alexander; and, more recently, the hymns of Christina Rossetti and Fred Pratt Green. Good hymns, like Scripture, have levels of meaning that allow appreciation by young and old alike.

(3) The writers of the best hymns for children consider the child's perspective. This often involves using the first person. Notice the following hymns, for example: "From Heaven on High" (Martin Luther), the final stanza of "In the Bleak Mid-Winter" (Christina Russetti), or "How Far Is It to Bethlehem" (Frances Chesterson). In each of these hymns the use of the first person perspective helps the child to personally and intimately identify with the birth of Jesus.

When a hymn makes use of the first person, some caution needs to be exercised, however.

One quick test suggested by Paul Schilling is to insert *we*, *us*, and *ours* in places that use *I*, *me*, and *mine* (S. Paul Schilling, *The Faith We Sing* [Philadelphia: Westminster Press, 1983], 181). The hymn that still makes sense will probably be of value to children. Children have a developmental tendency toward self-centeredness and an egocentric perspective. While the hymns they sing should often have a personal, direct appeal, we should not foster a spiritual egocentrism.

(4) The wedding of hymn text with tune is a crucial factor when choosing hymns for children. While there were problems of textual quality and theological depth in many of the hymns of the Sunday school era, many of the mediocre texts were sung and enjoyed because of their accessible tunes. The tune needs to enhance the character of the text. In some cases, it might be helpful to set older texts to new tunes.

Our predecessors in children's hymnody have provided us with a wealth of insight as we approach the task of hymn education today. Let us consider recent theological concerns as they have an impact on hymns as a teaching resource for children.

Theological Views for Children's Hymnody Today

While there is much to be learned from singing timeless hymns from the past, children also need hymns that articulate faith in today's language. Hymns that express a contemporary view of the world are essential to a growing faith. This issue is of vital concern to children and adults alike. What are some of the theological changes that have taken place in hymnody during the great revival of hymn writing of the last thirty years?

First, earlier views of God as awful and wrathful with occasional glimpses of benevolence have been replaced by a loving and caring God. Two texts by Fred Pratt Green illustrate this point.

Now praise the hidden God of Love,
In whom we all must live and move,
Who shepherds us, at every stage,
Through youth, maturity, and age.

(Fred Pratt Green, *The Hymns and Ballads of Fred Pratt Green* [Carol Stream, Ill.: Hope Publishing Co., 1982], 73)

For the fruit of all creation,
Thanks be to God;

For his gifts to every nation,
Thanks be to God;
For the ploughing, sowing, reaping,
Silent Growth while we are sleeping,
Future needs in earth's safe-keeping,
Thanks be to God.

(Ibid., 28)

A second area of contemporary change is the child's awareness of science, especially in hymns that refer to outer space. Only recently have hymn writers attempted to bring us into a post-Copernican view of the universe. Adults are slow to accept the changes in imagery, wishing to cling only to hymns like Watts' hymn that states, "I sing th'almighty power of God that made the mountains rise." Today's children grow up in a world full of space shuttles and daily scientific breakthroughs. They can help adults learn to accept a God, who continues the process of creation through the exploration and advancements of the crowning glory of Creation—humankind. Several hymns come to mind. I will refer to two.

Herbert Brokerlings' hymn, "Earth and All Stars" (*Lutheran Book of Worship* [Minneapolis: Augsburg Publishing House, 1978], hymn no. 558), literally hurls images of the modern world at the singer. Many of these refer to science in today's terms. These include "Engines and steel! Loud pounding hammers!", "Classrooms and labs! Loud boiling test tubes," and "Knowledge and truth! Loud sounding wisdom!" All of these "Sing to the Lord a new song!"

Catherine Cameron's "God Who Stretched the Spangled Heavens" is one of the best hymns in this genre. One stanza is quoted here.

We have conquered worlds undreamed of
    since the childhood of our race;
known the ecstasy of winging
    through uncharted realms of space,
probed the secrets of the atom,
    yielding unimagined power,
facing us with life's destruction,
    or our most triumphant hour.

(William J. Reynolds, ed., *Baptist Hymnal* [Nashville: Convention Press, 1975], hymn no. 150)

A third area that contemporary hymns explore is a view of gospel events as timely for today. The immediacy of the life of Jesus in contemporary hymns stands in contrast to the "long ago and far away" approach of hymns in earlier centuries. Brian Wren enables us to capture this spirit in his Easter hymn, "Christ Is Alive!"

Christ is alive! Let Christians sing.
    His cross stands empty to the sky.
Let streets and homes with praises ring.
    His love in death shall never die.

Christ is alive! No longer bound
    to distant years in Palestine
He comes to claim the here and now
    and conquer every place and time.

(Brian Wren, *Faith Looking Forward* [Carol Stream, Ill.: Hope Publishing Co., 1983], hymn no. 20)

Fred Kaan explores the nearness of Christ in his hymn, "Celebration Everywhere, and Time." Two stanzas are quoted here.

Christ is here and everywhere,
one with all his people,
but we make his whereabouts
with our Sunday steeples . . .

Give us grace to seize and use
every situation,
any time for worship, love,
blessing, celebration!

(Fred Kaan, *The Hymn Texts of Fred Kaan* [Carol Stream, Ill.: Hope Publishing Co., 1985], 12)

A fourth major contemporary change from past theological understandings that is just beginning to appear in many denominational hymnals is an awareness of hymns from differing cultures and worldviews. International hymnody, especially from third world contexts, breaks down the provincialism and nationalism that was a part of so many hymns of the past. One of the most popular hymns is from Ghana, with a text adapted by the Presbyterian missionary, Tom Colvin. A portion of the text from this hymn on servanthood is quoted below.

Refrain: Jesu, Jesu, Fill us with your love,
Show us how to serve the neighbors we have from
    you.

Kneels at the feet of His friends,
Silently washes their feet,
Master who acts as a slave to them.

Neighbors are rich folk and poor,
Neighbors are black, brown and white,
Neighbors are nearby and far away.

(Tom Colvin, *Fill Us With Your Love and Other Hymns from Africa* [Carol Stream, Ill.: Hope Publishing Co., 1983], 15)

Another advantage of using international hymnody is that these hymns break down the earlier perspective of what Lionel Adey calls the "Anglican conservative tradition of noblesse oblige" (Lionel Adey, *Hymns and the Christian Myth* [Vancouver: University of British Columbia Press, 1986], 170). The Anglican tradition acknowledged the poor in prayers and hymns, but there was often an awareness of class difference, a social self-consciousness about these expressions, and an appropriate maintaining of distance. Contemporary American society is not without its own traditions of noblesse oblige, class distancing, and ethnic isolation. I believe it is imperative that children learn to sing expressions of Christians from around the world, as a part of their Christian education. A broader worldview is called for in the Japanese hymn by Tokuo Yamaguchi, translated by Everett Stowe.

> Many are the tongues we speak,
> Scattered are the lands,
> Yet our hearts are one in God,
> One in love's demands.
>
> Even in darkness hope appears,
> Calling age and youth:
> Jesus, teacher, dwell with us,
> For you are the Truth.

(I-to-Loh, ed., *Hymns from the Four Winds: A Collection of Asian American Hymns* [Nashville: Abingdon Press, 1983], hymn no. 37)

A fifth area of concern to theologians and contemporary hymn writers is ecology. Children learn in school not only the advances of science, but also their responsibility to the earth as citizens of the world. The Latin word *colere*, meaning "to cultivate," implies a mutual responsibility between the farmer on the one hand and the land and animals on the other. If the farmer properly cares for or cultivates the land and the animals, the land and the animals will care for the farmer and the farmer's family in return. Hymns that reflect humanity's continuing role and responsibility in Creation should be a regular part of the Christian education of children. Brian Wren has provided a hymn that is being used in several recent hymnals. It combines thanksgiving to God with a confession of humanity's guilt in the irresponsible use of earth's resources.

> Thank you, God, for water, soil and air—
> large gifts supporting everything that lives.
>   Forgive our spoiling and abuse of them.
>   Help us renew the face of the earth.
>
> Thank you, God, for minerals and ores—
> the basis of all building, wealth and speed.
>   Forgive our reckless plundering and waste,
>   Help us renew the face of the earth.
>
> Thank you, God, for priceless energy—
> stored in each atom, gathered from the sun.
>   Forgive our greed and carelessness of power.
>   Help us renew the face of the earth.

(Wren, hymn no. 7)

A final area of contemporary concern has to do with the nature of Christ as found in contemporary hymns. Most historical hymnody for children described Jesus in Charles Wesley's terms as "Gentle Jesus, Meek and Mild." It is important for children in their Christian education to reflect in song on a well-rounded view of Christ's humanity. While several hymns quoted above offer help in this area, another example is appropriate. Timothy Dudley-Smith has written the following stanza communicating a fuller view of Christ:

> When Jesus lived among us he came a child to earth
> to wear our human likeness, to share our human birth;
> and after flight and exile, an alien refugee,
> return in peace and safety at last to Galilee;
>   through sunlit days of childhood a loving home to now;
>   in wisdom and in favor with God and man to grow.

(Timothy Dudley-Smith, *Lift Every Heart* [Carol Stream, Ill.: Hope Publishing Co., 1984), 165)

Jane Parker Huber has written a hymn that discusses the relationship between Jesus and God. This hymn on the Incarnation articulates a more complete view of Christ than many earlier hymns relating to Christ's childhood. In the third stanza quoted below, she expresses a view that stands in contrast to the Wesleys' hymns mentioned earlier.

> The baby in a manger tall
> Is God Incarnate for us all,

As God, true God, the only One,
Is born on earth as Mary's Son.

We cannot keep the Savior there,
For Christ is meant for everywhere,
Not just for shepherds' watchful eyes,
Nor for a wise man's valued prized.

As God's own person here on earth,
Christ came to show us human worth,
So Jesus cannot stay a child,
Dependent, gentle, meek and mild.

(Jane Parker Huber, _A Singing Faith_ [Philadelphia: Westminster Press, 1987], hymn no. 22)

Communicating contemporary theological concerns through hymns is an important task of hymns in the Christian education of children. The preceding section has discussed several concerns of contemporary theologies that have been articulated in recent hymnody. It is obvious that these illustrations were not from children's hymns, but were hymns for everyone. The hymns chosen as examples of current theological issues appeal to elementary-aged children, as well as adults. Much of today's hymnody is appropriate for nearly all ages.

Hymns, Scripture, and Worship

In addition to singing our faith in new ways, there are at least two other important areas in which hymnody relates to the Christian nurture of children. The first has to do with the relationship of hymns to Scripture. The editors of many recent hymnals are stressing the integral relationship between hymns and Scripture through improved and more thorough scriptural indexes of hymns. These guides, along with the inclusion of Scripture on the hymn page itself, are valuable aids in our understanding of this relationship. When the bond between specific hymns and Scripture is stressed, the potential for retention is increased. Other information, such as the background of the hymn writer, the circumstances under which the hymn was written, and the relevance of the hymn to the lives of children, further strengthen this bond and help to make hymns more a part of children's spiritual experience.

A second area relating to hymns and Christian nurture is that of teaching worship through hymns. It has been said that the Bible is a record of God speaking to humanity and the hymnal is a record of the Christian community's response to

God. Our Christian response in hymns takes place primarily during experiences of corporate worship. Hymn education is a significant part of worship education. Consequently, hymn education needs to be a regular part of the church school, as well as part of the children's choir. A brief list of resources in the teaching of hymnody to children is included in the article following this one.

Conclusion

Recall the story of the song of the Cambodian child at the beginning of this article. While we would find mind control through limiting the number of songs appalling in our society, the question must be asked whether we in the church teach hymns in a manner that expands a child's understanding of and relationship with God. Too often, I see well-meaning teachers teaching their students the same limited set of choruses that the teachers themselves were taught when they were children. If the hymnal is our response to God in song, than it is the responsibility of the church to teach children a variety of hymns that reflect both our heritage of faith and our understanding of God's work in our experience today. A brief historical overview of hymnody for children demonstrates many of the inadequacies of earlier attempts. Even a cursory view of the contemporary hymn scene shows, however, that the resources are available for developing the spiritual voice of the child through hymn singing.

C. Michael Hawn[8]

161 ♦ TEACHING HYMNS TO CHILDREN

Hymn education is an essential task of the children's music ministry. Good hymn education must be a carefully planned and intentional process. In this article, the author suggests resources and strategies for the children's choir leader or Sunday school teacher.

A Systematic Approach

In a recent issue of _The Hymn_, Mabel Stewart Boyter outlined a practical approach to "growing a hymn-loving church" (Mabel Stewart Boyter, "Growing a Hymn-Loving Church: An Interview with Mabel Stewart Boyter," _The Hymn_ 34:3 [July 1983]: 141–146). Mrs. Boyter makes hymn teaching the center of children's music education. I have been inspired to give some additional thought to this area based upon several personal discussions with Mrs. Boyter.

Systematic theology is having a significant impact upon our understanding of worship and hymnody. Two recent books are opening our eyes concerning what and why we sing in worship (Geoffrey Wainwright, *Doxology: The Praise of God in Worship, Doctrine, and Life* [New York: Oxford University Press, 1980]; S. Paul Schilling, *The Faith We Sing: How the Message of Hymns Can Enhance Christian Belief,* [Philadelphia: Westminster Press, 1983]). William Hendricks has applied this same systematic approach in order to understand how children view various theological issues (William L. Hendricks, *A Theology for Children* [Nashville: Broadman Press, 1980]). The major thesis of the initial section of this article is that we should intentionally develop a systematic theology through the teaching of hymns to children. The rest of this article gives suggestions in this direction.

The selection of resources for hymn study for children given below include approximately seventy hymns. Any list of this nature would need to be adapted in a variety of ways. Consider the following adaptations.

(1) Each denomination would want some hymns, which it would consider foundational. Reformed congregations would want additional Psalm paraphrases. Methodists would include additional Wesleyan hymns. Lutherans would need more hymns derived from the chorale tradition and later pietistic hymnody. Baptists would add several gospel hymns. It is very important that these additions be balanced with the more universal hymns suggested below and that they be fitted into a systematic theological framework in order to insure a more complete theological foundation for the child.

(2) Tune choices will also vary from congregation to congregation. While it is important to sing the most familiar tune according to local tradition, in some cases the children might learn a different tune to a familiar text, introduce this tune in turn to the congregation, and thus add new musical materials to the worship of a given church.

(3) The designations provided with each hymn as to their use with younger or older children are also somewhat relative to context. Much depends on how the children are grouped according to age and what the average age of the group is. Also be aware that individual stanzas of a hymn might be appropriate at a younger age, even though the entire hymn is only appropriate for when the child is older.

(4) A given hymn can illuminate and highlight several different theological truths. For instance, I have had a good experience teaching the hymn, "O Little Town of Bethlehem," within the context of the Trinitarian doctrine, with stanza two emphasizing Jesus; stanza three, God; and stanza four, the work of the Holy Spirit today. Others may use the hymn in a different context. Again, the important thing for the teacher to do is to guide the child to perceive the theological significance of the hymn.

(5) The teacher needs to be aware of the appropriate time to introduce specific theological concepts to children. This is an area of increasing importance and concern to those who work in spiritual formation of children. The heritage of various denominational traditions can make this difficult. However, most of the hymns I suggest for children are Christological. This is because our worship traditions are influenced in varying degrees by the events of Christ's life. Furthermore, it is much easier for the child to identify with Jesus as "friend," than with other persons of the Trinity. In short, the concrete nature of the Incarnation is most important in the spiritual formation of the child.

A second area I emphasize in the selection of children's hymns is God's creation and providence. In a world of nuclear armament, it is necessary to emphasize that, in spite of evil, this is God's world.

God, the Father, should receive much attention throughout the elementary age, although older children might give this theological area more attention. There are relatively few hymns available on the work of the Holy Spirit. These should probably be reserved for older children except as the Holy Spirit is included as a part of the Trinity.

The older child will find hymns on the nature of the Christian life, humankind and sin, the church as a body, and eschatological (last things) themes of increasing importance and interest. William Hendricks' book, *A Theology for Children,* should provide specific insight into this area for interested leaders of all denominational traditions.

(6) Finally, there are newer hymns and hymn writers that need our attention. Look closely at the more recent hymn additions in your denomination's hymnal and include the following hymns. Herbert Brokering's "Earth and All Stars" is an example of a recent hymn that falls under the category of God's creation and providence; it captures this theme in contemporary language which would appeal to a child. Other contemporary hymn writers include Brian Wren and Fred Pratt Green (see the resources at the end of this article).

Another source of hymns that appeals to children is drawn from traditional American materials. Hymnals are including texts and tunes from the Appalachian, black spiritual, and southern musical traditions in increasing numbers.

Third world hymnody should also be a part of the hymnological mix of today's child. Children today are much more aware of other cultures; and therefore, much more open to singing the worship materials from other cultural contexts. Little of this material has found a place in major denominational hymnals, but these hymns are available to those who will take the time to pursue obtaining them. Several sources have been listed at the end of this article.

Hymn Education for the Preschool Child

The preschool child finds hymns very interesting for several reasons. Hymn singing may be the first meaningful way, in which the preschooler can participate in worship. At this age, the child takes immense pleasure and satisfaction in learning and singing at least a few of the hymns known to the congregation as a whole. There are several hymns about God's world that the preschooler will enjoy, such as the first stanzas of "All Things Bright and Beautiful," "For the Beauty of the Earth," and "This Is My Father's World." At the same time, the preschooler can have contact with the larger body of hymnody by learning hymn fragments. Even knowing part of a hymn allows the child to feel a sense of unity with the congregation. The teacher needs to be aware that the preschool child's best pitch matching range is between D and A, above middle C. By pitching the fragments in this range, the hymn singing experience will also aid the preschooler's vocal development. The following is a brief list of hymn fragments that preschoolers can learn and enjoy.

General Hymns
- Come, Christians, Join to Sing (MADRID)—first two lines in F major
- For the Beauty of the Earth (DIX)—refrain in E flat or F major
- Joyful, Joyful, We Adore Thee (HYMN TO JOY)—first two lines in C or D major
- Now Thank We All Our God (NUN DANKET ALLE GOTT)—first two lines in C major
- Rejoice, Ye Pure in Heart (MARION)—refrain in C or D major
- Sing Praise to God, Who Reigns Above (MIT FREUDEN ZART)—last phrase in C or D major
- There Is a Name I Love to Hear (O HOW I LOVE JESUS)—refrain in D major
- When Morning Gilds the Skies (LAUDES DOMINI)—last phrase in F or G major

Advent/Christmas Carols
- Angels from the Realms of Glory (REGENT SQUARE)—refrain from F major (begin on the dominant chord, C major)
- Good Christian Men, Rejoice (IN DULCI JUBILO)—last two phrases in E major
- Go, Tell It on the Mountain (GO, TELL IT)—refrain in F major
- Hark, the Herald Angels Sing (MENDELSSOHN)—refrain in C major
- O Come, All Ye Faithful (ADESTE FIDELIS)—refrain in F major
- O Come, O Come, Emmanuel (VENI EMMANUEL)—refrain in C# dorian
- The First Nowell (THE FIRST NOWELL)—refrain in C major

These are suggestions. Other examples can be found by carefully examining your hymnal. Hymns can also be reinforced in the home of the preschooler by making parents aware of recordings that use children's voices. The finest examples that I know of in this category are two records produced under the direction of Ronald E. Nelson at Westwood Lutheran Church, St. Louis Park, Minnesota. The parents are encouraged to play one side of the record each day for the child. In this way, the child grows up hearing good hymns. The titles of the records are _Great Hymns for Children_ and _O Come, Little Children._

Also very useful is a recording of children produced under the direction of Mabel Stewart Boyter entitled _A Joyful Sound: Songs for Children_ (Waco: Word Records, W-3137-LP). By playing such recordings each day, the preschooler will learn both the quality of a child's singing voice and develop a growing knowledge of hymns. Other types of recordings include those that treat hymn tunes instrumentally (Terry Kirkland, producer, *Hymns for Quiet Times* [Nashville: Broadman, 1980]).

Selected Resources for Hymn Study with Children

The following is a modest list of resources that might be helpful in designing your own program of hymn study for the children of your church.

Contemporary Hymn Collections

Green, Fred Pratt. *The Hymns and Ballads of Fred Pratt Green.* Carol Stream, Ill.: Hope Publishing Co., 1982.

New Hymns for Children. Springfield, Ohio: Hymn Society of America, 1982.

Twelve New Hymns for Children. Springfield, Ohio: Hymn Society of America, 1965.

Wren, Brian. *Faith Looking Forward.* Carol Stream, Ill.: Hope Publishing Co., 1983.

Collections of Third World Hymnody

Colson, Howard S., comp. *Lead Us, Lord: A Collection of African Hymns.* Minneapolis: Augsburg, 1977.

Colvin, Tom. *Fill Us With Your Love and Other Hymns from Africa.* Carol Stream, Ill.: Agape, 1983.

I-to-Loh, ed. *Hymns from the Four Winds: A Collection of Asian American Hymns.* Nashville: Abingdon Press, 1983.

Routely, Erik, ed. *Cantate Domino.* New York: Oxford University Press, 1980.

General Hymn Studies and Collections for Children

Boyter, Mabel S. *My Favorite Christmas Carols.* Chicago: Carl Fisher, Inc., 1961.

———. *My Favorite Hymns of Praise.* Chicago: Carl Fischer, Inc., 1961.

Burdeshaw, Jane. *Funbook About Hymns.* Nashville: Convention Press, 1983.

Harris, Louis. *Praise-Hymns.* Waco: Word, Inc., 1973.

Hunnicut, Judy. *All Things Bright and Beautiful: Unison and Two Part Anthems with Handbells.* Minneapolis: Augsburg, 1979.

———. "Teaching Hymns to Children." Unpublished paper available from The Hymn Society of America, Springfield, Ohio.

Kemp, Helen. *Hymns Plus: for Junior Choristers.* Chapel Hill: Hinshaw Music, 1980.

Ramseth, Betty Ann and Melinda. *Take a Hymn: for Unison Voices with Instruments.* Minneapolis: Augsburg, 1982.

Additional hymn studies are available from the Choristers Guild, 2834 W. Kingsley Road, Garland, Texas 75041. These materials are available on individual sheets with the hymn on one side and a study on the opposite side. Usually, these were initially published in the *Choristers Guild Letters.* Over ninety hymns, covering the entire range of hymnody, are available.

C. Michael Hawn[9]

162 ◆ THE MINISTRY OF CHILDREN'S CHOIRS

Through participation in choirs, children are introduced to the meaning and significance of worship, learn the musical resources used in the worship of a given congregation, and serve the community as worship leaders. This article reflects on this important ministry and suggests how such choirs may be established.

What is the purpose of the children's choir in the worship life of a parish? The answer to this question will have profound influence on both the children and the parish. One parish may establish a children's choir primarily because other parishes have them, and the music program seems incomplete without one. Another parish may see a children's choir program as a means of outreach—a way of involving children and families who have not been active before. Still another may use the children's choir primarily as a presenter of the popular musicals—either staged or not staged on special occasions.

But these approaches may risk "missing the mark" of a primary focus for the choir. Children are often capable of far more maturity than we as adults imagine. For them to see the choir as a means of serving the Lord and the church in a very special way—as leaders of the weekly gathering of the parish family in worship—is probably the best motivating force for their participation.

How can such a focus be implemented? First, the publicity and recruitment involved in beginning a children's choir or in starting a new season for an established group should be appealing, but not misleading. The social aspect—the fun of participation—is not to be neglected or understated. But children need to know that they are also being given an important job to do. They are to be teachers of the congregation, in a sense; and thus are aware from the start that good training and hard work will be necessary. Does this mean less fun? On the contrary, it means much more because of the high standards and goals for which they strive.

On the other hand, a children's choir director could be so carried away with lofty goals that the individual child would lose importance and the social and fellowship aspects of choir, so beneficial to the growth of the child, would be crowded out of the picture by a no-nonsense policy from the time the singers enter the rehearsal room until they leave. The basic qualification of a children's choir director is a love for children, shown in concern for both the individual child and the developing relationships within the group. Social activities should occasionally supplement the rehearsals to achieve such balance.

We must also help children to develop an appreciation of quality. The following words by Robert Hovda (from _Signs, Songs and Stories_ [Silver Springs, Md.: Liturgical Conference, 1974]) are an important reminder about quality:

> Perhaps it is even more important when dealing with children, because children are open and in the process of formation. Children still have a chance of achieving a greater appreciation of beauty, authenticity, craftsmanship, skill, color and shape, texture, etc. Most adults are profoundly affected by our culture's general insensitivity and even blindness with regard to quality. . . . If many of us adults have been deprived of this kind of sensitivity, we owe our children an opportunity—by every means possible, including liturgical celebrations—for a broader and richer development of their human faculties.

We should insist on a relentless faithfulness to Zoltan Kodaly's reminder: "Only the best is good enough for a child."

But this may not be easy. A child may enter a choir program at age nine or ten—a child whose musical environment has been limited to television and pop radio—and be expected suddenly to appreciate the great musical heritage of the church. Imagine the confusion in the child's mind. This music is a foreign language, no more easily understood than a literary work in a strange tongue. How can the choir director provide a bridge to understanding and appreciation?

An Early Start

Suzuki and Kodaly have both insisted that musical education begins at birth, or before! It is time that the church take seriously the "mother tongue" learning method practiced by Suzuki and his teachers and students throughout the world. As an infant learns the native language by constant listening and repetition, so our children can learn the musical language of the church by constant exposure from birth. Children can "sit through" a liturgy without feeling excluded, if some of the music is familiar. Perhaps we need to place recordings of such music in the homes of infants for repeated (yes, even daily) listening. (In my own parish, such records are given as gifts at baptism.)

The new Alleluia Series published by Augsburg (studies in bible, worship, music and the arts from age three to junior high) has a recording for each student to take home. Parishes using the three-year lectionary will be especially interested in this series, since it follows that three-year cycle and may be used as enrichment for expanded choir rehearsals.

In addition to familiarizing children with the musical language of the church, such recordings can help them discover what the child voice is meant to sound like; and thus they will begin to imitate good quality singing. Of course, such benefits can occur only if the recordings use the best children's voices. (One that has been used for this purpose is "Great Hymns for Children" sung by the Westwood Choristers and available from Westwood Lutheran Church, 9001 Cedar Lake Road, Minneapolis, Minn. 55426.)

Good Church Music

A children's choir with a nucleus of those exposed to church music since infancy will make the job of maintaining quality much easier. But we cannot all be so fortunate—at least not at the beginning. We must meet our singers where they are, as they are, and lovingly guide them into the great wealth of church music that is their heritage. I believe that this can be done without compromising quality, but no one can claim the task will be easy. There is never quite enough time to search

The Cross Alisée Pattée. A cross inscribed within a circle.

for just the right materials for each group. There is good music of every style—including the style most familiar to the novice choir member—but in some styles it is harder to find. Composers such as John Rutter of England and Hal Hopson in the United States—to mention only two—have written quality music for treble voices (unison, as well as two-part) that is easy and in a style familiar to all children. Choristers Guild is one publisher dedicated exclusively to this goal.

How do we distinguish such music from the masses of "junk tunes" that flood the market in the name of giving children "what they like"? First and foremost, look for craftsmanship in both text and music. Texts may be childlike, but never childish. What does the text say? Does it reflect good theology? Does it have something new to offer, or is it simply a combination of rhymes and clichés designed to fit the tune? What is unique about the music? It need not be complex, but is it well put together? Does the melody sing well and wear well? Is the rhythmic treatment interesting—even exciting? What about the accompaniment? Perhaps by now, we have had enough of simplistic broken chord accompaniments and may expect more. One composer will take the easiest way out with such accompaniments, while another will make a real counter-melody out of what could have been a monotonous pattern of broken chords. The more a director studies and sorts in the selecting process, the more easily the wheat is separated from the chaff.

As the choir learns to sing well in familiar styles, the director may begin expanding appreciation for other types of church music. One goal of a year's repertoire should be a well-balanced diet of church music.

Thematic Planning

There is another important factor in selecting repertoire for the children's choir—and, in fact, for all choirs. With the consideration of quality and balance must go the thematic needs of the liturgical year. More words of Robert Hovda from the article quoted earlier need to be considered:

> . . . we have no "fillers" in a well-planned liturgical action. No part or element is introduced simply because we have to pass the time. We do not "throw in" a song because someone likes it, or interpose a gesture because it is familiar, or include a dance because we have a dancer . . . Anything that is to be part of a liturgy must pass the tests of quality and appropriateness.

The sight of a child's eyes widening as the words sung by the choir are quoted in the homily or sermon should be enough to convince a skeptical choir director that the children really do care! They have committed themselves to be servants of Christ and the church. The music they sing is also a servant—a bearer of God's Word. To enlist them in this service and then obscure its relevance by cloudy or nonexistent relationships to the theme of the day is to say we didn't really mean it.

Every choir director would do well to have all music and biblical or related texts filed according to the lectionary year. While many Sundays may remain with empty files for a long time, others will fill quickly with many possibilities. Chanting of the proper verses and psalmody should receive top priority. Even when a "general" anthem is used, care must be taken to avoid a conflict of moods. If a certain anthem doesn't fit in, postpone it and teach the congregation a new hymn instead.

The Teaching Choir

How can a hymn be taught? At least two ways come to mind, with many variations possible for each way. The congregation may rehearse the hymn before the service, with the choir singing it through first and then a "cantor" leading the congregation in repeating it with the choir. In most situations, it would be too much to expect the light children's voices to actually "lead" the people. Their leading is best done by alternations—either stanza by stanza or phrase by phrase.

This sort of teaching may also be a part of the liturgy, without previous rehearsal. Let the hymn be played through first—either by the organ or another instrument. Then have the children sing the first stanza, having heard the melody through twice. The organ may support them with melody only, if the tune is difficult. The choir may then do another stanza alone, with the congregation again following them. Let this hymn be included in the liturgy for several weeks in a row, if appropriate, so that learning can be reinforced. An organist working closely with the director will find other ways of presenting the tune during this period, whether in choral preludes or simply by using the hymnal setting as a prelude or voluntary.

The Voices

In addition to teaching the choir the music for their service in worship, the director has at least two other obligations to the singer. These involve the *skills* needed to do the most effective work as a choir. The first of these is the proper use and development of the voice. Children's voices have the potential of creating the most beautiful sound imaginable. But they cannot achieve this without help.

A big part of this help is in simply exposing them to the best sounds of children's voices. This is why recordings are so vital to the choir director, since these sounds rarely occur in the child's natural environment. While some parents will respond to the need of putting such sounds into the home, many will not. Therefore the rehearsal room must also feature good children's choir recordings. These can be played as the children enter the room or be given more attention as an integral part of the rehearsal. One rule to follow strictly in the latter alternative is while a recording is being played, no one talks or whispers. Boy choir recordings are especially useful in making boys aware of how they can and should sound, in contrast to the "macho male" voices some will try to emulate. Films such as Walt Disney's *Almost Angels* are readily available and will do much to accomplish the same thing.

But the director's own work with the choir is even more important in establishing good vocal quality. Beginning with downward vocalization from head tones in the upper part of the treble staff—sirens, "yoo-hoo," and other helps to discover "head tone"—and then striving for even color throughout the range (but as Helen Kemp says, "the lower, the lighter"), children will soon sense for themselves what sounds beautiful and what sounds "ugly" or "angry." Maintaining tall, but relaxed posture, with "loose" neck and jaw; breathing deeply and striving for a "tall tone," with mouth opening more vertically than horizontally; and working for phrases that climax on upper tones—these are only a few of the helps that will keep the voices growing in the most natural and beneficial way. It is beyond the scope of this article—if, indeed, at all possible—to present a comprehensive guide to the child voice. The conscientious director will attend workshops and observe the best local groups in rehearsal, as well as read as much as possible on the subject. The more a director learns about the child voice, the more that director becomes aware of how much more there is to learn.

Vocalizing can guarantee the exercise of the entire vocal range at each rehearsal, but another important factor is the selection of music which lies in the best part of the child's range. For too long children have been telling directors (and directors have believed them and told publishers) that they can't sing high. But directors must know better. A look at the great music of the church sung for centuries by children's voices will tell us that those composers knew that the loveliest and most effective tones of the child voice lie in the upper part of the treble staff, not the lower. The best writers for children today know this and will write accordingly. Avoid music that doesn't take the voice above its "middle." It will do nothing for the ongoing vocal development of your group and will only encourage forcing "gutsy" volume on middle tones. That will inevitably result in the upper tones becoming pale and remote by comparison and finally the kind of "break" that plagues many singers. Look at the music carefully. Do most of the notes lie between middle C and the G above, with a few climax tones going to the upper C? That is *not* a good range for children's development of their voices. If the whole scheme was transposed up a fourth, with most of the notes in the middle part of the staff and climaxes on upper tones, good use of the voice would be encouraged.

Reading Skill

The second skill needed is in music reading—sightsinging. How many hours of rehearsal time can be saved by a group that has at least a nucleus of good readers! The learning process can be cut in half, thereby opening new doors to more exciting repertoire and more time to "polish" and go beyond simply learning notes and words to actually expressing them. It seems that most public school music programs today simply do not have enough time in their schedule to teach music reading. Someone recently made a comparison between the time spent in language reading and music reading in the average elementary school. How well would Johnny and Joanne read, if they had spent only as much time with their reading as they spent with music reading? Of course, the comparison is laughable and makes one realize how absurd it is to expect competent sightsingers from such limited training. Perhaps, we in the church have a greater motivation for teaching music reading, since we have a greater message to sing.

A surprising amount of learning can take place if a few minutes of each rehearsal are devoted to sightsinging. The sightsinging flashcards created by Linden J. Lundstrom and now available from Choristers Guild (P.O. Box 38188, Dallas, Texas 75238) are an excellent resource for this purpose. They come complete with a teacher's guide for use for an entire choir year. The Alleluia Series mentioned above also includes sightsinging as a part of each lesson.

Expanding Horizons

Finally, then, what is the place of the children's choir in our liturgy? Except for its limitations as a strong vocal leader in congregational singing, its place can be the same as the adult choir. In fact, it is safe to say that many children's choirs are capable of greater enrichment of worship than adult choirs in the same parish. Children are often able to chant more easily than adults. (They haven't lived as long with metrical music.) Let them chant psalmody and other verses proper to the day as often as they can learn them well. Their teaching role in the congregation must not be neglected. Putting a children's choir opposite (in antiphony) an adult choir in a festival service can be most exciting. Their voices can soar in a descant to a familiar hymn. Anthems may be used as

preludes or they fit into the service thematically. Accompanying instruments, selected carefully for balance with the children, can enhance the lovely beauty of their voices. Processions are effective, especially for festival services, but must be carefully rehearsed—especially for body posture and speed (children will nearly always walk too fast). As rehearsal time permits, a cantata for a special occasion may be possible. This writer has found that, given an opportunity, a majority of choir members in grades five through eight will elect to belong to *two* choirs, spending up to five hours weekly in rehearsal and other class work. The additional choir is given to more intensive rehearsal, and therefore more challenging music. The excitement of such possibilities seems to be enough reward for the extra time given. Even singers with severe pitch problems have seen them quickly disappear in this "second mile" schedule.

Possibilities are truly limitless. The more comprehensive your program can become as it gradually takes shape and grows, the greater the satisfactions to your choir, to the congregation, and to you.

Ronald A. Nelson[10]

163 • A Method of Presenting the Bible to Children

The following article describes a method for teaching children the importance of Scripture and for developing their own natural spiritual sensitivity and openness. Whether followed exactly as described or adapted to local needs, this approach makes adults aware of the spiritual hunger and spiritual perception found in each child.

During the past year, our three-year-old became increasingly aware of crucifixes. Before a traditional representation, he often stopped, looked intently for a moment, and then reflected, "Jesus is dead." At first, I refrained from speaking, but soon realized his statement was a request; he was asking for meaning. Perhaps he is ready for the Good News, I thought. The next time he said it, I answered, "Yes, Jesus did die on the cross, but he rose from the dead. He is alive and with us still." This same dialogue was repeated on many occasions. I began to wonder whether it was making any impression. Would he believe what I said or what he seemed to be seeing?

Last week, it happened again. He saw a large, outdoor crucifix, and said, "Jesus is dead." Not knowing what to say anymore and feeling a certain embarrassment at the poverty of our representations of the paschal mystery, I responded only, "Yes, he looks dead." Whereupon he took my face in his hands and looked straight into my eyes. His own eyes were wide with the excitement of a sudden realization. He spoke in a hushed voice as if telling me a secret, "Maybe, they don't know he's alive."

It may take an adult to announce the kerygma, but it takes a child to receive it. If we have the eyes to see and the ears to hear, we will be astounded at the young child's natural and supernatural sensitivities. What looks like inattention can often be a profound attention to something else. What looks like dawdling can really be the child's way of absorbing and reflecting on reality. What sounds like naiveté can actually be a manifestation of the child's ability to see into the essence of things. Do not contemplatives urge us to slow down, to attend to one thing, to journey toward the heart of the matter? All this, the child does naturally, if the child is not tugged too quickly into the adult world. It is this capacity that makes the child so ready to receive transcendent reality. When presented with great religious truths and ultimately with God, young children open wide the doors of their souls.

Sophia Cavalletti has written eloquently of these matters in _The Religious Potential of the Child_ (New York: Paulist Press, 1988). She has studied children for over thirty years, she speaks with the authority of experience:

> All that we have been able to observe over these years, whether directly or through collaboration with former students, leads us to consider the child as a "meta-physical being" . . . who moves with ease in the world of the transcendent and who delights in—satisfied and serene—the contact with God.

When we consider presenting the Bible to children from three to six years of age, our estimation of their capacities will determine not only our selections, but our manner of presentation. If we feel children are only capable of relating to what they have experienced, we may choose passages that include children or animals or everyday occurrences. If we feel they will not be engaged unless presented with a story, then we will opt for passages with a strong narrative element. But if, like Cavalletti, we are convinced that they are capable of genuine religious experience, we will present those texts that point to Scripture's essence and open into an experience of the divine. And we will present them in a way that invites the child's own participation in the mystery of a relationship with God.

Cavalletti has come to just such a selection of Scripture, not only on the basis of her biblical scholarship, as she admits, but from her experience with children. She began hesitantly and with no preconceived theories. However by gradually presenting Scripture texts and observing the children's reactions, she and her collaborator, Gianna Gobbi, a Montessori educator, came to realize that certain passage called forth the same reaction—intense interest, desire for prolonged involvement, and, most of all, joy.

When these reactions recurred over a long period of time, then Cavalletti and Gobbi believed that this was an indication that the subject matter and the manner of presentation corresponded to the interests and needs of the children. And so an ensemble of elements—few and essential—was slowly delineated. The children demonstrated that they knew these elements, not in an academic way, but as if these elements were part of their persons, almost as if they had always known these elements.

As the work of Cavalletti and Gobbi spread to other socioeconomic areas in Rome, and then into parts of Africa, Latin America and North America, the same phenomenon was observed. Culture and geography made little difference. "It is this that led us to consider that we were not faced with the personal reaction of this or that individual child, but rather a phenomenon concerning the child."

The Context

Before outlining these few and essential themes, we must consider the context of these Scripture presentations. They are given to young children in a specially prepared environment known as an atrium, a setting that allows children to live their religious lives in a child's way and prepares them to take their places in the church.

The atrium is outfitted, in the manner of a Montessori room, with child-sized furniture, shelving containing materials for the children's meditative work, and centers of religious activity, for example, a miniature altar table. A place of prominence is always given to the prayer corner, where children may go at anytime during the approximately two hour meeting and where they often gather for communal prayer and paraliturgies. The children are shown how to walk slowly and speak softly, so an atmosphere of silence reigns in the room even though they are busy doing many things. In fact, children often say what they like best about the atrium is that it is so quiet and peaceful.

In this setting, three-to-six-year olds are put "in touch with those sources through which God communicates and reveals [God's self] in living form," i.e., Scripture and liturgy. They are initiated into the language of this symbolic communication, focusing on individual elements that are gradually combined over the years into a remarkable synthesis. Because of the inherent unity of Scripture and liturgy, to be able to read the signs of one is to be able to read the signs of the other.

The content of the catechesis follows the liturgical year; seasonal material is presented at the appropriate time, and more general material is offered during ordinary time. Each year, for example, infancy narratives are considered during the Advent-Christmas season, but the specific text differs in the course of the three-year cycle. Children thus become familiar with different kinds of biblical texts, experiencing both repetition and newness.

The Parable of the Good Shepherd

Central to this catechesis is the proclamation of the parable of the Good Shepherd (John 10:3-5, 11-16). Its manner of presentation is typical of other scriptural presentations. A catechist gathers the children around, sitting on their level near a low table, and begins by retelling the story, never adding elements, but drawing out those elements that are especially significant for the children.

The points on which a catechist lingers, for it is these points that most enchant the children, are above all the personal love and protective presence of the Good Shepherd. The Good Shep-

herd calls each one of the sheep by name, knows each intimately even if there are many sheep, calls the sheep and gradually they become accustomed to the voice of their Good Shepherd and they listen. In this way, a precious relationship is established; a thread of love binds the sheep always more closely to their Shepherd. The Shepherd's voice is powerful and supremely patient; it never tires of calling and reaches even to those sheep who are far away, beyond the sheepfold. Slowly, they too turn to hear the Shepherd's voice and they gather together into one great flock. The Shepherd knows the needs of the sheep and guides them to good pastures, walking ahead of them to show the way and to be the first to confront any danger should it arise. So the sheep are safe and peaceful with their Good Shepherd; they know there is someone to protect them even in danger.

The catechist then leads a communal meditation on the text, perhaps posing evocative questions that help the children enter into the parable's meaning. During one presentation, some children gradually realized that they themselves were the sheep. Whereupon a three-year old leaped to his feet, pointed at the catechist, and said, "And you're a sheep too!"

After a sense of entry into the text is established, a solemn reading of the parable takes place. Candles are lit, and these words of introduction are sometimes used, "Now we will read the parable just as it is written in the Bible." Often a period of spontaneous prayer, arising out of silence, will follow. At this point, the parable is presented with sensorial material that is typical of that which the room is filled: a circular wooden sheepfold, a two-dimensional figure of the Good Shepherd (in the style of Michelangelo's David, a strong young man with a sheep on his shoulders), and ten two-dimensional sheep.

As the parable is read again, the figures are moved to correspond to the actions in the text. These actions give children the basic idea of how to use the materials. However as they return to use them again and again in the course of the year, their own meditation will prompt them to make subtle changes in the movement, signaling to the observant catechist that they have personally appropriated the content of the parable. One little girl took the figure of the Good Shepherd in her hand and touched the head of each sheep. She then told the catechist, "He loves the sheep so much; he is giving them kisses."

Several important ideas are revealed in the children's reaction to this parable and the choice of this parable as the cornerstone of the catechesis by Cavalletti and Gobbi. "In our estimation," writes Cavalletti, "children should be initiated into present religious reality." What has happened in Jesus is decisive for our reading of the Hebrew Bible and, indeed, for the nature of religious experience. She advises initiating young children into the New Testament, especially the Gospels, "concentrating on the passages the theological meaning of which the child can penetrate." If children are able to feel even once their hearts burning within them as they hear passages from Scripture, they will be on their way to regarding the Bible as a book of life.

Second, the choice of this parable is wholly suited to the needs of the young child, who is in a developmental period, according to Maria Montessoir, that is especially sensitive to the need for protection. This parable can touch the young child's soul, providing the grounding for a trusting faith that integrates the affective dimensions of the personality and religious knowledge. For some children, this parable brings to mind memories of loving people in their lives, for the Good Shepherd image carries maternal as well as paternal associations. But for the child who has not known such love, the parable not only remains accessible, but can be supremely important, reorienting the child's life.

Third, the parable can be considered as a kind of creedal formulation.

> [It] introduces the child into the nucleus of the Christian mystery in its greatest content. . . . From a doctrinal point of view, the parable is a fundamental text that centers on the mystery of the person of Christ and His relationship with us, a relationship at once personal (the Shepherd knows each sheep by name) and communal (the sheepfold). It is the parable of providential love that reaches the ultimate sacrifice of life, and as such it is a paschal parable.

As Cavalletti is fond of saying: "The greatest realities are for the youngest children." When they are in possession of the vital nucleus, their religious development becomes a process of meditatively unfolding something they already know in their hearts, even, one could say, in their bones.

The Prophecies and Historical Narratives

If the parable of the Good Shepherd is the central scriptural passage, it is by no means the first presented during the catechetical year. It is proclaimed during Lent only after the children's awareness has been refined by other scriptural and liturgical works. For young children, Cavalletti limits her use of passages from the Hebrew Bible to a few prophecies, during Advent, that contain strong images and can be interpreted as pointing to the person of Christ, for example, Isaiah 9:2, Isaiah 9:6, Isaiah 7:14, and Micah 5:1. With their images of light or the little child, these prophetic texts are usually printed in beautiful script, illustrated, mounted, or framed. They are presented in the prayer corner by the catechist, who also leads a meditation. Often the children begin to pray spontaneously at this point, using the images of the prophecy.

The first of the historical passages are also represented in Advent. During each year of the cycle, one or two of the following are given: the Annunciation, the visitation, the adoration of the shepherds, the adoration of the magi, the presentation in the temple, or the flight to Egypt. Their presentation is similar to that of the parable of the Good Shepherd, containing a retelling of the story in the catechist's own words, a mediation, a solemn reading of the text, a prayer response, and a presentation of the parable. In this case, the sensorial material is somewhat different; the figures are always three-dimensional, instead of two-dimensional, and are moved about in dioramas that are as historically accurate as the catechist can make them. It is a treasured moment when a child in the atrium is heard to say to another something like, "Did you know that Jesus really lived?" The awareness of Jesus as a historical person is a significant achievement.

Yet these infancy narratives are not presented primarily as history, but instead as theological meditations.

> These are pages of exceedingly rich theological content; their theology is neither systematic nor explicit but one that is almost "hidden" in the text. We are dealing with a theology that is completely different from the textbook kind of theology; it cannot be learned through academic study, but rather through a prolonged "listening" to the text. It is a theology characteristically allusive.

If the catechist is able to meditate deeply on the mystery of the Incarnation, he or she will be able to bring a sense of wonder to the text which, like the biblical text, reveals to the children the importance of this child, the Son of God and the Son of Man. The catechist will also demonstrate that there is always more to be discovered in biblical texts, even ones we have heard many times. After the presentation of the Annunciation, a little boy, not quite three, took the figure of the angel, held it up to the face of the figure of Mary, and said, "No afraid; be happy; God!" If the essence of the text is presented in a few, well-chosen words, the text will become part of a child's very soul.

The events at the end of Christ's life are conveyed primarily through the model of the city of Jerusalem, rather than through a detailed reading of Scripture. The paschal character of Christ's death is conveyed through the presentation of the Last Supper (Mark 14:12-17, 22-24). For this, a small model of the upper room, a table, bread and wine, and three-dimensional figures of Jesus and the apostles serve the children's meditation.

At the end of the reading when the figures have been removed from the model room as if they are going to the garden of Gethesemane, the catechist announces, "There, he was taken, and later he died." The catechist then puts a miniature crucifix on the cenacle table, where the bread and wine from the Last Supper remain. This is followed immediately by the announcement of the Resurrection, "But, Christ rose from the dead." The catechist places two candles on either side of the crucifix and lights them, saying, "He is alive and with us still." Here, the link between Scripture and liturgy is clear, for the children, since the beginning of their time in the atrium, have been sitting at the miniature altar table, in just the same fashion as they now see the table in the upper room. The connection need not be spelled out; a deep silence of recognition often follows this presentation.

Cavalletti stresses the need to keep the proclamation of the death and the Resurrection together and in balanced proportion.

> We believe it is necessary to tie them together; we do not even pause temporarily on the death, considering perhaps it is a well-known fact that the death was followed by the resurrection. Yes, it is known, but . . . very often the accent is ap-

plied to the death and so it comes to assume a greater vividness, than the resurrection. The disturbing proclamation we give is of the resurrection, and it is on this that we should concentrate.

The Parables of the Kingdom

In the weeks after the close of the Christmas season, the children are presented with some of the stories Jesus told, in particular, the parables of the kingdom. These stories reveal Jesus as a poet and teacher, who saw in the natural world spiritual things. These stories call forth in both child and adult a sense of wonder: from the tiny seed of the Mideastern mustard—a tree; from the lump of dough—a loaf of bread! The kingdom of God is like these examples; it is born out of the small and is transformed into greatness by divine power. This same energy is at work in the children and manifests itself in their physical and spiritual growth.

The value of the kingdom is presented in Matthew 13:44-46, in the parables of the precious pearl and the hidden treasure. The essential element in these parables is the kingdom's supreme worth, not the renunciation involved in attaining it. Young children, in fact, do not even allude to the renunciation involved in these parables because they are so taken with the joy of finding. Cavalletti says it is not necessary to stress the moral dimension of these parables.

Barbara Schmich Searle

164 • BIBLIOGRAPHY ON CHILDREN IN THE WORSHIPING COMMUNITY

Ban, Arline J. *Children's Time in Worship.* Valley Forge, Pa.: Judson Press, 1981.

Barton, Anne. *All Age Worship.* Bramcote, Nottingham: Grove Books, 1993.

Berglund, Mary Catherine. *Gather the Children: Celebrate the Word with Ideas, Activities, Prayers, and Projects.* Washington: Pastoral Press, 1987.

Bernstein, Eleanor, and John Brooks-Leonard, eds. *Children in the Assembly of the Church.* Chicago: Liturgy Training Publications, 1992.

Buchanan, Colin Oglivie. *Children in Communion.* Bramcote, Nottingham: Grove Books, 1990.

Fortunato, Connie. *Children's Music Ministry.* Elgin, Ill.: David C. Cook Publishers, 1981.

Gobbel, A. Roger, and Phillip C. Huber. *Creative Designs with Children at Worship.* Atlanta: John Knox Press, 1981.

Halverson, Della T. and Barbara P. Garcia. *God's Children in Worship: Congregational Guide.* Nashville: United Methodist Church, Discipleship Resources, 1988.

Keithahn, Mary Nelson. *Our Heritage of Hymns.* Dallas: Choristers Guild, 1986.

Keithahn, Mary Nelson, and Mary Louise Van Dyke. *Exploring the Hymnal.* Dallas: Choristers Guild, 1986.

Lehn, Cornelia. *Involving Children and Youth in Congregational Worship.* Newton, Kans.: Faith and Life Press; Scottdale, Pa.: Mennonite Publishing House, 1982.

McGavran, Grace W. *Learning How Children Worship.* St. Louis: Bethany Press,1964.

Morris, Margie. *Helping Children Feel at Home in Worship.* Nashville: United Methodist Churches, Discipleship Resources, 1988.

Neufield, Bernie. *Worship in Youth and Children's Groups.* Newton, Kans.: Faith and Life Press; Scottdale, Pa.: Mennonite Publishing House, 1981.

Ng, David, and Virginia Thomas. *Children in the Worshiping Community.* Atlanta: John Knox Press, 1981.

Reformed Liturgy and Music 26:1 (Winter 1992). Issue's theme is on children as participants in worship.

Reformed Worship 12 (Summer 1989). Issue's theme is on children in worship.

Stewart, Sonja, and Jerome W. Berryman. *Young Children and Worship.* Philadelphia: Westminster Press, 1989.

Young, Daniel. *Welcoming Young Children to Communion.* Bramcote, Nottingham: Grove Books, 1983.

White, Jack Noble. *Everything You Need for Children's Worship.* Cincinnati: St. Anthony Messenger Press, 1978.

⚘ THREE ⚘

Women in Worship

The role of women in the ministry of the church has long been a controversial subject. The New Testament, for example, both records significant contributions of women and includes injunctions limiting their role. In recent decades, this subject has been addressed by Christians of many traditions. Many have begun to ordain women to positions of leadership within the church. This chapter will address the role of women in the assembly of God's people gathered for worship. Important issues in this discussion include the role of women as worship leaders, the nature of Christian ministry, and the language used in Christian hymns, prayers, and liturgical texts. This chapter will not solve these issues, but will provide both ideas and structures to stimulate discussion and a guide by which churches can evaluate their own practices.

165 • WOMEN AND WORSHIP

The contemporary women's movement has highlighted several issues of concern relating to women and the church's worship. These issues include questions on the presence of female leadership in worship, the use of inclusive language for humans, the language used for God, whether Judeo-Christian worship is fundamentally sexist, and the use of images of women in worship.

The current women's movement, like its nineteenth-century forerunner, has included in its critique an examination of the position of women in the church in general and in the church's worship in particular. Several issues have emerged as a result of this renewed awareness of the role that the church has played and continues to play in the oppression of women as a group.

(1) The contemporary concern of the women's movement for equal access for women in existing ecclesial structures dates back to the nineteenth-century women's movement. In relation to worship, this concern has focused especially on the presence of women as leaders in worship in general and as ordained clergy in particular. The struggle of women to gain official recognition of their ministry by the church has, in many cases, been successful. It has also generated extensive research and publications on the history and the-ology of women's leadership in the church. Moreover, this struggle characteristically has been motivated not only by a concern for the public recognition of the call to ministry of individual women, but also by the conviction that such a recognition would itself constitute a powerful witness to the fullness of a church of women and men, equal in the sight of God by virtue of their baptism. At the same time, the physical presence of women at the altar and the pulpit also challenges presuppositions about the nature of God and the adequacy of exclusively male language to speak of God.

(2) A more contemporary concern has been the use of language in such a way that women are, implicitly or explicitly, included. The conventional practice in English of using male referents as "generic," i.e., referring to the whole human race, has been sharply challenged by those who point out that such usage perpetuates the misconception that males are normative human beings and women are secondary, derivative, or deviant. While this critique is by no means universally accepted, the scholarly community in general and the publishing community specifically, especially in the United States of America, have adopted "inclusive" language more and more. All evidence suggests that this practice will eventually be accepted. The use of inclusive language in refer-

The Cross Fitchée. *Any cross in which the lower arm is drawn to a sharp point is said to be* fitched, *or pointed. This form of the cross is believed to have originated during the late middle ages. It is believed that Crusaders carried small pointed crosses with pointed arms so that they could be thrust into the ground at the time of daily devotions.*

ence to people in liturgical books, hymnals, resources, and Bible translations has growing support within many church bodies. Linguistic changes are beginning to appear in revised liturgical books and new translations of Scripture.

(3) Although often perceived as a part of inclusive language, use of language about God is most usefully treated as a separate (though not unrelated) issue. The predominantly (if not exclusively) male image of God, which is portrayed in the traditional language of prayer, Scripture, and hymns (to say nothing about visual images), raises questions about the extent to which women are created "in the image of God." Such androcentric language has also undoubtedly been used to reinforce the notion that men are not only normative representatives of the human race, but also more adequate than women as representatives of God. Proposals for change range from the elimination or avoidance of any gender-specific language about God, through the attempt to balance male and female language and titles, to the use of only feminine pronouns and titles for God. Efforts to alter masculine language encounter most difficulty with language referring to God as Father, references to Jesus, and Trinitarian formulae. The first difficulty is a problem not only because of the theological import of the term, but also because of its emotional resonance for many Christians. The second is a historical difficulty, and the third is a doctrinal and ecumenical problem. Solutions will require serious reexamination of the underlying theological issues in order to recast the language in a way that is accessible to contemporary sensibilities while remaining faithful to the tradition the church has received. The very understanding of "tradition" itself has, of course, been challenged on the basis of its exclusion and denigration of women. At the present time, there is no consensus about a solution among those committed to a change in traditional androcentric language about God. Indeed, there will be no easy solution.

(4) More fundamental, perhaps, even than critiques of language or admission to leadership, is the question of the ability of traditional structures of Christian or Jewish worship to tolerate the inclusion of women in full equality with men. For some, the Christian and Jewish traditions are fundamentally sexist; therefore, they must be rejected *in toto* by women and replaced by new feminist religions that appropriate traditions from ancient non-Christian goddess worship. Sometimes called *Wicca*, such worship includes meditation, trances, and spell-casting. This worship emphasizes the quality of all human beings and their continuity with the natural world.

Others deny that Christianity (and/or Judaism) is inherently and irreversibly sexist. These people are committed to the reformation of the church by the full inclusion of women and the recognition of women's contributions, both past and present. Some understand this position not as a reformist position, but as a "radical" position, i.e., calling the church back to its "roots," which have been revealed to have been far more egalitarian than has been assumed.

(5) For those who have remained in the church while critical of its treatment of women, yet another concern is the content of worship. These people are concerned, in particular, with the way references to or images of women are presented

in the worship service. They are concerned with negative images (Eve as originator of sin; Israel as harlot or unfaithful wife, and so on) and with positive images that reinforce the secondary status of women (Mary as docile and asexual; obedience to male authority as the primary measure of female virtue, and so on.). The avoidance in lectionary readings and preaching texts of scriptural material that depicts women as agents of God in history (Miriam; Hannah; Mary Magdalene as "first witness to the resurrection," rather than reformed harlot, etc.) is noted, as is the dearth of similar examples from more recent history. The Roman Catholic church, with its sanctorale cycle, has more resources for this than most Protestant churches, although even in the Roman Catholic church male saints predominate.

For relevant titles on this subject, see Carol Christ and Judith Plaskow, eds., _Womanspirit Rising,_ 1979; Rosemary Radford Ruether, _Sexism and God-Talk: Toward a Feminist Theology,_ 1983; and Elisabeth Schüssler Fiorenza, _In Memory of Her: A Feminist Theological Reconstruction of Christian Origins,_ 1983.

Marjorie Procter-Smith[11]

166 ✦ TOWARD A NEW UNDERSTANDING OF MINISTRY

Women have played a significant role in the life of the church throughout its history. In recent years, women have participated in more and more facets of the church's life, leading to new insights regarding the nature of Christian ministry. This understanding, outlined in the following article, emphasizes the importance of human relationships and the sharing of power.

Historical Considerations

From the time of Jesus, the participation of women in the public life of Jesus and his church has been documented. The Gospel accounts are replete with references to those women, who ministered to Jesus, who were delegated to announce the Good News, and who gave silent witness to his agonies.

Paul in his letters and Luke in Acts also note the activity of women in the early Christian community. Both the influence they exerted and the respect they received attest to the unquestioned role accorded to women who ministered to the early community.

Since that time and up to the present, the role of women in public ministry has waxed and waned. Little of this has appeared in most histories of worship. This may be understood as mirroring the larger culture, where the activities, contributions, and accomplishments of women have tended to be ignored or, at the very least, downplayed. The focus of religious histories has commonly been upon affairs of the institutional churches, precisely as institutions. The systematic exclusion of women from ordination and from positions of institutional authority guarantees that in these histories there is little or nothing about women.

The Face of Women in Ministry: Structural Implications

While neither ignoring the pain women have experienced as a result of their exclusion from many church structures nor affirming nor condoning the blatant sexism and sometimes subtle misogyny that have marked the Christian church's practices and structures, reflection on the consequences of that reality leads to some interesting observations. Having experienced exclusion from ministry in a hierarchical structure, gifted women have shaped alternative means to minister to the body of Christ and be Christ on this earth. Horizontal leadership based on mutual support, inspiration, and the convening of the community marked the public ministry of many women. Given their exclusion from institutional politics, some women were free to opt for a more prophetic style of public ministry than is usually possible for those who must accept the limits of conventional roles and institutional approbation. Finally for reasons already mentioned and often precisely because of their position in the church, women were often better able to notice and to attend to that which was left undone and to those who were overlooked, omitted, or excluded in the pastoral practice of the institutional church. Monika Hellwig has observed that, in such instances, the impact of women in public ministry has tended to be prophetic, radical in its long-term implications for the social structures of society, and, in terms of the social dynamics, a movement from below.

The Face of Women in Ministry: Psychological Issues

A key factor influencing the concept of women in ministry is to be found in the reality that the authentic involvement of women in ministry brings to ministry a potentially counter-cultural aspect. To better understand this, Anne Wilson-Schaef's identification of two operative "systems" in our culture is helpful. The first of these is the "dominant" system, typically characterized by current male-oriented values. The second is an "emerging" system, marked by what has been traditionally characterized as a feminine style. The shift that is currently occurring is the increased identification and acceptance of the emerging system. In this process, women and men are experiencing an enhancement of many styles of thinking and interacting that were previously not valued and are exploring the implications of these shifts in both their personal and professional lives.

This transformation has major implications for an understanding of ministry. To begin, it affects how the notion of ministry itself is defined and integrated into the life of the minister. Traditionally reflective of the dominant system, ministry and work were seen as fairly synonymous. John Futrell, for example, in writing on "The Challenge of Ministry," describes ministries as "human services performed in response to the human needs of people." In the emerging system, relationships, rather than work, are seen as a focal point; everything must go through, relate to, and be defined by relationships. Hence, ministry is construed in terms of relationship. It becomes that which one does with one's life in order to make sense of other aspects of one's life. Neither profit- nor power-oriented ministry takes its meaning from creativity, from bonding, from the inherent humanness of ministry touched by the reality of the Incarnation, or from a keen sense of service. Ministry is, in the emerging system, an expression of one's relationship with God, with others, and with oneself.

Other aspects to be considered in light of this shift in worldview and in terms of its impact on the notion of ministry include structure, power, healing, and various understandings of God and spirituality.

The structure of the dominant system is hierarchical, with no ambiguity in regards to accountability or control. God is superior to man, who is superior to woman, who is superior to animals, which is superior to things inanimate. Boundaries are clear, and dichotomous (either/or) thinking abounds. Ministry is something "done to" others, with the minister clearly in a superior stance as the one who imparts (grace, benefits, etc.).

The emerging system has a less clearly defined structure. Boundaries are fairly permeable; categories are less clear; and structures are more easily flexed to address the needs of all. "Neatness" is not a hallmark of such a system. Ministry in this context is a shared experience which reverences various needs of individuals. While roles are defined there is a giving/receiving dynamic that is consonant with the emphasis on relationship mentioned above.

Power is another critical concept. Jean Baker Miller defines power as "the capacity to implement." As such, power has two components: power *for* oneself, and power *over* others. With this in mind, the dominant system has traditionally seen the power of another person or group of persons to be dangerous. Either you control them, or they will control you. This is based, in part, on the assumption that power is a "zero-sum" entity; there is just so much power available. (If, for example, the amount of available power is twenty units, having twelve leaves only eight units available to others.) The dominant system, therefore, jealously guards power and sets deliberate limits, as regards to its use.

The emerging system provides another consideration of power. Here, power, like love, is assumed to be limitless. When shared, it regenerates and expands. Women and men need power to grow and develop. However with the greater development of each individual, the more able, more effective, and less in need of limiting or restricting others she or he will be.

Because of their place in the structure of the dominant system, many women have marked difficulty in coping with and appropriating power. Given their limited understandings, many have used power in the style of the dominant system. Others, fearful of such an outcome or distrustful of their own giftedness, have abrogated any power that is even rightfully theirs. Distortions of spirituality, where humility has become equated with actively avoiding the recognition of gifts and talents, also has discouraged individuals from appropriating their God-given heritage. Interestingly, references to the Spirit of God often reflect a gender difference that may be an indication of an even deeper power issue. Women refer to the "Spirit of love," and men invoke the "power of the Spirit."

There is another aspect to be considered in terms of power and the role of women in ministry. It comes in terms of weakness or powerlessness. For women, weaknesses are typically seen in terms of vulnerability, helplessness, and neediness. The dominant system encourages men to abhor these feelings in themselves, while it has encouraged women to cultivate this state of being. In reality, however, these feelings are common to all. Those who are better able consciously to admit to and tolerate these feelings have a ministerial "edge" in this regard since this ability puts them more closely in touch with basic life experiences. Having to defend less and deny less, they are in a position to understand and minister to weakness. As persons more comfortable with their own weakness, they are more readily able to illumine the path to wholeness for others.

As might be expected, "healing" in the dominant system is something done by the hearer, who is "certified" by the system. Failure in the treatment is most typically construed in terms of some deficit of the patient. Linear logic marks the thought construction of this system. In contrast, the emerging system views "healing" as a process that occurs within a person with the facilitation and help from the healer. This relationship between healer and patient is a key factor. Translating this understanding to the terms of ministry, it is easy to understand the existence of tensions in the church as regards the determination of who, for example, is "legitimately" a minister to a community and how that role/relationship is expressed.

In the dominant system, understandings of God and spirituality parallel the schema already outlined. The structure of most theological assumptions is a dominance-submission scheme. With the perpetuation of the belief that the suffering servant is the holiest of all, women and others found "lower" in the order of things have been encouraged to be suffering servants, thus achieving absolution for their status. God, the "prototype" of perfection of this system, is perfect, all-knowing, and unchanging. The role of the minister is to mediate between God and those lower in the hierarchy so that salvation might be accomplished.

The emerging system's view of God also parallels the emerging worldview. Here, God is viewed primarily in terms of relationship. Coming to know God is imaged as a deepening and broadening process, rather than one of climbing a ladder. Boundaries between the sacred and the secular, between what is holy and what is profane, are less rigid and apt to be informed by the lived experience of those who come to worship. The role of minister is to facilitate that identification process and to enable the community to encounter the holy in this way.

New and Old Directors of Ministry

What is it that makes the movement that is publicly acknowledging and incorporating women in ministry? While some might describe it as "tokenism" or a long overdue acknowledgment of the real contribution made by women, there also seems to be a subtle, yet discernible, shift in the understanding of what ministry involves. The affirmation of the emerging system described in the previous section attests to this shift. The shift might also be interpreted as the acknowledgment that the "works" or activities of women in public ministry, different as they have been from traditional or formally "sanctioned" works, are not only true expressions of ministry, but are also activities that are to be embraced by all in the church.

The image that best expresses one of the greatest contributions that women have to offer to the emerging understanding of what it means to be a public minister in the church may be found in that of pregnancy. For centuries, the male model of potency, impact, and discharge has dominated the cultural image of ministry. Filling empty churches, establishing flourishing programs, and erecting tangible structures were frequently the measures of effective ministry. The emergence of the women's movement, particularly in the United States, has brought with it some alternative approaches to these familiar activities of ministry. In contrast to the male style, the image of pregnancy depicts attitudes of trust, surrender, and receptivity. The pregnant woman is intimately connected to the new life within, yet is not in total control of either the ultimate outcome or many aspects of the process. She does not, for example, determine that on this day "we will work on the nervous system" and that at another time "we will develop fingers and toes." Yet, the woman who is pregnant cannot help but be mindful of the new life within and must direct a significant portion of her consciousness toward health and wholeness. While often finding herself in a stance of reverent reflection, she is an active participant in the process of forming this new life. At no point is the pregnant woman a passive observer.

The shift in the culture's attitude toward pregnancy also provides a fitting metaphor for the new understandings of the role and influence of women in ministry. It is not long ago that pregnancy and all it entails was marked by embarrassment, seclusion, and disfavor. Euphemistically referred to as being "in seclusion," women were typically excluded from the public eye. Only in recent years have pregnant women been "allowed" to continue and experience "public" roles. The condition of pregnancy no longer needs to be hidden. Hence, there appears an increasing readiness to acknowledge the value of the lessons of pregnancy, the lessons of that experience of actively waiting, in hope and in faith, with participation in the process, surrender to the mystery, and commitment to the product. Such might be wholesome attitudes to inform those who are committed to ministry in this age of transformation.

Miriam D. Ukeritis[12]

167 • Inclusive Language

Due to the lack of an inclusive third person singular pronoun in English and due to the traditional use of the masculine noun and pronoun for referring to a generic person, English-speaking peoples have through their language implied a secondary status for women. Recently, some churches have attempted to correct this androcentrism of the English language. Some have dismissed these alterations as trivial, while others have expressed concern about the intent of such changes, especially regarding those terms that convey our images of God. The growing importance of this issue ensures that lively debate will continue for some time.

The question of inclusive language in liturgy and biblical translation has been a subject of considerable controversy in the English-speaking church. The issue has been raised in connection with other languages as well. In the United States

and also in Canada where feminism has been advanced in the churches and theological seminaries and where increasing numbers of women are being ordained to the ministry, there has been particular attention to this issue. The definition of inclusive language depends on a perception of current English usage as characterized by androcentrism. The male is taken to be the normative human person; i.e., the word *man* connotes both the male and the human being as such. Male pronouns are used as generic pronouns. The term *woman* and female pronouns are never used as generic references for a human being, but are exclusive terms for females. This pattern of grammar is not a linguistic accident. It has developed under the influence of a patriarchal social order, in which the male head of family was regarded legally as the representative human person. On the other hand, women and other dependents could not represent themselves, but were included under the male head of family.

This patriarchal social pattern is further reflected in theological language by referring to the community of Christians as *brothers,* by referring to that same community, in relation to God, as *sons,* and by using images for God that correspond to male leadership roles, such as father, lord, and king. Male generic language renders women invisible as autonomous persons and conveys the implicit message that women are secondary and dependent beings, whose relationship to males is analogous to the relationship of human creatures to God. This pattern of male generic language has today come to be recognized as incompatible with the equal dignity of female and male as human persons.

The corrections of male generic language can be done either by using neutral generics, such as *person* rather than *man,* or by adding words that connote the female counterpart to the male term, such as *brothers and sisters* rather than *brothers.* Avoidance of male generic pronouns can be accomplished by repeating the noun, or by using either *he or she* or *them* in place of the generic *he.* The objections to this have often been the sense of the awkwardness of style, due to the lack of an inclusive third person singular pronoun in English. However, in liturgical usage, this awkwardness can often be avoided by substituting first and second person pronouns, *we* and *you* or *thou,* in places where such direct address is appropriate in the language of the prayer.

Such rewriting of the language of hymns, readings, and liturgical prayers has often been done on a local basis by church groups concerned about the issue. The most ambitious effort at developing inclusive language for church usage has been the _Inclusive Language Lectionary_ mandated by the Division of Education and Ministry of the National Council of Churches of Christ in the USA. Since 1980, a three-year cycle of lectionary readings in inclusive language has been in preparation for use by the member churches.

The committee of the _Inclusive Language Lectionary_ has undertaken to provide inclusive terms, not only for human beings, but also for God. Theologically, the committee understands its mandate for such inclusive language for God as based on the fundamental affirmations that God is, by nature, beyond gender and that all images for God derived from gender roles are metaphorical, not literal. To use exclusively male metaphors for God implies either that God is literally male or that males alone are the appropriate human images for God. Such an assertion implies that women are not truly theomorphic; that is, do not possess the image of God. If women are truly equivalent with men as images of God, then metaphors for God drawn from female roles should be as appropriate as metaphors drawn from male roles.

Consequently, the _Inclusive Language Lectionary_ adds the word _mother_ to that of _father_ as a metaphor for God's parental relationship to humanity. It also substitutes neutral generic terms, such as _sovereign_ or _ruler_, for terms of male leadership roles, such as _lord_ or _king_. In relation to Christology, the committee uses male nouns and pronouns for Jesus Christ's historical humanity, but substitutes inclusive terms for the divine Word or the second person of the Trinity manifest in Christ's historical person, such as _child of God_ for _Son of God_. The term _Son of Man_ as a messianic title has been replaced by the term _the Human One_, as a translation of the Hebrew term _ben Adam_, a term which, although male generic in form, means simply "a human being."

These changes of language, not only for humans, but also for God and Christ, have provoked profound anxiety and animosity among church members, as well as church leaders. Clearly, inclusive language is not simply an academic matter, but strikes deeply at people's emotional feelings about their sexual and social identity. Although inclusive language is sometimes decried as trivial, the depths of emotion stirred by this question suggests that the implications are complex and far-reaching.

Part of the anxiety comes simply from the sense of being deprived of familiar language, which has acquired great emotional resonance through usage in prayer and worship. For many, the word itself is the bearer of the realty to which it points. To have the words _father_ and _lord_ vanish from public worship to be replaced by _father and mother_ and _sovereign_ is experienced as a literal loss of the familiar divine presence for an alien divinity. For some, underlying this sense of the loss of familiar language is a deeper association of male generic language with the social and cosmic order and a fear that all right order is upset if male and female stand on the same plane socially and as metaphors for the divine. Thus, the question of inclusive language points to profound connections between language and the experience of reality, which have only begun to be explored.

Relevant titles include: _An Inclusive Language Lectionary: Readings for Year A,_ 1983; _Readings for Year B,_ 1984; Barbara A. Withers, ed., _Language and the Church,_ 1984.

Rosemary R. Ruether[13]

168 • THE NATURE OF INCLUSIVE LANGUAGE

For too long, speakers and writers have ignored how their language betrays a negative judgment against large segments of society, whether women, minorities, or the disabled. The following article defines inclusive language and suggests what issues the church must address in pursuing a just use of language in worship.

The term _inclusive language_ refers to words intentionally selected to redress the bias inherent in centuries-long use of language employed by the dominant culture. It refers to words, therefore, which remove women from the invisibility and inferiority imposed upon them by such terms as _mankind, brotherhood of man, the weaker sex,_ etc. It refers to the conscious substitutions of positive phrases in referring to people of color instead of vilifying expressions like _blackmail,_ *blackball, blackguard,* etc. And it refers to deliberately chosen words, which refer to those who suffer patently observable impairments, calling these people, *mute,* for instance, instead of *dumb,* or *differently abled* instead of *disabled* or *handicapped.*

Inclusive language emphasizes clarity and honesty. It proceeds from an overriding value judgment that one race or gender is not superior to another or that one is not less human for being sense-impaired. Inclusive language identifies the positive and equally important contributions of many different peoples and experiences. Inclusive language pertains to verbal and nonverbal images that describe both humankind and God.

Human or "Horizontal" Language. Discriminatory descriptions of women provide the most common illustrations of the need for inclusive language. Women are categorized as inferior to men. Such sexist or exclusive language evolved from the socio-cultural bias against women, where the nouns *man, men,* and *brothers* and the pronoun *he* refer to both women and men. This androcentric language clearly conveys that male is the norm and female is a subspecies of male. Inclusive language corrects this misconception through both gender-specific language and emancipatory language, i.e., words and images that acknowledge the distinctive contribution women make to the fullness of the human experience. In addition to concerns about gender, inclusive language is sensitive to all examples of implicit bias in language: race superiority (white is purer than black); physical ability (*rectitude* as a word describing right and *sinister* the left; sheep on the right, goats on the left); and a host of others.

History. A cursory glance at significant moments in linguistic history makes clear that the choice of male pronouns and nouns used generically was based on the patriarchal view of the ordering of society. As early as 1560, there is evidence that grammar was determined by the "natural" order, i.e., man precedes woman. By 1850, an Act of Parliament in England eliminated the use of *he or she* when referring to human beings, substituting *he* alone.

Since the beginning of the twentieth century, questions have been raised about androcentric words used generically for all humankind. The most serious challenges have occurred since 1960 in conjunction with the civil rights and women's movements. Linguistic scholars suggest that "true generics" implies equal application. This mutuality does not exist with words such as *man, brothers,* and *men* because no one understands *woman* to imply man, *sisters* to include brothers, nor *women,* men. Instead, the use of such language renders women invisible and implies inferiority. Inclusive language offers one of many necessary correctives for this situation.

Theological or "Vertical" Language. The patriarchal context that influenced "horizontal" language impacted the development of theological language as well. The primacy of male language for God also was fully acceptable. Recent linguistic and theological thinking raises serious questions about the "normative" character of male imagery for God. It offers fresh interpretations of biblical texts and theological positions long used to undergird traditional arguments for the sole use of male metaphors for God, predominantly Father, though also King, Lord, Master, and Prince. Male language limits the revelation of God and promotes idolatry (the worship of any image of God as though it were God).

Theologians throughout history understand their task as one of relating the nature of God to contemporary experience. Christological doctrines and Trinitarian formulas have emerged from such study and debate. In the ongoing explanation of these aspects of human/divine relationship questions appear. One such critique concerns the use of exclusively male metaphors for God. These metaphors inherently communicate that God is like a man (especially like a *father*), and that men are like God. Such implications undermine the power of women to be images of God, as well as to mediate God's grace.

Implications for Sacramental Practice. Invitations of God embodied in the process of preparation for and performance of the sacraments involve an offer of freedom, of access to inexhaustible divine mystery, and of a relationship of unimaginable love. This articulation requires utmost sensitivity and honesty. Language restrictions, which suggest some human participants in this sacramental encounter are more significant than others or that God's image is more concretely known through male metaphors rather than female ones, limit the fullness of the sacramental encounter. Examples span a spectrum from hymns, prayers, gestures, and models of leadership that do not express an integrated human community to "essential" theological formulas that use only male metaphors such as Father, Son, and Holy Spirit. (Though some suggest that the Holy Spirit has female referents, pronouns do not ordinarily confirm any such tradition.)

Concerns about inclusive language provide a serious critique of sacramental practice. They challenge the church to examine the theology and ecclesiology embodied in the celebration of sacramental liturgies, so that the significance of these moments reflects more honestly the fullness of the divine/human relationship.

Janet Walton[14]

169 ✦ Issues in Developing Inclusive Language for Worship

As the previous article suggests, the language the church uses in worship communicates important attitudes about the status of women in the church. Yet reforming the liturgical language of the church is no easy task. Reforms can easily be either insufficient because they retain an unjust use of language or too radical because they sacrifice valuable texts from the church's history and weaken the theological basis of the church's worship. The following article presents one strategy for reforming the church's language in a balanced way.

One of the most controversial issues in worship today is language. Many women and men in Christian churches are calling for inclusive language in hymns and worship resources, yet they may differ as to what defines "inclusive." Still others would prefer that language remain as originally written and that respect for the original text of a litany, a hymn, or Scripture be honored. Most people recognize that language is in continuous flux. The question is how to hear the desires of persons of varying viewpoints, as well as to answer the broad spectrum of needs for justice and equality.

Language has the power to shape our world and change our churches. It affects our thinking about one another, as well as our respect for each other. Hymnal committees find themselves spending many painstaking hours searching for ways to be responsible to biblical accounts and theological tenets, to historical integrity, to congregations, and to a vision of a world in which women and men are equal in the sight of God.

There is no one answer to the dilemma of inclusivity of language, for interpretation of the very word _inclusivity_ comes from many voices. Does inclusivity include the personhood of God as well as humanity? Is inclusivity achieved when metaphors and images are deleted, rather than expanded, especially when speaking of God? How do we as Christians respect the biblical words that refer to God and Jesus while, at the same time, break down hierarchical structures?

Consider the following issues:

(1) If radical change is made in historical texts, an important sense of history is lost. Therefore, traditional hymns and prayers of the Christian church may need to remain in their original form.

(2) Memory of an personal association with hymns contributes to the richness and integrity of worship. Therefore, we are called to respect the memory banks of sisters and brothers, even when the words of that memory may bring uncomfortable images to other brothers and sisters or to us.

(3) New hymn texts and litanies need to express our world today and our part in modeling the equality of persons, whatever their race, culture, or sex. Therefore, we include in worship "texts which enlarge and deepen our faith through their poetic expression in late twentieth-century terms" ("Statement of Policy on Language for the Hymnal Project," of the Church of the Brethren, the General Conference Mennonite Church, and the Mennonite Church in North America, October 29, 1987).

(4) No one biblical translation is solely God's voice. The "original" Bible is one which does not exist in today's worship, for it was written in Hebrew, Aramaic, and Greek. Therefore, the use of Bible readings from an inclusive language lectionary help to increase our understandings of biblical truth and are often closer to the original intent and meaning of the Bible.

Some of us struggle greatly with language that is not changed or made contemporary, while some of us struggle greatly with language that _is_ changed. Change might best happen when we respect the old while at the same time introduce the new, for newness is more possible when we approach it out of security.

Language is fluid, always undergoing change. The expression of our human nature and God's divine nature is best achieved when we increase our understanding of each other and our understanding of who God is. We need to do this by working at a multiplicity of images to describe men and women, as well as to describe God who embraces not only all that is male and female, but more. There is comfort in warm, parental images of God. To take out the male and female characteristics of God often has resulted in the depersonalization of God. Therefore, our concept of God must not erase the masculine entirely, but go beyond exclusively the masculine to include the feminine.

As we approach the twenty-first century, we are called to enlarge and deepen our faith through images and terms that give honest and creative expression to the Word and age in which we live. The language of our worship will hold us accountable to each other and to God.

Nancy Rosenberger Faus

170 ✦ Bibliography on Women in Worship

———— Biblical Lectionaries ————

An Inclusive-Language Lectionary. rev. ed. 4 vols. Atlanta: John Knox Press, 1986. This lectionary uses the cycle of readings derived from the "Consultation on Common Texts," an ecumenical group created by ICEI. This cycle was first approved in 1982 and proposed for use in 1983. The Bible version basically used in this lectionary is the Revised Standard Version, as emended to avoid exclusive language in words about human beings.

Ramshaw Schmidt, Gail, and Gordon Lathrop, eds. *Lectionary for the Christian People.* 3 vols. New York: Pueblo Publishing Co., 1986. This lectionary includes the readings assigned in the Roman Catholic, Lutheran, and Episcopal lectionaries. The Revised Standard Version text, emended, is used. This version tries to avoid some of the more radical changes made in the National Council of Churches' *Inclusive Language Lectionary.*

———— Books on Inclusive Language ————

Bloesch, Donald. *The Battle for the Trinity: The Debate Over Inclusive God-Language.* Ann Arbor, Michigan: Vine Books, Servant Publications, 1985. An evangelical theologian critiques many of the changes in language for worship and theology that have arisen out of feminist theology.

Clark, Linda, Marian Ronan, and Eleanor Walker. *Image Breaking, Image Building.* New York: Pilgrim Press, 1981. An examination of the role of the imagination in worship and the importance of encouraging feminine metaphors in worship, together with sample liturgical texts.

Criteria for the Evaluation of Inclusive Language Translations of Scriptural Texts Proposed for Liturgical Use. Washington, D. C.: United States Catholic Conference, 1991.

Duck, Ruth. *Gender and the Name of God: The Trinitarian Baptismal Formula.* New York: Pilgrim Press, 1991. A theological argument for broadening the range of images used to speak of God in Christian baptism in particular, with implications for Christian liturgy in general.

Emswiler, Sharon Neufer, and Thomas Neufer Emswiler. *Women and Worship.* San Francisco: Harper and Row, 1984. A guide to critiquing and developing nonsexist resources for worship, including hymns, prayers, and liturgies. Includes many sample texts.

Hardesty, Nancy A. *Inclusive Language in the Church.* Atlanta: John Knox Press, 1987. A practical guide that helps readers understand why exclusive language is a problem for Christians—and how to overcome this problem in language referring to God, to the community, and to the relationship between them. Concludes with a useful bibliography of "References" and "Resources" (103–109).

Henderson, J. Frank. "ICEL and Inclusive Language." In *Shaping English Liturgy,* ed. Peter Finn and James M. Schellman. Washington D.C.: Pastoral Press, 1990, 257–278. A comprehensive history and assessment of ICEL's ongoing efforts to respond to the call for inclusive language in English liturgical texts.

Plaskow, Judith. *Standing Again at Sinai: Judaism from a Feminist Perspective.* San Francisco: Harper and Row, 1990. A reevaluation of women's history and experience in the Jewish tradition. Combines a critique of patriarchalism with provocative new understandings of God,

Torah, the meaning of community, and the value of sexuality.

Russell, Letty M., ed. _Feminist Interpretation of the Bible_. Philadelphia: Westminster Press, 1985. A collection of essays that deal with a variety of issues: feminist consciousness; interpretation of familial biblical stories; and the formation of feminist critical principles.

Schneiders, Sandra M. _Women and the Word: The Gender of God in the New Testament and the Spirituality of Women_. 1986 Madeleva Lecture in Spirituality. New York: Paulist Press, 1986. A lucid and scholarly effort to find a creative, liberating vision of God and of Jesus—one that does not glorify masculinity at the expense of femininity and does not seek to justify the oppression of women by men.

Watkins, Keith. _Faith and Fair: Transcending Sexist Language in Worship_. Nashville: Abingdon Press, 1981. A practical, pastorally sensitive discussion of the need for a change in liturgical language, of the way to help congregations make such changes, and of the motives for making these changes. Concludes with a "Workbook for the Lord's Day Service" that provides examples and explanations of prayers in inclusive language.

Wren, Brian. _What Language Shall I Borrow? God-Talk in Worship: A Male Response to Feminist Theology_. New York: Crossroad, 1990. A discussion of the nature of language used in worship for God that argues for including feminine metaphors for God in hymns and prayers. Includes sample liturgical texts.

Psalters That Use Inclusive Language

Boersig, Teresa. _Companion to the Breviary: A Four-Week Psalter Featuring All-Inclusive Language_. (To order: PSALTER, 2500 Cold Spring Road, Indianapolis, IN 46222). A liturgical version of an inclusive language Psalter, arranged according to daily prayers times (Morning, Daytime, and Evening) over a four-week period, including antiphons, responsories, and prayers.

Chamberlain, Gary. _The Psalms: A New Translation for Prayer and Worship_. Nashville: Upper Room, 1984.

ICEL Liturgical Psalter Project. _Psalms for All Seasons_. Washington, D.C.: NPM, 1987. (Available from: Pastoral Press, 225 Sheridan St., N.W.,

Washington, D.C. 20011-1492; 202-723-5800; Fax: 202-723-2262). Provides _musical settings_ and inclusive language translations for many of the Psalms.

The Psalms. Chicago: GIA Publications, 1986. A revision of the well-known Grail Psalter, using inclusive language.

Schreck, Nancy, OSF, and Maureen Leach, OSF. _Psalms Anew: In Inclusive Language_. Winona, Minn.: Saint Mary's Press/Christian Brothers Publications, 1986. A _complete_ Psalter (text only, no music) in nonsexist language.

Liturgies and Other Worship Resources

Duck, Ruth. _Bread for the Journey_. New York: Pilgrim Press, 1981; _Flames of the Spirit_. New York: Pilgrim Press, 1985; and _Touch Holiness_. New York: Pilgrim Press, 1990. A variety of worship resources, written with special care for inclusive language.

Gjerding, Iben, and Katherine Kinnamon. _Women's Prayer Services_. Mystic, Conn.: Twenty-Third Publications, 1987. A variety of resources for worship, including calls to worship, litanies, and prayers.

I Will Pour Out My Spirit. Geneva: WCC Publications, 1988. A liturgy for celebrating the gifts of women to the church printed in four languages.

Morley, Janet. _All Desires Known_. Wilton, Conn.: Morehouse-Barlow Co., 1988. A variety of liturgical resources written from a feminist perspective, including lectionary collects and eucharistic prayers.

Morley, Janet, and Hannah Ward. _Celebrating Women_. Reprinted from _Women in Theology_. Wilton, Conn.: Morehouse-Barlow Co., 1988. An anthology of poems and prayers, many of which are appropriate for use in worship.

Winter, Miriam Therese. _Woman Prayer, Woman Song: Resources for Ritual_. Oak Park, Ill.: Meyer Stone Books, 1987.

———. _WomanWisdom: A Feminist Lectionary and Psalter: Women of the Hebrew Scriptures. Part I_. New York: Crossroad, 1991.

———. _WomanWitness: A Feminist Lectionary and Psalter: Women of the Hebrew Scriptures. Part II_. New York: Crossroad, 1992.

———. _WomanWord: A Feminist Lectionary and Psalter: Women of the New Testament_. New York: Crossroad, 1990.

❧ FOUR ❧

Handicapped Persons in the Worshiping Community

Though not intentionally, worship planners often fail to consider the needs of the disabled, hearing-impaired, and other physically challenged adults. This chapter attempts to redress this situation by presenting several thoughtful articles that consider disabilities in a scriptural light.

171 ◆ THEOLOGY OF MINISTRY TO PEOPLE WITH DISABILITIES

People with developmental disabilities are typically devalued by society. The Christian church, however, needs not only to reflect on what it means to be created in the image of God in relation to ministries and the developmentally disabled. In addition, it also needs to reflect on the meaning and implications of what it professes in its liturgy. For example, how does becoming part of Christ's body through baptism relate to ministries and the developmentally disabled? The following article will explain the theology of and the implications of liturgy to the church's ministries and the developmentally disabled.

To be developmentally disabled in the United States is to be marginalized and devalued. The more serious and numerous the disabilities are, the more extreme the marginalization and devaluation. Current legal and social policies notwithstanding, there is much pressure to merely warehouse persons with developmental disabilities. We as the authors make these claims categorically, but not without cause. We have worked with such persons in residential settings. And we know how easy it is to forget them. They are always last in line for all things, save one. When it comes to budget cuts, they lead the parade. "They" are the severely and profoundly disabled. They have mental retardation plus cerebral palsy; plus hearing, vision, and speech defects; and plus numerous other disabilities.

Here we shall refer to them as *persons with developmental disabilities,* an awkward term, but one that avoids most of the negative pitfalls of other labels.

Both of us operate from an unabashed Christian worldview. We invite non-Christian readers to accept our writing as a stimulus to their own thinking, knowing that we cannot possibly know how to assess the issues from the viewpoint of another faith. The questions raised here, however, are universal.

Most work that discusses the theology and ethics of ministry with persons with developmental disabilities begins with some type of discourse on what it means to be a human being. What does it mean that all of humanity is created in the image of God? Our consideration of the problem proceeds from this question. However, it is important to understand that this is only a beginning point. We as Christians need to be able to move from this type of discussion to realize that, in the church, we are called to evaluate who we are in relationship to those who are devalued by their mental disabilities.

This call can be explored through the liturgy of the church, as an ethical statement of our faith and Christian lives. In other words, while the basic premise that all human beings are created in God's image is an extremely important issue and must be discussed, the place where we as Christians must operate is from within liturgy, the "work of the people." How do we carry the symbols of

Christ and his church into the world? How do we live those ethical acts that we claim within the liturgy of our church?

What do we really claim, mean, and understand when we gather as God's people? What do we say, mean, and believe when we talk about baptism, the Holy Eucharist, confession, proclamation, intercession, and offering? These are the questions that must be asked and discussed if we are to understand the moral dilemma presented by Christian ministry and the mentally disabled.

Reflecting on Christian Beliefs

Focusing our attention on the religious needs of persons with developmental disabilities requires that we reexamine some of the beliefs we might have taken for granted. The general public, including deeply religious people within the Christian community, usually gets away with believing it has done everything possible for persons with serious disabilities when it has provided them with food, clothing, and shelter. Advances made in recent decades indicate how inadequate that belief really is. We will better serve persons with developmental disabilities, those who are devalued, and our Creator if we take time to reflect on those beliefs which underpin our actions. Let us look at four areas of concern: (1) our beliefs about human beings; (2) the meaning of serving others; (3) the nature of religious bodies; and (4) the peculiar nature of our own faith communities.

First, what do we really believe concerning *the nature of humankind.* One of the cornerstones of the Judeo-Christian tradition is the belief that humankind is created in the image of God. But to believe that every human being is God's image is to fly in the face of some powerful beliefs of the modern age. For we are told over and over again by powerful agents of belief, notably the entertainment media, that those who are beautiful are the most favored of all people. Another message, sometimes promoted by persons recognized by many as Christian leaders, is that we know we are blessed of God when we are successful. Beauty and success are modern marks of God's favor!

What are we saying about God, and about ourselves, when we define the pretty and the successful as God's chosen few? Certainly, those of us whose lives are lived in relationship with persons with disability have no excuse for succumbing to the heresy. We do have great reason to protest against

forces that seek to further alienate persons, who struggle on the margins of acceptance by others every moment of their lives.

Second, what we believe about *service as part of our calling* is equally as revealing as what we believe about humankind. One of the great weaknesses of the worldwide missionary efforts of evangelical Christians in the nineteenth and twentieth centuries was the seductive way, in which congregations could ease their collective conscience by sending money and personnel to the far reaches of the world, while they ignored the needs of alienated persons nearer their homes.

The same phenomenon occurs in disability ministries. A congregation can easily delegate a small group to assume responsibility for a disability ministry, while most of the congregation does not even know such a ministry exists. It is much more difficult for the entire congregation to become actively involved in service to persons with disabilities. Yet, at the heart of the Christian experience is the command to care for those who cannot care for themselves.

Personal involvement is at the heart of the issue. What is our mission to persons, who are at a disadvantage in the world? When is that mission best accomplished by mutual activity? When should someone else do it? And when must I personally become the servant of those in need? Even in the midst of a servant ministry, the needs, the options, and the commitments are vague. This alone calls us to stop and examine our own sense of service and mission to others.

Third, it is helpful to reexamine what we think about the *institutional church*. If we believe that the church is irrelevant, weak, or outdated, then we will have no difficulty allowing the needy in our midst to be cared for through government programs. If on the other hand, we believe the church is the living extension of God in the world, offering hope and comfort to those who need it, then we will become the instruments of that hope and comfort to those who need it, for in doing so our hands become the instruments of God's love for all persons.

Fourth and finally, we must consider our *belief*. There is a desperate need for ministry to persons with developmental disabilities which grows out of a centered faith. We need to know both what we believe as individuals and as congregations affiliated with a given religious body. There is a relationship between learning more and more about our own religious roots and the ability to minister with persons who are different from us. The more clearly we understand the differences, the sooner we can get on with the mutual ministry we, the Christian community, must claim as ours.

On Being Human

What does it mean to be "created in the image of God"? We must approach this issue with caution and care. We need to heed the words of Stanley Hauerwas.

> I think we should feel more the oddness of trying to determine this or that as the criterion that makes us human. The conditions of being human form a far too complex pattern to ever be reduced to something like criteria. Too quick appeals to the mystery of being human can be but excuses for cloudy and sloppy thinking that attempts to evade some of the hard issues we are confronting, but they may also be profound responses to the human sense that ultimately we are not our own creators. To be human is to be open to the call of what we are not, and there is therefore no chance that our humanity will be enhanced by excluding from our ranks those who do not understand as we. We must therefore approach the attempt to develop criteria of the human with the humility that recognizes that we would be less than human if we did not recognize that there are limits to what can be brought under our control. (Stanley Hauerwas, _Truthfulness and Tragedy_ [Notre Dame: University of Notre Dame Press, 1977], 162–63.)

It comes as no shock to some of us that whole classes of people were treated as nonpersons in the past. Women, children, slaves, and peasants have been treated as chattel. We do not have to go back very far into North American history to find Africans and Native Americans being treated as less than human. Yet, we profess that all are created in the image of God.

Creation in the image of God does not merely refer to the possession of special human faculties, such as the mind, the emotions, or the will, though these are essential to humanity's being. To be created in the image of God does not refer to the possession of the special characteristics of humans, though these are part of human life. To be created in the image of God means that hu-

mans have the possibility of relating to God and to other human beings as persons. The Creation account first of all states, "God created human beings in God's own image, in the image of God, God created them"(Gen. 1:27-28). The account then spells out what it means to be created in the image of God and what it means to be fully human. David Schroeder has written:

> To be fully human is to receive affirmation from others. It is important for us as humans to be accepted as persons, to receive love and acceptance from others, to receive from others feeling of worth. Not to receive this is both physically and emotionally damaging. Without this acceptance none of us functions properly; without it we feel assaulted, rejected and diminished in worth or esteem. (Alfred H. Neufeldt, ed., _Celebrating Differences_ [Newton, Kans.: Faith and Life Press, 1984], 2.)

One of the church's difficulties with ministering to persons with developmental disabilities and their families relates to the creation and the image of God, and also with the creation's image of God. In other words, we as Christians create preconceived notions of what God is and what God looks like before giving it any serious thought. In this dilemma, one of the points of liberation theology needs to be heard by the church. Frederick Herzog writes:

> This peculiar thing about Messiah Jesus is that for the church the new thought about God did not emerge via pure thought. In Messiah Jesus, God acted out of a way of being God unheard of before. (Frederick Herzog, _Justice Church_ [New York: Orbis Books, 1981], 3.)

This quote reminds us that we need to be careful, for, as it was in the person of Christ Incarnate, God may be different than what we often expect. Christ is the one who taught us that if we walk with the poor, the hungry, the lame, the downtrodden, the outcast, and the developmentally disabled, we walk with him. These people are the images of Christ; these people are the images of God.

The Liturgy for and Ministry to the Mentally Disabled: Greeting and Gathering

The most basis question we can ask at this point is why does the Christian community gather. Why is it that the Christian community comes together and what does it propose to do? It seems obvious that the Christian community comes together to worship God. However, it is also true that Christians gather in order that they give some evidence of who they are. Therefore, Christians gather so that they may know who they are. This is why the liturgy is so important to Christian ethics. Stanley Hauerwas writes the following:

> Christian ethics involves the extraordinary claim that by learning to be faithful to the way of life inaugurated by Jesus of Nazareth we have, in fact, become part of the shared history that God intends for his whole creation. [W]e as Christians have been given the means to recognize ourselves for what we are—historic beings who must begin our ethical reflection in the midst of history. For Christian ethics begins in a community that carries the story of the God who wills us to participate in a kingdom established in and through Jesus of Nazareth. No matter where it begins theologically, if it tries to do more or less than remind us of the significance of that story it has lost its way. (Stanley Hauerwas, *Peaceable Kingdom* [Notre Dame: University of Notre Dame Press, 1983], 61–62.)

Because Christian ethics begins in a community that has a common story, we as Christians should be able to observe ourselves when we gather as a church community. In doing this, it becomes important to be able to identify who we are. This process should not be a new concept in the ethical manner in which we relate to others. An example of this step in the ethical process can be seen in Moses facing God at the burning bush. God makes himself known by saying, "I am who I am," and thereby promising the presence of God. In much the same way we, as the church, need to pay attention to the need to let others see us as who we are. We are a particular people because we are called to be imitators of Christ. This concept applies directly to the issue of the church and the developmentally disabled. If we identify ourselves as Christians and invite others to be a part of the body of Christ, we can not exclude anyone, especially devalued persons.

Historically, those people who have gathered around Christ were a diverse people. These people included the healthy and the lame, the rich and the poor, and tax collectors and publicans. All gathered together to see and hear the Christ.

This fact is difficult for a homogeneous church to see. This fact significantly addresses the issue of the church's ministry to the developmentally disabled population. Because we as Christians have no direct experience of gathering with those with disabilities, we think they must not exist. The familiar phrase, "out of sight, out of mind," applies here. Because of the exclusion of the disabled within the institutional church, we must intentionally be inclusive when we gather as Christ's body. Ministry to the developmentally disabled cannot take place without it being intentional. Therefore, when we gather together as worshipers in Christ Jesus, let us gather because of our differences, rather than in spite of them. Let the church gather and bid others who are "different" to come and be a part of Christ's body.

Confession

From time to time, we need to address the place of confession in the Christian church, particularly as it relates to ministries to the disabled. Confession qualifies the moral life because when we prepare to confess our sin, we first must discover what sin is. We cannot confess our sins if we do not know them. Sins are identifiable and particular. We confess our sin so that we may be reconciled to God and to our brothers and sisters in Christ. We must understand confession as a redemptive act, as an act that reminds us of the broken state that exists in the community.

David Steinmetz, in his book *Memory and Mission,* gives a clear example of confession as a redemptive act:

> The saying of Jesus that the whole has no need of a physician is a saying that the Church has always had great difficulty in assimilating. It seems so much more reasonable to believe that God will be merciful to those people who meet certain prior expectations: the right ideology, the right sex or race, the right degree of devotion to the cause currently supported by the right elements in society. "But when we were right," Luther observed in one of his earliest writings, "God laughed at us in our rightness." God's quarrel is with the whole human race and not merely with certain factions in it. Judgment falls not only on the theologically heterodox but also on the theologically pure. The one absolutely indispensable precondition for the reception of grace is not to be right—not even in the sense of theological orthodoxy—but to be sick. The gospel is for real

sinners. God promises to give God's grace to "real sinners." Real sinners are people who are not merely sinners in fact (everyone, after all, is a sinner in that sense), but who confess that they are sinners. "Real sinners" conform their judgment of themselves to the judgment of God over them and by doing so justify God in God's Word of judgment and grace. Paradoxically, it is the "real sinner" who is justified by God and who knows both theoretically and experientially what repentance offers and demands. (David C. Steinmetz, _Memory and Mission_ [Nashville: Abingdon Press, 1988], 39–40.

It is difficult to ignore this type of reasoning when considering the problems that surround the Christian community's lack of intentionality in disability ministries. The church needs to realize the prejudicial nature of the exclusion that exists within its body. Only when the church can realize and confess its prejudice against devalued persons, can it become a healthy community. Stanley Hauerwas and Bonita Raine point out a good example of this type of realization and confession:

The [Catholic] bishops candidly acknowledge that the church's ministry to handicapped people has been sporadic and too often only at the urging of public opinion or circumstances, presumably from outside the church. Such an admission follows the bishops' reflections on the nature of prejudice and its relationship to perceptions of difference. It is not coincidental, we believe, that this observation about the church's activity is likened to the notion that we tend all to often to think of them as somehow apart—not fully "one of us." Our concerns about the nature of community, especially ecclesial community, are also addressed by the bishops. While they affirm Christians' obligations to seek with handicapped people justice in a wider society, the bishops suggest what it is the church should be if it is to.retain fidelity to the task to which Christ called it. They suggest that the notion of interdependence is critical and that openness to discovery in diversity or difference is vital. Such a community, they say, will actively work to make modern society. The bishops are nowhere more eloquent, however, than when they describe the warm acceptance with which handicapped people should be gratefully welcomed in the ecclesial community wherein we can all benefit from their spiritual gifts and the self-realization they share with the rest of us in the Christian community, namely, that "we all live in the shadow of the cross." That

shadow reminds us that we are all "marginal" people, and hence our need for mutual integration. (Stanley Hauerwas, _Suffering Presence_ [Notre Dame: University of Notre Dame Press, 1981] 187.)

Until this type of confession can be made, the broken nature of God's church cannot be healed through reconciliation and the sharing of the peace. In confession, the church and the people of the church can experience redemption from its own prejudicial practices.

Offering

The relationship between worship, liturgy, and ethics is a relationship in which we as worshipers share our lives through our worship in the liturgy. When the community of faith teaches us what Christ has offered to us, as well as how it was offered, offering in the liturgy qualifies the moral life. First and foremost, we need to understand this type of offering as one of sacrificial giving. We are called not only to give, but to give ourselves sacrificially. Paul states, "We are to offer ourselves as living sacrifices." We know how we are to give because we are able to see in the Scriptures that Christ loved the world so much that he gave himself as a living sacrifice for us, "the unlovable" ones. In considering offering as sacrificial giving of ourselves and of the community of faith, Dietrich Bonhoeffer makes a clear statement of the nature of this sacrificial giving:

Cheap grace is the preaching of forgiveness without requiring repentance, baptism without church discipline, communion without confession, absolution without personal confession. Cheap grace is grace without discipleship, grace without the cross, grace without Jesus Christ, living and incarnate. Costly grace is the treasure hidden in the field; for the sake of it a person will gladly go and sell all. It is the pearl of great price to buy which the merchant will sell all his goods. It is the kingly rule of Christ, for whose sake a man will pluck out the eye which causes him to stumble. It is the call of Jesus Christ at which the disciple leaves his nets and follows him. Costly grace is the gospel which must be sought again and again, the gift which must be asked for, the door at which a man must knock. Such grace is costly because it calls us to follow, and it is grace because it calls us to follow Jesus Christ. It is costly because it costs a man his life, and it is grace because it gives a man the only true life. It is costly because it condemns sin, and grace because it justifies the sinner. Above all, it is costly because it cost God the life of his Son: "Ye were bought at a price," and what has cost God much cannot be cheap for us. Above all, it is grace because God did not reckon his Son too dear a price to pay for our life, but delivered him up for us. Costly grace is the incarnation of God. (Dietrich Bonhoeffer, *The Cost of Discipleship* [New York: Macmillan, 1961], 47–48.)

This costly grace is the grace that calls us to submit to the yoke of Jesus Christ and follow him. This is what it means to offer something to God and our brothers and sisters in the world who are broken and devalued by most of our society. This is the type of offering of ourselves we are called to when we consider the church's ministry and persons with developmental disabilities. When Christ calls us, he bids us, "come and die."

Ministry and persons with disabilities can be understood, at least partially, in how we offer ourselves to others whom we consider "different" in our society and the church. This means that the church should teach its people to submit to the yoke that Christ has called them to, the servant ministry, and to offer themselves as living sacrifices to those who suffer from the church's own oppression. We can not merely say that Jesus Christ offered himself for each of us personally, but we also need to realize that Christ offered himself for all of God's people. Because of Christ's offering, how much more should we be willing to offer ourselves as a sacrifice in ministry and care to those whom we consider different than ourselves, persons with disabilities.

When we, the church, are able to accomplish this type of sacrificial giving of ourselves, we will then learn how to enter the difficult ministry of embracing suffering as we take up our crosses. John Westerhoff shows the meaning of embracing this type of suffering through a story a mother told him of sending her young son to the store. When her son didn't return as soon as she had anticipated, she ran out to look for him and found him skipping up the street singing! "Where have you been," she asked. "Well," he began, "Susie dropped her doll and it broke." His mother interrupted, "And you had to stay and help her pick it up." "No, mommy," he explained, "I had to stay and help her cry." This example illustrates how

we should offer ourselves in our ministry to the mentally disabled: we should suffer with them.

Scripture and Proclamation

In most of American Christian denominations, the reading of Scripture and preaching is central in most worship services. We need not to neglect the developmentally disabled when sharing this part of our liturgy. We often think that there may be too much of a gap between "us" and "them" in comprehension of the Word. In other words, we feel that preaching and Scripture cannot be understood in ways that many "normal" people might. So why should we spend the time to preach?

We should preach to persons who are developmentally disabled for any reason that we might preach to any other part of our congregations. First of all, we preach to tell the story of a community of faith and the history of that faith. But, we also proclaim the Scriptures to help shape and form the community of faith, so that as we hear the Word we are moved toward being new and renewed creatures in Christ's body.

Our concern should not always be that the proclamation of Scripture is understood, but we should also be concerned that the Word in some way shapes and forms the community as a whole. When this happens, a new bond will hopefully enable the community to live the Christian story in a covenant, or in our case, a new covenant relationship.

It is not enough that we concern ourselves with finding ways to minister *to* the persons with developmental disabilities. Our task is to learn how to share ministry *with* such persons who live and worship among us.

Baptism and the Eucharist

Finally, this discussion of the liturgy as an ethical norm of the church cannot conclude without emphasizing that baptism and the Eucharist are the most significant moral activities of Christians. The reasons for the significance of these acts are first of all grounded in the fact that Christ in the Scriptures commanded both of these acts. Second, baptism and the Eucharist are primary to Christian ethics because both acts member or remember the community of faith. Our baptism tells us who we are as individuals, but more importantly, who we are as a community of faith. Baptism states who we are as a particular people; and because of this, we are called to live within a moral community. Baptism and the Eucharist are efficacious because they are both a representation of what Christ does to us and for us. We do very little, if anything, to accomplish these moral acts. Will Willimon indicates this quite clearly:

> In contrast to the human-centered, human-conditioned, Enlightenment view of the sacraments, Christian theology has traditionally asserted that God is the actor, and we are the recipients of what God does through the sacraments. The efficacy of the sacraments does not entirely depend upon us, upon our ability to love God or to lead holy lives. In his infinite love, God has not left us alone. God continually, graciously, gives himself to us and makes himself available to us through touched, tasted, experienced, visible means. This God does (thank God) in spite of our best intentions. We do not have to (nor, in the final analysis, can we) make it happen. If we be loved and if we be healed and if we be saved, it is first and forever because of God's own active, self-giving, initiating love. As Calvin said, "He condescends to lead us to himself by these earthly elements, and to set before us in the flesh a mirror of spiritual blessings he imparts spiritual things under visible ones." (William Willimon, _Worship as Pastoral Care_ [Nashville: Abingdon Press, 1979], 150–51.)

Through baptism, we can come to know who we are because the church, as a moral community, can share its history of Christ with the catechumen. This is how we learn who we are as Christians. Baptism as well as the Eucharist brings us into the recognition of the truths of ourselves, of our sins, and the truths of Christ, in a way that we cannot know by any other means. The Eucharist is also primarily a moral act because we are remembered and reconstituted to Christ in such a way that we can know who he really is. This occurs because he has promised, in a covenant relationship, to be present in this moral act; and he has given us the physical signs in order that we can recognize him as who he is, the Christ. This eucharistic promise is the promise that he will be with us.

Therefore, baptism and the Eucharist have everything to do with the way we think positively or negatively about our ministry and worship with the disabled. When we are baptized, we become a particular people. This means that we are brought into a particular moral community that says particular things about the moral life. We are all baptized into one body, the body of Christ. Our Christ died for all people, not for just some. If baptism facilitates our recognition of ourselves as a Christian community, then we must be able to distinguish the difference between living a moral Christian life and excluding "outsiders" from a Christian community that lives a particular ethic within the liturgy. The issue is one of dissonance between what we say about baptism and how we relate to those whom we devalue as handicapped persons. That is to say, if we are really claiming that baptism is a celebration of the identity of the Christian community, then we must learn to fully accept our Christian response to minister to, minister with, and minister on behalf of persons with developmental disabilities. As Willimon writes, "In baptism the church is saying to the candidate: 'You are ours, and we are God's.' . . . we claim you and . . . God will make claims upon you. You are now a part of the body." (Willimon 157). The challenge to the church is that they remember their baptism as a communal event and begin to claim the persons with developmental disabilities as their own, for baptism calls us to this community.

If Christ is present and active in baptism and the Eucharist, then we must also recognize that Christ is present for all in his body and blood for he has certainly promised to be. Therefore, we must all become one though we are many, though we are different, because Christ has reconstituted us all as new beings of one body.

This paper grows out of our experience in working with persons with developmental disabilities. From largely our experience, we have concluded that the communal nature of the Christian faith must shape ministry to persons with developmental disabilities. This is to say, we must be able to look at the liturgy of the church and question what it is about the liturgy that shapes and forms a community of faith. However, we must understand that the liturgy calls us to respond to those things we profess. From this perspective, we realize that the liturgy is the ethical norm which calls us to a daily renewal of Christian life and ministry. We are called to rethink what we have said in the past and move on to the pressing present needs of ministry that meets the needs of the total community. John Westerhoff has written in _On the Threshold of God's Future_:

While the first duty of the church is worship, the primary responsibility of the church is to the world where its people live and work. Unlike other institutions founded for the benefit of their own members, the church is a community founded for the benefit of others. To be Christian is to be baptized and therefore adopted into a community called into life and to bear witness to how God's reign has come, is coming and will come. So everything we receive when we come to take Eucharist is immediately turned into a responsibility to live a eucharistic life. The church is to be a sign of God's forgiving, suffering, reconciling love as represented in this story and a witness to that love in society through the actions and words of its people, whose life stories have been transformed by God's story. The church must never become a place of escape or a sanctuary from the world. The world is God's and is good. It has been corrupted by God's creatures, who in their freedom distort and deny the truth about themselves and God's reign, who obscure the activity of God. Still God loves this world and creatively is acting within it to the end that the divine will is done and the divine reign comes. This same God in the mystery of creation has brought into being a community to be the sign of and witness to the continuing transformation of the world through suffering love. As that called community, we gather to worship God, to place our total dependence upon God and God's ways, to discern God's will, to receive the gift of power, to cooperate in God's saving work, to act with God and thereby illumine and enlighten the world to God's love, and to serve the world by joining God in ministering to its needs—especially those of the weak, estranged, poor, sick, oppressed, and downtrodden. As God has loved the world in Jesus Christ, so we as God's body love the world. To that ministry all of us who have been signed with the cross and marked as Christ's own forever are called and empowered. (John H. Westerhoff and Caroline Hughes, *On the Threshold of God's Future* [San Francisco: Harper and Row, 1986], 82.)

Ingram C. Parmley and Tresco Shannon[16]

172 • PLANNING FOR DISABLED PEOPLE

With at least 35 million people with disabilities in America, a worship committee needs to plan to include these people in worship. This process of including people with disabilities begins by determining whether the church building, including the worship space, is fully accessible. This process also involves attitudinal changes, considerations about worship language and worship leaders, and the commitment of the church to be inclusive. The following articles outlines some steps to take in this process.

Although I have spent the last ten years in a wheelchair, I have traveled extensively. I have discovered that there are two kinds of institutions that are least likely to be accessible to me and others like me who are disabled. These institutions are medical and religious buildings. Medical institutions assume that people are either healthy or sick and thus dependent. Clinics and office buildings for doctors are thus constructed with very little regard for people who cannot negotiate steps or get through narrow doorways. Religious institutions seem to be built upon the assumption that only persons who meet some agreed upon standard of normalcy are appropriately welcomed and included.

In a world that is increasingly open to people with disabilities, these two institutions stand out in contrast. Airlines, on the other hand, are very receptive. On almost any flight, I am in the company of other people with disabilities. Sometimes as many as four or five of us are on one plane. I frequently ask myself, "Where are these people on Sunday morning?" The painful answer is that the church sends out a message to people with disabilities that we really are not very welcome, that we make others uncomfortable, and that our presence may disrupt the orderly routine of the worship service.

Church buildings have generally been designed and built with the aim of directing the attention of those who enter to an exalted sense of the power and magnificence of God. High vaulted ceilings, great stairways at the entrance and at the chancel, and high arches and mammoth doors are all examples of such efforts. Height seems a characteristic way of focusing the attention of the people upon that which is above, beyond, and mysteriously removed from them. Even newly constructed church buildings seem to continue this traditional pattern.

Church buildings might just as well be directed toward the honor of human beings. We, as Christians, center our attention upon a God who became one of us, who is known to us as the

Incarnate Lord. Jesus Christ shared our flesh and, as the image of the invisible God, is the supreme revelation of God. This supreme revelation is of primary importance to us. All our images of God must be seen through this revelation; all ideas of God's majesty and mystery must be understood in the light of Christ.

Human beings are the reason for church buildings. Church buildings should not be grand monuments to God, but places in which the people of God gather to offer their praise, to hear the story of God's work in the world, and to share in the sacred meal which binds them together with the risen Lord. A church building should be constructed in order that it may primarily relate to people. The Incarnation itself is God's revelation in human terms. The central mystery, which we as Christians celebrate is the Christ, who "though he was in the form of God, did not count equality with God a thing to be grasped, but emptied himself, taking the form of a servant, being born in the likeness of men" (Phil. 2:6; RSV).

Therefore, the primary consideration for us, Christians, when planning for worship space is how does it facilitate the gathering of the community of believers? The sense of awe and mystery in the structure is only one of several necessary considerations. The sense of community in the structure and the way in which the space for worship is hospitable for human beings ought to equally considered.

A principle for worship used by the Reformers was that worship should be in the language of the people. That is to say, it is absolutely essential that people be encountered where they are. Language is one vehicle of human communication, but only one. Church buildings, which dwarf people, which make human communication difficult, and which inhibit the participation of people, are not buildings that reflect the Incarnation.

As we consider the human dimension of worship, we must begin to consider how worship space enhances or deters the ability of human beings to function and respond. We need to be primarily concerned with how real people fit in the space, how their needs to see and to hear are met in the space, and how the space makes them feel about themselves. A building, which is frightening or demeaning, which makes people feel small or insignificant, is a denial of the Incarnation. The designers of such a building do not take

seriously the New Testament image of the church as the body of Christ.

Most church buildings are a nightmare for many people. They present barriers to the full participation of many. They force people into a position of being outsiders, who must adjust to space that makes it very difficult for them to enter, to see, or to hear, or even to feel at home. The message proclaimed by such a church building is that the building is for those who are young, strong, agile, healthy, and acceptable; for those who understand some sacred mysteries; for those who are good enough, whole enough, mature enough, and robust enough. Church architecture can be, of itself, a means of excluding people who feel small and insignificant, unworthy and unwanted, unwelcome and unable.

The body of Christ cannot be fully realized when a great many of the people who should be part of that body are excluded; these excluded people include those, who are not strong enough to climb the many steps, who are not tall enough to reach the handle of the heavy doors, who are not agile enough to fit into the pews, and who are not able to hear or see in the great cavern which is the nave. Dim lighting and great distance may enhance a sense of mystery and awe, but at a terrible cost to people whose participation is made very difficult.

A primary question that we must ask ourselves, as we look at the space for worship which we have inherited or which we are about to design, is how it makes possible the full participation of the body, the full and whole body of Christ. How does church architecture enhance or deter the ability of human beings to function? Quite often this seems to have been the very last question asked, if it has been asked at all.

I realize that I approach this subject with a particular bias. I come to worship in my wheelchair. In the church in which I worship with my family, I am required to sit in a side aisle. Sitting in the center aisle would interfere with ushering, with processions, and with those who need to use that center aisle for movement. The design of the church building is such that there are rows of pillars which block my view. I must choose my place carefully on a given Sunday. I can choose to see the pulpit or the Communion Table. I cannot see both at the same time from the same location. Thus, my choice of location for my wheelchair on a given Sunday must be determined by what I anticipate as the primary setting for the action that day. In the chapel of the seminary where I am chaplain, I park my chair in the rear of the nave in the last row of pews so that I can move out of the way quickly when the center aisle is being used by others.

My situation is not unique. The point is that no one in the church seems to think about the position of anyone else. We as Christians seem to act as if the church was truly designed for God and not for us. How else does one explain the absence from public worship of those who, like myself, have physical disabilities, which are more apparent than the rest of the people in attendance? Even those who appear to be without obvious problems are willing to strain their necks, to peer around the heads of those in front of them, to sit in pews that defy the back muscles, to stand on floors that are slippery and dangerous, to sit in a space that is cold and drafty, and to try to hear sounds that are muffled by high ceilings or by acoustics that are terrible, all in the name of the honor of God.

If the Sabbath was made for human beings and not the other way around, then church buildings ought to be designed reflecting that principle. Churches are for the sake of flesh and blood people, who have needs and limitations. They are the people of God and members of the body of Christ, whose presence and full participation are essential for the health of the whole body. Yet we have these buildings. They are not going to go away. We can hope that new churches will be constructed which will not repeat the errors of the past, but what can be done about those which are already with us?

First, I suggest that every worship committee get in touch with people in the community, who represent various kinds of disabilities or limitations. Gather together those with visual impairments, arthritic limbs, paralyzed limbs; those who have difficulty in hearing; those who are small (children are excellent because they generally tell the truth); and those who are intimidated by the church. Have these people enter the space used for worship, and let them tell you how it feels and what the real problems are. If you can establish rapport with them, you may very well be surprised at what information you receive. For the first time, you may come to understand how thoroughly anti-human your church building is and how it keeps away many who wish to seek Christ.

Before you dismiss this idea as an effort to cater to a few cranks who won't come to church anyway, try it yourself. Take a seat on a Sunday morning. Ask yourself how comfortable you feel. Discover how the design of the space enables you to see, to hear, and to participate in the service. How does the space make you feel about yourself? Do you feel important? Do you feel included in what is happening? Are you related to those about you?

On a given Sunday, try to put yourself in the position of a person with a visual impairment. Cover your eyes or simply keep them closed for the duration of the service. How much of what goes on includes you? What good is the bulletin or hymnal? Furthermore, watch children around you. What does worship space do to them? How does it include their needs? Do they seem to feel included in what takes place?

These questions need to be faced and answered by all who have a role in the design of worship space. In most of our churches, the answers to these questions are negative. If we are serious about being an inclusive community, we will need to do more than install a ramp at the entrance to the building or mark one of the parking spaces with the symbol for the disabled. Indeed, these actions are important. They are symbolic of our desire to welcome all people, but they can also be terribly misleading if we stop there. There is nothing quite so discouraging as a church building which holds promise from the outside as fully accessible, but which turns out to be impossible for participation in worship after entering it, or which has met some needs, but which has not provided a toilet that is accessible for people in wheelchairs.

Planning for persons with disabilities needs to be done with full consideration of all persons and all types of limitations and needs. We need to remember that many types of disabilities exist and that many people are disabled because they do not fit the standard of normalcy. They may, for example, be too short for the planned worship space.

In addition, a congregation should take seriously the attitudes which have produced the building in its present shape. Why have we as a congregation been so inconsiderate of the needs of other people? What do we really think a church building is for? If we think that awe and mystery are essential, we may really have to admit that people who do not fit in, who are not "normal," may need to be excluded. We may even discover that we do not want people in our worship who disturb us or make us feel threatened. Our primary values may be such that we cannot really welcome with enthusiasm those who cannot accommodate themselves to our standards and ideals.

It is better to face this fact honestly than to pretend that we are open to all people, when, in fact, we are not. The honest confessions of our limitations and the recognition of our deepest fears are far more healthy, than dishonesty. Order and decorum may really be the primary values in our congregation. If that is so, then to encourage parents of a retarded child to bring that child to church will only be damaging in the long run. I know that I speak for many other people with various kinds of disabilities, when I say that I would rather know that I am unwanted then to have my welcome arise from guilt and take the form of pretending behind the mask of fear and shame. We, who already suffer from our physical problems and scars of life, do not want to be misled.

If we as Christians can determine that we are really open to an inclusive ministry and ready to pay a price for that inclusiveness, then we can begin to change. The most difficult of all barriers to an inclusive congregation are attitudinal. Once attitudes are changed, the path to full participation by all is one of means and methods.

There are many tools to help us proceed in our efforts to make our churches accessible to all people. We can determine, for example, how wide a doorway needs to be to make it possible for a wheelchair to pass through (thirty-two inches). Nearly every denomination has publications which help to outline those steps that need to be taken to ensure the full participation of all.

As a beginning, ask these questions:

(1) How could a person in a wheelchair enter our building?
(2) Is there a place for a wheelchair within the congregation?
(3) Are the rest room doors and stalls wide enough to admit a wheelchair?
(4) Do we have materials in Braille for use by those with a severe visual impairment?
(5) Do we have large print hymnals?

(6) Do we use the services of a signer for the benefit and inclusion of persons with hearing difficulty?
(7) Does our church have hand rails on all stairs?
(8) How safe are the floors for people on crutches?
(9) Do we have drivers who will pick up people unable to drive?
(10) Is there at least one washbasin no more than thirty inches high in the men's and women's rest rooms?

These are a few basic questions. If we can answer them, we have come a very long way toward making our church buildings fully accessible. The range of these questions touches upon many of the barriers, which keep persons with disabilities away from the church. The problem of transportation, for example, is a major barrier to many people, who can neither drive themselves nor ride in public transportation. They do not want to be put in the position of begging for rides, so they are quite likely to remain excluded, alone in their homes. To take the step to provide transportation by enlisting volunteers and then announcing this service so that all may hear is an important move in becoming an inclusive church.

Once the person enters the church, the next major obstacle is likely to be _the usher_. How does the usher welcome and assist the person with an obvious disability? Knowing when to lend an arm and when not to is a learned skill. How friendly is the usher to someone who is having trouble? Sometimes church ushers can seem unfriendly when they may be struggling with themselves and their own fears of being condescending. We need to remember that the usher is the first person met by the newcomer in the church. The usher thus represents the whole congregation.

Materials that can be given to assist the person with a disability may spell the difference between participation and exclusion. A Braille hymnal or a large print hymnal may be the way in which a person with a visual impairment can feel included and also participate in worship. The same is true of hearing devices for those who need assistance in overcoming their hearing impairment.

The _language of worship_ is, itself, a means by which many people may feel excluded from full participation. We are aware today of the power of exclusive language regarding women; and in most churches we are taking steps to respond to the desire of women to be fully included. The same situation exists for people with physical and emotional disabilities. How often, for example, do we use the word *blind* to refer to people who are insensitive, ignorant, or unwilling to perceive the truth? The word *deaf* is also used in the same ways. Some Sunday try to pay attention to the ways in which words describing various kinds of disabilities are used in worship. We may be uncomfortable with what we discover. The language of worship can exclude many people, especially when these people already feel that they are outsiders to the community of faith. An inclusive church pays close attention to its use of words.

The language of worship may also discriminate against those persons who are not highly verbal. A significant problem with worship in most churches of the Reformed tradition is the almost total reliance upon words for the proclamation of the message of the gospel. Many people, such as those with severe hearing disabilities, children, those with mental disabilities, and even those with limited educational backgrounds, do not use words easily and do not form conceptions primarily with words. These people respond to stories which are illustrated, to banners with color and symbol, and to movement such as dance. An inclusive church will make every effort to communicate the Good News in as many ways as possible so that all may encounter Christ and respond in love and obedience.

The *leaders of worship* may be important symbols to others. Again, we are slowly learning that the presence of women in leadership positions in worship is an important way of making clear that all are included. The same can be said of the presence of people with various disabilities or limitations. A Scripture lesson read by someone using a cane can do a great deal to symbolize the full inclusion of all. There is great power in the demonstration of the capabilities of those whose limitations are very obvious. When persons with disabilities are given opportunities to provide leadership in worship, they represent hope to all who feel that their abilities are unwanted or unappreciated.

All the attention and care to make a church fully accessible will not, by themselves, bring persons with disabilities to the church to be welcomed. After many years of feeling excluded and un-

wanted, disabled people will likely be hesitant to believe that the church really intends to welcome them. They may remember the times when their own pain was made worse by Christians who reminded them that perhaps the disability was their own fault, from a lack of faith or even a result of the punishment of God. These negative messages do not disappear easily; they are among the reasons that persons with disabilities are not to be found in the church on Sunday.

There are people in our congregations, who do not believe that there are a sufficient number of persons with disabilities "out there" to make it worth the expenditure of money and effort necessary to become a fully accessible church. These people will be especially vocal when, after some effort and expense to make the church accessible, persons with disabilities do not rush to attend. The absence of a dramatic response will confirm some people's belief that the effort was all a tempest in a teapot.

In his excellent book written for the guidance of congregations, *Creating the Caring Congregation,* Harold Wilke gives some figures which ought to be of concern to us all. Using data from agencies of the various levels of government, he estimates at least 35 million persons have various kinds of disabling conditions. In addition, he states, "their numbers are increasing. Medical advances have made it possible for a great majority of persons with severe spinal cord injury to continue a useful life" (Harold H. Wilke, *Creating the Caring Congregation* [Nashville: Abingdon, 1980], 71). Other groups are also increasing. With better care for newborns, there is an increase in the number of babies born with spinal bifida. The dramatic increases in life expectancy have resulted in larger numbers of aging persons. People with disabling conditions are a significant proportion of the total population.

The church must decide if it really wishes to include this large number of people in its ministry. It must come to realize that these people have gifts to give; that disability always carries with it a particular kind of ability that God uses. It is a tragedy that the church has often been an obstacle to the use of the gifts of persons deemed unable to participate because they are different.

It will take time and energy beyond the removal of physical barriers to include disabled people in the life of the church. Does the church make it clear in its advertising that the church is fully accessible? Such an announcement, now beginning to be seen in some newspaper ads, is a clear signal of the readiness of the church to receive and include disabled people in its life and work. But even this step will not be enough.

Every congregation has in its membership, families in which there is some form of disability present. The persons with disabilities may even have a tangential relationship with the congregation. Often these people have had negative experiences with the church. Perhaps they have had the devastating experience of someone coming up to them and saying, as they have said to me, "If you had faith, you would be well." It does not take very many of these experiences before disabled people decide not to risk contact with church people.

People who bear the scars of such hurt will need to be gently invited and encouraged. Perhaps they could be encouraged to attend and to participate in some small group activity so that they can become more comfortable before they venture into the arena of Sunday morning worship.

Because of the difficulties, a congregation, which has a vision of being truly inclusive, needs to keep that vision in view and to be persistent. There will be problems. There will be people, who do not agree with the intent. There may be unpleasant moments, when the congregation will wish that they had never begun to open their church and make it more inclusive. The call to be a fully inclusive church must stem from a deep faith in the Lord, who calls us to be his body and who promises that we will meet him as we encounter those who have needs.

Howard Rice[17]

173 ◆ INVOLVING PEOPLE WITH DISABILITIES IN WORSHIP

By neglecting to include persons with disabilities, the church impoverishes itself. Disabled persons complete the church body, have special gifts, and are called by God to minister to the church. Christians need to be concerned about their church facilities and their language in order to facilitate their unity with their disabled members.

Harold Wylie is an elderly and significantly retarded member of Grace Church. Though ambulatory, he walks with difficulty; his language skills are limited. Conversation with Harold consists mainly of a few stock phrases, the most frequent being "How ya doin' buddy," accompanied by a pat on the back. Harold speaks this line many times each Sunday, occasionally with a twist. Once I heard him greet our pastor with the words, "Hello, you devil you!" Only Harold could get away with that, though others of us are tempted to try!

One Communion Sunday, I came to understand the importance of Harold's presence in our congregation in new ways. The liturgy that day included what we have come to call "come forward" Communion. Small groups are ushered to the front of the sanctuary, where they assemble in a semicircle to receive the bread and the wine as the rest of the congregation sings softly. Harold was part of a group seated near the back, and the other members of his group had all moved to the front before Harold had made it even halfway down the aisle. His greeting, "How ya doin' buddy," could be heard easily as Harold stopped to pat the shoulders of friends he passed. An elder, noticing that Harold's group was nearly through being served, walked fifteen feet down the aisle and put his arm around Harold. Harold did the same, and together they walked to the front. At that very moment, the congregation was singing a verse from "We Are One in the Spirit." "We will work with each other, we will work side by side, and we'll guard each man's dignity and save each man's pride," we sang. It was as if it had been scripted.

Worshiping with Harold and others like him has taught members of our church much about the meaning of the childlike faith that Christ commends and about the nature of Christian fellowship. Yet many people with disabilities like Harold's remain on the fringes, never a true part of the worshiping family of God.

It's time for change.

Persons with Disabilities Make the Church More Complete

By neglecting to include persons with disabilities, the church impoverishes itself. Rev. Harold Wilke, a United Church of Christ pastor who, incidentally, happens to have no arms, says it this way:

A church is handicapped unless it has persons with handicapping conditions within it. Only when all of God's children are present are we truly the body of Christ. (Harold Wilke, "Keynote Address to Presbyterians for Disabilities Concerns Conference," 1989.)

Did you catch that remarkable idea? Without disabled people, the church itself is disabled!

The Christian church often has responded with compassion to the needs of those with disabilities; however, it is time to move beyond that. Christians today must learn that weak and strong together are needed in the church—that those who are imprisoned, hungry, or impaired possess precious gifts for the church.

What are these gifts? People with disabilities have many of the same gifts that people without labeled disabilities possess. Just because a person is unable to see print does not mean she cannot read from the Bible. The need to use a wheelchair does not silence a quality voice. Retardation does not diminish the genuineness of a person's public profession of faith. People with disabilities can and do use their gifts in worship in the same ways as others do.

They also have their own unique gifts. Jean Vanier, a French-Canadian philosopher and theologian, who has lived for years in community with persons who have disabilities, reminds the church:

The life-giving Jesus is hidden in them. He is truly there. If you become a friend of the poor, you become a friend of Jesus; you enter into an intimate relationship with Jesus and you will be led into the heart of the beatitudes. (Jean Vanier, *The Broken Body—Journey to Wholeness* [1988], 73)

Scripture also tells the church this:

Whosoever welcomes one of these, my brothers or sisters, welcomes me, and whoever welcomes me welcomes the One who sent me. (Matt. 25:40; author's paraphrase)

Does it seem possible that Jesus could be revealed in persons with disabilities? In contrast to Western culture, which glorifies health and athleticism and which canonizes achievement and productivity, the gospels depict life—Christ's and humanity's—as a mixture of strength and weakness.

Christ invites us as Christians to lives of discipleship in a world that is not, and among people who are not, intrinsically healthy. The presence of disabilities in members of the church is a reminder that although we all must live with brokenness, brokenness is not the last word. When the church welcomes individual differences, including those which are called "disabilities," we make it easier for each one of us to disclose our woundedness and to begin moving toward wholeness.

In worship we meet God. But it is not a meeting and a conversation between equals. We do not earn the right to enter into dialogue because of our excellence in singing, our eloquence in prayer, or our expressiveness in reading Scripture. When persons with disabilities participate in visible roles in worship, we are reminded that our great Lord condescends to meet with each of us in spite of our flaws. In worship, we meet the God of grace.

Worship with Persons Who Have Disabilities Calls Us to New Understandings of Communion

The celebration of the Lord's Supper is an act of remembrance; we remember who Christ is and who we are—the community of believers. In his speech to the "Merging Two Worlds Conference" in 1987, Parker Palmer taught me that the opposite of *to remember,* is not *to forget,* but *to dis-member*—to cut off from humanity. We live in a dismembering world that puts people into categories (retarded, mentally ill, alcoholic, or gay). In society and in the church, such labeling does violence to community, creating distance between people. How sad it is that often we know better how to divide, than how to unite.

Part of what happens at Communion is that we *re-member* who we are—one body made up of many parts. Harold Wylie taught me and other members of my church a great deal about *re-membering* that we are one in the Spirit—*all* of us, whatever our disabilities. He also taught us some important things about the Lord's Supper.

A deep truth about Communion is that in it the worshipers experience oneness with Christ and oneness with each other. It is communion *for* the saints, as well as communion *of* the saints. The sacramental ritual unites worshipers to Jesus Christ and unites people with and without disabilities to each other.

Persons with Disabilities Are Called to Ministry

Just as God called Moses to lead in spite of his speech problems and the apostle Paul to witness in spite of his "thorn," persons with disabilities are today being called to minister to those who are TABs (Temporarily Able Bodied). No doubt some of you can think of ordained pastors who are blind, who have cerebral palsy, or who are in wheelchairs.

The fact that God calls all kinds of people to ordained ministry has implications for seminaries and for the architectural design of churches, particularly the pulpit area. However, those issues go beyond the scope of this article. The point is that God does call less than perfect people to ministry—surprise, surprise!

God calls lay persons with disabilities to minister to and with us as well. Let me share a poem called "A Little While" taken from a wonderful book of free verse by a Dutch poet, Lize Stilma:

It's Easter.
Together, all flowers celebrate.
And the congregation with them.

Grace is there too.
Together with the members of the youth group she offers
flowers to the young people at their Confirmation.
Undaunted she steps to the front and says, "Here. Last year I did it. I loved it."
She repeats it twenty-two times.
Then her arms are empty.
It's Easter.
A celebration.
She knows it very well. Jesus died, but He lives.
That's why everybody is so happy.
Am I happy?
My positive answer clearly doesn't convince her entirely.
Do I really know what Easter means?
Shall she explain it to me?

Some things in life can only be said in a soft voice.
Close to the one for whom the words are intended.
Obviously this explanation is one of those.
She stands on her toes, puts her arms around my neck and says,
"When you die you go into a coffin.
Then people bury you in the ground.
But that's not so bad. It's only for a little while.

God takes you out again.
Do you know that?"
Yes, I do know that.
Only now I'm more certain.

That evening I walk in a cemetery.
Someone was buried there a week ago.
Someone very dear to me.
In a coffin.
In the loose sand.

To that grave and myself I said,
"It's only for a little while.
God will take you out again."

Those words were placed in my mouth by a little Downs syndrome girl.
Very softly.

She is called Grace.
That means "prophetess"!

(Lize Stilma, "A Little While," in *Portraits* [1985], 75–6.)

Some Good Policies and Practices for Involving Persons with Disabilities

Today as never before the doors of churches are opening to persons who have a variety of disabilities. Some of the following changes and decisions often come along with the open doors, making it possible for persons with disabilities to become full and active members of the worshiping community.

Inclusive churches make their sanctuary accessible. People must first of all be able to get into the sanctuary. Churches who wait to make changes until someone with disabilities joins their congregation will likely never attract such a person. Modifications to parking spaces, curb cuts, ramps, and elevators may all be necessary.

Inside the church still other changes may be needed—changes that remove barriers to sight, sound, and understanding. Interior modifications may include making available such resources as Braille and large print bulletins, amplification equipment, sign language interpreters, and spaces in the pews for wheelchairs.

A congregation that believes involving persons who have disabilities is important will do an assessment of barriers and seek to eliminate them. Many helpful resources exist. For example, the Christian Reformed Church's Committee on Disability Concerns has accessibility checklists for churches and offers consultation on architectural design.

Inclusive churches are careful about language. Self-advocacy organizations such as People First International ask that noun and adjectival constructions, such as *the blind* or *mentally retarded persons* be avoided. Instead, the *person* should be put first as in "persons who have hearing impairments" or "persons with mental retardation." Also, diminutive forms of first names, such as "Tommy" or "Kenny" should be avoided when addressing adults; and, on formal occasions at least, Mr., Mrs., Miss, or Ms. should be used.

Language and imagery that discriminates against handicapped people appears in some of our church music as well. Consider the metaphor in the lyrics of "Just as I Am, Without One Plea":

> Just as I am poor, wretched, blind.
> Sight, riches, healing of the mind.
> Yes, all I need, in thee to find,
> O Lamb of God, I come, I come.

This familiar juxtaposition of physical and spiritual poverty also appears in the hymn "Amazing Grace"; and, of course, it is found in Scripture. But, as Steward Govig so passionately indicates:

> Is it necessary to associate poverty and wretchedness with blindness? Many of us are acquainted with someone who is blind and is scarcely poor or wretched! How about using the words "Selfishness" or "Stubbornness" in place of blindness? "Healing the mind" may be desirable, but we need the forgiveness of our sins even more. (Steward D. Govig, *Strong at the Broken Places: Persons With Disabilities and the Church* [Louisville: Westminster/John Knox Press, 1989], 83.)

We must be sensitive to language. It is not only a matter of balance in perspective, but a matter of justice. With our words, we distance or bridge distances, we include or we exclude.

It's true that sometimes people with disabilities need to be protected, but where is justice when we fail to use language that speaks of their gifts? The way we talk about people reflects how we view them and shapes our interaction with them.

Inclusive churches use special environments only as a last resort. Most people with disabilities can participate in regular worship activities in the same environment as everyone else. When people with disabilities are grouped together in a separate environment for worship, everyone loses. If a person who is disabled cannot perform all parts of a worship activity, it is better to provide an assistant than to provide a different setting.

Thomas B. Hoeksema[18]

174 ♦ LITURGIES WITH DEAF WORSHIPERS

For deaf persons, liturgies need to communicate through gesture, action, sign language, drama, film, slides, overheads, and skits, as well as through speech and music. Such media are the vernacular for deaf people. The following article will offer some suggestions on how to make liturgy communicate to deaf people.

Music and sound, drama and poetry are closely linked to liturgical prayer, as indeed, most forms of worship are based on sound. For many people, worship is the spoken or sung Word. Sometimes music is added to the liturgy; and gestures and objects are part of the accompanying ceremonial. However, too often liturgists emphasize language only, citing the assembly's need to understand the service and to share in the proclamation of the Word. Severely deaf people derive little or no benefit, however, from this type of religious service; and they are unable to contribute much to it. For the deaf, the liturgist must change the emphasis from the auditory to the visual aspects of worship. It is less obvious, but of great importance to note, that this shift will also be helpful for people who can hear.

Sound, especially speech, is important for worship; it evokes an intellectual, emotional, and inspirational response from the assembly. Yet there are three theological problems with liturgies that only rely on sound to communicate. First, sound liturgies are based on the principle that faith comes by hearing. They do not seem to be based on the principle that God's Word is incarnate and should be proclaimed by seeing, touching, tasting, and smelling, as well as by speaking and listening. Second, the nature of human response also requires a larger vision. In Mark Twain's *Letters from the Earth,* the angel was astonished to discover that earth's people, most of whom could not abide music for any length of time, still imag-

The Cross Adorned. *Pictured is a Latin cross whose surface bears painted or carved lilies, Passion flowers, or other floral forms. Several variations of this cross exist.*

ined heaven to be entirely devoid of every pleasure not associated with harps and singing. It was obvious to Satan that the "church" was a plague to be avoided, so little did it have to do with the full range of people's capacity for life (Bernard DeVoto, ed., *Letters from the Earth* [1985]). Third, a liturgy that is too auditory fails to make even good use of sound, since silence and gesture as well as spoken language are parts of sound. These theological problems clarify an important point: a liturgy that is good for deaf people will be good for people with hearing also.

Men and women who have been severely deaf from birth or early infancy will generally have experienced great difficulty in acquiring language. Many have little intelligible speech, and their understanding of both spoken and written language is often limited. Where vocabulary is limited, the understanding of thought patterns takes on visual, rather than verbal forms. The poetry of biblical and liturgical language, as well as its theological significance, must be explained as far as possible; this means that communicators to deaf people must be more than translators—they must also be interpreters.

In a religious setting, we are dealing with words that signify abstract concepts and ideas, rather than words that lead to obvious concrete and pic-

torial imagery. During liturgy, Christians call forth praise, increase awareness of their brothers and sisters and their needs, and express their faith and relatedness to the Holy One. Deaf persons, as well as persons with hearing, need to experience this celebration in communion with the whole church. Involving everyone in this experience is a difficult challenge. To meet this challenge, we must develop and follow some general principles for planning liturgies that include the deaf.

Physical Surroundings

According to Eugene Walsh, S.S., five ministerial locations are necessary for the celebration of Mass. The assembly, the presiding minister, and the musician need identifiable places, as well as the altar and lectern needing a place. The space and place of each ministry must be so arranged that they help the assembly and its ministers to do their tasks effectively and graciously. There must be good light so that people can see each minister's face and hands clearly. No window should be located behind the minister; it would produce a glare for the congregation and cast the minister's face in a shadow.

The assembly space should assist people to gather around and to be in touch with one another. The other spaces should be in front and in full view of all members of the assembly.

The worship space, and especially its background, should be uncluttered. Statues, ornate decoration, and murals should not draw attention away from the presider. Only furniture that is actually being used should be in the celebration area.

Vestments and Other Decorations. The utensils and the elements of bread and wine should be chosen carefully for each celebration. A glass decanter of wine and a glass chalice allow persons to see the wine. Loaves of bread are more visible than unleavened bread. The altar is an important symbol; it should have on it only what is used when it is used.

Books, banners, flowers, vestments, and other decorations are secondary signs. They should not be distracting, but simple and bright, strong and wholehearted. No signs should be present that do not focus on the theme chosen for a particular celebration. A theme is not an addition to the lectionary. It is, rather, the specific idea or concept embodied in a particular liturgy. The more clearly it is understood, the easier it is to express.

Music and Speech. Too many elements incorporated into the liturgy are distracting and confusing. A good liturgical principle is to make the liturgy a visual or visible event. It should be shown, not said. What people can see is what happens in the liturgy. The use of the vernacular in liturgy extends beyond the use of the native tongue to include the use of sign language, drama, gesture, film, slides, overheads, and skits. Such media are the vernacular for deaf people.

Songs that are simple and repetitive can be used in liturgies for deaf people, especially if the music's purpose in worship is to promote celebration by the assembly. Songs must be capable of eliciting the participation of deaf persons; for example, a deaf person may choose and lead the signing of songs. Otherwise, deaf people will watch songs as an interpreter's performance, rather than as an occasion for their own participation. Sometimes, deaf persons enjoy watching a reverent rendition of a hymn and are led to pray by this experience. An occasional solo or sign choir performance can enhance the liturgy.

Some pastoral workers who teach signing songs to deaf choirs find the work a good opportunity for catechesis. Deaf persons, after discussing the meaning of the words, will choose the signs and motions that best express this meaning, invite participation, and elicit praise.

Some Concrete Suggestions

There are many possible ways to include deaf persons in the penitential rite. Slides can be used, for example, to illustrate failure to appreciate God's gifts or situations of interpersonal discord. All persons should sign after each picture, "Lord, have mercy," or another appropriate response. Penitential rites should always be simple—in keeping with their place in the overall structure of the celebration. If the use of slides overemphasizes this rite, they may be used at another time, perhaps during the prayers of the faithful.

The opening prayer in the sacramentary is a model prayer. The presiding minister may want to embellish it or adapt it to a specific congregation. When inviting the people to pray, the presider should pause and encourage the people to pray silently before proceeding with the official prayer.

Many pastoral workers with the deaf will use only one reading at the liturgy of the Word, because they do not believe the average person (hearing or deaf) can pay attention to and assimilate three readings. Although this is not always the case, the Constitution on the Sacred Liturgy makes provision for special liturgies when it states, "The revision of liturgical books should allow for legitimate variations and adaptations to different groups, regions, and peoples" (par. 37). Drama by deaf persons is a very effective presentation of the readings; filmstrips and slides are also good. The *New Testament for the Deaf* published by Baker House will assist those who need assistance in simplifying the language.

The use of all three readings ensures that the gospel is presented in relation to the whole of Scripture, and it provides a more ample opportunity for deaf lectors to participate. Lectors should always practice well ahead of the ceremony to ensure that a clear expression of the message is given.

Short and simple homilies are usually good ones. Charts and visual aids are especially effective for younger audiences. Adults too will remember ideas that are visually illustrated.

The prayer of the faithful is an important and comforting aspect of celebrating the Eucharist. It can be a time to invite spontaneous petitions from the congregation. An appropriate response could be signed, for example, "Father, for your gifts, we thank you."

Action and gesture speak more than words, during the presentation of the gifts. People bring a decanter of wine and a basket with unbroken bread to the presider, who accepts them and places them on the altar. The prayers of preparation are said silently and quickly with the priest holding the decanter and basket together in a single, simple, reverential gesture. No music or song should be permitted at this point as it might distract from or prolong what is taking place. Possibilities for interpreting the various eucharistic prayers have been developed and are available from the National Catholic Office for the Deaf.

When the distribution of Communion is complete, the empty baskets and goblets are placed on a side table to await purification after the service. Once again the altar should be clear. A quiet meditation with slides can be used during this time. An appropriate short reading, adapted psalm, or a spontaneous thanksgiving litany could serve for this meditation. In a variation of the thanksgiving litany, a representative from each family may come forward and mention a specific blessing for which that family is thankful.

The closing song will be simple, repetitive, and joyous.

I have presumed that the planners and ministers of liturgies are comfortable with the language of the deaf and are sensitive to the special needs of this group. Specific materials may be ordered from the National Catholic Office for the Deaf, which publishes _Signs for Catholic Liturgy and Education_ and a bimonthly journal _Listening,_ which features specific liturgies for various seasons of the church year.

Another type of situation occurs when a few deaf persons are part of a congregation in which most can hear. Then an interpreter, rather than the celebrant, signs the words of the celebrant, readers, and singers. In this case, the interpreter must follow the established format. Since the celebration will probably proceed at an accelerated pace, the interpreter must be well-prepared and should have consulted with the minister about where to stand and where deaf persons will sit in order to see clearly. Before the service begins, the interpreter will study the readings, the song words, and the homily, if the celebrant has a copy. Often song words are not clearly articulated and so the interpreter will need to rely on written lyrics. Those who appreciate the difficulty of interpreting hymns and who need assistance in signing, should see "Interpreting Hymns for Deaf Worshipers" in _Listening_ magazine (Sept.-Oct. and Nov.-Dec. 1983).

With careful preparation, an interpreter can be the link connecting deaf people to the celebration, allowing them to take their rightful place in a worshiping assembly. Sometimes persons who can hear may also sign parts of the liturgy. At such times, deaf persons will feel a true sense of care, concern, and unity within their parish.

M. Alverna Hollis[19]

175 ✦ BIBLIOGRAPHY ON DISABLED PERSONS IN THE WORSHIPING COMMUNITY

Access: A Bibliography of Resources Related to _Barrier-Free Environment._ New York: National Council of Churches, 1978. A list of material available to aid churches in building or renovating structures.

Bernadin, Joseph. _Access to the Sacraments of Initiation and Reconciliation for Developmentally Disabled Persons._ Chicago: Liturgy Training Publications, 1985.

Costello, Elaine. _Religious Signing._ New York: Bantam Books, 1986. A complete glossary for signing biblical, religious, and liturgical terms, including both a description and sketch of the gestures for each.

Govig, Steward D. _Strong at the Broken Places: Persons With Disabilities and the Church._ Louisville: Westminster/John Knox Press, 1989. A treatise on the role of persons with disabilities in churches in North America today, along with several proposals for including them more fully in the life of the church.

Harrington, Mary Therese. _A Place for All: Mental Retardation, Catechesis, and Liturgy._ Collegeville, Minn.: Liturgical Press, 1992. A brief essay on the importance of including the developmentally disabled in the process of church education and in the worship of the church. Written from a Roman Catholic perspective.

Hogan, Griff, ed. _The Church and Disabled Persons._ Springfield, Ill.: Templegate Publishers, 1983. Essays on a variety of disabilities and how the church can minister to those who have them, with special attention to religious education.

Müller-Fahrenholz, Geiko. _Partners in Life: The Handicapped and the Church._ Geneva: World Council of Churches, 1981. A variety of articles that describe the theological basis for ministry to the handicapped and current practices in a wide range of churches around the world.

Newman, Gene and Joni Eareckson Tada. _All God's Children: Ministry to the Disabled._ Grand Rapids: Zondervan, 1987. A variety of practical insights for ministering to persons with a wide range of disabilities, along with a comprehensive list of resources to support ministries to the disabled.

Ohsburg, H. Oliver. _The Church and Persons with Handicaps._ Kitchener, Ontario, and Scottdale, Pa.: Herald Press, 1982. An overview of the church's ministry to handicapped persons, with both a discussion of the theological principles that support this ministry and proposals and suggested resources for developing this ministry.

That All May Worship: An Interfaith Welcome to People With Disabilities. Washington, D.C.: National Organization on Disability, 1992. A brief, practical guide to making the local church a place that welcomes and embraces persons with disabilities.

Van Opzeeland, Okhuijsen and Cees. *In Heaven There Are No Thunderstorms: Celebrating the Liturgy with Developmentally Disabled People.* Collegeville, Minn.: Liturgical Press, 1992. A book that presents imaginative ways of engaging developmentally disabled persons in Christian worship. Contains many suggestions for various services in the Christian year.

❧ FIVE ❧

The Worshiping Community and Its Cultural Context

Every expression of worship is shaped by the culture that shapes those who worship. Every person inherits styles of language and music, conventions of communication and greeting, and patterns of thinking and feeling from the culture in which he or she lives. These are inevitably reflected in countless ways in worship: The style of language of hymns and prayers, the ways worshipers greet each other or pass the peace, and the types of physical expression deemed appropriate are all shaped by culture. As Christianity moves into new cultural settings or as culture changes in settings where Christianity has had a long history, worship leaders and planners must consider how liturgical texts and actions can remain faithful to the Scriptures and be authentic expressions of worship from within culture. This challenging task, which is often described by the term inconturation, demands that liturgists be thoroughly knowledgeable about what is essential in Christian worship and what is authentic for a given culture. This chapter will introduce readers to the fascinating subject of liturgical inculturation and provide some basic guidelines for thinking about this important subject.

176 ◆ A History of Cultural Adaptation in Christian Worship

Although the challenge of swiftly changing cultures is especially characteristic of recent years, the cultural adaptation of Christian worship has a long and fascinating history. This article identifies many of the most important adaptations of worship through the early history of the church.

As the expression implies, *liturgical adaptation* refers to the process by which the liturgy is modified in such a way as to render it "more suitable," "more appropriate," "more meaningful" to a given group of worshipers in a given context. While the term *adaptation* has been criticized as connoting an overly timid and even paternalistic attitude toward this process, the documents of the Second Vatican Council and the revised liturgical books use this word in a variety of contexts to express a range of nuanced ideas: from the most superficial kinds of rubrical changes to the creation of new

liturgical forms springing from the genius of a particular culture. A careful reading of these documents, especially *S.C.* 37–40, will reveal that the term *adaptation* when applied to the liturgy variously refers to concepts borrowed from the social sciences, such as *localization, acculturation, contextualization, indigenization,* and *inculturation,* as well as the more theological expression *incarnation.*

Examples from the History of the Liturgy

Liturgical adaptation, however, while a relatively new expression in the liturgical lexicon, is not a new phenomenon in the history of the liturgy. As the *Constitution on the Sacred Liturgy* itself points out, the liturgy "is made up of immutable elements, divinely instituted, and of elements subject to change" (*S.C.* 21). Even a cursory review of the history of Christian worship illustrates that the church both consciously and unconsciously adapted these "elements subject to change" not only from one generation to the next but also from one culture to another in order to express and celebrate the mystery of Christ in a meaningful way.

Given the Jewish background of the first generation of believers, it is not surprising that the earliest forms of Christian liturgy were profoundly rooted in the ritual patterns of first-century Judaism. The most obvious case in point is the reinterpretation (one could say adaptation) of the Passover meal from a domestic memorial of the Exodus of Israel from slavery and oppression, to the Christian Eucharist, the memorial of the "Passover" of Christ, celebrated in homes by small groups of believers. Just as the Hebrew Scriptures were reinterpreted by the early church in a Christological light, so basic Jewish ritual actions, such as the laying on of hands, baptismal washing, and anointings, were given new meanings in the context of the Christ event. Both the New Testament and extrabiblical witnesses to early Christian worship patterns, such as the *Didache* (9, 10) and the *First Letter of Clement* (59–61), betray a marked indebtedness to Jewish forms of prayer and blessing rooted in the Hebrew Scriptures, though now refocused on Jesus, the servant of God. This characteristic influence of the Hebrew Scriptures and the cultural worldview expressed by them would never be totally lost by the church as it moved from one culture to another down through the centuries.

As the new church attracted more and more converts from paganism, it also entered into a dialogue with the dominant Greco-Roman culture, which also affected the church's worship. While this dialogue was often polemical, characterized by a total rejection of cultural expressions based on polytheism, practices that were not intrinsically linked to pagan worship were incorporated into the Christian liturgy and usually interpreted in light of the Hebrew Scriptures. Thus, we find in the *Apostolic Tradition* of Hippolytus that after the newly baptized received the Eucharist for the first time, they were given a drink of milk and honey. Hippolytus explains the significance of this action as "the fulfillment of the promise God would give them a land flowing with milk and honey" (*Apostolic Tradition* 21 [London: SPCK, 1968]). Yet this type of drink would not have been unfamiliar to a Christian neophyte, since it was ancient Roman custom to give a similar drink to

newborns as a sign of welcome into the family and to ward off evil spirits (Anscar Chupungco, *Cultural Adaptation of the Liturgy* [New York: Paulist Press, 1982], 16). Clearly what is at work here is an adaptation of a welcoming rite practiced in the surrounding culture to illustrate the significance of full initiation into the church imaged as the family of God.

Once Christianity was made a legal religion in 313 by Constantine and then the official religion of the Empire during the reign of Thedosius (379–395), the church's dialogue with Greco-Roman culture became progressively more positive. This was a period of great creativity and the era that saw the gradual birth of the liturgical families of rites in the East and the West. Each one of these developing rites was marked not only by the theological controversies and political instability of the age but also by the pastoral concern to adapt the church's worship to the needs of the huge influx of new converts through the assimilation and reinterpretation of cultural symbols drawn from the religious and political usages with which the new Christians were already familiar.

One aspect of this adaptation can be seen in the worship space of the Christian assembly. The simple house church or house of the assembly *(domus ecclesiae),* which was able to accommodate only a small number of worshipers, was transformed into an imperial basilica, capable of holding vast throngs of the faithful. While maintaining the image of the church as the "household of God," this image became progressively more stylized in the appointments of the new Christian basilicas. The apse, where the emperor or magistrate was enthroned, became the place where the bishop presided from his chair, or *cathedra,* surrounded by his council of elders, or *presbyterium*. Not surprisingly, the liturgy itself became more stylized and formal. It began to reflect the new position of the church vis-à-vis the political and social order, borrowing elements of imperial court ceremonial from the now-Christian emperor, for whom the bishops became funtionaries. Liturgical vesture in the East and the West, which has undergone numerous changes down through the centuries, still reflects the formal dress of imperial officials of the late empire. It is also important to note that while the liturgy is still very deeply rooted in the Scriptures, the patristic authors of this period began to legitimate the now more formal liturgical practices through recourse to the cultus of the Jerusalem temple as described in the Hebrew Scriptures and the New Testament, especially in the letter to the Hebrews. A "sacralization" of both the persons ministering to the community and the place where it gathers to pray gradually took place, paralleling religious attitudes toward the sacred found in both Judaism and paganism.

Significantly, it was during the fourth century that the very language of worship of the Roman church was adapted to a changed cultural situation. It must be remembered that the Roman church, until the third century, was predominantly Greek-speaking. It was just before the reign of Pope Damascus in the middle of the fourth century that Latin, the contemporary language of the majority of the Christians of Rome, definitely found its way into the liturgy of the church of that city. While this change was essentially a pastoral one to enable the faithful to understand what was being prayed, the form of the Latin adopted for Christian worship was in many ways stylistically similar to that employed in the pre-Christian, Roman cultures. Both responses, _Libera nos, Domine_ and _Te rogamus, audi nos,_ derive from the pagan Roman practice of invoking the gods with a series of intercessory acclamations. The typical Roman concern for juridical precision through the piling up of synonyms in sacrificial formulas also became a feature of the liturgical prayer of Christians. A recent Roman convert from paganism would have been very familiar indeed with the stylized expression specifying the gifts presented at the Eucharist, such as _have dona, haec munera, haec sacrificia illibata_ appearing in the _Te igitur_ section of the Roman Canon and reflecting the hieratic language of the pagan Roman cultus.

This adaptation extended beyond just the verbal. A gesture of reverence still prescribed today in the Roman liturgy, kissing the altar and the book of the Gospels, also finds its origin in the pagan Roman custom of venerating the sacred with a kiss. Moreover, the development of some aspects of the liturgical year would be incomprehensible without a knowledge of previous pagan celebrations, such as the Mithraic celebration of the _dies natalis solis invicti,_ celebrated at the winter solstice and reinterpreted by the Christian church into the annual celebration of the birth of Christ, the "sun of righteousness" spoken by the prophet Malachi. These and many other examples illustrate the church's constant (and sometimes unconscious) attempt to adapt its worship to its changed cultural context through the reinterpretation of religious, social, and political customs already extant in the world in which it lived.

This era of the "classic Roman liturgy," which extended from the fourth to the seventh centuries, is a crucial one from the point of view of liturgical adaptation because the reforms of the liturgy that took place after the Second Vatican Council were very much influenced by the liturgical movement of this "classic" period, which was a kind of blueprint that guided the liturgical renewal of the Roman rite. In effect, the cultural values or "genius" of Roman culture in this period was "simplicity, practicality, a great sobriety and self-control, gravity and dignity" (Edmund Bishop, "The Genius of the Roman Rite," in _Liturgica Historica_ [London: Oxford, 1918], 12). These values have served in subsequent periods of liturgical reform as a kind of yardstick by which such reforms were measured. These values played a key role in the liturgical renewal of the Second Vatican Council: "The rites should be marked by a noble simplicity; they should be short, clear, unencumbered by useless repetitions; they should be within the peoples' power of comprehension and as a rule not require much explanation" (_S.C._ 34).

As Frankish and Germanic peoples, centering around the area of what was the old Roman Empire, were evangelized, it was only natural that their worship, too, was influenced by their particular culture. In the period prior to the ninth century, when the Roman rite was imposed on the Frankish kingdom by Pepin and Charlemagne, Western liturgical rites developed quite independently from the Roman rites and reveal very different approaches to Christian worship. One can easily see in the style of the prayers found in the various non-Roman sacramentaries of this period a reflection of the challenges, that beset these local churches, expressed in a style proper to the particular national "genius" of these people. In Ireland, where the harp of the wandering troubadour still functions as national symbol, the prayers of the Celtic rite excelled in lyrical compositions and hymnody. In the face of serious Arian opposition to orthodoxy, the formerly thoroughly romanized province of Spain, especially in Toledo and Braga, produced the so-called Mozarabic, or Visigothic, rite, which combined a refined Latin erudition with a special concern for orthodoxy of expression. The more "barbarian" province of Gaul produced prayers with tended to be prolix, moralizing, and emotional, but also to liberally incorporate quotations from the Scriptures. Though all of these rites employed Latin in worship, their style is unmistakably different from the more restrained and abstract Roman genius.

The See of Rome, however, being the center of pilgrimage to the shrines of the apostles Peter and Paul and the only patriarchate in the West, commanded enormous respect in the West. Many of these pilgrims returned home to incorporate liturgical practices that they had witnessed at Rome into their own worship. It was also to Rome that Charlemagne turned in an astute political move to unify his kingdom by means of imposing uniform liturgical observances on his dominions. While the liturgical unification he promoted used the liturgy of the city of Rome as its base, his borrowing of Roman liturgical forms was not wholesale. Under Charlemagne's auspices, a supplement to the Roman sacramentary, which he had received from the pope, was composed, and it included the blessing of the Easter candle (the present *Exsultet*), as well as ordination prayers, blessings, and formulas for consecration of churches and exorcisms—all of which reflect the characteristic Franco-Germanic verbosity coupled with a love of Scripture. This supplement was eventually incorporated into the Roman section of the sacramentary and was brought back to Rome and became, with a few alterations down through the centuries, the Roman missal used by the Roman rite until the reforms of the Second Vatican Council.

It was also about the same time, during the reforms of the papacy undertaken by the Ottonian emperors in the ninth and tenth centuries, that we see the influence of the early medieval culture on liturgical practice. The Roman-Germanic pontifical of the tenth century, a fusion of the ancient *Roman Ordines* (guides to liturgical celebrations) with material from northern Europe, contains dramatic evidence of the influence of feudalism; for example, six sections of the book are dedicated to the *Indicia Dei,* or "trials by ordeal." While

these "barbaric" ceremonies were dropped by subsequent pontificals, feudalism continued to influence the liturgy. The gesture of fealty used by a knight to his liege was introduced into the ordination rite for presbyters by the end of thirteenth century in Rome. When the ordinand placed his hands between the hands of the bishop to promise obedience, he is imitating that feudal gesture of homage given by a vassal to his lord.

Although there was an attempt under Gregory VII (1073–1085) and Innocent III (1198–1216) to return to what was perceived to be the traditions and practices of the ancient Roman fathers, these reforms were impeded by a lack of documentation and historical sophistication. The Roman liturgy therefore evinced not only the sobriety and gravity of ancient Rome but also the allegorism, moralization, verbosity, and flair for the dramatic, which characterized the people of northern Europe. It was this essentially hybrid liturgy, purified of abuses by the Council of Trent, that is contained in the Missal of Pius V promulgated in 1570.

The Reformers of the sixteenth century approached the problem of adaptation from another point of view. Instead of adapting the liturgy in light of what was perceived to be the ancient practices of the Roman church, they made a conscious attempt to look at worship as presented in the Scriptures. One of the problems they perceived in medieval worship was that it was monopolized by the clergy and was unintelligible to the people because it was celebrated in Latin. It therefore needed to be translated into the vernacular, purged of what they regarded to be Roman error and superstition, and firmly based on the Word of God. Luther, Zwingli, Bucer, Calvin, and, later, Cranmer all produced new vernacular liturgies that attempted to return to the worship of the early church. While these revisions were successful insofar as they once again made the words of worship comprehensible to the people, they were unable to "turn the clock back" to the first century because the New Testament contains no formal worship services and hence no pattern to emulate. As with the attempted reform of Gregory VII in the eleventh century, historical study and theological reflection was not sufficiently developed in the sixteenth century to do anything more than to create worship services shorn of direct references to Catholic doctrines problematic to the Reformers, such as eucharistic sacrifice. While they were assiduous in translating both the Scriptures and prayers used in church, the Reformers produced liturgies that very much reflected the cultural ethos of northern Europe during the late Middle Ages. Although their services emphasized the primacy of the Word of God interpreted by every Christian, a Word that was accessible to a much broader section of the population through the invention of the printing press, their liturgies also reflect the strong penitential emphasis and the interest in subjectivity already present in the late Middle Ages in such spiritual movements as the *devotion moderna.*

The apparent rejection of centuries of liturgical tradition by the Reformers, as well as what was perceived to be their deviations from doctrinal orthodoxy, led the participants in the Council of Trent to reaffirm what they regarded as ancient tradition. The rite of the Mass was protected from any change or modification by canonical regulations by this council, which legislated absolute compliance to the most minute rubrical detail under pain of sin. The four hundred years between the promulgation of the Missal of Pius V in 1570 and that of Paul VI in 1970 is a history of rigid liturgical centralization and uniformity in the Roman Catholic church, largely immune to any attempts at adaptation. It was during this period that, having no outlet to modify the liturgy as such, both popular devotions and a manifest theatricality increasingly began to frame the eucharistic liturgy and other rites of the church. Medieval practices—such as processions and expositions of the Blessed Sacrament, novenas to the saints, the rosary, and the dramatizations of biblical stories performed both inside and outside the church—were maintained, especially in the Spanish part of the Catholic world. While the rite of the Mass itself could not be changed, its celebration was peripherally embellished by full orchestras and choirs performing complex musical compositions. The churches built during this period resemble theaters, where the faithful, like an audience, "attended" the various ceremonies of the church "performed" in a dramatic setting designed to inspire feelings of devotion and awe. During this age of divine-right monarchs, it is also not by chance that many churches resembled throne rooms where the great King of heaven present in the blessed sacrament held

court, enthroned in an ornate tabernacle on the main altar, surrounded by candles, flowers, and incense.

Ironically, these four hundred years also corresponded to a period of great missionary outreach by the church to peoples of different cultures in the Americas, Africa, Asia, and Oceania. One notable exception to this Roman insistence on uniformity was an experiment promoted by Matteo Ricci, a Jesuit missionary in China, that became the object of controversy from 1610–1742. Ricci obtained important indults from the Holy See to adapt the Mass, liturgical vestments, and language of the liturgy to Chinese culture. Moreover, he also urged that the practice of the Chinese to honor their ancestors by bowing before ancestor tablets, derived from Confucianism, not be interpreted as idolatry or superstition but be permitted to Chinese converts by the church as a cultural expression that was an integral part of Chinese identity. These attempts at rooting the gospel and the worship of Chinese Catholics in their own culture were met by serious opposition from other missionaries, notably the Dominicans, who accused Ricci and the Jesuits of promoting idolatry. In a very interesting instruction to the Vicars Apostolic of the Far East issued by *Propaganda Fide* in 1659, the idea of transplanting Europe to China as necessary for evangelization was labeled as absurd. The instruction clearly draws a distinction between the faith and its European cultural expression, and states that the faith does not demand that rites and customs of non-Europeans be repudiated or destroyed in order for them to become Christian. Indeed, the faith wills that these rites and customs be preserved intact in order to serve as vehicles for evangelization, provided they are not "depraved" ("Instruction Vicariorum Apostolicorum and Regna Synarum Tonchine et Cocinnae Profisiscentium," in *Collectanea Sacrae Congregationis Propaganda Fide*, I [Rome, 1907]). This instruction, therefore, lays down the principle of liturgical adaptation, which would be echoed in Pius XII's encyclical *Summi Pontificatus* of 1939 (*Acta Apostolica Sedis* 31 [1939]: 329) and in the *Constitution on the Sacred Liturgy* of the Second Vatican Council (37).

Unfortunately, the insights of both Matteo Ricci and *Propaganda Fide* were lost in the intervening years. Chinese performance of ancestral rites was condemned by the bull *Ex quo singulari* in

1742, which "spelled the loss of China and Indochina to the church" (Chupungco, *Cultural Adaptation*, 38). It became clear to many potential converts outside of western Europe that to become Christian meant to become European.

Mark R. Francis[20]

177 ✦ Liturgical Adaptation in the Roman Catholic Church in the Twentieth Century

One of the most significant developments in Roman Catholic worship in the twentieth century has been the increasing sensitivity to the cultural setting in which worship is offered. The landmark decision of the Second Vatican Council, which called for all worship to be offered in the vernacular language, is only one example of important developments in the process of liturgical inculturation. This article describes the process, concentrating on the important decisions of the Second Vatican Council.

Prior to Vatican II

The fifty years prior to the Second Vatican Council witnessed a renewed interest in matters liturgical and in making the liturgy truly the prayer of the church. Prompted by both the liturgical movement and the liturgical reforms of Pius X, Pius XII, and John XXIII, the liturgy once again became the object of serious study by theologians, historians, and missionaries. Since it was also during this period that the church was wrestling with the modernist controversy, which discouraged the open questioning of any aspect of church life that was considered traditional, it is not surprising that these studies most often revolved around a return to the sources of the Roman rite as it was practiced in the city of Rome from the fourth to the seventh centuries. The effort was to recapture the valued "Roman genius" of the liturgy and to clearly distinguish the classical forms from the medieval and baroque accretions, which, in the mind of many in the liturgical movement, tended to blur the true nature of liturgical celebrations.

Thus, it was on the basis of historical precedent that a call went out to adapt the liturgy to the needs of the day. Like the liturgical reform attempted by Gregory VII in the eleventh century, one could characterize both the papal reforms of the liturgy and the approach of liturgists during this period as a "repristinization" of the Roman rite: a return to the simplicity, sobriety, and clarity of expression characteristic of the classic Roman genius in order to render the worship of the church more accessible to the faithful, especially to those in mission lands. It was on the basis of historical precedent, then, that the restoration of the Easter Vigil (1951) and Holy Week (1955) by Pius XII was undertaken. Masses were promoted by some in the liturgical avant-garde in both Europe and the United States. It was also on the basis of historical research into the liturgy that the period just prior to Vatican II began to hear more and more calls for the use of the vernacular in worship.

Because of the groundwork done by liturgists and historians in the years prior to Vatican II, the Preparatory Commission on the Liturgy established by the pope in 1959 was in a position to quickly draft a schema of the document on the liturgy. It reflects the advanced state of the research on the liturgy prior to the council that this schema became the first order of business of Vatican II.

Vatican II

The norms for liturgical adaptation to the customs and traditions of peoples are outlined by Vatican II (*S.C.* 37–40). These articles clearly move beyond what many critics had labeled an "archaeological" approach that characterized much of the preconciliar research on the liturgy, and they open the way for real adaptation of the liturgy based on a reformed Roman rite characterized by a "noble simplicity, brevity and clarity" (*S.C.* 34). While the council proposes the Roman rite as a "universal" rite, it does so fully aware that there will have to be important differences in the way in which it is celebrated in cultures as diverse as those found in Africa and Asia.

Article 37 of *S.C.* announces the general principle governing liturgical adaptation and is based on Pius XII's encyclical *Summi Pontificatus*. This article opens the door to true liturgical pluralism within the Roman rite by stating:

The church has no wish to impose a rigid uniformity in matters which do not affect the faith or the good of the whole community; rather, the church respects and fosters the genius and talents of various races and peoples.

Clearly, the principle enunciated in this article reflects the historical reality lived by the church down through the ages, except for the anomalous period after the Council of Trent. It is the faith itself that constitutes ecclesial unity and not a rigid uniformity in the cultural expression of that faith in the liturgy. The article further establishes two general criteria for admitting elements of a particular people's way of life in the worship of the local church. One is negative: "that anything not indissolubly bound up with superstition and error" may be admitted into the liturgy. The other is positive: that these elements be "in harmony with the true and authentic spirit of the liturgy." Both of these criteria require interpretation that is not exhaustively provided by *S.C.* and that will become the object of subsequent debate after the council.

Having stated these general principles of adaptation, *S.C.* 38–39 then moves to more concrete proposals regarding their implementation and to what could be termed the first level of adaptation of the Roman rite. It provides for "legitimate variations and adaptations to different groups, regions, and peoples" in the revision of the liturgical books. These revisions and adaptations are to be done "especially in mission lands," although the sense of the word *especially* (*praesertim*), as explained by the conciliar commission, while emphasizing the need for adaptation in mission lands, does not mean to exclude the possibility of adaptation in countries where Christianity and the Roman rite have known a long history.

S.C. 37 sets a limit to these adaptations with the expression "provided the substantial unity of the Roman rite is preserved." The expression "substantial unity of the Roman rite" is nowhere defined by *S.C.*, but is most probably referring to article 39, which speaks of adaptation within the limits set by the *edition typica* of the liturgical books. This means to say that the unity of the Roman rite is safeguarded when the norms for adaptation, written into the official liturgical books issued by Rome, are observed. These norms give some limited freedom to the "competent territorial authority," i.e., a national conference of bishops, to adapt the liturgy to local needs. It

should be noted that if the liturgical books provide for it, the bishops' conferences may institute modifications in the liturgy, that go beyond simple cosmetic changes and that even restructure the rite itself. Article 39 further states that this kind of adaptation is to be applied "especially in the case of the administration of the sacraments, the sacramentals, processions, liturgical language, sacred music, and the arts." This mandate is reiterated in article 63, which calls on the bishops' conferences to prepare new rituals adapted "to the needs of the different regions."

Thus, the approach to adaptation taken by these articles (*S.C.* 38–39) could be described by the term *acculturation,* defined as an initial encounter between the Roman rite and the local culture. While maintaining the nucleus of the Roman rite, a translation of those elements that are contingent on Western culture would be recoded or reinterpreted into the particular forms and expressions of the "receiving" culture in order to make them more expressive of the faith.

Article 40 deals with a more radical form of adaptation, which can be rightly called *inculturation*. While the norms proposed for acculturating the liturgy as found in the revised liturgical books might be sufficient for renewing the liturgy in a European country such as Italy, the council wisely foresaw that in areas of the world that are not heirs to an exclusively western-European cultural tradition, the need for adapting the liturgy would require not only more profound modifications of the Roman rite, but a real inculturation of the liturgy. This inculturation of the liturgy can be defined as an ongoing process of a reciprocal, critical interaction and assimilation between the Roman rite and the local culture. Although the initial draft of the first part of this article specifically mentioned the missions, this reference was dropped in the final redaction of the document in order to allow the application of this article to other "places and circumstances" not considered "missionary" ("Typis Polyglottis, Vaticanis" in *Schema Constitutionis de Sacra Liturgia* [1962], 27).

S.C. 40 spells out the nature of these adaptations and the procedure that is to govern their implementation in three paragraphs. The first paragraph stipulates that the "competent territorial ecclesiastical authority" is "to carefully and prudently weigh what elements from the traditions and culture of individual peoples may be appropriately admitted into divine worship." The adaptations judged opportune should then be submitted to the Holy See's approval. The second paragraph deals with the Holy See's granting the bishops' conferences the authority to direct "preliminary experiments" for a specified length of time and within certain groups so that "the adaptations are made with all the circumspection they demand." Finally, the third paragraph speaks of the technical assistance of experts, "particularly in mission lands," where the problems associated with this kind of adaptation would presumably be more complex.

While articles 37–40 of *S.C.* mark a revolutionary departure from the centuries-old Roman resistance to any kind of liturgical adaptation, they should also be read in the context of other articles that speak of more general principles of liturgical reform such as article 24, which emphasizes the importance of the liturgy being thoroughly grounded in sacred Scripture. Also, article 23 reflects a more cautious attitude toward both liturgical adaptation and the unity of the Roman rite. It states that even after careful "theological, historical, and pastoral investigation," as well as a "study of the experience derived from recent liturgical reforms, . . . there must be no innovations unless the good of the church genuinely and certainly requires them; care should taken that any new forms adopted should in some way grow organically from forms already existing." The same article warns against "marked differences between rites used in neighboring areas." While these caveats might seem today to be overly cautious, they reflect the "compromising nature" of a document drafted to assuage the anxieties of some of the more traditional conciliar participants, who feared not only ill-considered innovation but the wholesale destruction of the Roman rite.

Articles other than 37–40 of the same document, however, speak in very specific terms of the possible need for the radical adaptation or inculturation of the liturgy in "mission lands," especially in the celebration of the sacraments of initiation and marriage. Article 65 proposes that "besides what is part of Christian tradition, those initiation elements in use among individual peoples, to the extent that such rites are compatible with the Christian rite of initiation" be allowed. In much the same spirit, article 77, which speaks of the revision of the marriage rite, states

that "the competent, territorial ecclesiastical authority . . . is free to draw up . . . its own rite suited to the usages of place and people."

This call for adaptation expressed by the *Constitution on the Sacred Liturgy* becomes even more insistent and sophisticated in subsequent conciliar documents, that treat the relationship between the church and culture, especially the *Decree on the Missionary Activity of the Church* (*A.G.* 9–11, 21–22) and the *Pastoral Constitution on the Church in the Modern World* (*G.S.* 44, 58). These documents, along with the *Dogmatic Constitution on the Church* (*L.G.* 13, 17, 23) and the *Declaration on the Relation of the Church to Non-Christian Religions* (*N.A.* 2), being the product of a more mature degree of conciliar thought on the question of adaptation, help to describe in more detail the relationship of the church to culture and hence clarify some of the ambiguity noted in the documents relative to liturgical adaptation.

One of the most important theological constructs proposed by the council to describe the relation of church to culture is found in the *Decree on the Missionary Activity of the Church* (*A.G.* 10). This article proposes the Incarnation of Christ as the paradigmatic way in which the universal church relates to local cultures. The *Pastoral Constitution on the Church in the Modern World* defines this relationship as reciprocal; it is not simply a question of the church "translating" into another cultural idiom the datum of the faith, whose western European expression is considered somehow normative. Rather, citing the historical relationship between the church and culture, it belongs to the church itself to again profit from the "riches hidden in different cultures" and "to learn to express the Christian message in the concepts and language of different peoples" through fostering a "vital contact and exchange between the church and different cultures" (*G.S.* 44). Moreover, "the church has been sent to all ages and nations and, therefore, is not tied exclusively and indissolubly to any race or nation, to any one particular way of life, or to any customary practices, ancient or modern" (*G.S.* 58).

These teachings of the council clearly have implications for the more radical adaptation or of the liturgy as described in *S.C.* 40 in groups and nations that are not heirs to the western European cultural tradition.

Postconciliar Developments

The period just after the council saw intense activity on the part of the various commissions established to revise and translate the new liturgical books into modern languages. It should be pointed out that the very translation of the official Latin *edition typica* versions of the liturgical books constitutes an adaptation. The instruction *Comme le prevoit* of 1969 on the translation of liturgical texts for celebration with a congregation (*D.O.L.* 838–880) clearly enunciates principles and norms that emphasize that the text, "as a ritual sign, is a medium of spoken communication" (*D.O.L.* 842) and discourages a literal fidelity to the Latin text. This instruction opts for the principle of "dynamic equivalence," whereby the concepts expressed in the Latin text are rendered in a modern language by proposing an equivalent concept drawn from the culture where the language is used. Realizing the complex nature of this enterprise, the Consilium also wisely notes that the mere translation of texts is "not sufficient for a fully renewed liturgy. The creation of new texts will be necessary" (*D.O.L.* 880).

Looking at the introductions and ritual directions in the revised and translated liturgical books, the word *adaptation* is applied to the liturgy in two distinct ways. The first kind of adaptation concerns the alternatives provided by the liturgical books themselves to be selected by those who prepare the liturgy so that the celebration might "correspond as fully as possible to the needs, spiritual preparation, and mentality of the participants" (*General Introduction to the Rite of Mass* 313). The *Actio Pastoralis* instruction on Masses for special groups and the *Directory for Masses with Children,* issued by the Congregation for Divine Worship, make further provision for this kind of adaptation of the eucharistic celebration based on number, age, and spiritual needs of those who make up the assembly. The revised rites of initiation, for example, also contain articles, that provide guidelines for the presider's adaptation of the celebration (RCIA 67; *Rite of Baptism for Children* 27–31; *Rite of Confirmation* 18).

A second kind of adaptation proposed by the postconciliar documents already enunciated in *S.C.* 38 and 39 falls within the purview of national bishops' conferences deputed by *S.C.* 63 to compose their own rituals "adapted to the needs of their specific regions," which were to be confirmed by the Holy See. Elements from the local culture that substitute or illustrate the Roman ritual can be incorporated into the liturgy. This acculturation of the liturgy parallels to some degree the principle of dynamic equivalence at work in the translation of verbal texts. Much of the postconciliar work on adaptation, especially in Africa and Asia, has used this method. The recent "Roman Missal for the Dioceses of Zaire" approved by the Congregation for Divine Worship in 1988 ("Le Missel Romain pour dioceses du Zaire," *Notitae* 24 [1988]: 454–472) is a good example of the use of this approach. This missal "interprets" the Roman Missal in the cultural idiom of this region of Africa, restructuring the rite, adding local gestures, and proposing alternate prayers that reflect deeply held values in Africa, such as respect for ancestors.

The third and most radical form of adaptation, inculturation, is not provided for by the liturgical books, except in the case of marriage. The *Introduction to the Rite of Marriage* speaks not only of assuming elements from the local culture to illustrate what is contained in the Roman ritual (*O.C.M.* 13–16) but of the creation of a whole new rite based on the culture of the place, as long as the presence of the minister who witnesses the vows is safeguarded and the nuptial blessing is given. In this case, the Rite of Marriage seems to be in genuine dialogue with local cultures, a dialogue that presupposes a real reciprocity by encouraging the use of marriage customs and traditions originating in the pre-Christian culture. However, in general, there seems to be a marked hesitance on the part of the Roman authorities to implement fully the possibilities inherent in article 40 of the *Constitution on the Sacred Liturgy*.

On the one hand, there seems to be a fear that adaptation would lead to a total disintegration of the Roman rite, whose theological and formal characteristics are deemed worthy of retention, even in very different cultural contexts. On the other hand, not very much time has elapsed for this to take place. As we know from history, it took several centuries for the Christianization of the Roman Empire to get to the point where the church felt comfortable in adopting formerly pagan customs into Christian worship. Although conciliar documents like *Nostra Aetate* 2 speak of a real openness and respect for non-Christian religions, it seems that a similar process needs to take place in non-European areas before the liturgy can truly be described as having inculturated elements from non-Christian religions, that are an integral part of the cultural identity of these countries.

As the previous pages have demonstrated, liturgical adaptation is not a new phenomenon. Since the liturgy is the self-expression of the church, it has and must continue to adapt itself to the different and changing cultural environments in which it finds itself or risk becoming irrelevant. Much more is at stake than simply making people feel more "at ease" in worship; the very mission of the church to preach the gospel to all nations is compromised when adaptation does not take place. As Anscar Chupungco notes, "The refusal to adapt amounts to a denial of the universality of salvation" (Anscar Chupungco, *Cultural Adaptation of the Liturgy* [New York: Paulist Press, 1982], 87). The challenge that faces all local churches at present, especially those in non-European settings, is essentially one of evangelization, of proclaiming and celebrating the message of the gospel and the mystery of Christ in a way that is meaningful to the many cultures of the human race. This can only be done if local churches are allowed to continue on the road to true liturgical inculturation indicated by the Second Vatican Council. Paul VI indicates:

> Evangelization loses much of its force and effectiveness if it does not take into consideration the actual people to whom it is addressed, if it does not use their language, their signs, and symbols, if it does not answer the questions they ask, and it does not have an impact on their concrete life. (*Evangeli Nuntiandi* 63)

Mark R. Francis[21]

178 ✦ LITURGY AND CULTURE: FOUR PARADIGMS

The following article introduces the reader to four different approaches to liturgical inculturation and to the variety of scholarly disciplines that can aid liturgists in thinking about the relationship between worship and culture.

Modern discussions about the cultural adaptation of the liturgy are related to fundamental theological convictions about the relationship between the Christian tradition and human culture. In general, four paradigms to the faith/culture relationship appear to be operative in modern American Catholicism. These are the conservative, liberal, radical, and neoconservative.

The conservative paradigm maintains an absolute commitment to the inherited shape of Catholicism and has very little openness to modern culture. While conservatism often manifests strong commitment to traditional cultures in which religion and social life were integrated, it generally regards modern culture as inimical to authentic religious life and practice. Among the more notable examples of the conservative paradigm is the integralist movement in French Catholicism in the earlier part of this century. Archbishop Marcel Lefebvre, founder of the Society of St. Pius X, remains the most notable representative of the conservative position today.

The conservative paradigm places strong emphasis on the cultural integrity and autonomy of Catholicism. The church, accordingly, is viewed as a perfect society, and conceptions of doctrine and ecclesiastical practice generally have a classicist character, which fails to account for change and development within the tradition.

In liturgical matters, this paradigm generates strong opposition to liturgical change or adaptation. It precludes the possibility of significant use of non-Christian ritual elements and symbols in the liturgy. Indeed, it takes a generally hostile attitude towards non-Christian religions, regarding them as defective vehicles for the gospel.

The conservative position is represented by those who reject or merely tolerate the liturgical revisions initiated by the Second Vatican Council. Adherents of this view generally opt for the normative character of the so-called Tridentine Mass and deny that the liturgy should be adapted or changed for cultural or pastoral reasons.

Cultural adaptation of the liturgy in this mode tends to be superficial and incidental. The project here is appropriately characterized as *accommodation,* whereby some local or native artistic elements or customs are allowed a minor role in liturgical celebrations. The principal concern, however, remains the integrity of the Latin rite in all its elements and expressions.

The liberal paradigm in modern Roman Catholicism is characterized by a commitment to intensive dialogue between the gospel and human culture. It has a strong openness to the religious significance of modern culture and the revelatory character of ongoing human experience. It seeks to overcome the rupture between Christian tradition and the modern world and tends to be optimistic about the congruence between the gospel and culture. It is enthusiastic about cultural pluralism, interreligious dialogue, and the emergence of a world church incarnated in diverse cultures.

In liturgical matters, the liberal attitude is strongly committed to cultural adaptation. It is confident that Catholic liturgy can be extricated from its Roman and European forms and expressions. The project here is appropriately described as _inculturation_, whereby local ritual and symbolic forms are invested with Christian meaning. The goal is to create styles of worship that are authentically Christian, yet structured around the ritual and symbol systems of the particular culture. The project typically involves attempts to "baptize" some non-Christian rites, particularly those associated with passage and transition.

Liturgical inculturation is not, however, free from considerable ambiguity. The attempts to identify and adapt non-Christian ritual and symbolic forms as vehicles for Christian expression can easily be compromised by the internal dynamics and semantic tenaciousness of the forms themselves. Accordingly, the liberal project to wed Christian meanings and cultural forms has a tendency to underestimate the complexity of the project involved.

The radical paradigm is distinguished from the liberal by its commitment to a substantial reformulation of Christian faith. In general, radicalism has a limited and selective commitment to the inherited tradition and generally allows a hermeneutic of suspicion a central role in the appropriation of that tradition. The interest is not so much in opening the gospel or the Christian tradition to cultures as it is in generating a critique of both the gospel and human culture and establishing a new religious/cultural order. Accordingly, the radical project is often apocalyptic and millenarian. Radicalism favors a pluralistic view of religion, allowing other religions equal or similar status to Christianity and asserting the possibility of a number of Christ figures, or saviors. For these reasons, it is not committed to upholding the uniqueness of Christ or of the Christian faith.

The radical dialogue between Christianity and other religions is appropriately described as _in religionization_, whereby Christianity undertakes a self-emptying into non-Christian religions so that a new religious order will emerge. What Christianity has to offer other religions in this paradigm is not particular forms, doctrines, or an institutional order but a liberating dynamic for self-expression and freedom.

The radical approach is operative in some strands of Christian feminist thought and practice, which seek a reconstruction of Christian tradition in order to overcome perceived structures of patriarchy, sexism, and oppression. Some feminists, critical of both Christian tradition and patriarchal culture, promote a process similar to in religionization, whereby Christianity enters into dialogue with non-Christian feminist and utopian traditions and generates new ritual and symbolic expressions.

In the radical paradigm, adaptation brings about a profound reconfiguration of inherited liturgical forms. It favors local religious elements and symbols and rejects those imported from other cultures. It accords scriptural status to nonbiblical

The Cross Fleurettée. _A decorative cross used with altar or pulpit vestments during the season of Pentecost. The ends cut off in three graceful petals symbolize the Holy Spirit._

readings and gives narrative and mythic expression to minority or "suppressed" voices.

The neoconservative paradigm shares with the conservative an absolute commitment to the priority of the Christian tradition, but is distinguished from it by a more sophisticated appreciation of change and development within the tradition. This paradigm shares with the liberal an appropriation of the positive values of human culture and the need for the church to have a credible presence in diverse cultural environments. However, it incorporates a fundamentally critical and cautious attitude toward modern liberal culture and is aware of the danger to Christian faith in a wholesale embrace of liberal values and philosophical schemes. Accordingly, neoconservative scholarship is acutely attentive to social-scientific analysis of the anti-institutional, atomistic, and individualistic character of modern culture.

These four paradigms of the faith/culture relationship are not, of course, rigidly self-contained or mutually exclusive. Considerable overlap is evident in theory and practice; and depending on the issue, there is considerable movement back and forth.

Developing Methodologies

The study of the relationship between liturgy and culture is carried on today in a variety of ways and incorporates methodologies developed in a number of different fields. The philosophical and scientific study of religion (Otto, Eliade, Van der Leeuw), philosophy (Ricoeur, Langer), psychology (Freud, Erikson, Jung), and sociology (Berger, Palmer, Bellah) have been usefully appropriated in the study of Christian rites. Of particular importance are the methodologies and findings of ritual studies, the study of popular religion, and the literature of cultural criticism.

Ritual studies is a relatively new field unifying the study of ritual traditionally carried out in the fields of anthropology, sociology, psychology, and art criticism. Though the methodologies employed in ritual studies remain quite diverse, they share a common appreciation of the highly dynamic role of ritual and symbol in cultural and religious communities. Much of the work in the field is carried on through minute study of the internal dynamics of official elements and systems. An increasing number of liturgists have begun to attend to the operations of Christian liturgy through the insights that are gained from the field of ritual studies. Among the theorists whose work is relevant to liturgical studies are Victor Turner, Mary Douglas, Clifford Geertz, and Ronald Grimes. Liturgical scholars are, as yet, however, only at the beginning of the process of developing an adequate methodology for the application of ritual studies to the study of Christian liturgy.

An area of study that provides significant insight into the culture/liturgy relationship is that of folk or popular religion. Here attention is not so much upon non-Christian religious communities but upon traditional Catholic societies where a fusion of Catholic ritual and pre-Christian rites and customs has long been effected. While study in this area has traditionally embodied the conviction that folk religion represents a corruption of Christian practice and an unhealthy syncretism, more recent study has come to regard popular or folk religion as expressive of a positive and pastorally appropriate concretization of the gospel in particular cultures.

Impetus for a more positive appreciation of popular religion in Latin America was provided by the meetings of CELAM at Medellín in 1968 and at Puebla in 1978. The study of Hispanic folk religion has since then become an important feature of church life in both Latin America and North America. Considerable attention has also been devoted to the insights for liturgical adaptation that may be gained from the study of Filipino Catholicism, black Christianity in North America, and analyses of Polish, Spanish, and Italian Catholicism.

The literature of cultural criticism also provides important elements of reflection for liturgical scholars concerned about cultural adaptation in modern secular societies. American culture critics (Lasch, Sennett, Meyerowitz, Bloom) have analyzed the individualistic, subjectivist, and atomistic character of American culture and have generated caution among some theologians and liturgists about the prospect of an indigenized American Catholicism. The compatibility of American culture with Roman Catholicism has been the source of debate among neoconservatives, with some (Schlinder, Olsen) arguing for fundamental incompatibility and others (Weigel, Novak, Neuhaus) arguing for a fundamental compatibility, despite the present disorder of American culture.

M. Francis Mannion[22]

179 ❖ A ROMAN CATHOLIC APPROACH TO LITURGICAL INCULTURATION

Roman Catholic liturgical inculturation begins with the texts that are approved for use in Catholic parishes around the world. Liturgists are charged with discerning how those texts and related ritual practices may be appropriately expressed in various cultural settings. Key issues include the translation of liturgical texts and the development of indigenous arts, music, vestments, and gestures.

Our concern is not with inculturation _and_ the liturgy but inculturation _of_ the liturgy. The focus will be on the processes, methods, attitudes, and persons involved in assuring that the liturgy truly reflects the culture of those who celebrate it. While many aspects of the church's liturgy deserve attention, we will reflect for the most part on the eucharistic liturgy.

The larger _context,_ however, for a discussion of the inculturation of the liturgy must be the question of authentic living, giving witness to and celebrating the Christian faith. The liturgy is surely a privileged area of inculturation, one most tangible. But liturgy is the public celebration of the faith of a particular people. Unless that lived faith is inculturated into the customs and culture of that people, the liturgy will remain foreign or even imposed, rather than flowing from the lives of the people.

The _goal_ desired in inculturation of the liturgy is a eucharistic celebration that is vital, challenging, and liberating. The worshiping community is confronted and comforted by the Word of God, which is explored in a homily that relates the Word to the community's particular context. Then, the community members are sacramentally linked with the paschal mystery of Jesus Christ and strengthened to go forth and live that mystery in their situation. The Eucharist, if truly inculturated, is indeed the source and summit of Christian life and impels those who actively participate to go forward to witness to that life in the marketplace.

The _problem_ of inculturation of the liturgy arises precisely because, in at least the most recent history of the liturgy, there has been in the Latin Catholic church an emphasis on preserving the unity of the church's liturgy, often at the expense of its catholicity. The Tridentine rite had been the predominant form of worship in Latin Roman Catholicism from Trent until the breakthrough of the Second Vatican Council. This meant that even as the church expanded from Europe to North and South America, to India, to the Far East, and more recently to Africa, it was this same Roman rite that was uniformly celebrated.

In the movement towards full inculturation, authors speak of _degrees_ or _stages_ of inculturation. A first stage, which is really the absence of inculturation, is _imposition_, where the theology and liturgy of Europe, for example, is exported to the Americas or to Africa with no input from the receiving culture. A second stage or degree is _translation_, where at least the local languages are employed in catechesis and liturgy. A third stage would be _adaptation_ or _accommodation_. Here minor changes are allowed, and at least some attention and respect is given to the local culture. This is explored by the Second Vatican Council in _S.C._ 37–39. Finally, true _inculturation_ can occur where the local culture is seriously studied and supplies new creative impetus and input for liturgical celebrations. _S.C._ 40 speaks of this deeper or more radical adaptation. Yet in reality, one must admit that there are only a few examples of such true inculturation, e.g., in the liturgy of Zaire and in certain Indian churches.

Vatican II was clearly part of the recent trend to appreciate cultural diversity and richness. The _Constitution on the Sacred Liturgy,_ with its fostering of the vernacular language in the liturgy, is simply one small beginning in the more difficult and unexplored moves to inculturation in the liturgy. The _Pastoral Constitution on the Church in the Modern World_ presents a new appreciation of culture and impels the church to dialogue with the modern world, rather than withdraw from it. So too, the _Decree on the Missionary Activity of the Church_ indicates that mission flowing from the Incarnation must take place in every culture on this earth. The seeds of the Word _(semina Verbi)_ are present in all cultures, and thus the missionary treads on holy ground when he or she encounters another culture. All of these provide a foundation and impetus for inculturation in all areas of Christian life, including in a special way the liturgy.

How does this inculturation take place? What are the attitudes that must be present in church leadership and in the people of God for it to occur? Who actually carries out the challenging task of inculturation of the liturgy? We will attempt to address these key questions through the employment of the pastoral circle. Imagine a circle with three points on its circumference and with arrows pointing back and forth between the points on the circumference. The first point of the circle represents the rich liturgical traditions of the church, going back to the New Testament. This would also include contemporary official church teaching on the liturgy, as in Vatican II, as well as the rich diversity of liturgical expression found throughout the Catholic church today. The second point of the circle represents the local community in its particular cultural situation or context. This might be in New York, Nairobi, or a small village in India or in Africa. The third point refers to the pastoral or liturgical leadership of that local community—those in charge of planning and celebrating the liturgy.

To assure that a liturgy is truly local and hence inculturated and yet to assure that it is truly Christian and Catholic, the liturgical leaders need a familiarity with the various possibilities of liturgical expression and symbolism offered by the Christian tradition (the first point on the circle). They also need to be immersed in their local culture, so that they know how that particular community gathers, prays, sings, and expresses its faith most in accord with their cultural heritage (the second point on the circle). The leadership must of course not act on its own, but always in dialogue with the larger church and with the authorities of the church. And the leadership (the third point on the circle) must realize that it will succeed only to the extent that it calls forth and involves the gifts, talents, and sensibilities of the community for which it is responsible. Liturgy is indeed the public prayer of the people of the local community, and it must be an expression of their faith and their struggle for a life of justice, their living the kingdom vision. Thus, in the moving to a truly inculturated liturgy, it is the entire community that must eventually take responsibility for the liturgy; even if in its formative stages, this will depend heavily upon the liturgical leaders and their collaborators.

Inculturation of the liturgy thus must occur in every local church and not simply be thought of as applying to Africa or Asia. As a matter of fact, the need for inculturation can be seen most clearly in non-Western cultures. But the need for it can also be seen in a black or Hispanic parish in the United States. So too, a liturgy for children or youth should have a different tone than one for adults; and a liturgy in the heart of New York City must be somewhat different from one in a rural area of Montana. Thus, every Christian community has the challenging task of celebrating the liturgy in a manner that is faithful to the Christian tradition (represented by the first point on the circle) and appropriate to its particular context (the second point on the circle).

There are several areas of inculturation of the liturgy, just as there are degrees of inculturation. One might begin with the language of the celebration or with liturgical vestments that better reflect local culture and clothing. The music might be adapted to employ local instruments. Yet these are only small beginnings. Every aspect of liturgy must be creatively examined, including the time and space for the celebration, the gestures and postures (sitting rather than kneeling), the forms of prayer (more use of litany/responses), the art and architecture (local or imported stations of the cross), the images and symbols that grow from the religious and cultural sensibilities of the people, and the mode of leadership (individual or communal, male and/or female). Even the basic elements of the celebration, the food and drink, become part of the search of the local community for ways in which to liturgically live and celebrate its Christian faith. If this community, led by the Spirit, with the help of liturgical expertise and in union with the universal church, creatively and faithfully expresses its faith, then it will in turn be contributing to the growth of the catholicity of the church. One sees this already occurring through the church in Zaire and through the possibilities it offers both to African Catholics and to the universal church.

How did this creative new liturgical expression originate? One must first recall that the Roman rite, even at the time of Vatican II, was only one, although a very important, rite of the church. One must see that the form of liturgy as brought to Africa by the missionaries is indeed one form and one that can be developed in accord with liturgical principles and guidelines from church authorities. And even within the present rite, there is space for and a call for adaptation and limited flexibility. Celebrants should take advantage of the various options now possible for the entrance rite and for the introduction to the Lord's Prayer, to cite two examples. Then through catechesis and discussion, one begins to encourage the local community to explore its own religious heritage and move to an authentic inculturation of the liturgy for that local community. The local community must keep in dialogue with the larger church. The fact that progress can be made is attested to in the evolution and approval of the Zairian liturgy for certain parts of Zaire. But one must immediately admit that the liturgy of Zaire is the exception rather than the rule and that, for 99 percent of Africa, the process of inculturation of the liturgy has scarcely begun.

Inculturation of the liturgy must be seen therefore as a key part of the ongoing process of any local Christian community in its attempts to truly live and witness to its Christian faith. It is universal and ongoing, that is, called for in every local church and in every time. Cultures are changing. The forces of technology and modernization are offering new possibilities and challenges to Christian communities. Unless the Christian remains in dialogue with these new developments, his or her faith life and subsequent liturgical life will be out of touch and will have no creative impact on these developing cultures. The mission of the church will suffer.

Finally, and this flows from all we have said, inculturation should become something natural, not added on. It simply is the creative living and celebrating of Christian faith in particular contexts. The fact that at present we must single out and focus on inculturation is an indication that we have failed to be engaged in the ongoing inculturation of the liturgy. Our efforts now are corrective. We look for the time when these corrective efforts are no longer necessary, when every local Christian community takes seriously its charge and challenge to be truly Christian and be truly local, faithful to and yet not uncritical of its particular culture.

Peter Schineller, S.J.[23]

180 • CHRISTIAN CULTURAL ENGAGEMENT AND LITURGICAL INCULTURATION

The following essay situates the issue of liturgical inculturation in terms of the larger question of the relationship between the church and culture, attempting to highlight both the inevitable shaping of the church by its cultural environment and the important mission of the church to work for the transformation of culture. Unlike some recent Roman Catholic approaches to inculturation, which often begin by discussing how the text of the liturgy should be adapted to a given cultural situation, this essay describes a framework in which all aspects of worship can be considered in their cultural context.

The greatest challenge facing liturgists today is arguably the challenge of inculturation. The expansion of the church into every neighborhood of the global village and the cultural ferment characteristic of our age challenges the church on every continent to reconsider the relationship of its institutions, theological formulations, and corporate worship to its cultural context. With respect to worship, a bevy of recent publications have addressed the cultural dimension of Christian liturgy, arguing either to bolster traditional liturgical practices threatened by contemporary culture or to censure traditional practices in favor of enticing alternatives. These often animated arguments are frequently advanced in the context of difficult dilemmas that face local parishes. To what extent should Roman Catholic worshipers in Zaire adhere to prescribed Roman rubrics? Should the Protestant community church in any town in America implement a seeker-sensitive alternative worship service? It is an understatement to assert that the passion involved in such debates usually emits more heat than light.

What is needed is a far-ranging model for conceptualizing the problems of inculturation. Participants in these passionate debates need a balanced, even dispassionate, framework both to negotiate between entrenched and conflicting perspectives and to sense the implications of their eventual decisions. Such a model must reflect both rigorous theological thinking and a passion for the church's mission in the world. It must offer a balanced, multidimensional view both of liturgical action and of the culture in which the liturgical action will take place. This essay attempts to define some important dimensions of such a model. Its task is thus synthetic. At many levels, this paper is dissatisfying because of it; complex issues and theories are addressed in only a cursory fashion so as to observe their interrelations. The goal of this essay, then, is not to answer any specific liturgical issue, but rather to propose a framework that will guide the asking of future questions about the relationship of worship and culture.

The implicit thesis of this analysis is that liturgists have not always addressed cultural questions with either an understanding of the cultural dimensions of liturgy or a passion for the church's mission in the world. Likewise, missiologists and evangelists have not always appreciated the significance of Christian liturgy both as a central act in the church's life and as an important means for initiating God's children into the full life of the church. This paper is offered to promote resolution of these often clashing interests.

Christian Cultural Engagement

The relationship of the Christian faith and human culture is a question that has both haunted and inspired the Christian church since its inception. The first Christians faced innumerable questions about how to live Christianly in pagan Hellenistic culture. Post-Constantinian Christians faced questions about the identification of the church with the monarchy. In recent generations, Christians in the West have again needed to discern how to engage a pagan, secularized culture, while fast-growing Christian communities in third world countries face the challenge of working out the implications of their faith in their cultural context for the first time. Human culture has and will always provide the context in which the church both lives and defines its identity.

Throughout the Christian tradition, many strategies for relating to culture have been practiced and identified. These range from the affirmation of the world by liberal Protestantism to the denial of the world by some forms of Fundamentalism. The variations along this spectrum have been classified by various scholars, from the seminal work of Ernst Troeltsch to the most famous of its progeny, H. Richard Niebuhr's *Christ and Culture* (New York: Harper and Row, 1951). This scholarly conceptualization, perhaps most discussed by social ethicists, is an immensely important work. It crystallizes the most significant theological commitments of various traditions and sets them on the brink of praxis, where they function to motivate and guide Christian communities.

Equally interesting are the ongoing efforts of individual Christians and Christian communities to live out their faith in culture. This praxis both precedes and is later shaped by this scholarly reflection. Christians throughout the centuries have made valiant attempts both to come to grips with the culture around them and to find ways of relating to that culture that are consistent with their faith.

Roughly two broad strands of such efforts can be identified. The first strand consists of efforts within cultures where the church is already established. Whether or not Christian values are dominant within a culture, these efforts find support from a church already largely inculturated. In such contexts, Christians have produced scholarship and participated in the political and economic life of the community, reflecting their faith commitments in each area of life. The second strand consists of missionary enterprises to establish Christian churches in new cultural contexts, such as early Jesuit missionary efforts to Native Americans or current efforts to evangelize various third world countries. These two strands of cultural involvement are rarely considered together. The former is typically the domain of social ethicists; the latter the domain of missionaries and missiologists. But what is significant for the discussion of liturgical inculturation is the striking similarity between these two tasks, for each requires an assessment and evaluation of the cultural context and the development both of a posture to relate to that culture and of strategies with which to engage it. In each of these efforts, Christian believers and Christian churches are addressing an aspect of human culture and are doing so in a self-consciously Christian way. Liturgists considering cultural issues must learn from the insights of both missiologists and social ethicists.

The Role of Christian Liturgy in Cultural Engagement

Strikingly absent from most discussions about the Christian faith and culture is any mention of liturgy. Although liturgy is arguably the most public act of the church, although it includes the central acts of proclamation and sacramental celebration—constitutive dimensions of the Christian church in almost every ecclesiology—and although corporate worship is the single act for which more time and energy are spent than almost any other activity in the history of the church, liturgy is largely ignored in Christian social ethics and missiology. Yet what the church does in its worship, I will argue, both reflects and shapes its attitude toward culture. Since this suggestion is not self-evident to many Christians, especially Protestant ones, some apologetic is needed for taking liturgy seriously when thinking about Christian cultural engagement.

First, liturgy inevitably mirrors both the cultural context and the particular strategies for cultural engagement of any given worshiping community. As Michael Warren has observed, "The worship of the assembly actually does truly embody and express the lived commitments of the group, whatever these are" (*Faith, Culture, and the Worshiping Community* [Washington, D.C.: Pastoral Press, 1993], 59). In the nineteenth century, for example, the "Christ against culture" orientation of the Cambridge ecclesiologists and the "Christ of culture" orientation of mainline Protestantism is given no more eloquent testimony than in their respective worship practices.

Second, Christian worship is an essential dimension of the *missio dei* (mission of God) in the world. The very act of worship by the royal priesthood of God declares the praises of God to the world (1 Pet. 2:9). And one essential dimension of the Lord's Supper is its role in "proclaiming the Lord's death until he comes" (1 Cor. 11:26). Unfortunately, the relationship of worship and mission has not always been appreciated. Rarely have missiologists and liturgists been collaborators in theological discussions or ecclesiastical structures. This was observed as early as thirty years ago by J. G. Davies, who nevertheless urged his readers to "seek to understand worship outwardly in terms of mission" (*Worship and Mission* [London: SCM Press, 1966], 7). Liturgy and mission are not dialectical sparring partners. In the words of Patrick Kiefert, "Effective evangelism and liturgical worship belong together in a mutual apostolic mission" (*Welcoming the Stranger: A Public Theology of Worship and Evangelism* [Minneapolis: Fortress, 1992], 5).

Finally, liturgy has a powerful role in forming individual Christians and the Christian community in their appropriation of a cultural environment. Christian worship forms participants by means of narrative and proclamation, prayer and sacrament, so that they will approach their day-to-day lives in ways that reflect deeply biblical patterns of thought and action. It is one occasion where the church's distinctive vocabulary, narratives, and rituals are developed and enacted. If the church wants to exercise any initiative in its engagement with culture while remaining faithful to the gospel, then it must not neglect the liturgy. For liturgy, more than any other dimension of the church's life, shapes the "lived theology" of a given worshiping community. It writes what might be called the theology of the heart, the theology by which Christians live, think, and pray. In *Constructing a Public Theology: The Church in a Pluralistic Culture* (Louisville: Westminster/John Knox Press, 1991) Harvard theologian Ronald Thiemann indicates:

> [Liturgy] has been one of the most important teaching tools throughout the history of the church. Text, ritual action, liturgical movement, and visual images intertwine to manifest the living faith of the Christian church. For today's Christian, who participates in the life of the Christian community primarily through its Sunday morning worship, liturgy continues to be the primary setting in which the beliefs and practices of Christianity are communicated.

Similarly, as Mark Searle observed, "Celebrating the liturgy should train us to recognize justice and injustice when we see it. It serves as a basis for social criticism by giving us a criterion by which to evaluate the events and structures of the world" (Mark Searle, "Serving the Lord with Justice," in *Liturgy and Social Justice* [Collegeville, Minn.: Liturgical Press, 1980], 29). Corporate worship is an opportunity to model an honest and balanced form of cultural engagement, to awaken in worshipers a deeper sensitivity to matters of justice, and to form worshipers in deeply biblical patterns of thought and action.

The Process of Liturgical Inculturation

Christian cultural engagement has been a central concern for the church throughout its history. Christian liturgy is a dimension of the church that cannot be ignored in this important activity. But how ought liturgy to engage culture? How should liturgists charged with planning and leading worship take into account their cultural context? Following its intent to chart broad conceptual territory, this essay will now propose three tasks in which liturgists should be engaged. These are not intended to be a tidy three-step solution to the problem of cultural engagement, but rather three areas for constant attention in the ongoing challenge of planning and leading Christian worship.

Conceptual Task. The first task is conceptual and theological. Its goal is the refinement of a model in which the questions of cultural engagement can be asked. This task involves proposing definitions for culture, the church, and liturgy, and suggesting how these entities relate. At the very least, this conceptual task demands answers to at least three important questions.

First, what should the Christian posture be toward culture? Quite obviously, consensus among Christians on this question has never been achieved. Answers to this question are both irreconcilable and entrenched in centuries-old traditions, ranging from the affirmation of culture by various liberal Protestant groups to the abnegation of culture by various Anabaptist communities.

What is important for liturgists to understand is that this posturing by Christians of every age and tradition reflects deep theological commitments. If creation is highly valued and seen to include the potential for human culture, then Christian cultural engagement will likewise be highly valued and believed to contain great potential for good. If creation is devalued or subordinated to redemption in a larger theological scheme, then culture will undoubtedly be viewed skeptically. Likewise, the theology of the Incarnation is a theological construct often used as model for Christian cultural engagement, whereby Christian cultural engagement is understood as a mirror of Jesus' simultaneous full participation in culture and his critique and transformation of culture.

Also important for liturgists to understand is that both any given culture and the Christian message are too nuanced, rich, and complex to admit any simplistic, monolithic strategy. At a given time and place, Christians may need to participate vigorously in some forms of cultural life, seek to transform others, and avoid still others. The complexity involved can not be overstated. Modern culture exerts influence on several levels of meaning and is itself comprised of a host of diverse subcultures. Blanket statements about either culture as a whole or the nature of Christian cultural engagement are very dangerous.

Among liturgists, there appears to be consensus that the extremes of either identifying with or spurning a given culture are to be avoided at all costs. Identification with culture, among other things, threatens the meaning of Christian symbols. In the words of Langdon Gilkey, "Religious symbols that lose a special judgment and a special promise over against culture also lose their life and reality" (Langdon Gilkey, "Symbols, Meaning, and the Divine Presence," *Theological Studies* 35 [1974], 253). The denial of cultural elements, in contrast, fundamentally calls into question the very human quality of the liturgy itself.

Perhaps the greatest perceived threat to liturgists today is the mutation of traditional liturgical worship into presentation and even entertainment evangelism. Quentin Schultze observes:

> Across the Protestant and Roman Catholic spectrum, local congregational worship seems more and more like a Hollywood production. Although the televisional influence is not the only one, show-business elements are unmistakable in contemporary worship. The key words used by advocates are "relaxed," "informal," "interesting," and "relevant." . . . (Quentin J. Schultze, *Televangelism and American Culture* [Grand Rapids: Baker Book House, 1991], 221)

The reasons behind this development and its implications for the life of the church are significant and complex, to be sure. But in analyzing this trend, liturgists—and church leaders of every type—must realize that it represents nothing less than a radical identification with culture.

The second question concerns the *goal* of Christian cultural engagement. Some Christians limit their vision, believing that personal evangelism is the only way in which they should relate to their larger cultural environment. Others expand their vision to include a host of cultural activities, proposing that Christians bring their particular insights and values into the public square. This task must be informed by theological insight, particularly by eschatology and missiology. Each of these disciplines in its own way presents a grand portrait of the kingdom of God both as anticipated in the future and realized in the present. In their classical form, each militates against a reductionistic view of mission, which concentrates solely on individual salvation and claims proselytism as its highest goal, while still emphasizing the importance of individual conversion to God. Suffice it to say that throughout its history, the church has tended to emphasize one to the exclusion of the other.

The third question to be addressed regards the role liturgy should play in cultural engagement. This question is particularly important, given the significance of worship in defining and forming the Christian community. Like the others, this conceptual question must be approached theologically, this time from the discipline of the theology of liturgy. Any adequate theology of liturgy teaches that Christian liturgy is a multivalent entity. It is worship, but it is more than worship; it is prayer, but it is more than prayer; it is sacrament, but it is more than sacrament; it is witness and proclamation, but it is more than witness and proclamation. Christian liturgy is also at once the activity of God and the actions of the worshiping community. The community gathers, listens, sings, prays, and eats. And yet it is God who is present, Jesus Christ who perfects the priestly offerings of the community, and the Spirit who effects this presence and groans within individuals of the community—as in all of creation—as they pray. Christian liturgy properly resists being reduced into an evangelistic platform on the one hand or being disembodied from the body of Christ on the other hand. Articulating these basic themes in a theology of liturgy helps to suggest how liturgy in any worship tradition could be understood as a means to cultural engagement. Specifically, it challenges any effort to limit liturgy from cultural engagement on the one hand and to reduce cultural engagement to liturgical expression on the other hand. Meanwhile, it argues that worship must maintain an independent integrity in the life of the church, having its own unique purposes, methods, and modes of participation.

These three conceptual questions suggest that, in addition to other important and proper roles, a liturgist must be a theologian. This involves the lovely and enviable task of imagining the fullness of the kingdom of God, of dreaming of that ideal world yet to come, and of fending off every effort to reduce or limit that vision.

Task of Assessment. If the first task concerns an ideal or idyllic world, the second is oriented to the real world, to real problems, and to the day-to-day worship of the church. This second task is assessment. Christian liturgists who plot strategies for cultural involvement need to be studious observers of both the culture(s) in which they work and the liturgies they plan and lead. This suggests two types of assessment.

The first is _assessment of the local cultural context._ Liturgists must be skilled cultural observers. Fortunately, liturgists have many mentors and fellow workers in this task, given the huge industry that supports the description and criticism of culture. Cultural pundits, advertising strategies, and sociological studies all teach us about the defining characteristics of life and culture in the twentieth century. Even the church is blessed with sophisticated sociological analysis of its life. These are voices to which liturgists must listen and listen discerningly.

Perhaps the greatest trap into which Christian liturgists may fall regarding such analyses is the temptation to oversimplify the trends and values of contemporary culture. Recent social and anthropological theory has moved away from a vision of a given culture as a unified whole. Instead, it distinguishes structural and improvisational dimensions at work in any given cultural setting. With regard to life in the United States, for example, consider the many terms that could claim to define the current cultural climate: individualism, privatism, modernism, postmodernism, pluralism, secularism, subjectivism, multiculturalism, cynicism, populism, consumerism, narcissism, entertainmentism, violent, politically correct, ritually incompetent, post-Christendom, and becoming intimatized, politicized, and bureaucratized. Each of these terms identifies an important feature of modern North American culture. The sheer number of these and related descriptions calls the attentive student of culture to resist simplistic analyses.

Also problematic is the assessment of any one of those terms for its import for Christian worship. With regard to the subjectivism, for example, M. Francis Mannion is quick to observe that it will lead to a "bitter harvest" in which worship degenerates into "therapy," becomes disengaged from its role in social transformation, and—along with the Scriptures and the church itself—becomes a slave to "inner realities and personal dispositions" (M. Francis Mannion, "Liturgy and the Present

Crisis of Culture," *Worship* 62 [March 1988], 105–107). In contrast, Michael Aune considers this assessment "needlessly inflammatory" and proposes that precisely this sort of subjectivism may lead to a realization of the new potential for appropriating the objective meaning of liturgical action (Michael B. Aune, "Worship in an Age of Subjectivism Revisited," *Worship* 65 [May 1991], 224–238). Any prominent cultural value may have simultaneous potential for good and evil with respect to worship. Liturgists must be vigilant for liturgical strategies that will foster the good without reaping the evil.

The second task of assessment is *assessment of current liturgical practice.* This is an art that liturgists have always practiced to some extent. Every effort to analyze the relative strength of the worship life of a community is a part of this task. But liturgists must go beyond a simple evaluation of their goals and relative strengths and learn to view their own community as if they were from the outside. Particularly instructive are methods of cultural anthropologists and other students of human ritual who attempt to observe religious rites with the goal of interpreting or of hypothesizing about the relationships they express and the theological commitments they imply. These methods attempt to distill what may be the hidden cultural assumptions of a given Christian community. This sort of assessment turns liturgists into students of themselves and their community, heightening self-consciousness about the far-reaching implications of even mundane liturgical choices for the theological integrity of the worshiping community. Observing who leads liturgical celebration, for example, provides a clue to the particular vision of leadership and community that a given church espouses. Observing what style of music is employed in liturgy is indicative of the social and cultural setting of a given community and of its implicit relationship with local culture. Every liturgical action is a cultural icon that teaches the attentive observer a great deal about the cultural values and theological commitments of a worshiping community. Liturgists must be constantly vigilant about these indicators and must become adept at carefully scrutinizing local liturgical practices as such an icon.

The Liturgical Task. A third ongoing task for Christian liturgists is one of *liturgical contextualization.*

This task permeates every aspect of planning and leading Christian worship, each of which inherently involves issues of contextualization within culture. Every anthem, hymn, or bit of service music; every banner, parament, or vestment; every spoken prayer, homily, or rubric is a cultural artifact. The goal of the conscientious liturgists should be not only to describe this phenomenon but also to prescribe liturgical practices that adequately reflect a community's cultural context and theological commitments. This third task is carried out in light of the conceptual- and assessment-oriented tasks described above. This task is particular to each worshiping community. No universally applicable approach nor any universal solution to a given set of liturgical questions can be recommended in this brief essay. What can be said is that its largest challenge is to both remain faithful to the gospel of Jesus Christ and to be appropriately responsive to the cultural context in which it is placed. The twin dangers it seeks to avoid are "cultural capitulation" on the one hand and "cultural irrelevancy" on the other hand (Kenneth Smits, "Liturgical Reform in a Cultural Perspective," *Worship* 50 [1976], 98).

Final Comments

This essay has proposed that liturgical inculturation be attempted in light of a complex web of theological and cultural analyses. The three tasks described above complicate what otherwise may have been conceptualized as a comparatively simple task of, say, translating a given liturgy into a new vernacular language or adopting a new style of music.

But what is the benefit of this complex scheme? First, it alerts liturgists and anyone else who will listen to their formative role in the church. Liturgists who plot changes in liturgical practice along cultural lines are never changing only the order or style in which a Sunday morning service takes place. In a much broader and significant way, they are rewriting the church's approach to social ethics and theology; they are rewriting and adapting the church's strategy for cultural engagement.

Second, a more expansive frame of reference exposes unwitting inconsistencies in the church's life and work. It is paradoxical, for example, that conservative Protestant evangelicals, who have long been wary of cultural engagement, eagerly embrace a sweeping mélange of cultural forms in their liturgical life. It is similarly telling that many worshiping communities with a strong liturgical tradition are now questioning nearly every aspect of their worship life. Not even the most cherished liturgical texts, music, and visual symbols in the most traditional communities have escaped cultural critique. It is important that this evaluation not take place in a overly simplistic discussion that ignores the complexity of modern culture.

Third, by discussing cultural engagement, evangelism, and liturgical inculturation in the same context, each is given its own identity while remaining open to insights gleaned from the others. Without each other, each produces an unnecessarily narrow vision of Christianity. Evangelism without social ethics is mere proselytism; social ethics without evangelism is mere activism; social ethics and evangelism without inculturation, is cultural chauvinism; and inculturation without social ethics and evangelism is merely cultural capitulation. Any divorce of these concepts from each other renders both Christian cultural engagement and Christian worship impoverished.

Fourth, this scheme reminds liturgists that they will inevitably err. Liturgical inculturation is fraught with dangers on every side. One decision that absolutizes culture may be followed by one that sells out an enduring and integral aspect of the Christian faith. One decision that shores up the church's identity and criticizes a local cultural context may endanger the church's survival in that context and vice versa. This is not to deter the effort from being made, for liturgical inculturation is inevitable. To not attempt to control or shape liturgy is to be left open to the warp and woof of a culture. Rather, this scheme calls liturgists to a certain sobriety for their task.

Thus, the task of liturgical inculturation is never to be underestimated. If carried out oblivious to a culture milieu, apathy to larger theological issues, and strong-headed self-confidence, this task can and will paralyze both the mission and the liturgy of the church for generations to come. But if handled with sociocultural poise, theological acumen, and prayer-filled common sense, this task can invigorate the mission of the church on every level.

John D. Witvliet

181 ✦ BIBLIOGRAPHY ON LITURGICAL INCULTURATION

Arbuckle, G. A. "Inculturation Not Adaptation: Time to Change Terminology." _Worship_ 60 (1986): 551–520.

Aune, Michael B. "Worship in an Age of Subjectivism Revisited." _Worship_ 65 (May 1991): 224–238.

Bevans, Stephen B. _Models of Contextual Theology._ Maryknoll, N.Y.: Orbis Books, 1992.

Bibby, Reginald. _Fragmented Gods: The Poverty and Potential of Religion in Canada._ Toronto: Irwin, 1987.

Chupungco, Anscar. _Cultural Adaptation of the Liturgy._ New York: Paulist Press, 1982.

———. _Liturgies of the Future: The Process and Methods of Inculturation._ New York: Paulist Press, 1989.

———. _Liturgical Inculturation: Sacramentals, Religiosity, and Catechesis._ Collegeville, Minn.: Liturgical Press, 1992.

Conn, Harvie. _Eternal Word and Changing Worlds: Theology, Anthropology, and Mission in Trialogue._ Grand Rapids: Zondervan, 1984.

Collins, Mary. _Worship: Renewal to Practice._ Washington, D.C.: Pastoral Press, 1987.

———. "Liturgical Methodology and the Cultural Evolution of Worship in the United States." _Worship_ 49 (1975): 85–102.

Daly, Robert J., ed. _In All Things: Religious Faith and American Culture._ Kansas City: Sheed and Ward, 1990.

Davies, J. G. _Worship and Mission._ London: SCM Press, 1966.

Dawson, Christopher. _Religion and the Rise of Western Culture._ Garden City: Image Books, 1958.

Diekmann, G. "Is There a Distinct American Contribution to the Liturgical Renewal?" _Worship_ 45 (1971): 578–587.

Doran, Carol, and Thomas Troeger. "Reclaiming the Corporate Self: The Meaning and Ministry of Worship in a Privatistic Culture." _Worship_ 60 (May 1986): 200–209.

Ellul, Jacques. _The Subversion of Christianity._ Grand Rapids: Eerdmans, 1986.

Fleming, Bruce C. E. _Contextualization of Theology: An Evangelical Assessment._ Pasadena, Calif.: William Carey Library, 1980.

Francis, Mark R. _Liturgy in a Multi-Cultural Community._ Collegeville, Minn.: Liturgical Press, 1991.

———. "Adaptation, Liturgical." In *New Dictionary of Sacramental Worship*, 14–25. Collegeville, Minn.: Michael Glazier/Liturgical Press, 1990.

———. "Liturgical Inculturation in the United States and the Call to Justice," in *Living No Longer for Ourselves: Liturgy and Justice in the Nineties*, eds. Kathleen Hughes and Mark R. Francis. Collegeville, Minn.: Liturgical Press, 1991.

Gilliland, Dean S. *The Word Among Us: Contextualizing Theology for Mission Today*. Dallas: Word Publishing, 1989.

Gusmer, C. "A Bill of Rites: Liturgical Adaptation in America." *Worship* 51 (1977): 283–289.

Gy, P. M. "The Inculturation of the Christian Liturgy in the West." *Studia Liturgica* 20 (1990): 8–18.

Hauerwas, Stanley, and William H. Willimon. *Resident Aliens*. Nashville: Abingdon Press, 1989.

Hesselgrave, David J., and Edward Rommen. *Contextualization*. Grand Rapids: Baker Book House, 1989.

———. *Communicating Christ Cross-Culturally: An Introduction to Missionary Communication*. Grand Rapids: Zondervan, 1978.

Kavanaugh, Aidan. "Liturgical Inculturation: Looking to the Future." *Studia Liturgica* 20:1 (1990): 70–80.

Keifert, Patrick R. *Welcoming the Stranger: A Public Theology of Worship and Evangelism*. Minneapolis: Fortress Press, 1992.

Kraft, Charles H. "The Church in Culture—A Dynamic Equivalence Model," in *Down to Earth: Studies in Christianity and Culture*, eds. John R. W. Stott and Robert Coote. Grand Rapids: Eerdmans, 1980.

———. *Communication Theory for Christian Witness*. Nashville: Abingdon Press, 1983.

———. *Christianity in Culture: A Study in Dynamic Biblical Theologizing in Cross-Cultural Perspective*. Maryknoll, N.Y.: Orbis, 1979.

———. "Interpreting in Cultural Context." *Journal of Evangelical Theological Society* 21 (December 1978): 357–367.

Larkin, William J., Jr. *Culture and Biblical Hermeneutics: Interpreting and Applying the Authoritative Word in a Relativistic Age*. Grand Rapids: Baker Book House, 1988.

Leith, John H. *From Generation to Generation: The Renewal of the Church according to Its Own Theology and Practice*. Louisville: Westminster/John Knox Press, 1990.

Lingenfelter, Sherwood. *Transforming Culture: A Challenge for Christian Mission*. Grand Rapids: Baker Book House, 1992.

Mannion, M. Francis. "Liturgy and the Present Crisis of Culture." *Worship* 62 (March 1988): 98–123.

Martinez, German. "Cult and Culture: The Structure of the Evolution of Worship." *Worship* 64 (1990): 406–433.

Mayers, Marvin K. *Christianity Confronts Culture*. Grand Rapids: Zondervan, 1987.

Montefiore, Hugh. *The Gospel and Contemporary Culture*. London: Mowbray, 1992.

Myers, Kenneth A. *All God's Children and Blue Suede Shoes: Christians and Popular Culture*. Wheaton, Ill.: Crossway Books, 1989.

Newbigin, Leslie. *Truth to Tell: The Gospel as Public Truth*. Grand Rapids: Eerdmans, 1991.

———. *Foolishness to the Greeks: The Gospel and Western Culture*. Grand Rapids: Eerdmans, 1986.

———. *The Gospel in a Pluralist Society*. Grand Rapids: Eerdmans, 1989.

Nicholls, Bruce J. *Contextualization: A Theology of Gospel and Culture*. Downers Grove, Ill.: InterVarsity, 1979.

Nida, Eugene A. *Customs and Culture: Anthropology for Christian Missions*. New York: Harper and Row, 1954.

———. *Message and Mission: The Communication of the Christian Faith*. New York: Harper and Row, 1969.

Niebuhr, H. Richard. *Christ and Culture*. New York: Harper and Row, 1951.

Postman, Neil. *Amusing Ourselves to Death: Public Discourse in an Age of Show Business*. New York: Penguin Books, 1985.

Phillips, James M., and Robert T. Cole, eds. *Toward the 21st Century in Christian Mission*. Grand Rapids: Eerdmans, 1993.

Saunders, George R. *Culture and Christianity: The Dialectics of Transformation*. New York: Greenwood Press, 1988.

Schmemann, Alexander. *For the Life of the World*. Crestwood, N.Y.: St. Vladimir's Seminary Press, 1963, 1988.

Schultze, Quentin J. *Televangelism and American Culture—The Business of Popular Religion*. Grand Rapids: Baker Book House, 1991.

Senn, Frank C. *Christian Worship and Its Cultural Setting.* Philadelphia: Fortress Press, 1983.

———. *The Witness of the Worshiping Community: Liturgy and the Practice of Evangelism.* New York: Paulist Press, 1993.

Shaw, R. Daniel. *Transculturation: The Cultural Factor in Translation and Other Communication Tasks.* Pasadena, Calif.: William Carey Library, 1988.

Stackhouse, Max L. *Apologia: Contextualization, Globalization, and Mission in Theological Education.* Grand Rapids: Eerdmans, 1988.

Stott, John R. W., and Robert Coote. *Down to Earth: Studies in Christianity and Culture.* Grand Rapids: Eerdmans, 1980.

Thiemann, Ronald F. *Constructing a Public Theology: The Church in a Pluralistic Culture.* Louisville: Westminster/John Knox Press, 1991.

Van Engen, Charles. *God's Missionary People: Rethinking the Purpose of the Local Church.* Grand Rapids: Baker, 1991.

Van Engen, Charles, Dean S. Gilliland, and Paul Pierson, eds. *Good News of the Kingdom: Mission Theology for the Third Millennium.* Maryknoll, N.Y.: Orbis Books, 1993.

Warren, Michael. *Faith, Culture, and the Worshiping Community.* Washington, D.C.: Pastoral Press, 1993.

Webber, Robert E. *People of the Truth: The Power of the Worshiping Community in the Modern World.* San Francisco: Harper and Row, 1988.

———. *The Church in the World.* Grand Rapids: Zondervan, 1986.

White, James F. *The Worldliness of Worship.* New York: Oxford University Press, 1967.

———. *Protestant Worship: Traditions in Transition.* Louisville: Westminster/John Knox Press, 1989.

———. "Worship and Culture: Mirror or Beacon." *Theological Studies* 35 (1974): 288–301.

❧ SIX ❧

Cultural Diversity in the Worshiping Community

This chapter explores the changing cultural context of North America and calls for a new sensitivity its emerging ethnic and cultural traditions. The white Anglo-Saxon domination of American culture will likely continue to be replaced by a cultural mosaic that includes Hispanic, African, and Asian cultural traditions. These developments will have significant consequences for the future of the church; already many worshiping communities have become multicultural. An understanding of the Asian, African, Hispanic, Caribbean, and Native American traditions of Christian worship will help the churches prepare for the changes that will take place.

182 • THE EMERGENCE OF A MULTICULTURAL SOCIETY

Ethnic diversity and the aging of Western societies have dramatically changed the potential composition of the church. Religious organizations will become ineffective if leaders conduct their pastoral care and evangelistic outreach in ways not relevant to the twenty-first century. For some denominations, the rapid pace of change seems to preclude long-range planning; crisis intervention has become both a personal and a church management strategy. However, demographic statistics that portend the shifts in population growth, composition, and geographic distribution provide a foundation for flexible and intelligent planning.

—— Race and Ethnic Demographics ——

Demographers project that the proportion of the United States population that is white and non-Hispanic will decline from the present 83 percent to 65 percent of the population by the year 2010. The 12 percent of the population that is African American will remain steady; Asian and other groups will increase to 5 percent of the population; and the Hispanic population will double in size to 18 percent of the total population. According to the 1990 census, Hispanics in-

creased by 7.7 million—more than twice the number of people added to the African-American group in the same period. The Hispanic addition was larger than the entire 1990 Asian and Pacific-Islander population ("The Top Findings from the 1990 Census," *Population Today* [July/August 1991]: 3–4). This increase reflects the high fertility and immigration rates of Mexican and Puerto Rican groups. Hispanics are also disproportionately young, meaning that a greater percentage of this population is in, or is entering, their prime childbearing years. *American Demographics* reports that the YUMies (young urban Mexicans) are eager to take the places of the American Yuppies (young urban professionals) The data clearly suggest that the United States will become a Spanish-English bilingual country in the twentieth-first century.

When business leaders in the European Economic Community are asked which languages will likely become standard in the new political unit, many have surprisingly included Spanish along with English. South America is seen as a burgeoning market for European goods and services. Business interests in the United States recognize the Latin factor; the church needs to heighten its awareness as well. In fact, some American churches have begun Spanish-as-a-second-language training for their members. These church leaders are well-informed and accurately planning for the multi-cultural future.

Social scientists have identified a demographic "70-30 tip-point" which affects relations between population groups. For example, when in a changing neighborhood the arriving ethnic group has increased to 30 percent, intergroup conflict often results. At the present time, several cities of the United States contain more than 30 percent Hispanic populations:

Large Metros with Highest Percentages of Minorities

Metro Area	1990 Percent Minority	Change Since 1980
San Antonio	55.7	+ 2.8
Miami	52.2	+13.2
Los Angeles	50.2	+11.1
Houston	42.1	+ 7.3
San Diego	34.6	+ 8.5
Dallas-Ft. Worth	30.3	+ 6.1

Source: "Are Two Americas Emerging?" *Population Today* [October 1991]: 6–8.

Reflecting "tip-point" anxieties, eighteen states have discussed and passed "English only" legislation. Fractious church divisions may also result from changes in the ethnic composition of the church group. Church leaders have one of two choices: either discover ways to celebrate diversity within a unified congregation or create homogeneous, but socially marginal, enclaves.

The African American population will not increase their percentage of the population over the next several decades, but their numbers will continue to grow. The Asian population, although not large, is the fastest growing ethnic grouping. Filipino, Korean, Chinese, Vietnamese, and Asian Indian are the predominant groups (Bryant Robey, "America's Asians," *American Demographics* [May 1985]).

Each Asian group differs from the others with regard to language, economic status, and level of education. As recent arrivals in the country, these groups welcome involvement with social organizations, including the church. Religious institutions are uniquely able to respond to immigrants' needs for pastoral care, social relationships, and orientation to American culture. This is a "window of opportunity" for Christian ministry; it would be unfortunate indeed to ignore such an opportunity.

——————— **Age Differentials** ———————

Life expectancy has increased. The older population of eighty-five plus years has increased 165 percent in the past twenty-two years. By the year 2050, life expectancy for women will reach ninety years and for men, eighty-eight years. Designations for the elderly are divided into three categories to recognize differences in seniors' general health and social participation. The young-old are those aged sixty-five to seventy-four; the old-old are those seventy-five to eighty-four; the feeble-old are those eighty-five and older. According to the 1990 census, about 12.5 percent of the nation's population (31 million) were young-old; 10 million were old-old; slightly more than 3 million were feeble-old (twice the proportion of the very old people in 1960) (*New York Times*, Nov. 10, 1992). By far the fastest growth in the elderly population has been among the feeble-old.

The young-old are mobile, active, and generally healthy. This group is beginning to express dissatisfaction with the response of the church toward them based on assumptions about their supposed lack of capacity for energetic and intelligent participation. With 76 million baby boomers on the way toward senior status, by the year 2015 approximately one fourth of the American population will be young-old. Changed assumptions, new programs, and shared leadership with today's comparatively few seniors will be practice for the elder boom tomorrow.

In addition to the numbers of persons living longer, a decreasing birth rate has enlarged the proportion of those over age sixty-five (Ben J. Wattenberg, *Birth Dearth: What Happens When People in Free Countries Don't Have Babies.* New York: Pharos Books, 1987). Macro-level changes in the proportions of young and old in society will create similar changes in proportions in church congregations. Fewer babies mean adjustments in the church nursery, Sunday school, and family programs. Churches have often measured their effectiveness and hope for the future on the numbers of young people in the congregation. New definitions of a "healthy" church membership will be required.

A serious imbalance in the dependency ratio of children and elderly to the economically produc-

The Passion Cross. The distinct feature of the Passion cross is the ends that have been cut to points. It is often pictured arising from a chalice. The cross represents the agony of Jesus in the Garden of Gethsemane

tive is anticipated as the baby boomers approach retirement age. In 1950, there was roughly one elderly person for each seven persons of working age. By the year 2030, the ratio is projected to be one elderly person for every two and a half persons of working age. Nursing home populations will more than double by 2030. Over half those residents will be eighty-five or older (*American in the 21st Century: Social and Economic Support Systems* [Washington, D.C.: Population Reference Bureau, 1990], 20).

Important questions are being raised in the debate over rationing health care for the handicapped and the feeble old. The church cannot remain uninformed or absent from such discussions. Significant and moral decisions are being made now which will affect large percentages of the population in the decades ahead.

Religious groups are a natural resource to help share the emotional and familial burdens for the dependent young as well as the old. Current housing and ministry responses to the elderly are a step in the right direction. Increased emphasis from the church on the social obligations of all citizens can mitigate the overwhelming individualism of the culture.

Business leaders are concerned about the size

and educational level of the next generation's labor force. With the exception of Hispanic groups, the age cohorts following the baby boomers are much smaller in number. Because Hispanics are, on average, less educated than the non-Hispanic white population, the educational challenge to provide skilled and learned workers in the next decades will be enormous (John H. Ralph and Mary J. Frase, "Drop-Outs: Doing It By The Numbers." *Population Today* [April 1992]: 5–6). The church should confront the challenge by providing substantive mentoring/tutoring assistance to Hispanic youth within each local area.

The challenge of the twenty-first century for the church is to be an integral part of the growing mosaic and ethnic richness of American society.

Sondra Lindblade

183 • WORSHIP AND MULTICULTURAL DIVERSITY

Cultural diversity has characterized the Judeo-Christian tradition from its earliest history. While the Bible and the church's liturgies show those actions that are central to faith, cultural and social factors have shaped practice in profound ways in each worship setting. This article briefly outlines those actions and beliefs that are central to Christian worship and the corresponding practices shaped by culture and society.

The notion that North America, and particularly the United States, is a "melting pot" of cultures is no longer a valid metaphor to describe the American cultural landscape. Immigrants of the early part of the twentieth century are often surprised by the fervor of their children, grandchildren, and great-grandchildren to reclaim the cultural heritage of their ancestors. The fact that the cultural history of our forebearers shapes our identities as individuals and communities is undeniable. Parents and students from Native American, African American, Hispanic, and Asian heritages are no longer pacified or satisfied with versions of history told from Anglo or Western European perspective. Literature departments in major universities are being torn apart by debates about the "canon" of texts students should read. Textbook revisions in history and science are increasingly difficult for publishers to get approved in state departments of education. North American society and the societies within the continent are increasingly culturally diverse. At times, the level of diversity threatens the very nature of national identity and cohesiveness.

The church, as one element of North American social life, naturally, is prone to the stresses caused by cultural diversity. Finding appropriate processes to guarantee equal partnership in leadership, policy making, and forming the church's mission for those peoples who were once evangelized has been difficult for the predominantly Caucasian churches of North America. Perhaps the reality of cultural diversity has been most difficult to manage in worship. Differences in language, customs, ceremonies, aesthetic sensibilities, social decorum, and theological emphases have often made cross-cultural worship impossible. The problem is solved in many places by forming congregations of one ethnic or racial type, isolated from the mainstream. However, in many urban centers and in areas where churches have sponsored Asian and Hispanic refugees, worshipers from different cultures are meeting together more regularly. Certainly, worship in denominational conference settings brings the joys and frustrations of cross-cultural worship home even to those whose local congregation is culturally homogeneous. By attempting to look beyond our desires for uniformity and familiarity in worship practice, we as Christians will likely experience a new kind of unity through diversity. And if this should happen, we may discover deeper truths about the nature of Christ's body, the power of the Holy Spirit, and the immense love of God.

———— Worship as a Culturally ———— Specific Activity

Culture is created through language, symbols, ritual, myths and stories, art forms (such as music, dance, painting, sculpture, etc.), and beliefs that show a people's understanding of themselves and their relationship to the natural and spiritual worlds. These building blocks profoundly shape the ways in which we think and live daily. Society more explicitly describes the natural patterns of human interactions or prescribes the means by which human interaction can be accomplished. Class stratification may illustrate a natural evolution of skills, knowledge, and resources into a hierarchical pattern; however, such stratification

may eventually evolve into rigid class structures or castes that are protected by law or strong social sanction. In modern history, societies often have been judged by how well their patterns of interaction provide for the needs and rights of all those living under their power.

Jewish and Christian worship have always taken place in specific cultural and social contexts. Practices have both shaped the social world in which they took place and have been shaped by the prevailing culture around the worshipers.

Jacob built an altar after encountering God to mark the place of this theophany or revelation, a practice common in his cultural context. David and Solomon dreamed of building a temple for God because in their cultural and social setting kings built temples to their deities. The synagogue pattern of worship and study emerged when Jews were exiled in Babylon and separated from the temple geographically. It continued after they resettled Jerusalem and preserved the Jewish legacy when the temple fell a second time.

Christian worship grew out of the Jewish context of the eastern Mediterranean and only later was influenced by Hellenistic Judaism. The early Christians continued practicing the Jewish forms of worship they had learned prior to their encounter with Jesus: they gathered to hear the Scriptures, to pray, and to share a ritual meal. Only later in the first century did more distinctly "Christian" patterns emerge as the tensions between the Jews and Jewish Christians increased. Many of the difficulties that Paul addressed in his letters to the Corinthians reflect the class and cultural patterns of that Greek society, particularly with regard to worship.

As Christianity spread throughout the Middle East, Africa, and southern Europe during the second to fourth centuries, various regions with bishopric oversight began developing distinctive liturgical styles. Liturgical scholars have identified seven liturgical families, which form during these years: Alexandrian, Western Syrian, Eastern Syrian, the liturgy of St. Bail, Byzantine, Roman, and Gallican (including Ambrosian, Mozarabic, and Celtic liturgies). Simply reading the prayers contained in these liturgies composed throughout their years of development reveals differences in worldview, rhetorical style, and central metaphors. For example, the Gallican rites can be described as being more "flowery" or effusive in tone than the more austere Roman rite. The Mozarabic rites display influences of the culture of the Moorish invaders. The church of the East presents an imagistic, poetic, sense-absorbing liturgy.

The Reformation brought crises in social, political, philosophical, and theological realms to the fore. In Germany, Switzerland, and England, liturgical reforms needed to have the approval of the local and state political authorities. The possibilities and limits of liturgical reform were directly governed by social and cultural constraints.

Missionaries throughout the church's history have directly faced issues of cultural diversity and inculturation. Paul's address to the Romans in Athens shows the need for "translating" the truth known in one society in certain cultural forms into the cultural forms of another society. Roman Catholic mission work in the Far East during the fifteenth, sixteenth, and seventeenth centuries confronted different understandings of father-son relationships, shame and guilt, and forgiveness, all of which had implications for their methods of evangelism.

British and North American missionaries of the nineteenth and twentieth centuries encountered similar problems in Africa, Asia, and Latin America. The issues of inculturation are unavoidable in worship because much of the church's worship life is carried on at symbolic and metaphoric levels.

In contemporary North American culture, the media and social justice issues are shaping the church's worship life. Beginning with televised evangelistic crusades in the 1950s, television and radio have become increasingly important in the presentation of the gospel. Media and publishing empires have been built to keep the Christian message continually floating across the airways. These industries are changing the character of worship in many settings, particularly with regard to music, to the hearing of the Word, and to the size of congregational gatherings.

The realities of injustice, racism, exploitation, physical abuse, drug dependence, and homelessness announced daily over television and in newsprint illustrate the decaying moral infrastructure of North American society. Often these conditions exist in larger proportions in immigrant populations or in populations that have been marginalized from the power bases in social life. In the last decade, greater attention has been given to these sins through prayers of confession, prayers of intercession, hymns, special observances for recent martyrs, and increased attention to service in the world and in worship.

These examples are meant to illustrate briefly that Christian worship has always been culturally diverse and socially embedded. Worship does not float above the shared mediums of language, symbol, gesture, metaphor, artifact, or relationships of social life, but is shaped by them and expressed through them. As ethnic communities and their cultures gain greater identity in North America generally and in the church specifically, issues of cultural diversity in worship will create opportunities and frustrations for denominations at national and local levels. Conflicts over style, interpretations of symbols, stories, and metaphors, leadership, and differences in socially accepted forms of interpersonal interaction will remain central points of challenge for the church's ability to value the differences represented by each culture and to continually discern truthful practice.

One Body—Many Members

Paul is explicit in the first letter to the Corinthians about the nature of the church as a body, specifically the body of Christ.

> For just as the body is one and has many members, and all the members of the body, though many, are one body, so it is with Christ. For in the one Spirit we were all baptized into one body— Jews or Greeks, slaves or free—and we were all made to drink of one Spirit. (1 Cor. 12:12-13)

While this text is often taken as a description of the local congregation since it is in the section of the letter addressing the issue of spiritual gifts, Paul's missionary work itself implies that he understood the concept of the body beyond the limits of a specific local gathering. Paul addresses the subject again in Colossians 1:18 and 3:15; the writer of Ephesians speaks in a similar mode (Eph. 2:16; 4:4-13, 16). For those communities influenced by Paul, the body imagery is of central significance.

Churches in North America readily acknowledge belief in this metaphor of the church as Christ's body at the abstract level, but struggle to realize its truth at the concrete level. Living as a body in culturally mixed conversations, in mutual sharing, and in a commitment to caring has not characterized church life in general. Congregations most frequently operate on commonly shared assumptions relating to their worldview, the role of humanity in the world, sinfulness, guilt, salvation, power, and grace. Until recently, conversations about a person's experience of these and other "theological" terms in daily life were rarely heard in church. Where such intense sharing has occurred and is occurring, do worshipers see their commonalities and their differences in cultural and social experience? The body, then, is no longer a disassociated set of members, but a group of members communicating continually about the body's well being and its relationships with its head.

Inherited Actions and Beliefs. All Christian congregations and worldwide bodies have inherited certain liturgical actions and beliefs through Scripture and tradition. These fundamental practices and beliefs identify a congregation as being Christian in practice, and therefore different from other religious traditions:

(1) God is sovereign over all time, is known personally through Jesus Christ, and guides and ministers to the church and to all believers by the power of the Holy Spirit.

(2) God's purpose is the salvation of the entire creation, a gift that will eliminate all sin, heal all brokenness and disease, deal justly with all peoples, and bring to completeness all that God created.

(3) God's Word in Christ and in the Scripture reveals God's nature (e.g., God's love, freedom, majesty, transcendence, closeness, etc.), God's saving acts (e.g., God's judgment, redemption, forgiveness, etc.), and God's demands (e.g., faithfulness, righteousness, truthfulness, obedience, etc.).

(4) Jesus Christ, the Son of God, is the Savior of the world and the model for Christian life.

(5) The Holy Spirit leads nonbelievers to faith, sanctifies the church and all who believe, draws believers more deeply into fellowship with Christ and with God, manifests gifts for building up the church, and comforts believers in times of suffering and temptation.

(6) The church is the primary agent for God's saving activity in the world.

(7) The church's worship is characterized by gathering as a body around God's Word and by sharing the meal Christ ate with his disciples and gave to the church as a sign of covenant. Singing, praying, offering, and exhorting surround these primary acts.

(8) Baptism, confirmation, ordination/orders, anointing, reconciliation, and marriage are actions governed by this church for the sake of discerning the body and expressing essential dimensions of God's relationship with God's people.

While these beliefs and actions are held by all Christian traditions, their practice varies from church to church due, in part, to the historical circumstances shaping a particular tradition and to the cultural realities in which a tradition took root. Words or texts that have become associated with the rites or practices of a particular tradition often express the shared meaning of the action. A brief perusal of liturgical texts from various traditions reveal differences in theological emphases or in understandings of the purpose of practice. Often, work for ecumenical consensus begins with the attempt to find commonality in the wording of texts that can point to common understandings of the act and its shared meaning.

Central Symbols. The central symbols of worship shared by all Christian traditions are Scripture, bread, wine/cup, water, oil, and the gathered body. Through these things, the Holy Spirit makes God's presence known in worshipers' lives in a way that is significantly different from the way God is known through the natural world or through private prayer. While the emphasis on these symbols varies slightly or radically from tradition to tradition, they are found in the orthodox practice and theology of all Christians.

Most traditions have used the vernacular language of the worshipers in their liturgies for centuries; the Roman church has used the vernacular since the Second Vatican Council. The subtleties of language itself make it a fascinating aspect of liturgy. Because of the different possibilities and limitations offered by the Spanish and English language in expressing relationships, shades of meaning, which may be different from an English speaker's experience, enter a Spanish speaker's experience even though both worshipers experience the same set of Christian symbols. While language differences are clearly a barrier to communication at the practical level, we are often not aware of differences of interpretation and understanding below the surface. No translation from one language to another can be literal, in the same way that no person's experience in one place can be literally "translated" or transferred into another time and place. Translations may be truthful to the spirit of the meaning of the original language, but they are never exact.

Because words, bread, wine, oil, water, and the body are culturally rich symbols outside of the church, it is not surprising that the church's practice has been influenced by local sociocultural practices. For example, in societies where wine is not a cultivated product and thus has little social meaning, the celebrative and fellowship aspects of the Lord's Supper may be diminished when wine is prescribed. In some cases, missionaries and bishops opted for a more meaningful indigenous substitute; in other cases, wine was imported. These are the kinds of circumstances with which missionaries, pastors, and congregations working cross-culturally must contend. What is usually at issue is not whether one cultural understanding of these central symbols is truthful and the other is false. What is at issue is whether the life-giving power of these symbols can encompass the multitude of sociocultural meanings surrounding them and still remain consonant with the church's experience of God's purpose and character witnessed in Scripture and through the traditions.

Secondary Acts and Symbols. Everything else that surrounds the central acts and symbols of worship are secondary in importance. The arrangement of the worship space, the colors used, the specific hymns sung, the arrangement of leadership, vestments, the church calendar, etc., are not ends in themselves, but point out the central symbols of faith and practice. Furthermore, they point to God in Christ. This is not to imply that secondary acts and symbols are insignificant. Indeed, they help worshipers unfold the mystery of God communicated through worship in a specific location at a specific time. In the secondary acts and symbols, cultural uniqueness is seen. Ethos or group feelings of worship is best communicated through them. How the sanctuary is arranged and decorated; what hymns are sung (and in what language); what stories are told and how they are told; what instruments are needed to accompany

the music; what colors are used; what style of public prayer is used; how children are involved in worship; how to move from one place to another; how objects are used, all these and a multitude of other aspects are shaped by the culture and society in which worship takes place. In cross-cultural settings, pastors and worship leaders must know the cultures represented in their congregations so well that they can remain focused on what is central (hearing God's Word and sharing at the Table), while encouraging various cultural interpretations and meanings to elaborate or penetrate the central ones.

This last point suggests that pastors, worship leaders, and congregational members cannot expect to learn enough about other cultures represented in their body on one hour each Sunday morning. Cross-cultural understanding comes only through sharing in each other's daily lives, asking questions when further knowledge is sought, seeking forgiveness when miscommunications and misunderstandings arise, and genuinely valuing the truth and wisdom found in cultures other than one's own. Cross-cultural understanding takes time, patience, and the guidance of God's Spirit.

Signs of Unity in Cultural Diversity

Several international organizations have worked directly with cross-cultural diversity in worship with the hope of drawing the body of Christ into fuller unity. Other local efforts to build community have influenced worshiping congregations in other parts of the world. The following list is intended to illustrate the types of work encouraging cross-cultural worship and communication.

Lima Liturgy. The Lima liturgy was celebrated for the first time at the World Council of Churches Faith and Order Commission meeting in Lima, Peru, January 1982. It was created to "illustrate the solid theological achievements of the Faith and Order document, *Baptism, Eucharist and Ministry*" (Max Thurian and Geoffrey Wainwright, *Baptism and Eucharist: Ecumenical Convergence in Celebration* [Grand Rapids: Eerdmans, 1983]). It was also used on three occasions prior to the World Council of Churches' meeting in Vancouver, British Columbia, 1983. While this text hammers out basic theological agreements on the meaning of Eucharist across most all of the world's Christian traditions, its celebration was an opportunity for cross-cultural worship. The Lima liturgy received a great deal of attention during the years following the Vancouver meeting by liturgists around the world. While all agree that the liturgy is not yet perfect, many also agree that it is the closest thing to a liturgy representing consensus across Christian traditions.

What is most interesting about the text of the liturgy is that it does not reveal anything that could be construed as cultural diverse in and of itself. Its outline and texts are drawn from historical sources. An attempt was made to be theological consistent with all participating traditions. It is, essentially, a reformation of the text, keeping central the primary acts of Word and Table. No rubrics are given, regarding the style of celebration or the use of secondary acts or symbols.

While the text of this liturgy is set, the music weaving through the liturgy is not set. With the support of the assembly's worship book, *Jesus Christ—the Life of the World* (Geneva: WCC Publications, 1983), a rich tapestry of musical sounds could be woven.

> In order to respect the diversity of people, languages, and traditions present, ecumenical worship relies increasingly on symbols and music, movement and color, silence and shades of light rather than words, abstractions, explanations and argument. When it gets too complicated to speak about God in any detail, you're forced to leave silence and space and to let God fill them, leaving people to hear what they will hear. . . . After all the words are forgotten, the images of ecumenical meetings like this one linger on. At the Vancouver assembly these were a yellow tent, a native Canadian canoe, a black baby brought to the altar, a totem pole, a haunting kyrie chant, a multicolored cloud of balloons for peace released by children. (Bluck, *Canberra Take-Aways: What the Assembly Offers a Local Congregation* [Geneva: WCC Publications, 1991], 3, 26.)

Whether the Lima liturgy continues to gain greater acceptance across the Christian church or provides an encouragement for other such liturgies to emerge remains to be seen.

It must be stressed that the World Council of Churches is working ecumenically across cultural identities and not specifically with the problems of cross-cultural worship in the local congrega-

tion or denomination. Yet, the experience of those who have served in this organization, particularly on the Worship subcommittee, can provide invaluable guidance for treading the peaceful and turbulent waters of cross-cultural communication.

Ecumenical Prayer Cycle. *With All God's People: The New Ecumenical Prayer Cycle* (Geneva: WCC Publications, 1989) was compiled by John Carden and published by the World Council of Churches unit on Renewal and Congregational Life. The orders cover the seasons and feasts of the church, in addition to services of thanksgiving, the communion of saints, suffering and healing in the world, justice and peace, human rights, people of other faiths, and the affirmation of baptism. While these orders were prepared specifically for ecumenical settings, the prayers, resources, and music provided are from around the world. This prayer cycle would be of somewhat limited use in a cross-cultural congregation, but praying with these resources impresses on the worshipers that the body of Christ is diverse and heightens their respect for the miracle of communion in this body.

Taizé Community. The Taizé community in France has become a spiritual retreat center for hundreds of pilgrims each year. The community has developed a simple worship pattern and a simple, yet deeply moving, style of music that accommodates itself to its numerous visitors. Many of the congregational responses are in Latin, honoring the first language of the Western church. However, many other ostinatos, canons, and responses are in English, Spanish, French or German. Instrumentals and accompaniments are outlined for most melodies, but are not played strictly; parts weave in and out of the congregational and solo parts of a piece giving it a fresh and improvised quality each time. The intent of Taizé worship and song is not to accommodate cultural diversity as such, but rather to move the experience of worship to a different plane, where believers of different cultural backgrounds can unite.

Hymnal Publishing and Worship Resources. Several North American denominations have enriched their hymnody by publishing new hymnals or supplements devoted to the hymnody of a particular cultural group. The United Methodists have been particularly conscientious in supplementing their standard repertoire with hymns and songs from African-American, Asian, and Native American sources. _Cantate Domino_ (Geneva: WCC Publications, 1980) greatly influenced the hymnal revision work of many denominations in the late 1980s and early 1990s. This collection brought together melodies from around the world and paired them with ancient or modern texts.

Jesus Christ—the Life of the World directly supported daily prayer at the World Council of Churches' assembly in Vancouver. The collection contains hymns and songs from across the continents (intended to supplement the resources found in _Cantate Domino_ [1980]) and other written resources from various worldwide bodies. _In Spirit and in Truth_, created for the World Council of Churches' meeting in Canberra in 1991, contains similar musical and written resources.

The World Council of Churches' subunit on Renewal and Congregational Life has sponsored workshops around the world to develop skills in congregational and denominational musicians and worship leaders in order to strengthen ecumenical and cross-cultural worship at local levels. While many congregations find the rhythms and tonalities of some non-Western European music difficult (or impossible) to perform, the benefit of learning hymns and songs from other cultures opens the soul to the heart of another people. To praise in a soft and austere melody or to lament from the soles of one's feet offers an entirely new perspective on the wonder and passion of God.

Praise and Worship Singing. The prevalence of electric guitars, keyboards, and drums on radio and television airwaves has created a sound that transcends many cultural boundaries in North America. The sound is almost a cultural commodity. As a result, praise and worship music that imitates this electric music has crossed many cultural boundaries. The intense energy of the music is particularly appealing in cultures that are naturally physically and emotionally expressive. Since the texts of praise and worship songs are usually simple and repetitive, they can be translated easily into other languages or learned aurally by people from other language groups.

Christian Base Communities. The Christian based community movement of the third world (particularly in South and Central America, and the Philippines) has not directly changed worship in North America, but it has influenced the way in which many congregations gather around the Scriptures and share in fellowship. As members of these communities brought their experiences of suffering, exploitation, and joy to the study of Scripture, they discovered an increased awareness of God's justice and of their own solidarity. As their stories and prayers were recorded and made available to the larger church in the world, they were heard in North American congregations in sermons or in prayers of confession or intercession. Worshiping cross-culturally requires that the body of Christ not only enjoy the gifts of different cultural perspectives, but also share the pain and suffering presently found in the cultures represented in the body of Christ locally and globally.

Here from All Nations, All Tongues, and All Peoples

The image of all peoples of the earth gathering in worship has prevailed throughout much of Judeo-Christian history. Psalms (e.g., Ps. 66; 148), Hebrew Scripture prophecies (e.g., Isa. 2:3; 51:11; 60:14; Jer. 31:8; 50:5; Zech. 2:11), and Revelation 7 joyously proclaim this hope. The church throughout much of its history has understood itself theologically to be a unity of culturally diverse assemblies around the world enduring over time. The reality at the end of the twentieth century in North America is that our local communities are effected by cultural diversity in one way or another. Biblical visions and mandates for justice, peace, and salvation require us to take seriously the realities of our cultural strengths and biases that express themselves in religious forms. It will not be enough to tolerate each other in the body, while privately complaining about how hard it is to respect different cultural views. Our worship and our lives will be changed when we come to know God more fully through the expressions of faith by another people. Whether by moving our bodies to new rhythms, by exploring the significant symbols and metaphors of Scripture through another language and culture, and by hearing the experiences of suffering Christians in other ways, we will glimpse briefly in our lifetimes the biblical vision of the world's nations gathered around the Lamb's throne united in praise in God's eternity.

Writing about an encounter he had an ecumenical meeting, Alexandros Papaderos says:

I hurried off to the section meeting accompanied by Theodoros Stylianopoulos who, a little earlier, had delivered his plenary address on the Assembly theme. Orthodox bishops and theologians embraced and congratulated him: "Brother, you spoke as a true *Orthodox!* " Arriving shortly afterwards in my study group, I heard a Brazilian saying with delight: "You know, this Orthodox spoke in a truly *evangelical* way, taking a thoroughly biblical line!" Other Protestants agreed with him. And I realized that ecumenism is first and foremost the simple yet magnificent experience of *recognizing oneself in others!* (Alexandros Papaderos, "Ecumenism as Celebration," in *Faith and Faithfulness,* ed. Pauline Webb [Geneva: WCC Publications, 1984], 34.)

To recognize our common faith is the goal of worship in culturally diverse settings as well. Such a recognition is prompted by God's Spirit moving through our congregations and denominations, uniting the diverse parts of Christ's body. However, the Holy Spirit can work with us only as we are willing to listen to others' experience of God's love, willing to recognize ourselves in other Christians, willing to learn other ways of expressing ourselves to God, and willing to confess our dependence upon the Holy Spirit to create God's church in the world.

Rebecca Slough

184 ✦ TOWARDS GLOBAL WORSHIP: BEYOND THE HEADLINES

How much worship gets directed beyond local or even individual needs? Does worship declare the congregation's concern for the world that God so loved? This article offers suggestions on how to go beyond merely praying for the people in the newspaper headlines towards worship that is truly global in its outlook and practice.

God chose a poor vehicle to open my eyes to God's purpose and work in a world, larger than my country's church or even my country. In vacation church school, a mission story was read. These stories were more entertainment than truth. Snakes and witch doctors haunted every corner, so did racism and cultural imperialism. But one result was that we prayed for people far from us—people whom we did not know and with whom we had no connection, except that God

loved them as well as us, even if they were heathens.

This summer, I worshiped at this church. Throughout the whole service, not one mention in the sermon or prayers was made of any event or person outside those directly connected to the congregation. The world was stranded outside. Even general prayers for the sick were displaced by individualized concerns. God had become a local deity big enough to take care of only those assembled and their loved ones. At another church, a pastor reinterpreted the Gospel of John. "Children," he said, "when you read 'God so loved the world,' think 'God so loved me.'" I wondered at this reductionism. The world had been reduced to "me." Worship was reduced to an "us," no larger than the "family church."

In such a climate, to have someone pray for those events mentioned in the headlines would be a big improvement. To have a preacher relate the biblical word to world events and connect both to the lives of the congregation would be extraordinary. But worship often gets only as far as the media leads. I would like to offer possibilities beyond the headlines toward worship that is truly global in its outlook and practice.

Embracing the Larger Community

The headlines have two major inadequacies, as a source for global worship. The first is that the news media do not present the whole world—only the part that sells advertising. Some events get almost monotonous attention, but other things are left unmentioned. How much is known about the conflicts in Mozambique, Sri Lanka, or El Salvador? How much is said about the terrifying epidemic in Peru or the total devastation of African villages by the AIDS virus? To have worship that is global means to pray for those whom the media chooses to ignore—to worship a God larger than the boundaries of our knowledge or compassion and larger than the compass of CNN. Global prayers are not bound to the compartmentalized time slots, which chain so much of our concern.

A simple plan can help start the process. The World Council of Churches publishes an ecumenical prayer cycle, *With All God's People.* Two or three countries are named each week, so that all nations are remembered in a year. Use of the liturgical resources from these countries enrich the possibilities available for worship. Other options include prayer calendars for missionaries. To pray for a country about which one knows nothing is only a start. It poses some questions: Where is this country? How do the people live there? What role do Christians play in the culture? Church networks, particularly mission magazines, can be a source of information, so that the prayers can be as informed as possible.

Every morning, the World Council of Churches begins with prayer. One day, the leader of the prayers asked us to name people we knew from the country about which we were praying. At the World Council, where people do much traveling, many names surfaced. This made our prayers more concrete and vital. These personal connections may not happen very often in local settings, but there may be more possibilities than first imagined. Someone may have a relative or friend living overseas. Increasing numbers of persons are going to mission work camps. The telephone or fax could also be exploited as a means to connect churches. Calls could be made to mission partner churches and prayers be said for these churches. Technology will certainly provide other methods. One person could be designated to do some basic research and write a petition for intercessions (a petition, not a travelogue or geography lesson). The missions committee might regularly offer prayers for missionaries and then go on to pray for those whom they serve and who serve them. To pray for the world is not difficult. To desire to include the world, or more specifically the people of the world, in our worship is more difficult. As people travel they might consciously seek other Christians, whose names and ministries they could bring back to the local congregation for prayer. In this way, the local congregation is expanded. Prayer goes beyond the big names and issues to people, but these people are not centered in one local community. They span the globe and have strange sounding names. Then, worship will have gone beyond the headlines to embrace a larger community.

Receiving Gifts from Neighbors around the World

There is a second reason that headlines are inadequate as a base for global worship. Most often, these headlines present the world as a problem to be solved or a mistake to be corrected.

But, worship is not just about problems. Worship is meeting God and discovering God's gifts. Global worship goes beyond the headlines because in Christ we find our sisters and brothers who have great gifts to share with us.

In former times, the missionaries were sent out to preach the gospel to those who had never heard about Jesus Christ. In many places, that faith has taken root; and presently, the Christian faith is shedding its cultural captivity to Western forms. People are bringing their faith to their culture and their culture to their faith. These non-Western peoples have developed ways to reach their own people. These forms from these peoples are now available to the whole church. These gifts can let us see again the markings of a vital faith.

Music. One of the most vibrant gifts that demonstrates the vital faith of these cultures is music. _The Presbyterian Hymnal_ is filled with songs from other cultures. These musical gifts are waiting to be sung. But they will not communicate the vitality of other peoples' vision, unless they are sung well.

One of the first clues is to use imagination with instrumentation. For some music, the drum is the most important accompaniment. Rhythm instruments are not just for the children's choir anymore. Guitars are often a part of music from Latin America (but are part of folk American and European music). Asian music often uses a flute or recorder to support the singing of the melody. Finger cymbals can provide color to the sound. Instrumentation does not require the resources of a large church. In most every community, someone owns a snare drum. Borrow the drum and the drummer. Increasingly, synthesizers that easily produce a wide variety of sounds are available. Cultivate church musicians with enough imagination to find the sound of another culture and bring that sound into the sanctuary. There is no quicker way than in music to illustrate and to enliven global Christianity to congregations and, if done well, no better way for them to receive the gifts that world Christians have to offer. In worship, one door to the world is through sounds.

A beginning point could be the singing of carols from around the world at Christmas. The Chinese hymns, no. 65, "Midnight Stars Make Bright the Sky" and no. 33, "Sheng Ye Qing, Sheng Ye Jing," could be accompanied by flute, recorder,

The Maltese Cross. This cross resembles four spearheads with the points touching. The eight outer points are a well-known symbol for the eight Beatitudes.

or violin on the melody. Instead of the printed keyboard part, a drone on the tonic and dominant would provide variety. A plucked sound, similar to a harp, could be used from a synthesizer. From Malawi, there is no. 55, "That Boy-child of Mary." Have a leader sing the verses, with everyone joining on the refrain. Add light drums along with a recorder on the melody. This hymn could be sung without the book because of its simple chorus. The Hispanic carols, no. 45, "A La Ru," and no. 64, "De Tierra Lejana Venimos," could both use guitar and percussion, particularly claves and maracas. In "De Tierra Lejana Venimos," the first verse could be sung as a duet using the accompaniment as a guide for the alto part. There are other international carols as well. These simple suggestions can be expanded so that the cultural uniqueness of the songs are presented.

Songs from Christians of other lands call us to a new faithfulness and a new hope, such as this song from Argentina:

May the God of hope go with us every day,
Filling all our lives with love and joy and peace.
May the God of justice speed us on our way,
Bringing light and hope to every land and race.
Praying, let us work for peace, Singing, share our joy with all,

Working for a world that's new, Faithful when we hear Christ's call.

(*Presbyterian Hymnal*, no. 432)

And calls to faithfulness and hope is also in this song from Central America:

You know that I own so little,
In my boat, there's no money nor weapons,
You'll only find there my nets and labor.
O Lord, with Your eyes You have searched me,
And, while smiling, have called out my name.
Now my boat's left on the shoreline behind me,
Now with You I will seek other seas.

(*Presbyterian Hymnal*, no. 377)

Then, there is this song from Korea:

Whatever talent God has given me
I pledge to use in service and in love,
Joined with my God to lift my neighbor's load,
New strength and hope are given from above.

(*Presbyterian Hymnal*, no. 410)

Christian songs from other lands also call us to greater unity, such as this song from Japan:

Many are the tongues we speak,
Scattered are the lands,
Yet our hearts are one in God,
One in love's demands.

(*Presbyterian Hymnal*, no. 465)

And calls to unity issue forth from this song from Ghana:

Jesu, Jesu, fill us with Your love,
Show us how to serve the neighbors we have from You.

(*Presbyterian Hymnal*, no. 367)

Finally, the same theme is continued in this song from the Hispanic community:

Like the grains which become one same whole loaf,
Like the notes that are woven into song,
Like the droplets of water that are blended in the sea,
We, as Christians, one body shall become.

(*Presbyterian Hymnal*, no. 518)

The material in *The Presbyterian Hymnal* has one disadvantage. The songs are usually too long to attempt to sing them in their original languages. One of the breakthroughs that worship leaders for the World Council of Churches have discovered is the value of short liturgical pieces. One resource is *In Spirit and Truth,* the worship book from the Seventh Assembly of the World Council of Churches. There is also an audio tape of the Assembly's worship, which gives important clues about how the songs can be sung. In addition, there are a series of books gathered from regional music and worship workshops. These include *African Songs of Worship, Asian Songs of Worship, Todas Los Voces,* and *Brazilian Songs of Worship.* These are available from the World Council of Churches, 475 Riverside Dr., New York, NY 10015. One other resource deserves special attention. It is *Sound the Bamboo,* a comprehensive collection of Christian music available through the Asian Institute of Liturgy and Music, P.O. Box 3167, Manila 1099, Philippines.

Many Christians may not be used to service music beyond the *Doxology* and the *Gloria Patri.* In the "Service for the Lord's Day" on page twelve of *The Presbyterian Hymnal,* there are many possibilities for including liturgical songs from other regions. A vibrant Alleluia between the second lesson and the Gospel can set the Gospel apart as a special hearing. The parts of the Eucharist can be sung. Intercessions can be undergirded by interspersing Kyrie eleison. The Taizé community from France has many responses, which can bear meditative repetition. Two examples are no. 567, *Gloria, Gloria,* and no. 599, *Jesus Remember Me.* The Iona community from Scotland also creates these. Christian composers all over the world are making use of these forms. This can be a simple and exciting way to bring global gifts into worship.

Bodily Movement. Musically, there is one thing still lacking. To receive the musical gifts to the fullest, we as Christians need to become free enough to move our bodies in worship. Africans in particular have discovered the freedom to praise God with their whole selves—their feet as well as their voices. I was taught to sit still in church. Africans are teaching us that our praise is less than full until we praise God with everything that we are and that includes shoulders, knees, and hips. This takes a good leader. The best method is to invite an African musician to church, but few still have this opportunity. People can learn to move. I usually invite persons first to move their feet up and down to the beat. Then, I invite them to swing their arms or clap their hands. I try to do this in the context of prayer for the first time. A good starting song is *Wa Wa Emimimo* from Nigeria.

I ask people to wave the Spirit down, along with moving their feet. The next step is to turn this motion into prayer. This is difficult for those of us used to silence and stillness as the mode of prayer. But for some, this becomes a new opportunity to experience connection with God.

Visual Arts. The visual arts are another way to bring global gifts to worship. Third world shops carry items appropriate for worship: materials for stoles, sculpture, bells, paintings, and crafts. Again, tourists can be encouraged to seek products that could be used for the praise of God from the countries they visit.

Including in Worship the World that God So Loved

The world can enter our worship through actions which enable other cultures to pray. For instance, Asians put great emphasis on light. They often have a lamp at the center of worship. They may approach the light and place their hands in its heat and then rub their face. This is a way of symbolically putting the light of Christ inside. Some Orthodox traditions sprinkle water as a special sign of blessing. A service of blessing the water will be included in a book of worship services, available in 1992, from the Canberra Assembly and other World Council meetings. A variety of instruments can call a congregation to worship: a conch shell from the Pacific, drums from Africa, a sitar from India. These ideas are not complex, but they bring to worship the variety that God has given us.

In stewardship campaigns, we ask people to look at the way they spend their money as an indication of their values and their faith. Might we look at our prayers and our music to get a sense of our deepest liturgical goals? How much of our worship gets directed beyond local or even individual needs? Does our worship declare our concern for the world that God so loved? Have we lost faith that God is active in the world? Although the Berlin wall has crumbled and the Soviet coup has failed, have we lost the ability to see God at work in the large strokes of history, so we pray for individual boons, where the miracles are easier to handle and less threatened by continual ambiguity? Bringing the world into our worship also brings in all the hungry, the destitute, and the refugees searching for safety. It brings in the abused women and children. It includes the people that the headlines exclude.

Terry MacArthur[24]

185 ✦ Cartigny Statement on Worship and Culture: Biblical and Historical Foundations

The Cartigny Statement on Worship and Culture was prepared on October 1993 by the Lutheran World Federation's study team focused on this topic. In this first consultation, the team focused on the biblical and historical materials relating to the relationship between worship and culture in the church. The team's inquiry focused on what is cultural, countercultural, and transcultural in Christian worship.

Preface

This statement was prepared at the first consultation of the Lutheran World Federation's study on Worship and Culture, held in Cartigny, Switzerland, in October 1993. Those invited to participate comprised the LWF's ongoing international study team for the project; the participants represented all continents of the world. At this initial consultation, the study team focused on the biblical and historical (early church and Lutheran Reformation) foundations of the relationship between worship and culture. The study team will meet again in March 1994, in Hong Kong, to explore contemporary issues and questions of the relationship between culture and liturgy, church music, and church architecture. Following the Hong Kong consultation, it is envisioned that the study will move into a regional phase, in which regional study teams will encourage and assist in the identification and exploration of particular issues related to worship and culture as they exist in the LWF's regions, sub-regions, and member churches. This exploration is to be at the pastoral, as well as the theological level. Phase III of the study is to synthesize and reflect globally on the regional findings; phase IV is to conclude the study with a wide variety of seminars and

workshops to implement the results of the study, as each region and LWF member church decides what is helpful.

The contents of this Cartigny Statement, therefore, are conclusions only of the study team's initial consultation, with its specific focus on biblical and historical foundations. It is not a final statement on the topic as a whole.

(1) Introduction

(1.1) With gratitude to God, the LWF study team on Worship and Culture acknowledges the efforts of the church throughout the ages to adapt to current and local situations. We ourselves are also particularly grateful that the Lutheran World Federation and its member churches have given us a mandate to begin a new study on this central aspect of our Christian life.

(1.2) We began our work with the conviction that even during our own times the Word of God must be interpreted within the context of a changing world. Through the Holy Spirit, Jesus Christ is present in our own diverse cultural contexts today, just as his presence was incarnated in the life situation of the first century.

(1.3) We acknowledge the need in our time to make worship both authentic to the Word of God and relevant to given cultures. The church is called upon to continue the on-going task of reformation, so that the Gospel might faithfully be proclaimed among the various cultures of today's world. In the final analysis, the church is an assembly of believers in a given place and time where the Word of God is preached according to the Scriptures and the Sacraments administered following the letter and spirit of the Gospel (cf. Augsburg Confession 7). It has been our Lutheran tradition—indeed, it belongs to the Christian tradition as a whole—that the Word of God should be rendered understandable to all and that the Sacraments should be accessible to all believers. This is understood in the context of God's grace and what Christ does for us.

(1.4) In the incarnate Christ, the witness and service of congregations become meaningful to our societies. The church in its worship, which is the central expression of celebrating our life in Christ, should be seen as an ongoing incarnation of the Gospel.

(2) First Questions

(2.1) As member churches of the Lutheran World Federation from across the world begin to explore how the Gospel can be rooted in cultural patterns, it is clear that such an exploration is not a luxury, but an imperative. Further, it is clear that the process of localizing worship is not something new, but rather is an age-old ecclesial inclination attested by well-known examples from the past.

(2.2) But the rich and complex record of the faith compels us to take more than a cursory look at the past. It seemed right, then, to engage ourselves in a more comprehensive search for the roots and methods which could provide directions and energy for present opportunities and challenges.

(2.3) The process for the first consultation grew from a profound recognition that Jesus Christ himself is God incarnate in human culture. This preeminent inculturation led us first to the New Testament where we could discover how the liberating Word for the world met culture. Then we were propelled into a study of the early church, where the Word continued to be incarnated in several different cultures; and finally the consultation focused on the Lutheran Reformation as a particular time when that creating Word was experienced anew, challenging and transforming culture. The ecumenical importance of this process led to the involvement in our deliberations of several non-Lutheran participants.

(2.4) A sense of the dynamic life-giving relationship between worship and culture derives from more than an examination of theological development. Therefore, this study by definition searches for illumination from the histories of liturgy (text and action), church architecture, and church music as well, giving the study that kind of breadth required by current cultural contexts.

(2.5) The deliberate intent to discover how the church in the past has sorted out the issues and processes attending the worship/culture dynamic has yielded considerable insight and prospects for future fruitful interaction. Examples: (A) The church, as a continuing incarnation of Christ in the world, is always taking root in culture as that place where Christ can be experienced anew. To recognize the cultural component of the church's worship, however, is to reckon the rich presence of God's diverse creation in the references and materials of Christian worship. A focus on the cultural leads the church toward a more responsible relationship with creation itself. (B) Asking inculturation questions of the church's history has made it clear that there are identifiable core elements of Baptism and Eucharist which perdure through nearly every time and place. (C) The church's liturgy is most authentic when it resists crystallization by permitting the Gospel to interpret and direct the contextualization process.

(2.6) The focus on history, therefore, quite naturally draws attention to contemporary issues, as Christian communities live the Gospel in worship in their various cultures. At the Hong Kong consultation in 1994, the study team will turn toward specific contemporary concerns, seeking to find common methods and mutual encouragement as the churches carefully attend to these issues.

(3) Models and Methods

(3.1) An examination of the history of the church, from its inception in the Hellenistic-Jewish milieu to the current modern contexts, reveals that it has struggled continually with how to relate Christian worship to the cultures in which it is located. The process of understanding and answering this question has been alternately called contextualization, indigenization, localization, and inculturation. Each of these terms has been used in different ways, in different places in the world; and it should be noted that no one single term adequately expresses the process.

(3.2) Nonetheless, it remains the case that the Christian assembly for worship, with its music and its spatial environment, stands at the intersection of Christian faith and cultural patterns. Out of this complex interplay of Christianity and culture, three areas for consideration readily become apparent—the cultural, the countercultural, and the transcultural. The task of relating worship and culture, then, involves asking the following three questions.

(3.3) First, what are the cultural elements in Christian worship (including liturgical texts, gestures, vestments, furnishings, art, music, and architecture) which give expression to the particularity of the gathered people? Cultural elements have been used in worship throughout the history of the church (for example, the adaptation of basilican architecture in the Constantinian church) to help engage Christian worship with a particular context, while yet remaining faithful to the Gospel. In the same way, the churches in every generation and in every context must ask what cultural elements can/should be used in their worship in order to help locate the worshiping community in its particular cultural context.

(3.4) Second, what are the countercultural elements in Christian worship which challenge the culture in which it is located? The church throughout its history, by its faithful proclamation of the gospel, has challenged the status quo and the social injustices of its day (for example, Christ and his disciples sharing meals with the socially unaccepted people of their day). In the same way, the churches in every generation and in every context must ask what in their worship can/should be countercultural, challenging the culture in which it exists and ultimately facilitating its transformation.

(3.5) Third, what are the transcultural elements in worship which place it clearly within the universality of the Christian liturgical tradition? The church throughout its history has consistently observed certain core elements within its worship as a way to identify itself with the universal tradition of the church which transcends time and place (for example, the use of water in Baptism). In the same way, churches in every generation and in every context must ask in what ways their worship practice can/should transcend their particular culture, placing them within the universal Christian tradition.

(3.6) Therefore, the task of relating worship and culture is ultimately concerned with finding the balance between relevance and authenticity, between particularity and universality, while avoiding eclecticism and/or syncretism. While it is clear that each church in its cultural context will need to ask these questions for itself and find answers appropriate to its own situation, it is also clear that this inquiry will require each church to attend to the experiences of the other churches and to the treasures of other cultures.

(3.7) An examination of the tradition, from the biblical witness, the early church, and the Lutheran Reformation, reveals the core of Christian worship to be Word, Baptism, and Eucharist. The pattern, or ordo, of entry into the community is teaching and the baptismal bath. The pattern of the weekly gathering of the community on the Lord's Day is the celebration centered around the Word and the eucharistic meal. These core elements are clearly evident in the historical witnesses of the Christian worship tradition. Further, it is evident that the purpose of this pattern of worship is faithfully to receive and faithfully to proclaim the gospel of Jesus Christ.

(3.8) One helpful model, then, which is evident throughout the history of the church, is found where the worshiping community is able to receive and use the important elements of the culture (and thus be localized in a particular context), while at the same time critically shaping these elements so that they may bear witness to the gospel of Christ, who transcends and transforms all cultures (and thus be rooted in the universal Christian tradition). "See, I am making all things new" (Rev. 21:5, NRSV).

(4) Prospects

(4.1) The consultation studied processes of interaction between worship and cultural settings in the New Testament, the early church, and the Lutheran Reformation. It identified the use of different models and methods and recognized in these patterns an on-going process.

(4.2) The study team wishes to invite the churches to join in this study of the common roots of Christian worship, believing that study offers important tools for the analysis of their worship (liturgy, music, architecture, art, and so on) within their various cultural settings.

(4.3) The study team will continue its work by examining contemporary relationships between worship and cultures. In specific topics for further consideration, the study will seek to clarify the interrelationship between form and content in liturgy; the use of language, gestures, symbols, and music in varying cultural contexts; and the shaping of worship space, with the goal of the inclusive participation of all people—exploring what is cultural, countercultural, and transcultural in these elements.

(4.4) The sacramental practices for baptism and the Eucharist need to be examined and adapted to recover their full meanings, within the churches' current diverse cultural contexts, in order that the gift of God's grace may be offered to all.

(4.5) The churches are challenged to be creative as they develop forms of worship which are both authentic and relevant, responding both to their cultures and to the gospel. Through the power of the Holy Spirit, the churches can find for themselves and offer to the many societies of the world an alternative model of life.

Lutheran World Federation

186 • Vox Populi: Developing Global Song in the Northern World

With the increase in the number of Christians in other parts of the world other than the Northern (or Western) world, the church of the Northern world should learn from the musical geniuses of these different peoples. In this article, the author suggests what African music, Asian music, and Central and Latin American music offers Northern people.

An African Experience

In the fall of 1989, I spent five months in Africa, primarily in Nigeria, teaching at a seminary in the southern region of the country populated primarily by the Yoruba people. Since transportation was readily available, I made every attempt to visit as many local churches as possible on Sunday mornings and experience the vast variety of Nigerian worship. There was one congregation in particular that I enjoyed and I visited them on several occasions. It was not too far from the city of Ogbomosho, where I was living. Just as I drove into the rural area on the eastern edge of the city, there is a sign to the Promised Land. This land had been "promised" some years ago to a colony of lepers, who, with their families, lived, farmed, worked, and worshiped on this piece of property. I always arrive early when visiting a church in order to greet people and have plenty of time to get a sense of my surroundings. At first glance, it looked like any other Yoruba village; but upon closer observation, I started to note differences. There were many more folks on crutches than I would normally see. Some people walked on padded knees because of a lack of feet. Friendly folks extended an often fingerless hand to me in greeting. While the transmission of leprosy is still a mystery, I had been assured that casual contact would not be harmful. There were many lepers with their families, who did not appear to have the disease. The sounds of children playing and singing filled the air, just as it would in any other village.

Worship was always special with these people. The hymn singing was varied and vibrant. Very few owned hymnals. They were expensive. Not everyone could read. The favorites were always memorized and when new material was learned, "lining out" proved to be an effective technique. In this community, there was the additional problem that many of its residents were not able to hold or turn the pages of a hymnal because they lacked fingers necessary for such an intricate task. The songs ranged from traditional Western hymns translated into Yoruba, e.g., "Work for the Night Is Coming," and "What a Friend We Have in Jesus," to indigenous expressions of their Christian faith. Regardless of the source or origin of the style, the ubiquitous West African drum ensemble always accompanied the group.

I had grown accustomed to hearing drums at almost every service that I attended. If the truth were to be known, I really experienced a percussive void in worship when I returned to the United States. While the trap sets of the United States and Europe were making some headway in the urban situations, the indigenous four- or five-person West African drum ensemble provided an intricate carpet of sound, offering a foundation for all congregational hymns that gave not only a sense of momentum to the music, but encouraged the singers. Indeed, it was quite often that the congregation augmented the praise of the drummers with their own spontaneous polyrhythmic hand-clapping. (Keep in mind that their hands were not occupied with hymnals.) The drummers at the Promised Land were especially thrilling to watch. They all lacked fingers. Drumming was one of the few means of expression that was still open to them; and they savored it with joy.

It is customary for Nigerian choirs to process into the sanctuary as a signal that worship is beginning. The choirs always enter and exit singing—the first of the worship leaders to arrive and the last to leave. It is as if the Spirit will only come in with a song. I remember the processionals of the Promised Land choir vividly. Some members were physically whole and marched in to the beat; others hobbled in on crutches with no less vitality. The proud director led the way. Because he had no feet, however, he led the processional and directed the group from his padded knees. It was a paradox to see so much joy on the face of a man who was forced to assume a position of humility. Such were the many paradoxes of the Promised Land.

The *Why* Question

My experiences in Nigeria and Kenya during 1989 and subsequent visits to Haiti, Nicaragua, Mexico, and Cuba are full of such stories. As a student of cross-cultural liturgy and music-making, the question arises, what music and liturgy from non-Western settings might inform and enrich worship in the United States? But perhaps, I am ahead of myself. Maybe the first question is not *what*, but *why*. Why should worshipers in the United States be interested in using non-Euro-American materials? After all, our market is thoroughly saturated with "our own" music already, isn't it? Asking *why* is worth the effort if materials from non-Euro-American cultural contexts are going to be used effectively and with integrity in the service of liturgy.

The Proverbial Elephant. My first response to the *why* question is a reference to the proverbial elephant surrounded by several blind people. Upon being asked to discuss their experiences, each described the elephant in the context of his or her relationship to the elephant. The person closest to the trunk or the tail had a much different description than the person touching a massive leg or the person riding on the back of the elephant. Euro-American musical tradition has had a profound impact upon the worship of the global community. Indeed, everyone is interested in learning songs from this tradition. My travel has not to this point taken me to very many places where Euro-American songs have not had some impact—albeit in varying degrees and adapted in some way to local musical customs. But, when it comes to expressing the nature of God through congregational song, we, Euro-Americans, are finally learning that even the splendor and diversity of the Euro-American musical tradition does

not begin to describe "the elephant." Robin Leaver has expressed the situation very well:

> In the nineteenth and earlier twentieth centuries, the export of hymnody was entirely one-way: *from* Europeans *to* Africans, Asians, or to whomever. Instead of being taken as examples of how the Christian faith can be incarnated within a particular culture, European hymns were taken to be the only valid vehicles of faith: instead of using them as signposts pointing out possibilities for the creation of new expressions of the faith from within a different culture, only mirror images were produced. (Robin A. Leaver, "Theological Dimensions of Mission Hymnody: the Counterpoint of Cult and Culture," in *The Hymnology Annual: An International Forum on the Hymn and Worship,* ed. Vernon Wicker [Berrien Springs, Mich.: Vande Vere Publishing Ltd., 1991], 40.)

To carry the analogy a little further, we are discovering that we do not know as much about the elephant as we thought. So the first answer to the *why* question is that the Euro-American view of the world and Christianity is but one of many worldviews.

Things Are Not Like They Used to Be. The second response to the *why* question acknowledges the changing face of Christianity. Walbert Bühlmann, a Roman Catholic theologian, helps us see some of these changes in his book, *With Eyes to See: Church and World in the Third Millennium:*

> In 1900, 85 percent of all Christians, and 77 percent of all Catholics, lived in the Western, or Northern, world–Europe and North America. Over the last few decades, however, the historical situation has changed radically. With the baby boom and new conversions in Latin America, Africa, Asia, and Oceana, by 1970 51.86 percent of Catholics lived in the third world. Based on this trend, I predicted at that time that by the year 2000 some 70 percent of Catholics would be living in the third world. By 1985 the proportion had already risen to 59.80 percent, an increase of 7.94 percent. Were this rate of increase to hold steady over the next fifteen years, the proportion would be 67.74 percent by the year 2000. Correcting for some probable acceleration, the actual figure will indeed doubtlessly be around 70 percent. (Walbert Bühlmann, *With Eyes to See: Church and World in the Third Millennium,* trans. by Robert R. Barr (Maryknoll, N.Y.: Orbis Books, 1989), 6.)

Bühlmann suggests that when Orthodox and Protestant Christians are included in the equation, third world Christians will outnumber Christians of the Northern world, 60.2 percent to 39.8 percent by the year 2000 (Bühlmann 7).

To bring it a little closer to home, I recently attended an interfaith service at Temple Emanu-El in Dallas, where the gathering of at least fifteen hundred was addressed by Ann Richards, the governor of Texas. The major theme of her address was the changes in population in the state of Texas. Soon after the turn of the century, the Anglo population will be in a minority in Texas. One of the highest priorities of her administration is the placing of minorities in governmental positions of responsibility in an effort to avoid a leadership vacuum among minorities in the next century. It appears that even the Northern world will be in for many changes within a few decades. So, the second answer to the _why_ question is a pragmatic one, "the times are [ecclesiastically and politically] changin'."

Liturgical Renewal: We Are Still Looking for Answers. As important as the theological, ecclesiastical, and political realities are, I do not find these as compelling as the liturgical reality. During this century, movements for liturgical renewal have searched for new materials and forms in a variety of places. Historical liturgies and practices, the arts, ecumenism, and the marketing strategies of the church growth movement are but a few of the means promoted for revitalizing worship. Each approach offers a new perspective on liturgical life. There is some evidence in recent hymnals and worship books that another movement is vying for recognition among liturgical renewal movements. I am borrowing a term suggested by Harold Best in his recent book, _Music Through the Eyes of Faith_ (San Francisco: HarperCollins, 1993). Best suggests the term _musical pluralism_ (see chapter 3). His rationale has many facets, but is similar in part to an idea mentioned above: "Since no one culture can 'say it all,' how fitting it is for Christians to want to join the creative ways of other cultures, for no other reason than to fill out their praise!" (Best 68). Another facet of Best's argument for musical pluralism may be tied to a classic definition of the term _liturgy_ as "the work of the people." Perhaps this is inherent in Best's approach when he says:

Musical pluralism does not begin with aesthetics but with people. No matter how favorable or objectionable their music might be at first blush, it is of primary importance that the music makers are honest-to-goodness people who must be loved first of all as such. The next step is to understand that they honestly love the music they make or they would not have made it to begin with. (Best 68.)

Included in Best's discussion of musical pluralism are not only musics from non-Western cultures, but diverse musics within our culture. Central to his thesis, however, is the vitality that could be brought to worship life in the United States through musical pluralism. Drawing from the visitation of the Holy Spirit, Best reminds us that "Pentecost tells us that one artistic tongue is only a start and thousand will never suffice" (Best 67).

Living beyond Culture. It is important to ask _why_ when pursuing a musical course that may change the face of liturgy during the next half century. In searching for a shorter, direct answer, I find John Blacking's argument the most compelling. Although Blacking speaks as an anthropologist, his thesis is most relevant to the church musician looking to the future. In his book, _How Musical Is Man?_ (Seattle: University of Washington Press, 1973), Blacking is concerned about the provincial blinders that a single culture places on the perception of the musician:

An understanding of [the] processes involved in the production of music may provide us with evidence that men are more remarkable and capable creatures than most societies ever allow them to be. This is not the fault of culture itself, but the fault of man, who mistakes the means of culture for the end, and so lives _for_ culture and not _beyond_ culture. (Blacking 7.)

This is not primarily a discussion of the future of church in the twenty-first century. If it were, I would borrow Blacking's idea and say that the future of church music is dependent upon the ability of church musicians to lead their congregations to live _beyond_ their inherited culture. If the Christian message is to be incarnate in the music and liturgy, we share in the future. We must seize the possibility of living beyond our primary cultural contexts. Indeed, the life and ministry of Christ might be viewed from the perspective of the accounts, in which he lived beyond the cultural norms of his day. Whether dealing with a suspect minority group like the Samaritans, relating to women, choosing his followers from among the powerless of his society, assuming postures of humility and servanthood as a model for leadership, teaching the elders at the age of twelve, cleansing the temple of some early capitalists, or preaching a gospel that threatened the established political and religious orders, Jesus lived beyond the cultural expectations of a poor Jewish man of his day.

The *What* Question

Having considered to some degree the question of *why*, I want to approach the question of *what* global music might offer to those of us in the Northern world. Let us dismiss immediately the tokenism of a few new musical selections that will add a little variety to our preset musical agendas. If the discussion above has any validity, tokenism will not suffice. The church music community has done some preliminary thinking in this area in the report of *The Milwaukee Symposia for Church Composers* (Washington, D.C.: National Association of Pastoral Musicians, 1992). In the section on "Cross-Cultural Music Making" (paragraphs 56–63), there are excellent points for our consideration as we pursue a response to the inclusion of multicultural materials in liturgy. Perhaps a few quotes from this document might help focus our thinking:

> Cultivating the cross-cultural dimension of the Christian life in worship does not mean simply borrowing ideas from some distant culture or language. (par. 57)

> Beginning the cross-cultural diversity by recognizing the diversity in our own midst does not mean that we can limit ourselves to attending to the cultural diversity in our own community. The call to mission, implicit in every celebration of Christian liturgy, requires that we recognize the needs of those beyond our local horizons. (par. 58.)

> Developing an authentic cross-cultural perspective requires that this issue live at the very heart of the liturgical preparation process. (par. 59.)

> From a musical perspective, accepting the challenge of cross-cultural worship requires addressing the ethnocentrism that has marked Western Christian music for the last millennium. (par. 60.)

> Even in linguistically and ethnically homogenous communities, singing the music of another culture means entering into their world. (par. 63.)

Tokenism is not implied by these statements. In spite of the brevity of this document and the section on cross-cultural music-making, the seeds of an agenda for the future are there, ready to be sown. Time does not allow a broader commentary on each of the statements extracted from this document. Please allow me to offer some commentary on the final statement. What does the music of other cultures offer to a linguistically and ethnically homogeneous community?

My limited experience in the liturgical and musical life of cultures outside the Northern world and the use of global materials within predominately Anglo liturgical settings suggests some potentially radical changes that might occur. I have chosen for the sake of time to limit my discussion to the broad geographical areas of Africa, Asia, and Latin and South America, although this approach might be taken with various musical cultures within the United States. In general terms, the continental regions of Africa, Asia, and Latin/South America each contain a diversity of musical expression from the profoundly simple to the significantly complex. Each region contains music that expresses feelings from the deepest sorrow to ecstatic joy. Yet, in the midst of such great musical variety within each continental region, there are primary semblances of musical experience that characterize the diverse musical expressions on each continent. I wish to propose what I consider to be a *primary semblance* in the diverse musics of Africa, Asia, and Latin America that might be of significance to liturgy in the predominately Anglo liturgical communities of the Northern world. The term *semblance* is borrowed from the writings of Susanne K. Langer, where she states that ". . . what art expresses is *not* actual feeling, but ideas of feeling; as language does not express actual things and events but ideas of them [i.e., semblance]" (*Feeling and Form: A Theory of Art* [New York: Charles Scribner's Sons, 1953], 59). It is not my intention to reduce the broad range of musical expression of each continent to one simple statement. The purpose is to chose a salient musical semblance from each broad cultural region that might liturgically offer ethnically homogeneous Anglo congregations in the United States a way to learn to live and worship *beyond* their primary culture.

A Primary Musical Semblance of Africa: Communal Music-Making

The opening narrative came from a scene in a rural Nigerian village. While the fact that this village was a leper colony offered some variance from the norm, a primary semblance of African music-making was still there in abundance. For me, this semblance is the sense of community that is fostered by and through music. Music-making in Africa is participatory—not a spectator sport. There is very little distinction between those that sing in the established choir and those who are a part of the congregation. When, on occasion, I was asked to sing a solo, I soon learned that the congregation demonstrated their appreciation for my singing by humming, clapping, or swaying with my music, rather than passively listening. When it comes to music-making, the individual soloist is important only inasmuch as that person prompts or facilitates the singing of the group. In this regard, the solo musician in most African worship has much in common with the role of the cantor as discussed by Paul Westermeyer in his book, *The Church Musician* ([San Francisco: Harper and Row, 1988], 13 ff). The call-and-response form punctuates all aspects of liturgy from the prayers and hymns to the reading of Scripture and the sermon. The leader is a prompter in the primarily oral liturgical tradition of Africa. Notice in the following prayer of thanksgiving from a Nigerian African church, the frequency that the congregation punctuates this Yoruba prayer with an "Amen." They do not wait until the end, but offer encouragement all along the way.

> Creator of Heaven and earth, accept our praises—AMEN!
> Messiah, accept our thanks and accept our praises—AMEN!
> As young people and adults, accept our thanks and praises—AMEN!
> As male and female, accept our thanks and praises—AMEN!
> On this Sunday accept our thanks and praises—AMEN!
> On all days accept our thanks and praises—AMEN!
> Let not the mouths which we thank thee become sour—AMEN!

> Let us not give thanks in sorrow—AMEN!
> Let us not give thanks in tears—AMEN!
> Let us not give thanks in regret—AMEN!
> Let us not be thankful half-heartedly—AMEN!
> Accept our thanks and praises, O Lord, make us useful to Thee— AMEN!
> Hear us O Ruler of Heaven, through Jesus Christ our Lord—AMEN!

(John Carden, comp., *With All God's People: The New Ecumenical Prayer Cycle* [Geneva: WCC Publications, 1992], 190–191.)

While in Nigeria, I studied the Yoruba talking drum, an instrument capable of making different levels of pitch, simulating the tonal changes in pitch of the Yoruba language. Each morning in the chapel worship at the seminary where I taught, a different drum ensemble was featured—five in all. In one conversation with my drum instructor, I asked him who was the best drum player in the seminary. After some time, he told me in a polite way that I had not asked a relevant question. The question was not, "who is the best drum player?" but "who is the best drum ensemble?" An individual drummer was of little musical significance without an ensemble of drummers. Skill in West African drumming is demonstrated in the process of interacting with other drummers. Drumming, indeed like most music-making, is realized in community.

I read of an analogous situation in Vincent Donovan's book, *Christianity Revisited* (Maryknoll, N.Y.: Orbis Books, 1978). Donovan was a Roman Catholic missionary working among the Masai people of East Africa. After some months of discussing the essence of Christianity with the elders of a particular group of Masai, they decided to accept Christianity. Donovan encouraged them to write a credo that expressed their new-found faith. Once again, Donovan discovered that the question was wrong. The Masai wrote not a *credo*, but a *credemos*. It was unthinkable to write, "I believe." The Masai creed emphasized repeatedly, "we believe." Other changes included a shift from the traditional Masai belief that there was no afterlife to a belief in eternal life. When someone dies, the deceased is carried to the bush and the hyenas do the rest. Let us read together the Masai *credemos*:

> We believe in the one High God, who out of love created the beautiful world and everything

good in it. God created people and wanted them to be happy in the world. God loves the world and every nation and tribe on the earth. We have known this High God in the darkness, and now we know God in the light. God promised in the book called the Bible, the word of God, that all nations and tribes of the world would be saved.

We believe that God made good this promise by sending Jesus Christ, the Son of God, a Jew by tribe, born poor in a little village, who left his home and was always on safari doing good, curing people by the power of God, teaching about God and people, showing that the meaning of religion is love. He was rejected by his people, tortured, and nailed—hands and feet—to a cross and died. He lay buried, but the hyenas did not find his body, and on the third day, he rose from the grave. He ascended to the skies. He is the Lord!

We believe that all our sins are forgiven through him. All who have faith in him must be sorry for their sins, be baptized in the Holy Spirit of God, live the rules of love, and share the bread together in love, to announce the good news to others until Jesus comes again. We are waiting for him. He is alive! He lives! This we believe. Amen! (Vincent J. Donovan, *Christianity Revisited* [Maryknoll, N.Y.: Orbis Books, 1978], 200.)

I suggest that the primary African musical semblance that the Northern world needs to experience is community. The musical and liturgical forms that support this semblance in corporate worship would be most helpful in the narcissistic, self-centered, individualistic worship of many predominately Anglo churches. The question so often voiced—"Were my needs met?"—would be unthinkable in the midst of African worshiping communities. Strength for the individual is found in what strengthens the community.

A Primary Musical Semblance of Asia: Mystery and Silence

When it comes to the myriad forms of Asian worship, I am at a loss for first hand experiences. My thesis of a primary musical semblance for this part of the world is especially tentative. It is grounded in two things—the students from various parts of Asia to whom I have had the privilege of teaching over the years (including students from Korea, Japan, China, Singapore, Tonga, and the Philippines) and the musical materials from various parts of Asia, especially those provided

through the work of I-to-Loh and Francisco Feliciano at the Asian Institute for Liturgy and Music in Manila. Among the most valuable of these materials is the hymnal, *Sound the Bamboo*, published under the auspices of the Christian Council of Asia. Based on this limited experience, I venture the thesis that the primary musical semblance of the diverse traditions represented in Asia that is most needed in the Northern Anglo world is that of silence and mystery. While a full range of emotional experience is expressed through Asian music, the sound of a Japanese *koto* or *shakuhachi* or the Chinese *p'ip'a* seems, at least to my Western (or Northern) ears, to leave space for the contemplation of the Mystery that created and sustains us. Perhaps the following prayer from the Buddhist/Christian Center in Hong Kong illustrates this point:

> With all my heart I take refuge in God,
> the Lord of all things, the Creator of the universe,
> the Source of all good.
>
> With all my heart I take refuge in Christ,
> the Remover of all sin,
> the One who re-establishes our pure nature within us,
> the perfect revelation of the eternal Word of God.
>
> With all my heart I take refuge in the One
> who embraces the whole universe
> and has myriad ways and means of influencing souls,
> the pure and tranquil Holy Spirit. Amen.
> (Carden 198.)

The predominately Anglo church has much to learn from Asian Christians about the truth that emerges from silence and the reality that appears in the space of contemplation. Protestant Christians, in particular, feel that a thought is not complete until it has been verbalized and the more words—the better. Asian Christians understand the beauty of mystery and the value of waiting for "the still, small voice." As a student friend from Singapore said to me recently, "It is all right if we do not understand God completely. Western systematic theology is fine as long as it doesn't expect to answer all the questions, and in attempting to do so, put God in a box."

A Primary Musical Semblance of Latin and South America: Fiesta

In some ways it is easiest to identify the primary musical semblance of Latino music and its use in worship. Pablo Sosa and others have identified the spirit of the _fiesta,_ especially as it is revealed in the Eucharist, as the most significant Central and South American contribution to world liturgy. Some of the mass settings from Central America articulate this very well. The _Misa Popular Nicaragüense, Misa Campesina Nicaragüense,_ and _Misa Popular Salvadoreña,_ all are a remarkable synthesis of the prophetic and the celebrative. Once again, my experience is limited, but I have noted an inverse relationship between the level of human suffering and the degree of _fiesta_ spirit manifest during the Eucharist. In other words, the less that the people have in material wealth, the greater the sense of celebration and thanksgiving that takes place during the Eucharist. There are many other aspects of the music from our neighbors to the south that would enrich Anglo worship, e.g., the use of movement, songs on the theme of hope, the connection between the rural communities and the love of nature, the rich agrarian metaphors in the congregational songs, etc., but liturgical renewal movements in this country would benefit the most from the vital role of the sacraments in Latino liturgy.

The following questions still remain:

(1) How do we educate church musicians in the art of cultural/musical pluralism, i.e., to live beyond culture?

(2) How do pastors and musicians learn to integrate these materials in to the fabric of a given liturgical tradition?

(3) How do we change the conventional Northern view of the choir versus congregation to a view that emphasizes a musical partnership between choir and congregation?

(4) How do we prepare for the theological questions that will arise from cross-cultural music-making and liturgy?

(5) How do we move beyond treating the liturgical and musical offerings of our Christian sisters and brothers as quaint, and see them as substantive and meaningful (for indeed, these cultures recognize the many musics of the Northern world as significant)?

(6) Are we ready to listen to the musical voices beyond the Northern world (these would include some voices within the boundaries of the United States), i.e., are we ready for missions in reverse?

In conclusion, I place much of my hope for the future of church music in the twenty-first century in the development of congregational song within liturgy. The task for the predominately Anglo church is to incorporate the diverse voices of the global community into the sung faith of our worshiping communities. If we can _sing_ beyond our culture, maybe we can begin to _live_ beyond our culture.

I close with a benediction found on a church wall in Mexico:

Give us Señor, a little sun, a little happiness and some work.
Give us a heart to comfort those in pain.
Give us the ability to be good, strong, wise and free
so that we may be generous with others as we are with ourselves.
Finally, Señor, let us all live in your own, one family. Amen.
(Carden 254.)

For Additional Reading

Best, Harold M. _Music Through the Eyes of Faith._ San Francisco: HarperCollins, 1993.

Blacking, John. _How Musical Is Man?_ Seattle: University of Washington Press, 1973.

Bühlmann, Walbert. _With Eyes to See: Church and World in the Third Millennium._ Trans. Robert R. Barr. Maryknoll, N.Y.: Orbis Books, 1989.

Carden, John, comp. _With All God's People: The New Ecumenical Prayer Cycle._ Geneva: WCC Publications, 1992.

Donovan, Vincent J. _Christianity Revisited._ Maryknoll, N.Y.: Orbis Books, 1978.

Leaver, Robin A. "Theological Dimensions of Mission Hymnody: the Counterpoint of Cult and Culture," in _The Hymnology Annual: An International Forum on the Hymn and Worship,_ ed. Vernon Wicker, 38–50. Berrien Springs, Mich.: Vande Vere Publishing, 1991.

Langer, Susanne K. _Feeling and Form: A Theory of Art._ New York: Charles Scribner's Sons, 1953.

I-to-Loh, ed. _Hymns from the Four Winds: A Collection of Asian-American Hymns._ Nashville: Abingdon Press, 1983.

———. _Sound the Bamboo: CCA Hymnal 1990._ Manila: Christian Conference of Asia and the Asian Institute for Liturgy and Music, 1990.

The Milwaukee Symposia for Church Composers:

A Ten-Year Report. Washington, D.C.: The National Association of Pastoral Musicians, 1992.

Vigil, José María, and Angel Torrellas, eds. *Misas Centro Americanas.* Managua: CAV-CEBES, 1988.

Young, Carlton, ed. *The United Methodist Hymnal.* Nashville: United Methodist Publishing House, 1989.

C. Michael Hawn

187 ✦ CARIBBEAN WORSHIP

Although Christians have worshiped on the Caribbean Islands for many decades, patterns of worship that reflect local culture have only arisen in recent years. This article describes this process and calls for further attention to cultural issues and provides both a brief introduction to worship in this cultural tradition and a helpful point of comparison for churches that are struggling with cultural issues in other settings.

Contemporary Caribbean worship is an adventure of the spirit. But the road to an indigenous form of Caribbean worship has been arduous. The European colonizers brought to the West Indies (as well as to the rest of the world) their cultural heritage. There was only one-way cultural communication: from the rich and dominant Europeans to the backward and primitive non-Northerners. The mores of the Arawak and Carib Indian, and even more those of the African slaves, were denigrated and European things were promoted and idolized. The former were considered pagan, the latter were to be emulated. Thus the slaves and natives learned to dress, eat, speak, and worship like their masters. They desired to have children, whose complexions were as light as possible. There was a cultural miscegenation. African and Indian traditions were subsumed. Christianity and Westernization became synonymous. The church was used by the oppressive colonists to maintain their dominance. Thus all religious expressions indigenous to the slaves were viewed negatively, suppressed, or devalued. An nineteenth-century anonymous writer while describing a funeral ceremony displays a typical negative attitude toward the slaves' musical culture:

> During the whole of the ceremony, many fantastic motions and wild gesticulations are practiced, accompanied with a suitable beat of their drums, and other rude instruments, while a melancholy dirge is sung by a female. . . . This species of barbarous music in indeed more enchanting to their ears than all the most exquisite notes of a Purcell or Pleyel, and however delighted they might appear to be with the finest melody of our bands, let them but hear at a distance from the one to enjoy the other. (cited on page 7 in Prince, from *An Account of Jamaica and its Inhabitants* [London: Longman: 1808], 250–251.)

With the advent of independence, beginning with Jamaica in 1962, Caribbean nations have become more sensitive to their African heritage. The Jamaican national hero, Marcus Garvey, had chided black ministers decades before for not teaching people to appreciate their African cultural heritage. Now many Caribbean people have begun to ask questions of identity, while moving away from the attitude that whatever is foreign is superior to that which is indigenous. The colonial umbilical cords are being cut.

A number of churches have been attempting to decolonize their theology. As part of the process, attempts are being made to decolonize the liturgy. It is recognized that the Caribbeans have a unique, distinctive, peculiar, and historical experience, which is not reflected in their worship because they have adopted the modes of life from Europe and America and have become extensions of such. Some Jamaicans and Jamaican religions have long retained some vital cultural heritages from their African roots. Many have been syncretized with Christian European tradition and developed a unique indigenous form as is evident in Revivalism (e.g., Pocamania) and Rastafarianism. However since 1962, mainline religious traditions such as the Anglican church have liturgically evolved and are making slow but steady progress in indigenizing their worship, incorporating more participation, gestures, and body movements, which all are vital components of the everyday life of the people.

Yet a recent survey suggests that the gap between Caribbean culture and Christian worship remains wide. The inherited traditions "disaffirmed the indigenous and glorified the 'emigrant' [sic]," said one respondent. Davis noted that "there was a feeling that there was a . . . sincerity gap between the rites and ceremonies and real life"—something not unique to the Caribbean (Kortright

Davis, *The Caribbean Church—To Change or to Stay? Just a Simple Survey* [Barbados: CGSRS, 1982], 19). To be truly indigenous in its theology and liturgy, the church must "take seriously and responsibly the cultural milieu and environment in which it finds itself thereby recognizing the cultural and social experience of that milieu" (see Knolly Clarke, "Liturgy and Culture in the Caribbean: What is to be Done?" in *Troubling of the Waters,* ed. Idris Hamid [Trinidad: Rahaman, 1973]). Indigenization will take into account not only the realities of the peoples' Afro-European heritage, but the total realities of Caribbean societies: "hunger, disease, ignorance, illiteracy, unemployment, frustrations, and the struggles of people for liberation, justice, and peace" (cited in page 7 of Prince, from *An Account of Jamaica and Its Inhabitants* [London: Longman, 1808], 250–251). All these realities must be expressed in the church's music, language, dance, and symbols.

Local Caribbean music has been looked upon as sacrilegious, sensual, ungodly, and carnal because of its rhythmic idiom. But the Caribbean person is a rhythmic being. Iris Hamid sees rhythm as a key phenomenon in communications in the Caribbean (Iris Hamid, *In Search of New Perspectives,* 18, cited in Donovan L. Grant, "Towards a Ministry of Music: An Examination of the Ministry of Music in the Roman Catholic church of Jamaica and the United Church of Jamaica and Grand Cayman" [Unpublished paper, University of the West Indies, 1985], 8). Rhythmic music has existed in the Jamaican Christian worship for decades. But it was found among the sects, such as Revival and Pocamania, and the "lower class" churches, such as the Pentecostal and the Church of God. These churches transformed Western hymns into a neo-African form. Noel Dexter, the Director of Music at the University of the West Indies, has noted that more and more youth want more rhythm, a mode a person can clap to. For them, the straightforward metrical hymns are boring. Yet Marjorie Whylie (Director of Studies, Jamaica School of Music) argues that even the traditional hymns lend themselves to rhythm. The problem is that the mode in which the music is set is European. "What we need to do then is to apply it to our own arrangement. Normal Jamaican common rhythmic patterns are all double and quadruple for the most part. . . . Therefore those hymns that are written in simple double can be arranged so as to bring in certain rhythmic components" (Richard O. Ramsey, "The Relationship Between the Church Music and Songs Used in the Main-line Churches in Jamaica and the Jamaican Culture and Social Classes" [Unpublished paper, United Theological College of the West Indies, n.d.], 8).

Not only rhythm, but instrumentation must reflect the West Indian experience. The organ has been the traditional instrument of preference. But as Althea Spencer noted this instrument is suited to the smooth plodding of European hymns. It is unnatural for people whose bodies are rhythmic. Thus instruments, such as drums (especially the congo drum), guitars, mouth organs, tambourines, shakers, steel pans, violin, flute, bango, rumbo boxes, and maracas, etc., evoke a more natural response in the people.

Although the instrumentation allows us to express the physical in worship, the lyrics are as much an important component in the indigenization enterprise. Ralph Hoyte has demonstrated how folk songs have been the spontaneous expression of the human spirit—its philosophy of life, its joys and sorrow, its religion. Folk songs define and articulate the meaning of existence. This is true also of indigenized religious songs and hymns. Instead of hymns which cater to the class of Caribbean people, whose experience has a North American or European orientation, there is blossoming a new hymnody, which focuses on the historic and present experience of the majority of Caribbean people—their poverty, their oppression, the injustice they face, and the pain they bear. Victor H. Job's "Lord God of All the Nations," which can be sung to the tune of "Lead on O King Eternal," is illustrative (All songs cited in this article are from *Sing a New Song,* vol. 3 [Barbados: Cedar Press, Caribbean Conference of Churches, 1981]):

Lord God of all the nations and these Caribbean lands,
Look now on your creation with mercy and with love;
We need your consolation as never before;
Grant us your free salvation, and guide us safely home.

Our islands are divided by land, by air, by sea;
By race, by creed, by culture, political decree.
The Church too is fragmented and full of enmity;
But God calls us together to work for unity.

Your people are surrounded by hatred, greed,
and lust,
By poverty, oppression, injustice and mistrust.
With God who is our Healer we'll cure the
wounds and pain;
We'll give them food and shelter and bring new
life again.

For we have seen your guidance through changing scenes of life,
Your help and your deliverance from tyrannies
and strife,
You broke the chains and shackles and set your
people free
To save our lands and people from sin and misery.

Give to us that new vision that clearly we may
see;
A new determination onward to strive with you
To fight for human justice, for love and liberty
For unity and concord and human dignity.

O God of our salvation our Hope, our Strength,
our Trust!
We pray for all the nations for all our deeds unjust.
In our tribulations, we know you'll see us
through,
And when life's journey's ended we'll just rest in
peace with you.

Not only do the Caribbean people need more
hymns that conceptually treat the large issues of
tyranny, oppression, injustice, pain, and deliverance, but hymns and songs that do not prolong
the colonial ethos. For example, Marjorie Whylie
notes that snow-capped mountains is completely
foreign to the Caribbean experience and appre-
ciable only to those who travel (Ramsey 8). More
hymns like Hugh B. Sherlock's, "God of the Earth
and Sky," is more meaningful to Caribbean
peoples' experience.

God of the earth and sky, Lord of our hills and
plains
Ruler of night and day, bright sun and cooling
rains—
Great Elohim! To thee we raise our harvest hymn
of joyful praise.

'Mid dancing azure seas, upheld by thy command,
Our lovely islands rise in tropic splendor planned.
And we are stewards of thy grace, unless we see
thee face to face.

Thine is the fruitful field, the broad-leaved plan-
tain thine,

Banana, slender cane, tall palm and lowly vine.
Thine own, O Lord, we bring to thee of all thy
bounty rich and free.

Star-apples, purple-dyed, their leaves of bronze
and green
With ackees scarlet-hued, gay citrus gold is seen.
Thou matchless Artist! Here may we thine own
eternal beauty see.

More and more hymns are being written which
reflect the daily experiences and cultural norms
of the people. Much of the contextualizing of theology, tunes, rhythms, lyrics, and performance
have been done by Catholics (see Grant 20; and
Ramsey xvi–xviii). Father Richard Ho Lung has
been at the forefront of this enterprise. He argues
that "spiritual truths must be conveyed through
Jamaican local images. For example, struggle for
labor, survival" (cited in Ramsey 18). His "Communion Feast" is illustrative of this theme of
struggle:

Come pray, Kushu, we go long to watch we papa
a reap.
Come here, Kushu, come pray bredda where
Sammy a nail zinc to cover we head
You're there Savior, I don't mean maybe.
De big girl a cook calaloo in a soup, she help
Die but your rise, yes, you rise a Savior-love.

CHORUS
Come we Mavis, come we children, celebrate in
the feast of love.
The worry and the hurry and the work can pro-
vide our prayer.
Come we Sammy, come we children celebrate in
the feast of love
The sharing and the caring bring the bread of our
Savior's life.

You're there Jesus, we go wash de children for
school,
You're there Jesus, I don't mean maybe Alphy a
cut sugar cane fi a job,
You're there, Jesus, we know you Jesus our Father above send you down to the earth to love,
You come here and you live here and you die as
a Savior
Die but you rise, yes, you rise as a Savior-love.

We're home, Jesus, your body and your blood
they nourish and heal,
We're home, Jesus, we're home, Jesus, We work
and we strong and we worship in song
We're home, Jesus, I don't mean maybe.

Your Father above send you down to the earth
   our home,
You come here and you grow here and you die as
   a Savior,
Die but you rise, yes, you rise as a Savior-love.

Here, I am arguing that hymns such as this and Caribbean music with its rhythmic and other idiomatic components must be the mainstay of Caribbean worship. Caribbean worship and thus Caribbean liturgical music must be incarnational. It must come closer home to the twenty-four hour cultural experience of the people. Thus, it must be indigenous. It is not good enough to relegate the rhythm, the clapping, the physical portions, and the indigenous instrumentation to the evening services and crusades. These elements ought to be incorporated into the worship experience. They should become the common currency of the people. The challenge for the diaspora Caribbean community is to create a worship experience, which does not ignore Caribbean history, but speaks to the unique presence of the Caribbeans in an adopted society.

Pedrito V. Maynard-Reid

188 ✦ ASIAN WORSHIP

The following article briefly describes a variety of worship practices on the Asian continent that have grown out of a desire to be both faithful to the Christian tradition and reflective of local culture. Each of these examples provides a thought-provoking case study regarding the interplay of Christianity and culture, giving readers both a window into worship on the Asian continent and a perspective from which to evaluate their own worship practices. Readers should bear in mind that the Asian churches represent many cultural and denominational traditions and that specific examples should not be taken as representative of worship on the whole continent.

Many Asian liturgies and forms of worship are replicas or imitations of those practiced in their mother churches in Europe and the West. Although there are vast national and denominational differences in liturgical practices in Asia, one may group Asian liturgies into four traditions: the Mar Thomas tradition in South India, the high church liturgical tradition, the free church tradition, and the recent charismatic tradition. The Mar Thomas church is believed to have been established by St. Thomas, one of Jesus' disciples. Their liturgies are, therefore, closer to those of the Orthodox tradition. Both the high church tradition, such as Episcopalians, and the free church tradition, such as Presbyterians, were introduced to Asia from Europe and the West during the last two centuries. The charismatic tradition entered Asia mainly from the United States after the second World War. All liturgies and music from these four traditions have been adopted and translated into Asian languages. Although one may find minor changes in their orders and in their wordings of contents of prayers, the shapes and the theologies of Asian worship are basically the same as those of their mother churches.

The current trends of liturgical revival from the West, the new awareness of Asian identity, and the new interest in Asian cultures have contributed greatly to the renewal of worship in some Asian churches today. While local congregations still maintain their traditional Western forms of worship, some seminaries in South India, Taiwan, the Philippines, and Indonesia, to name only a few, have been developing contextual liturgies and music that are gradually gaining acceptance. Ecumenical conferences and international gatherings in Asia over the last decade have also inspired many innovative worship forms. Furthermore, the publication of _Sound the Bamboo: CCA Hymnal 1990_ will undoubtedly play a significant role in adding dynamic life to Asian worship. This collection, which contains 2280 hymns from 22 Asian countries, is published by the Christian Conference of Asia. One should also mention a group of community churches in Issaan, northeast of Thailand, which have developed native forms of worship that utilize local hymns. An ordinary Sunday worship service, which is conducted in family churches (they do not build churches), consists of the following order:

Prelude (native ensemble of mouth organ, lutes,
   flutes, and drums)
Call to Worship (in song and dance)
Reading of the Scriptures
Bible Study or Sermon
Prayer of Confession
Holy Communion
   Apostle's Creed (sung)
   Words of Institution (1 Cor 11:23-26)

> Prayer
> Distribution of the Elements (sticky rice
>   loaves and rosselle tea)
> Communion
> Singing of Communion Hymn and Dancing
> Prayer of Thanksgiving
> Offering (with song and dance)
> Prayer of Intercession
> Postlude (native ensemble)

Although Asian churches seem to show little creativity in their liturgies, some of them have begun to explore various cultural expressions, symbols, and symbolic acts, and to utilize them in their worship. The following is a brief description of some of these acts in their liturgical contexts.

Call to Worship

Conch Shells. Conch shells symbolize longevity; they are believed to have magical powers. In many rituals, they are used to call for rain and the spirits of ancestors. They also announce the arrival of a chief or an important person, thus marking the beginning of an important event. It is natural that the Christians in Moluccas, Indonesia use the conch shells on Sunday morning, as a call to invite people to worship God.

Greetings and the Sign of Peace

Namaskar. Namaskar is an Indian way of greeting, where both palms are folded in front of one's face, followed by a slight bow and by the saying of "Namaste!" as a greeting. This posture represents humility, respect, and reverence. It has become a general greeting for Christians, especially as a sign of peace during worship services.

Thai Christians have adopted this posture, but with the hands placed near the heart accompanied by a greeting of "sawatee." Since hand shaking and embracing may be too intimate in some Asian culture, the Namaskar sign is very well suited for an Asian context. One can find the same in northern Sumatra, Indonesia.

Holding palms together is also a popular sign of reverence among Buddhists, Taoists, and to a certain extent, among Confucians. It is a posture for praying, and for paying homage to gods and respected sages. Christians in Thailand have naturally adopted this sign of reverence in their prayers. Instead of responding "amen," they further bow their head to touch the tip of their fingers, as a sign of "so be it."

Hongi. The traditional way of greeting guests for the Maori is to hold each other's arms and rub each other's noses together a few times, while looking into each other's eyes warmly. This tradition has been adopted in the church not only as a common greeting, but as a sign of peace as well. In practicing the Hongi, people go around and greet everyone present at the church. Care is taken that no one in the room has been left out in this friendly ritual.

Paying Obeisance to God

Parikrama. Some of the churches in South India have created a particular ritual during their worship service to pay obeisance to God. First, they set up a *mandala,* a place in the sanctuary decorated with a cross, pebbles, vase, and lotus flowers (a sign of purity). The mandala represents the Holy of Holies, thus acknowledging God's presence. Then, the worshipers bring gifts of flowers or any objects of God's creation and walk slowly in a meditative posture around the mandala three times, each time placing one gift on the mandala and doing the sign of Namaskar. This action also symbolizes thanksgiving, praise, and offering of self to God. After this action, the worshipers return to their seats (on the floor) and continue their meditation (cf. ATESEA, *Doing Theology with People's Symbols & Images,* Occasional Papers no. 8, ed. Yeow Choo Lak and John C. England [Singapore: ATESEA/PTCA, 1989], 21).

Penitence

Coconut Smashing. The Tamil Indians in Malaysia are mostly Hindus. In their festive processions, some would smash coconuts (symbolizing their hearts) along the road to express their penitence for sins they have committed. Since the hard skin of the coconuts have already been removed, the impact causes the coconut to break into small pieces. The juices and the fragments of white meat splash all over the place. This symbolizes the resolution of the "sinner," as if he or she were saying, "May I perish like this coconut, if I commit the same sin again!" Then, they would pick up one or two pieces of the kernel, symbolizing the pure heart or conscience and peacefully go home. Some Christians have adopted this practice in the church. After confession of sin, they smash the coconut; and after the assurance of pardon, they pick up a kernel as a sign of peace of heart. (cf.

ATESEA, Occasional Papers no. 8, 19). Here, one can see the inculturation of a pagan ritual to a new Christian context with powerful effect.

Sugar Cane Breaking. In Papua New Guinea, a host breaks sugar cane into pieces to share with his guests as a token of welcome and as an assurance of breaking any possible barrier between them. Christians have utilized this custom in their worship. After the confession of sins, they break sugar cane and distribute the pieces to all participants, as a sign of breaking the wall of division, of mutual forgiveness, of total acceptance, and of unity in one Lord.

Mat Covering. When a Pacific Islanders want to show their regret for having offended someone, they pick up a large piece of straw mat, go sit in front of this person's house covered with this mat as a sign of sorrow and repentance. They stay that way until the offended person shows forgiveness by coming out to remove the mat and invite the penitent into his or her house, thus restoring their broken relationship and accepting the penitent as a friend again. This sign of penitence has been accepted into the liturgy of Pacific Island Christians.

Fern Furling. The Maori of New Zealand have a ritual, which Christians have adopted for their worship service. After the prayer of confession, the congregation walks in line slowly forming the shape of a furling punga frond and silently confessing. When the line forms a crowded circle, the assurance of pardon is pronounced. Then, they turn around, unfurling, as a sign of being relieved from the burden of sin. With new life, they walk faster in joy, sing a song of praise, and return to their seats.

Proclaiming God's Word

Batu Pamali. Batu pamali are "sacred stones" originally placed in front of the _Baeleu_, the ancestor's house in the Moluccas culture of Indonesia. These stones are living signs of the presence of their ancestors' spirits; they represent promises, as well as taboos and punishment. The people would make a promise in return for a wish, with the stones as their witnesses. If they broke the promise, the stones would punish them through various disasters.

In Moluccas, the Christians build the pulpit with stones, upon which is placed the Bible. They pray to God and preach God's Word in front of these stones, with the authority and the confidence that God is their witness. They are responsible for preaching the truth. The Communion Table is also built with these sacred stones. They conduct Holy Communion on these stones, as a powerful witness that God-in-Christ is in their midst making a new covenant.

In the same region, pulpits are also constructed in the shape of a large conch, from which God's Word is proclaimed loud and strong and from which the gospel is spread to all.

Hindu Symbols Adapted to Christian Preaching. Some priests of the Roman Catholic church in South India have adapted Hindu expressions by wearing an orange robe, sitting in a "yoga" posture, with the right hand making the "ok" sign, which symbolizes speaking truth in preaching. They even put coconut oil, a lamp, and flowers on a plate as an offering, which is then raised by both hands and circled vertically three times while chanting "shanti, shanti, shanti" (peace). All of these are cultural adaptations whose significance can easily be identified and understood by some Indians, although others may be offended.

Receiving the Light

The Lamp. When a Hindu prays in a temple, the devotee may hold a small copper lamp with three tiers; the upper tier has five wicks that can be lit. Christians in South India have adapted this custom by giving this lamp a new identity. First of all, a pagan symbol on the top of the lamp has been replaced with a cross. The light, which had symbolized enlightenment, wisdom, and knowledge has now been reinterpreted according to Christian faith. Jesus Christ is the Light of the World, without him, there is no life. In a worship service, after listening to the Word, the congregation is invited to come forward to receive the Light and to pray for wisdom in understanding. This is done by feeling the flame and by praying for wisdom in understanding. First, the worshipers feel the flame with both hands and then touch their foreheads to symbolize intellectually receiving God's Word and/or Christ into their heads. A second touch on the eyes symbolizes a prayer for illumination of the mystery, for seeing the Light and understanding the truth. Finally, the third touch is on the heart to indicate the receiving of Christ and his Word into their hearts with emotion, feeling, and love. Again, this is a meaningful inculturation of an existing rite into a Christian rite.

The worship service in traditional Protestant churches tend to put too much emphasis on passive cerebral understanding of the Word. But by encouraging worshipers to come forward and to touch and feel the warmth of the flame, as though they are touching Christ and his Word, faith comes alive. Many, who have participated in this symbolic act in some ecumenical service, have witnessed this uniquely uplifting experience.

Holy Communion

Coconut Meat and Juice. Coconuts are probably the most popular and most important subsistence for people in Southeast Asia and the Pacific regions. Millions of people rely on the coconut and its products for a living. The Filipinos have made use of the coconut in their Communion service. One can easily understand the implication of this symbolic act within the Holy Communion service: one coconut, being broken, with meat and juice coming from the coconut to nourish the people. Traditional elements for Holy Communion, bread and wine, were originally an integral part of the Jewish, as well as the Western meal. Since neither of these are part of the Asian meal, coconuts become meaningful substitutes for bread and wine.

Rice Loaves and Roselle Tea. Sticky rice is the most important staple food for the agrarian people in northeastern Thailand. The Christians, therefore, use sticky rice baked in the shape of a loaf to be broken and shared during their Communion in the house church. They also drink a red-colored tea made of rosselle leaves to represent the blood of Christ. The rosselle juice is a kind of herbal tea, which is believed to have a healing effect for the body. Thus in the Communion service, it signifies spiritual healing as well. During or after the partaking of the elements, the communicants may stand up and dance freely to show their joy and thanksgiving for the spiritual food and Christ's salvation. This cultural adaptation into the eucharistic liturgy is so meaningful and powerful to the Issaan people that the church has grown astonishingly in the region.

Rice Cakes. Rice is the most important staple food. Life without rice is unimaginable in Asia. The

famous Korean poet, Kim Chi Ha, considers a community eating rice together at a table as a spiritual experience. Japanese theologian, Takenaka Masao, writes that God is rice rather than God is bread, in the sense that rice is the symbol of life in Asia, just as bread is the symbol of life for in the West (ATESEA, *Doing Theology with Cultures of Asia*, Occasional Papers no. 6, ed. Yeow Choo Lak and John C. England [Singapore: ATESEA/ PTCA, 1988], 65). So on various occasions, Asian Christians in Taiwan, Korea, the Philippines, etc. have used rice crackers or rice cakes for Communion with powerful effect.

Sweet Potatoes and Rice Wine or Oolong Tea. Sweet potatoes used to be the main staple food for the poor in Taiwan. The physical shape of the island also resembles that of a sweet potato. Furthermore, recent political oppression and religious persecution have given rise to a sense of pride and self-identity in Taiwanese Christians. Hence these Christians use the sweet potatoes, as a symbol of their faith. A recent poem uplifting such a Taiwanese spirit reads:

Sweet potatoes, fearless about being rotten beneath the earth,
only yearn for the sprouting of leaves and branches for generation after generation.

The efforts of spiritual reconstruction and contextualization of theology and liturgy have inspired Christians to use sweet potatoes as the "bread" for Communion: a baked whole potato is broken into pieces for people to share. The meaning of sacrifice, as implied in the poem above, reflects the words of Christ, "unless a grain of wheat falls into the earth and dies . . . it bears much fruit" (John 12:24). Thus, the potato is suitable for taking the place of "bread." Since grape wine is foreign to this culture (although imported grape wine is available), rice wine, a popular liquor for feasts as well as general cooking, or oolong tea, the best and most popular brand of Taiwanese tea, are served as the "cup" for Holy Communion. Thus both "bread" and "wine," being native elements closely related to daily life, become intimate and meaningful celebrations of the Lord's Supper within the Taiwanese culture.

Chicken Meat. It is almost unthinkable to substitute chicken for bread in Communion. But Indonesian Christians have used it with the following rationale:

(1) Chicken is the most popular meat for general consumption.

(2) No matter how beautiful chickens are, they only live for people, sacrificing themselves to nourish human beings.

(3) A rooster reminds us of the weakness in human nature and our possible denial of Christ as did Peter.

(4) Chickens remind us of God's love as shown in Jesus' lamentation for Jerusalem: "how often would I have gathered your children together as a hen gathers her brood under her wings . . ." (Matt. 23:37).

Furthermore, chewing the chicken during Holy Communion makes people savor its taste, as if they are actually making the effort to digest the body of Christ, not just letting the "bread" melt in the mouth.

The above experiments may have gone far from Western traditions. It is hard to know how well they will be accepted into the official liturgy of any mainline Protestant church. They, nonetheless, represent the conscious effort of some Asian Christians to search for ways of interpreting their faith and for forms to worship God. Some of these cultural perspectives may give us insight and encourage us to seek for meaningful Christian expressions in our own contexts.

I-to-Loh

189 ✦ Worship in Evangelical Hispanic Churches

Hispanic worship can be divided into four main expressions: Catholic, evangelical Protestant, Pentecostal, and spiritist. This article briefly describes the primary emphases of worship in the evangelical and Pentecostal worship traditions.

The evangelical Protestant church in Hispanic countries grew out of the evangelical missionaries, who labored among the masses to bring them into the Protestant or Reformation tradition of Christianity. These evangelical groups ranged from denominations like Methodist, Presbyterian, Baptist, and Lutheran to independent non-aligned missionaries. Many of the new members of these churches were either former Roman Catholic Christians or were a part of formerly unevangelized Indian tribes in remote jungles and mountains. The evangelicals brought a distinct pattern of worship to the Hispanics. Worship was centered on the preaching or teaching of the sacred Scriptures. The preacher or pastor became the focal point of the church and of the worship experience, although lay participation was also encouraged, especially in singing, praying, and sharing of special talents. The climax of the service was the encounter of the worshiper with the Word of God.

Due to its strong European ties and its literal adherence to the written Word, evangelicals have not been as open to syncretism as has Roman Catholicism. Evangelicals rejected anything that was not biblical. The negative side to this approach is the rejection of Hispanic cultural norms in favor of European and North American norms. Those groups that have rejected Hispanic culture more intensely have had a difficult time gaining acceptance and many have disappeared, when their European or North American connection weakened or disappeared.

The evangelical Protestant worship tradition gave birth to the Pentecostal or charismatic tradition. Around the turn of the century, a new system of worship arose in North America characterized by distinct manifestations of the Holy Spirit in the form of ecstatic utterances (speaking in tongues), the baptism of the Spirit, the presence of sign gifts of miracles and healings, and the liberation of women in the worship experience. Pentecostalism swept across Latin America like a fire attracting people from Roman Catholic and evangelical churches, as well as indigenous peoples. Traditional Pentecostal denominations like the Assemblies of God, the Foursquare church, and certain holiness groups were responsible for the spread of Pentecostalism.

Pentecostal worship is marked by personal expression. Although the preaching of the Word is important, the manifestation of the Spirit in the form of praying in tongues, healings, slaying in the Spirit, and prophecies occupy an important part of the worship experience. Pentecostal worship is unstructured, spontaneous, eclectic, and unpredictable. The people come for an encounter with God.

Hispanic evangelical and Pentecostal worship is informal as compared to Catholicism. Rituals are noticeably absent. People attend the worship service for God to do something or say something, but God cannot be tied to a set program in these traditions. The ritual is not as critical as the relationship the worshipers have with each other and with God. There is also a sense of community. The worshiper does not "go to church;" he or she is the church. The interrelationships are highly pronounced and encouraged.

The worship is indeed a *fiesta,* a festival. The worship time is warm and enthusiastic. There is interaction, corporate singing, even audible corporate prayers. The worshipers erupt in hand-clapping, raising of hands, loud hosannas and amens. The key is participation. The priesthood of all believers is the doctrine that permeates the worship experience. Hispanic worship in evangelical and Pentecostal traditions takes this doctrine to its logical conclusion: everyone can participate.

Pentecostal Hispanic worship may take the same form as the evangelical, but with different emphases and forms of expression. Pentecostal worship is usually louder, more emotional, more spontaneous, and more unpredictable. The song service may continue for some time unabated. The people are free to clap and dance. Some bring tambourines or maracas to aid in the worship. Most of the music is comprised of *coritos,* not traditional hymns. The aim of the worship service is to stir the emotions and to gain participation, not necessarily impart doctrine through sacred hymns.

There is also spontaneous and prolonged periods of prayer. A portion of the service may involve a call to prayer, with people making their way to the "altar" to seek God in prayer. The sermon is designed to move people to action, not necessarily to expound a text. The preacher wants to bring the worshipers to an *encuentro con Dios* (an encounter with God). The climax here is the manifestation of the Pentecostal experience of the second chapter of Acts upon the congregation in the visible display of the coming of the Spirit upon the people. The worshipers come expecting to be baptized by the Spirit, to be healed of disease, and to be "slain by the Spirit." The typical worshiper leaves with a sense of emotional release and spiritual rejuvenation.

Hispanic worship is by no means staid. It is in constant flux. Churches are including the latest developments in technology in their worship. Some evangelicals are borrowing from the Pentecostals; and some Pentecostals are becoming less

spontaneous and more sophisticated. Yet, they still continue to reflect in their worship the Hispanic culture.

Alex D. Montoya

190 ✦ Music in Evangelical and Pentecostal Hispanic Churches

As in every worshiping tradition, music in Hispanic churches today represents a blend of the old and the new and of indigenous and imported musical styles. This article describes this interplay in Hispanic churches, observing the main genres and accompaniment styles involved.

In the past, music in the traditional Hispanic evangelical church was of two types. Part of its hymnody consisted of Spanish translations of traditional songs imported from the United States and England. Since the worship service of the past was patterned after the North American model, the use of these hymns was a logical and natural outcome. Such hymnody, though not indigenous to the culture, served a major purpose of communicating doctrine and meaning to the church. European hymns are steeped in doctrine that helps to establish the believers in the faith. Popular hymns, like "At the Cross," "The Old Rugged Cross," "How Great Thou Art," "Holy, Holy, Holy," and many others comprise a large portion of Hispanic evangelical hymnody. Latin Americans have also contributed their portion of hymns patterned after the North American style.

The other type of Hispanic music is the popular choruses or *coritos,* as Hispanics call them. These are usually short spiritual songs played to lively music, usually music that is Hispanic in flavor. These *coritos* are extremely popular since they are easy to memorize and are what are called "heart songs." They speak of the Hispanic experience of suffering, persecution, and the cost of discipleship. A personal love for Jesus Christ is a popular theme. Being set to local melodies further adds to the popularity of these songs. Since many churches cannot afford standard hymn books, these *coritos* are set to memory or condensed into small paperbacks, which individuals purchase for themselves. The ballad or *corrido* is also found in Hispanic hymnology. The *corrido* is an indigenous style of communicating a story via music. Story-telling is quite popular among believers, as among unbelievers. The gospel lends itself naturally to this style of music.

The basic instrument of the Hispanic church is the Spanish guitar, which is used to play both hymns and _coritos._ It is unsurpassed in its versatility, convenience, popularity, and ease of mastery.

The piano is also quite popular, limited by its cost and the lack of skilled accompanists. Some Hispanics have developed a new style of accompaniment characterized by the repetition of key chords. This approach produces a lively style, which fits in nicely with the culture. Most churches prefer the "playing by ear" approach over the "playing by note." The organ is not very popular for the obvious reasons of the cost and the lack of skilled musicians.

Some churches include a number of other musical instruments that are peculiar to Hispanics, such as the tambourine, the bongos, _maracas_, and different types of guitars. The accordion is also a popular and adaptable instrument, which combines the range of a piano with the rhythm of a guitar. It is not unusual to see the people accompany the song leader with hand tambourines, beating them against their legs or against the palms of their hands over their heads. _Maracas_ are used in the same manner. Putting all these instruments into any size congregation naturally makes for a lively and exciting song service.

Hispanic evangelical and Pentecostal churches also make use of church choirs, ensembles, and solos. Very few church choirs approach the polished style of North America with their range of voices. Hispanic choirs exist more for encouraging participation in music than for an exhibition of personal or corporate talent. The same is true of quartets and ensembles. Soloists are sought out and are in great demand.

Congregational participation is very important since Hispanics are a music-loving people. A typical worship service has lots of music, not only solos and duets, but congregational singing. It is not unusual for a congregation to stand and sing continuously for fifteen to twenty minutes. The singing is usually loud, emotional, and accompanied by hand-clapping, tambourines, and hand raising. Some songs make provision for congregational interaction, which adds a special dimension to the worship service. Singing really

becomes an expression of the human soul.

There are significant trends today in music. More and more congregations are using electric guitars and electronic synthesizers. This reflects the impact of modern music upon the culture. There is some resistance to this trend, but it is not as vehement as in past decades. There is also a greater use of special choruses that reflect the new emerging subcultures and the blending of cultures. The American music movement is having a profound impact upon Hispanic artists, especially when some of the music is bicultural. The trend is refreshing and continues to enhance traditional melodies and styles of worship. Still other churches have grown in sophistication and are making ample use of the organ and piano, mimicking North American expressions.

A recent worship experience in a Hispanic service revealed a special style, which reflected the old and the new coming together. Temple Calvario of Santa Anna, California makes use of guitars, electric guitars, a piano, a synthesizer, a set of bongo drums and percussion drums, three lead singers, and trumpets. In a unique blend of old _coritos_ and new choruses, the worship team leads a bilingual audience in a song service in both English and Spanish. The song leader uses an overhead projector to lead the congregation in singing the hymns. Here is an example of the latest combination of the traditional and the contemporary technical approach.

The traditional style of worship still prevails among many of the Hispanic evangelical churches. The closer one is to North American influence, the greater the similarities in worship. There is a refreshing wind, however, blowing across the churches, an indigenous, uplifting, God-honoring expression of Hispanic devotion to the Lord Jesus Christ.

Alex D. Montoya

191 ✦ INDEPENDENT AFRICAN WORSHIP

Worship on the continent of Africa has a rich history, dating back to the earliest period of the Christian church. In recent years, however, new and exciting developments have occurred in sub-Sahara Africa. This article describes these recent developments and the worship of independent African churches. These practices are particularly *interesting, as examples of how the Christian faith interacts with local culture.*

The history of Christianity in North Africa begins in the very first century of the Common Era. The bishops and theologians of Egypt played a decisive role in the early years of Christianity. The desert Fathers and monks exerted a monumental influence, particularly in the arena of Christian spirituality. Orthodox traditions were established in Egypt and Ethiopia; and Christians courageously survived the Islamic expansion of the seventh and eighth centuries that engulfed and cut them off from the rest of Christendom. These Orthodox traditions continue to worship with liturgy rich in symbols and actions—ancient, apostolic, and African.

However, it was not until very recent times that Christianity made significant inroads into sub-Sahara Africa. Except for a brief foray into the Congo in the sixteenth century under the rule of a converted monarch, King Alfonso Mvemba Nzunga, Christianity's success came in the wake of flourishing colonial expansion in the latter part of the nineteenth century. The religious practices of churches, which were directly formed or grew out of the missionary activities of this period, vary widely. Some churches continue a faithful repetition of actions passed down by missionaries. Others use liturgy, which is essentially the same, with the addition of distinctive African elements. And many of those who fall under the general classification of the African independent church have developed rituals and liturgy, which seem predominantly African with only traces of the influence of European missionaries.

Of those who retain relations with mission organizations, the traditional body which brought Christianity to them, a significant difference can be observed between more formal, liturgical churches (i.e., Roman Catholic and Episcopalian) and informal, predominantly Protestant groups. Liturgical churches have historically been more tolerant of native ritual traditions, due, in part, to their own emphasis on a rich variety of symbolic actions. Therefore, Roman Catholics had little difficulty understanding and accepting the practice of "ancestor veneration" in the context of the Christian veneration of saints. Pope Paul told the African bishops in Kampala, Uganda, in 1969, "You may and you must have an African Christianity."

On the other hand, Africans already possessed a sophisticated and highly developed sense of sacrifice, a ritual of central importance to the Christian church; and therefore Africans readily accepted actions associated with concepts of sacrifice.

Liturgical traditions also emphasized counterparts to traditional "rites of passage" concerning birth (infant baptism), initiation into adulthood (confirmation and baptism), marriage, and death. These counterparts did not simply replace native traditions. Catholic missionaries were encouraged to adopt elements of the local rituals to enhance interest in Christian worship. For example, some local traditions bestowed a new name on children who underwent initiation into adulthood, as a sign of new life. In areas where this was practiced, the Catholic church encouraged priests to bestow Christian names at baptism.

Of special interest, however, are those churches who have asserted their independence from mission support and control, particularly radically new churches founded by native prophets and healers. In these churches, creative adaptations of texts and rituals central to Christian worship, such as *The Book of Common Prayer*, the Eucha-

St. Julian's Cross. This beautiful decorative cross is made of four crosses that meet in the center. This symbol may speak of the power of the cross, which extends to the four corners of the earth.

rist, baptism, and ordination, were made. Also, entirely new rituals and ritual objects appear in worship. For example, some churches make extensive use of flags, staves, spears, and elaborate robes, often designed and employed in accordance with the visions of the founder and/or influential members.

One liturgical element which has had a profound impact upon independent African Christianity is *The Book of Common Prayer*. Harold Turner, in his first attempt at analyzing material from an African independent church, examined "The Holy Litany," published by one of the West African independent churches. This particular church represents "one of the many similar bodies that have emerged from the Anglican church in Nigeria." This African litany begins with a three-fold pattern, but without explicit reference to the Trinity. It also employs a distinctly African metaphor that appears at several key junctures in the text.

PRIEST: We use our mouths like broom before Thee.

CONGREGATION: **Good Lord, have mercy upon us.**

PRIEST: We use our mouths like broom before Thee.

CONGREGATION: **Good Lord, have mercy upon us.**

PRIEST: We use our mouths like broom before Thee.

CONGREGATION: **Good Lord, have mercy upon us.**

PRIEST: We great sinners humbly supplicate before Thee.

CONGREGATION: **Good Lord, forgive us.**

This portion divides the litany into three sections and provides the conclusions. In the first section, a series of confessions and requests for deliverance from various evils follow the "broom theme." In a direct application to the African situation, these evils include witches, wizards, poisonous locusts, flies, drought, black butterflies, and birds. This African litany also expands, what is originally a single reference to the day of judgment into a series of six versicles "based on biblical language drawn from apocalyptic passages."

The second section contains a long "victory" passage, in which a series of twenty-seven versicles proclaim victory over a variety of evils. Turner points to the "peculiarly African development of two related themes" represented by the phrases, ". . . hear us, that those evils which the craft and subtle of the devil or of man worketh

against us, be brought to nought," and "From our enemies defend us, O Christ." Turner concludes that "even where the African litany might seem to depart most widely from the form and content of its original, it still keeps company with it in spirit and intention." The concept of God emerging from this litany is clearly "in control of all society, nature, death, and evil powers including Satan." He is also a God who "will act to reveal his control both now and in the future consummation."

This leaves the matter of the image found in the "broom theme." Turner found various explanations of the meaning of this phrase. It appears to originate from an act performed as a sign of humiliation and penance, either voluntary or commanded as punishment, before a Yoruba king. Others pointed to a direct revelation received by a founder of the church as the origin of the phrase. A prominent leader also connected it with the story of Isaiah 6:5 concerning his unclean lips which needed "sweeping." Turner concludes, "that here we have an introductory element, representing both reverence and humiliation before God, and also the need for cleansing, before proceeding to the prayers."

Liturgical innovation in African independent Christianity extends to the actions performed in worship. For example, the Cherubim and Seraphim Society, founded in 1925 in Lagos, Nigeria, by Moses Orimolade Tunolase, exhibits a wide range of religious practices: some borrowed, some transformed, and others clearly created. Rituals borrowed from European-based churches include Sunday worship, baptism, Communion, confirmation, marriage, burial, ordination, and some important anniversaries and saints' days. Of particular importance is, once again, *The Book of Common Prayer*. Often the particular services held on these occasions are wholly or in part taken from mission churches. However, when they use another church's service, they usually add elements from traditional religions or from revelations received by members.

One of the religious forms peculiar to the Cherubim and Seraphim Society is that of festivals. Festivals create a calendar for the life of the church and celebrate important days in the history of the organization. For example, members celebrate festivals for the anniversaries of St. Michael and St. Gabriel, the spiritual founders of the society, the Cherubim and Seraphim bands, and the Founder's Memorial anniversary. Festivals established their prominence in the early days of the founding of the society, when members would celebrate traditional ceremonies in their respective churches and only come together as a society on these festival days.

Holy Michael's anniversary is celebrated on September 29. Two special lessons are read. One lesson is from Daniel 12; and the second lesson is from Revelation 12. The climax of the service involves "the bearing of swords by three leaders who raise them as they stand at each of the four corners of the building and shout three times 'The Sword of the Lord,' while the congregation responds 'the Sword of St. Michael.'" A prayer is offered for the sword of St. Michael "to descend as a victory over our enemies and a shelter over the members of the Society." A closing hymn is sung and a final prayer spoken.

J. Akinyele Omoyajowo describes the Anniversary of the Cherubim Band, celebrated on the last Thursday of May.

> Special dresses are worn at the service. Before the sermon a short ceremony is performed: Four leaders stretch forth spears. The most senior of them faces the east and shouts: "The Star." The whole congregation, standing, then answers: "The Morning Star." This is repeated seven times after which the congregation kneels, and the leader says a short prayer for the guidance of the Star and for salvation and victory for the whole Cherubim and Seraphim Organization. Two special lessons are read after which the Grace is said and the *Te Deum Laudamus* chanted.

At the anniversary in Memory of the Founder, a vigil is kept at the founder's grave from 10 P.M. on the eighteenth of October until 3 A.M. the next morning. A memorial service is then held on the nineteenth at the grave and in every house of prayer on the following Sunday.

Other special liturgical elements employed by the society include the idea of sacred places and objects, taboos and robes of office, dancing, clapping, and stamping. Robert Wyllie has documented several "spiritist" services held by Christian congregations in Southern Ghana. One of these was a meeting of the Cherubim and Seraphim. This congregation employed several distinct areas of worship, the building proper and an area known as the mercy ground. The mercy ground, situated in front of the building, consisted of a sandy area

surrounded by a low wall, in the middle of which stood a white wooden cross. Inside of the building, a low, wooden partition divided the space into a large main room and a smaller "sanctuary" at the further end. In the sanctuary, there was a chair and table, on which were "seven lighted candles, two vases of flowers, a bell, and a wooden crucifix. In front of the sanctuary were two large drums painted bright red."

The service began at 9 A.M. with the soft and slow singing of a hymn, while the captain and another man played the drums. Someone else kept time with the singing by ringing the hand bell. After the singing of this hymn, the pastor (bishop) entered the sanctuary area, knelt on the floor, and led the congregation in a prayer. The congregation then sang several more hymns as the captain circulated among them with the censer. The pastor returned to the sanctuary to offer prayers for the leaders of the society and government, and for those present. More hymns were sung and the pastor once again entered the sanctuary, this time to pray for "divine light, so that the faithful might better understand God's Word," and for the peace of the souls of the departed faithful.

The service continued with readings from the Bible, hymns, prayers, a relatively short sermon, and testimonies. Enthusiasm seemed to die down until the offertory, which was accompanied by a lively song:

> Power, O Lord!
> Power, O Lord!
> Power, O Lord!
> Power, Power, Power, O Lord!

This was sung as the members filed, dancing and swaying, past the offering bowl. The pastor and the captain manned the drums, beating furiously upon them with their hands. Two women began to spin, with outstretched arms, before the sanctuary; another ran up and down the length of the church, leaping from bench to bench; yet another hopped on one leg in front of the drummers before falling to the floor. The captain seized the thurible and ran swiftly around the church, leaving a trail of incense in his wake. Two men hurriedly pushed aside some of the benches, as several women began to throw themselves around, knocking over the benches as they fell or stumbled.

The pastor circulated throughout the room

carrying a metal rod, which he used to lightly touch the foreheads of participants who knelt at his feet. Assistants touched these same people with a small wooden crucifix and rubbed the abdomens of two childless women with water from a bottle. The climax came when the captain "began to shudder and shake, slapping himself repeatedly upon the face." He proceeded to turn somersaults on the floor, his left eye closed and his right rolling "wildly in its socket." Then the captain shouted, accusing the pastor of not having fasted. He was taken out onto the mercy ground to recover.

Many of these elements are found in other independent African churches. Wyllie attended the Christian Church, popularly known as "Taylor's church," across the street from the Cherubim and Seraphim. Here the pastor's table held a candle, a hand-bell, two Bibles, two hymnals (Methodist), and two alarm clocks. To the side of the table stood a large drum.

The service followed the reading of John 13:30-36, during which the pastor walked among the worshipers gesticulating enthusiastically while the congregation occasionally interrupted him by singing verses from a hymn. John 1:1-11 was read and was followed by more preaching, singing and dancing. During the hymns, the pastor would beat the drum furiously or join in the dancing. The sermon ended and the pastor and two other men beat the drum vigorously. "The singing ceased and the assembly converged in a semicircle around the dancers, clapping their hands and shouting 'Praise the Lord!' and 'Praise Him!'"

After more singing, praying, and dancing, an offering was taken and the healing portion of the service began. While the people kneeled and prayed aloud, the pastor moved among them laying hands on them and praying over them. Suddenly, he seized one woman and cast her to the floor in the center of the circle and began to perform cartwheels around the inner part of the circle. One woman stood over her fallen companion while the others danced around with arms held on high. The woman on the floor began to twitch and shudder as she lay on her side with her arms behind her back. A few minutes later, she was joined on the floor by five more women and a young man, all of whom rolled around, writhing and kicking.

At a third church, Dugan's Church, Wyllie observed a similar service on a Sunday morning. Again a table with hand-bell, Bible, candles, and an alarm clock stood at one end of, in this case, an enclosure. The service consisted of singing, dancing, hand-clapping, and drumming. Once again, members of the congregation experienced the power of the Holy Spirit in very physical ways.

> In the space of a few minutes no fewer than fifteen women were throwing themselves around, spinning with outstretched arms, and hitting their bodies so violently against the wooden uprights of the enclosure that the whole structure shivered and shook. At one point we had to move our chairs back to avoid the women as they fell over benches or rolled writhing as they did so. After about five minutes of this frenzied activity, the music stopped and most of the women staggered back wearily to their places on the benches.

The role of the leader at Dugan's Church introduces a new element to the list of central ritual elements in independent African Christianity. He is referred to as "the Prophet." After the offertory, the prophet proceeded to walk among the participants and "read 'messages' in the hands of some members."

> He paced jerkily around the enclosure, throwing a darting glance at this palm or that, never looking closely at any one hand. After such fleeting glances he would turn and look in several different directions in quick succession, stabbing his feet rapidly on the ground as he did so. At the same time he kept exclaiming "Ha!" "Ai!" and "Jesus!" and rasped out such orders as "Fast for three days!"

Prophets and healers also figure prominently in the independent churches among the Zulus of southern Africa. Again, we see the themes of visions, power for healing and divination, and the transfer of this power within the context of spirited corporate worship. Bengt Sundkler observes that the "Zulu prophet is not the terminal receiver of his message but always a channel for the message to be transmitted to the church, and this message is in the process amplified by the participating mass experience."

Not only is the leader's calling often communicated to him or her in a dream, rituals performed in worship can also originate in visions and dreams. These rituals can then share not only holy knowledge, but dreams and visions with the participants. Worship opens the door for the individual to share the dream experience. Sundkler sees a "beautiful solution of the tension between corporate participation and the individual's experience. The dream experience is the individualized and interiorized continuation and adaptation of corporate worship."

The liturgy among the Zulus also includes a strong emphasis on music and a tendency toward response and interplay between the leader and the congregation. Sundkler observed the following in 1969 during a service led by Archbishop Sikakana.

> The Archbishop would sing one line, with strong emphasis. The congregation would respond with the same vigor; then—and this had a very moving effect—the Archbishop would repeat the singing of the words with a soft voice, as if whispering a great secret, and his wife and the congregation followed him. With innate discipline, they would enter into the secrecy of these holy mysteries and corporately whisper their joy at the Angels and Creatures and Elders, invisibly but certainly present, moving their wings softly.

As we saw in the Cherubim and Seraphim service, in which the captain challenged the pastor, "many specifically 'African' homiletic situations include an element of an almost electrifying 'give and take', a challenge and response between preacher and local group."

For all the importance attached to preaching, praying, singing, healing and prophesying, the foundation of the spirituality found in independent African churches still remains the sacraments, particularly baptism. Baptism, for the African Christian, stands as a key moment of decision and a source of power, both at the time of baptism and later as the believer recalls the experience. Gerhardus C. Oosthuizen has written about baptism as a purification ritual in the African independent churches, particularly those churches in which the "healer-prophet" style of leadership is prominent.

> Whatever the reasons for the tremendous development of the AIC (African Independent Church) may be . . . one of the many reasons lies with the interpretation of baptism as a sacrament and a means of obtaining grace and numinous power. This symbol assists those who take part in it to receive the benefits for which it stands, namely, to be in the transcendent world which manifests

itself through various benefits bestowed generously on them, if they fulfill the necessary requirements such as fasting, attending the preceding nocturnal revival service, and confessing their sins.

As one stands on the shore of the Indian Ocean near Durban and watches a leader of a group of Zionist Christians repeatedly hurl a believer into the pounding surf the stark differences between this and European/American baptisms become apparent. As groups of these worshipers gather on the beach, surrounded by circles of wooden staves and poles with flags fluttering in the strong wind, the question arises, "What is Christian about these rituals?" Yet in some sense, in their white robes with dark crosses stitched on the back, these Christians are claiming a portion of the power associated with baptism in the early church.

What happened at the River Jordan and the Sea of Galilee during the time of Jesus is repeated today at the river and the sea. As a result of the symbolic repetition of the original, those taking part in the ritual at the Durban beach become part of early New Testament history.

> Because baptism is the AIC symbol of transcendence, not primarily of being initiated into the church, initiants are assured of the victorious outcome of the struggle of the divine powers against the demonic powers of darkness. They receive life through the removal of sins effected by baptism; they receive "the Spirit" because they have been cleansed and "the Spirit" is a source of strength.

The traditional African emphases on purification and power actually recapture elements of the ritual of baptism that were of critical importance to the early Christians. Through purification and a ritual identification with the death and resurrection of Christ, the believer becomes a participant in the powerful victory of Christ over death and the forces of evil. The reenactment of this crucial cosmic occurrence empowers the initiate to battle the forces of evil in his or her own world.

Marlin Adrian

192 ✦ AFRICAN-AMERICAN WORSHIP

Featuring vital and profound music and the energetic interchange of the spoken word, African-American wor-

ship is emotionally charged and integrated with all of life. All of the senses and many forms of expression are used to lament the trials of life and to celebrate the power of God in Christ.

Of all the cultures which make up pluralistic society of the United States, the African American may capture best the wholistic view of worship. The African American worship service evokes all the ingredients of the human personality. Both in music and the spoken word, African Americans have resisted the taming of the senses and have allowed their worship to be a reflection of their entire existence—not merely a "spiritual" phenomenon that occurs in worship and is unrelated to everyday living.

In order to understand the African American worship phenomenon, one must understand its history. It was religion that sustained the African American throughout the centuries of slavery and continues to sustain to a great degree up to the present. "It served as the organizing force around which life was structured" (Geneva Southhall, "Black Composer and Religious Music," _The Black Perspective in Music_ 2 [Spring 1974]: 50). Church and religion was not disconnected from other aspects of daily life. The Western dichotomous view of life was not adopted. The church served as school, forum, political arena, social club, art gallery, and conservatory of music. It was and is the place where fellowship and interaction with fellow human beings and with God takes place. The interrelatedness of such worship is what gave the black person the strength to endure. The liturgy and expressions of worship were reactions and response to life's trials, tribulations, and hope.

——— Spirituals and Gospel Music ———

More and more, we all are beginning to recognize that the Negro spiritual is not a simple, nice slavery tune. Rather it is a powerful musical medium that holds a key to the slaves' description and criticism of their living environment and a positive answer to that situation. These songs, notes Geneva Southhall, "represent the unconscious efforts of the slave to make sense of a shattering life situation. In the songs, the slave expresses in words, nuances, and melody his weariness, loneliness, sorrow, hope, determination and assurance" (Southhall 50).

In the twentieth century, a new black musical art form has dominated the worship services of the African American church. Black gospel, like its predecessor the spiritual, also grew out of the difficulties, trials, and tribulation of a disinherited people. As blacks from the rural South emigrated to Northern urban settings following Reconstruction, they felt the need for a type of music that was relevant to their peculiar problems, particularly the suffering, oppression, desolation, and disinheritance of their new life. The black gospel song is "a song of faith which rallies the hope and aspiration of the faithful in the face of devastating social conditions" (John Michael Spencer, _Protest and Praise: Sacred Music of Black Religion_ [Minneapolis: Fortress Press, 1990], 199; see also Wyatt T. Walker, _"Somebody's Calling My Name": Black Sacred Music and Social Change_ [Valley Forge, Pa.: Judson, 1979], 127). In a tribute to Thurgood Marshall and Thomas Dorsey, the father of gospel music, _Newsweek_ observed that in gospel music, "out of deep despair comes transcendence." It is precisely out of such despair that Dorsey's most famous gospel composition, "Precious Lord, Take My Hand" arose (Jerry Alder, "Their Amazing Grace," _Newsweek_ [February 1993], 58).

Musical lyrics such as these continue to help African Americans surmount the difficult circumstances of their existence. Throughout black gospel, Jesus is seen as the alternative to the depressing and degrading social situation. How appropriate that this idiom should be called gospel—"it attempts to relate the 'Good News' of Jesus Christ primarily to the existence of black folk in this country" (Louis-Charles Harvey, "Black Gospel Music and Black Theology," _The Journal of Religious Thought_ 43 [Fall–Winter 1986–87]: 26).

Black gospel has, however, been criticized by whites and blacks alike. This unsympathetic view is due to a number of factors. One is that it is seen as entertainment utilized by opportunists. But the same can be said of any musical form. Another factor for the rejection of gospel music as a worship form is that it has its roots in the musical idioms of African Americans at the turn of this century. Both types of gospel music grew out of each peoples' history and culture. Each root is different. To condemn one and uphold the other is crass ethnocentrism!

A word also needs to be said about instrumentation, particularly the drum—an instrument which is creeping back into many churches. John Michael Spencer, one of America's foremost African American musicologists, asserts that the diaspora "de-drummed" the African in this country. Although the drum was abandoned here, it continued in the West Indies and South America in spite of restrictions. Legal restrictions were stringently enforced in North America because the drum was perceived as pagan, sinful, and evil. This prejudiced perception of the drum became so ingrained in the religion of the enslaved, that the instrument that once was held in the highest sacred esteem, soon lost its sacredness. Although African Americans were "de-drummed" (and only temporarily), they were not "de-rhythmized." "With the drum banned, rhythm still endured as the essential African remnant of black religion in North America . . . it empowered those who possessed it to endure slavery by temporarily elevating them out of the valley of oppression up to a spiritual summit" (Spencer 199; quoted from *"Somebody's Calling My Name,"* 127).

The Spoken Word

As we have seen thus far, music—vocal, instrumental, and rhythm, all play an essential role in the African American worship culture as it relates to the very basic existence of the worshiper. This is also true with regards to the spoken word.

Craig Dossman, a famous African American Adventist preacher, has noted that in the black church preaching is the central feature of worship (Craig A. Dossman, "Don't Forget the Bridge," *Ministry* [October 1991]: 25). However, preaching in this culture is not limited to a one-way spoken word. There is intonation by the preacher, response by the congregation, instrumental interruption and interjection by the organist and other musicians, etc. The segment of the service dubbed "preaching" is a continued demonstration of high emotional and cognitive drama experienced thus far in the service.

It must be admitted that in part the effectiveness of the black sermon lay in the preacher's tone of voice, the dynamic and rhythmic nuances, and the emotionally charged oratory, rather than the preacher's vocabulary and intellectual message. However, contemporary university-trained black preachers combine an intellectual approach with the traditional style of their forebearers. The traditions of the scholar and the folk preacher are melded.

The interaction between the preacher and the congregation is the most folksy part of black worship. This interaction between "preacher in the pulpit" and "preacher in the pew" is natural because of the shared experiences of African Americans. The congregation feels free to respond vocally and physically, as the preacher enumerates the issues at hand through Scripture, stories, and skilled symbolism. The drama, the musical and performative power of black preaching with its theatrics, moves the congregation and causes natural reactions, such as nodding of the head, waving of hands, shedding tears, singing, and humming aloud. Dossman notes that "many Black preachers have developed the habit of eliciting responses with such interjectory remarks as 'Have I got a witness?' or 'You ought to say amen!' And Black congregations respond with a variety of expressions: 'Tell the truth preacher' 'Yes, Lord' 'Help him Lord!' 'Preach the Word' 'Praise the Lord!' 'Amen, amen!'" The dramatic pauses and empty spaces in the sermon delivery all aid in eliciting congregational response, as well as emphasizing particular points (Dossman 25; cf. Spencer 225–243; Southhall 49).

Most outside of the African American culture have found it difficult to grasp the significance of the mechanics of such a worship service. We need to recognize that every aspect of the service, every action of the worshiper, is fundamental to the filling of the spiritual need. Worship is a catharsis for the oppressed. It allows their pent-up anxieties and emotions to be released through singing, moving rhythmically, percussive clapping and shouting, and responding with elation. In this sense, the African American worship service is one of "total communal intimacy" (Southhall 49) with God, one another, and the individual.

Melva Costen

193 • NATIVE AMERICAN WORSHIP

Christian Native Americans bring to worship the riches of the Christian tradition, as well as a worldview shaped by their own rich cultural history. This article describes how these two influences shape worship in some Native American Christian communities.

——— **Worldview: the Basis of Ritual** ———

Ritual may be defined as an external expression of an internal reality. Ritual, which in Native American culture takes the form of elaborate ceremonies, is intimately related with the land. Our "traditional" ceremonies are founded in our myths, which narrate the way we as humans view the creation. Our ceremonies and stories show us how we are a part of the whole family of creation and how and why we act as we do.

The spirituality of our people has to deal, first of all, with the "worldview" of our people, on which all ritual must be based. The worldview of a person, or a society, is the basic view of the reality that is around that society or person. It touches the how and why things came to be as they are and the how and why they change. It is the theology of the individual and of the society. A worldview of an individual judges and evaluates the values and goals of society. It is the bases from which a person thinks about the supernatural (Charles Kraft, _Christianity in Culture_ [Maryknoll, N.Y.: Orbis Books, 1979], 55–57).

A worldview gives meaning to a host of life experiences: birth, death, illness, puberty, marriage, planting and harvest, uncertainty and elation. This is often experienced through ritual or ceremony, in which many people participate—some by prayer, some by trance. The society is provided security and support for their behavior. A worldview integrates, systematizes, and orders a person's or society's perception of reality. It shows what reality should be like. It understands and interprets the many events of life. In all this, it establishes and validates basic premises about the world and men and women's place in it. A worldview also relates the striving and emotions of each person to his or her perceptions of reality.

How we as individuals look at reality determines how we approach God and how we see God. It also determines how we are going to celebrate this relationship to God in our daily lives as individuals, as a community or as a society.

In Western culture, which brought the truth about Jesus and Christianity, there is a worldview of creation and land that describes the relationship of humans to it as a subservient and dominant relationship. The worldview of Native American individuals and society, in contrast, describes this relationship as a relationship of equals. The world and all of creation is a family

together. Creation is not to be controlled, but empowers us in our daily life and relationships. The sacred history of Native American peoples contain many creation stories, which Christian spirituality and ritual has to deal. There are not many teachings, in all the tribes, that are similar. How each tribe celebrates these teachings differs.

——— **Native Ritual: Native Ceremony** ———

For the native person, ceremonies are not occasions for display; instead they are a necessity. The prime reason for having a ceremony is to restore or ensure the health of an individual. The mystical spillovers from the ritual benefits the health of everyone who attends. The ritual heals the spirit as well as the body. It heals the community, drawing those in attendance together into the mystical body of the people. The description of ceremony brings out a worldview of a people, who have a close relationship with the land.

Liturgy (ritual and ceremony) has to do with the expression of ourselves and our way of being religious. It draws us to become who we really are in relationship to God and to each other as a community. It is the external expression of our internal relationship to God and neighbor. This external expression of our internal relationship should both assist us and empower us to become who we are to be in the family of creation. In our native ceremonies, therefore, we allow our relatives of the world to assist us. We do not use the "things" we use in our ceremonies as objects. We pray in thanksgiving as with a relative who shares of self and life to empower us to become who we should be in relationship to God, to self, to community. Even when we go to gather the medicines (our prayer objects) of the people, we give thanks for the life of what we have picked. We pray for the continuance of the life of the family of the sweet-grass, the tobacco, the sage, and the cedar. I mention these because these are four of the medicines that I use when I pray. Every tribe has medicines that are proper to their ceremonies.

Ceremonies in our tribes are owned by certain people. The person who has the right to conduct a certain ceremony is gifted with this or that ceremony by the people because of a certain respect they have in the community. Among the Navajo, as in many of our tribes, it takes a lifetime of prayer and learning to own even one ceremony. It requires, as one author noted, "an incredible feat of memory to hold clearly in mind to the last detail the symbols and their position, the colors and materials of the dry paintings, the equipment, the elaborate rituals, the dances, the hour long chants."

Certain people are given the right to conduct a sweat, to carry a pipe, to perform the many ceremonies of our Native American life. In all the ceremonies, there are different people who have the right to do certain ceremonies that make up the total ritual. Take for example, my medicine lodge. There are certain people who drum and sing, certain songs to be sung. There is the *oshkahawis*, who is the helper in the ceremonies. There is the *botaweinini*, who is the fire tender. There are the teachers, the elders. Each person has special ceremonies which are proper to each thing he or she does.

Ritual: Our Way of Being Christian

Richard McBrien says that Christian spirituality is "the cultivation of a style of life consistent with the presence of the Spirit of the Risen Christ within us and with our status as members of the Body of Christ. Christian spirituality has to do with *our way of being Christian*, in response to the call of God issued through Jesus Christ in the power of the Holy Spirit" (*Catholicism,* vol. 2 [San Francisco: Harper, 1980], 1057ff).

Western Christianity has been brought to the Native American in the Western worldview and has done violence to the spirituality of the native peoples of the Americas. The rituals that have been given to us are foreign to how we as Native Americans experience our view of the world. Perhaps this is why we see the great dichotomy of 80 percent of some tribes being baptized Catholics and only 5 percent living the sacramental life of the church. How can the native peoples respond to "this call of God issued through Jesus Christ. . . ?"

In the document on liturgy, the council fathers clearly state:

[Liturgy] is made up of unchangeable elements divinely instituted, and elements subject to change. These latter not only may be changed but ought to be changed with the passage of time, if they have suffered from the intrusion of anything out of harmony with the inner nature of the liturgy or have become less suitable. . . . Christian people, as far as is possible should be able to understand them with ease and take part in them fully, actively, and as a community. (*S.C.* 21.)

The elements of Christian liturgy that can be changed need to be translated into the worldview of the Native American people.

I have explained some aspects of ritual, ceremony, as it exists among our Native American peoples. This is not an exhaustive treatment of the subject. There are many different ways of existing and many possible rituals that can be drawn from the many tribes of the Indian people. One example of a Christian use of Native American ceremony can be found in the native ceremony of purification, which can easily be used as the reconciliation rite in the Eucharist (see John Hascall, "Native American Liturgy," *Liturgy* 7:1 [1988]: 34–39).

Native American Ritual

Spirituality is the heart of the struggle of our native people to be strong and proud as individuals and as a people. This spirituality is closely tied to the land and to all of creation. The land gives us strong religious experiences, which nurture and renew our experience of God and our relationships with each other. In the past, we have been forced to separate from our reality what spirituality is. What was sacred to us was seen as pagan. The loss of a strong spirituality among the native peoples can be attributed to our being alienated from the land and being put on reservations. Many have rejected their spirit ways and are now lost in the rapidly changing world. Instead of full, conscious, and active participation in the rituals of the church, which the council fathers envisioned, we see alienation. Those people, who try to adapt their worldview to this new worldview, struggle in their faith.

If we as Native Americans are to come to this "understanding with ease and taking part fully, actively, and as a community," there has to be sincere dialogue between the two worldviews of reality. We must search the rituals, ceremonies, myths, and legends of the native peoples and find Jesus, who is the truth, find Christ, who is already present in the ceremonies and teachings of our peoples. We must look at the sacred history of all the tribes of our peoples to see how our reality of God has taught us and led us to worship, which is the purpose of all religious ritual. We must search the ceremonial celebrations of life that are already present in the native peoples' lives and draw forth the Christ, who is already there. I cannot tell what these rituals will be or who will perform these ceremonies. That is in the future. What can we do today to allow the people to grow into that which the Father wants us to be?

John S. Hascall[25]

194 ✦ BIBLIOGRAPHY ON WORSHIP AND CULTURAL DIVERSITY

———— Worship in Africa ————

AMECEA Pastoral Institute. _Living Worship in Africa Today_. Eldoret, Kenya: Gabe Publications, 1980.

Fashole-Luke, Edward, ed. _Christianity in Independent Africa_. Bloomington, Ind.: Indiana University Press, 1978.

Johnson, Walton R. _Worship and Freedom: A Black American Church in Zambia_. New York: Africana Publishing Company, 1977.

Okure, Teresa, ed. _Thirty-two Articles Evaluating Inculturation of Christianity in Africa_. Eldoret, Kenya: Gabe Publications, 1990.

Omoyajowo, J. Akinyele. _Cherubim and Seraphim: The History of Christianity in Africa_. New York: Nok Pub. Int., 1982.

Turner, Harold W. _History of an African Independent Church_. 2 vols. Oxford: Clarendon Press, 1967.

Tovey, Phillip. _Inculturation: The Eucharist in Africa_. Bramcote, Nottingham: Grove Books, 1988.

———— Worship in Asia ————

ATESEA. _Doing Theology with Cultures of Asia_. Occasional Papers no. 6. Edited by Yeow Choo Lak and John C. England. Singapore: ATESEA/PTCA, 1988.

———. _Doing Theology with People's Symbols & Images_. Occasional Papers no. 8. Edited by Yeow Choo Lak and John C. England. Singapore: ATESEA/PTCA, 1989.

I-to-Loh. _Rak Phra Jao, Rao Pen Thai (The Love of God Sets Us Free): A Collection of New Thai Hymns_. AILM Collection of Asian Church Music no. 14. Manila: Asian Institute for Liturgy and Music, n.d.

———. _Sound the Bamboo: CCA Hymnal 1990_. Manila: CCA/AILM, 1990.

———. _Ka Goa Siong-chan (Teach Us to Praise: In Search for Contextual Church Music)_. Tainan: Jen-kuang Publishing House, n.d.

———— Cultural Diversity in ———— Worship in America

Costen, Melva. _African American Christian Worship_. Nashville: Abingdon Press, 1993.

Costen, Melva, and Darius L. Swann. _The Black Christian Worship Experience_. Black Church Scholar Series, vol. 4. Atlanta: ITC Press, 1992.

Francis, Mark R. _Liturgy in a Multicultural Community_. Collegeville, Minn.: Liturgical Press, 1991.

I-to-Loh, ed. _Hymns from the Four Winds: A Collection of Asian American Hymns_. Nashville: Abingdon Press, 1983.

McClain, William B. _The Soul of Black Worship_. Madison, N.J.: MultiEthnic Center, Drew University, 1980.

———. _Come Sunday: The Liturgy of Zion_. Nashville: Abingdon Press, 1990.

Plenty Good Room: The Spirit and Truth of African American Catholic Worship. Washington, D.C.: United States Catholic Conference, 1991.

Rivers, Clarence Joseph. _This Far By Faith: American Worship and Its African Roots_. Washington, D.C.: National Office for Black Catholics, 1977.

PART THREE

Worship and Ministries within the Worshiping Community

Part of the blessing and joy of participating in a worshiping community is found in the various ministries that community extends to each of its members. When the church gathers for worship, Christ's love is extended; pastoral care is demonstrated; the truth of God's Word is taught; and personal spirituality is directed. While each of these ministries finds its appropriate expression outside of public worship—in church education sessions and pastoral care ministries, for example—corporate worship is the foundation of these ministries as well as being an important occasion for pastoral care, spiritual direction, and church education in itself. This section explains the vital relationship between worship and each of these ministries. It is not intended to provide a complete guide to these vital ministries, but it will explore how they relate to worship.

✤ SEVEN ✤

Worship and Pastoral Care

As the center of the life of the church, the gathering of the community for worship is the foundation of every aspect of the church's life. The ministry of pastoral care is rooted in common worship, for genuine sensitivity to mutual needs naturally develops as Christians hear God's Word, celebrate in the sacraments, and join in common prayer. Further, worship itself is an important opportunity for ministering to the needs of hurting people. The acts of naming an affliction, of turning a sorrow into a prayer, and of proclaiming the hope that Christians have in Christ all minister to the those who suffer. In worship, Christians rejoice with those who rejoice and mourn with those who mourn, ministering to each other in Jesus' name.

195 ✦ A CHRISTIAN VIEW OF SICKNESS

A large portion of pastoral care, including the portion addressed in Christian worship, is directed to those who battle sickness in some form. Every culture and worldview has a unique way of thinking about sickness, with important implications for how care is administered. The following article describes one way of viewing sickness from a Christian perspective.

Most religious traditions have attempted to make sense of illness and disease. The interpretative frameworks they employ involve elements of medicine, religion, and magic; and in some religions all three elements are totally intertwined. The basic question frequently dealt with is the cause of illness, though this is scarcely adequate. A theological and pastoral approach to illness can not be reduced to questions of origin and cause; it must answer the question of the significance of illness in the economy of creation and salvation. This significance is closely tied with the meaning of suffering in human existence.

Illness is a complex reality. It is a physical, spiritual, psychological state with deep social and cultural consequences. Emphasis in the recent past has been put on the physical causes of illness and on the necessary science and technol-ogy to eradicate illness. Today, however, there is a greater awareness of the social and cultural factors affecting health and illness and a deeper understanding of the interactions of the physical and emotional.

Given the concept of health as a structural and functional wholeness, disease can be defined as the breakdown of such wholeness and integration. Illness represents a disharmony of many forces and fronts. A common denominator of serious illness is the radical disruption of one's ordinary life. Sickness modifies the ordinary patterns of a person's existence, sets the person out of the ordinary sphere of his or her social activities and roles, and brings about a new personal world. Such an occurrence can be accompanied by melancholy, confusion, anger, outrage, depression, and a variety of other confusing feelings. The collapse of one's ordinary world often leads to passivity and a sense of helplessness.

Because religion is a basic shaper of attitudes and dispositions, Christianity as a religious tradition can profoundly inform the way believers perceive and respond to illness, and can provide a significant resource for coping with it. The relationship between the experience of illness and faith is a two-way street. If Christian faith can help form interpretations of sickness, sickness itself can alter the shape of one's faith. Severe illness often leads to questions about God and involves a reevaluation of one's whole faith-stance.

Illness in the Hebrew Scriptures

The Christian stance towards illness has been shaped by a long faith tradition with roots in the Hebrew Scriptures. Judaism is marked by its monotheism. God is the Creator of everything and the existence of everything including man and woman depends totally upon God. Everything is subordinated to God, even evil forces. Furthermore, God is characterized as a God of justice and compassion, attributes revealed in God's covenantal relationship with Israel. Within that theology, illness cannot be attributed to a god of evil, such as the spirit of darkness in Zorastrianism. In the Hebrew Scriptures, a close relationship exists between sin and illness, illness being God's punishment for sinfulness. In Deuteronomy 32:39, God affirms: "I kill and I make alive; I wound and I heal." Both health and sickness are under God's control. The acknowledgment of and repentance for sin is necessary for the restoration of health (Ps. 32:3-5). Sickness is finally not simply vindictive punishment, but a corrective, a possibility for spiritual growth.

Illness in the New Testament

In its approach to illness, the New Testament reflects the greater influence of Persian thought than earlier Jewish writing. We find in the New Testament a certain modified dualism. Within God's creation, which is basically good, there exists certain evil powers such as Satan who insinuate evil into the world. A real struggle between such forces and God is taking place in the world.

Jesus himself, whose ministry is characterized by healing, appears to break through the understanding of illness as a consequence of sinfulness and thus posits illness in a very different light (John 9:31; 11:4; Luke 13:1-11). Jesus does not declare that illness contributes to one's salvation nor does he interpret illness as divine punishment. God does not provoke illness, either as a reprisal or to put women/men to the test. Illness is seen as going against God's compassionate love and as a contradiction to God's plan for creation.

Illness in the Church's Tradition

The development of New Testament material in the early church took various directions. It seems that the Alexandrian and Capadocian Fathers, especially Basil, were the first to develop a theological doctrine of illness. Their positions were influenced by their understanding of original justice and original sin. Women and men were created to image God, a God understood as impassible and unchangeable. So whence illness? Illness can only be seen as a consequence of original sin, the product of human sinfulness.

Basil offers various reasons why Christians are affected by illness. Illness can have a corrective effect. It can be seen as punishment for sin. It can test one's faith and provide a way to develop detachment and the acceptance of death. Discerning the cause or reason for illness was important since it determined whether one should seek possible relief from a physician. Only when sickness is the result of natural causes or is a corrective should a physician be summoned. When sickness is discerned as punishment, it should simply be accepted. Some of this understanding could still be found much later in the church. In 1829, for example, Leo XII declared, "Whoever allows himself to be vaccinated ceases to be a child of God. Small pox is a judgment of God, the vaccination is a challenge toward heaven."

Throughout the history of Christianity there has always been a degree of tension between theology and medicine. In certain positions, recourse should be to God alone since God is the source and also the healer of ills for others. In other positions, physicians can be understood as God's instrument in healing the sick. Because of these differing positions, the relationship between the cure of the soul and the care of the body has often been conflictual. A canon promulgated at the Fourth Lateran Council in 1215 (22 *Decretales* 5:38, 13) affirmed the physician's obligation to call a confessor before taking care of the patient.

Following the practice recommended in James 5:14-16, the early church employed a ritual for physical healing, which later came to be used almost exclusively for anointing the terminally ill and for a preparation for death. Compassion for the sick found expression in other ways as well. Already in 372, we find the establishment of a charitable institution, the *Basileias*, which became the prototype of Christian hospitals. Gregory of Nazianzus in his panegyric on St. Basil refers

refers to this institution as a place "where disease is regarded in a religious light . . . and sympathy put to a test" (*On St. Basil*, 63). St. Jerome also recounts the establishment of a hospital in Rome by a lady friend, Fabiola. He narrates how she gathered the abandoned sick and nursed them (*Epistle* 77.6, 1–2).

Such institutions as anointing the sick and the establishment of hospitals follow Jesus' example of compassion, whose object was not only the soul but also the body. Moreover, the visitation and the care of the sick has always been encouraged and understood as a basic expression of one's love for God (Matt. 25:35-40).

Christian Attitude Toward Illness

What meaning, what attitude should a Christian have toward illness? Contemporary existentialist thought has pointed out several important elements of sickness as state of being. Sickness reemphasizes the experience of contingency and the fragility of human existence. Sickness, with all the limitations it imposes on the body, can bring about a deeper grasp of human freedom. Recovery from sickness often entails a greater exercise of one's freedom. Every illness is a limitation upon freedom and an opportunity to transcend such limitation. While illness often tends to isolate, it also leads to a greater sense of dependence upon the "Other." The meaning of every illness is dying; and in a real way every healing is resurrection. In a sense, illness is always a passage point, the threshold between dying and living. Sickness is liminal. Sickness is the enemy of life.

The Christian response to illness is a stance of acceptance and of refusal. Acceptance is necessary since illness is the consequence of our finitude and the precariousness of our existence. Refusal is also necessary, for sickness, which is a negative element in life, is often an impediment to human development, weakening one's capacity for spiritual development and self-understanding.

Pastoral Approaches

Conflicting views on the cause, nature, and meaning of illness have made a pastoral approach to illness difficult. In the medical approach, there is more focus on the illness than on the ill person. In the religious approach, in contrast, there is more attention given to the afflicted person than to the affliction. A holistic pastoral approach would have to pay attention to both the illness and the person.

Many contemporary illnesses such as hypertension, cancer, and AIDS do not easily lend themselves to one single pastoral approach. These illnesses are deeply related to stress, to lifestyles, and to relationships. Illness itself affects a person's relationships to God, to oneself, and to one's family and friends. In many cases, sickness is correlative to sin, not in the sense that it is sent upon an individual as punishment, but as a result of personal decision or action. The etiology of many diseases can be directly related to the lifestyle individuals have created for themselves. There is clearly personal responsibility and possible guilt. A pastoral approach to illness must recognize the tendency of afflicted persons either to perceive their sickness as punishment or to excuse themselves completely from responsibility. Furthermore, a pastoral approach must recognize the need to emphasize Jesus' attitude toward the sick. To exhort a sick person to offer her/his suffering to God would imply that there is some virtue in remaining unwell. Jesus never questions the afflicted person's desire for healing. He in fact encourages it. Illness is not meant of itself to "sanctify" us, to test our faith. It serves to invite us into the mystery of God's own suffering. What the paschal mystery reveals to us is not the necessity of suffering for salvation, but the great truth that, although sickness tends to isolate us and cause us to withdraw, God is our companion, a fellow-sufferer with us.

Lucien J. Richard[26]

196 ✦ A Christian View of Healing

Both the Old and New Testaments are filled with references to the healing of disease. Healing is an important metaphor for understanding the nature and significance of God's love for us and of salvation in Christ. This article describes healing from a biblical point-of-view and lays the foundation for imaging the role that liturgy has as a vehicle of pastoral care.

Healing is no stranger to the Judeo-Christian tradition. In the Hebrew Scripture, God affirms, "I am the Lord, your physician" (Exod. 15:26). A central description for God's work in creation is that of healing. Healing is one expression of God's special care for people: "I am the Lord, your healer" (Exod. 15:26b). God orders people with power and destroys enemies and deceivers. God's will for the people, a will that is not without condition, is imaged through that of God as healer. Both disease and health originate with God: "I kill and I make alive; I wound and I heal; and there is none that can deliver out of my hand" (Deut. 32:39).

God relates to people both positively and negatively. In Hosea, God is represented as being in despair over Israel's seeming incurableness. In Jeremiah, Yahweh affirms, "Your hurt is incurable, and your wound is grievous. There is no one to uphold your cause, no medicine for your wound, no healing for you" (Jer. 30:12-13). Yet God's compassion is infinite; God simply cannot abandon Israel. Both the discipline and the healing of Israel is from God, "Yet it was I who taught Ephraim to walk, I took them up in my arms; but they did not know that I healed them" (Hos. 11:3).

Yahweh heals the diseases, which have their origin in God and are the consequences of human infidelity and sinfulness. Often the situation of Israel is compared to someone who is left without medical help. "Is there no balm in Gilead? Is their no physician there? Why then has the daughter of my people not been restored?" (Jer. 8:22). While many texts refer to the healing and the sickness of individuals, the healing from Yahweh is primarily for the reconstitution of Israel. The importance of these various texts lies in the fact that Yahweh is represented as the restorer and orderer of human life.

In the New Testament, Jesus' miraculous healings are presented as the signs that the Messiah has arrived and the kingdom of God is in our midst. Among the powers of the Messiah is the power to heal the sick (Luke 7:21; also Matt. 11:4-6). Jesus' healings are presented in the Gospels as the product of his charismatic power.

From a historical point of view, Jesus stood in the tradition of Jewish charismatic healers. Touching is a very important aspect of Jesus' ministry of healing. In fact, in the Hebrew Scriptures, the language of the senses is used to express God's compassion. God is the one who sees our afflictions, who hears our cries, and who feels our pain. The ministry of Jesus represents God as a salvific God, a God of life.

Jesus' ministry of healing is in line with his con-stant emphasis upon compassion. The root meaning of compassion is "being moved by" another's situation at the very core of one's being. Not only does compassion characterize Jesus' ministry and is the basic ground for his deeds of healing; but for Jesus, God is also the compassionate one. Jesus invites his disciples to be imitators of God's compassion: "Be compassionate, even as your Father is compassionate" (Luke 6:36). Jesus' movement must be characterized by compassion. In fact, Jesus sent his disciples out to continue his ministry of healing (Mark 6:7-13; Matt. 10:5-10; Luke 9:1-6). In the letter of James, we find the classic New Testament text on the implementation of this ministry (5:14-16).

Jesus performed healings on the Sabbath in defiance of the law (Mark 3:1-6). He healed individuals, who were considered on the margin of society, such as a tax collector (Luke 19:1-10). He healed individuals outside the land of Israel (Mark 7:31-37). In his healing, he rebuked the forces that seem to make people sick (Luke 13:16). Illness is viewed by Jesus as a destructive and deteriorating force. Any attitude that would glorify sickness is alien to Jesus' attitude. Jesus as the Savior is the great physician (H. Beyer, *Theological Dictionary of the New Testament*, 130).

Toward a Theology of Healing

While healing is an important element of Jesus' ministry and redemptive work, it has never been a major concern of theology. A theology of healing is quite absent from the Christian tradition. Developments in many areas of theological concern and the rediscovery of the importance of the healing ministry in the charismatic movement demand a theology of healing.

Such a theology presupposes first of all a definition of health. Health is often understood as merely the absence of disease or infirmity. Yet the preamble of the charter of the World Health Organization attempts to convey a holistic view of health: "Health is a state of complete physical, mental, and social well-being and not merely the absence of disease or infirmity." To this definition, one should add a spiritual element. The root of the word implies completeness, wholeness. Yet unlike disease, which is frequently recognizable, tangible, and rather easily defined, health is a more nebulous reality, difficult to define and never in a state of perfection.

A theology of healing must emphasize the centrality of the concept of personhood and the principle of totality. Health must be defined in such a way as to encompass the total good of the person. Christianity insists that we see healing and disease with the eyes of faith. It offers the triadic framework of Creation, Fall, and redemption as its basic worldview. The framework can be expressed in the following way:

- *Creation:* original blessing, light, freedom, integrity, peace, health;
- *Fall:* deprived human condition, blindness, bondage, brokenness, estrangement, disease;
- *Redemption:* restored human potential, enlightenment, liberation, reintegration, reconciliation, health.

A theology of healing must be anchored within this framework; the major operative elements have to be a theological anthropology and an anthropological soteriology.

From an anthropological perspective, all forms of dualism have to be avoided. The body-soul unity is a necessary implication of the doctrines of the Creation and the Resurrection. The human spirit lives in and through expressive embodiment because the human person is a psycho-physical unity. Within this anthropology, woman and man should not be considered as a composite of several levels, such as body, soul, and spirit, but as a multidimensional unity. Different dimensions of human reality do not lie one alongside the other. In every stage of life, all dimensions are potentially or actually present.

Salvation itself can be described as an act of healing. In many languages, the root of the word *salvation* indicates this. The Greek word *soteria* comes from *saos;* and the German word *heiland* from *heil.* All of these different roots mean "whole, not yet split, disrupted, or disintegrated." Ultimately healing in the sense of salvation implies victory over death itself.

In the New Testament, the concept of salvation implies the deliverance of human beings from all forms of evil, from sickness, from mental illness, from demonic powers, and ultimately from death. The concept of reconciliation emphasizes the restoration of a broken relationship. Redemption connotes freedom from various forms of bondage; the term *salvation* is a rich and complex one and cannot be restricted simply to the restoration of broken relation with God. It encompasses the total good of the person; and in that sense it connotes the process of healing.

There can be no total dichotomy between eschatological salvation and salvation in this world, between "secular" history and salvation history, between healing for eternal life and healing for this life. For salvation to be truly human, salvation must have some experiential dimensions. It must reflect at least partially what salvation implies. To indicate this mystery the Greek Fathers spoke of the divinization of woman and man.

No human techniques of healing can ever remove fully the various forms of suffering that afflict humanity. Victory over suffering is essentially partial and limited. It would be false to understand salvation uniquely as meaning perfect wholeness, for such wholeness means ultimately liberation from finitude and basically from mortality. Ultimate salvation does not in any way imply that salvation comes to humanity simply from outside. Salvation is from within, from what occurs here within our human context. The New Testament gives us an expression of this: one is judged ultimately according to one's compassion (Matt. 25:34-40).

According to the New Testament, salvation involves two movements that are not to be separated: a movement beyond the world, eschatological in nature; and a movement within this world, towards wholeness in life through the gifts of the world, such as medicine, rest, and friendship. While within the Christian perspective there are values higher than life, life in and of its dimensions is of real value.

Jesus' ministry of healing continues in the church and takes place in charitable, charismatic, and sacramental ways. Healing takes place in the tradition in the church of caring for the sick in hospitals and other institutions. The charismatic ministry of healing is very much present in the contemporary church. The sacramental ministry of healing, while expressed in the Eucharist and penance, is most fully operative in the sacrament of the anointing of the sick. The evolution of this sacrament is indicative of the many problems involved in developing a theology of healing. In the early church, the sacrament was understood primarily as an unction for healing. But step-by-step, this was transformed into unction as a preparation for death and had more to do with forgiveness of sins than with bodily healing. It was eventually perceived as the final sacrament for the dying. The healing intended was a spiritual healing.

In the *Constitution on the Sacred Liturgy* (*S.C.* 73ff) and in *Pastoral Care of the Sick: Rites of Anointing and Viaticum* (Collegeville, Minn.: Liturgical Press, 1983), the original purpose of the unction is restored as a sign and prayer for the return to physical health. The new rite is intended to help us understand human sickness in the context of the whole mystery of salvation. Here the gift of bodily health is looked upon as ancillary to the good of the soul. Yet the restoration of physical health remains uncertain. It must be admitted that the ultimate triumph over sickness and evil is achieved eschatologically (Rom. 8:18-20). Sickness and suffering are not unqualifiedly contrary to the will of God. The mystery of God's will for life remains paschal in nature; the suffering of Christ, in light of the Resurrection, was not a defeat of God's will. Yet the church's ministry of healing is an affirmation of the primacy of life and its ultimate victory over death, a victory proleptically achieved in the resurrection of Jesus. All healing then must be understood as originating in God as the giver of life. No healing can be effective in separation from the structures of life itself.

Finally, a contemporary theology of healing must address the basic question of addiction as a pervasive situation. Any addiction is a limitation of the freedom of human desire. It involves the severe loss of willpower and brings about a radical distortion of reality.

Now the basic metaphor used in the Scriptures for sinfulness is that of bondage or slavery, from which one must be delivered into freedom. Addiction is related to sin. It is the bodily and psychological dimension of sinfulness. Deliverance and healing from addictions is a freeing of the will in its journey to God. Our addictions hinder our seeing the truth. Healing of addictive behavior is freeing, an experience of God's salvific presence. It is the relived experience of the Exodus, the experience of spiritual deliverance.

Lucien J. Richard[27]

197 ◆ MINISTRY TO THE SICK

Offering care and solace for those who are sick are essential ministries of every Christian pastor and of the whole Christian community. The sick need the healing news of Christ and the power of the Spirit to both fight against disease and to find comfort and hope. The Christian community, likewise, needs the sick to teach what is most important in life and to witness to the power of the gospel.

Human life is permeated with paradox. The joy and pleasure of the act of conception result in the risk and pain of childbirth. The rich process of physical, mental, and spiritual development is pervaded by the anxiety that accompanies all human growth. And the grand promise of youth and health must eventually come to terms with the experience of limitation, illness, debilitation, and ultimately death. Promise and pain bracket human life at every turn.

The Creation story of Genesis reveals that God did not intend the great gift of human life to be experienced in this way. In Genesis, suffering and death are shown to be intruders in the Creator's original design. They reveal humanity's separation from God, the result of our fallen state. By human choice, sin entered the created order, and with it, death.

Jesus Christ, the Word incarnate, was sent by

The Cross Potent. This cross, also known as the Jerusalem cross, is designed from four tall crosses whose lower ends meet. The crosses resemble ancient crutches and symbolize Christ's power to heal.

God into this ruptured creation to reclaim it and humanity for God. Jesus suffered. Jesus entered into the very heart of the paradox of human life by willingly embracing death on the cross. By raising him to life, God overcame death and restored humanity within the original, creative design revealed in Genesis. This does not mean that suffering and death have been removed from human experience, but that they have been conquered and made salvific, the very means of eternal life.

It is within the context of the mystery of Christ's dying and rising that Christians who are sick are seen to have a ministry to the community of faith and to the world as a whole. With Christ, they stand in the center of the paradox of life, the grandeur of its promise and the inclination to hopelessness with which it is rife because of suffering and the certainty of death. On the one hand, by their active struggle against illness, the sick members of the community of faith witness to the fact that sickness and suffering are evil and alien to God's plan for creation. In this, they proclaim the goodness, the gift of life, and the greatness of humanity's place within the created order. As the introduction to _Pastoral Care of the Sick_ states: "Part of the plan laid out by God's providence is that we should fight strenuously against all sickness and carefully seek the blessings of good health, so that we may fulfill our role in human society and in the Church" ([Collegeville, Minn.: Liturgical Press, 1983], 3).

On the other hand, by their willing acceptance of the suffering that they cannot avoid, Christians who are sick experience and witness to the reality and mystery of suffering: "their faith helps them to grasp more deeply the mystery of suffering and bear their pain with greater courage" (_Pastoral Care,_ 1). In the heart of this mystery, they discover that the experience of suffering need not be one of futility and despair. In union with Christ's own suffering and death, these old enemies of the human race, these strangers to God's creative intent have been transformed into the means of grace and salvation. "From Christ's own words they know that sickness has meaning and value for their own salvation and for the salvation of the world" (_Pastoral Care,_ 1). By embracing the suffering that is theirs as members of a flawed yet beloved race, the sick unite themselves with the sufferings of Christ and help witness to and achieve the restoration of all in Christ: " we should

always be prepared to fill up what is lacking in Christ's sufferings for the salvation of the world as we look forward to creation's being set free in the glory of the children of God—see Colossians 1:24; Romans 8:19-21" (_Pastoral Care,_ 3).

Christians, who are sick, minister to the well first and foremost by being witnesses to and embodiments of these fundamental truths of Christian revelation. It is in this sense that _Pastoral Care of the Sick_ says "the role of the sick in the Church is to be a reminder to others of the essential or higher things. By their witness the sick show that our mortal life must be redeemed through the mystery of Christ's death and resurrection" (3). By their struggle with illness, they recall the community of faith to its belief in the fundamental good of created life as a gift of God. And by associating themselves "willingly with the passion and death of Christ"(_Pastoral Care,_ 5), they share with him the cost of redeeming that mortal life.

By facing the reality of sickness, the weakness, dependency, and fear that it entails, the sick Christian can help the Christian community and society as a whole acknowledge and accept the fundamental frailty of human nature that all people experience, whether or not they are sick. The denial of this reality can succeed only temporarily and is not without cost both for the individual and for society. In the individual who attempts it, this denial can result in an incapacity to deal with the changes and chances of life and one's own weaknesses. It can also mean an unwillingness to see change in others and can result in anger at the sight of one's own unacknowledged weaknesses reflected in others. These characteristics can also be evident on a larger stage in societies, where frailty and the nonproductivity associated with it are viewed as having no value. In such a society, the infirm and aged are relegated to the margins of the normal life of the group and even may be viewed with disdain. They are potentially painful reminders of a fundamental frailty that no one wants to admit within a social structure where measurable productivity is the gauge of personal worth.

The tendency in each of us and in the society we inhabit to deny human weakness and dependency is the outcome of fear, a fear which has its roots in an abiding sense of our mortality. Sickness puts us in touch with mortality, our own and others', in a direct and inescapable way. And those who are sick can minister to the well by showing them first of all that this fear is not to be denied, that it has positive value and rests on a true intuition that things were not meant to be like this. Second, the sick can help the rest learn that this fear can be faced and thereby become the way to hope and healing, the occasion for coming to an acceptance of our full humanity.

The sick are not then, in a marginal relationship with the rest of human society. Even less so are they on the periphery of the Christian community. They have an essential role at the very heart of the mystery of Jesus, dead and risen. The Gospels portray Jesus as having a constant concern for the sick and the infirm, whom he sought out, consoled, and healed. Jesus recognized that in their weakened or impaired condition the sick were allowed only a marginal existence in society. Some were considered outcasts Jesus' ministry to them was at one and the same time an affirmation that such suffering was the result of an evil completely opposed to his Father's design and a proclamation of the kingdom that he came to inaugurate, a kingdom heralded by Jesus' own divine compassion and healing. And in his utter self-giving on the cross, Jesus suffered fully the effects of the evil loose in the world. In Jesus, we see the face of a God who is forever at one with the abandoned, the destitute, the victim, and all who experience hopelessness. The whole of Jesus' life, death, and resurrection show us a God passionately attached to us, to the restoration of all creation.

The community of faith needs those who are sick to teach it about the vulnerability of God in Christ, who "is still pained and tormented in his members, made like him" (*Pastoral Care*, 2). The sick teach the community about Christian hope found paradoxically in human vulnerability when united to Christ, the suffering servant. In the face of a society, which can view the sick only as those who are in need and for whom so much must be done, the Christian community proclaims the place and dignity of the sick by the very way in which it loves, cares for, and depends upon them. And even as the community encourages them to offer their sufferings in union with Christ, it relies upon them to pray, in the privileged way that is theirs by virtue of this union, for the whole church and for the entire world, for peace in the world, for the many needs of the church, for indi-

viduals and families in crisis, and for all those caught up in the mystery of human sufferings, whether in body, mind, or spirit (see *Pastoral Care*, 56).

James M. Schellman[28]

198 • DEFINING PASTORAL CARE AND LITURGICAL RENEWAL

Pastoral care is often thought to involve one-on-one listening and counseling. Yet this is only one setting where pastoral sensitivity and guidance may be shown. For genuine pastoral care involves living and expressing God's presence in all aspects of life, including pastoral counseling, spiritual direction, and liturgical ministry. Worship leaders can effectively develop their pastoral sensitivity by considering themselves pastoral caregivers.

Whatever work we do in liturgy, we must begin to identify it with the work of pastoral care. Whether we are a leader of renewal, a member of the assembly, or a servant of it—presider, music minister, eucharistic minister, cantor, hospitality minister, altar server, environmental minister, lector, cross-bearer—we are involved in pastoral care. In all these roles, we will accomplish nothing if we are not first and always centered in God. A look at pastoral care will provide us with the framework to do just that.

In whatever we do for and with each other, there is a specific, underlying essence that is shared by all. St. Paul names this essence clearly: "There are different gifts but the same Spirit; there are different ministries but the same Lord; there are different works but the same God accomplishes all of them in everyone" (1 Cor. 12:4-6). This essence is present in all ministry work, including pastoral and liturgical ministry, spiritual direction, and pastoral counseling. The appropriation of the servant role transcends any specific ministry; we are all called to love and serve in whatever capacity we are able. All ministry has this underlying essence, and an unifying goal as well: increasing human wholeness centered in the Spirit. Howard Clinebell believes that "each function (ministry) can be an instrument of growth and healing, a channel of pastoral caring."

In reviewing definitions of pastoral care, many authors seem to classify it as a separate area of ministry, on a horizontal plane that includes spiritual direction and pastoral counseling, liturgical and pastoral ministry. But I contend that pastoral care is not something separate, above, or side by side other ministries. It is not another type of ministry. *Pastoral care is the awareness and expression of the essence of God that permeates and informs all areas of ministry.*

When we understand ourselves to be pastoral care-givers in whatever we do, we must be guided by this essence, the presence of God. This understanding also recognizes the initiating action of God. When this presence and action are both tacitly and overtly expressed in and through the components of pastoral care—community, mutuality, inclusiveness, vision, orientation toward growth, support/challenge, and reflection—Christian qualities and virtues will become increasingly visible in our work. St. Paul sees these qualities and virtues very clearly:

> Because you are God's chosen ones, holy and beloved, clothe yourselves with heartfelt mercy, with kindness, humility, meekness, and patience. Bear with one another, forgive whatever grievances you have against one another. Forgive as the Lord has forgiven you. Over all these virtues put on love, which binds the rest together and makes them perfect. Christ's peace must reign in your hearts, since as members of the one body you have been called to that peace. Educate yourselves to thankfulness. Let the Word of Christ, rich as it is, dwell in you. In wisdom made perfect, instruct and admonish one another . . . Whatever you do, do it in the name of the Lord Jesus. Give thanks to God the Father through him. (Col. 3:12-17)

This passage sums up some of the most important components of pastoral care. An understanding of these components and their corresponding Christian virtues and fruits needs to be brought into all of our efforts of liturgical renewal. We also need to be willing to bring them into our own lives. When we clothe ourselves with the mind of Christ, which is what Paul is describing in this passage, we become more effective ministers, be it in one-on-one relationships or in working with the community.

Community and Covenantal Promise

When we gather, we form not just a community, but a community in covenant with God. A deeply rooted sense of covenant brings a rich dimension to community, whether it be as large as a five hundred member assembly that has come together to worship or as small as two persons, who meet for spiritual direction or counseling. God's promise and invitation to us to be the covenant community is revealed in the Hebrew Scriptures: "I will sprinkle clean water upon you . . . I will give you a new heart . . . I will put my spirit within you . . . you shall be my people and I will be your God" (Ezek. 36:25-28).

The Christian Scriptures broaden the vision of this community: "Where two or three are gathered in my name, there am I in their midst" (Matt. 18:20). Within community is the promise of renewal in the real presence of Jesus. It is the will of God that forms this community; it is the presence of Christ that guides it; it is the gift of the Spirit that empowers it.

Mutuality and Humility

According to Robert W. Hovda, "The church teaches and shares its corporate wisdom through many different ministries. But the church is also taught by the child, the adult, the neophyte . . . Mutuality is a characteristic of every ministry." No ministry is one-directional. In virtually every situation, at some level and in some way, everyone is ministered unto. "In the measure you give, you shall receive, and more besides" (Mark 4:24). The person who is giving care has a need to be of help, a need that is met through those in their care. Beyond basic needs, there is an entire level of exchange: those who teach are taught; those who listen, learn; those who give, receive. This sense of mutuality gives birth to the humility that Paul asks of us. It also gives birth to a healthy respect and appreciation of the other that often gets lost when we are feeling overwhelmed by the demands of our ministry. It counters the burnout and frustration that are often experienced on many different levels.

Inclusiveness and Reconciliation

Our Scriptural tradition clearly articulates the sense of inclusiveness that we should carry into all of our ministry work. "There is but one body and one spirit, just as there is but one hope given all of you by your call. There is one Lord, one faith, one baptism; one God and Father of all, who is over all and works through all, and is in all" (Eph. 4:4-6). There is no mention of exclusion for any reason here, no mention of a system which judges some as less worthy of invitation.

Our ability to openly include and accept is possible only when there has been reconciliation, only when we have been able "to bear with one another and forgive whatever grievances we might have." As we receive this forgiveness and reconciliation, we learn to be more forgiving and reconciling. Barriers and impediments to relationship fall away. We are moved to accept and then to include. Jesus' own example of inviting the most lowly to share at table with him can serve as our own example. "If Jesus ate with sinners as a witness to God's offer of reconciliation, how can his Church do any less?" (Regis Duffy, *Real Presence* [New York: Harper and Row, 1982]). We must "reach out creatively to the 'unacceptable' and the 'undesirable'" as part of our call to serve.

Vision and Prophecy

A faith-inspired vision of Christ living in each of us is crucial in our work. This vision is neither complicated nor sophisticated. Its very simplicity baffles most. In the words of St. Paul, "The life I live now is not my own; Christ is living in me. I still live my human life, but it is a life of faith in the Son of God, who loved me and gave himself for me" (Gal. 2:20).

How different we would feel, how different would our actions be if we could see this potential and be fed by that vision. The vision of community is one of the body of Christ: "members may be concerned for one another. If one members suffers, all the members suffer with it; if one member is honored, all the members share its joy. You then, are the 'body of Christ'" (1 Cor. 12:25-27).

As pastoral care-givers within liturgical ministry, we have a responsibility to treat each member of the community according to that vision. When we greet each person, it is Christ whom we greet as well. "God is not to be found in isolated individualism then, but in others," writes Walter Conn in *Christian Conversion* (New York: Paulist Press, 1984). To treat the community as the body of Christ will increase our reverence of and respect for the group which has come together in Jesus' name. The vision becomes a self-fulfilling prophecy. As we treat each other as Christ-like, we become more Christ-like. The prophetic call

that we are to become Christ-like and to become the body of Christ achieves reality for an ever-increasing number of people. In so doing, we spread our faith in a subtle, self-fulfilling way.

Growth and Transcendence

Orientation toward growth and transcendence enables us to view the people with whom we work as people in search of a different way of being. This orientation sees the human being as a creature in search of the transcendent. In working in liturgical renewal, we must begin to look at all the various needs, tasks, and issues as opening into growth, not as demands to be met and pathologies to be corrected. It is generally believed by most of the developmental theorists that the movement from place to place is often precipitated by crisis, a concept which the Chinese understand as including both danger and opportunity. Liturgy, by its very nature, brings us into the heart of this opportunity over and over again. It does this by asking us to be more honest, by asking us to see who and where we are now and who and where God is calling us to be. Resolution of the crisis brought about by this soul-searching often leads us to a place in our journeys that is more transcendent than the previous one, to a place where we live in greater awareness of and harmony with God.

As pastoral care-givers, the view of crisis resolution as a potential for growth can positively affect our view of the work that we do and the people we serve. Perception (negative and positive) tends to be contagious and self-fulfilling.

Support, Challenge, and Liberation

Our ability to support and at the same time to challenge is one of the many paradoxes that are a part of living a life based on the Christian faith. As ministers, we support those whom we serve. But at the same time, we also need to promote a liturgical environment in which there is freedom for self-evaluation and challenge from others when feelings and behavior appear to be inconsistent with the gospel message.

This component of pastoral care involves support as people struggle to understand and then answer God's call to them as individuals and as a community; it also involves challenge when they grow complacent and satisfied with ritual alone.

In Jesus, we have the perfect example of support through his healing and his love. He also gives us a perfect example of challenge through his many exhortations to the people to take up their crosses (Mark 8:34), sell their possessions and give to the poor (Matt. 19:21), and serve (Luke 22:27).

When we respond to loving support and challenge, we move beyond our concern with material possessions and self-absorption into loving service to others. What we experience is liberation from past wounds and from current values that are false and misleading. No longer as wounded and no longer as obsessed, we become more free to experience the transforming power of the gospel through Christ and the Spirit.

Reflection and Wisdom

Reflection upon our life experiences is like fertilizer in the soil—it will bring the experience to its greatest life and purpose. It allows the experience to bear its fruit, the wisdom hidden within it. This is as true about our liturgical experiences as it is about other experiences. It is only through _reflected experience_, which constitutes our meaning-seeking, that our faith can be deepened and strengthened and our ministry become effective.

We must begin to understand what our own experience is before we can work with and for others. We must take time to reflect what is meaningful to us for it is through this process that our own faith is formed, transformed, and enlivened; it is through this process that our passion is reclaimed and rekindled. We can learn various facts about Christian tradition and ritual, but these, in and of themselves, will not constitute faith. When we reflect on experience in the light of Scripture and tradition, deeper faith and wisdom are born. Wisdom "knows all and understands all things, and will guide me discreetly in my affairs and safeguard me by her glory" (Wis. 8:11).

Liturgical Renewal

The embodiment of these components is a lifetime process. It does not happen all at once. However, becoming aware of each of them will enrich our work and inform our approach to all ministry. We must keep in mind that fruit and virtues arise through God's initiative and ongoing action in our lives and work; they are a gift.

How do these components and their fruits and virtues work in the area of liturgical renewal? In our renewal efforts, we assume many roles: as models of prayer, reflection, or sharing; as teachers of content, doctrine, or tradition; as leaders of eucharistic liturgy and other forms of communal worship. Applying to these roles the components of pastoral care we have just examined will help us rekindle the passion in liturgical renewal.

As Models. We serve as models when our renewal efforts are directed toward helping people to reflect on their experience of liturgy, to share those reflections, and to enter prayer more deeply. This reflection, which is really a deep savoring of all that is, breathes new life into our liturgies. A sense of _mutuality_ certainly is necessary here; we do not model from above, but among. As we give, so do we receive. Grateful for all those with whom we work, able to see them as contributing to the process in different, but equally significant ways, mutuality brings the gift of humility to our work.

The component of _inclusiveness_ also is necessary. When we model reflection, sharing, and prayer, we are in a place where we can make everyone feel equally welcome and accepted. If we incorporate a willingness to accept _support and challenge_ when we model reflection, sharing, and prayer, we will encourage others to do the same. Our willingness to accept, support, and challenge will liberate us from complacency and the status quo.

As Teachers. When our renewal efforts are directed toward instruction, purpose, and doctrine, two components of pastoral care are critical. First, are we faithful to God's call to be not just a community, but a _covenant community_, a community bound together by God's promise? Second, do we believe in the _prophetic vision_ of ourselves as the body of Christ? In our teaching of liturgy, we need to communicate how liturgy informs and strengthens this covenant community, the body of Christ, and how the community informs and strengthens liturgy. They are inseparable. Our vision works hand in hand with God's prophecy. As we see ourselves as the body of Christ, as we see the Christ within each of us and the Christ among all of us, so it is that we become Christ among all of us, so it is that we become Christ for one another. This prophetic vision will help those we instruct to see liturgy as a living sacrament, liturgy as a sacred gift from God that reveals the Christ within and among us.

As Leaders. When renewal is directed toward prayer, we may function as leaders of the that prayer in the community we serve. In leading, we must incorporate the component of *inclusiveness*—all must be lovingly encouraged to come to the Table and to be reconciled. This component of pastoral care is perhaps the most important one when we lead—no one must be forgotten. As leaders, we are the instruments, who guide our assemblies, who prepare an environment in which real communal prayer, relationship with God, will thrive. The component of *reflection* is also essential. It is often in our own reflections, in our savoring, in our willingness to simply be in the experience of worship that this intimate relationship with God is revealed and wisdom is born. This "wisdom made perfect" becomes the silent, steady hand in our leadership. When we lead others in prayer, this gift of wisdom will be our guide as we guide.

From the outset, our renewal efforts will be informed by a certain attitude and approach, whether the effort is involved with prayer, reflection, or sharing; programs or projects; liturgical praxis, gestures, symbols, music, environment, or catechesis. If this approach and attitude is one of *orientation toward growth*—an orientation that all humans possess by their very nature—the process will be greatly enhanced and facilitated. An orientation toward growth, a way of seeing every effort as an effort that originates from an unspoken desire to come to rest in God, points us into the light of the risen Christ.

It is a forward-looking orientation, rather than an orientation arising out of sin, darkness, and a need to fix. The difference is subtle, but significant. Every renewal effort arises from the desire to support human beings in their journey toward becoming one with the God who so loves them. Arising from this desire, our renewal will be about wholeness and holiness, about passion and life, about involvement and commitment to all that God has created us to be.

Susan Jorgensen[29]

199 ✦ SPIRITUALITY AND PASTORAL CARE

Genuine pastoral sensitivity arises out of the pastor's own spiritual life and the pastor's experience of God's presence. Whether pastoral care is demonstrated through counseling or liturgical leadership, it must be grounded in faith and permeated with prayer.

Working as a pastoral psychotherapist, I am increasingly captured by questions of pastoral identity. Who am I as I sit in this room with struggling and suffering persons? Why am I here? How do I envision and embody my role here? The explicitly *pastoral* dimension of these questions also includes how all this connected to my experience of prayer and faith? In responding to these questions, I have found it helpful to return to those basic experiences which are foundational in my life—personal experiences of healing and salvation.

In this article, I would like to invite others into a conversation about such personal experiences. The invitation involves dialogue about the relationship of spirituality to our pastoral work. The contemporary literature of pastoral care and counseling emphasizes theological reflection and dialogue with Christian sources (Scripture, tradition, confessional communities) as ways of insuring an appropriate pastoral identity and practice. While acknowledging the value of these proposals, I submit that they are insufficient. Over the years, I have become convinced that pastoral identity and practice need to be rooted in personal prayer and spirituality. It is in the crucible of a personal encounter with God that pastoral identity is born and progressively integrated. In exploring this living relationship with God, we can approach with freshness the deep religious roots of our ministry.

The task requires some personal revelation and reflection. I will present here an exercise, exploring certain prayerful experiences that have aided me in addressing questions of pastoral identity. They are important factors in the spirituality which undergirds my ministry. *Spirituality,* as I use the term here, is a way of living in explicit relation to God and neighbor. Listening, discernment, and responsive action nourish this way of life. It is a vital union of spiritual experience, vision, and praxis.

I will present a spirituality of "grateful response" that has become the force behind my pastoral ministry and guides my sense of how ministry can be performed. The unfolding of healing metaphors in personal experience with God will be the path for reflection and will lead into a discussion of qualities of pastoral sensibility, as well as a view of Christology that may ground pastoral work.

The Starting Point

In _The Practice of Spiritual Direction_, William Barry and William Connoly suggest that any exploration of spiritual life can profitably begin with personal experience: "What are people's spiritual lives actually like and what has helped to develop them?" ([New York: Seabury Press, 1982], viii). As a Catholic priest and member of the Society of Jesus, my spiritual life is formed and shaped by the _Spiritual Exercises of St. Ignatius_ and the ongoing development of Jesuit spirituality (Louis J. Puhl, trans., _The Spiritual Exercises of St. Ignatius_ [Chicago: Loyola University Press, 1951]). Jesuits and others who follow this spiritual way maintain personal contact with Jesus the Christ, through contemplation of his life via Scripture and liturgy and discernment of his calling in contemporary "signs of the times" and in the continuing experience of the people of God (William A. Barry, "The Experience of the First and Second Weeks of the Spiritual Exercises," _Review for Religious_ 32 [1973]: 106). In pursuing elements in a spirituality for pastoral care, I will draw on my own experience and style of prayer. Certainly, this is only one way of proceeding. It is one pastoral counselor's attempt to articulate some of the deep roots of his ministry. Hopefully, this exercise will invite others to similar exploration and dialogue.

Two metaphors come to mind, both from times of personal retreat and quiet prayer. One metaphor arises from the setting of a mental hospital. In a large, dark room sits a young male patient, bound in a "jacket." He is isolated and alone, cut off not only from human companionship, but from silent company of clear perceptions and images as well. He is unkempt, unshaven, and wild-eyed. Most painfully, he has a clouded mind. Stresses, frustrations, and terrors seem to be assaulting him from within; and he feels defenseless before the onslaught. He knows it has not always been like this. The cloudiness and lack of clarity paralyze and frighten him; he feels beset, overmatched, defeated. "Who will rescue me from the pit?"

The setting for a second metaphor is a medical hospital at the bedside of an accident victim. He is paralyzed from the neck down and bandaged. He cannot see through the bandages nor can he hear beyond vague distortions. When he rises above the stupor of shock and medications, he is aware of feeling cut off, out-of-touch, disoriented. He does not seem able to hold on to reality, but slips in and out of contact. In lucid moments, amid the loneliness and fear, he wonders what could possibly bring light in to this darkness. He wonders, "Who can save me in this time of trouble?"

Until someone grasps his hand! This, he can feel. This sudden connection has warmth and strength, resolve and compassion in it. He feels flooded with hope and love.

Each of us utilizes metaphors for the articulation and deep appropriation of our experiences and their meanings. Metaphorical language is a way in which we can articulate our experience and comprehension of ourselves, of others, of creation, of God. Metaphors reveal, and offer the potential to reinterpret, our ways of being and acting in the world. They offer a path for seeing linkages in who we are, what we do, and why and how we do it.

These two metaphors which arose for me in prayer—the mental patient and the accident victim—acted as "lenses" to aid me in interpreting various aspects of my life. They were given to me during retreat in prayerful moments of reflection on my own woundedness and sinfulness. Within this context, they aided me in seeing the alienation and isolation that are part of illness and sin. They functioned as indicators of inner estrangement and disorientation, catching the essential neediness that can arise from one's own wounds and sin.

These metaphors become nodal points for me, drawing to themselves memories, affects, and understandings of both patterns of disorder or sinfulness and its effects, and also a deep sense of my own need for healing and salvation. They also became central, organizing metaphors for my sense of pastoral identity and motivation for involvement in a "healing" ministry. They helped to convey a kind of "felt knowledge" that has affected my view of reality and my actions and reactions within it.

The Desire to Serve

James Fowler has reminded us that "call and response" to God lie at the heart of Christian life and ministry (James W. Fowler, _Faith Development and Pastoral Care_ [Philadelphia, Pa.: Fortress Press, 1987]). I suggest that the "call" of God often comes to us in experiences of a personal encounter with God's healing grace and leads in gratitude to a "response" of offering oneself for healing ministry. Personal healing becomes the occasion for a desire to follow and serve, to respond to God's gracious activity by mediating a similar healing for others.

The two metaphors I've described spoke to the alienation and disorientation that often accompany illness and the effects of sin. As these experiences unfolded in prayer, there came an experience of contact, of shared strength, of "being grasped." Into the midst of isolation and confusion, there came a healing touch. I felt the presence of God in Christ grasping me and breaking into my closed world. The experience of "being grasped" emerged as a surprising and revelatory event. It evoked a surprising affective and attitudinal response. I encountered the grace of God, healing and saving me in the midst of my wounds and sinfulness.

The experience of "being grasped" by God's grace became a felt sense of being accepted, of being a "loved sinner." It also led to being a "wounded healer." William Barry states:

> Many experience tears of joy as they feel themselves to be loved sinners . . . The knowledge is a deep, abiding, felt kind of thing (*knowledge* in the way John means the word in his Gospel). It is the kind of knowing that leads to action and desire, the kind of knowing that wants to be shared and spread. It is "Good News."

Grace that heals and liberates is grace which calls for service.

The experience of being saved becomes the catalyst for both gratitude and love. This in turn brings a desire to respond, to "follow" and reform one's life. A deep spiritual dynamic is dictated here. Such a reformation of life may very well include decisions about the form and style of discipleship one envisions and embarks upon to actualize a response to that call. Reformation of life leads to a "lifestyle response" to God's healing activity. In following the "healing Lord" through a personalized style of discipleship and ministry, one hopes continually to meet him, be with him, and serve him. The style of ministry and discipleship, as a personalized and grateful response to being healed, becomes a way of encounter and a way of salvation.

I am proposing a model of "grateful response" as the basis for healing ministry. As we return to our own experiences of being accepted, of being healed, these experiences function both to anchor and to enliven our understanding of, and involvement in, specific forms of ministry. Such deeply religious experiences in our own lives lie, I believe, at the root of our desire to serve. They operate at the heart of our desire to be "disciples," to follow Jesus and serve at his side. The "deep gladness" they engender leads to grateful response. Pastoral care and counseling become both an actualization and a continued refinding of the Lord's gracious presence, through being and finding his presence with those whom I serve.

Sensibility and Pastoral Relationship

In moments of gracious approach by God, personal and lively contact allows us to grasp a life-giving pastoral vision and sensibility. Experiences of "grateful response" to God function as guideposts and touchstones for one's *style* of ministry. Drawing to themselves associations, memories, and feelings, they communicate a "felt" sense of how one can and should be in the world. They become bases for pastoral sensibility and for how one envisions one's pastoral role. A dynamic of "grateful response" leads to pastoral vision.

The minister aware of his or her own connection with suffering and neediness is a minister truly open and caring toward suffering and needs in others. Such ministry flows into three essential qualities of pastoral sensibility: compassion, steadfast love, and faithfulness. These three biblically-based qualities, reflective of the Lord's stance toward a broken world in need of redemption, are indispensable for ministry in general and for pastoral care and counseling in particular. In contemporary clinical parlance, we might speak in a parallel way of "empathy," a "holding environment," and the "therapeutic alliance" (Walter Brueggemann, "Voices of the Night Against Justice," in *To Act Justly, Love Tenderly, Walk Humbly: An Agenda for Ministers,* ed. Walter Brueggemann et al. [New York: Paulist Press, 1986]). I am not proposing here a one-to-one correspondence between these religious and clinical terms. Complex nuances and linguistic contexts inform and contextualize each of them. Rather, I am suggesting a softer kind of correlation, a more general stance and attitude of persons, interestingly similar across the range of "helping professions."

A basis of "grateful response" in the healing ministries, rooted in personal experience, is preeminently empathetic. Being grasped and healed holds within it the possibility of compassion. Grounded in a sense of self as a "loved sinner" and a "wounded healer," ministries of pastoral care and counseling ought to envision themselves as "walking with" and "standing alongside" troubled or wounded persons. In vital touch with his or her own pain, the minister notices and cares about the pain of others. Understanding the gracious and healing approach of God in her or his own regard, the minister resolves to be present to souls as a living mediator—an "incarnation," if you will—of God's grace; that is, to be the presence of God's kingdom breaking through, as Jesus himself was.

The minister comes to a sense of identity as a "fellow pilgrim," walking with those in need of grace. To be sure, the minister is catalyst and guide along the way, but she or he is fellow-traveler as well. This is the key to a empathic basis for ministry. Empathy, or the ability to "love tenderly" (Micah 6:8), is to love "with an awareness of the capacity of the other to be wounded, to suffer pain, and to be dependent upon relationship with others" (Sharon Parks, "Love Tenderly," in _To Act Justly, Love Tenderly, Walk Humbly: An Agenda for Ministers,_ ed. Walter Brueggemann et al. [New York: Paulist Press, 1986], 30). It is the ability, rooted in one's own wounds and healing, to understand and care about the situation of another.

Again, ministry in touch with its roots of neediness and healing comprehends well the necessity for "steadfast love." God's response to sinful and suffering people is characterized by _hesed,_ a steadfast and fierce devotion to their health and their good. As Sharon Parks points out, such a stance on the part of God understands both our vulnerability and our innate possibilities, our best good. Consequently, God's gracious love toward us is both "tender" and "tenacious" (Parks 39). The kingdom of God, the centerpiece of Jesus' mission and ministry in God's name, provides both a "holding environment" for human vulnerability and a context of hope, calling persons to a new and more healthy being. It is the kingdom or "reign" of God that is the ultimate environment

which holds client, counselor, and the healing enterprise.

Such a holding environment is essential for the reconstruction that is the goal of pastoral therapeutics. "When one's faith and self come apart to come together again, there must be a supporting, nurturing environment that 'holds' us" (Parks 34). Fowler speaks similarly in his discussion of "reconstructive change" in the face of failure or spiritual struggle, legacies of woundedness, or deficiencies from the influence of others' or our own choices. In his view, the movement into "reconstructive change" requires a holding environment—an "ecology of care and vocation"—for successful passage (Fowler 103–116). Pastoral care and leadership involves attentiveness to the nurturing of healing and "holding" environments.

The third critical quality of pastoral sensibility is its valuing of faithfulness. YHWH, the Faithful One, made a covenant of unshakable fidelity to persons. For the Christian, Jesus in his person is the Incarnation of this faithful word of promise, the new covenant of healing and salvation. Pastoral sensibility understands the value of faithfulness from its own experience of being saved and healed, not just once, but again and again. It understands that God's loving stance toward persons is ever-gracious and therefore seeks to make such faithful love its own.

Pastoral care and ministry take their cue from the experience of God's trustworthy stance toward the people of God. As Nagy and Krasner have suggested, "trustworthiness" is an essential element for healing and loving relationships (Ivan Boszormenyi-Nagy and Barbara R. Krasner, "Trust-based Therapy: A Contextual Approach," _American Journal of Psychiatry_ 137 [1980]: 767–775). And, as counselors of various schools can attest, the trustworthy faithfulness of the "therapeutic alliance" is an indispensable element in the healing of persons.

Empathy, holding, alliance—all these clinical notions have their parallels in biblically-informed pastoral sensibility—each speak to the necessity of _relationship_ in healing endeavors. Pastoral care and counseling are ministries of healing and loving relationships. The metaphors I've proposed in our "conversation" are relational metaphors. True, each began with isolation and estrangement; each was striking because of its relationship deficits. Yet, the healing encountered came by way of "being grasped," of being approached in relationship. Relational presence and intervention became the way of healing and salvation.

My own path of growth in pastoral identity and work has proceeded in this way. For me, it is important to provide compassion, steadfast love, and faithfulness in the therapeutic relationship. It has become equally important to envision myself as a catalyst for these qualities in my clients' wider relationship network. Healing and recovery occur (and are maintained), not only in the therapeutic relationship, but in the wider relational surroundings as well. An additional issue, which is directly related to care and counseling that are *pastoral,* involves the connection to the spiritual relationship that holds and supports pastoral work. Ministry with persons occurs within the ambience of relationship to God and the kingdom of God. All ministry done in Jesus' name involves, at its depth, relationship with him, as God's offer of healing and reconciling grace. Pastoral ministry is inherently Christological.

Finding the Christ

Here I can only indicate what must—for the present—remain suggestions of a "healing Christology," as it relates to the ministries of pastoral care and counseling. Earlier I spoke of the "grateful response" to the experience of "being grasped." I suggested that this could inform one's life and the possible choice of a healing ministry, as a way to both actualize one's gratitude and continue following the Lord. Pastoral care and counseling could, I suggested, further specify one's discipleship, as a participation in the church's ministry in Jesus' name.

What I would like to point toward here is that such a response may discover itself continually *finding* the Lord in its ministry. Moreover, such encounters with the Lord are the primary means for nourishing such demanding ministries over the long term. This Christological element is the wellspring for Christian pastoral care and counseling's spirituality and identity. It is true enough to say that what makes counseling *pastoral* is its rootedness in the ministry of the church. Nevertheless, a full exploration of what this means must take into account the Christology which grounds *both* the church's sense of itself and the minister's pastoral identity and motives. Here the church's living contact with its original experiences converges with the counselor's own. At its heart, the church's self-identity and the pastor's identity and spirituality are Christological.

For the ministries of pastoral care and counseling, I envision—and in no way are these to be seen as exhaustive—three Christological dimensions: being his presence, finding his presence; and being in his presence. All three dimensions are inherent in pastoral relations and are constitutive of a spirituality for pastoral ministry.

Our ministry as Christian pastoral agents, as well as the church's mission and ministry, is guided and shaped by Jesus Christ, as a metaphor of God's healing and salvific love, as a parable of the kingdom of God (Sallie McFague, *Metaphorical Theology: Models of God in Religious Language* [Philadelphia, Pa.: Fortress Press, 1982]). Jesus becomes the original, foundational metaphor which grounds our identity, pastoral motives, and way of being, both collectively and individually.

As Sallie McFague has indicated, it is possible for a person to be and act metaphorically (McFague 67–68, 108–111). Looking back into our own lives, we can recover memories of people, who served as role models for us. Their words, causes, and behavior became guideposts and catalysts for our emerging sense of self. Their life stories functioned as guiding metaphors for us, revealing and interpreting some of the mysteries of our lives, grounding and articulating some of the dreams which helped to form us as persons. In the way of metaphor our familiarity with aspects of their story helped to illumine the unfamiliarity of ourselves and our stories.

From this vantage point, it is a small step to the experience of ourselves as metaphorical figures in the lives of our parishioners and clients. As I've reflected on the two metaphors, which have become part of our conservation, it is clear to me that they form my sense of being healed and grasped by God's healing love. In the experience, which funded these two metaphors, it was Jesus the Christ, God's healing-in-person, who approached and grasped me. More to the point, these metaphors also image for me my approach in a healing ministry to those I serve.

For at least some of my clients, I have become a concrete embodiment of God's kingdom of love and healing. In this view, pastoral care and counseling can be seen as a "personalizing" of Jesus' presence and ministry, an incarnation of the Lord's own stance toward sinful and suffering people. Pastoral care and counseling become incarnations of God's continual offer of salvation and healing, mediated through my ministry. The counseling situation becomes a possible encounter with, and discovery of, God's forgiveness and Jesus' ministry of reconciliation and healing in the midst of broken, alienated, and wounded living. The pastoral counselor becomes for the client a personalized point of meeting with God's gracious activity and discovers (often surprisingly) herself or himself _bringing God's presence._

Further, the richness of prayerful spirituality also allows a sensitive pastoral agent to discover the Lord's presence in her or his client. In the New Testament, Jesus' own identification with the poor, the struggling, and the sinner allows—in fact demands—such a vision. As pastoral agents labor to break the barrier of alienation that shackles clients, to heal life's wounds, and to restore this person to the possibility of free partnership with God, they encounter the suffering and crucified One, calling from the midst of the client's pain and struggle. Finding the crucified, the friend of tax collectors and sinners and of widows and orphans, endows their work with a sacred quality.

Finally, as each of us plumbs spiritual resonances of our work and ministry, we find our faith and our prayers calling us to labor alongside the crucified and risen One. That is, we discover that, as we work with God's people, we minister within the ambience of God's presence and grace; we find ourselves _being in God's gracious presence._ Here the kingdom of God, as the sacred ambience for client, counselor, and the healing relationship, comes to the fore. The ultimate environment for our lives and ministry is seen to be God's gracious and healing love. Ministry itself is "grasped" by God; in God, we live, move, and have our being.

These three Christological aspects of pastoral care and counseling—being God's presence, finding God's presence, being in God's presence—require more reflection and prayerful study, to be sure. Precise elaboration of them will be an important future task. I propose them here as part of our "conversation," because they have emerged in my own reflection on experiences which ground my pastoral ministry. They have also become part of my experience of prayer, as I try to maintain and nourish spiritual rootedness for min-istry, which is funded by my sense of call to partnership in what God is doing and inviting. It is my hope that others, joining this conversation through exploration of their own experience, will contribute to our understanding of the Christological basis for a spirituality of pastoral care and counseling.

A Practical Consideration

It may prove useful for the reader to have some sense of how such a spirituality might operate in the concrete. An example, I refer to often is the case of "Rob."

Rob is a twenty-six year old, white, male, graduate student. He initially came for pastoral psychotherapy in order to address issues of depression, estrangement from his family, and social isolation. The details of this young man's life and symptoms are not as important as the process that ensued between us.

Rob's was a story of unremitting loneliness and schizoid withdrawal, yet it was a narrative laced with desire for warmth and relationship. His presentation, however, was anything, but helpful. He would sit for long periods of silence during sessions. His responses to questions were both brief and guarded, followed by relapse into withdrawal. He periodically expressed frustration at his inability to relate more appropriately, but seemed incapable of doing more. His self-presentation demonstrated the loneliness and isolation that characterized his life. I, for my part, could feel both the loneliness and the desire for closeness in the room. I could feel the frustration as well. A number of sessions continued in this way.

It is my habit to pray regularly for my clients and to search in times of prayer for generative ways to be with them (Oliver J. Morgan, "Pastoral Counseling and Petitionary Prayer," _Journal of Religion and Health_ 26:2 [1987], 149–152). Actively bringing clients into my relationship with God in prayer helps me to keep in perspective the _pastoral_ dimensions of my work. It should be no surprise to state that I was beginning to feel depressed, bored, and resentful toward Rob. Being with him was making me feel helpless and paralyzed. I began to dread our time together each week, as I felt more isolated and my presence seemed futile. Nevertheless, I brought Rob and our situation to prayer. I needed something to help me break the logjam.

I was unprepared for what happened. In the midst of trying to speak about my dilemma in prayer, a strong sense of "companionship" enveloped me. In rapid succession, a series of "understandings" came to me. I had felt this loneliness and inability to "break through" in my own life. In those moments, God had reached out and "grasped" me. God longed to do the same for Rob, and perhaps could do so through my ministry. I need not carry all the burden of this task myself; God's grace enveloped both of us and our work together. And, I understood something else, too. Rob's brokenness and struggle wore the visage of Christ and his sufferings. The Lord was appealing to me through Rob's suffering.

With the dawning of this knowledge in prayer, much of my own frustration and paralysis drained away. The task had been given new meaning and vision. I was able to identify emphatically with Rob's struggle, I was able (at least to some extent) to entrust our time together to God's grace as the environment for our work. And, I decided to take a risk with our fragile alliance as a way to build trust.

Our next session began with the usual silence. In contrast, however, to my previous inner attitude, I prayed calmly and felt again quiet assurance of God's companionship. After a brief time, I shared with Rob my previous frustration, my sense of the feelings in the room, and my desire to understand him and be helpful. Abruptly, the mood in the room changed. Rob began to talk, hesitantly at first, but with genuine effort to "make contact." Something powerful had changed in our relationship. I do not intend to convey a dramatic change in our relationship or course of treatment. There was much hard work to do and periodic relapses into withdrawal. However, our therapeutic work over the next year and a half was significantly affected by the growing trust and alliance that began on that day. The pastoral vision and sensitivity evoked in prayer were crucial elements in the ministry that was our therapeutic work together.

Conclusion

It has been my intention to stay close to personal experience and reflection in this "conversation." I believe that such an "experience-near" exercise can be helpful in approaching questions of pastoral identity. I believe, too, that such an approach can be a fruitful starting point for contemporary pastoral theology.

I have stated here that attention to one's personal experiences of healing and salvation can invigorate both vision and practice in pastoral ministry. These experiences can often function as keystones for a spirituality that underlies and nourishes pastoral action. As we come toward the end of our conversation, a few summary words are in order.

Earlier, I defined "spirituality" as a lively blend of vision and praxis, a stance or posture that combines prayerful listening, discernment, and decision-making in an intentionally God-ward and neighbor-ward way. As the "conversation" proceeded, I spoke of personal metaphors of woundedness and healing as touchstones for an experience of "grateful response." In our exploration, I noted that qualities of compassion, steadfast love, and faithfulness arose in ministries rooted in such personal experience. I noted as well a Christological basis for both ministry and identify; Christology anchors both personal and ecclesial spiritualities for ministry.

The notion of a spirituality for ministries of pastoral care and counseling has received scant attention in the literature to date. Our "conversation" has been an attempt to begin a dialogue about this important issue. To be sure, such "spirituality" needs further elaboration. The interrelations of personal metaphors with the root metaphors of the Christian tradition will need further clarification, as will the relationship between theology and the practice of ministry. Other forms of spirituality and ways of prayer need to be discussed. Nevertheless, I believe we have made a start by discussing some personal, experiential roots for theology and ministry. It is my hope that such an exercise will evoke continued reflection, dialogue, and prayer, guided by living contact with God's call and our own personal responses.

Oliver J. Morgan[30]

200 • RITUAL IN PASTORAL CARE

The author gives a concise definition of ritual, its meaning and origin, and looks at the pastoral care aspects of liturgy, stating that "for many Christians, the sacraments are the primary meeting place of ritual and pastoral

The Triparted Cross. A decorative cross with three vertical and three horizontal limbs interwoven, all of equal length. The intersections of such crosses resemble the patterns made in basketweaving.

care." He concludes with a look at the use of ritual prayer in the traditional one-on-one counseling relationship.

Many serious students of pastoral care, and of ritual, find any positive relationship between the two, dubious at best. To begin a consideration of ritual pastoral care, therefore, we need to remember the recent nature of these mutual suspicions.

Until about fifty years ago, rituals of church life were closely intertwined with pastoral care. The history of pastoral care paralleled the history of ritual (it could even be said that at times it *was* the history of ritual), for pastoral care was expressed, more often than not, in ritualized forms. After the apostolic era, pastoral response to critical life situations took on, in many case, a ritualized and formal character; pastoral responses to human situations were often judged appropriate or inappropriate by how faithfully they clove to established forms. That pattern held sway for much of Christian history. (John T. McNeill's monumental *History of the Cure of Souls* [New York: Harper, 1951] makes the shift from the personal to the formal in pastoral care very clear. But the shift from personal to formal did not originate with Christianity.)

The last half-century has seen a major change, traceable to at least three influences. Culturally, there has been a growing mistrust of forms and of the authority they appear to represent. In psychological theory, Freud and his followers linked ritual to obsessional neuroses—although ritualized practices were and are clearly visible in many aspects of psychoanalytically-oriented treatment. In religious practice, in pastoral care theory, and especially in clinical pastoral education, there has grown up an insistence that ritual ignores the particular, in favor of the general; and that the use of rituals permits ministers to avoid dealing with difficult interpersonal situations.

In the Presbyterian seminary I attended, pastoral care was taught as a series of formalized behaviors. In situation A, the pastor should engage in activity A; in situation B use B, and so on through the catalogue of human crises. I saw only a few years later that the forms—pastoral care rituals, worship rituals, and even formal clerical clothing—so valued in the Department of Practical Theology at that seminary were avoided and even despised by those most deeply grounded in pastoral care and counseling.

Today specialists in pastoral care, in fact, present no consistent picture in terms of the use of ritual. At a recent conference among such specialists, I spoke with a pastoral counselor who rigorously refused to conduct worship in any such setting, where one of his clients might be attending worship. In addition, I spoke with another who used ritual both in church worship services and in her counseling practice.

Pastoral care specialists have been lax in examining the relationship between pastoral care and ritual in a disciplined way. (A significant and exciting exception is Elaine Ramshaw's *Ritual and Pastoral* [Philadelphia, Pa.: Fortress, 1987].) There is, however, a growing consciousness that pastoral care and church ritual are far more deeply related to each other than has been ordinarily assumed.

Paul W. Pruyser, the late psychologist of religion, who for many years directed the Department of Education at the Menninger Foundation, was troubled by the disuse of ritual in church life. In an essay written for a 1969 *Festschrift* in honor of Seward Hiltner, Pruyser discussed a particular aspect of ritual—benedictions and blessings—in his typically pungent style:

Over the years, in attending worship services, I had gradually become accustomed to ministers terminating their services with a rushed and hardly audible benediction, uttered on the way out from the back of the sanctuary where nobody could see them. And if the benediction was pronounced from the pulpit, audibly and visibly, the spectacle for the beholders was often little more than a slovenly gesture, consisting of only one arm, raised half-heartedly and only half-way up, against the force of gravity to which that poor limb would quickly succumb again. [This experience is evidence] that there has been a steady decay in Protestantism of once powerful and wholesome symbols, or . . . the replacement of symbols by mere emblems. (Paul W. Pruyser, "The Master Hand: Psychological Notes on Pastoral Blessing," in *The New Shape of Pastoral Theology,* ed. William B. Oglesby [New York: Abingdon, 1969], 353.)

Pruyser saw, more clearly than many of his contemporaries, the intimate, subtle relationship between pastoral care and ritual. In tracing that relationship, our first task is to understand more clearly the nature of ritual.

The Nature of Ritual

[A ritual is] an ordered or patterned sequence of interpersonal behavior, often occurring in connection with a particular event or circumstance, performed in the same (or a very similar) way each time it occurs, sometimes embodying a reference to a historical event, and symbolizing—pointing beyond itself to—a value or belief commonly held by the individuals or groups who perform it.

This definition encompasses a wide variety of religious and nonreligious behaviors, from the "Minnesota farewells" affectionately lampooned by Garrison Keillor to the most formal religious ceremonies. It includes the ways a particular family celebrates holidays, birthdays, and anniversaries. It includes such sacramental gestures as the laying on of hands at an ordination or in the giving of a blessing, the joining of the hands of a marrying couple, or the breaking of the bread at a eucharistic celebration. It excludes certain behaviors which, though sometimes called ritualistic, grow out of a particular person's need for defense against unwelcome experience (e.g., the "ritualized" counting or handwashing engaged in

by people suffering from compulsive disorders).

In church bodies with a strong liturgical consciousness, the proper performance of ritual may be carefully defined and described by the church and great value may be placed on performing the ritual properly. In other churches, rituals are equally present, but tend to be considered informal or even casual, rather than formally prescribed. Even such supposedly informal rituals tend to have considerable power, however; and those who develop them will often resist very vigorously any attempt to alter them. Those who deviate may suffer unpleasant social consequences. Any group of people regularly interacting with each other tends to attach to rituals feelings that, to an outsider, seem far more intense than an objective evaluation would warrant. Anthropologist Edward T. Hall calls this *formal* behavior, behavior based on an apparent assumption that there is no other way to do things (Edward T. Hall, *The Silent Language* [New York: Doubleday, 1959]).

Functions or Meanings of Ritual

Rituals provide at least three things felt by those who participate in them to be valuable.

(1) They offer a sense of identity, of "we-ness" which cements the bonds among members of a particular group. People, who can say of themselves that "*we* do things *this* way," have a means of saying who they are and what they hold in common. The traditions of families, the liturgies of churches, and the customs of nations and ethnic groups, all serve this function.

(2) Rituals offer to participants a sense of living in a regular, reliable, trustworthy world. The Christmas decorations are put away with the confidence that these same ornaments and wreaths will be used to decorate the house and the tree, next year. (In many families, the ornaments are put away on the same day each year, perhaps New Year's Day or Epiphany).

(3) Rituals in many cases symbolize a deeply felt reality, a truth about God, self, or life. They take on a kind of life from that reality. Theologian Paul Tillich argued that rituals, like all symbols, participate in the reality of that which they symbolize, and die if the reality behind them dies.

The Formation of Rituals

Any piece of behavior which someone finds

useful, valuable, or even merely pleasant may be "nominated" to become a ritual, but the process is not as conscious as the word _nominated_ might suggest. At first, it may be repeated merely because it has been experienced as appropriate, meaningful, or simply gratifying. Through repetition, the behavior takes on power. Meanings are often added by accretion, collecting over the years. Rituals formed in this way often bypass conscious processes of formation, and (partly because the process is kept out of conscious awareness) take on considerable psychological power. Here the meaning of ritual resembles the function of religion as C. G. Jung saw it: to allow people to be in touch with their in most depths without being overwhelmed by them.

There are other processes of formation. It is possible to invent a ritual by consciously seeking ways of symbolizing a felt reality. Rapid changes in a society and its patterns of relationship may prompt people to create rituals that express, or help to manage, feelings arising in reaction to the changes. Such conscious inventions are attempts to perform a function, which simply accrues or develops in a less intentional process.

In the mid-1970s a committee of the United Methodist Church wrestled with issues of change and produced a book called _Ritual in a New Day: An Invitation_ (Alternate Rituals Editorial Committee of the Board of Discipleship of the United Methodist Church, _Ritual in a New Day: An Invitation_ [New York: Abingdon, 1976]). It included rituals for the dying, for the ending of marriages, and for other beginnings and endings. The strength of the book lay in its approach to previously uncharted areas; its weakness lay in its wordiness. It is characteristic that many consciously invented rituals, including those in the Methodist book, place heavy reliance on the spoken word. Other behaviors are not entirely omitted; one divorce ritual includes removing a wedding ring from the divorcing woman's left hand and placing it on the ring finger of the right hand, thus making the ring "reconsecrated to her freedom" (_Ritual in a New Day_, 92). But the principal reliance is on words; and all too often, the carefully chosen words lack the rhetorical power which frequently seems to come with the words of a ritual that has gradually evolved. (The heavy reliance on words in consciously constructed ritual often narrows or forces the meaning of the ritual.)

In some cases, new conditions and changed circumstances have been well-served by the adaptation and application of an already existing ritual originally evolved for a somewhat different purpose. Such rituals tend to have the emotional power of the original, but they run the risk of making misstatements about the nature of the situation to which they are being applied. If a ritual has been used in one situation and is now applied to another, participants tend to regard this new situation as a mere variant of the first, rather than as something new and different.

Rituals also take on a life of their own, in a process closely akin to what Gordon Allport called "functional autonomy." This may mean that the ritual in question becomes so far removed from its origins that many would call it dead. Long after a ritual has ceased to fulfill the third function cited earlier, it may still fulfill the first two functions. Perhaps one might say that even when theologically dead in Tillich's sense, a ritual may for a time remain alive psychologically.

Ritual and Pathology

Many psychotherapists tend to hold ritual of any kind in contempt. Much psychoanalytic thought has adopted Freud's old assertion that there is a profound connection between obsessional states of mind and religious ritual. Therapists of various persuasions have expressed suspicion of ritual, warning us to be wary of any behavior on our own part that we regularly repeat. They have a valid point; many ritual behaviors can be used as defenses.

At the same time, most therapies and therapists have developed rituals of their own, differing from locale to locale and from one theoretical approach to another. American psychoanalysts tend to avoid the "handshaking ritual" prevalent in our society, while those in Europe tend to shake hands formally with analysts at each session. The ritualistic aspects of analytic meeting rooms, with their "icons of the saints," have frequently been notified. So has the highly stylized language that therapists tend to use to identify members of their own "clubs." In one center where family systems theory is dominant, the use of the word _transference_ is ritualistically avoided.

Psychotherapists often use ritual settings, ritualized language, and even ritualized postures and body movements—largely to keep anxiety at a minimum.

Ritual is not in itself anti-therapeutic. However, using it unconsciously, using it without knowing why one is using it, or using it as a means of exercising power and control can all be anti-therapeutic. Therapists' clients will often ascribe some kind of power to any ritualized behavior; and it is quite possible for a therapist to use rituals of some kind to take the edge off the therapists' own feelings of powerlessness or insecurity, at some cost to the client.

It is clear that some uses of ritual have a pathological basis. Rituals do in some ways serve as defenses against unwanted experience. Defenses, however, are not in themselves pathological, and often serve quite positive purposes. It becomes pathological when defenses are misused or overused.

Pastoral Care Aspects of Liturgy

Many aspects of familiar liturgies have particular meaning for pastoral care. Specialists tend to be more interested in the way ritual may be used in pastoral care and counseling, but an approach "from the other direction" may be more important to parish pastors.

Liturgy in General. Calls to worship, assurances of pardon or absolution, benedictions, and other common elements in a worship service are likely to evoke a deep response from worshipers, even when they are not consciously aware of it. Not long ago, a member of a congregation returned to Sunday morning worship after having been hospitalized for a major heart attack. After the service, she said to the minister, "The opening hymn was wonderful! Everybody sang so enthusiastically, and I felt like I could really lift up my heart and rejoice." The minister properly understood her comment to mean that pastoral care had been extended to this woman through the choice and singing of the hymn.

Among the great figures of the past half-century in pastoral care and counseling, Seward Hiltner was for many years the principal articulator of contemporary pastoral theology. One of his legacies—perhaps his greatest—is his perspectival approach, which affirms that there is no such thing as an instance of pastoral work that has only one meaning (Seward Hiltner, *Preface to Pasto-*

ral Theology [New York: Abingdon, 1959]). All pastoral care among Christians involves, however subtly, a proclamation of the gospel; pastoral care among Jews involves, however subtly, an exposition of Torah. What concerns us here is the way a "shepherding" perspective shows up in rituals primarily intended for some other purpose. The word *shepherding* has been controversial ever since Hiltner decided to use it. Many resent the implications of stupidity or willingness to be part of a herd, which they believe they see in the word. Hiltner's original choice was of course not predicated on those implications but upon biblical imagery and upon the caring, self-giving qualities long associated with such imagery. But the negative implications of the metaphor are undeniable.

Consider again Paul Pruyser's comments upon the way a benediction is delivered. Liturgical theology and pastoral theology are likely to come to similar conclusions about such gestures. In some churches, one can see a benediction delivered with hands at waist height, palms turned upward. In the history of liturgical theology that gesture is a beseeching attitude, the posture used for a prayer of petition. It is quite different from the classical posture for blessing advocated by Pruyser, in which it is clear that the "blesser" is giving something to someone. From the point of view of liturgical theology, the petition gesture does not say that the leader is delivering a blessing. The pastoral theologian would probably conclude that the minister has rejected the idea of delivering a blessing in the first place. Contained in that shift is a profound reshaping of the understanding of the nature of ministry.

As William Willimon has pointed out, "every element of the worship service has some potential use as pastoral care" (*Worship as Pastoral Care* [Nashville: Abingdon Press, 1979]). Sermons may grow out of particular pastoral concerns. (When psychologist Harry Levinson worked at the Menninger Foundation, he defined a pastoral sermon as one which adequately described a hurt, put a label on it, and suggested clearly what could be done about it. From a Christian perspective, one might alter that slightly to include what God has already done about it.) Pastoral prayers may come to grips with issues and feelings. Postures, gestures, and ways of handling sacraments may touch upon issues too deep for words.

Sacraments. For many Christians, the sacraments are the primary meeting place of ritual and pastoral care. Many sacraments are symbolic reenactments of some event in the life and ministry of Jesus. (I use the term _sacrament_ also to include what in various denominations are otherwise called "sacramentals" or "ordinances.") Although words accompany and to some extent give specific meanings to sacramental acts, sacraments convey meanings "too deep for words." One act may "contain" a very wide variety of meanings simultaneously.

The Eucharist, in particular, speaks to people in countless different ways about a variety of ideas and themes central to their faith and their lives. Because it is primarily a congregational sacrament, it often conveys the idea of membership, incorporation in a community, which may be powerfully felt by persons temporarily isolated by illness or other circumstances. Because its symbols are common food and drink, it usually conveys the idea of sustenance. Because, unlike baptism, it is repeatable, it is available to believers at a wide variety of times in life. To administer the Eucharist is thus often a powerful act of pastoral care (even though, it is many other things, as well).

A consideration of the pastoral care aspects of the sacraments includes the recognition that their use is not without risk. The use of the Eucharist with the sick must be very carefully planned and needs prior interpretation. Every hospital chaplain has seen hospitalized believers terrified at the appearance of a minister with the elements of communion—it has felt to them like an omen of impending death. An almost converse risk is that ritual may be interpreted by more naive congregants as an act of magic, with _automatic_ saving power, as if God could be manipulated by it. Such an interpretation gravely undercuts its value as an aspect of pastoral care.

The Use of Ritual in Pastoral Care and Counseling

Pastoral counselors and counseling agencies surround their clients with rituals. The routines of the office, the waiting room setting, the patterned way of beginning an hour, and other such regularities all form rituals, in which client and counselor alike participate. To be sure, such rituals are of a slightly different sort than those we have been discussing, but they convey similar meanings. In particular, the rituals used in a counseling office provide a sense of identity and regularity, which may be reassuring or annoying to the client. (More often it is reassuring.)

When we approach the use of ritual in pastoral care and counseling, we are treading on more difficult ground. It may be useful to cite two concrete incidents, one in the context of pastoral counseling, the other of pastoral care.

The first took place in the context of a pastoral counseling center, where a counselor was working with a middle-aged client, whom we shall call Eloise. In one session, the hour was almost over. Eloise, frightened about her immediate future, was talking about her fears. Part of the fear came from her own past and her unusual childhood; part of it came from real dangers she was facing. She got up to leave, reached the door, and turned to stare at the pastoral counselor with a particularly intense look. The counselor remembered how often Eloise had spoken of her attachment to Zenna Henderson's "people" stories.

The client, whose relationship with her own congregation was conflictual, would have rejected a "church" ritual, although she was a woman of faith. The counselor touched her forehead, and quoting a line of blessing from a Zenna Henderson story very familiar to Eloise, said, "Go under the Protection." Months later, as the work was terminating, the client asked the counselor if she remembered the moment, and the counselor said, "Yes." "That," said the client, "was what turned everything around. I knew then that I could make it."

The other story comes from a theological seminary, where a professor of New Testament took a strong pastoral interest in his students. Birgit, a student in her mid-thirties, realized with dismay that her marriage was irretrievably lost. She secured a divorce, but for more than a year afterward went about her work in the classroom crippled by guilt. She undertook a summer quarter of clinical pastoral education, but her supervisor reported similar "crippling" in that setting. When she returned to school, the professor provided pastoral care for her in several conversations. One day, after a conversation with his colleague in the Pastoral Care Department, the professor decided to offer a ritualized form of care to Birgit. Student and instructor planned the brief ritual together, but the professor told her that he wanted to be free to handle some aspects of the event in his own way.

The professor, in alb and purple stole, stood with Birgit and a dozen of her friends in the seminary chapel. The group read a prayer of confession in unison, and the professor read an assurance of pardon. Then he handed her a canvas book bag, which she held open. Into the bag, the professor and the friends dumped pictures, books, and other items connected with her marriage. Then they stood silently for a few moments as Birgit held the now very heavy bag.

Then one of Birgit's friends took one handle of the bag and shared the weight. Again they stood that position for a few moments, and then the professor reached over and drew Birgit's wedding ring (which she had put on for the ritual) from her finger, and dropped it in the bag. Again, in silence, they held their positions. Finally, in what to Birgit was a surprise, the professor brought out a large pair of garden shears and severed the handles of the bag. It dropped to the stone floor with a thud.

Birgit knelt, and the group gathered around in silence, laying their hands on her head. After silence, the professor said, "Go in peace," and the group quietly left the chapel. The difficulties did not disappear overnight, but Birgit later said that this ceremony had marked the beginning of her healing.

Several issues connected with the use of ritual in pastoral care and counseling are visible in these two stories. Whether what was done in either case was wise or valid will of course depend upon the point of view from which one starts. For example, a pastoral counselor working from a psychodynamic perspective will probably find the blessing given to Eloise a problem. What was the meaning of the client's intense stare? Is it not probable that her look was an expression of transference, that she wanted her counselor-mother to save her from her anxiety? That, of course, is quite possible.

The counselor saw it differently. Though not unaware of transference issues, she knew that Eloise saw her and knew her as a clergywoman of Eloise's own denomination. She had already preached and baptized a baby in a worship service, where Eloise was in attendance. More than anything else, she saw her primary identity as that of pastor and chose to function with the ascribed power of the pastoral role. A far more urgent question in the counselor's mind was whether Eloise could accept and integrate any blessing. In retrospect, it seemed clear that the blessing and the "protection" were used by the client to provide a firm "working place" from which to wrestle with a number of anxiety-provoking issues.

It is interesting to contrast the scene in the counselor's office with the one in the seminary chapel. The post-divorce ritual was an instance of pastoral care in ritualized form, extended in a group setting (involving the recipient's relevant community of faith), while the "Henderson blessing" took place in a pastoral counseling context and involved only counselor and client. Those are significant differences. Transference, though present in the teacher-student relationship, was not an issue or a problem in the ritual; and the professor's standing as a representative figure in a faith community was made even clearer by the invitation to other members of the faith community to be present.

A useful principle can be surmised from this discussion. In a pastoral care context, the minister is functioning as a figure representing a faith community, and members of the community may even be present. In a pastoral counseling context, the relationship is more personalized and almost never are representatives from the community present. This does not necessarily mean that a pastoral counselor should never use a ritual of some sort; but it is a caution against careless use that can easily be misinterpreted.

Prayer

The single most frequent question raised about ritual in pastoral care and counseling has to do with prayer. Typical is the instance of the client in a church-sponsored counseling center. She was a moderately active member of a congregation that called itself evangelical; the counselor was a minister in the same denomination, but not connected with her particular congregation. After several months of satisfying work, she suddenly reported to the counselor that some of her friends were advising her to terminate work with him because he was not praying with her at every counseling session.

Typical, too, is this story of the recently ordained minister, who regularly prayed with everyone he visited in homes and hospitals. He was astounded when one of the elderly women he called on asked him _not_ to pray with her. He was inclined to attribute the request to a supposed lack of religious conviction on her part, until she pointed out that the things he prayed about were seldom her real concerns.

These two true stories serve as a caution that _always_ and _never_ are dangerous words to use in any instance of pastoral care. Those who always pray or who never pray (aloud) run the risk that we always run when we substitute routines for thinking. Prayer in pastoral care situations need to be based on the attitudes and needs of the parishioner.

That caution extends to the way in which prayer is offered. Nico ter Linden tells the story of an uneducated, deeply religious Catholic, who on his death bed pleaded with his priest, "Cain't ya please stop prayin' out of book?" (_In the Lord's Boarding House_ [Nashville: Abingdon Press, 1985]). But he also tells of one of his own Dutch Reformed parishioners, who insisted that the Christmas Eve service was not complete unless the minister used the ancient Latin formula, _Puer nobis natus est._ Ministry to particular individuals depends on the pastor's knowledge of those individuals' particularities.

In pastoral counseling, there are likely to be fewer situations, in which prayer will seem appropriate, primarily because people struggling with difficult issues often have a tendency toward the use of prayer, either as a defense or as magic to avoid facing difficult problems or to alter situations magically. The underlying principles are the same, however. Always praying or never praying are both loaded with dangers. There is no substitute for being aware of, and thinking carefully about, the particularities of the individual one is working with.

We often long for rules, which will tell us specifically, definitively, what we should and should not do. That longing is built, by the way, on the same dynamic foundations as the neurotic use of rituals of which psychoanalysts are so suspicious. No absolute rules can be offered. But we are in a position to set down some general principles which can guide counselors and caregivers.

Any given ritual may have a meaning for the person who decides to use it different from meanings held by other participants. Thus it is impor-tant that the participants make sure that their use of the ritual has a similar meaning to all involved.

Rituals which involve only two people are likely to carry with them more dangers, than those which involve other representatives of a community. Whenever a community puts in the hands of some representative person the authority to conduct particular rituals, that person will be seen as having some kind of power. Psychologically, this process is akin to the transference; sociologically, it involves what is called ascribed power. Situations involving transference or ascribed power always carry the possibility of misuses, a possibility which is decreased when more than two people are involved. This is particularly true of rituals involving body movement and/or touch.

Nevertheless, the value of touch is very great, particularly in situations involving anything approximating a blessing. Praying with sick or grieving folk and offering them a blessing or a benediction ought whenever possible to involve touch. Pruyser writes, "most pastors . . . do [this] almost instinctively, because they know 'in their bones' that tragic situations always call for some kind of touch, some kind of effortless self-giving, some direct, primitive, unreflected, spontaneous spilling over of affect into the motor system" (Willaim B. Oglesby, ed., _The New Shape of Pastoral Theology_ [Nashville: Abingdon Press, 1969], 362).

Although rituals may be constructed for a specific situation, it is valuable to make use of already existing rituals whenever possible. Sometimes it isn't possible. No ritual exists for a given situation; or the ones that do are inadequate. But in general something that is done once to meet a specific need (a) is not a ritual in the first place, and (b) will probably be constructed with too little regard for principles underlying good use of words or of movement.

Pastoral care is deeply and powerfully associated with ritual, a fact that we are only recently beginning to recover. There exists—there has always existed—danger that rituals will be misused, but principles do exist for the guidance of pastors and counselors. Meanwhile, there are dangers ever deeper in avoiding and neglecting this fundamental pastoral resource.

Kenneth R. Mitchell[31]

201 ♦ HUMAN SITUATIONS IN NEED OF RITUALIZATION

Ritual responds to the human need to negotiate times of change, to reaffirm the world of meaning in tragic and meaningless situations, and to mark transitions in life's journey. Yet some of our rituals do not seem to reach far enough; and there are still other situations for which there is no ritual at all. This article looks at shortcomings in ritual and offers some suggestions about how ritual might better support situations of pastoral care.

The story is familiar.

John and Mary have long awaited the birth of their first child, only to have the delivery end in stillbirth. Distraught, they summon the chaplain and request the stillborn child be baptized.

In this case and a hundred more like it, people engaged in pastoral ministry are confronted with a dilemma. How can we honor the deep need people feel for ways to ritualize what they are experiencing, when the only ritual at hand is theologically inappropriate or pastorally inadequate or when there is no ritual at all? Continuing efforts to find appropriate rituals for difficult cases, such as stillbirth and divorce, reflect the urgency of this pastoral question today. There are other areas of pastoral need for ritual as well, such as puberty or coming-of-age, leave-taking, grieving, and significant transitions in self-understanding. The recent series on *Alternative Futures for Worship* not only reconsiders traditional sacraments, but also includes a set of alternative rituals as a point of departure for discussion (Bernard J. Lee, ed., *Alternative Futures for Worship* [Collegeville, Minn.: Liturgical Press, 1987]).

This pastoral need for ritual is being felt at a time when rethinking old ritual ways has opened the possibility of a fresh approach to the need for revised or new rituals. The fields of liturgy and pastoral care share a revival of interest in ritual and its role in the society around us. There is, it would seem, a widespread interest in the return to ritual. This article has two purposes: to offer some preliminary reflections on that return to ritual and what it implies, and then to suggest several questions for the continuing discussion of situations in need of ritual.

Return to Ritual

Beginning in the late sixties, long-standing traditions were questioned in some segments of our culture. Received rituals that had embodied and sustained the central values of the culture and our individual and collective sense of identity within it were set aside. It happened in the society at large, but it also happened in the Roman Catholic church. It was an uncertain time as the church left behind long-standing ritual forms and practices and adopted revised liturgical rites. In the society and in the church, there were those who insisted that ritual is contrary to the freedom of the individual because it tends to standardize experience. Others believed they had outgrown the need for ritual.

But even as ritual ways of the culture were being significantly altered or even discarded, the need for ritual continued to reassert itself. The human potential movement soon learned to create its own set of rituals; protest movements quickly ritualized their songs, chants, and marches; liberation movements developed greeting rituals and other rituals that fostered collective commitment; and those outside the church found ways to celebrate significant moments in human life with revised religious rituals. While it was a time of great upheaval and change, the change was more apparent than real. Traditional rituals were discarded, only to be replaced by what

The Cross Patonce. A beautiful decorative cross often found in needlework and church bulletins.

Hine has called "self-generated rituals."

We are, then, at something of a watershed. Even though traditional rituals have been abandoned or significantly altered, the human need to ritualize has survived and is finding new ways of expressing itself. As old ritual undergrowth is cleared away, new ways of ritualizing are being shaped for life in a changing world and church. What is even more significant is that we have rediscovered a wider human need for ritual in all aspects of life. And that discovery has opened up new opportunities. The recognition of the pastoral need to help people ritualize significant moments like stillbirth or leaving home comes at time of new-found freedom from old ritual forms.

The disciplines of pastoral care and liturgy have also gained new insights and resources from psychology and anthropology for revitalizing ritual. Not too many decades ago the reigning attitude in psychological and psychoanalytic circles, following the lead of Freud, was that ritual is either a form of pathological compulsion or a repressive mechanism used to avoid the growth-inducing ambiguities and tensions of life. Credit for reversing this negative assessment of ritual belongs primarily to Erik Erikson. He developed a theory of ritualization that regards ritual behavior as a normal, normative part of healthy human growth and development. For Erikson, ritualization is "an agreed-upon interplay between at least two people who repeat it at meaningful intervals and in recurring contexts," an interplay which had "adaptive value for both participants." Various aspects of the capacity to ritualize are acquired step-by-step, from infancy into adulthood; and ritualization is itself key to coming to full psychosocial development as a mature individual capable of bonding and generativity.

This revived appreciation of ritual did not stop with Erikson. Interest in the social aspects of individual dysfunctions in general and of pathologies such as schizophrenia in particular, led to a study of systemic, ritualized patterns of verbal and non-verbal communication in families and other groups. More recently, the emerging literature in family systems theory has focused more broadly on the role ritualization plays in the life of human systems, not only for its diagnostic or therapeutic purposes, but also for the positive contribution ritualization makes to the healthy functioning of the group. These developments in the social sciences are reflected in the field of pastoral care. There is an increasing recognition of the human need for ritualization in the process of conversion as people mature in faith within the community of believers.

Liturgical interest in ritualization has also revived during the past two decades. The Second Vatican Council renewal set Roman Catholic liturgy free from the absolute hold of received ritual forms and called for more attention to the human, communicative dimensions of the rites. Liturgists turned to anthropology for their first dialogue partners on the role of ritual in human life and discovered the work on rites of passage pioneered by Arnold van Gennep and developed more recently by Victor Turner (van Gennep [1960]; Turner [1969; 1972]). The triple pattern of separation-transition-reincorporation identified by anthropologists gave liturgists a new way to look at the sequence of every celebration. Moreover, liturgists have discovered in this pattern a paradigm which places liturgy in a larger context. Rites of passage lead from daily life into a time of transition, or liminality, and back into daily life. In a broader sense, when life is understood as process or journey, rituals serve to mark significant moments of transition. In the same way, liturgical celebration is not an isolated event; it is related to life outside the liturgy. Like all rituals, liturgy marks and facilitates the significant transitions of individuals and community, making their lives a continuing journey of faith and conversion.

This liturgical interest in ritual process became much more pastoral and concrete after the promulgation of the Rite of Christian Initiation of Adults (RCIA) in 1973. The restored catechumenate has provided a phased ritual process which closely parallels typical rites of passage. The RCIA describes the initiatory process as an inner spiritual journey of faith and conversion marked outwardly by periodic ritual celebrations (_Roman Ritual_ [1988], 4–6). Pastoral implementation of the rite has spawned a growing body of literature on the journey of faith and conversion to unfold within the ritual process of the RCIA. Furthermore, the RCIA has helped theologians to see that sacraments are not isolated events, but part of a larger ritual process. Taking the RCIA as a paradigm, liturgists are now exploring process models for other sacraments as well.

As a result of these new insights into ritualization from anthropology and the social sciences, liturgy and pastoral care now have new resources to offer pastors in dilemmas like the one presented by the request of John and Mary to baptize their stillborn child. Faced with people who need to express their human experiences of growth and transition spiritually in situations where there are no traditional rituals, pastors now have a new opportunity and an awesome freedom to draw on the resources of tradition and the human sciences to meet those pastoral needs in a new way. There are, however, complex questions that accompany this new freedom. I intend to explore briefly three such questions concerning human situations in need of ritualization. What is a ritual? How can we identify situations in need of ritualization? And what strategies and resources do we need in order to respond pastorally to those situations?

What is a Ritual?

Discussion about situations in need of ritualization usually focuses on specific cases, rather than on prior questions about ritualization. We assume that we already know from experience what ritual is and how it functions in our lives. The aim of the discussion is then to identify the potential need for ritualization and to determine what kinds of ritual are on hand to meet those needs. I would like to reverse that procedure and start with our assumptions about ritual.

What is ritual? Though definitions vary widely, several themes are common enough to describe ritual for our purposes. Ritual is a patterned series of symbolic actions, which members of a group use repeatedly, especially in critical, significant moments of life, to express and enact the story out of which they live, the hopes that give them purpose, and the shared beliefs, values, and sense of meaning that shape their world and their lives in it. Because its words and actions are highly symbolic, ritual speaks more to the heart than to the head. Ritual is born for communication; it is made to be shared.

With slight alterations, religious ritual fits this same description. Religious ritual is used by a particular community of faith. The community believes that it performs the ritual in response to God's call or because it believes that the ritual, at least the words and actions which form its core, has been given to it by God. Those gathered for the ritual believe that God is actively present with them through the ritual as they tell and enact their story, affirm their hope for the future, and commit themselves to the shared values and meaning which are to mark their life in the world.

Why do we ritualize? There are at least three functions that rituals perform. First, ritual serves to invest a situation with meaning or create and maintain a world of meaning for us. We need ritual both when the ambiguities and paradoxes we experience in life seem to render our world meaningless, when its meaning is so apparent that it cannot be left unsaid, and also when its meaning is so overwhelming that it cannot be said in ordinary speech. A second function of ritual is to help individuals and groups negotiate times of transition. We need ritual to provide us with a sense of identity, particularly in significant moments of change. A third function is to bond a group together by the repeated sharing of a common story, meaning, identity, and purpose. We need ritual to survive and flourish as a community.

Religious ritual functions in a similar fashion. It affirms that life is truly invested with the meaning ascribed to it by the community's faith. It sustains participants in their identity as believers, helping them to see life transitions as moments of transformation in a journey of faith. And finally, ritual gathers people in God's presence, making of them a people called to be God's own.

An interplay between continuity and change runs throughout this understanding of how rituals function. Rituals help individuals and groups negotiate moments of transitions. The outcome we most commonly expect from ritual is that of continuity. Rituals reaffirm the meaning of life, maintain individual and group identity in the midst of change, and keep the community stable and cohesive. But there can be another outcome as well. Discontinuity, rather than continuity, with the past may be the outcome when an individual or a group undergoes more radical change and adaptation to new situations. There are, then, two major theoretical orientations toward the function and purpose of ritualizing, one seeing ritual as "a mechanism of continuity, a way of countering change" and the other regarding ritual as "affording change via adaptation or integration."

This opens into a final, more troublesome question about ritual. Both of these theoretical orientations assume that ritual remains constant, untouched by the changing situations it helps us to negotiate. But what if ritual itself is caught up in change? Ronald Grimes has recently noted that rituals do change, contrary to our popular assumption. In addition to the well-established, mature forms in which we normally experience our rituals, they also have their nascent and senile stages. Nascent ritual, in particular, often escapes our notice. To allow for the growth and development of ritual, Grimes rightly suggests that we speak of ritualization, rather than of ritual.

This question is particularly pertinent in our day, when time-honored rituals and ritual ways have been discarded and new rituals generated in their staid. What is the function of such changing ritual? Should we shape our ritualizing to promote stability and continuity in an era of transition or to foster individual and group adaptation against the conservative pull of tradition? How can we identify and nurture nascent rituals? And for the purposes of our discussion, should we then reverse the sequence we are following and attend first to particular situations of need, since they may in fact call for a kind of ritualization that does not yet exist? These questions deserve a larger discussion than we can afford here. At a minimum, however, we ought to heed Grimes' recommendation and attend to the need for ritualization, leaving open the possibility for nascent ritual and the particular forms it might take.

Situations Needing Ritualization

How can we identify the situations in which people are in need of a way to ritualize what they are experiencing? What clues are there? What criteria can we use? I believe there are a least four criteria that might help us identify such situations.

First, there will probably be a need of ritualization in moments of significant transition. In negotiating such moments, people are wrestling with issues of continuity and change. Two cases help to illustrate this.

(1) Though Dan and Julie, soon to be married, are both college graduates, they seem to be so young to their parents. Julie is the baby of the family, the last to leave home. Dan is also the youngest child; his four brothers and sisters are unmarried, though his oldest sister was married and is now divorced. Dan and Julie have asked that their wedding ceremony include a parental blessing, a customary ritual in his family.

Both Dan and Julie have struggled with their changing relationships to their families of origin. Ordinarily the various blessings of the wedding ceremony focus on the couple's joining together to form a new family unit; the ritual is a public seal of the private process of marital bonding that has taken place and will continue. At the same time, however, another process has been silently unfolding for Dan and Julie in relation to their families of origin. They have become aware that their preparations for marriage have intensified for them the process of leaving home in a new and final way. Because they wanted to ritualize both processes, Dan and Julie asked that the liturgical rite which blesses a critical moment in the coming-together process include a parental blessing of this significant moment in the leaving-home process. We need to recognize in our wedding rituals that getting married is often an experience of discontinuity, as well as continuity.

(2) Bill and Ann, the parents of three pre-adolescent children, have gone through a long and bitter separation now ending in civil divorce. Despite their attempts to shield them, the children are taking the break-up of the family badly. Separately, both parents have asked the pastor if anything can be done to bring about some measure of healing.

In this case, the transition to be ritualized for Bill and Ann was one of radical change—the departure from their married state. They needed a symbolic statement to acknowledge the separation; they also needed to ritualize the reality of forgiveness in the midst of separation and grief. The hoped-for outcome for their children, in contrast, was one of continuity in the midst of the terror of separation and the dread of abandonment. The children needed the assurance of a continued parental relationship. Although a single ritual of healing may not satisfy both needs in such situations, it is important that we continue to explore ways of symbolizing continuity and discontinuity in the same ritual.

Second, ritualization will be required when there is a significant need to express or discern the meaning of our lives. This is only natural, since the rituals we perform and the stories we often tell as part of our rituals, codify life's meaning for us. The need may manifest itself in either two situations. In the first instance, we need a ritual expression when our life is filled with a sense of meaning and purpose, as in the following case.

In response to a call in the parish bulletin, Greg and Karen, a young couple, volunteered to help staff a newly formed youth ministry. Fresh from a series of training weekends and an optional course in adolescent psychology at a local college, they have just taken up their ministry without any fanfare. But it seems strange to them to begin this ministry without some public celebration of their new undertaking.

For Greg and Karen, the absence of ritual acknowledgment seemed to diminish the significance of their ministry. Ritual can lift up the meaning, we already experience in life events and place a public seal on it. The case of John and Mary given above points to another need—the need to ritualize in times of ambiguity, when life seems meaningless. Parents like John and Mary, who have experienced the death of an infant, clearly understand meaningless suffering and instinctively look to ritual to help them live through the experience and search for its meaning.

Third, there will be a need for ritualization in situations which call for personal commitment and group support. Rituals provide members of a group going through major transitions a safe place to face both the risks and the new possibilities inherent in such moments. Commitment is most easily made in the context of mutual support. Greg and Karen, the young couple entering youth ministry, needed the support of their parish community to sustain their commitment. Furthermore, as experience with the RCIA has shown, a reversal of roles often occurs and those making the commitment can become a source of challenge and support to the rest of the community to recommit themselves.

In the early years of their marriage, absorbed by career demands and the cares of raising two young children, Laura and Tom had drifted away from the church. The serious insistence with which their oldest child requested first Eucharist caught them unprepared to face their own religious commitment. They asked the pastor if their daughter could receive first Communion during a home Eucharist, before the public celebration for her class in church.

The commitment of their child was a challenge to Laura and Tom, and they needed to draw strength for their own recommitment from her first Communion. Though first Eucharist is the completion of initiation into the community of faith, the pastor recognized that Laura and Tom also needed a way to ritualize the return to active membership to which their daughter had called them.

Fourth, when a significant experience unfolds over a period of time, there will be a need to mark the important thresholds ritually. As study of the rites of passage suggests, we need rituals to name a journey as we enter into it, to nurture and sustain the journey as it unfolds, and to seal and mark the journey at its completion. For Dan and Julie, their wedding ceremony had to mark important thresholds in the simultaneous processes of leaving father and mother and cleaving to a spouse. Greg and Karen also needed to mark their entry into a youth ministry in their parish.

These criteria have been stated rather generically, since both human and religious rituals can be of help when people have a need to ritualize their experience. A liturgical variation on these criteria is apropos, however. There will be a need for liturgical ritualizing in situations where the religious meaning and commitment of one's life need to be discerned or expressed. In those moments, the meaning of our life journey needs to be revealed in God's Word and enacted in a saving deed.

Finally, we should note the apparent inadequacy of existing liturgical rituals to address certain aspects of the experience fully in the cases of the stillborn child, the bride and groom, and the first communicant. To identity situations needing ritualization is only a first step. What strategies and resources do we have to meet these needs? In exploring this question, I will distinguish between situations for which there are established rituals and situations for which no rituals exist.

Strategies and Resources

Where there are existing rituals, the first strategy might be to attend more carefully to the pastoral care opportunities present in each ritual situation. Established rituals of the church are often significant family events as well as rites of passage for an individual in his or her faith journey. As people prepare for a sacrament and celebrate it, there are many occasions to elicit the human story to be marked in the sacrament. Thus, the baptismal naming of a child can also be a moment of story-telling and a symbolic act of the family traditions that helps the parents become aware of hidden hopes they have for the child. Good pastoral care can be attentive to the mid-life transitions that are often taking place in the parents of those receiving first sacraments or confirmation. Enabling people to tell their story during rites of pastoral care of the sick, wakes, and funerals is a way of bringing closure to a particular life and creating a cherishable memory for those who survive (Anderson and Foley [1988]). Ritualizing the experience of leaving one's family of origin adds a significant dimension to the celebration of marriage. Thus, in the case cited above, Dan and Julie each shared a private moment of blessing and farewell with their parents during the rehearsal; and there was a joint parental blessing of the new couple during the wedding. Pastoral sensitivity to such opportunities surrounding the ritual cannot help but have an impact on the ritual itself. Eliciting the stories and needs of people as we work with them to prepare the liturgy will inevitably shape the homily, the choice of texts, and the decisions for pastoral adaptation available in most rites.

Flowing from that, a second strategy is to see the liturgy itself as a public act of pastoral care. A wooden celebration of a sacrament "according to the book" can be an uncaring celebration, with only scant attention to the people who have come to celebrate God's presence in their lives. Liturgical renewal has stressed often enough the elements that are critical in preparing a liturgy in which the people experience care for them in their particular needs. Those elements are attention to the assembly and its active participation, concern that the rite and its symbols are hospitable and fully human, and a prayerful awareness of the presence of God suffusing the assembly and its rituals with holiness. Liturgy celebrated in this spirit ritualizes the need people feel for the presence and companionship of God in the midst of the pain and ambiguity of their lives. Together, these first two strategies offer pastors a way to use traditional liturgical rites to address human needs, which a more "theological" approach to administering sacraments only as a "means of grace" can fail to satisfy.

A final strategy may be to take a cue from the RCIA and explore the possibilities of expanding an existing sacramental ritual into a phased ritual process spread over time to accompany the human journey of people. There are already proposals along those lines for a Lenten process of reconciliation (Hart [1987]; Keifer [1980]), for a more integrated process of caring for the sick and dying (Anderson and Foley [1988]), and for a phased ritual process for marriage (Stevenson [1987], 190–194).

Situations for which there are no existing rituals, such as stillbirth and divorce, present more difficult pastoral choices. The first and most difficult decision, for both individual pastoral ministers and for a church or congregation as a whole, is whether or not to allow and encourage the emergence of nascent ritual in situations for which there have been no liturgical rituals. In wrestling with that decision, it is not helpful to make our ritual choices absolute, e.g., private _or_ public, religious _or_ human, liturgical _or_ non-liturgical. We would do better to envision a continuum of possibilities between these extremes. Situations like miscarriage and rape, for which rituals have been suggested, seem far too personal for a fully public ritual; but a ritual expressing the care and support of a small group in a private setting may be appropriate. Other situations, like divorce, may not be apt for a fully sacramental liturgy. A public liturgical ritual on a par with marriage could appear to negate the meaning a church community sees in the sacrament of marriage; but must a divorce ritual be a "marriage in reverse?" Can we not find room in our pastoral repertoire for liturgical rituals which are both human and religious, which can be more or less public, according to the circumstances, but which stop short of the fully public celebrations we call sacraments? A sacramental theology which holds that the sacramental is larger and more basic than the seven sacraments offers a theological starting point; and the rich tradition of the "sacramentals" provides a paradigm for filling out the continuum. A range of celebrations would allow greater pastoral flexibility in addressing the needs of people.

If a church or an individual pastor does decide to foster new forms of ritualization, what rituals are they to use in the meantime? Waiting for nascent rituals to develop would force people to put their immediate needs on hold. What other resources might we have at hand? A short-term strategy would be to look to our ritual tradition itself for rituals that could be recovered or adapted. For example, it would be possible to ritualize marriage in stages by recovering betrothal ceremonies and other forms of blessing found in earlier tradition or by using the ritual blessings for engaged and married couples often found in a church's occasional services or ritual books, such as the Roman Catholic *Book of Blessings*. These books often contain a wide array of blessings, which can be used or adapted for a variety of circumstances. Experience with rituals for the catechumens in the RCIA suggests that we might easily adapt ritual gestures, such as signing of the senses, blessing, and anointing to other situations.

Finally, if part of a long-term strategy is to encourage new ritual forms to address situations in need of ritualization, we can still look to tradition for a number of ritual patterns to help us give nascent rituals a familiar shape and feel. Ritual tradition has much to teach us about the components of effective ritual, such as symbols, gestures, movements, and patterns of ritual language. Rituals typically begin by summoning the gathered people into God's presence; they unfold in both word and gesture; and they end with a blessing and sending. The words of liturgy are spoken and sung, with interspersed silence. There is a constant dialogue; every address, reading, and prayer dialogue, both ritualized and informal, evokes a response. Ritual prayer expresses the community's memory and hope, in a recital of God's past deeds and application for God's future help. Rituals use communicative action, gesture, posture, and movement. The core actions are drawn from among our most common everyday actions, like touching, bathing, feeding, and lighting a lamp. And finally, like the staged pattern of rites of passage, rituals show an affinity for the great moments of transition in life and easily expand into a ritual process to mark the journey. We do not have to invent the ritual pattern anew each time we face a new situation of pastoral need.

Conclusion

John and Mary, who requested that their stillborn child be baptized, expressed a need to ritualize a tragic moment in their life. The pastoral dilemma in responding to their request is this: to baptize the dead child as a way of ministering to the parents or to withhold the baptism as a way of preserving the integrity and public meaning of the ritual itself. There are honest reasons for both choices. But are these the only choices? In a time

of return to fresh ways of ritualizing the important moments of human need, resourceful pastors are discovering that baptism need not be the only ritual choice in the situation of a stillbirth. Other rituals can be devised from existing ritual resources to help the parents affirm their relationship to the dead child and to enable the process of separation and grieving to take place. Thus, for example, we might fashion a ritual by borrowing the naming ritual from the rite of infant baptism, a gesture of commendation and farewell from the funeral rite, and, from either ritual, prayers placing the child in God's care, such as the prayer in the revised Order of Christian Funerals for those who mourn a stillborn child (*Roman Ritual* [1989], no. 339). The solution is not neat, but it may be the only pastoral choice available, while we wait for churches and those experienced and gifted in pastoral care and liturgy to nurture the growth of nascent rituals more suited to such human situations.

Gilbert Ostdiek[32]

202 • THE CHURCH'S RESPONSE TO ABUSE

The abuse of women is one of the most tragic social problems of modern society and is found both outside and inside the church. The following article describes the staggering proportions of this problem and offers guidelines for the church's response to it.

Before you finish reading this article, twenty-four women in the United States will be battered by a husband, father, boyfriend, or uncle (i.e., one every fifteen seconds). One-fourth of those battered women are pregnant; their batterers typically attack the woman's abdomen, whereas non-pregnant women are most commonly beaten on the face and breasts. Physical violence by family members is the single largest cause of injury to women in the United States. A study in a Connecticut hospital found that almost half the women in the emergency room were treated for beatings by male companions or family members. Estimates are that somewhere between three and four million women each year in the United States are beaten by their husbands, ex-husbands, or boyfriends. By the end of the day, four women will have died of their injuries.

Before you finish this article, a woman in the United States will be raped, most likely by a friend, an acquaintance, a date, or a family member (i.e., one every six minutes). At this rate, almost one-half of the women in the U.S. will be raped in their lifetime. Many of these rape victims are children. Researchers estimate that one out of three girls in the United States will be sexually assaulted or abused by the age of eighteen. Ninety percent of the abusers know their victim: father, stepfather, uncle, grandfather, family friend, babysitter, teacher, minister, priest. One out of seven married women are raped by her husband.

A Fear That Changes Everything

No woman is exempt from the threat of personal violence. We as women all learn to adapt to this reality at the habitual level. We lock doors, check the back seats of cars, and avoid going out at night alone. We avoid making eye contact when walking on public streets. We monitor how we dress, how we move, how we sit. By a thousand such small, deeply internalized habits, we constrict ourselves, restrict our movements, limit our lives out of fear.

Many of us learn, to our everlasting pain and rage, that in reality these measures do not protect us. We are not safe. The lesson that our self-protective behaviors serve us about as well as throwing salt over our left shoulder is a painful one. We learn it by personal experience of violence, by the violation of someone we know, or by intentional confrontation with the literature on the subject. We feel angry; we feel betrayed. It is especially painful for us to think that men we know or love commit this violence.

Nor do we find that our religion or our church protects us from this violence. Difficult as it is for us to believe it, these statistics are true for our church, our parish, our congregation. Violence against women takes place at every socio-economic level, at every educational or professional level, across racial and ethnic lines, in all religions. In every congregation, every parish, are survivors of sexual violence and rapists, women and children who are beaten regularly in their home, and violent men. Yet the church and its leaders are, more often than not, silent. Pulpits do not thunder with denunciations of violence against women and children. Church leaders do not write pastoral letters crying out against woman-battering and

sexual violence. There is no commandment that says, "Thou shalt not rape."

It is more common for batterers to quote Scripture to justify their abuse and to claim that their authority over women is God-given. Religion often silences battered and raped women through instructions from leaders to submit to male authority, to suffer in silence and make no protests, to find spiritual value in their suffering, and to forgive their persecutors. Religion often blames women by associating women with sin, sexuality, and evil. This makes us responsible for violence inflicted on us by someone else. For faithful Christian women, this use of our own spirituality against us is unspeakably painful and provokes a deep crisis of faith.

What change of heart, of life, is needed? True repentance requires the acceptance of responsibility of one's sin. First the batterer or rapist is to be held accountable for his violent behavior and its consequences. This in turn means that it is the church community's responsibility to hold him accountable by a process of repentance and reconciliation. Studies of battering men report that the most effective response to battering is to call the police and file charges. Any other response increases the likelihood that the abuse will be repeated. Therefore, church processes of repentance and reconciliation should not short-circuit legal processes, nor should they offer easy forgiveness. The church should refuse to protect the violent man from the consequences of his actions, demand he make restitution to his victims, and require his participation in intensive training to help him learn a non-violent way of life.

On the institutional and the personal level, the church must be an advocate for women. It must make clear in a variety of ways that any form of violence against women is unacceptable and contrary to the teaching of the church.

It must reinforce these pronouncements with action by training church leaders to recognize and deal with violence against women; by providing and supporting shelters for women and children; by insisting that the use of violence by one partner in a marriage (including rape) breaks the marriage vows; and by refusing to protect men who batter or rape from the consequences.

Friends or ministers of a woman who has survived physical or sexual violence can make themselves available to her for support and help. They can encourage her to take care of her safety and support her if she decides to report the assault to the police. Both clergy and laity need to be informed about the legal rights of battered and raped women. They need to be prepared to support women through the often grueling legal processes. Local congregations can provide safe temporary housing among their members for a woman who chooses to leave an abusive man.

Marjorie Procter-Smith[33]

203 • BIBLIOGRAPHY ON WORSHIP AND PASTORAL CARE

Duffy, Regis. *A Roman Catholic Theology of Pastoral Care.* Philadelphia: Fortress Press, 1983. The basic premise of this book is that "commitment to gospel tasks and responsibilities is a key factor in effective pastoral care." The author looks at the model of the catechumenate as a working foundation for the development of pastoral care. He also looks at Jesus as a *medicus* or "doctor of the soul," suggesting that we adopt this as our model for pastoral care. Although the author does not tie pastoral care and worship together, the focus on commitment, which we hear at the end of each and every liturgy, provides a solid link and much food for thought.

Fowler, James. *Faith Development and Pastoral Care.* Philadelphia: Fortress Press, 1987. Although this book is primarily about faith development and pastoral care, as the title suggests, the author has some excellent chapters that look at pastoral care within the context of the covenant community and its public life. The final chapter of the book looks at how pastoral care is informed and strengthened by the public church: "the vocation of the church, and the vocation of Christians, is to align our efforts as responsible selves, as much as we can, with the purposes and work of God." This is both the stuff of worship and pastoral care.

Green, Robin. *Only Connect: Worship and Liturgy from the Perspective of Pastoral Care.* London: Darton, Longman, and Todd, 1987. This book describes the vast importance of the symbols of Christian worship in shaping and ministering to all people who worship. Such symbols

help persons come to understand both God and themselves and are a vitally significant component of a full-orbed pastoral care program.

Keene, Jane A. *A Winter's Song: A Liturgy for Women Seeking Healing from Sexual Abuse in Childhood.* New York: Pilgrim Press, 1991. A liturgy for a service of healing, together with an introduction to the significance of such a service. The liturgy includes prayers and related texts that could be adapted to a variety of related uses.

Nouwen, Henry J. M. *Creative Ministry.* New York: Doubleday, 1971. This book articulates a spirituality for all types of ministry. The author sums it up by saying that, "whatever form the Christian ministry takes, the basis is always the same: to lay down one's life for one's friends." The author looks at five forms of Christian ministry: teacher, preacher, counselor, organizer, and celebrator. Taken as a whole, the book offers a good foundation for all pastoral care, some of which unfolds during communal worship.

Ramshaw, Elaine. *Ritual and Pastoral Care.* Philadelphia: Fortress Press, 1987. In the series forward, the editor of the series, *Theology and Pastoral Care*, remarks that "we have a book that stands nearly alone in the effort to unearth the pastoral care dimensions of the liturgical life of the church." The author takes a thorough look at ritual in two contexts: as an act of care within the context of community and as an act of care within the context of the individual. She uses concrete, down-to-earth stories to illustrate her points. She concludes by looking at ritual and care for the world.

Stone, Howard. *The Word of God and Pastoral Care.* Nashville: Abingdon Press, 1988. The author's goal is to correlate theology and pastoral care. Although his audience is primarily those who are engaged in pastoral counseling, his treatment of the Word of God, the priesthood of all believers, acceptance and suffering has important implications and parallels for worship and ritual.

Willimon, William H. *Worship as Pastoral Care.* Nashville: Abingdon Press, 1979. The author's premise is that "the pastoral care that occurs as we are meeting and being met by God in worship is a significant by-product that we have too often overlooked." The author discusses the historical separation of pastoral care and worship and what worship is. In addition, he looks creatively at resistance to worship. He then looks at specific forms of worship: the funeral, the wedding, baptism, and Communion. His final chapter examines liturgy and leadership.

EIGHT

Liturgies for Worship and Pastoral Care

Although pastoral care may be extended in every gathering of Christians for worship, there are occasions when particular needs may be addressed by a gathering called to pray for a specific concern or to celebrate a specific occasion. This chapter presents sample liturgies for such occasions. They may be adapted for use in local churches.

204 ◆ A LITURGY FOR THE LONG-TERM SERIOUSLY ILL

This liturgy is designed as a communal celebration of the sacrament of the anointing to take place within the context of a eucharistic liturgy. Family, friends, and, if possible, caregivers are invited to gather with the seriously ill in a place suitable for worship. The primary community of worship, however, remains the ill persons themselves. Care should be taken that the liturgy not be celebrated in such a way that the sick persons become passive observers because of a pace set by the healthy. Care should be taken too that the sick persons gathered achieve some sense of relationship among themselves, in addition to their relationships with family and friends.

Gathering for Worship

As the people gather in the space set aside for worship, music which is soft and inviting and yet which proclaims the presence and comfort of God should be playing. It may be recorded music or music sung by a small group of singers.

As the people gather, the presiding celebrant greets each of the sick in a personal manner and also welcomes the accompanying families and friends. When all are gathered, the presiding celebrant and ministers go to the front and begin the service.

Call to Worship

PRESIDER: My brothers and sisters,
welcome to God's house.
I wish you peace and healing
and the deep strength of our
common faith
in God and in Jesus Christ.
You who are sick especially
are honored guests in God's house.
And we who join you in prayer
are honored to be with you.
May the peace and blessing of God
our Father
and the Lord Jesus Christ be with you.

ALL: **And also with you.**

(The presider goes now to each of the sick and asks in these or similar words:)

PRESIDER: [Name], as you come into God's presence this day, what special prayer do you bring to God?

(Each of the sick is invited to name a special prayer. When all have been given an opportunity to do so, the presider addresses all the sick:)

PRESIDER: You have each named a special prayer of your own, and have heard each other's special prayers. Will you pray for each other that God may bless you all?

(Some word or gesture of assent is invited, for example:)

THE SICK: We will.

(The presider then addresses all who are gathered:)

PRESIDER: And you who gather in love with this blessed community of faith and hope, will join in prayer for all the sick that God will heal them and give them peace?

ALL: **We will.**

Opening Prayer

PRESIDER: Then let us now pray:
Good and gracious God,
in your Son Jesus Christ,
you reach out to the sick
and touch them with your healing power.

Be with us now with this same healing power.
You hear the desires of our brothers and sisters
who come before you in hope and in trust.
You see us all gathered in love before you.

Show yourself once more
a God who blesses and cares and gives peace.
We ask this through Christ our Lord.

ALL: **Amen.**

────────── **Liturgy of the Word** ──────────

PRESIDER: And now let us listen and take comfort in the word God speaks to us.

Reading
(Isa. 43:1-4a)

Responsorial Psalm
(Ps. 63)

REFRAIN: My soul is thirsting for you, O Lord my God.

Gospel Acclamation
(cf. James 1:12)

Alleluia.
Blessed are they who stand firm when trials come;

when they have stood the test,
they will win the crown of life.
Alleluia.

Gospel
(Matt. 11:25-30)
Other appropriate readings, psalms, and verses may be chosen.

Homily

Intercessions

────────── **Liturgy of Anointing** ──────────

Instruction

PRESIDER: My brothers and sisters,
we come now to the time of special grace,
the time of anointing.

The apostle James asked:
"Are there people sick among you?
Let them send for the priests of the church,
and let the priests pray over them,
anointing them with oil in the name of the Lord.
The prayer of faith will save the sick,
and the Lord will raise them up;
if they have committed any sins,
their sins will be forgiven them."

My brothers and sisters
who are sick among us,
it is our privilege as a priestly people
to pray God's healing and anointing upon you.

Know that it is in your power
to offer even your sickness
as a gift of worship to God.
In God's power may you be healed.

Laying on of Hands
Joined by some of the friends and family, the presider goes to the sick one by one, places hands on each of them, and prays silently.

Anointing
(The presider then anoints the sick on the forehead and hands, saying: [anointing the forehead])

Through this holy anointing may the Lord in his love and mercy help you with the grace of the Holy Spirit.

ALL: **Amen.**

PRESIDER: [anointing the hands]
May the Lord who frees you from sin
save you and raise you up.

ALL: **Amen.**

Prayer after Anointing

(When all have been anointed, the presider invites the sick to join hands, if this is possible, during the following prayer:)

PRESIDER: Good and gracious God,
God of love, ever-caring,
we give you praise and thanks
through your Son, Jesus Christ.

In him you show us how much you
love us;
In him you have tasted
the beauty and the pain of all human
life.

Those who were sick came to him
and found healing.
Those who had sinned asked of him
and found your forgiveness.

With oil that is blessed
and hearts that are humbled
we have anointed our sisters and
brothers
here present.

With us at their side
they offer to you
their fears and their doubts,
their suffering and pain,
their human lives, fragile and broken.

Send our own spirit of love upon
them.
Speak the healing words of your Son
to them.
Give them the grace of your loving
presence.

Keep their eyes fixed firmly upon you
in the eager hope and expectation
that with you, and with you alone,
their lives will be transformed.

Where sin and death will be no more,
where sickness and sorrow will be
overcome,
there may we know together

that you are our God,
and we the people you call your own.

All glory be to you, Father,
and to your Son,
and to your Holy Spirit,
now and forever.

ALL: **Amen.**

(If this service of anointing takes place apart from the Eucharist, the Lord's Prayer and a final blessing follow. If it takes place during the celebration of the Eucharist, the liturgy continues as usual:)

Liturgy of the Eucharist

(If possible, while the gifts are brought to the altar or table, some personal effect of each of the sick is also to be brought forward. This serves to unite their own sickness and suffering symbolically with the offering of Christ enacted in the Eucharist.)

(At the sign of peace, where it is possible, the sick extend the greeting to each other.)

(The following orations are suggested:)

Prayer over the Gifts

PRESIDER: Lord our God, giver of all good gifts,
from among the many you have given
to us,
we bring bread and wine to give you
thanks and praise.

In simple gifts we bring all that we are
and all that we hope for.

Look with special kindness
on our brothers and sisters who are
sick among us.
Give them healing and peace.

Be pleased with us and the offering
of our lives.
Unite us to Christ
and his own sacrifice of praise.
We ask this through Christ, our Lord.

ALL: **Amen.**

Concluding Prayer

PRESIDER: Lord Jesus Christ,
you are the beginning and the end
of all God's creation.

You have gone before us to prepare
the way.

Yet you remain among us as companion and friend.

As you have nourished us with your
 food of life,
help us to be strong in faith,
a source of courage to each other,
and a gift of praise
to the God you have revealed.

We ask this in your name,
 for you live and reign forever and
 ever.

ALL: **Amen.**

Pastoral Note

There will, of course, be some who will not be able to participate in this communal form of anointing. For the long-term ill, the regular enactment of this anointing will serve as the *context,* the "world remembered," when they no longer can participate with the others. For these, it would be helpful if some of the "community of the sick" join in the prayer of the anointing. For others too, it would be helpful if some continuity with this communal celebration could be established so that the witness it represents may be a ministry to all who are anointed in whatever circumstances it proves necessary to anoint them. It might be helpful to conclude the communal service with a "dismissal" that sends those who have been anointed to minister in some way to those who were not able to attend. The anointing of these others would then be held as part of the communal celebration itself.

Gerald Calhoun and Peter Fink

205 ✦ A Liturgy for the Families and the Community of the Terminally Ill

The following liturgy is designed for use of those who suffer along with the terminally ill. It is designed both to allow for prayers to be offered for the sick and their families or support communities and for the hope of Christ to be proclaimed.

Introduction

Settings. There are several possible settings for a ritual of this type. They include but are not limited to the parish, the hospital, and the home.

Parish Setting. Staff members associated with the parish health-care ministry will probably not be familiar with the persons for whom and with whom these rituals might be celebrated. Such persons could be invited to participate in a celebration of the sacrament offered only for people confronted with the terminal illness of a loved one. They in turn might be encouraged to invite friends and associates.

Another alternative is to announce the celebration of the sacrament to the entire parish community so that as many persons as possible might be present in prayerful support of those facing the loss of a loved one. This would also allow for participation of persons whose own personal grief may not be generally known. As in the first instance, persons associated with dying patients might be given a more personal invitation to attend.

The ministers in the community ought to be especially mindful of the needs and sensitivities of those for whom the anointing is being offered. It may happen that some will refuse the invitation. This should not be interpreted negatively as, for example, lack of gratitude or weakness of faith. More likely, it will be indicative of the style or stage of coping operative in the grieving persons. In such cases, other pastoral alternatives might be required.

Hospital Setting. Parish ministers assigned to a health-care chaplaincy or pastoral-care personnel might arrange for a celebration of the sacrament for the families and friends of the sick in the hospital chapel or some other appropriate place. Again, participation could be encouraged either by personal invitation or by general announcement. In hospitals and other health-care environments, such as nursing homes, doctors and nurses could likewise be invited to participate. In some situations, it might be appropriate to design a ritual for these helping professionals, who must daily contend with the loss of patients through death.

Home Setting. In some circumstances, it might be advantageous, even necessary, to provide for the celebration of the sacrament in a more private setting. The pastoral awareness and sensitivities of the health-care minister concerning some patients and their families might indicate a need for a personal, intimate ceremony on familiar home territory. The parish or hospital minister might have to suggest such a celebration, rather than wait for the family or friends to request it.

Environment. The specific space designated for the ceremony should be as comfortable and aesthetically pleasing as possible. Creating attitude and atmosphere is essential. Quiet music, soft lighting, and tasteful artifacts, such as candles, plants, flowers, vessels, and table coverings, all contribute their beauty to the graceful celebration of the rite. In the face of sickness and death, the total celebration of the ritual—word, silence, gesture, and environment—must unite in offering healing, hospitality, and hope to participants.

Size. It is probably safe to assume that most celebrations of this ritual would be small. Thus, it is possible, and even desirable, to foster a certain level of informality. Compassion, gentility, and warmth are important qualities. Informal though it may be, however, it is never intended that the ritual be casual. Care must be exercised to ensure a delicate balance.

Tone. A contemplative tone is important to the ritual enactment. Creating a "space before God" in which the participants can simply "be with" God, themselves, their emotions, and one another is best served by a contemplative atmosphere. A gentle, alternating rhythm between sound and silence is to be encouraged.

Length. If for no other reason than the physical and emotional fatigue associated with grief, the length of the service should be approximately one half hour. Celebrations for larger groups may require additional time. However, care should be taken to avoid taxing the already strained energies of the participants.

The following ritual sample is intended to be *both* a single celebration of the sacrament of anointing for family and friends of those who are sick *and* a ritual structure that may be adapted according to the Kübler-Ross stages of death and dying. For this reason, an appendix to the full ritual offers alternative texts for the instruction and Scripture reading to be used at each stage.

Gathering for Worship

Gathering

The presider and other participating ministers greet the assembly at the entrance to the worship space to extend an initial sense of hospitality and welcome. When all are assembled, the ministers enter in procession, accompanied by instrumental music.

Call to Worship and Greeting

PRESIDER: My brothers and sisters:
In the name of our Lord Jesus Christ
I welcome you.
I invite you to come to him who says
to the wary, the burdened, and the sorrowing:
"Come to me and I will give you rest."
Place yourselves now in Christ's compassionate presence.
He desires to share your pain
so that he may sorrow with you
and grant you peace.

May the Lord be with you.

ALL: **And also with you.**

Opening Song

Opening Prayer

PRESIDER: Let us pray.
God of all comfort and consolation,
be with us now in our prayer.
We suffer with those who suffer;
we die with those who die.

Touch us in the deepest recesses of our grief,
in those hidden places we fear to acknowledge
or give to your keeping.

Help us to be compassionate
toward those who are sick.
Help us to be gentle with ourselves.

May we come to understand and accept
the mystery of sickness and death,
which holds our loved one(s) in its grip.

In the fullness of time and in the slowness of our hearts,
speak to us your word of comfort and your word of peace.
We ask this in the power of the Spirit
and in your Son, Jesus Christ, the Lord.

ALL: **Amen.**

Instruction

PRESIDER: The journey of life brings each of us,
at one time or another, to a place of
pain.
Without our will we are brought into
life;
against our will we are forced to confront
the pain of sickness and the sorrow
of death.

Each of you knows the pain associated
with the sickness and death of those
you love.
Your concern is for them,
and yet your own hearts are torn
apart.
Your own lives are disrupted.

This pain and disruption you may
nobly try to deny;
yet it is there. It may bring your anger,
or lead you to bargain with God and
with life
"if only things could be different."
Or it may make you very, very sad.

Yet, however you feel at this moment,
the healing power of Christ seeks to
touch your hearts.
He seeks to lead you to accept and
embrace
this life with all its mystery,
and to discover his love for you
in the midst of this sadness and grief.

May we spend a few moments in quiet
reflection
before our God, and allow ourselves
to experience honestly
and with reverence the feelings that
are uniquely our own.
Let us express ourselves to God in
truth, without fear or shame.

Reflective Silence

_____ **Liturgy of the Word** _____

Reading
(Matt. 26:36-46)

Homily

(The homily is usually given by the presider or by
some other person invited to provide this ministry. In some situations, however, it may be appropriate to invite the participants to share their
reflections on the Scripture reading in the format
of a dialogue homily.)

Psalm/Song of Hope and Trust
(At the end of the homily, some form of common
prayer or song is appropriate as both a conclusion to the Word and a transition into prayers of
petition.)

Prayer of Petition

PRESIDER: My brothers and sisters,
the God to whom Jesus prayed for
deliverance
invites each of us to be healed.
In Jesus we find the hope that makes
us whole
and the promise that life is forever.

God is no stranger to our human pain
and suffering.
In Jesus God has embraced our own
human life
even to the point of suffering and
death.
In Jesus God has become companion
to us
in our own journey through life.
"Behold, I am with you always";
"I make my abode with you."

Unite then your sorrow to the dying
and rising of Christ.
Believe and your faith will make you
whole.
In faith and in hope be companion to
those
with whom you keep vigil,
your loved ones for whom we now
pray:

(All in the assembly are invited to pray in
their own words for their loved ones and for
themselves. If it is helpful, the presider may
form the first several petitions. After the petitions:)

PRESIDER: Loving God,
Lord of all health and wholeness,
you are source of our life
and fulfillment of our death.

We come to you now with varied
  needs.
Into your gentle care we place ourselves
and our loved ones who are ill.

Be for us now
light to brighten our darkness,
strength to transform our weakness,
and comfort in the midst of our pain.
We ask this in the power of the Spirit
through Christ, our Lord.

ALL: **Amen.**

Rite of Anointing

Anointing

PRESIDER: My brothers and sisters,
as a sign of our faith
and in hope for the healing embrace
  of God,
come forward now
to be anointed with holy oil.

May Jesus Christ,
who is infinite compassion,
touch you and bless you,
and give you his healing grace.

(As each member of the assembly comes forward, he/she is anointed on both forehead and hands. The presider prays the accompanying prayer:)

PRESIDER: [anointing the head]
May God heal your own wounds
as you stand in hope
with [Name], who is ill.

[anointing the hands]
May God give you
eyes to see and ears to hear
and hands that you may touch
and bless and understand.

(When all have received the sacrament of the anointing, there follows a brief period of silence.)

Common Prayer
(Ps. 23)

(The service concludes with Psalm 23 recited or sung in common. If desired, the Lord's Prayer or a suitable prayer of praise and thanksgiving may be prayed instead.)

Dismissal

PRESIDER: Signed with the cross of Christ,
and touched with his healing grace,
go forth now from this place
to serve God's people
in compassion, kindness, and love.
ALL: **Thanks be to God.**

Closing Song

Appendix: Alternative Texts for the Stages of Death and Dying

The suggestions that follow are intended to serve in the adaptation of the above ritual to the various stages of death and dying as cited above. Both instruction and Scripture text are to be inserted within the above ritual in their designated places.

ALTERNATIVE FOR STAGE 1: DENIAL

Instruction

The human confrontation with sickness and death almost always meets with some form of denial, at least in its initial stages. We seek to pretend it away. "It can't be happening; it can't be true." This is true for those who fall sick. It is equally true of those who love them.

Our prayer today invites you to look squarely at your own deep reactions to the sickness that has come upon people you love. It may be hard to believe it is happening to them. But since their own sickness reveals how deeply your lives are connected to theirs, you may find it equally hard to believe it is happening to you.

To deny sickness in those who are sick is a refusal to accept them as they now are—especially at a time when they most need to be accepted. To hide your own fears and denial behind well-intended words that promise "all will be well" is in fact a denial of truth and a rejection of those whom you love.

Now more than ever, they need you to be true. Now more than ever you need to be true. Both they and you need to speak in truth, for only in truth will faith be able to speak, hope be able to serve, and love be able to deepen.

Christ does not hide from the deepest truth of our lives. He loves us when we sin; he embraces us when we are sick. Let us spend a few moments in quiet reflection before Jesus Christ and let the truth of what is happening to our loved ones and to ourselves come deeply into our hearts. And let him who is Truth itself comfort us and bring us deep peace.

Reading
(Matt. 16:21-23: Peter denies Jesus' impending suffering and death.)

ALTERNATIVE FOR STAGE 2: ANGER

Instruction
On days when all is well, it is easy to be happy with God. It is also easy to ignore God, or simply to take God for granted. When all is not well, when sickness strikes us or someone we love, we are much more likely to feel betrayed by God and to become very angry.

And our anger goes not only to God, but in so many directions: to the one who is sick ("Why are you doing this to me?"); to the doctors and givers of care ("Why can't you do more?"); to others in the family ("Why don't you do your share?"); and to just about anyone else who may happen to come our way.

Jesus himself was angry in the face of his death: at Judas, who was impatient to betray him; at Philip, who was slow to understand; and at Peter, whose pretended bravery was but a form of denial. And he was angry at God, his Father, who demanded much and yet seemed to abandon him.

If anger fills your hearts this day, place it with him who has known anger and yet passed beyond its grip. Place it with him who quiets all anger and fear with a glance, a touch, a silent word.

Reading
(John 18:10-11: Simon Peter, angry at Jesus' arrest, draws a sword.)

ALTERNATIVE FOR STAGE 3: BARGAINING

Instruction
There is a game we play in the face of sickness and death, perhaps as a retreat into denial or a defense against anger. We bargain with God, with life, with ourselves.

We bargain with the past and fill ourselves with false regrets that we should have done what we did not do. "If only I had . . . ," the bargain goes.

We bargain with the future, making all sorts of promises, equally false, of what we will do "if only . . ."

The irony is that we waste the time that is ours looking for time that is not ours and will not be. And the precious time that is ours, to speak and to care and to love, quickly passes us by.

This time is given to each of us, not to pass it in idle wish or vain desire, but rather:

> to speak, as perhaps we have not spoken before;
> to care, as perhaps we have not cared before;
> to love, as perhaps we have not loved before;
> and to believe deeply and to trust in the ways of God.

This time is given to those you love. This time is given to you. Take it and use it well.

Reading
(Luke 22:41-46: Jesus prays for the cup of suffering to pass from him.)

ALTERNATIVE FOR STAGE 4: DEPRESSION

Instruction
The passage of sickness can be long and tedious, wearing away at all the resources to cope, bear with, endure. A vigil with those who are sick can likewise be long and tedious and likewise wear away one's personal resources. In the end we can grow very tired of it all, and simply sad.

Such sadness or depression can leave us locked

The Cross Pattée. This is one of the most beautiful and widely used of the decorative crosses. It may be used in vestments and church bulletins.

in our own world, a world that has grown smaller as all avenues of escape seemed to close. It is hard to minister to those who are depressed. It is hard to minister when we ourselves are without hope.

In your own vigil with your loved one(s), no doubt your energies have been spent, well spent, yet spent. And if you are sad, it is a sadness you need to understand if you will help someone else to pierce its deep, dark mystery.

You will seem to be surrounded by silence. Yet deeper than silence, and within the silence itself, there waits a word to be heard. A word of courage and a word of hope.

In the silence of your hearts, listen now to the whispers that alone will redeem the sadness. Let the Lord, who has gone before us all, speak gently, yet powerfully, where you need him most to speak.

Reading

(Matt 17:22-23: Jesus speaks to his disciples of his coming suffering.)

ALTERNATIVE FOR STAGE 5: ACCEPTANCE

Instruction

In the Garden, and again on the cross, Jesus gave his life and his sufferings over into the hands of his God. It was not a "giving in," nor even a "giving up." Jesus gave himself over to another, who lovingly and graciously received his gift.

So often we are counseled to accept what is given to us. Perhaps from time to time we counsel others to do the same. But in that word we all too often forget the gift and the giving that acceptance involves. To see suffering, my suffering or the suffering of one I love, as a precious gift I can give in love to my God is the deepest secret of all human pain.

God is not far away from those who are sick nor from those who keep vigil with the sick. God is present most deeply within the pain and the sorrow and the sadness, yearning to make of it all a gift of praise and glory. It takes deep faith and hope and love to give even pain as a gift to God. But such a gift reveals pain's deepest meaning and deepest possibility.

Look at your own pain and the pain of those you love, and listen. From deep within a voice may be heard, even now: "You are precious in my eyes, and honored, and I love you."

Reading

(Luke 23:44-46: Jesus commends his spirit to God.)

Mary Francis Duffy

206 ✦ A LITURGY FOR A PERSON SUFFERING FROM ADDICTION OR FROM SUBSTANCE ABUSE

The problems of addiction and substance abuse are among the most severe problems facing our culture today. Whereas some worshiping communities have remained silent about members who may be faced with these problems, worship services, such as the one outlined here, that identify the problem, offer prayers on behalf of those who suffer, and proclaim the hope that Christ embodies may be important occasions for healing and renewed commitment for those who suffer and for the whole community.

Gathering for Worship

(When the community has gathered, a suitable song may be sung. After the singing, the minister says:)

> In the name of the Father, and of the Son, and of the Holy Spirit,

(All make the sign of the cross and reply:)
Amen.

(A minister who is a priest or deacon greets those present in the following or other suitable words, taken mainly from sacred Scripture:)

> The Lord be with you.

ALL: **And also with you.**

(A lay minister greets those present in the following words:)

> Let us praise God our Creator, who gives us courage and strength, now and forever.
> Amen.

(In the following or similar words, the minister prepares those present for the blessing:)

> God created the world and all things in it and entrusted them into our hands that we might use them for our good and for the building up of the church and human society. Today we pray for [Name], that God may strengthen

him/her in his/her weakness and restore him/her to the freedom of God's children. We pray also for ourselves that we may encourage and support him/her in the days ahead.

____ **Reading of the Word of God** ____

(A reader, another person present, or the minister reads a text of sacred Scripture:)

Brothers and sisters, listen to the words of the second letter of Paul to the Corinthians 4:6-9: We are afflicted, but not crushed.

For it is the God who said, "Let light shine out of darkness," who has shone in our hearts to give the light of the knowledge of the glory of God in the face of Christ.

But we have this treasure in earthen vessels, to show that the transcendent power belongs to God and not to us. We are afflicted in every way, but not crushed; perplexed, but not driven to despair; persecuted, but not forsaken; struck down, but not destroyed.

(These texts may also be read:)

Isaiah 63:7-9—He has favored us according to his mercy.

Romans 8:18-25—I consider the sufferings of the present to be as nothing compared with the glory to be revealed in us.

Matthew 15:21-28—Women, you have great faith.

(As circumstances suggest, one of the following responsorial psalms may be sung or said, or some other suitable song.)

Psalm 121

I lift up my eyes toward the mountains;
whence shall help come to me?
My help is from the LORD
who made heaven and earth.

May he not suffer your foot to slip;
may he slumber not who guards you:
Indeed he neither slumbers nor sleeps,
the guardian of Israel.

The LORD is your guardian; the LORD is your shade;

he is beside you at your right hand.
The sun shall not harm you by day,
nor the moon by night.

The LORD will guard you from all evil;
he will guard you life.
The LORD will guard your coming and your going,
both now and forever.

[or]

(v. 2) Our help is from the LORD who made heaven and earth.

[or]

Psalm 130:1-2, 3-4, 5-6, 7-8

[or]

(v. 5) My soul trusts in the LORD.

(As circumstances suggest, the minister may give those present a brief explanation of the biblical text, so that they may understand through faith the meaning of the celebration.)

_____ **Intercessions** _____

(The intercessions are then said. The minister introduces them, and an assisting minister or one of those present announces the intentions. From the following those best suited to the occasion may be used or adapted, or other intentions that apply to the particular circumstances may be composed.)

MINISTER: Our God gives us life and constantly calls us to new life; let us pray to God with confidence.

PEOPLE: **Lord, hear our prayer.**

ASSISTING
MINISTER: For those addicted to alcohol and drugs, that God may be their strength and support, we pray.

PEOPLE: **Lord, hear our prayer.**

ASSISTING
MINISTER: For [Name], bound by the chains of addiction/substance abuse, that we encourage and assist him/her in his/her struggle, we pray.

PEOPLE: **Lord, hear our prayer.**

ASSISTING
MINISTER: For [Name], that he/she may trust in the mercy of God, through whom all

things are possible, we pray.

PEOPLE: **Lord, hear our prayer.**

ASSISTING
MINISTER: For the family and friends of [Name], that with faith and patience they show him/her their love, we pray.

PEOPLE: **Lord, hear our prayer.**

ASSISTING
MINISTER: For the Church, that it may always be attentive to those in need, we pray.

PEOPLE: **Lord, hear our prayer.**

(After the intercessions the minister, in the following or similar words, invites all present to sing or say the Lord's Prayer:)

Let us pray to our merciful God as Jesus taught us:

ALL: **Our Father . . .**

(This may be followed by one of the following intercessions:)

For addiction

God of mercy,
we bless you in the name of your Son, Jesus Christ,
who ministered to all who came to him.
Give your strength to [Name], your servant,
bound by the chains of addiction.
Enfold him/her in your love
and restore him/her to the freedom of God's children.

Lord,
look with compassion on all those
who have lost their health and freedom.
Restore to them the assurance of your unfailing mercy,
and strengthen them in the work of recovery.
To those who care for them,
grant patient understanding and a love that perseveres.
We ask this through Christ our Lord.
Amen.

For substance abuse

God of mercy,
we bless you in the name of your Son, Jesus Christ,

who ministered to all who came to him.
Give your strength to [Name], your servant:
enfold him/her in your love
and restore him/her to the freedom of God's children.

Lord,
look with compassion on all those
who have lost their health and freedom.
Restore to them the assurance of your unfailing mercy,
strengthen them in the work of recovery,
and help them to resist all temptation.
To those who care for them,
grant patient understanding and a love that perseveres.

We ask this through Christ our Lord.
Amen.

(As circumstances suggest, the minister in silence may sprinkle the person with holy water.)

(A minister who is a priest or deacon concludes the rite by saying:)

May God give you light and peace.
Amen.
May God raise you up and save you.
Amen.
May God give you courage and strength.
Amen.

(Then the minister blesses all present:)

And may almighty God bless you all, the Father, and the Son, and the Holy Spirit.
Amen.

(A lay minister concludes the rite by signing himself or herself with the sign of the cross and saying:)

May our all-merciful God, Father, Son, and Holy Spirit, bless us and embrace us in love forever. Amen.

207 ✦ A LITURGY FOR A VICTIM OF CRIME OR OPPRESSION

Crime and injustice afflict every worshiping community. Some congregations are afflicted on a daily basis by the *injustices perpetuated by our culture. The following service allows for prayers to be offered on behalf of those who suffer and proclaims the hope of Christ. Adapt as necessary to local needs.*

Gathering for Worship

(When the community has gathered, a suitable song may be sung. After the singing, the minister says:)

> In the name of the Father, and of the Son, and of the Holy Spirit,

(All make the sign for the cross and reply:)
> **Amen.**

(A minister who is a priest or deacon greets those present in the following or other suitable words, taken mainly from sacred Scripture:)

> May the grace and peace of Christ be with you.

ALL: **And also with you.**

(A lay minister greets those present in the following words:)

> May the Lord grant us peace, now and for ever. Amen.

(In the following or similar words, the minister prepares those present for the blessing:)

> Throughout history God has manifested his love and care for those who have suffered from violence, hatred, and oppression. We commend [Name] to the healing mercy of God, who binds up all our wounds and enfolds us in his gentle care.

Reading of the Word of God

(A reader, another person present, or the minister reads a text of sacred Scripture:)

> Brothers and sisters, listen to the words of the holy Gospel according to Matthew 10:28-33. Do not fear.
>
> Jesus said to his disciples: "Do not be afraid of those who kill the body but cannot kill the soul; rather, be afraid of the one who can destroy both soul and body in Gehenna. Are not two sparrows sold for a small coin? Yet not one of them falls to the ground without your Father's knowledge. Even all the hairs of your head

are counted. So do not be afraid; you are worth more than many sparrows. Everyone who acknowledges me before others I will acknowledge before my heavenly Father. But whoever denies me before others, I will deny before my heavenly Father."

(These texts may also be read:)
Isaiah 59:6b-8—The Lord is appalled by evil and injustice.
Job 3:1-26— Lamentation of Job.
Lamentations 3:1-24—I am one who knows affliction.
Lamentations 3:49-59—When I called, you came to my aid.
Luke 10:24-32—The Good Samaritan.

(As circumstances suggest, one of the following responsorial psalms may be sung, or some other suitable song:)

Psalm 140

> Deliver me, O LORD, from evil men;
> preserve me from violent men,
> from those who devise evil in their hearts,
> and stir up wars every day.
>
> Save me, O LORD, from the hands of the wicked;
> preserve me from violent men
> who plan to trip up my feet—
> the proud who have hidden a trap for me;
> they have spread cords for a net;
> by the wayside they have laid snares for me.
>
> Grant not, O LORD, the desires of the wicked;
> further not their plans.
> Those who surround me lift up their heads;
> may the mischief which they threaten overwhelm them.
>
> I know that the LORD renders
> justice to the afflicted, judgment to the poor.
> Surely the just shall give thanks to your name;
> the upright shall dwell in your presence.

[or]

Psalm 142:2-3, 4b-5, 6-7

[or]

Psalm 31:2-3a, 4-5, 15-16, 24-25

(As circumstances suggest, the minister may give those present a brief explanation of the biblical text, so that they may understand through faith the meaning of the celebration.)

──────── **Intercessions** ────────

(The intercessions are then said. The minister introduces them, and an assisting minister or one of those present announces the intentions. From the following, those best suited to the occasion may be used or adapted; or other intentions that apply to the particular circumstances may be composed.)

MINISTER: Let us pray to the Lord God, the defender of the weak and powerless, who delivered our ancestors from harm.

PEOPLE: **Deliver us from evil, O Lord.**

ASSISTING MINISTER: For [Name], that he/she may be freed from pain and fear, we pray to the Lord.

PEOPLE: **Deliver us from evil, O Lord.**

ASSISTING MINISTER: For all who are victims of crime/oppression, we pray to the Lord.

PEOPLE: **Deliver us from evil, O Lord.**

ASSISTING MINISTER: For an end to all acts of violence and hatred, we pray to the Lord.

PEOPLE: **Deliver us from evil, O Lord.**

ASSISTING MINISTER: For those who harm others, that they may change their lives and turn to God, we pray to the Lord.

PEOPLE: **Deliver us from evil, O Lord.**

(After the intercessions the minister, in the following or similar words, invites all present to sing or say the Lord's Prayer:)

The Lord heals our wounds and strengthens us in our weakness; let us pray as Christ has taught us:

ALL: **Our Father . . .**

Prayer of Blessing

(A minister who is a priest or deacon says the prayer of blessing with hands outstretched over the person to be blessed. A lay minister says the prayer with hands joined:)

Lord God,
your own Son was delivered into the hands of the wicked,

yet he prayed for his persecutors
and overcame hatred with the blood of the cross.
Relive the suffering of [Name];
grant him/her peace of mind
and a renewed faith in your protection and care.

Protect us all from the violence of others,
keep us safe from the weapons of hate,
and restore to us tranquillity and peace.

We ask this through Christ our Lord. Amen.

(As circumstances suggest, the minister in silence may sprinkle the person with holy water.)

(A minister who is a priest or deacon concludes the rite by saying:)

May God bless you with his mercy,
strengthen you with his love,
and enable you to walk in charity and peace.
Amen.

(Then the minister blesses all present:)

And may almighty God bless you all,
the Father, and the Son, and the Holy Spirit.
Amen.

(A lay minister concludes the rite by signing himself or herself with the sign of the cross and saying:)

May God bless us with his mercy.
strengthen us with his love,
and enable us to walk in charity and peace.
Amen.

(It is preferable to end the celebration with a suitable song.)

From *The Book of Blessings*[34]

208 ✦ A PRAYER FOR THE HEALING OF MEMORIES

In any worshiping community, there are persons, perhaps many persons, who suffer each day because of persistent memories of traumatic events in their past.

Whether abused by a close relation, injured in war or in an accident, or rejected by a given person or group, memories can be a source of perpetual pain and afflic- tion. The following prayer addresses such painful memo- ries. Adapt or shorten as local situations may require.

We are grateful, Lord Jesus. Grateful that there isn't any time in your world. Grateful that you can walk back through our lives—all the way back to the very moment we were conceived, and you can heal us even then. You can free us from all those things that may have caused us difficulty at the moment of our conception, whether we were con- ceived in an act of love or whether we were an accident.

And as we were being formed within our mother's womb, you were there, to heal and lib- erate us from any disturbing impressions that may have touched us from our mother or from the cir- cumstances of our parents' lives. For whatever reason, there may not have been an atmosphere of love. Perhaps this environment was a result of poverty and discord; perhaps as each of us was carried within our mother's womb, she was over- worked. For whatever reason, there was a lack of harmony and love, and our spirits picked this up long before we were ever delivered. And already then we wanted to withdraw; we preferred not to emerge, not to be exposed, not to be known.

We pray, Lord Jesus, that you would now sup- ply all those things that have been lacking within us, and that you would remove from our spirits any anger, any resentment—whatever has been in our spirits, Lord, that is not of you. We thank you, Lord Jesus, for doing this.

And we praise you too, Lord Jesus, that you are healing us also of the trauma of being born. For many of us, our mothers had to labor for hours, perhaps days, and we know the effect this has upon an infant. Perhaps someone here was a blue baby, a breech baby, or born by instrument. And so we pray, Lord Jesus, that you would heal us of the birth pains, the trauma, whatever it was we went through in being born. Remove any doubt, any fear, any feelings of insecurity, we may have incurred when passing from our mother's womb. Rid us of any guilt we may be burdened with in having caused another to suffer because of our coming into this world, especially if we perceived we were neither wanted nor loved.

We pray, too, Lord Jesus, that you dispel any

disappointment we may have been to our parents because they so much wanted a little boy and we were born a little girl, or because they expected a daughter and the doctor announced "your son." We pray, Lord Jesus, that any disappointment, any frustration we may be carrying within our spirits because of our having been born the "wrong" sex would be healed and that from this day on we would be allowed to become the men and women you have destined us to be. Lord Jesus, we pray that whatever pain our coming into life may have caused another, especially our mothers, you would remedy now with your most precious blood.

Lord, we pray a healing upon each one of us in this room for that particular time in our lives, and we thank you, Lord Jesus, that you were there as we were being born, to receive us anew within those same hands. Lord Jesus, we thank you.

We thank you too that you were there during those early months of our infancy, during those times when we were most in need of you. There are those who needed more love during those first months; and there are those who never received this love because they'd been separated from their mothers through illness, separated through di- vorce, separated through death. And so there were times when we didn't have a mother's love surrounding us that would have helped us feel stability and strength.

We pray, Lord Jesus, that you would now sup- ply within us what has been lacking since those times when we needed to have our mothers hold us very close, when we needed to have our moth- ers rock us, when we wanted our mothers there to tell us stories, but they couldn't be there. We ask, Lord Jesus, that all those things that only a mother could do would be done now in the very depths of our being that any one of us who may have felt neglect during those first months might experience now an overwhelming sense of mater- nal love.

There are those, too, that lacked a father's love. Perhaps some among us never knew their father because he was away fighting in a war. Perhaps he never came home. There are many who have been separated from their fathers through divorce; and there are many more of us who have been sepa- rated from our fathers through death.

Whatever the reason for the void, we pray, Lord Jesus, that you would now fill in that part of our lives with the strong, tender love that can come only from a father. When we needed to have those strong arms around us and a daddy to love us, when we needed a father's advice, when we needed to feel his strength and the security of his love, and he wasn't there—oh, Lord, if only we could have experienced all of this. You do that for us now. Let us know that we have not been abandoned, that there are strong arms to lean on, that we do have someone watching over us and caring for us, even when we aren't aware of it. Lord Jesus, as a father stoops to raise his child to his cheeks, we ask that you would now take us in your embrace and that the warmth, the strength, the tenderness of this embrace would heal us. Lord Jesus, we thank you for what you are now doing.

And Lord, we pray a healing for us as we were growing up. Some of us were born into very large families, and so there wasn't much time for us as individuals. We can understand this and we can even accept this, and yet—there is a part of us that never felt loved. And so we pray that today, Lord Jesus, you would let us know that each of us is a very important person in your family, that each of us is a very unique and distinct individual and

that you love each of us in a very tender and in a very special way. We pray too that you would heal any hurts that may have come to us because or relationships within the family: the brother or sister who didn't accept us, who didn't understand us, who didn't show us the love or the kindness that we needed to receive from him or her and from no other. A part of us never felt loved because of it.

Lord Jesus, we pray that you would allow us right now to reach out with forgiveness to that brother or sister, whom over the years we've never quite been able to accept because he or she hasn't accepted us. Lord Jesus, you do that, launch out into the depths of our hearts and forgive them through us. And give us that extra measure of love for them so that the next time we see them it will be with such an overwhelming feeling of love that all the things that have stood between us over the years will have passed away, and behold, you will have made us new. Praise you, Jesus.

Lord, we pray a healing for us as we went off to school. Perhaps the first real trauma in our lives came when we left for school for the very first time. Perhaps we had never before been separated from our mothers or from our homes, and the experience seemed unbearable. Some of us, Lord, were very sensitive and shy, and it was extremely difficult to be with that unknown teacher, with those unfamiliar kids and in that cold classroom. There were things that were expected of us; and things that were done to us by teachers who were unkind, by classmates who didn't understand us and didn't accept us. Maybe our parents thought our *C*s should be *B*s and our *B*s should be *A*s, and so we grew up thinking we couldn't possibly, ever, be good enough for anything.

Lord, we pray a healing on all those years we spent in the classroom. Some of us began to withdraw; and we began to fear speaking out in groups because we'd been ridiculed, because we'd been criticized in classroom situations. We stopped speaking out, Lord, because it was just too painful. But now we pray a healing on that, and we ask that the door within the hearts of each of us might be opened up, that our tongues might be loosened, and that you would allow us to relate to one another in a more open and free way.

Lord Jesus, we ask that you heal those years we spent in adolescence, when we began to experience sexual maturity and it frightened us; it

The Cross Triparted Fleurée. This decorative cross is made of three parallel verticle segments and three horizontal ones. The ends bear leaf-like ornaments.

embarrassed us and it caused us pain. Some of us have never forgotten the experiences that were ours in learning about ourselves and what it meant to be a person. And so we pray a healing on those years we spent as teenagers. We pray a healing on our doubts, our fears, and our insecurities. We pray too for those times when perhaps we were hurt in interpersonal relationships, when we were put down by others, when perhaps we were taken advantage of, or laughed at—Lord Jesus, all of those incidents that have caused us suffering or embarrassment. Enter into our hearts and transform all those experiences so that we remember them no more with shame, but with thanksgiving.

Help us to appreciate the difficulties young people face in growing up. Aware of our own time of conflict, our own time of seeking and searching, somehow may we be able to help young people understand themselves. As we are now being covered with your most precious blood, as we are now being made as white as snow, we pray that somehow we could convey to young people that you do understand them, that you do wait for them. Though we fall, we will rise; and though we sit in darkness, you are our Lord and light. We thank you, Lord, for all that you're doing within us.

General Conclusion

As we emerged from that period of our lives and we began to enter into the vocation to which you called us, we pray a healing on the difficulties that came upon us—when we failed to become professional in areas where we wanted most to succeed; for the dreams and expectancies that we held before us, but were never realized. Lord Jesus, we hold up to you all of those longings.

Some of us have been called to be wives and mothers, husbands and fathers; some of us have been called to the religious life; and others of us have been called to be single lay persons. In whatever way you have asked us to follow you, Lord, there has been suffering and there has been pain. There is no career or vocation on earth that doesn't entail some difficulty, some adjustment, some problem deep inside of us that needs to be healed. And so we pray, Lord Jesus, that you would heal us in the state of life we find ourselves in today and all that has meant to the world around us.

We pray today that with each other, we would not fear to break the bread of ourselves, that with each other we would not fear to share our cup of weaknesses—a sharing of life built not on a false ideal, but on real hope, with faith in ourselves and with trust in each other. We pray, Lord Jesus, that the life we share might be your life. We thank you, Lord, for the words spoken to us through the prophet Isaiah:

> Remember not the events of the past,
> the things of long ago consider not;
> See, I am doing something new!
> Now it springs forth, do you not
> perceive it? (Isa. 43:18-19)

Lord Jesus, as your love flows over this room, as your love flows over these pages, and as each of us finds within his or her heart those things that need to be healed, to be set free, we praise and thank you, Lord, because we know it is being done. There is no power in heaven or earth that can stop it from being done because it has already been accomplished. Lord Jesus, you said on the cross, "It is finished."

First Conclusion for Religious (Members of Monastic Communities)

As we emerged from that period of our lives and we began to enter into the vocation to which you called us, we pray a healing on the difficulties that confronted us. We pray especially for all your religious—your priests, brothers and sisters—that your healing hand would be upon them and that it would touch each of the religious and diocesan communities they represent. We pray that we would come to know the deep personal love you have for each of us, because without this love we are incapable of loving others; without your love, we are incapable of loving even ourselves.

Wipe from our eyes any tear; remove from our hearts any pain, any suffering we have ever known. There are many who have experienced the sudden change of assignments, the sudden change of superiors. We pray that you would heal the wounds that have been inflicted upon us so that in remembering not the events of the past, the barriers of hostility that keep us apart—the barriers that separate us from our superiors, our pastors, our bishops, our parishioners, and our students; the barriers that divide us from each other; but more especially, the barriers that keep us distant from you—might be torn down. We pray that today we be lifted up to a new dimension of love—transformed—and that the Good News of your love would spread throughout our land. So may your people know it is you who love them in and through us. We pray that your glory may be made manifest and that unity may be made complete, that today we may go forth with a newness of purpose and with a boldness that can come only from your anointing.

Lord Jesus, as your love flows over this room, as your love flows over these pages, and as each of us finds within his or her heart those things that need to be healed, to be set free, we praise and thank you, Lord, because we know it is being done. There is no power in heaven or earth that can stop it from being done because it has already been accomplished. Lord Jesus, you said on the cross, "It is finished."

Alternate Conclusion for Religious

There are those whom you are calling to be the prophets of today, calling them into exile within and without community, so that your Spirit may be freed. There are those whom you are now preparing and calling to do a special work like Abraham, Joseph, Moses, and Ruth—to lay their lives on the line as broken bread and poured-out wine for your people. For these leaving means far more than just a physical transfer from one place to another; it means leaving and letting go of a familiar context of life, with its own pattern of thinking, values, and viewpoints—leaving and letting go with the assurance that your protection would be forever with your chosen people. Lord Jesus, we stand on that promise, and we ask that we may go forth with a newness of purpose and a boldness that can come only from your anointing.

Lord Jesus, as your love flows over this room, as your love flows over these pages, and as each of us finds within his or her heart those things that need to be healed, to be set free, we praise and thank you, Lord, because we know it is being done. There is no power in heaven or earth that can stop it from being done because it has already been accomplished. Lord Jesus, you said on the cross, "It is finished."

Conclusion for Married People

As we emerged from that period of our lives and began to enter into the vocation to which you called us, we pray a healing on the difficulties that came upon us. We pray especially for husbands and wives and for their marriages, that you heal those things that have passed between them, the hurts and frustrations that can come between two people who are trying to live together and to learn about one another in a very close relationship. It is you who are our peace, and it is to you we turn, asking that you make each couple one by tearing down the walls of hostility that keep them apart. Cleanse each of these marriages so that they might begin again as new, freed, and healed.

We pray that with each other, we would not fear to share our cup of weaknesses. Aid us toward a sharing of life built not on a false ideal, but on real hope, with faith in ourselves and with trust in each other. We pray, Lord, that the life we share might be your life. We pray that your life within us might be extended, that as we open the doors of our hearts you would heal the wounds, the frustrations, the misunderstandings that have been ours with our mother-in-law, our father-in-law. We pray that we might open not only the doors of our hearts, but the doors of our homes, and that your love within us would be extended to include and to embrace them. We thank you, Lord Jesus, for the words spoken to us through the prophet Isaiah:

Remember not the events of the past,
the things of long ago consider not;
See, I am doing something new!
Now it springs forth, do you not
perceive it? (Isa. 43:18-19)

Lord Jesus, as your love flows over this room, as your love flows over these pages, and as each of us finds within his or her heart those things that need to be healed, to be set free, we praise and thank you, Lord, because we know it is being done. There is no power in heaven or on earth that can stop it from being done because it has already been accomplished. Lord Jesus, you said on the cross, "It is finished."

Some Scripture Passages on Healing

Hear me, O house of Jacob,
all who remain of the house of Israel,
my burden since your birth,
whom I have carried from your infancy.
Even to your old age I am the same,
even when your hair is gray I will bear you;
it is I who have done this, I who will continue,
and I who will carry you to safety. (Isaiah 46:3-4)

At sunset, all who had people sick with a variety of diseases took them to him, and he laid hands on each of them and cured them. (Luke 4:40)

A leper approached him with a request, kneeling down as he addressed him: "If you will do so, you can cure me." Moved with pity, Jesus stretched out his hand, touched him, and said: "I do will it. Be cured." The leprosy left him then and there, and he was cured. (Mark 1:40-42)

As they were going, a women who had suffered from hemorrhages for twelve years came up behind him and touched the tassel on his cloak. "If only I can touch his cloak," she thought, "I shall get well." Jesus turned around and saw her and said, "Courage, daughter! Your faith has restored you to health." That very moment the woman got well. (Matthew 9:20-22)

The apostles on their return related to Jesus all they had accomplished. Taking them with him, he retired to a town called Bethsaida, but the crowds found this out and followed him. He received them and spoke to them of the reign of God, and he healed all who were in need of healing. (Luke 9:10-11)

When they arrived at Bethsaida, some people brought him a blind man and begged him to touch him. Jesus took the blind man's hand and led him outside the village. Putting spittle on his eyes he laid his hands on him and asked, "Can you see anything?" The man opened his eyes and said, "I can see people but they look like walking trees!" Then a second time Jesus laid hands on his eyes, and he saw perfectly; his sight was restored and he could see everything clearly. (Mark 8:22-25)

Paula Van Horn[35]

209 • A Liturgy for Survivors of Abuse

The following liturgy is designed for use by survivors of abuse. It allows for the pain and suffering of the abuse to be turned into prayers that seek healing from God. This service may be adapted for use in local congregations for other acts of personal injustice.

———— Gathering for Worship ————

Call to Worship: *Psalms/Now* (Leslie F. Brandt) (Read by the worship leader. Perhaps this might also be danced as it is being read:)

O God, my life is cluttered up with conflicts.
And there are times when you seem so oblivious to it all.
The pitfalls before me, the weakness within me—
all this is most depressing.
I feel as if I am groping in utter darkness.

Break into my darkness, O God.
Set me free from my hang-ups.
May these daily pressures that threaten to strangle me
drive me to your fountainhead of grace.
Then night will give way to the dawn,
depression shall resolve into joy,
and I shall sing your praises once more.

O foolish spirit, why do you fret over so many things?
God is here!
God knows all about your troubles and trials.
Renew your faith in God, and rejoice.

I shall rejoice.
No matter how black the night,
God is my ever-present and eternal Hope.

Statement of Welcome
(read responsively by the pastor and the survivors:)

PASTOR: God loves you. God created you. You are a child of God.

SURVIVORS: Today we come together in worship in the full knowledge that we are survivors of abuse. We cannot change that fact about our experience. However, we can chose to not let that fact be the only identity we have. We were not created to be abused. We were created to be children of God.

PASTOR: God loves you. God has called you. God welcomes the childlike choices of your life. God offers you a life of childlike peace within.

SURVIVORS: The fact that we are survivors has controlled how we have made responses to the world in which we live. Now we can make the choice to let healing begin, or continue, so that our ways of making choices can change. We were not created only to hope, but to have life and live it abundantly.

ALL: We are wonderful results of cre-
          ation, unique, and special in very
          many ways. We have every right to
          honor the special people we are,
          our behavior, and what has brought
          us to this point in our healing where
          we seek reconciliation. We ask God
          to join in our prayers, our songs,
          our readings, our worship. We ask
          God to be with us in our pain and
          our joy, our hopes and our fears.

─────────── **Rites of Confession** ───────────

Preparation for Confession

PASTOR: As we prepare for a time of confes-
          sion, we must remember to come as
          children. We must come simply and
          openly. We need to remember that we
          must not bear the guilt of the sins of
          others. We are children who have
          been affected by the choices of oth-
          ers. God is a gentle parent who wel-
          comes us.

Litany of Confession
(Adaptation of Psalm 44:)

SPEAKER 1: Lord, I have heard of how you have
          been with your children through-
          out history. They assumed you
          were with them even in their afflic-
          tions. You were with them in the
          crises of their lives.

SPEAKER 2: I long to behold your face. My tears
          drip into my food day and night.
          Where were you, God, when I felt
          abandoned?

SURVIVORS: Forgive me, O God, when I couldn't
          even call upon your name.

SPEAKER 1: You have watched over me in the
          midst of my conflicts. You have en-
          abled me to overcome many of the
          obstacles of my life. Even when I
          failed, you directed me to the
          course you wanted me to follow.
          You helped me learn to cope with
          most things.

SPEAKER 2: But I am aware of how much I need
          you, God. I am incapable and in-
          adequate at times. I struggle to
          believe you have been with me in
          my deepest pains and longings.

SURVIVORS: Forgive me, O God, when I couldn't
          even call upon your name.

SPEAKER 1: But where are you now, O God? I
          cannot reach you. You have gone
          from me and left me with my bag
          of pain.

SPEAKER 2: My cry for help is only an echo
          within me. I find only insurmount-
          able walls and the darkest of cor-
          ners. No one seems to speak to me
          with love or concern.

SURVIVORS: Forgive me, O God, when I couldn't
          even call upon your name.

SPEAKER 1: The shame and the pain are too
          deep to bear. No one can help me.
          If others knew of my problem, I am
          sure they would only shun me.

SPEAKER 2: I am in deep trouble, and there is
          no one to turn to for help. I have
          not forgotten you, O God.

SURVIVORS: O God, listen to me. Respond to
          my cry for help. You can deliver me
          from this terrible conflict before it
          destroys me. Help me to sense
          your loving concern. Save me be-
          fore it is too late. Forgive me, O
          God, when I couldn't even call
          upon your name.

PASTOR: The God who can hear your crying
          before your silent tears are shed;
          the God who can hear your calling
          when your voices cannot speak;
          the God who can give you shelter
          when you are abandoned and alone
          is the God who does understand
          your coping, forgives your wrongs,
          and upholds you in your healing.

SURVIVORS: The child in us wants to be for-
          given, yet the pain of our tears still
          burns on our cheeks.

PASTOR: Water can be in the form of tears,
          but it can also wash away the tears.
          As the bowl of water comes to you,
          hold it for the neighbor who passed
          it to you. They will use a finger to
          get a drop to wash under each of
          your eyes, and then dry the cheeks
          with the towel. Then, passing the
          bowl, wash the tears away for the
          next person. As you do this act of
          washing, tell the person, "Feel the

cool water of forgiveness wash the salt of your tears away."

(After the entire group has washed away tears, the pastor continues:)

PASTOR: Your tears are washed away. You are forgiven. You are loved. You are precious children.

ALL: **Amen.**

Hymn of Loving
"What a Friend We Have in Jesus"

Scripture
Matthew 18:1-5

Pastoral Message

Communal and Pastoral Prayer

Call to Prayer
(from *The Wounded Healer*)

When we are not afraid to enter into our own center
and to concentrate on the stirrings of our own soul,
we come to know that being alive means being loved.
This experience tells us that we can love
only because we are born out of love,
that we can give only because our life is a gift,
and that we can make others free
only because we are set free by God,
whose heart is greater than ours.
When we have found the anchor places for our lives
in our own center,
we can be free to let others enter into the space
created for them and allow them
to dance their own dance,
sing their own song,
and speak their own language without fear.
Then our presence is no longer threatening and demanding
but inviting and liberating.

PASTOR: Are there any joys or concerns you wish to bring at this time? When an individual shares a joy or concern, will another volunteer to pray for that which is brought to our prayer? (Allow time for the exchange. Then begin the prayer, let others share, and close at the appropriate time.)

Offering
We have sung. We have read the Word. We have shared the spoken word. We have prayed. We now come to the time of offering. Ours is a symbolic offering of the child within, an offering of light joining with the light of life in others; with the light of the precious ones to whom redemption is promised; with the symbolized light of creation of which we will sing. Join the dancers at the end of the song in celebration that today your child is welcomed again by the Lord as Jesus promised.

(This song would be beautiful with four dancers interpreting the directions of the earth, bringing forth the symbols of light. In addition, each person would be given a candle. The survivors then could have the opportunity to join in the dance, bringing forth their candle and lighting it from the fire of the day. They would set them into a pan of sand so that each candle would add to the light as an offering of their child's shining face.)

Rising from the East, women bring the dawn;
hear our waking song arising.
Shining from the South, women bring the day;
earth at work and play all shining.
Praising from the West, women bring the evening;
fire gives the light for praising.
Dreaming from the North, women bring the starlight;
darkness births the dancing and dreaming.
With her wings unfurled,
we are gathered in and blessed in our rising.
("Rising" by Colleen Fulmer)

Celebration of Silence
(At the end of the lighting, we will join in a moment of silence to give the child peaceful welcoming within and peaceful acceptance without.)

Song of Welcoming the Lord's Joining Our Child
"Come My Way, My Truth, My Life" (Vaughan Williams)

Benediction
PASTOR: You have risked in coming here. May God the Creator bless your departing from this place.

SURVIVORS: Amen.

PASTOR: You have risked in opening yourself in prayer. May God the Christ bless and welcome your child in love and healing.

SURVIVORS: Amen.

PASTOR: You have risked in celebrating who it is that your child is. May God the Holy Spirit enable you to continue to feel the power of redemption as you live life in the richness of the present moment and anticipate the joy of eternity to come.

SURVIVORS: Amen.

Katherine Lawrence

210 ✦ A LITANY OF THANKSGIVING FOR WORK

Work is part of the lives of many person in every worshiping community. Offering prayers of thanksgiving for meaningful work and for those who do it is an important act of pastoral care, which reinforces the important connection between corporate worship and the everyday lives of God's people. Adapt to local needs or customs, perhaps with references to work carried on by individual members of the worshiping community.

LEADER OR CANTOR: We give thanks, O God, for the work of our lives.

PEOPLE: **We praise you, God.**

LEADER OR CANTOR: For the work of our hands,

PEOPLE: **We praise you, God.**

LEADER OR CANTOR: For the work of our minds,

PEOPLE: **We praise you, God.**

LEADER OR CANTOR: For the work of our hearts,

PEOPLE: **We praise you, God.**

LEADER OR CANTOR: For the enlightening work of teachers, librarians, students, and coaches,

PEOPLE: **We praise you, God.**

LEADER OR CANTOR: For the healing work of doctors, nurses, and counselors,

PEOPLE: **We praise you, God.**

LEADER OR CANTOR: For the creative work of artists, musicians, painters, and sculptors,

PEOPLE: **We praise you, God.**

LEADER OR CANTOR: For the precise work of engineers, scientists, and computer specialists,

PEOPLE: **We praise you, God.**

LEADER OR CANTOR: For the nurturing work of homemakers, parents, and guardians,

PEOPLE: **We praise you, God.**

LEADER OR CANTOR: For the wise work of retirees and grandparents,

PEOPLE: **We praise you, God.**

LEADER OR CANTOR: For the proclaiming work of writers, photographers, editors, and publishers,

PEOPLE: **We praise you, God.**

LEADER OR CANTOR: For the trustworthy work of accountants, bankers, lawyers, politicians, and salespeople,

PEOPLE: **We praise you, God.**

LEADER OR CANTOR: For the faith-filled work of ordained, religious, and lay ministers,

PEOPLE: **We praise you, God.**

LEADER OR CANTOR: For the protective work of police, firefighters, and military personnel,

PEOPLE: **We praise you, God.**

LEADER OR CANTOR: For the dedicated work of secretaries, receptionists, and bookkeepers,

PEOPLE: **We praise you, God.**

LEADER OR CANTOR: For the compassionate work of volunteers,

PEOPLE: **We praise you, God.**

LEADER OR CANTOR: For the judicious work of managers, administrators, directors, and supervisors,

PEOPLE: **We praise you, God.**

LEADER OR CANTOR: For the fruitful work of farmers, fishers, growers, and gardeners,

PEOPLE: **We praise you, God.**

LEADER OR CANTOR: For the steadfast work of those who manufacture products,

PEOPLE: **We praise you, God.**

LEADER OR CANTOR: For the constructive work of builders, surveyors, architects, masons, and carpenters,

PEOPLE: **We praise you, God.**

LEADER OR CANTOR: For the efficient work of those who transport people and things by bus, train, plane, taxi, truck, and boat,

PEOPLE: **We praise you, God.**

LEADER OR CANTOR: For the hospitable work of cooks, waiters and waitresses,

LEADER OR CANTOR: cashiers, and hotel and motel workers,

PEOPLE: **We praise you, God.**

LEADER OR CANTOR: For the clarifying work of television, radio, and news media workers,

PEOPLE: **We praise you, God.**

LEADER OR CANTOR: For the dependable work of telephone and postal workers,

PEOPLE: **We praise you, God.**

LEADER OR CANTOR: For the good work of all other workers,

PEOPLE: **We praise you, God.**

LEADER OR CANTOR: For our work, that sheds light on the darkness,

PEOPLE: **We praise you, God.**

LEADER OR CANTOR: For our work, that creates order from chaos,

PEOPLE: **We praise you, God.**

LEADER OR CANTOR: For our work, that builds peace out of hostility,

PEOPLE: **We praise you, God.**

LEADER OR CANTOR: For our work, that helps others,

PEOPLE: **We praise you, God.**

LEADER OR CANTOR: For our work that serves others,

PEOPLE: **We praise you, God.**

LEADER OR CANTOR: For our work that empowers others,

PEOPLE: **We praise you, God.**

LEADER OR CANTOR: For our work that inspires others,

PEOPLE: **We praise you, God.**

LEADER OR CANTOR: For our work that builds your kingdom,

PEOPLE: **We praise you, God.**

211 ♦ A LITURGY FOR RETIREMENT FROM WORK AND REDIRECTION IN VOCATION

The following liturgy may be used at the occasion of a retirement. It expresses thanksgiving for the blessings of work, petitions for God's continued direction, and promises of commitment to future service in God's kingdom. This service may be adapted for use in the local parish.

——— Introduction to the Service ———

Major transitions in the lives of individuals are marked in every culture; usually they are termed "rites of passage." Both the individual and society need support during times of traumatic change. The retirement from regular employment is one such change. The Christian faith proclaims the hope that work roles can be let go and life can continue with meaning and vocation. The church invites persons retiring to share this moment with the community of faith.

Prior time should be allowed by the person retiring to meet with the chief minister of the rite to discuss life in retirement. A part of this counseling would include planning the liturgical celebration with special attention given the direction of life in service to Christ and the world. This redirection is contained in the commitment to Christian service and includes a statement of specific responsibility to the parish or community. This act concludes with the renewal of baptismal vows.

A priest or a bishop normally presides at the Celebration of Retirement and Redirection, because such ministers have the function of pronouncing blessing and celebrating the Holy Eucharist. When both a bishop and a priest are present and officiating, the bishop should pronounce the blessing and preside at the Eucharist.

A deacon, or another assisting priest, may read the Gospel, deliver the sermon and charge, and perform other assisting functions at the Eucharist. With no participating bishop or priest, a deacon may use the service that follows, omitting the blessing.

It is desirable that lay persons from the family, the workplace, and friends of the person retiring read the lessons from the Old Testament and the Epistle and lead the Litany of Thanksgiving for New Vocation.

In the gathering statement (at the symbol [N.N.]), the full names of the retiring person are stated. Subsequently, only the person's Christian name [Name] is used.

Following the declaration of retirement and during the liturgy of the Word, the person retiring is seated with family and friends until the presentation. Everyone remains standing until the conclusion of the collect.

At the offertory, it is desirable that the bread and wine be presented to the ministers by the retiring person, family, and friends. They may remain at the altar to receive Holy Communion before other members of the congregation. Communion is always offered to every baptized person present.

The most appropriate hymns for the Celebration of Retirement and Redirection may be hymns that offer thanksgiving for the blessings of work and promise continued service to God's kingdom, as well as those familiar and favorite ones of the person retiring.

Whenever possible, immediately following the rite, a reception, dinner, or other gathering is held to encourage sharing important events in the retiring person's life by family, faith community, friends, and coworkers.

The Service

At the appropriate time, the person retiring assembles with the family, friends, and coworkers in the church or other suitable place.

For the entrance, a hymn, psalm, or anthem may be sung, or instrumental music may be played. The person retiring enters during this procession.

When everyone is assembled, with the retiring person facing the celebrant, the celebrant addresses the congregation, saying:

Dear friends, today we have gathered in the presence of God to give thanks for the accomplishments of work and to celebrate a new vocation in retirement. When God had accomplished his work of creation, he looked upon his completed work, proclaimed that it was very good, and instituted Sabbath rest. The Sabbath rest of God is a pattern for retirement life. The Creation was completed, but the loving, active care of God for his creation continues to this moment. Our Lord Jesus Christ completed his earthly work of salvation on the Cross declaring, "It is finished," after which Scripture and our own faith witness to the hope of eternal life through Christ's resurrection life. We rejoice in the work God the Creator has given to us to do; but we also affirm that the value of a person is based on more than work done through gainful employment. Baptism made us members of God's family and gave us intrinsic worth. Our work always is a means of joining in God's creative purpose for life. Yet the promise of a Sabbath from employment is not the end of living or usefulness. Retirement calls for commit-ment to redirecting life to the service of God, humanity, and creation. Therefore, retirement life is entered by reaffirming baptismal membership in God's family and offering to God a new vocational commitment.

[N.N.] has come today to celebrate retirement and commitment to redirected living. With the ending of full-time employment, there is new opportunity to offer service to God. [Name], retirement is a moment of giving up activities that have provided definition for too much of your life. However, from baptism we understand that ultimate significance in life is in relationship with God and service to him and his world. Will you redirect your life to new ways of God's service?

(The person retiring responds:)
I will, with God's help.

(The celebrant then addresses the congregation, saying:)
Will all of you witnessing this commitment support [Name] in retiring from employment and redirecting his/her life to a new vocation?
PEOPLE: **We will.**

The Ministry of the Word
CELEBRANT: The Lord be with you.
PEOPLE: **And also with you.**
CELEBRANT: Let us pray.

Eternal God, Creator and Renewer of life, you continually call us to a rhythm of work and Sabbath rest. In the Sabbath rest of retirement, may we discover new meaning for life and new opportunities for serving you. We offer thanks for [Name] and his/her years of faithful work. May your Spirit bless his/her coworkers and continue work done through you, even as he/she now retires. Give him/her a fulfilling redirection of life committed to you; through Jesus Christ, the beginning and ending of life. Amen.

(Then one or more of the following passages from Holy Scripture is read. A period of silence may follow each reading. The reading of a passage from the Gospel always concludes the readings.)

Genesis 1:26–2:3—God turns from work to rest.
Genesis 12:1-7—Abram and Sarai arecalled to new life.
Deuteronomy 8:1-10—Future fulfillment is with the Lord.

Ecclesiastes 3:1-11—There is a time for all of life.

Jeremiah 29:11-13—promised hope for the future

Romans 12:1-8—Conform gifts to God's transformation.

1 Corinthians 12:4-13—varieties of gifts and services

Ephesians 4:1-8, 11-16—growing to full maturity

1 Timothy 5:3-10—dedicated living for elder women

1 Timothy 6:5-12—Faith is the source of enduring riches.

2 Peter 1:3-11—God provides for the full life.

1 John 5:13-15—strength in assurance of eternal life

Revelation 7:13-17—joy in following Christ

Revelation 21:1-7—God constantly renews.

(Between the readings, a Psalm, hymn, or anthem may be sung or said. Appropriate Psalms are 23; 46; 92:1-4, 11-15; 121; 128; 145:13b-21; 148.)

> (Then all stand, and the deacon or minister appointed says:)
>> The Holy Gospel of our Lord Jesus Christ according to _____.
>
> PEOPLE: **Glory to you, Lord Christ.**

Matthew 7:7-12—Seek and God provides.

Matthew 16:24-28—continuing to follow Christ

Mark 12:28-34—the full life of loving God and neighbor

Luke 12:22-34—Don't be anxious; trust God.

Luke 19:1-10—Jesus finds inherent worth.

John 3:1-8—new birth at any age

John 13:1-5, 12-17—commitment in Christ's service

John 15:8-17—bearing the lasting fruit of love

> (After the Gospel, the reader says:)
>> The Gospel of the Lord.
>
> PEOPLE: **Praise to you, Lord Christ.**

The Sermon

(At the conclusion of the sermon, the person retiring stands and is addressed in these or similar words:)
> My brother, [Name], at baptism every Christian accepts Jesus Christ as Lord and Savior of life, a life committed to serving God the Father through the strengthening presence of the Holy Spirit. As a Christian, you are called in all circumstances, by word and example, to bear witness to the Good News of God in Christ. As a Christian, in accordance with the gifts you are given, you are to carry on Christ's work of reconciliation in the world. Also, you are called to continue to take your place in the life, worship, and governance of Christ's church. The conclusion of this commitment is that in our Christian journey, Christ is leading us into a pilgrimage in which we leave the familiar to engage a new life direction.
>
> Are you prepared to retire from your present employment and redirect your life toward opportunities that God presents?

(The person retiring says:)
> I am prepared, with God's help.

The Retirement

CELEBRANT: [Name], you have been assured of support in the opportunities of your retirement living. Each of us at baptism is given gifts by the Holy Spirit for the community's good. These gifts do not diminish or end with retirement from employment. As we have given thanks for the accomplishments of the past, we now look to the future as you offer yourself to your new way of life in this act of commitment.

(Facing the congregation, the retiring person makes a commitment to the service of Christ, undertaking special responsibilities in retirement living. Included in this act should be the giving of a work symbol, representing the end of employment, to persons of the former place of employment. Also, a symbol of the new commitment may be presented to the person retiring by representatives of the new service or the congregation. The act of commitment concludes with the following committal act and the renewal of baptismal vows.)

(The person retiring kneels and says:)
> Almighty God, you have sustained me throughout my employment; and now I thank you for the strength you have given to have reached retire-

ment and the opportunity to redirect my life in new ways of serving you and the community. As the future unfolds, may all my fear be set aside through deepening trust in your daily grace; through Jesus Christ, the Lord of Life. Amen.

(After this act, the retiring person stands and the celebrant says these or similar words:)

In the name of this congregation, I commend you to this new life, and pledge you our prayers, encouragement, and support, through God the Father, Son, and Holy Spirit.

PEOPLE: **Amen.**

The Renewal of Baptismal Vows

CELEBRANT: Let us stand and join [Name] in renewing our baptismal life. Do you reaffirm your renunciation of evil and renew your commitment to Jesus Christ?

PEOPLE: **I do.**

CELEBRANT: Do you believe in God the Father?

PEOPLE: **I believe in God, the Father almighty, creator of heaven and earth.**

CELEBRANT: Do you believe in Jesus Christ, the Son of God?

PEOPLE: **I believe in Jesus Christ, his only Son, our Lord. He was conceived by the power of the Holy Spirit and born of the Virgin Mary. He suffered under Pontius Pilate, was crucified, died and was buried. He descended to the dead. On the third day he rose again. He ascended into heaven, and is seated at the right hand of the Father. He will come again to judge the living and the dead.**

CELEBRANT: Do you believe in God the Holy Spirit?

PEOPLE: **I believe in the Holy Spirit, the holy catholic church, the communion of saints, the forgiveness of sins, the resurrection of the body, and the life everlasting.**

CELEBRANT: Will you continue in the apostles' teaching and fellowship, in the breaking of bread, and in the prayers?

PEOPLE: **I will, with God's help.**

CELEBRANT: Will you persevere in resisting evil, and, whenever you fall into sin, repent and return to the Lord?

PEOPLE: **I will, with God's help.**

CELEBRANT: Will you proclaim by word and example the Good News of God in Christ?

PEOPLE: **I will, with God's help.**

CELEBRANT: Will you seek and serve Christ in all persons, loving your neighbor as yourself?

PEOPLE: **I will, with God's help.**

CELEBRANT: Will you strive for justice and peace among all people, and respect the dignity of every human being?

PEOPLE: **I will, with God's help.**

The Prayers of God's Gifts in the New Life

CELEBRANT: Please rise and let us pray together in the words our Savior taught us.

PEOPLE AND CELEBRANT: **Our Father in heaven, hallowed be your Name, your kingdom come, your will be done, on earth as in heaven. Give us today our daily bread. Forgive us our sins as we forgive those who sin against us. Save us from the time of trial, and deliver us from evil. For the kingdom, the power, and the glory are yours, now and forever. Amen.**

(If Communion is to follow, the Lord's Prayer may be omitted here. The deacon or other persons, such as family, coworkers, and friends, lead the following litany:)

DEACON: Let us pray.

Eternal God, creator and preservers of all, giver of the grace to be coworkers and the hope of meaningful living: Continue the saving work of your Son through your Spirit in our midst, particularly for [Name], who comes seeking your blessing in his/her retirement.

PEOPLE: **Give grace to your servant, O Lord.**

DEACON: Grant that his/her retirement be an

instrument for serving the common good and a witness against casual human abuse in work or leisure; and may the personal increase in leisure become a time for opening to new growth.

PEOPLE: **Give grace to your servant, O Lord.**

DEACON: Give him/her, as he/she leaves the accomplishments and frustrations of the workplace, a sense of gratitude for those who have shared his/her journey.

PEOPLE: **Give grace to your servant, O Lord.**

DEACON: Grant him/her wisdom and understanding in the ordering of his/her retirement life, that aging may be seen as a vital part of your eternal order; that he/she may be blessed with a hopeful perspective to guard against a narrowing of life; that his/her aging may be valued as a time to be a bridge to past, present, and future gifts.

PEOPLE: **Give grace to your servant, O Lord.**

DEACON: Grant that as his/her aging compels the conserving of personal energy, he/she may see the need to revere the resources of nature and, rather than wasting them, find ways of working with you in creation, so future generations may enjoy your abundance.

PEOPLE: **Give grace to your servant, O Lord.**

DEACON: Give him/her thankfulness for all who have made the life journey with him/her thus far, especially _____ (family, friends, and coworkers may be named); and as we remember that your Son Jesus taught that all who do your will are related, may you keep this family in your continual care.

PEOPLE: **Give grace to your servant, O Lord.**

[Optional]:

DEACON: [Make his/her marriage to N., who has shared his/her life, a source of deepening oneness, friendship, encouragement, understanding, and love.]

PEOPLE: **[Give grace to your servant, O Lord.]**

[Optional]:

DEACON: [Give him/her continuing joy in the gift and heritage of his/her children (Names may be used; and, if appropriate, grandchildren, also with names). As parent (and grandparent), may he/she find satisfaction in caring, and may the children respond with honoring love.]

PEOPLE: **[Give grace to your servant, O Lord.]**

DEACON: Grant him/her a vision of Christ's eternal hope that, as more and more of those he/she cares for leave this earthly city, no desolation may overcome him/her and that his/her soul may be nourished and strengthened with the bread of your presence for the rest of his/her pilgrimage.

PEOPLE: **Give grace to your servant, O Lord.**

DEACON: Grant that all who have witnessed this retirement and redirection of life, especially the retired and those nearing retirement, may find their future encouraged and their faith confirmed. May the eternal strength of Almighty God support us until the evening of our life comes and retirement activity ends; then in the grace of God the Father, Son, and Holy Spirit may we be granted a safe lodging, a holy rest, and peace at last. Amen.

The Blessing of the Retiring Person

(The people remain standing, while the retiring person kneels and the priest says the following blessing:)

Let us pray.

Eternal God, the beginning and end of life: We give you thanks for [Name]'s work among us; may he/she remember this labor with satisfaction. Bless his/her new commitment, and grant him/her courage and vision, joy and hope, patience and wisdom in retirement. May God the Father, God the Son, and God the Holy Spirit bless, preserve, and keep you; may the Lord mercifully look upon you with his favor, and fill you with spiritual benediction and grace; that you may live faithfully now, and in the age to come have life everlasting. Amen.

The Peace

(The celebrant may say to the people:)

> Let us share in the joy of [Name]'s retirement and greet each other in the peace of the Lord.
>
> The peace of the Lord be always with you.

PEOPLE: **And also with you.**

(The newly retired person exchanges greetings with family, friends, and throughout the congregation.)

At the Eucharist

(The liturgy continues with the Offertory, at which the newly retired person and selected others may present the offerings, which may include symbols of the new vocation and gifts previously given, along with the bread and wine. During the offertory, a Psalm, hymn, or anthem may be shared.)

(The Communion continues with the Great Thanksgiving, using the selected eucharistic prayer.)

(For the preface the following is used:)

> For as you turned from the good work of creation to Sabbath rest; and your Son completing his earthly work of salvation opened the heavenly way for us; by the Holy Spirit you bless us in retirement and guide our redirection in eternal hope.

(At the Communion, it is appropriate for the newly retired person and selected others to receive Communion first, after the ministers. Also, during Communion appropriate hymns and anthems may be sung.)

The Postcommunion Prayer

(In place of the usual postcommunion prayer, the following is to be said:)

> Almighty God, we give you thanks for binding us together in these holy mysteries of the body and blood of your Son Jesus Christ, and for uniting us to the saints at work and at rest. Grant that by your Holy Spirit, [Name], now retired, may continue faithfully in word and action, in love and patience, and in hope and joy in his/her new commitment and obtain those eternal joys promised to all who are born of the Spirit; through Jesus Christ your Son our Lord, who lives and reigns with you and the Holy Spirit, one God, now and forever. Amen.

(The service concludes with the blessing and a dismissal, which may be in these words:)

> Let us go forth living for Christ.

PEOPLE: **Thanks be to God.**

As the newly retired person leaves, a hymn, psalm, or anthem may be sung, or instrumental music may be played. The celebration may continue with greeting the newly retired person.

Without Eucharist

(When Communion is not to follow, the service concludes with the blessing and a dismissal, which may be in these words:)

> Let us go forth living for Christ.

PEOPLE: **Thanks be to God.**

A hymn, psalm, or anthem may be sung, or instrumental music played as the newly retired person leaves. The celebration may continue with greeting the newly retired person.

Commentary on the Liturgy

The title of this liturgy attempts to incorporate three important elements common to rites of life passage: first, a separation from the old lifestyle; then a period of transition and recognition; and finally, there is incorporation into the new lifestyle. The wedding service is a very clear model of this pattern.

For marriage, two persons are presented, and with them come their very distinct family traditions. Through the public declaration of vows, a commitment to oneness in a new life is established. So too in this retirement rite, many diverse components of an individual's life gather, as symbolized by the gathering of coworkers, family, friends, and believers. Through this rite, public witness is made to the movement away from employment and toward a commitment, under God's guidance, to a vital new lifestyle.

Lay Involvement. Participatory worship is a hallmark of Anglicanism; therefore, rather than having the clergy perform, with the laity simply observing, opportunities for lay leadership are encouraged. The lay reading of Scripture is significant. A principal act of the Reformation was to return the Bible to the people as trustworthy sharers in receiving God's Word. Whenever possible, lay persons should participate in proclaiming the Word of God.

Once again, not only is the retiree honored by

bringing forward the elements for Communion, but the importance of the total community—clergy and laity—participating together is emphasized. This is a reminder that a priest or bishop cannot celebrate the Eucharist alone. The elements for Communion represent our total lives being offered to Christ's service; this point is even more evident when the elements come forward from the body of the congregation.

Hymns. Hymn singing is one of the most effective ways to involve the total congregation in the worship of the church. Even though there be gifted choristers and musicians available, this important people's part of the worship should be included if at all possible. There is a list of suggested appropriate hymns; however, the retiring person's selection of particularly meaningful hymns can add to the special significance of this service for all who gather. The music chosen offers another way of celebrating the uniqueness of the retirement event.

Following the Liturgy. With time constraints and other realities, not everyone who wishes to speak can be given time and everything desirable cannot be said during the liturgy. So, even though a retiring person may want to keep what seems to be "fuss and bother" to minimum, the total community needs a time following the service to gather and share further. This gathering need not be elaborate or costly. The fact is that, whether the gathering be a simple reception or elaborate dinner, the people come to be with and express their care to the retiree.

Rubrics. This service presumes that an active Christian would expect this celebration (as with other high points in life) to naturally belong in one's home church. There the familiarity and hospitality shared among family and Christian brothers and sisters can be extended to the larger community of friends and work associates. Of course, for good reason, the service may need to be held at home or in another location; however, celebrating this event in the church offers a natural aspect of witness in bringing work associates and non-church friends to the "faith-home."

A sense of continuity, of belonging to a greater fellowship than employment affords, is gained within the observance in the home church with familiar clergy and parishioners. Being "at home"

among the familiar contributes to the celebrative, supportive atmosphere, as at a baptism, a wedding, or even a funeral. The hope is that just as the expected place for a wedding now is in church, in the future the normal place for Christian retirement rites will be in the church.

Service Music. Music gathers us—hearts, minds, and spirits. Hymns sung together further community feeling and encourage participation throughout the liturgy. Of course, other forms of music may need to be used. Whatever form the music takes, the person retiring should be involved in the selection. Just as the entrance of the retiree focuses attention on the observance of a personal relationship with God, the music selection can help particularize this event. This service, from the entering to the leaving, lifts before God this individual's retirement and the significance of this transition in life.

Gathering Address. The gathering statement makes no presumption about the faith commitment or worship familiarity of the congregation. In fact, the service assumes that the congregation is made up of persons who first are there to witness and support the individual's retirement and redirection. However, this event differs greatly from secular retirement observances, which tend to simply provide a closure for work life. From their entrance into the church, the gatherers are reminded of God's presence and the eternal nature of what is taking place. Of course, the expected celebration of the accomplishments of work takes place. However, there is also a new element; those gathered will also witness the retiring person's commitment to a new direction, a new vocation within retirement. This service is a resounding *no* to suggestions of "rocking to death" in six months.

The emphasis here is that human beings are not simply producers, that they are valued beyond work. Within this liturgy, participants are recalled to the point where initial worth is established—baptism. For most people, baptism is a time of total dependence. God acts through baptism to give us value, when we can be only receivers of God's grace.

From the start, this liturgy offers opportunities to honor past work and also to focus on a future of hope-filled living based on a new commitment to God.

Commitment to Retirement. The public declaration of a willingness to retire brings the issue of closure to the surface. It is important that the retiree consciously consent to this act of leaving; and the public declaration of that consent establishes the retiree's new position. This response recognizes that successful retirement living is not just individual will and effort; God is to be counted on—"with God's help"—as in other transitions in life.

Congregational Affirmation. Faith in the incarnation of God is witnessed by directing attention to the congregation as the body of Christ. Trusting in Christ's presence in the midst of this event is a key difference from secular observances. The congregants are not just spectators. They are called to be witnesses and to actively support the retiree in establishing a new lifestyle. By directly involving the congregation, the hope is that everyone present will reflect also upon the personal nature of retirement, whether their own retirement has already occurred or is in the distant future.

Scripture Selections. As with other aspects of living, the Bible gives insight into issues connected with retirement and the redirection of life. By thoughtful Scripture selection, the retiring person can share with others the pattern of God's call to his or her future living. The opportunity to involve laity in reading should be encouraged. Participative support is enacted by those who read; also, through this action they can gain further understanding of the service. A variety of people participating here and throughout the service is a clear call for retirement to be lived in community. Since this service is one of proclamation of Christ's presence, a Gospel lesson always concludes the readings.

Sermon. The sermon is not expected to be a eulogy. Illustrating the proclamation of God's Word with meaningful moments from the retiree's life would give specificity to this occasion; however, this time is to preach Christ. With a congregation including a variety of faith commitments, some emphasis could be given to proclaiming the difference between secular and Christian retirement. The sermon might stress the continuing benefit of having the Lord's supporting presence and guidance, thus giving signs of hope to the retiree and others. The continuing relationships within the church can be especially helpful when much of what gave meaning to day-to-day living has changed.

The concluding statement of the sermon directly addresses the retiring person. To conclude this way is similar to the practice at ordination services; and in this connection, it serves to declare that this service paves the way for a new vocation. The charge is based on the catechism and suggests that the Christian way of life is for all ages. These statements serve to remind the retiree that the issue is not retirement from living but retirement to a new lifestyle. To encourage awareness of the reality of this moment, the retiring person is given a personal call to face retirement directly and turn to a new vocation. The time to lay aside present employment has come. And the response to this call—"I am prepared, with God's help"—indicates forethought for this moment and for life ahead. Also, acknowledgment is given that for this believer, the redirection is not "solo." Our God gives promises that can be counted upon.

The Retirement. To further localize this event, the service moves to a public act of retirement. Just as our God became flesh and dwelt among us, the moment of retirement is "fleshed-out," incarnated in real time. The retiring person is not left to peruse this moment alone. The support of the community is represented by selected family members and former work partners who accompany the retiree to the altar.

The retiring person stands at the altar before the celebrant, who represents the solemnization of this event in God's presence. The celebrant expressly invites Christ's support for the future. Congregational support already has been shown by the accompanying persons. However, they are encouraged to be even more expressive by commenting on the retiree's accomplishments and how much he or she will be missed. Also, symbolic gifts of appreciation, representative of the work being left, may be presented. Of course, if there are many gifts, just a few are selected for this time, with the others saved for the events following the service. This action provides a valuable opportunity to publicly let go of the work relationship. Now the possibility is open for other commitments.

With the turn made toward the future, the celebrant reminds everyone that, for the Christian, personal worth does not depend on the products of the work world, but on the baptismal moment of birth into God's family. *All the rest of life is a response to God's gracious declaration of our worth*. And although this value may be given special meaning thorough engagement in the marketplace, retirement is an opening of yet another valuable stage.

The Act of Commitment. This act makes clear the move from the workaday world to retirement living. The retiring person commits to this very important step in words and acts carefully crafted during the preretirement counseling and a time of personal reflection. The wedding service stresses that none should enter marriage "unadvisedly or lightly," and this same strong emphasis must be made in anticipation of successful retirement.

As with the exchanging of wedding rings, the new status may be symbolized by giving and receiving objects. The finality of departing the workplace is acknowledged by the retiree giving a symbol to a representative of the former employment. For example, an architect may return her blueprint or a teacher may return his class attendance book. Hopefully, this symbolizing will be in a more positive spirit than suggested by the associate who said, "Great! Give 'em back their clock!"

Stepping into retirement can be celebrated by representatives of the new commitment giving a symbol; for example, a person becoming a lay visitor at a hospital could be given a stack of patient cards. This presentation comes just before the retiree kneels to seal the commitment in prayer to God. Again, a significant difference exists between this rite and a secular retirement, where emphasis is on closure and where "gallows humor" generally prevails when the future is contemplated. Instead of looking only to the past, the retiring person reaches toward the future, trusting in a partnership with God.

The "solemnization" of this commitment is then declared by the celebrant and responded to by the congregation. Here, too, the retiree is assured that he or she does not walk alone. There is definite intention to continue in relationship with God and the community.

The Renewal of Baptismal Vows. Whenever a new venture is taken, the way is made easier by familiar accompaniments. Hopefully, this renewal of vows will be one of these "accompaniments." The baptismal vows were part of our new birth in Christ; and since that event on many significant occasions (even annually at Easter), a renewal of baptismal vows has taken place. Now this renewal is the first action in retirement—witnessing a belief in God and commitment to Christian living. Personal faith is affirmed. However, this renewal is not private; the total community also acclaims this time of retirement and redirection as a moment of reaffirmation of faith. What could have been simply a private affair thus becomes an opportunity for community renewal.

The Prayers. A natural response to sharing a special event in life with someone is giving a gift, as with birthdays and weddings. For Christians the best gift is intentionally praying for someone. The prayer portion begins with the Lord's Prayer as a summary of all our concerns before God. Personal preference is encouraged by providing a choice of the traditional or ecumenical form of the prayer. It is significant that the first prayer spoken in retirement by the person and congregation is encouragingly familiar and opens the way for the unique prayers and blessing.

The prayer "gifts" for this occasion are then given. An important opportunity for involvement is afforded when these prayers are offered by persons close to the retiring person. The litany form also encourages active participation by the whole congregation. Participatory prayers underscore the congregation's important role as an active witness, rather than a disinterested audience.

Themes important to retirement and redirection are offered in each litany segment. The congregational responses stress God's grace, so vital for all living, as the key ingredient here. Significant to these prayers are the options to include the spouse, children, and even grandchildren. Since quite often the retiree is accompanied by the spouse of many years and by adult children, it is as important to include them as any other aspect of work or retirement would be included. And for many people, the "jewels" of this stage in life are grandchildren, who may be remembered in prayer. This litany gives thanks for accomplishments, seeks guidance and strength for the future, and concludes with the comforting assurance expressed by John Henry Newman.

The Blessing. The primary difference between this service and a secular celebration is the enjoinment of God's blessing upon the retiring person. Hopefully, as this service invites God's partnership now and in retirement, the uniquely positive atmosphere created by our Lord's presence at the wedding in Cana may be experienced. The hope is that future participation in sacred celebrations of retirement will establish positive outcomes such as those seen when comparing "church" and "civil" weddings. We trust God's blessing to reverberate from this moment through the rest of life.

The Peace. The natural desire to express joy for and with the retiring person is released in the ancient Christian practice of sharing "the peace." Some may have the feeling that they are about to "explode" at this moment. So the liturgy frees everyone up for a celebrative encounter. Of course, the hope is that sharing the peace will be expressing the joy of Christ. However, the risk of missing the significance is the same risk taken in the first instance of having this liturgy. God's special blessing of the retiree now spills over onto all.

The Eucharist. Continuing the liturgy with Communion presents the opportunity for the completeness of our Lord's promise to nourish us with his presence. From baptismal birth throughout growing up, with accomplishments and crises, the Supper of the Lord has been there. At the end of employment, there is the tradition of the banquet; even more appropriate at this celebration is the eucharistic banquet. Of course, Christ's inclusiveness as Savior comes in the invitation for all baptized persons to receive Communion.

The symbolizing of the new vocation in the offertory should be done and done with forethought. The retiring person has a unique opportunity to lay his or her self on God's altar saying, "Here I am, Lord; send me." This act could be a profound witness to nonbelievers. For the retiree to be joined by family, coworkers, or friends in presenting the gifts is to share the blessings. This time can be a particular tribute of thanks to God for the companionship of a spouse throughout the work life.

If the messages of the various eucharistic prayers are studied before a choice is made, the prayer selected can offer another unique moment. The specific preface recalls God's works of salvation and encourages trust in the guidance of the Holy Spirit right now.

Postcommunion. As with other milestone celebrations, a specific postcommunion prayer of thanksgiving is provided. A final reminder is given of our union with all the saints through partaking in the Eucharist. Significantly, the retiring person is named and the reason for the gathering is proclaimed once more.

Blessing and Dismissal. God's blessing sends the congregation to their livings, especially the retiring person to the new life. In addition to those already provided, a specific dismissal is provided which stresses continuing the active life in Christ. The retiring person joins in recessing so that he or she may be ready to greet those who have shared this very special time. Also, the retiree could invite others, who have been important to the work journey, to join the recessional.

Without Eucharist. For the active communicant, Holy Communion normally will be a part of the retirement service, just as it will continue nourishing the rest of life. However, good cause may preclude the Lord's banquet. In this case, a simple prayer service ending is provided, which includes a special dismissal. Here also the recessional points to a time of greeting the newly retired person.

Following the Service. At the conclusion of the service, a reception or dinner is strongly encouraged as an occasion for celebration. The number of participants is limited in the structure of the service; thus, there is the distinct possibility that others wishing to add congratulations and blessings would be disappointed without some forum. Many times only a sampling of gifts and mementos can be presented during the service. So this after-service gathering time is very important for closure to the retiree's employment and opening to the future. How this time is structured should be the choice of the retiring person; but, whether a simple reception in the parish hall or an elaborate banquet in a restaurant, the point is to honor the very real need of those attending the service. In addition to further expressions to the retiree, this time also affords due recognition of the spouse, other family members, and special persons who have supported the honoree throughout the work years.

David Cottrill

Worship and Pastoral Care: A Charismatic Approach

An emphasis in the pastoral care ministries of charismatic churches has been spiritual healing. This aspect of pastoral care has embraced, not only prayer for physical healing, but also healing from sin and sinful patterns, "inner healing" or healing of memories, and the ministry of deliverance from demonic oppression. This chapter will introduce the reader to healing in the charismatic tradition and discuss its implications for Christian worship.

212 • PASTORAL CARE AND DIRECT DIVINE HEALING

The ministry of healing has been a central aspect of the Christian faith, beginning with the work of Jesus and the apostles. Throughout Christian history, the church has pursued several approaches to the ministry of healing: hagiographical, incubational, revelational, soteriological, and confrontational.

Adolf Harnack, eminent historian of the early church, observed early in the twentieth century:

Deliberately and consciously [Christianity] assumed the form of "the religion of salvation or healing" or "the medicine of soul and body," and at the same time it recognized that one of its chief duties was to care assiduously for the sick in body. (*The Mission and Expansion of Christianity in the First Three Centuries,* 2nd ed. trans. and ed. James Moffatt [New York: G. P. Putnam's Sons, 1908], 108.)

Harnack thought this was one of the church's crucial strategic decisions, and he continued, "Christianity never lost hold of its innate principle; it was, and it remained, a religion for the sick" (Harnack 109).

Through the centuries, care for the sick has characterized those who have identified themselves with the main ideas of traditional, historic Christianity. Usually this concern has been expressed through the practice of medicine. However, not infrequently, it has appeared in extraordinary forms which can be called "divine healing," wherein the restoration of health comes through the direct intervention of God.

In any discussion of divine healing, the question of the verification of miracles must be raised. Ren Latourelle suggests three criteria that should be applied before accepting an event as miraculous. First, there must be solid historical proof that it occurred. Second, it must be something medically unusual or difficult to believe. Third, it must have occurred in a setting of prayer and holiness (*The Miracles of Jesus and the Theology of Miracles,* trans. M. J. O'Connell [New York: Paulist Press, 1988], 310–313).

According to the biblical record, healing was a major feature of Jesus' ministry. He was God's ultimate response to the spiritual, natural, social, and personal disorder caused by human sin. For those who had "eyes to see," the physical, emotional, and spiritual healings wrought by Jesus were signs that the kingdom of God had appeared among human beings. These signs of the kingdom continued after the ascension of Jesus, and on throughout the church age until the present day. This study will examine some approaches to divine healing that have occurred in the history of the church.

The Hagiographical Approach. The name *hagiography* is derived from the Greek *hagios*, meaning "saint." Hagiography is the written record or study of the lives of saints. This approach to healing emphasizes the holiness of the healer, based on the fact that the first New Testament healers were Jesus and his apostles. During the second and third centuries the church developed the idea that Christian martyrs and especially holy people had somehow attained an exalted position of influence with the deity and could intercede with God on behalf of the sick and needy. Relics such as items that belonged to these saints, or even parts of their dead bodies, were thought to have inherent healing power.

Modern examples of the hagiographical approach are the healing ministry at St. Joseph's Oratory in Montreal, which originated with the ministry of Brother Andre and the miracles occurring at Medjugorje, in the former Yugoslavia, where it is claimed that the Virgin Mary has been appearing daily since June 1981. In both places, the emphasis on Jesus Christ and the thoroughness of documentation indicate that some of the healings are authentic.

The Incubational Approach. In the early centuries of the church various locations were designated as "shrines" where it was thought healings were likely to occur. More recently, two ministries that developed in Switzerland claimed that people who came to stay in their residences and were prayed for over a length of time could be healed. One is the Elim Institution in Mannedorf, south of Zurich, founded by Dorothea Trudel in the mid-nineteenth century. The other was established in the 1930s by Charles and Blanche de Siebenthal and Marguerite Chapuis in Yverdon-les-Bains, north of Lausanne.

Both of these ministries based their practices on James 5:14-16, committing themselves to persevering prayer until healings took place. They welcomed whoever came with whatever disorder and assumed that healing would eventually occur in each case.

The Revelational Approach. The revelational approach to healing is based on Scripture passages such as the story of Ananias and Sapphira in Acts 5 and the mention of the word of knowledge in 1 Corinthians 12:8. Both of the passages indicate that God gives supernatural revelation.

William Branham, associated with the Latter Rain revival of the 1940s, practiced the revelational approach to healing and became a model for many other North American ministries. Branham allegedly received information about people's illnesses from an angelic messenger, who stood by him as he ministered to the sick. Miracles were a hallmark of the Latter Rain revival, and a great many have been attributed to Branham.

Kathryn Kuhlman's ministry extended from the late 1940s until her death in 1976. Miss Kuhlman disavowed any part in the healing process, insisting that her role was simply to announce what God had already done as God made her aware of it. As a result of the spectacular healings associated with her ministry, she became a well-known American religious figure.

The Soteriological Approach. By the late nineteenth century, a number of people from major denominations had begun to practice healing. Based on Matthew's assertion that Jesus fulfilled the prophecy of Isaiah 53:4, "He himself took our infirmities, and carried away our diseases" (Matt. 8:17), these people taught that as a person is saved through faith in the atoning work of Christ, that person can also be healed through such faith. This doctrine came to be known as "healing in the atonement."

In the mid-twentieth century, Oral Roberts and other members of the Pentecostal movement adopted this concept of healing. Roberts toured the nation with a revival tent from 1947 to 1968, laying hands on thousands of people for divine healing.

The Confrontational Approach. J. C. Blumhardt, who died in Germany in 1880, and John Wimber, founder of the Vineyard churches in southern California, both exemplify confrontational healing. Central to this philosophy is the idea that Jesus has engaged the powers of darkness in battle and has defeated them, inaugurating the victorious kingdom of God. His victory makes it possible for Christians to maintain victory over the sickness and demonic activity that characterize the kingdom of darkness.

Blumhardt did most of his praying in the privacy of his Kurhaus in Bad Boll, while Wimber ministers to large crowds in public. He also employs the gift of knowledge in his exercise of the gift of healing. Wimber is unique among those with dramatic healing ministries in that he has devoted much time and energy to teaching others how to pray for the sick.

Conclusion. The healing ministry of the church through the centuries has featured both the ordinary and the marvelous. Countless testimonies of healing verify that God sometimes chooses to respond to human need by direct intervention. There is no formula that guarantees healing; nor does the occurrence of healings or miracles authenticate the doctrinal philosophy of the healer. Healing is God's prerogative, and God remains sovereign.

Ronald Kydd

213 • FOUR BASIC TYPES OF HEALING

Effective healing ministry involves an understanding of the basic types of conditions that require healing, and the appropriate prayer methods by which each condition may be addressed.

A real problem in the ministry of healing is the tendency to oversimplify—the making of one's own limited experience into a rule or doctrine. In the past, priests and ministers were often trained to treat most problems as though they were moral problems that could be solved by _will power,_ through the help of grace. A better understanding of various types of healing is essential to an effective ministry in this area.

There are four basic kinds of healing, differentiated by the kinds of sickness that afflict us and the underlying causes of those sicknesses. Unless we know these differences, we will not be able to help most people. We might, in fact, harm them by insisting on a particular diagnosis and a particular method of prayer, when a different diagnosis and type of treatment and prayer are needed.

In praying for the sick, then, we must understand that there are three types of illness, each requiring a different kind of prayer: (1) sickness of spirit caused by personal sin; (2) emotional illness and problems (e.g., anxiety) caused by past hurts; (3) physical illness caused by disease or accident. In addition, any of the above can be caused by demonic oppression.

As a consequence, there are at least _four basic prayer methods_ that must be understood in order

to exercise a complete healing ministry: (1) prayer for _repentance_ from personal sin; (2) prayer for _inner healing_ or "healing of memories" for emotional problems; (3) prayer for _physical healing_ from physical illness; and (4) prayer for _deliverance_ (exorcism) from demonic oppression.

Sometimes a person will need all of these forms of prayer. For example, a middle-aged woman may ask for prayer for arthritis (physical healing), who was deeply hurt by her father when she was young (inner healing), has never forgiven him (repentance), and has not been able to relate properly to her husband (inner healing). In her search for answers, she has attended séances or consulted a "spirit-guide," who has given her guidance through automatic writing (deliverance).

Sacraments and Rites. In sacramentally oriented churches, sacramental acts are used for these same four types of healing. (1) The sacrament of _reconciliation_ (formerly termed penance) effects repentance. (2) The sacrament of _reconciliation_ can also effect inner healing. (3) The sacrament of _anointing of the sick_ effects physical healing. (4) The rite of _exorcism_ effects deliverance from demonic oppression or possession.

Medicine. God's healing can also come through the ministration of the medical profession. In the past, there seems to have been a division in the minds of many Christians between divine healing and natural or medicinal healing. Such a division is unnecessary and can be damaging to the patient, who may be reluctant to consult a physician because he or she thinks that depending on medicine or therapy indicates a lack of faith. The truth is that all healing derives ultimately from the Creator God and is under the control of God's sovereign will.

Francis MacNutt[36]

214 • HEALING OF SIN

Physical and emotional illness is often related to underlying patterns of sinful attitude and behavior. In such situations, genuine repentance is an essential component of healing.

The first and deepest form of healing that Christ brings is the forgiveness of sin. Salvation from sin is healing at the deepest level.

Even though a person has been forgiven and received into the family of God, the practice of sin in his or her life is often related to physical and emotional illness. The Lord promises Israel that if they keep the commandments God will not bring on them the diseases God brought on the Egyptians (Exod. 15:26; Deut. 7:15). Paul warns the Corinthians that failing to properly recognize the body of Christ will result in physical ailments and even death (1 Cor. 11:29-32).

The connection between sin and sickness has been noted by psychologists and physicians. Howard R. and Martha E. Lewis write:

> Even cancer has recently been linked to emotion. Researchers are finding that cancer victims are often people who have long felt hopeless, who have believed that their lives are doomed to despair. The onset of the disease in many cases is associated with a series of overwhelming losses that make the person finally give up entirely. (*Psychosomatics: How Your Emotions Can Damage Your Health* [1972], 7.)

The Gospels record that in some instances Jesus responded in anger to illness. When told that Peter's mother-in-law was sick, Jesus is said to have rebuked the fever (Luke 4:39). This is a distinctively different attitude from that of some Christian writers, who see illness as redemptive. Rather than being redemptive, physical sickness can be a sign that a person is falling apart at a deeper level.

The realization that physical illness can symbolize a deeper sickness caused Dr. Paul Tournier to abandon the merely physical treatment of his patients and to incorporate both prayer and psychology, in attempting to heal his patients at all levels.

It is sometimes helpful to initiate a prayer of repentance for inner healing before praying for physical healing. When Jesus healed the paralytic, who was let down through the roof, he first pronounced forgiveness on the man. In this case, the physical healing was a sign that spiritual healing had occurred.

People have been known to be healed spontaneously after participating in a prayer of forgiveness for those who had wronged them. On the other hand, a lack of forgiveness appears to be a major obstacle in receiving healing. This may be why Jesus links the forgiveness of one's enemies with answers to prayer (Mark 11:24-25). A person who refuses to forgive what others have done is closing himself or herself off to another person, and in so doing is rendered incapable of opening himself or herself to the Lord. Jesus said that loving one's neighbor is closely related to loving God; it is in doing both that a person fulfills the Word of God (Matt. 22:38-40). James' classic statement on healing includes a directive to "confess your sins to each other, and pray for each other so that you may be healed" (James 5:16).

Francis MacNutt[37]

215 • INNER HEALING OF EMOTIONS

Inner healing is a process through which the background causes for dysfunctional behavior and emotional distress are discovered and dealt with through prayer. A recognizable sequence of events often occurs in the effective ministration of inner healing.

Many sincere Christians remain defeated in their personal and emotional lives in spite of repentance and the exercise of will power. When priests and pastors find they cannot help them, the sufferers are referred to psychiatrists. In many cases, the only result of this kind of therapy is that the patients acquire a vocabulary to describe their problems.

Intractable emotional problems usually produce a profound sense of guilt in the Christian, who knows that a believer's life is supposed to be an example of God's power and victory. Christians should experience inner *peace and joy,* delight in the knowledge that *God loves them,* relate to others in *community,* and live a life *free from anxiety.* Yet a depressed person can do none of these things. In some cases, God becomes the enemy because it appears that God is refusing to respond to the earnest prayers and efforts of the emotionally disturbed person.

The Rationale for Inner Healing

In 1966, Agnes Sanford published a book entitled *The Healing Gifts of the Spirit* (Philadelphia: Lippincott, 1966) in which she introduced the concept of "healing of the memories." Mrs. Sanford explained that many people are affected not only by what they themselves have done, but also by the sins of others and by entrenched evil in the world. For example, a child who is deprived of love will lose the ability to love and trust other people or even God. As an adult, the person may deeply desire these relationships, but be unable to achieve them.

The basic concept of inner healing is that the Jesus who healed during his earthly ministry, and who is "the same yesterday and today and forever" (Heb. 13:8), can remove the poison of past hurts and resentments, heal the wounds thereby inflicted, and fill the injured person with his love. In such cases, there will be a need for repentance and possibly also for deliverance.

Prayer for inner healing should be considered any time a person becomes aware that he or she is in some way incapacitated or bound by old hurts. This bondage may evidence itself in feelings of worthlessness, erratic periods of anger or depression, anxiety and unreasoning fears, compulsive sexual drives, and other similar problems.

The Process of Inner Healing

The process of receiving inner healing involves asking Jesus Christ to take us back in memory to the time of the emotional injury and to free us from its effects. This involves two steps: (1) _bringing to light_ the things that have hurt us, and (2) _praying_ for healing. It is usually best to talk through our hurts and their possible cause with another person, since exposing the incident can sometimes render it powerless and facilitate healing. In prayer, we ask the Lord to heal the wound and nullify its effects.

Some psychologists now believe that many of a person's deepest hurts are sustained at a very early age, sometimes before birth. It is thought that a mother's rejection of the unborn baby or her anxieties can have an emotional effect on the child. Adult patterns are usually set in the first three years of life, before the child is capable of understanding what is happening to him or her and before a person is free to make personal decisions. If a person has always felt unloved or unlovable or is chronically restless or fearful without apparent reason, it can be helpful to examine those early years for emotional injuries.

The Setting for Prayer

Because the revelation of painful and sometimes shameful memories can be difficult and embarrassing, it is best to arrange a private setting for this activity. The afflicted person must never be forced to pray about personal matters in a large group or with someone with whom he or she feels no affinity. Given the sensitive nature of the matters that could be disclosed, he or she should be able to select persons with whom to pray. Sometimes this can be done in the confessional setting, with the sacrament of reconciliation being extended to include the prayer for inner healing.

In any case, the one who is called upon to minister inner healing should be qualified by a gift of the Spirit, should have knowledge of psychology, and should be sensitive. The prayer counselor should not initiate prayer for inner healing, but should wait until the hurting person volunteers information concerning a need and indicates that help is desired. This can take place in very informal settings, such as at morning coffee with a friend or neighbor.

In cases of depression, the sufferer will probably not feel that he or she has sufficient faith to believe God for healing. It is possible that the sufferer has prayed about the problem previously and is convinced that God does not care about the situation. The counselor must not require a demonstration or statement of faith from the person, but must assume that if faith is required it will come from the one who is ministering the healing. It is important to allow enough time for the problem to be confessed and for the prayer to be unhurried. Arrangement should also be made for follow-up.

Excising the Wound

Before praying it is often helpful to ask a few specific questions. For example, in order to locate the origin of the hurt one might ask, "Did you have a happy childhood?" If the answer is "no," an explanation of the reason usually reveals the basic problem. If "yes," one can ask when things first began to go wrong. As a general rule, the problem will date to childhood.

Another question that can be asked is, "Do you have any idea _why_ this happened to you?" The answer to this question may reveal broken relationships with parents through neglect, harshness, or even death. When hurting people do not know what happened to cause their symptoms, the counselor should pray for God's revelation or wait until such time as the painful event comes to consciousness. If people can remember how the problem began and why it occurred, they should ask Jesus to walk back into the past with them while the counselor describes the Lord's healing of each of the principal emotional hurts they have sustained. Because it is the inner child of the past who is being healed, the prayer should be couched in a simple, childlike style.

When a person reveals his or her inner hurts, they may sound inconsequential to an adult mind. However, they were probably very traumatic to the immature victim. Both the counselor and the one for whom prayer is offered should attempt to experience the pain as a child would have done in the situation.

——————— Filling the Void ———————

After the prayer for healing of the hurt, a prayer should follow for the filling up of the empty places the traumatic early experiences may have left in the life. Such a prayer usually involves asking for a filling with God's love, since a perceived lack of love is almost always the root of the original problem. In many cases, it is the love of the child's father, which psychiatrists now recognize is vital for healthy self-esteem and emotional development that was missing. Jesus prayed that the love with which the Father loved him could be in the disciples (John 17:26); this is the essence of the prayer that should follow healing of memories. The prayer can be personal and graphic. For example, the counselor might ask God to hold the hurting child in his arms or take him or her by the hand and assure the person of God's love and care.

Francis MacNutt[38]

216 ◆ PHYSICAL HEALING

The ministry of prayer for physical healing involves a process of listening, physical contact where appropriate, and prayer with confidence and thanksgiving.

It is probably more difficult to believe God for physical healing than for any other type. Christians are sure that prayer can bring people to repentance or change a person's character, but many are reluctant to pray specifically for physical healing. Such prayer requires spiritual cour-

age. It is, however, a simple process and usually takes less time and preparation than prayer for inner healing.

(1) Listening. The first step in praying for healing is to listen in order to find out the nature of the problem. There are two specific things for which to listen: (1) what the person perceives as the problem; and (2) what God might disclose about the problem through the word of knowledge. One ear should be tuned to the sick person and the other to God. Sometimes the knowledge from God comes in the form of definite mental images or verbal impressions. In many more cases it comes in a form similar to intuition. The person praying receives a sense of what is causing the problem.

In addition to insight about the problem, God gives other direction when we are careful to listen. Among those things we learn to listen for are *whether or not to pray*, and *what to pray for*.

There are multitudes of sick people. Some of them are not ready to be healed, even when they ask for prayer; perhaps we are not the right people to pray for them. We should pray only for those persons to whom God directs us. One indication that God's healing power is present is a sensation of warmth, similar to a gentle flow of electricity coursing through the hands. Sometimes there is an inward assurance that we are to pray for a particular person. Certain people experience a sense of peace or joy when they are supposed to pray and a feeling of heaviness or darkness when they are not. Agnes Sanford writes:

> It is not the duty of every Christian to pray for everyone. Our prayers will help some and will not help others, for reasons beyond our understanding or control. Only the Holy Spirit can safely direct our healing power. And if we will listen to the voice of God within, we will be shown for whom to pray. God directs us most joyfully through our own desires. The impulse of love that leads us to the doorway of a friend is the voice of God within and we need not be afraid to follow it. (*The Healing Light* [Plainfield, N.J.: Logos International, 1976], 86.)

Even when no clear guidance is received, it is appropriate to pray for healing. If a person asks for prayer, it can be assumed that he or she has been prompted by the Lord to request this help. Also, when we sense compassion rising in us toward the person requesting prayer, we should respond to his or her need.

When listening to the person describing the problem for which he or she desires prayer, we should be alert to the possibility that healing may be needed at a deeper level than the level the person is expressing. There may be a need for repentance; and the sufferer may wish to take part in the rite of reconciliation. If the listener discerns that the person needs deliverance, it is best to request the help of several people experienced in this kind of ministry.

In addition to listening to the person describe his or her symptoms, it is important to hear what the Holy Spirit might tell us about the nature of the affliction. The conviction that Jesus Christ and his Spirit are the ultimate source of the life to which we are about to minister can give us confidence that our Lord will enlighten us about how to pray effectively for that person.

(2) Laying On of Hands. Laying hands on the sick is a traditional Christian practice. Jesus promises that those who believe in him "will place their hands on sick people, and they will get well" (Mark 16:18). If the person for whom you are praying objects, it is best to respect his or her feelings and maintain a slight distance. However, both the Bible and practical experience verify that healing power often flows from the person praying to the person for whom he or she prays through physical touch. Jesus sensed that healing virtue left him when the woman with a hemorrhage touched the hem of his robe (Luke 8:46).

On a purely human level, physical touch can be therapeutic. Love and concern are more tangibly expressed with touch than with words.

(3) The Prayer. Prayer for the sick can be spontaneous or prepared in advance. One can assume any comfortable position—sitting, kneeling, or standing. The object is to put both parties to the prayer at ease in order that they can forget themselves and concentrate on the presence of God. Ordinarily the prayer for healing involves (1) the _presence of God_, and (2) the _petition_. Knowing that only the Lord can heal, we focus our spiritual consciousness on him and his love for us.

The prayer for healing should be as _specific_ as possible. Visualize clearly what we are asking God to do. For example, when praying for the healing of a bone, we can ask the Lord to remove infection, stimulate the growth of the cells needed to restore the bone, and fill in any breaks. Being specific in making request has the added benefit of enlarging the faith of the person praying as he or she sees in his or her imagination the healing taking place.

The prayer should be _positive_. Instead of emphasizing the state of illness, focus on the body as it will be when it has been healed. Positive prayer encourages the sufferer and builds faith.

(4) With Confidence. Jesus taught that a person who has no doubt in his heart can command a mountain to fall into the sea and it will obey him (Mark 11:22-23). Faith to believe for healing is a spiritual gift. However, the Bible does not teach that only those with this gift should pray for healing. Jesus assured his disciples that if they asked, believing that they had their request, it would be theirs (Mark 11:24). Knowing that it is Jesus' nature and his desire to heal, we can ask him to do so with confidence.

(5) With Thanksgiving. Paul exhorts believers not to worry about anything, "but in everything, by prayer and petition, with thanksgiving, present your requests to God" (Phil. 4:6). Thanksgiving finds its source in the assurance that God hears and answers prayer. John writes:

> This is the confidence we have in approaching God: that if we ask anything according to his will, he hears us. And if we know that he hears us— whatever we ask—we know that we have what we asked of him. (1 John 5:14-15)

Thanking God for the answer as a part of the healing prayer can nurture faith and encourage the sick person to believe God for healing.

(6) Prayer in the Spirit. In some situations, it is difficult to know how to pray. At these times, we can turn our prayer over to the Holy Spirit and pray in tongues, knowing that "the Spirit himself intercedes for us with groans that words cannot express" (Rom. 8:26). When time constraints do not allow the minister to speak personally with each person who has come for prayer, he or she can lay hands on each person in turn, praying in the Spirit, trusting the Spirit to direct the prayer. This can also be done when the sick person speaks another language and cannot indicate the nature of his or her problem to the person praying.

Francis MacNutt[39]

217 ♦ DELIVERANCE AND EXORCISM

Deliverance ministry is intended to heal through setting people free from demonic influence over their behavior and emotions. This entry presents specific guidelines and cautions with respect to the conduct of deliverance ministry.

Within the Roman Catholic church, a distinction is made between *exorcism* and *deliverance.* Exorcism is a formal ecclesiastical prayer to free a person *possessed* by evil spirits and requires the permission of the bishop. *Deliverance*, on the other hand, frees a person from oppression by evil spirits and is a relatively common occurrence. In the Protestant community, the term *exorcism* is rarely used, but some charismatic ministries are known for their emphasis on deliverance.

Deliverance ministry is more often avoided than pursued by the clergy. It is much easier and less frightening to pray for healing than to command evil spirits and do battle with supernatural powers. However, there are some people who cannot be helped without being delivered from the power of demonic oppression.

Jesus did not draw back from dealing with Satanic powers, nor did his disciples. The one who ministers in Jesus' name cannot refuse to follow his example and fight the demonic whenever it presents itself.

Indications That Deliverance Is Needed

Our society has tended to diagnose various personality problems as neuroses and psychoses, but such labels do not reveal the root causes of the problems. They merely describe symptoms. It is not legitimate to assume that evil spirits afflict every person who suffers with these conditions. On the other hand, those who are closed to the possibility that such problems as schizophrenia can be caused by demonic intervention may be refusing the patient what could be his or her only opportunity for a cure.

Three basic guidelines can be used to determine when deliverance ministry is appropriate:

(1) Is there a history of compulsive behavior? When a person is unable to change destructive behavior in spite of repeated attempts to employ self-discipline, either prayer for inner healing or prayer for deliverance (or both) may be the an-

swer. Common compulsions include drug addiction, alcoholism, attempted suicides, and overeating.

(2) Does the person asking for prayer state that the problem is demonic in origin? This is not to suggest that every person who thinks he or she is beset by demons is correct. However, such a person's testimony should be seriously considered by the minister.

(3) Does the prayer for inner healing appear to be ineffective? Because this kind of prayer usually has a positive, visible effect, the fact that it does not, in some cases, should alert the minister to the possibility that the problem is demonic in origin and deliverance is required.

Persons who are under demonic oppression are often guilt-ridden and consider themselves unworthy, unlovable, and destined for failure. These same symptoms can be produced by psychological wounds from a traumatic or unhappy past. Chemical imbalance in the body can sometimes cause depression and feelings of guilt. The spiritual gift of discernment is necessary for determining what kind of prayer—whether for deliverance, inner healing, or physical healing—will be most effective in the situation. It is wise to enlist the

The Cross of Iona. This distinguished-looking cross with the circle representing the Trinity is the traditional Celtic or Irish cross.

help of people known to exercise this gift whenever possible.

The Prayer for Deliverance

The prayer for deliverance differs from prayers for healing in two specific ways: (1) whereas prayer for healing is addressed to God, in prayer for deliverance, the minister addresses the demons directly; and (2) whereas prayer for healing is ordinarily a petition, prayer for deliverance is a command.

For a person who has the gift of faith, prayer for healing can also be a command—"In the name of Jesus Christ of Nazareth, walk!" (Acts 3:6b)—but prayer for deliverance is always a command, ordering the demonic forces to depart in the name of Jesus Christ. When delivering the soothsaying slave girl, Paul said to the evil spirit, "In the name of Jesus Christ, I command you to come out of her!" (Acts 16:18b).

Prayer for Protection. As the prayer begins it is wise to pray for _protection_. Ask God to surround and protect every person in the room with the power of the blood of Christ. Pray that no evil force will be able to harm anyone in the room—or anywhere else—as a result of demons being cast out. That this kind of harm can occur is evident in the biblical record in Acts 19:15-16:

> The evil spirit replied, "Jesus I know, and I know about Paul, but who are you?" Then the man who had the evil spirit jumped on them and overpowered them all. He gave them such a beating that they ran out of the house naked and bleeding.

In this instance, the exorcists, the sons of Sceva, apparently did not have the spiritual authority needed to perform the exorcism. Similarly, problems can arise for us if we do not pray for God's help and are not called to this ministry, which deals with powerful spiritual forces.

Binding the Enemy. After praying for protection, we should ask in the name of Jesus that the force and power of any demons _be bound_ and lose their power to resist. This kind of prayer seems to help the deliverance take place more quickly and with less effort. For example, during prayer for deliverance, some persons feel as if they are being choked by an invisible hand; they may be thrown to the ground; or they may suddenly go blank. The demons may begin speaking through the person, saying things such as "You will never drive us out; we are too many and too strong for you." All of these manifestations temporarily interfere with the prayer until they are dealt with. Praying that the powers of evil be bound can avoid some of these unpleasant occurrences.

Identifying the Oppression. It is helpful to determine _the identity_ of the demon with whom we are dealing. Usually demons are identified by their predominant activity; e.g., a spirit of self-destruction or a spirit of fear. This may sound strange to those who have never dealt with demonic forces, but demons do seem to have identities and names, which they reveal to us in several ways:

(1) The person asking for prayer knows what the demon is or its characteristic activity is.

(2) Through the gift of discernment, the persons doing the praying know the identity of the demon(s). This does occur, but it is unusual.

(3) Through commanding the demons to identify themselves, their names or characteristics are discovered. Often they will speak through the oppressed person or he or she will receive a strong mental picture or idea of the nature of the demon.

Renunciation. If an area of demonic interference is recognized, the person should _renounce any sin_ connected with it. If, for example, a spirit of hatred identifies itself, then the person should forgive any persons who have ever wronged him or her, and thus cut away the sin or wound that has given the demonic force a hold on the sufferer's life. In addition, one can _renounce the spirit_ of hatred or whatever else it is. If the evil spirits do not have a profound hold upon a person, self-deliverance is a real possibility. If the person has been involved in spiritualism or other forms of occult activity, he or she should renounce by name each one of these activities.

Casting Out the Demon. The next step is to ask the tormented _person himself or herself to cast out_ the demon by a prayer of command. Sometimes this is enough to cause the demonic force to depart.

If the demons have not yet departed, the minister should pray for deliverance. This deliverance prayer has several definite components:

(1) "In the name of Jesus Christ . . ." It is not by our authority that we cast these demons out,

but we name the power to which all principalities and powers must bow. "'Lord,' they said, 'even the devils submit to us when we use your name'" (Luke 10:17).

(2) "I command you . . . " (looking directly into the eyes of the person for whom you are praying). This is a prayer of authority, not of entreaty. The person commanding can speak quietly, but must really believe that the authority of Christ will rout the forces of evil.

(3) "the spirit of . . . " Identify the spirit, if possible, by name, "spirit of hate," "spirit of despair," or whatever else it is.

(4) "to depart . . . "

(5) "without harming [the person being freed] or anyone in this house or anyone anywhere else, and without creating any noise or disturbance . . . " There have been occasions when other people have been attacked by the demons leaving; or the person being prayed for has been needlessly tormented. These problems can all be precluded by praying for God's protection. Since deliverance tends to be a spectacular or ugly performance if the demons are unchecked, it is advisable to command them to be quiet and not to create any disturbance.

(6) "and I send you straight to Jesus Christ that he might dispose of you as he will." Some practitioners prefer to command demons to "return to the abyss," but it is better to leave their destiny to the wisdom of Christ. "But even the archangel Michael, when he was disputing with the devil about the body of Moses, did not dare to bring a slanderous accusation against him, but said, 'The Lord rebuke you!'" (Jude 9).

After the prayer for deliverance, there is often a transforming change that takes place in people who have not been helped by any other means. They may say things like, "I just felt something leave" or "I feel a tremendous weight being lifted off me."

If there are many demons, the person seems to know when they have all gone. There is a sense of freedom and joy; at times, there is actual physical relief, such as the removal of some gripping pain.

Often the demons come out with a struggle. Sometimes they cry out or throw the person to the floor (phenomena mentioned in the Gospels) or they come out in a fit of coughing or retching. All of these symptoms are unpleasant and make the work of deliverance an unsavory task. If these phenomena become too exhibitionistic, the minister can command the demons to keep quiet, to stop tormenting the person, or to cease whatever else they are doing.

After praying the prayer of deliverance, it is helpful for the leader and others to praise God or to sing (and for those who pray in tongues to do so). This kind of prayer goes on until the demon releases whatever hold it has upon the person and leaves. If there is no change, the person leading the prayer needs the discernment to know how to proceed from there.

Following the Deliverance

In order to prevent a return of oppression, three procedures should be followed after a deliverance.

(1) Immediately after the deliverance the minister should pray inviting the Lord to fill the person with his love and grace. Any area left empty by the departure of demons should be filled by the presence of Jesus.

(2) The person should be taught to break the habitual behavior patterns that led to the original demonic infestation. If the problem was in the area of despair, for example, some kind of spiritual discipline is needed to combat the area of human weakness that caused the problem in the first place. In addition, the person should be taught how to rebuke any forces of evil and keep them away, once they have been driven out. "Submit yourselves, then, to God. Resist the devil, and he will flee from you" (James 4:7).

(3) The person who has been delivered should adopt a regular schedule of prayer, of reading the Scripture, and (if he or she belongs to a sacramental church) of receiving the sacraments of the Eucharist and of reconciliation.

(4) Ideally, the person should then become part of a Christian community. Just as alcoholics have found that they cannot, for the most part, remain sober without the help of people who understand and care (such as members of Alcoholics Anonymous), so people who have been delivered need the prayer and loving support of community. Churches should make a concerted effort to provide such interaction and support.

Who Should Pray for Deliverance

For a variety of reasons, the ministry of deliverance should be reserved for those who have been called to it. Because deliverance requires a prayer of authority, those who feel uncomfortable in situations of authority—who are timid or insecure—are not suited to this ministry. They will either be so frightened that nothing will happen through their prayer or they will mask their insecurity by false posturing that will only discredit their ministry.

On the other hand, because deliverance is a confrontational ministry, persons with aggressive tendencies may feel called to this work, when in reality they are working out their own aggressions. Since their motivation is ambiguous, the results of their ministry are likely to be the same and can result in damage to the sensitivities of the person to whom they are attempting to minister.

Because of the need for sorting out the complexities of good and evil and knowing when to pray, what to pray for, and how, the deliverance minister must be experienced, wise, and discerning. People with a simplistic mentality, who tend to see issues in terms of black or white, often seem drawn to a deliverance ministry in which they help some people while they harm many others. This often gives deliverance a bad image, frightening away the very persons who might be qualified to exercise a discerning ministry of deliverance.

Francis MacNutt[40]

❧ TEN ❧

Worship and Spiritual Formation

The church is increasingly aware of its responsibility to provide spiritual nurture to all who participate in its life. Further, the actions, institutions, and teachings of the church have significant influence in shaping an individual's personal spiritual life. A person's understanding of God's nature, ability to experience the presence of God, and awareness of God's actions in the world are all influenced by such things as the type of language used in worship, the attitudes and actions encouraged in worship, and the patterns of communal support expressed in the worshiping community. These actions are often more influential in shaping personal spirituality than any official teaching or doctrine. Thus, worshiping communities have a great responsibility to consider the implications and influence of their patterns of worship and to take great care that their worship life provides a strong foundation for personal spirituality that is both vigorous and faithful to the Scriptures.

218 • WORSHIP AND SPIRITUAL FORMATION

Every aspect of liturgy shapes the faith of the worshiping community, altering its understanding of both God and the Christian life. This article explores some of the ways in which this occurs and suggests ways in which the church's worship can more adequately reflect the fullness of the gospel.

Definitions

It is a truism that worship has something to do with spiritual formation and direction. Actually defining the relationship between the two, however, involves considering a number of factors not evident upon a surface consideration of the topic. For instance, the term *spiritual direction* often evokes images of a spiritual mentor counseling a neophyte charge in matters concerning the ascent of God. This individual-centered model of how one grows in God continues today in the ancient contemplative monastic orders of the West and even is beginning to be utilized in various forms in a number of Protestant churches. Within that tradition, there are authors, such as Thomas Merton, who have attempted to relate liturgy to the practice of spiritual mentoring.

What concerns us here, however, is not the classical institution of spiritual direction. Instead, what follows is an introduction to the relationship between Christian worship and what can be termed spiritual formation. The question is how worship can be and is related to ongoing spiritual growth, which is a part of Christian life. That process obviously goes by different names in different ecclesiastical traditions: sanctification, holiness, even divinization (Greek *theosis*). This diversity of terminology reflects the variety of linguistic, historical, and sociological factors involved in how Christians describe and attempt to understand the very mystery of salvation itself.

Many congregations and denominations have come to realize that the Sunday service of worship can act as a powerful means of shaping the spiritual development of individual Christians. This liturgical influence upon spiritual formation probably does happen and ought to happen indirectly; i.e., only by conscious reflection upon the actions of Christian worship will it become clear how worship nourishes the individual in her or his life in God. Below, we will examine four components of Christian worship in light of their role in spiritual formation: the Word, the Eucharist, baptism, and the liturgical calendar.

General Considerations

Before considering these four elements of Christian liturgy, it is necessary to make a few general remarks about the relationship between worship and Christian life. Existence in Christ cannot, of course, be reduced to participation in worship services. As Paul makes clear, the offering made by Christians is their life; that is, their service (Rom. 12:1). Occasions for communal worship are privileged times in which the Christian community gathers to proclaim and celebrate through word, action, and symbol the saving action of God in Christ.

Worship can provide a means by which the meaning of Christian life is symbolized, articulated, interpreted, and critiqued. In this sense, liturgy can operate hermeneutically. For that function fully to take place, however, worship must take its place as one, but not the only, element of the community's life in Christ. If worship stands as the only (or even the primary) element of a congregation's life, it runs the danger of losing its openness to critique in the light of the gospel's demands. In such an isolated position, worship is capable of losing any relationship to the life of the community.

Congregational worship calls forth the best efforts of all in the community to interpret its rich field of symbols in order to make available to the present the diverse and multivalent liturgical tradition. It is vital that all members of the church share in this tradition. It is vital that all members of the church share in this interpretive project by bringing their own experience of life in Christ to the community gathered for worship. In too many Christian communities, the responsibility and authority for interpreting the symbols of worship is left up to the pastor alone or to a very small group within the church.

For the formative power of worship to emerge, all Christians must actively make the experience of worship a part of the interpretive cycle of Christian life. The mechanism for interpreting the actions and symbols of worship will vary from congregation to congregation: church school; share groups; informal settings, such as meals; or more structured occasions, such as perhaps the occasional churchwide retreat. Whatever form the vehicle for reflection and interpretation takes, the imperative element is the involvement of as many congregation members as possible. The ultimate goal, of course, is the establishment of a critical piety (for want of a better term) for all the baptized, a life in Christ *semper reformanda* (always reforming).

For such a critical piety to be nourished by worship, the symbols of worship (i.e., the material elements of the sacraments, the congregational liturgical actions, the structure of services, and above all, the biblical symbols that confront worshipers as they hear the Word and receive the sacraments) must be made as accessible for interpretation as possible for each worshiper. This is the task of those responsible for planning and conducting worship services. This task requires a solid understanding of the history of Christian liturgy and of the ethos of the congregation. If knowledge of history is lacking, the service runs the risk of being subject to the latest liturgical fad. If the ethos of the congregation is not grasped, the congregation may be alienated from its own service. In both instances, the formative power of worship is lost.

The Word: Hearing in the Context of Worship

Most Christian congregations no longer rely upon the Word of God delivered through the mouths of prophets, although prophecy does occur in some Pentecostal, charismatic, and African independent church services. Even in those settings, however, the Word of God as revealed in the Scriptures of the Old Testament/Hebrew Bible and the New Testament takes precedence, at least in theory. It is the reading, hearing, and preaching of the Word that stands in a primary, fundamental relationship to Christian worship. The Bible cannot be expected to supply a blueprint for worship; its writings only hint at the liturgical practices of the communities it represents. Instead, the Word of God has a more basic authority for Christian worship. Its proclamation of the gospel ought continually to challenge the churches to a greater conformity, in loving obedience and service, to God, who has spoken in Christ. The challenge the gospel poses to the life of the church ought to find expression in the church's liturgical acts. If it does not, worship not only loses its formative power but may actually hinder discipleship.

Two examples of this authority of the Word concern the persistence of racism and sexism in North

American congregations. Martin Luther King, Jr., called the Sunday worship hour "the most segregated hour in American life." Although Christians proclaim that in Christ "there is no Jew or Greek, male or female, slave or free," their liturgical assemblies often legitimate the exclusion of women from the gospel story and paper over the chasm separating Christians of different races. Any adequate theology of the Word of God in worship and spiritual formation must include an acknowledgment of the word of judgment that continues to address the "solemn assemblies" of contemporary Christians. A willingness to hear that Word and to act upon it helps legitimate what Christians have to say in other settings about the power of God's Word.

At least since the nineteenth century, American Protestant worship has not included a tremendous amount of Scripture. One learns from studying the witnesses to ancient Christian worship and preaching that Scripture directly and indirectly composed a major portion of worship. The great liturgies of the ancient sees (St. Mark in Alexandria, St. Basil and St. Chrysostom in Constantinople, St. James in Jerusalem, and several others) every Sunday included readings from the Law, the Prophets, the Epistles, Acts, and the Gospels. Ancient Christian prayers and hymns constantly quote and allude to Scripture passages. For example, the hymns of Ephrem the Syrian (d. 373) weave together scriptural allusion and imagery into masterpieces of poetic and theological expressions. They were sung in Ephrem's church and constitute one of the greatest poetic treasures of all Christianity.

Through the hearing of Scripture in the service, individuals can begin to relate the narratives of their lives to those of the people God called in Israel's history and in the ministry, death, and resurrection of Jesus. The question is how the church service can expose the congregation to most, if not all, of the Scriptures over the course of a given period of time. It is historically the case that, in mainline Protestant denominations, not much Scripture has been read or sung in the Sunday service. The advent of the ecumenical three-year lectionary produced under the auspices of the Consultation on Common Texts (most recently revised in 1992) has helped to change that situation, at least for some churches.

The CCT _Revised Common Lectionary_ is accompanied by a liturgical calendar into which the three-year cycle of readings fits. Thus this ecumenical lectionary makes possible the reading of a substantial portion of the Old Testament/Hebrew Bible and the New Testament over a relatively short period of time. In the process, the congregation using it experiences the biblical witness of God's saving actions through the prism of a year-long celebration of the birth, ministry, death, and resurrection of Jesus. In short, the lectionary and calendar "refract" the light of the gospel into its many components.

Of course, a lectionary provides only one means among many for achieving the goal of reading more Scripture in the Sunday service. Other churches choose to read entire books of the Bible over a number or Sundays. This method, known as _lectio continua_, appears to have been practiced in some ancient churches and was advocated by several of the sixteenth-century Protestant Reformers. The advantage of this approach versus that of a lectionary seems clear: One reads through entire biblical works, not simply the selections chosen for the lectionary. The disadvantages of _lectio continua_ include a potential loss of any wider context in which to place the work being read; there is always the danger that the congregation will lose sight of the wider canonical and historical context of the Sunday readings.

It does not necessarily follow, however, that a church that elects to follow this practice must abandon a liturgical calendar. Indeed, the construction of a scheme for the reading of entire biblical books that corresponded with the celebration of the Christmas and Easter liturgical cycles could make a challenging and rewarding exercise for a congregation willing to invest the time and energy to do so.

The Eucharist: Context for Spiritual Formation

The Lord's Supper is rooted in the actions of Jesus, who ate with tax collectors and sinners, who miraculously fed multitudes of people who came to hear him, who ate with his disciples a final meal before his execution, and who sat down to meals with them after his resurrection. The church's celebration of the Lord's Supper appears to have drawn upon these meals Jesus held and above all upon the Last Supper, with its dominant paschal imagery of covenant, sacrifice, and freedom.

Last Supper and Lord's Supper. Too often in Protestant services, the Lord's Supper has been interpreted solely in light of the Last Supper. While the cross certainly stands at the center of the Lord's Supper, its proclamation is incomplete if it does not include the Good News of the Resurrection and of the freedom from sin and death it effects. The recovery of the Lord's Supper in many Protestant churches will entail a recovery of the proclamation of the fullness of the gospel. As it proclaims the Good News of freedom, new life, holiness, and victory over sin and death, so also can the celebration of the Lord's Supper contribute positively to spiritual formation.

It can be argued that the Eucharist (or Lord's Supper) functions as the fundamentally stable element of the Sunday service. Other portions of the weekly times of worship can and do change according to the time of the liturgical, civic, or agricultural calendar. Each Sunday, the service proclaims a different facet of the saving love of God, and the changing readings, hymns, and sermons reflect that fact.

For those churches that celebrate the Lord's Supper each Sunday, the Eucharist provides a counterpoint, a context for the seasonal portions of the service. It proclaims the larger context for the church's gathering together: the saving death and resurrection of Jesus. Several advocates of liturgical renewal have spoken of the Great Thanksgiving at the Lord's Supper as the creed par excellence of the church, for in it the saving acts of God on behalf of humanity are remembered in thanksgiving. As it does so, the Great Thanksgiving provides a constant reminder, a context for reflection and action in Christ's name.

The Lord's Supper can most adequately contribute to spiritual formation when it is celebrated often, preferably every Sunday. Some may consider that a weekly celebration of the Lord's Supper is "too Catholic" or somehow indicates crypto-Anglicanism. It is worth pointing out that frequent or weekly celebration of the Eucharist was practiced not only by the sixteenth-century Protestant Reformers (Luther, Calvin, and Simons) but also by the seventeenth- and eighteenth-century forebearers of the "free church" denominations, English and Scottish Presbyterians and Congregationalists, and English Baptists. A recovery of frequent celebration for these churches will entail a rediscovery and interpretation of their own traditions' thought on and practice of the Lord's Supper.

Nourishment and Challenge. At its best, the celebration of the Lord's Supper proclaims the gospel through its material elements (bread and wine) and its actions (thanksgiving, offering, and receiving). The Lord's Supper nourishes believers; Christians speak of receiving the body and blood of Christ in the rite. Yet there is more to the Lord's Supper than nourishment; the action of gathering about the Table of the Lord who invited all sinners to the Table ought to play a role in spiritual formation. Thus, liturgical action can inform the process of growing in Christ.

Christian Initiation: Burial and Rebirth

The classical biblical images for baptism speak of death and burial with Christ (Rom. 6) and of new birth and the descent of the Spirit (John 3; Mark 1 and parallels). There is, of course, a communal dimension to baptism; through it, women and men enter the body of Christ. These basic meanings of baptism are rich in potential for spiritual formation if they are made accessible to contemporary women and men.

The history of Christian initiation reveals a multiformity in baptismal rites, which to some extent can be traced to the predominance of one or the other of the above biblical paradigms. Given this historical diversity in the rites of initiation, it is impossible to recommend as normative any one manner of performing and structuring this act. Whatever framework of baptismal practice a congregation uses, it will best facilitate the spiritual formation of the individual if it makes explicit the rich imagery for baptism found in the New Testament and in the Christian tradition.

In recent years, many churches have begun to recover or reemphasize the role of the Spirit in baptism. Liturgical and theological traditions throughout history have not always agreed about the precise relationship of the Spirit to water baptism, nor has a consensus existed concerning the most appropriate means of symbolizing that relationship. In this century, Pentecostal and charismatic churches have emphasized the role of the Spirit in an experience of spiritual maturity or renewal subsequent to water baptism, an event known by a variety of names: baptism of the Spirit and the second blessing, to name two.

The challenge today is to make explicit and accessible the rich symbols that have been attached to baptism throughout the ages. This task implies several things on the level of the celebration of the rites themselves, for example, emphasizing the physical element of water by using the method of immersion or pouring. Or else the candidate's profession of faith or the profession of faith made on behalf of the candidate can be constructed in ways that emphasize the communal nature of that act.

For women and men who belong to twentieth-century Western cultures, perhaps the most important dimension of baptism to recover is the communal dimension. Baptism represents the abandonment of one life and the beginning of another; this new life is marked by existence in Christian community with other followers of Christ. The church as the communion of disciples is the body of Christ in the world and serves as the family in which God nurtures women and men into full maturity in Christ.

The connections between baptism and spiritual formation can be made most explicit precisely when congregations emphasize the acts of repentance and entrance into a new life in community, which make up an important part of the baptismal rites. The form of those acts will, of course, vary from congregation to congregation. Some churches may wish to form a catechumenate (whether or not that term is used) in which persons desiring to repent and turn to God can learn (over the course of days, weeks, or months) about the meaning of life in the body of Christ and thus prepare for their baptism.

The Liturgical Year: Refracting the Light of Christ

The round of special seasons, Sundays, and days in the liturgical calendars of many churches reflects the human incapacity to comprehend the depth and richness of the fact of salvation in Christ on a daily basis. In addition, most Christian calendars reflect the interconnectedness of contemporary Christian communities with other cycles that give meaning to human life: the educational calendar (beginning in early September), the agricultural cycle (to which the educational calendar is still tied, at least in the United States), the astronomical cycle, the round of civic and national

holidays, even (and perhaps most strongly of all) the commercial calendar.

Incarnation and Resurrection: Two Foci. Making sense of this jumble of festivals and seasons can seem a daunting task for anyone who wishes to make the liturgical calendar a help to Christian formation. In actuality, the liturgical calendar is simple. It revolves around the celebration of two events in Christ's life: his birth (Christmas-Epiphany) and resurrection (Easter). These two cycles, in turn, stamp the services of every Sunday, which fall in their orbit with their particular character. For example, both Christmas and Easter came eventually to be preceded, in both East and West, by a period of preparation (Advent, Lent).

The entire purpose of this arrangement of festive time is to make possible the proclamation of the gospel, to explicate and enunciate the riches of what Christians believe God has done for the world in the Christ. Thus there is in the liturgical calendar an interplay of proclamation, celebration, and commemoration. The value of the liturgical year for spiritual formation lies precisely in its ability to make readily available for Christians a broader, deeper, and richer proclamation of the Good News than they might avail themselves of on their own.

Sunday: The Feast Par Excellence. It is not an exaggeration to suggest that Sunday is the most neglected feast day of the entire calendar. Yet Sunday is the foundation for the entire liturgical cycle. It is the day of Resurrection, the day of light, the eighth day, which is a sign of the eschatological rest that awaits all God's people. As such, it is an anticipation of the joy God will bring to fruition for the entire creation at the eschaton.

The celebration of Sunday in its fullness, therefore, offers perhaps the best opportunity for providing Christians the proper theological, existential, and eschatological framework for spiritual formation. The theological value of Sunday lies in its identity as the day of Christ's resurrection, the day of the event on which all Christian hope lies. Sunday celebrates the "new creation" wrought by Christ, the new life given to women and men through the death and resurrection of the Lord. Finally, the day of Sunday looks forward to the completion of God's intention for the world's salvation, a foretaste of which has been given in the resurrection of Christ. This eschatlogical dimension of Christian faith, although sometimes neglected, is an essential component of spiritual formation, for it makes possible the attitude of vigilance in hope that marks all the Christian's life.

When the Sunday service is permeated by the festive character of the eighth day, then it can succeed in conveying the theological and communal values that must inform Christian life every day of the week. Again, the manner in which Sunday worship articulates these values will vary from congregation to congregation, according to the liturgical tradition embraced by the congregation.

Liturgy and Contemplation. The connection between liturgy and contemplation or meditation has traditionally been made in the monastic communities of East and West, in which the daily recitation of the Psalms formed the core of individual and communal prayer life. In the twentieth century, some ecumenical communities (especially the Taizé community) have introduced opportunities for contemplation within communal worship through the use of silence and repetitive song. The Taizé services and music have found wide acceptance among Protestants and Roman Catholics alike, for they offer a means of structuring space for meditation into a variety of worship services. The ecumenical potential for the use of the Taizé resources is great.

Some Protestant congregations have begun to celebrate morning prayer and vespers, in which the reading of Scripture, psalmody, prayer, and silence contribute to a liturgical setting for individual meditation and prayer. The rise of small group movements within a variety of Protestant denominations (for example, the "covenant discipleship" movement in the United Methodist Church) may make possible new liturgical environments for meditation and contemplation.

The classical "unprogrammed" Quaker meeting, in which all are silent unless prompted to speak, is popular among Christians who belong to liturgical churches but who at the same time desire the liturgical silence necessary for prayerful meditation and contemplation. The use of silence certainly provides a powerful counterpoint to the often noisy, wordy character of much Christian worship. It can provide a wholesome context in which women and men can begin to journey toward the goal of all spiritual formation: lives that themselves are constant prayers to God.

Grant S. Sperry-White

219 ✦ Worship and Spirituality

This author suggests that Christians reexamine the specific nature of worship and spirituality. Worship has to do with interiority and with patterns of living that are shaped by the living, dying, rising, and coming again of Christ. In worship, the emphasis is less on the mind and more on the spirit. In spirituality, the emphasis is less on rules by which we live and more on the formation of the person.

Until fifteen years ago, my spiritual pilgrimage was within the context of a Protestant intellectual Christianity. The emphasis in this tradition was on believing the right things and doing the right things.

In this context, the relationship between worship and spirituality was tied to the sermon. The sermon was the main event and everything else was regarded as a preliminary. A major purpose of the sermon was to clarify right belief and to inspire the congregation to live by those beliefs.

In the early 1970s, I came to a dead end in this intellectual tradition of worship and spirituality. I believed that the worship had to be something more than singing a few hymns, saying a few prayers, and listening to a long sermon that was frequently tedious and uninteresting. I also believed that spirituality had to go beyond rule keeping. So I went on a search. My search took me into the early church, into the ancient tradition of worship and spirituality.

Obviously, the ancient tradition does not reject a Christianity rooted in an intelligent understanding of the faith. Nor does it deny the importance of a moral life. Where it differs from worship and spirituality today is in its specific understanding of the nature of worship and spirituality. It goes much deeper than a mere intellectual tradition. It has to do with interiority and with patterns of living that are shaped by the living, dying, rising, and coming again of Christ. In worship, the emphasis is less on the mind and more on the spirit. In spirituality, the emphasis is less on rules by which we live and more on the formation of the person. Let me explain.

Worship in the Early Church

Worship in the early church may be defined as telling and acting out the Christ event. What was of supreme importance was not the sermon nor the experience of the worshipers but the event that called the church into being, the event that it now actualized in its celebration.

In order to understand how worship was related to spirituality in the early church, we must first understand the nature of worship among these ancient Christians. Therefore, I will summarize early Christian worship in three basic principles; then I will relate these principles to the development of spirituality.

Worship Celebrates Christ. The focal point of worship was Christ—not the window to the father of liberalism nor the isolated satisfaction theory of Fundamentalism.

The Christ that was celebrated in worship was Christ the Creator, Christ the Incarnate one, Christ the inaugurator of the kingdom, Christ crucified, Christ risen, Christ ascended, Christ coming again to renew and restore the universe. In the early church, it was the whole Christ—the Alpha and Omega, the one in whom all things had been created, the one in whom all things consisted, the one in whom all things were reconciled—that was worshiped.

But this worship was not an intellectual presentation of Christ. It was a celebration: a celebration of his victory over the power of evil, a celebration of his resurrection—a celebration of his coming again to put evil away forever and to renew the world.

Like the worship celebration of the Jewish roots from which it sprang, the Christian celebration of Christ was characterized by three things:

Primarily, _worship celebrated the Christ event._ Early Christianity rejected Gnosticism with its implication that the living, dying, and rising again of Jesus was an apparition. Rejecting such mythical ideas, early Christians insisted that worship celebrated a significant event that took place in time, space, and history.

Next, early Christians believed that through celebration _the historical event of Christ became contemporaneous._ It was not an event that was imprisoned in history. But, like the Passover, which celebrated the Exodus and made it present in the experience of Israel, the celebration of the

The Cross Bottonnée. The ends of this striking form of the cross form trefoils. This cross, once frequently stamped on the cover of hymnals, is now widely used as a decorative cross on vestments, cornerstones, and church bulletins.

Christ event made Christ and his saving action present in all its original power to the worshiping community that gathered in his name.

Finally, _the means by which this event was made alive was through story_—story told, story acted out. In the reading and preaching of the Word, the story was told. In the celebration of the Eucharist, the story was acted out. Thus, in the telling and acting out of the Christ event, worship happened.

In Worship, a Divine Encounter Takes Place. In the ancient church, the assembly of people for the purpose of worship was seen as something distinctly different from a secular gathering. In worship, something supernatural happened. In the gathering of worship, the church was actualized. The body was formed. The eschatological vision was momentarily realized. Earth was brought up into the heavens and gathered around the throne together with the cherubim, the seraphim, and all the angels.

For example, in the opening acclamations of worship, the Gloria in Excelsis lifted up the worship to the heavens as did the Sanctus in the eucharistic prayer. In these actions, the worshiper was encountered by the living God seated on the throne, surrounded by the myriad of angels singing, "Holy, Holy, Holy." This was not mere ritual or a mouthing of words. It was an experience of eschatological glory, a fleeting moment in the realty yet to be revealed.

An encounter with God also occurred through the reading and preaching of the Word. In the kerygma, the Word proclaimed became realized. The kerygma actualized a moment of covenantal community in which, like in ancient Israel, the agreements were reiterated and acknowledged again.

But the supreme moment of the liturgy, the climax, the summit toward which the entire movement of worship was directed was the eucharistic action. Here, common bread and wine became, by the word of consecration, the body and blood of Christ. Christ became present in the action, present to bring salvation, healing, and restoration, which he brought at the cross and which he finally brings in the eschaton. This was no mere memorial. It was a divine action in which the words of Jesus, "Where two or three are gathered, there am I in their midst," were fulfilled.

Divine Action Is Realized through Human Response. Nowhere among the early fathers or in the liturgies of the early church does one find the late-medieval idea of *ex opere operatum*. Divine action does not automatically take hold and reshape a human life without a response born from within, however faint. But response is not a one-time action taken here or there. It punctuates the liturgy, occurring at every stage of encounter with the divine.

For example, the response to the Gloria, to extolling God in the fullness of glory, is like that of Isaiah's "Woe is me for I am a man of unclean lips—mine eyes have seen the glory of God." The Kyrie is the proper heartfelt response: "Lord have mercy."

Similarly, the response to the Word read and preached is "Thanks be to God." This acclamation is not to be mouthed as mere external words, but as the experience of the heart. Thanks be to God, who enters our history; thanks be to God, who becomes one of us; thanks be to God, who will restore and renew the whole creation in the consummation.

But the ultimate thanksgiving is the response to the eucharistic action itself. By taking the bread and the wine in the mouth, saying "amen," and swallowing it into the stomach, the worshiper is saying "yes," "so be it," "that is for me."

But now we must ask how does this understanding of worship relate to spirituality.

The Effect of Worship on Spirituality

A summary of worship as understood and practiced in the early church will help to build the bridge between worship and spirituality. That summary is this: *Worship reenacts the Christian vision of reality. Therefore in worship, a relationship with God is established, maintained, repaired, and transformed.* But when does this take place and how?

The Sunday Liturgy Viewed as a Rehearsal of Relationship. The Sunday liturgy, which tells and acts out the Christ event in word, eucharistic prayer, and song, is the context in which the worshipers' life is continually brought back into the story of Christ. Worship from the divine standpoint is "Tell me the old, old story." Worship from the human standpoint is "Just as I am without one plea." The divine and human encounter that occurs between God and God's people again and again and again is the context in which the worshiper is formed after the image of Christ.

True Christianity is not "believism," "liturgism," or "legalism," but the formation of character. What forms, shapes, and molds our person, our values, our character, our integrity is the frequent encounter with the living Christ in the liturgy.

This encounter is no mere intellectual idea, nor can it be reduced to an emotional experience. It is an encounter within community. And insofar as the community truly seeks to be formed by the Word, the individual is drawn up into that formation. What God is about in history is the formation of the body of God, the people within a people, the society within a society, the fellowship in faith.

This family is stamped by a character—the character of Christ delivered by the Spirit, especially in worship. From a human standpoint, this means that spiritual formation occurs not merely from being *at* worship, but allowing the vision rehearsed in worship—the vision that sweeps from ·

creation to re-creation—to become the vision out of which and by which each worshiper lives.

The Church Year and Spiritual Formation. In the early church, a relationship with God through Christ not only occurred in the liturgy of every Sunday, it also occurred daily through the church year.

The power of the church year is that it provides an external organization of time through which an internal experience of the Christian vision of reality is experienced. It serves as an elongated service of worship that stretches across the year. Each portion of the annual cycle is an aspect of the Christ event, drawn from the Sunday worship and applied to the life of the church and the individual.

In Advent, the church enters the Old Testament experience of longing for the coming of the Messiah and the promised restored earth where swords will be turned into plowshares. At Christmas, the people of God reflect with awe and wonder on the Incarnate one—God with us. And at Epiphany, the church witnesses the manifestation of Christ to the whole world.

Then, during Lent, Christians travel the road of death through Holy Week into death itself. They let their sins be nailed to the cross and buried in the tomb. Then on Easter, Christians experience the Resurrection as a living reality. Finally, Pentecost becomes the experience of the Spirit, the outward mission of the church toward the world.

These examples cited above describe how corporate spiritual formation, which occurs primarily through Sunday worship and extends through the year through sacred time, becomes the impetus for daily spiritual formation. Every day has its meaning rooted in the event that broke the powers of death, shifted history into the end times, and shaped God's people toward the end of history, the new heavens and the new earth.

But what about us? What are we to do today to bring worship and spirituality together again? Let me make four suggestions:

(1) Restore a Christocentric focus to worship. Some pastors and worship committees begin by asking, "What does worship accomplish?" They conclude that worship should accomplish education, evangelism, spirituality, or some other well-intended result. They then organize the service around that purpose. Judged by the early church, this is a fundamental mistake. The initial question is not, "What does worship accomplish?" but, "What does worship represent?"

Worship represents Jesus Christ. The whole theme of heavenly worship envisioned in Revelation 4 and 5 centers on Christ. Christ is worthy to receive glory and honor and power because he "created all things" (Rev. 4:11); he is worthy because he was "slain" and has "redeemed us to God" by his blood (Rev. 5:9); he is worthy because he has made us "kings and priests to our God and we shall reign on earth" (Rev. 5:10). Worship centers on the Christ who defines existence from creation to consummation, the Christ who has created a people, the Christ who gives meaning to all of life. Christian spirituality is rooted in this vision of life and must therefore grow out of it. Christian spirituality is fundamentally a life lived out of this vision. It is not a mere do-goodism or a head belief, but a life lived in the conviction that the Christ of the Bible is the meaning giver, that all things, including one's whole life, is of him, through him, and to him.

(2) Restore an order for worship that tells and acts out the fundamental story of human existence. Many Protestant churches have lost the meaning of order. These churches' emphasis on "doing things from the heart" frequently ignores the axiom that *external order organizes internal experience.* Therefore, we Protestant churches must find an external order in worship that tells and acts out the story so that our internal experience of being encountered by the story will be maximized.

The rule of thumb for order in worship is rooted in the nature of worship. If worship tells and acts out the story, then the order must be the servant of the message. The ancient order of worship was a single four-fold action:

(1) Preparation to worship
(2) Encounter through the Word together with response
(3) Encounter through Eucharist together with response
(4) Dismissal

This order organizes the internal experience of

(1) Coming before God
(2) Listening to God speak and responding to this spoken Word
(3) Receiving Christ through the symbols of bread and wine
(4) Dismissal to live in Christ's name

The worshiper who comes to worship with an intelligent understanding of worship and with intentionality is carried through an actual rehearsal of her or his relationship to God through the order for worship that organizes that relationship. Worship is then the context in which a meaningful encounter with God actually takes place. In the preparation, forgiveness of sins known and unknown is made; in the Word, God addresses the worshiper with the saving message; in the Eucharist, Christ encounters the worshiper in a healing way. While this relationship may happen on a subliminal level without understanding and intention, the probability of its occurrence is increased when the worshiper understands what is happening through the order and chooses to make it happen through intention. The consequence of this choice is an intensified spirituality.

(3) Restore more frequent celebration of the Eucharist. The norm of early Christian worship is Word and sacrament (Acts 2:4). The Word rehearses revelation while the Eucharist is the rehearsal of the Incarnation. God not only spoke in history, God became one of us in Jesus Christ. Worship that stops short of the full action of God in history withholds from the worshiping community the full story and a chief means of spirituality.

Beginning with the primitive Christian community, the church has always and everywhere recognized that Christ becomes mystically present in his saving and healing power at the Eucharist (except for Protestant rationalism). The ancient *anamnesis* (remembrance) was not seen as a mere memorialism, something we *do* with our memory. Rather, the remembrance is an action of God in which Christ's saving action becomes present. The *epiklesis* (invocation) done over the bread and the wine is the symbol that this bread and drink becomes the body and blood of our Lord. Calvin rightly insists that Christ is not contained in bread and wine, but like contemporary thought, recognizes that the bread and wine conveys the saving action of Christ to heal our wounded spirits, to bind up our broken hearts, to forgive our sin, and to reinvigorate our journey.

If this is true, the neglect of a regular eucharistic spirituality is to our own spiritual peril. On the other hand, a regular encounter with Christ at the Table is a source of spiritual renewal. Each time we come to the Table and stretch forth our hands to receive the bread of heaven and lift our lips to receive the cup of salvation, our vision of life in Christ is re-conformed. Consequently there is an urgent need among Protestant churches to restore weekly Communion. Together with the restoration of weekly Communion, however, there must be an attending instruction in its meaning and a call to intentionality from the worshiper.

Music plays a significant part in the entire service by accompanying the order and actually moving it in its various parts. At the Lord's Table, the restoration of song that captures the meaning of the encounter taking place with God is of paramount importance. Modern Taizé music, such as "Jesus, Remember Me When You Come into Your Kingdom," strikes the theme of Christ's action and our response.

(4) Restore the church year. The church year is one of the most important sources available to the Christian for an ongoing spirituality. It not only links Sunday to Sunday, but provides a Christocentric daily spirituality for the worshiper. The neglect of the church year by Protestants has left us without a significant external order for the annual organization of a spiritual pilgrimage linked with worship.

The church year marks times for us Christianly. We have many ways of marking time. We organize time personally around birthdays, anniversaries, and other special events. We mark time nationally around Memorial Day, Independence Day, Labor Day, Thanksgiving, and the like. We mark time around the academic year with the opening and closing of school and vacation. But how do we mark time in and through Jesus Christ on a day-to-day basis?

The church year celebrated through a daily devotion marking of Advent, Christmas, Epiphany, Lent, Holy Week, Easter, and Pentecost is the Christian way of sanctifying time, thus bringing time under the lordship of Christ. To neglect this Christian marking of time is to succumb to a secular calendar. To restore this Christian concept of time in the church corporate and in individual daily devotion links worship and spirituality in a way that no other discipline can match, for it links every day of life with the story that gives meaning to all of life.

Finally, let it be said that recovering the relationship between worship and spirituality outlined here is no mere gimmick. It reaches back into a tradition by which a multitude of Christians have lived for centuries. It has staying power. But unless it is vitalized by true faith in Christ living, dying, and rising again for the salvation of the world, it becomes a dead ritual. Ritual is important because it organizes experience. But what we want is a ritual accompanied by faith. This is the kind of ritual that brings depth to our relationship with God, provides us with significant religious experience, and shapes our spirituality.

Robert E. Webber [41]

220 ✦ SPIRITUAL FORMATION AND THE LITURGICAL TRADITION

A service book is the primary carrier of the church's liturgical tradition and, as such, is a rich treasury of the prayer of the church. A service book is also a fundamental expression of what the church believes, since the church's prayer and belief are inseparable. In communicating the faith of the church, the forms provided by a service book are an important means by which Christians are rooted in the faith and, therefore, an important component for spiritual formation.

As the primary carrier of the church's liturgical tradition, a service book embodies the church's corporate memory. The services express the way in which the community of faith remembers the faith story. In remembering that story, we as the community of faith are engaged in God's saving acts and discover the meaning of our lives before God. In that memory, we find direction and hope.

More than simply being a reminder of the past or a dramatic reenactment of past events, the liturgy _engages us in the faith_. We become participants in the saving acts of God. We are engaged by the God who acted in the past, who has dominion over all things, and who in the end will have the last word over all evil. The liturgical tradition embodied in a service book is therefore _a living tradition_ that joins us with the faith story and moves us into the future with fresh vision of God's ultimate purpose.

As an expression of this living tradition, the _Book of Common Worship_ (1993) breathes with the way Christians have celebrated the faith across time and so is very old. It embodies the church's liturgical tradition that is rooted in the earliest centuries of the church's life, has been developed and reformed over time, and is now appropriated in a form that is accessible to Christians today. While it took thirteen years to produce the 1993 edition of the _Book of Common Worship_, it is more accurate to say that this book was in preparation for nearly two thousand years.

It is important to keep covenant with the past. We ignore the past to our own peril. Valid forms from the past continue to teach us. In the revision of service books, old symbols are given new life. Forms that have served the church well in the past are made alive and fresh so that they can contain new vision. Eternal truths are expressed for a new culture.

Service Book—Catholic and Reformed. This service book transcends sectarian boundaries. The _Book of Common Worship_ embodies forms of worship that are a living expression of the one, holy, catholic, and apostolic church.

This is in accord with how the Reformed tradition understands the church. The Reformation sought to reform the church, not to establish a new church. To be faithful to the spirit of the Reformation is to always seek to reform the church in accordance with the Word of God, _Ecclesia Reformata Semper Reformanda_ ("the church reformed, always to be reformed"). This focus on the reform of the church catholic has set the Reformed to enter the ecumenical movement. In its best moments, the Reformed tradition has eschewed sectarianism.

Therefore, service books within the Reformed tradition, if they are faithful to that tradition, will be reformed catholic. In each service book adopted, Presbyterians have sought to be faithful to the tradition of the church catholic and have sought to be truly reformed.

Service Book and Spiritual Formation. Because a service book puts us in touch with the church's faith tradition, it can be an important foundation for spiritual formation. Although provided to shape corporate worship, a service book can ensure that our growth as individual Christians is grounded in the story of faith and is sustained within the community of faith.

As a treasury of prayer, the church's service

book merits a place in spiritual contemplation. When the church's service book claims a prominent role in personal piety, it will be an important element in forming our lives in the faith of the church. Familiarity with the prayers used in the church's services will result in a greater sense of participation in corporate worship and being in unity with the church in every time and place. The *Book of Common Worship* should not be reserved for use only by ministers and planners of liturgy, but should find a receptive place in personal devotion of all the faithful.

Use of the service book may be expected to shape our spiritual development in a number of ways.

To God Alone Be Glory! A service book will draw us away from dwelling upon ourselves and our own feelings, so that we may focus upon God. Christian piety centers upon God and the experience of God in our lives. The Shorter Catechism begins with the reminder that our main purpose is to glorify God, whom we are to enjoy forever. Worship in the Reformed tradition is characterized by an invocation that points us beyond ourselves:

> Our help is in the name of the Lord,
> who made heaven and earth. (Psalm 124:8)

Allowing the language of prayer of the service book to permeate our minds and hearts will engage us in prayer that is centered more fully upon God.

Based in Community. The service book represents prayer that is shared in *common* with the whole church of Jesus Christ in every time and place. The *Book of Common Worship* therefore sets forth what its name implies, worship orders and prayers that *unite* a people with each other, with the whole Christian family in every place, and with the faithful of every age since Christ rose from the dead. As a carrier of the liturgical tradition, a service book is a living link with the saints, prophets, and martyrs who have gone before us. The service book contains not only prayers that are written in our time but prayers that have been cherished across the ages. These are prayers that led our ancestors in the faith into God's presence and shaped the way they responded in serving God.

Cherished prayers from the past, like hymns,

can effectively engage us in an encounter with God. It is important therefore to understand that corporate worship is corporate *prayer.* When we gather on the Lord's Day, we gather to pray. We correctly call the place where we worship a "house of prayer." In song and word, we offer our prayer to God, praising and giving thanks, confessing, interceding, and offering our supplications.

Personal and Communal. Spiritual growth for Christians has its base in the community with which we worship and serve and in that company of the faithful in every land and from every age and with whom we are joined in baptism.

While a service book embodies the prayer of the faith community, communal prayer is foundational to personal prayer. A Christian in private prayer is not alone with God, but is joined in prayer with the whole family of God of which that Christian is a member. Even private prayer is therefore in a very real sense communal. By making the prayers provided for the church's communal worship our own prayers, personal piety is rooted in the community of the baptized.

Claiming the Saving Acts of God. By preserving the liturgical tradition that proclaims the saving acts of God, the service book can effectively root us in the faith. This is particularly true as we celebrate the formative event of the Christian faith— the crucifixion and resurrection of Jesus Christ. Each Lord's Day brings us together to celebrate Christ's rising from the dead. In the proclamation of the Word and in the breaking of bread, we are claimed by God, know Christ's healing presence, and are called to respond in faith. Celebrating the dying and rising of Christ in the great three days— Maundy Thursday, Good Friday, and Easter—has great power to transform our understanding of the faith. In the Easter Vigil that climaxes those three days, the story is told once again, beginning with Creation, recalling the Exodus, proclaiming Christ's dying and rising, and celebrating with hope the coming of the new age of God's reign. New Christians are baptized, and the baptismal covenant is reaffirmed by all the faithful, who then gather about the Table to celebrate the Eucharist in anticipation of the messianic banquet at the end of time.

Keeping time with the liturgical calendar is not simply a memory of the past and certainly not a reenactment of it, but rather a claiming of the saving events as transforming events for our lives. Making the prayers of the church our own prayers can help ensure that our spiritual growth will be rooted in the saving acts of God.

Rooted in Baptism. Spiritual formation that is shaped by a service book will recognize the important place that baptism has in Christian piety. We are beginning to rediscover that baptism is primary in the Christian experience. In the waters of baptism, we are

> buried with Christ in his death, raised to share in his resurrection, reborn by the power of the Holy Spirit. (_Book of Common Worship_ [_BCW_], 410)

Baptism marks our birth into the family of faith. A prayer in the new edition of the _Book of Common Worship_ reinforces this understanding:

> O God Most High,
> you have made the font of baptism
> to be the womb from which we are reborn
> in the waters of life. (_BCW,_ 472)

Baptism signifies our turning _from_ the ways of sin and turning _to_ Jesus Christ by calling us to renounce evil and its power in the world and to give allegiance to the triune God. Baptized by water and the Spirit, we are assured that the Holy Spirit is present to guide us into the ways of Christ. All that the Christian life is about is centered in the act of baptism.

The daily life of the Christian is marked by a turning from evil and a turning to Christ. Each day, Christians claim the promise of cleansing from sin and live in the confidence that the Spirit is present, healing our brokenness and guiding us into all truth. Each day, Christians die with Christ and rise with Christ in the new life. Our spiritual growth as Christians will be stronger when we recover the place of baptism in our lives, claim God's promises of which baptism is a sign, and embrace the power of baptism as a continuing reality in our lives until our baptism is completed in death.

Nurtured in the Eucharist. A Christian formation that is shaped by a service book also recognizes the centrality of the Eucharist in Christian piety.

Born into the family of God through baptism, we gather together at the family Table and feast on and with Christ in the Eucharist. All that baptism signifies is reaffirmed for us in the Lord's Supper. Made one with Christ, we are made one with those who in every place "share this feat." Once again, in the living tradition embodied in a service book, we are linked with the faithful who have gone before us.

The feast becomes the base for ministry as we pray in a Great Thanksgiving in the new _Book of Common Worship:_

> As this bread is Christ's body for us,
> send us out to be the body of Christ in the world.
> (_BCW,_ 129)

We anticipate the day of final victory as we pray:

> Keep us faithful in your service
> until Christ comes in final victory,
> and we shall feast with all your saints
> in the joy of your eternal realm. (_BCW,_ 73)

And in another prayer in the _Book of Common Worship_, based on a second-century text, we pray:

> Creator of all,
> just as this broken bread
> was first scattered upon the hills,
> then was gathered and became one,
> so let your church be gathered
> from the ends of the earth into your kingdom.
> (_BCW,_ 75)

Spiritual formation will be rooted in meeting Christ in the Eucharist as we thankfully remember the saving acts of God and invoke the Holy Spirit to act in and among us that we may feast upon Christ and be lifted into the presence of God.

Shaped by a Daily Discipline. Service books ordinarily provide resources for daily prayer. The _Book of Common Worship_ includes orders and prayers and suggests Psalms and Scripture readings for daily use by individuals, families, or particular groups of Christians.

Daily prayer provides a discipline of prayer that centers on prayers for the Psalms, silent prayer, reflection on Scripture, and prayers of thanksgiving and intercession. Daily prayer fulfills the injunction of Paul to "pray without ceasing" (1 Thess. 5:17). Spiritual growth will depend upon a discipline of daily prayer. In addition to morning prayer and evening prayer, the _Book of Common Worship_ provides for prayer at midday in the course of a day's work and an order of prayer at the close of day. Daily prayer will help make all of life a thanksgiving and every deed a prayer offered to God.

Formed by Scripture. Spiritual formation that is shaped by a service book will be rooted in Scripture. A service book provides lectionaries. The new *Book of Common Worship* contains the revised Common Lectionary, which engages congregations in a systematic reading and proclaiming of Scripture. The new *Book of Common Worship* also includes a daily lectionary, which offers a discipline for reading and reflecting upon the Scripture each day, enabling those who use it to read through the entire Scripture systematically on a regular basis. Spiritual growth will be nurtured in the Scripture. Reading and reflecting upon the Scripture will be an occasion of listening for what the Spirit is saying to us today and discovering what is required of us to be faithful in our times.

Related to Life. In using liturgical forms of a service book, we are prompted to bear the concerns of this broken world for which Christ died. Spiritual formation must in some way be engaged with human need. The service book preserves the tradition of Christian prayer in and for the world. We are prompted to pray for "the church universal, the world, those in authority, the community, persons in distressing circumstances, and those with special needs."

If we earnestly and sincerely pray for the world, we will seek to join Christ where he is present among us, healing life's brokenness and making peace. The Christian life is worldly in the sense that it takes the world into its very heart, both in prayer and in deed.

By preserving for us the living tradition of the faith, the service book can ensure that our spiritual growth is firmly rooted in that faith to which the faithful have given witness down through the ages. It can contribute to growth into maturity as it keeps us focused on the essentials of the faith. It can rekindle within us a fervent hope for the fulfillment of God's reign.

Harold M. Daniels[42]

221 • THE FORMATIVE POWER OF PUBLIC WORSHIP

Corporate worship forms a community into the body of Christ and has great influence in shaping the spiritual-ity of its members. Every worshiping community has a great responsibility for how this influence is wielded. Communities that take seriously their corporate worship life will find great benefits in the spiritual growth and vitality of individual members. This article describes how worship forms the faith of the community and provides suggestions for how communities can do this more effectively.

The public act of Christian worship (the liturgy) is the single most formative event in the life of the Christian community. Men and women are transformed into the image of Christ through the means of grace; and nothing is so significant in this respect as the regular, consistent participation in corporate worship. It is for this reason that worship has always been seen as the central life of the Christian community. Other components or dimensions of our common life together flow out of this event.

Yet Christians often underestimate or fail to appreciate the formative power of the liturgy. St. Paul stresses that in worship all things are to be done for edification (1 Cor. 14:26). Many thus conclude that worship can only be justified if it produces immediate results. Some are looking for visible, tangible signs of change in people's lives; and the liturgy seems to produce little if any change. From all appearances, the worshiper leaves the church on Sunday much the same person they were when they entered. Worship is readily seen to be a ritual of little inherent significance and value.

This conclusion leads to different responses. Some give up on worship. That is, they decide that since worship does not produce the desired result, worship is of no consequence. And so they downgrade the liturgy and make it but another event in the life of the community, one that is expendable if other more attractive or more useful events can be found. Or they begin to call just about anything that the church does worship. Christians may come together, may sing a few religious songs, may take an offering, and may have a talk from the pastor. But in effect, this is nothing more than a religious gathering.

On the other hand, there are those who affirm worship, but argue that the routine, the ritual or consistent order of worship, is not in itself helpful. They conclude that we need to supplement the liturgy or make something happen to justify worship—for it is inferred that the act of worship alone is meaningless. Some try to make it an educational event, stressing the importance of learning. Others add an altar call, thinking that if worshipers are called to a specific act of the will, the event as a whole is somehow more useful. The irony, when this happens, is that they then tend to overstate the potential of worship for spiritual transformation. When the worship event becomes educational or focused on an altar call, it is often expected to bring about radical or immediate change because learning took place or because someone genuinely responded to the preached Word with a decision or prayer. But the reality is that the human predicament is profound and complex and is not resolved in single dramatic or even decisive moment. On the other hand, the persistent and continued celebration of the liturgy has the capacity, over time, to affect real change that results in spiritual transformation.

A potential harm occurs when worship leaders in a sense force the hand of God by seeking to make the worship event educational or by supplementing it with a call to action. The value or significance of worship as a transforming event is often undermined because its true nature and goal is bypassed.

The liturgy is formative. The consistent practice of a simple order of worship that is designed to enable the people of God to bring blessing to God and to hear God's voice does encourage the Christian believer to experience the transforming grace of God. It is edifying. But its formative influence is subtle, quiet, and, as often as not, imperceptible. To appreciate the transforming power of public worship, we must resolve to consistently and simply worship in spirit and truth with a commitment to bless God and allow God to speak. Only then is worship formative. Only then is the common act of public worship an event that enables Christian believers to know the grace of the living God.

The Liturgy as a Transforming Event

The act of public worship brings transforming grace to the believer in a variety of ways.

First, the liturgy as a whole is redemptive in that worship itself is the purpose for which humanity has been created. In worship, we fulfill our identity, purpose, and fundamental orientation. The liturgy, then, forms the individual Christian believer by providing a structure, setting, and context for fulfilling the end for which the Christian was created.

Second, the different components within worship are individually formative. The Christian believer is called to worship and provided a forum for meeting and hearing God in the company of fellow men and women. The structure may not serve every believer equally well, but a good worship event incorporates the tradition and wisdom of a community such that any willing worshiper can respond within the framework provided and find God. And there is no suggestion that every aspect within worship is equally formative or of equal importance to each participant. Some will find some aspects of worship more significant on some occasions than others. We overload worship with our own expectations of immediate significance and consequence when we begin to think that every aspect of worship should be meaningful or fulfilling to each person present. Some will be on the fringe, observing. Others will be fully engaged. Few, if any, will be fully and equally engaged in each aspect of the worship.

But when engaged, the believer will find the structure, encouragement, and the means by which to respond to God, meet God, hear God, give offerings to God, and know the benediction of God. The gift of the church to its members is simply that of providing a regular, consistent, and accessible occasion by which God can be found.

One of the formative aspects of the liturgy is that it brings a discipline to the life of the individual believer. Through the regular celebration of the liturgy, the community as a whole makes disciples of one another through the discipline of corporate worship.

Third, the event of public worship restores hope. Each gathering of God's people represents another victory, another proclamation, verbal and nonverbal, that despite the headlines in the daily newspapers and despite the discouragement each Christian faces in the world—either in making a home, in fulfilling an occupation, or in the frustration of failure, unemployment, or death—Christ Jesus remains on the throne of the universe, still forgiving sins, still speaking truth, still filling his people with his Spirit, and still granting his benediction upon all who call upon his name. Worship, then, can and must be an event that brings encouragement and hope—thus empowering the individual to effectively be in the world and fulfill a vocation.

Fourth, public worship focuses the lives of believers on the death and resurrection of Christ Jesus—in effect fulfilling the exhortation of St. Paul that having received Christ Jesus as Lord, they be rooted and built up in Christ (Col. 2:6-7). Through worship, Christians call one another back to the central articles of faith. We call one another to remembrance that the death and the Resurrection might be central in our thinking, enabling us to live in its light. But more, worship actually roots us in the Christ event such that our lives are informed and actually transformed by the events. The cross and the Resurrection become immediate to our lives.

Finally, the event of worship humbles Christians. We are humbled in that the liturgy draws us into a grand and sacred heritage. We stand with every other believer in history; and we worship in communion with all other believers, affirming one gospel, worshiping the same Triune God, and submitting to the same preached Word. Each time, we are in some respect enabled to see that we do not stand alone as spiritual hermits.

But this humbling is actually more immediate. For each time we gather for worship, we are lead in worship by another human. It is but a mere human who preaches the Word of Christ; and it is but another mortal that administers Holy Communion. We are forced again and again into the reality that God's grace is mediated through frail instruments, reminding us of our own failure and weakness.

The central and most significant events of worship are the Word and the sacrament. All Christians recognize the formative power of the Word; and those Christians within more liturgical traditions appreciate that the grace of God is mediated through the Lord's Supper. The preached Word may not appear to have immediate effect. Christians, like all other people, are bombarded daily with words, words, and more words. Whether it is the verbal barrage of the radio, the television, or just the intense verbal context in which we live and work, words dominate our lives. With such an onslaught, words lose their meaning and power.

The recognition of the power of the preached Word lies in an appreciation of the potential of God's Word—God's creative and redemptive Word. Through God's Word, God brings all things into existence; through this same Word, all things are redeemed. And the preached Word, the consistent exposition of Scripture, is this Word. It transforms; it has inherent power. When found within the context of worship, it needs no supplement. It fulfills its purpose. God is at work when God speaks.

We may actually undermine the transforming work of the Word when we elicit a response prematurely. The preaching of the Word definitely includes the call for response, conversion, and obedience. But we are not transformed by our actions of response. The Word redeems; the preached Word transforms. But this Word effects radical change slowly, subtly, and, as often as not, imperceptibly—perhaps over the course of a lifetime, even a generation. The preacher is called to faithfully preach the Word. As people hear, listen, and obey, they are transformed not by their actions in response but by the Word itself.

The sacrament of Holy Communion, when it accompanies and complements the Word, is the means by which Christ is present among his people, bringing them to an awareness of the forgiveness of their sins, to his nourishment, and to his empowering grace. Christ graces his people through word and deed.

The basic assumption that lies behind the celebration of public worship is that not one of us is capable of sustaining his or her own spiritual life. We only grow up in Christ Jesus as we are integrated within a Christian community and only as, within that community, we participate in the fundamental act of worship. The liturgy is the gift of the community to each of its members—a gift that is the most fundamental reference point for the Christian experience of being in and following Jesus Christ. We need each other; more to the point, we need to worship together, for only then will we, together, grow up in our faith and know the transforming grace of Christ. And when we do, we find that public worship is the most formative event in the life of the people of God.

Having stressed the importance and potential of worship, I must also emphasize that worship is formative when it does not stand alone. Men and women who are formed through the event of worship are those who have incorporated other individual and corporate disciplines of the spiritual life into their experience, such as solitude and personal prayer, study and the devotional use of Scripture, and service in the world. Though worship is the central feature of the life of the church, the liturgy itself is the center, though not the whole, of the life of the Christian believer.

The Task of Those Who Care for and Lead Worship

What makes the worship event formative? How can a worship leader most effectively allow the celebration of praise itself to be the occasion in which God graces and transforms the people of God?

(1) The worship event is most helpful when the order of worship no longer is the focus of attention. C. S. Lewis once noted that if the liturgy is regularly changed, then the worshiper is observing the order of worship rather than worshiping. There should be enough consistency in the order of the worship event so that the worshipers do not need to think in terms of "what's next this morning?" but can instead, freely give themselves to worship.

(2) The worship leader must of necessity always recognize that a true servant is a shepherd or midwife, not an emcee. Effective worship leadership enables men and women to address their praise to God through the structure of worship itself. There is no need to imitate the emcee of the television variety show. Also, there are few things that violate the quality of the liturgy as worship leaders who cajole worshipers into a level of engagement or participation for which the worshiper is not ready. That is, sometimes the leader calls for an emotional reaction or a physical expression that the worshiper is not prepared to welcome. The genius of good worship leadership is that the worshipers are able to participate on various levels, including the physical.

(3) Effective leadership in worship is characterized by as few peripheral, nonessential words, actions, and forms as possible. Worship leaders provide a disservice to their people if they are constantly interrupting worship with brief exhortations, casual comments of no direct bearing on the worship. The worship leader is most effective, also, when the temptation to explain, introduce, and clarify is resisted. Each hymn does not need a verbal introduction; each event in the worship does not need to be explained again. We can assume two things: a basic intelligence in the worshipers and that each worshiper desires to meet God.

(4) Worship is formative when the order or structure of worship takes account of two factors: the need for consistency, order, and tradition—for each worshiper stands in an historical community—and the need for cultural relevancy. The worship event links the Christian with a tradition or spiritual heritage. This brings strength and depth to the worship event. But worship must be contemporary, for we do not worship in a historical or cultural vacuum. The language, forms, and symbols of both song and prayer, of entering and leaving worship, and of giving our offerings must all have meaning and significance for the worshipers within their cultural, historical, and social setting. The worship will be in the vernacular (in the broadest sense of the term).

Perhaps nothing else so threatens to drive the worship agenda and tempt the worship leader as the persistent demand for worship to be entertaining, informative, fun, and novel. We have this idea that people will return and our ministries will grow if we have something exciting for them to return to. But the most fundamental need of the people of God is a worship event that is consistent, is orderly, and through predictable forms enables them to meet God and hear God's Word. Never for a moment is this a justification for boring worship. It is merely intended as a release from the pressure to make people feel good. We can affirm that the deepest needs of God's people are found not through good feelings or entertainment but through the consistent act of worship wherein the great hymns of the faith are sung, sins are confessed, the faith is affirmed, the Word is preached, the Lord's Supper is celebrated, the offerings are collected, and the benediction given.

If the Word is preached in a manner that is concise and clear and the Lord's Supper administered in a way in which the worshiper can understand and easily participate, then God is indeed met. That very encounter with God is, by definition, formative. As such, the most significant and life-transforming event that happens every week is the quiet, consistent act of Christians worshiping the living God. It is not mentioned in the headlines of the daily newspaper, but it is the most crucial event in the life of any town or city. For in a quiet, unobtrusive way, God is bringing about a revolution.

Gordon T. Smith

222 ✦ THE RELATIONSHIP BETWEEN PRIVATE AND PUBLIC WORSHIP

Genuine worship and prayer is extremely difficult in the hurried pace of everyday life. Stress and busyness reduce not only the time we spend in prayer and worship but also the attention and energy we bring to it. This article reflects on the importance of opening ourselves to the awareness of God's presence in both private and public worship.

Most of us in the Protestant tradition have learned that worship and prayer mean addressing God. Whether saying prayers or singing hymns of adoration, confession, or supplication, we tend to think of prayer and worship as isolated actions. This understanding grows out of our experience within our faith tradition and our culture, and informs how we view both communal and private worship. Rather than being the initiators and sole doers of prayer and worship, the Scriptures and our experience inform us that God is the great initiator. God created us, began the relationship; and throughout the Scriptures we discover God continuing to be the initiator. Our worship and our praying, then, are responses to the God who has already invited us, drawn us, spoken to us, and desires to be in relationship with us (Matt. 1:23; John 14:23; Rom. 8:14-16; Rev. 3:20).

This brief discussion of congregational and private worship grows out of this assumption: that God, the great Creator, Lover, Redeemer, Healer, invites us home to himself. Worship and prayer arise from within our deepest hope and longings that we have a place to be at home (Luke 13). This same Lord God shows up among us in Jesus Christ (John 14:8-9). Since Pentecost, God is the self-giving participant, coming through the mysterious but concrete presence of the Holy Spirit, joining to our spirit and assisting us in our presence before God as we pray and worship (John 4:23-24; Rom. 8:15-16,26).

_____ Sabbath Rest _____

While I am not advocating any legalistic obser-vation of the Sabbath, the Scriptures do carry God's repeated invitations to rest from work. God is not against work. God is the Creator and giver of fruitful labor (Gen. 1:28; 2:15), but God also invites us to cease the productive mastery that work involves in order that we may relocate ourselves and be reminded of who we are: children of the loving Creator-Redeemer God. Our work moves us by necessity into various roles: pastor, professor, baker, bricklayer, mother, father, doctor, and so on. So also the various roles we embrace designate what tasks and responsibilities are ours to fulfill. God's invitation to Sabbath rest is to cease from defining ourselves in terms of roles and what we do, and to simply be. In the presence of God, we are all children of God, children who are dependent on God as Creator and Sustainer. This willingness to cease from our roles and our work and all the significance and self-importance we attach to them is what Jesus talks to his disciples about: "Truly I tell you, unless you change and become like children, you will never enter the kingdom of heaven" (Matt. 18:3). During prayer and worship, we experience this profound shift, a coming home to who we truly are in the image and in the presence of God through the saving work of our Lord Jesus Christ.

___ Being Attentive to the Presence of ___ God in the Gathered Community

This presence to ourselves or to God is not encouraged or assisted by the world's compulsive pace, which drives and controls that addictive part of ourselves—our old nature. The desire of God is to indwell the people of God through the Spirit of Christ (John 14:16-17); God is present, but often we are not at home. We are absent from ourselves. The pace of our culture, and often of our church life and of what we call ministry, blurs our senses and dulls our awareness as we spiral downward into anesthetized exhaustion. Once there, we seek to numb the pain and stress loaded upon us through such compulsive living by escaping into television, video games, eating, and so on. In that state of mind, we view vacations as a further chance to escape and may tend to think of "doing devotions" as intrusive or tainted with religious effort and drudgery.

We would do well to remember that as we and others join the gathered community to worship, we often become jostled, overstimulated, overworked, and overinformed by that constant stream of sound bites that speed endlessly forth from modern technology's addiction for information. To assist our awareness of the presence for God and our sense of being part of the gathered body, we need a gentle invitation to be present to ourselves, to come home to ourselves. The move may be consciously or unconsciously painful, for most of us do suffer some kind of pain from the feverish life we live. This life is destructive to that deep and genuine bonding in the Spirit of Christ. Silence, quiet music, hymns, and acts of coming or gathering are those forms of communal spiritual disciplines that can assist us in this journey from absence to presence. The Psalms, or some modern version of the psalmist's experience, can be a guide. Over half of the Psalter is some form of lament or complaint, words given to clothe our pain and stress so that in its naming and owning we are guided into the gracious, listening presence of God.

The invitation in all the movements of worship is to open ourselves to the God who is present: "For where two or three are gathered in my name, I am there among them" (Matt. 18:20). Attention needs to be paid during the leading of worship to those words or acts that assist the presence of God and to that which kidnaps a person out of that presence. Worship leaders who are mindful of their own sense of God's presence will be better able to assist the gathered community in developing the same sense. When we are involved with God at the deepest level of our being, then casual or rote ritual is impossible, whether our ritual is formal liturgy or the spontaneous prayers of the free-church tradition.

Such attention for God requires time and space. It cannot be rushed or coerced. However, it can be encouraged and assisted. We are often timid, like deer stepping gingerly into a clearing, always alert for danger. Meeting God in the open space of worship can be marked by fear, especially if the authority figures in our life have been demanding, legalistic, or abusive. Even the disciples needed time and special help in understanding what God is really like. "'Lord, show us the Father, and we will be satisfied.' Jesus said to them, 'Whoever has seen me has seen the Father'" (John 14:8-9). We may know this in our head, but in our actual experience we may be reluctant to open ourselves to God. The continual retelling of the Good News, the story of our salvation by grace through faith in the Lord Jesus, gradually stills our fears. We enter bit by bit into the Sabbath grace and the rest of worship (Matt. 11:28-30; Heb. 4:14-16). We come home.

What assists one in his or her awareness of God's presence may not assist another. Jesus stands among us, knocking at the door of our awareness (Rev. 3:20). For one, the door may be music; for another, the Scripture reading; and for another, prayer or silence. We can be expectant for God comes to us through all the doors and paths of the soul. As we gather in this awareness, we can be more patient and compassionate toward those who do not seem to enjoy or embrace those forms of worship that seem so vital to us. We may also seek to open ourselves more fully to all parts of the worship experience, even those parts that seem to bore us. Sometimes boredom is a device of our dysfunctional and old nature that helps it to avoid being present to God, to ourselves, or to others. Allowing nonhurried space and silence for meditative attentiveness and presence can be gradually introduced into our gathered life. Some guidance can be helpful, rather than leaving persons to wander around in their thoughts in an empty silence. This can become a problem in an age where silence is viewed as a waste of time or as an empty space that needs to be instantly filled with something—preferably sound.

Presence for God is not always accompanied by rich or marked experience. Such experiences do happen. Peter, James, and John were overwhelmed by their experience as God addressed them: "This is my Son, the Beloved; with him I am well pleased; listen to him!" (Matt. 17:5). Peter wanted to stay with that experience on the mountain. Although the experience was rich, powerful, and full of wonder, God directed the focus of the disciples through that experience to Jesus: "Listen to him!" In the same way, Jesus redirected the focus of the seventy after they reported on the way they had experienced God's power in casting out demons: "Do not rejoice at this, that the spirits submit to you, but rejoice that your names are written in heaven" (Luke 10:20). Again, he points to God's realm and the work of salvation he is accomplishing for them. Just so, as we worship, the experience we receive of God is a wonder and a consolation. But the experience is part of our ongoing transformation into the image of

Christ and an invitation to gaze upon our Lord Jesus, to have our focus redirected so that God fills our horizon. Then worship arises within us, and we adore in spirit and in truth.

Being Attentive to Presence in Solitude

While the retelling of the acts of God through Scripture, liturgy, drama, sacrament, or the spoken Word holds a central place in the worship of the gathered community, those retellings can deteriorate into dry ritual and form unless the individual members of the community are open and attentive to God's presence within them and among them. This attentiveness on the part of each individual is a vital link between congregational and private worship.

The gathered community encourages each individual to remain faithful to God in the solitude of their lives and vocation in the world. And the day-by-day presence for God on the part of the individual breathes an open space into the heart, where worship with the gathered community resounds and echoes with God's lively presence.

Jesus modeled a pattern for his followers, a rhythm of private prayer and worship that flowed into fruitful activity among people. This pattern weaves its way throughout his life and finally the lives of his disciples. In Mark 3:13-15, Jesus trekked up the mountain to a place apart and then called to him "those whom he wanted, and they came to him . . . to be with him, and to be sent out to proclaim the message, and to have authority to cast out demons." We have paid much attention in the church to being sent out and to proclaiming the message but very little attention to leaving our daily activity and turning aside to simply be with Jesus. Private worship is this simple but profound act of being with.

Jesus offered a simple pathway to solitude: "Whenever you pray, go into your room and shut the door and pray to your Father who is in secret; and your Father who sees in secret will reward you" (Matt. 6:6). This turning aside from the daily activity, coming into that chosen place, and shutting the door to all the other voices and influences that seek to mold and mark our life is part of the rhythm. Again, we cease the labor of our various roles and rediscover our identity as children in the gracious, listening presence of the God who sees.

Jesus delighted in explaining what God is like to the persons who gathered around him from abusive, dysfunctional familial, national, and religious systems. In this Matthew passage is an echo of Hagar's experience of God in Genesis 16. The Egyptian slave girl was caught up in the struggle of Abram and Sarai, who decided to start doing God's work for God rather than waiting on God to act. However, Sarai found herself hostile and anger towards Hagar, especially when the slave girl became pregnant with Abram's child, something Sarai had been unable to do. Sarai dealt harshly with Hagar, and the slave woman finally ran away. Pregnant, rejected, alone, she wanders in the wilderness. But God sees her and helps this woman, who had been used and abused, to find her way back home. Out of this experience, Hagar knows who God is for her: *El-roi,* God who sees. We may not always come into the room in our house feeling like a child who is welcomed and embraced by a loving God who sees us in secret. We may feel more like Hagar, an alien and a wanderer, discounted and at risk. But the God who sees is present. As we come into the place, we are desiring to be found.

No private prayer or act of worship is truly disconnected from the larger praying community. As each of us grow in our faithful response to God, so the gathered community is gradually transformed in its faithfulness to God and God's purposes. This transformation is assisted as we can give ourselves to the practice of spiritual disciplines, both corporate and private.

Spiritual disciplines also assist us in our presence for God, both in the place of solitude and as we act in our vocation in the world. Today a growing number of books are available to help us rediscover what the early Christians knew and practiced in their lives of worship and discipleship. Each spiritual discipline is simply a pathway into the presence of God and can be evaluated in that light. Does this prayer form assist me in my presence for God or block my spiritual attentiveness? Different disciplines suit different persons because of personality type, of religious background and experience, and of where a person is in their journey of discipleship and friendship with Christ. There is a growing awareness of the need for spiritual friends or directors who are gifted and trained in assisting that necessary discernment between the movement of God's Spirit in a person's life and the response of that person to God's presence and work, within oneself and in relationship with others.

Sometimes in the solitary space, alone in God's presence, the prophetic voice emerges. The faithful worshiper is given discernment and wisdom for the guidance of the gathered community. Also, in the presence of God, we become aware of our true humanity and our humility, and can speak wisdom with grace, meekness, and poise rather than with force, arrogance, and defensiveness.

Congruence between Personal and Corporate Worship

I have begun to wonder how much congruence exists between how persons experience worship in private and how they are assisted in worship as they gather in a community. I also wonder if the congregation and the persons responsible for planning worship stop to question how they are assisting others in their awareness of God's presence as they plan the sequence and content of the worship service. While we cannot program God's revelation of himself to us, we are invited by God to be attentive and present to God. Those of us who are helping to plan and lead the various elements of worship could begin by paying quiet attention to our own experience of God. What assists us to be present and attentive to God? And what prevents us? A worship-planning committee that spends a prayerful hour or two reflecting on these questions can be more attuned to where we as a congregation are. They can be more attuned to those elements that help us as we gather in community to be aware of the presence of the living and loving Christ within and among us.

Wendy Miller

223 ✦ LIVING THE EUCHARISTIC PRAYER

The author of this article explores the eucharistic prayer and asks how we as Christians can live this prayer and how we can be formed by this prayer. The author hopes to illustrate how the weekly ritual of assembling around Christ in prayer for the world will form in Christian people the mind of praise and the habit of service.

It is difficult to describe how liturgy forms the faithful in the spiritual life. Yet throughout the world's liturgical movement, liturgists desire for participation in the liturgy to form the faithful into the community of God. But we who are eager for the formation of persons as Christians must beware that we do not merely gun our engines on the theory that more and better liturgy, like more gasoline, will get this church moving. For we know that there are countless people who regularly participate in Christian liturgical celebrations whose lives appear to be untouched by the experience.

We speak autobiographically. Or we probe Christian history. Or we interpret studies. But we do not know how and when the liturgy is experienced as the vehicle for God's Spirit. We speak to one another only our hopes that the liturgy, which has brought grace into our lives, will do the same for others, children and adults alike. Many of the techniques for formation that are popular among newly converted adults are inappropriate for my daughters, still young children who were baptized as tiny infants. Yet I can hope that their weekly participation in the Eucharist will form in them an attitude of praise, prayer, and service that will join them to other Christians even in an increasingly secular culture.

Simply said, here is the liturgical logic: The weekly ritual of assembling around Christ in prayer for the world will form in Christian people the mind of praise and the habit of service. Prayer is to shape us by giving us hope for compassion. Unfortunately, much of the prayer written by white, middle-class, North American Christians has been so dwarfed by psychological rhetoric that intercession has more in common with personal therapy than with baptismal formation. The nineteenth-century faith in Jesus as personal Savior has met the twentieth-century human-potential movement. This results too often in prayers about how I can be more fulfilled this week. To find a prayer for Christian formation, let us look to the classic Western eucharistic prayer with its elements of praise, remembrance, and petition. Let us ask together how to live the prayer.

A Good and Joyful Thing

It is right, and a good and joyful thing
always and everywhere
to give thanks to you,
Sovereign of the Ages
You created all things
and called them good.

(In this article, I am using the form of the eucharistic prayer found in *Holy Communion,* Supplemental Resource no. 16, Service 20 [Nashville: Abingdon, 1987], 46–47. Copyright by The United Methodist Publishing House. Used by permission.)

Aristotle said that a story needs a beginning, a middle, and an ending. But the literature of this century indicates a world in which such naive order has been destroyed. Stories begin in the middle, proceed with a logic all their own, and stop without concluding. In many novels, the calendar day is the only shape given the protagonist's tale. The death of the omniscient narrator suggests a world in which we can speak only a private vision of personal values. The incoherent violence of recent movies seems to cement in American consciousness, rather than purge away, the terrible pattern of Vietnam, where our highest ideals began questionably, proceeded dishonestly, and ended, in the words of T. S. Eliot, "not with a bang, but a whimper." Adopted children in a mythic search for origins locate their birth parents, discovering only one or two slight, middle-aged aliens. Like digital clocks, we live minute by minute, the sweep of life obscured by the orange flashing figures, numbers as isolated as we ourselves are.

What would it be like if we were formed by the beginning of the eucharistic prayer?

In the first place, we would have assembled on the Sabbath. Endless orderless time would be benevolently laid before us in units we could grasp. We would give priority to the first day of the week, by assembling with others who shared this calendar of grace. Like the disciples in John's Gospel, we would gather on the first day of the week with sure knowledge that at such a weekly meeting God would be present to bless us. This communal affirmation of a human order to the universe, this peaceful acknowledgment that our time begins together in God, and this shared value that from such an assembly flows life in abundance is no small thing. Assembling on Sunday is like acting out Genesis 1. In the beginning, the universe, rather than mindlessly expanding into more vacuum, is benevolently ordered for the good of humankind by God. Thus merely to assemble with the baptized on Sunday is to re-create the modern universe, giving it a beginning in God and a

middle in grace, with hope for an end in fulfillment and peace.

The eucharistic prayer, like the Sabbath, situates the community in a graceful world. We begin by praising God. We acknowledge God as an *Abba* God, the loving parent who arranges the nursery to the child's best advantage, who protects the infant from evil, who nurses, instructs, and chides better than all the human parents and all the mythic gods and goddesses who fill our lives and storybooks. We state that God created the world. We form our community around this assertion that the world has its meaning in and from God. Since we are in God, we participate in its meaning. We state that God saves the world. We form our assembly around this belief that contrary to appearances, evil has been overcome by and in God. Since we are in God, we together are saved. Were the assembled community to enter fully into this opening paragraph of praise, our formation as Christians would have made a substantive beginning.

In Remembrance of These Your Mighty Acts

> Holy are you,
> and blessed is your eternal Word,
> who became flesh
> and came to dwell among us
> in Jesus Christ.

"Humankind cannot bear much reality," wrote T. S. Eliot. One way that we protect ourselves is to forget. The old saying is true, women do not quite remember the pains of childbirth. That I was in pain, I remember. What the pain was like in order to made me scream so wildly, I cannot recall. We forget the sufferings of the race, assassinations in our country, and quarrels in the family. We try to relax in an easy chair with earphones gently playing only New Age music.

Another way that we protect ourselves is to overlook. There is a man lying on the train platform crying out in pain, but I am in a hurry. I must not miss my appointment; it might even be a setup. It is as if each person has a certain capacity for pain, and this capacity is usually filled to the brim. Whether our pains be personal, familial, social, or political, there is no room for the suffering of others.

To pray the eucharistic prayer is to be the community that focuses on the Suffering Servant. In the center of the prayer, we remember Christ, the one who heeded the cry of the man on the platform even to his own death. We call to our remembrance, making the memory alive and well, that God is among us as one who serves the suffering ones. God sees human suffering and remembers it. And God's response to the cries in the emergency ward and around the world is to bind up our wounds, pouring on oil and wine. To pray this prayer together is to take on the mind of Christ, to don with the name _Christian_ the lifestyle of the Servant. Let the church be the donkey on which Jesus lays the wounded man; we are to carry those who are newly anointed and communed. To pray this prayer is to recall, even against our self-protective amnesia, the death of Christ and to hear, in spite of our headset, the cries of all in need. John's Gospel teaches us that the meaning of the Last Supper is seen in Jesus' washing his disciples' feet. So we come to the Table ready to serve.

One in Ministry to All the World

By your Spirit, make us one with Christ,
one with each other,
and one in ministry to all the world,
until Christ comes in final victory
and we feast at Christ's heavenly banquet.

Our culture is exhausted by its frantic search for community. No wonder, our children are enchanted by reruns of _Little House on the Prairie_ with its evocation of a mythic time when small neighborhoods lived with shared values in communities marked by friendliness and concern. The reformed drug addicts visiting our schools eagerly petition everyone to join their enthusiastic campaign for a drug-free society. I see in their fervor the old delight in group identity: "We are reformed addicts; we call you to our mission." Such a sense of group identity, such shared goals, such communal responsibility and support are increasingly rare in a society that seems overwhelmed by trying to embrace too much too fast. Now we do not look any longer to the pages of the _National Geographic_ for pictures of foreign patterns of life. We see them across the hall of our apartment building.

To pray the eucharistic prayer is to invoke God, the Paraclete. In this prayer, we pray for the Paraclete to come among us, to make us one, to

bring all the needy into the heavenly city. We pray that the Paraclete will continuously voice our concerns before God's throne, that there might finally be some action toward mercy and renewal. Together we pray for communion and even in the prayer begin to enjoy the communion we seek. But the communion of God's mind is so far beyond our own that always in the eucharistic prayer we are drawn to a deeper sense of what human communion is. It is not wearing similar clothes or seeking the same entertainment, but discovering a bond of love that God alone can create.

We are formed by our culture to live in chaos without praise, in the moment without sympathy, and in a lonely search for communion. To pray the eucharistic prayer is to praise God for a world mercifully saved, to remember the suffering ones as a faithful servant would, and to petition together so heartily for communion in this world that our lives naturally follow our prayers. Thus, we learn not to molder away our lives watching television, with its sound blocking out the needy world and its emptiness a symbol of our own barren lives. We join with a community that on Sunday morning sings hymns, that remembers Christ, and that hears the needy. We join a community that in praying for communion becomes a community of servants.

All Glory and Honor

Through your eternal Word Jesus Christ,
with the Holy Spirit in your holy Church,
all honor and glory is yours,
Almighty God, now and for ever.

The eucharistic prayer forms us by bringing us to God. God is the _Abba_, ordering the world in mercy; God is the Servant, identifying with all the needy; God is the Paraclete, forming us into a community. The doctrine of the Trinity need not be an archaic and sexist way to draw silly pictures of God. For Christians, the doctrine of the Trinity hints at the mystery of God and calls us into a human existence made in the image of this mysterious and merciful God. The institutional church is always buying some new method for catechesis and some new theory of education. Prophets on the edge of the church are always calling out their prescriptions for conversion and reform. Yet no sooner have we sold our decade's soul to a method or a cause than we see our convictions and methods as limitations. The doctrine of the Trinity, which classically provided the church with its outline for eucharistic praying, also offers to the church a program for catechesis and its inspiration for amendment of life.

What would our catechesis and conversion be if it was formed by the doctrine of the Trinity? Here are some suggestions for congregational education and service committees. The families of the newly baptized infants would recommit themselves to regular eucharistic praise and service. Our children would learn the Bible stories of God's benevolent love and would hear the lives of the saints, who are coservants with us, part of the community for which we strive. Mystagogical catechesis would be revived among us, with adults growing more deeply each paschal season into the mystery of life with God. Rather than mirror the aimless race of contemporary culture, congregational life would be marked by the beauty of hospitality and peace. The "least of these" would be the most honored in our midst, as we remember with St. Lawrence that the treasures of the church ought not be the new copes in our sacristy, but the homeless in our cities. We would see every need, every sorrow, every stranger with the eyes of a servant. We would stand together to support one another in the pain of seeing. We would break through the solipsism that sets in after the evening news by choosing one or two people who need our care, by choosing one or two cooperative efforts, and by working for the communion for which we pray.

These are only several suggestions, merely starters, for the church's formation by the liturgy. We are to be formed by the church's prayer to become, such prayers in the world, such instances of praise, service, and community, such personifications of joy, sympathy, and hope. We are so formed not by successful church programs or popular media techniques but by the Spirit of God, who draws us by God into God. May God, *Abba,* Servant, and Paraclete, teach us so to pray.

Gail Ramshaw[43]

224 • Worship and Spirituality in the Jewish and Christian Traditions

Christian corporate worship grew out of Jewish liturgi- *cal practice. Understanding the unique spirituality of* *Jewish worship can suggest both how the first Christians approached their own worship and how Christians today can more fully integrate their own spiritual pilgrimage with corporate worship.*

Jewish Liturgical Spirituality

Jewish liturgical spirituality is the lived awareness that all of life can be a means of becoming holy as God is holy. For a devout Jew, all of life can be liturgy. The prayer of blessings and praise *(berakah)* enables everything to be a source of remembering who one is in the presence of the All Holy One.

The living Word of God, the Torah and cultic liturgy, are central to the living of a liturgical spirituality. Together, Torah and cultic liturgy encompass the life of the community in its ongoing journey into the heart of God. Both foster communion with God, which is expressed through actions similar to those of God. To be holy as God is holy is the purpose both of Torah and of cultic liturgy (Lev. 19:2). Though the two are intimately related, they can be considered separately.

Torah has varied meanings. Torah can refer to the first five books of the Jewish Scriptures (Pentateuch), the entire Hebrew Scriptures (Tenakh), the scholarly exposition of the Scriptures as these apply to changing times, and the meditative study of God's living Word by the people.

Torah, God's living Word, is a creative dialogue of God with the chosen people. Because Torah is God's Word, the community will never hear that Word in its fullness. At the same time, Torah is addressed to the heart of the community who will hear and have their lives informed by it. The changing contours through which the Word of God is heard means there must be ongoing interpretation of that Word (halakha). The ongoing interpretation is no less God's Word, than the written Word.

God's Word addresses the heart of the community in many ways. The community must discern the meaning of the address at its place and time in history. Because God's Word is greater than human hearing and interpretation, there is no need for everyone to agree on meaning, as the rabbinical schools attest. As long as the people are living the commandments of loving God and loving others, their interpretation is a valid one.

Commandments are an essential part of God's living Word, for commandments unite the doer with the heart of God. Commandments are not fulfilled in merely doing what is specified as religious deeds. Commandments are only fulfilled if the doing somehow unites the doer with the heart of God and neighbor. To have 613 commandments in Torah is a blessing, not a burden. What other people have so many ways to be united with God?

Commandments guide the covenant community in a way of life that helps them remember who they are as God's people. There are many commandments because all of life, whether eating, drinking, celebrating, journeying, searching, weeping, or working, can reveal the living God. To remember is to know the living presence of God; to forget is to become lost in meaninglessness. Whom God remembers, looks upon, or hears has life. Whom God forgets descends into darkness. Commandments are a means of remembering blessings that further communion.

Those who fulfill commandments will be known by the fruits of communion with God and with others. To be a blessing and not a curse, to be a means of life for all, is a sign that the spirit of the commandments is being lived. Because the spirit is what gives and sustains life, not the literal living of the 613 commandments, the meaning of the commandments has been summarized throughout Jewish history. David reduced the meaning of the commandments to eleven (Ps. 15). Isaiah reduced the number to six (Isa. 33:25-26). Micah reduced the meaning to three (Mic. 6:8). Amos reduced the number to one (Amos 5:14). The rabbi, Jesus Christ, will also do this.

What this points to is that the purpose of Torah and its commandments is communion with the source of life that is known through how one lives. The living Word of the living God is an ongoing dialogue with a living and historically conditioned people. Because the Word of God is spoken to the heart of the community, there can be no authentic interpretation without the entire community discerning the meaning. The fullness of Torah lies ahead, not behind, so there is room for differences on the journey toward that fullness. The Word will not return empty, but it may return with a fullness greater than human interpretation could hope or dream or imagine.

God's living Word is known not only through Torah but also through cultic liturgy that has Torah as a vital part. Cultic liturgy provides expression, identity, and life direction for the Jew. The daily, weekly, and seasonal celebrations of the covenant people are central to Jewish liturgical spirituality. Life's liturgy is given direction through cultic liturgy that provides the sacred space for the community to remember its call to become God's people.

In the morning and evening, the devout Jew remembers the history and mystery of Creation, redemption, and covenant. This daily prayer recalls the past, reflects upon the present through the images of Creation, redemption, and liberation, and expresses hope for ongoing liberation from all that is not holy. "Help me to be awake to this day . . . alive to beauty and love, aware that all being is precious, and that we walk on holy ground wherever we go" (_Gates of the House_ [New York: Central Conference of American Rabbis, 1977], 3). In the morning and evening, the creed (Shema; Deut. 6:4) is recited as well as a variety of blessings that enable the people to remember, who they are and can yet be.

The Lord's Day (Shabbat) is a time to remember that rest is as sacred as work, if it is the creative rest that God intends. Keeping the Sabbath is doing the work of God. The workers who refuse to do God's work, which is to be re-created on Sabbath, will remain unprofitable servants. Sabbath begins on the eve as God's compassion is recalled, "As we being this day of holiness, we shall not forget the words of your prophet who called us to share our bread with the hungry, to clothe the naked, and never to hide ourselves from our own" (_Gates of the House_ 29). The ritual of candles, meal, and blessings begins the Sabbath time, which will not ritually end until the next day's evening service.

Seasonal festivals provide rhythms for liturgical life. In fall, the days of awe usher in the new year with an eight-day period extending from Rosh Hashanah to Yom Kippur. On this holiest day of the year, prayer, fasting, atonement, and forgiveness are the means of furthering the kingdom in this time and receiving blessings in the year ahead. Days of thanksgiving, Tabernacles, are celebrated for seven days in later fall. In winter, a feast of light, Hanukkah, celebrates a variety of accumulated meanings with gifts and joy.

A major festival, Passover, marks the spring season. This festival is kept as a night different from other nights. The ritualized meal provides a clear expression of the past, present, and future meanings of God's liberating of the covenant people. Seven weeks after Passover, Pentecost celebrates the receiving of the law of God with new wine and leavened bread.

Jewish liturgical spirituality is guided by the ritualized meanings of that spirituality. Though the whole life of the devout Jew can be called liturgy, Torah and cultic liturgy are central to the formation and expression of liturgical spirituality. There is a need to remember who the covenant people are called to be. Torah and cultic liturgy are means for remembering and for living a liturgical spirituality.

Worship and Spirituality in the Christian Tradition

For Christians, Jesus Christ is Torah and the source of a new and eternal covenant. Cultic liturgy is a means for Christians to remember who they are as a new creation in Christ. Liturgical spirituality is formed by the ritualization of the memory of Jesus Christ, who asks his people to remember by doing what he did and continues to do through the Spirit. The early church ritualized this memory as the Lord's Supper. Some early meanings of this memory can be located in the way Christian Scriptures describe this new and eternal covenant.

The New and Eternal Covenant of the Lord's Supper. Though the Last Supper was probably not a Passover meal, the scriptural accounts structure the meaning of the meal in a framework of a Passover ritual. A summarized comparison of the meaning of the Passover cups is one way to illustrate the new meaning that early Christianity assigned to the Lord's Supper or Eucharist.

The Passover ritual was opened by blessing this day as one of hope, by a washing, and then by an offering and sharing of a cup of joy and blessing. The New Testament accounts present Jesus as being joyful for the celebration and washings that occur. The ritual dipping of foods in the dish served as an hors d'oeuvre, with the main meal to follow. The departure of Judas fits in well here (John 13:2-15, 21-30; Luke 22:24-27; Matt. 26:20-25; Mark 14:17-21).

At the Passover ritual, a second wine cup was mixed, blessed, and shared. The ritual meal was served. The youngest child asked the question, "Why is this night different from every other night?" The story of Passover (Haggadah) and its application to the present was then told by the leader. Two psalms of praise and a prayer over the bread were recited. The bread was broken and shared, as was a third cup of blessing at the end of the meal.

For the disciples gathered with Jesus Christ, the night of this Last Supper is a night "different from all other nights." On this night, bread and wine are symbols that have new meaning in a new covenant. The covenant blood of Jesus Christ will be poured out for all so that sins can be forgiven (Matt. 26:29). The radical nature of Jesus telling the disciples to drink his blood can escape contemporary hearers. For the Jews, blood symbolized life, and life belonged only to God. Whoever drank blood was acting as God and would be cut off from the covenant people (Lev. 2:12; 7:27; 17:10-14; Gen. 9:3-5). Now whoever does not eat the flesh and drink the blood of Jesus Christ will not have life (John 6:53). The intimacy of this new covenant with its sharing in the life of God is a dramatic change in religious imagination.

A fourth cup of Passover was a cup poured and drunk for the completion of the Hallel (Psalms 114–118). The participants could eat or drink no more after drinking this cup, for they must continue to taste only the mystery of Passover through the night. To fully taste the mystery of Passover, Jesus Christ will experience a cup of suffering. He prays that this cup be taken away (John 18:11; Matt. 26:39-44; Mark 14:36-39; Luke 22:42-44). When the cup cannot be taken away, it will be accepted and those who poured it will be forgiven (Luke 23:24).

The fifth cup of Passover is a cup of the future. Some name it Elijah's cup, for Elijah was expected before the fullness of God's kingdom would come. As this cup was poured, the door was opened as a symbol of readiness for the kingdom to come. This cup would not be drunk until the kingdom came. The Passion accounts make interesting references to this symbolic cup and to Elijah (Matt. 27:47,49; Mark 14:36; Luke 23:37). In the two accounts of the death of Jesus that have been influenced by Psalms 22, the cup is not drunk (Matt. 27:48; Mark 15:36). In a third account, the fifth cup is drunk as Jesus announces his life is over. He breathes forth the spirit of the kingdom (John 19:30). In a fourth account, the risen Christ gathers with the disciples of Emmaus to eat and drink the meal of the kingdom, for the kingdom is here (Luke 24:32). All accounts point to the kingdom that has come in Christ, who now eats and drinks with his friends, who are part of that new creation.

The apostles appear on Pentecost as those who know of this new wine of the kingdom. For the Jews, Pentecost celebrated the receiving of the law of the covenant with new wine and leavened bread. Christian Scriptures point to the transformed meaning of Pentecost. Jesus Christ is the living Word of the living God. The apostles are ridiculed for being filled with new wine (Acts 1:2-13). The new creation of which Peter speaks has its first fruits in the life, death, and resurrection of Jesus Christ. All can be baptized into this new creation, for there shall be no further distinctions between slave and free, Jew and Gentile, male and female. The Spirit gives gifts to whomever the Spirit chooses.

The Lord's Day was a celebration of the new creation ushered into time through the life, death, and resurrection of Jesus Christ. The community who gathered to "do this in memory of me" were called to conversion and critiqued for areas of nonconversion. The hope of God for the world had been revealed in Jesus Christ, whose life was given for all. The Lord's Supper celebrated the infinite and intimate dimensions of reconciliation in Christ. It was formative of a liturgical spirituality, whose embrace was to be as cosmic as that of the Lord Jesus.

S. Shawn Madigan[44]

225 • CONTEMPORARY MODELS OF WORSHIP AND SPIRITUALITY

A variety of recent publications and programs have rethought how Christians can express their faith and develop their spiritual life in the modern world. This article identifies seven unique approaches to Christian worship and spirituality, and describes their commonalities and differences, providing a thought-provoking perspective from which individual Christians and particular churches or denominations can reconsider their own expressions of faith.

Since the late 1960s, there has been a virtual explosion in the area of Christian spirituality. In the beginning, it started in terms of a recovery of lost spiritual traditions. This was especially true in the Roman Catholic church, which has been the home of numerous schools of spirituality, usually in terms of some religious order. One thinks of Franciscan, Dominican, Carmelite, or Ignatian spiritualities. Many of these communities discovered once again the charisma of their founders, placed this originating experience in the contemporary context of the various biblical, ecumenical, and liturgical movements, and sometimes radically changed their practices of prayer and their pursuit of the spiritual life. The obvious changes were registered in retreat houses, where there was a growth of the individually directed retreat. Spiritual direction became an essential part of anyone's serious desire to grow in their relationship with God.

The Protestant churches, because of a certain wariness that much of this might be a form of works righteousness, were slower to join this

The Cross Amsata. A cross believed to be of ancient Egyptian origin. The configuration is frequently a tall cross or a Latin cross with a loop above it. The loop symbolizes life, particularly the new life that is in Christ.

movement of Christian spirituality. But as individual members of these churches sought for a deepening in the spiritual aspects of their lives and as they became more aware of the richness of their own traditions in the area of spirituality, they have tried to enter fully in the mainstream of spiritual practices.

But in the meantime, other factors have brought about changes in the direction of this spirituality movement. Spirituality is now seen in a broader context and not as something that can be monopolized by Christians. The convergence of the Eastern and Western traditions has added greatly to Christian spirituality on both the reflective and the practical level. And within the West itself as people have not found their spiritual resources in the churches, they have turned to what can only be called secular forms of spirituality, such as the many twelve-step programs and practices inspired by the human potential movement and transpersonal psychology. Now one is more likely to find the enneagram as part of the program of a retreat house than something explicitly liturgical.

Finally, much of spirituality has been defined in terms of the professional religious person, such as the clergy person. Today, lay movements have claimed spirituality in a way never before. And while many lay people find certain of the traditional brands of spirituality congenial, still another way of viewing Christian spirituality has become imperative. Thus, the use of models to deal with diversity. Models have been found quite useful in other area of theology, especially the theologies of the church and of the liturgy. In fact, one can view the Christian spiritual life through the same lens as one views the Christian liturgy. This is no surprise since the liturgy is the articulation of the Christian community's spirituality. It is the church's form of spiritual direction.

The Institutional Model

Because the institutional model stresses the importance of the visible and concrete in our lives, in terms of the Incarnation, it sees the spiritual life as something that requires structure and procedure. It is not possible to have a purely spiritual or invisible spirituality. A relationship with God that lacked the visible dimension would be inhuman. But if there is visibility, then there is procedure and structure.

According to this model, one would expect the spiritual life to have clear times for prayer and worship. Spiritual reading, meditation, and various spiritual disciples would all be part of what it means to grow in union with God. When people gather together and center their attention around the Bible, a cross, a lighted candle, or around their breathing and certain bodily practices, such as tai chi, we are seeing the institutional model at work.

When this stress on the perceptibility of one's spiritual life becomes dominant, a certain rigidity enters in. There is the danger of a work righteousness being present. One cannot become holy by satisfying certain rules. The spiritual life needs to be more elastic, so that personal creativity can remain a part of it. There can be no question of simply doing something in order to get grace. This is as true of extreme Catholic sacramentalism as it is of the Protestant work ethic. God's presence is found in all of creation, and not only where some authority says it is.

The Mystery Model

Spirituality from a mystery perspective does not mean the life of union with God is mystifying. Rather, one's spiritual life is wholly centered around the Christ event, especially the death and resurrection of Christ. Here the Resurrection is not simply God's approval of what has been done in Christ or some kind of "frosting on the cake" of the life of Christ. Rather, the Resurrection is *the* saving event. The cross has no value in itself if the Resurrection is not its purpose.

To be a spiritual person according to this model is to develop oneself so that one participates fully and concretely in the life of Christ, not the life of the historical Jesus, but in the life of the risen Christ. Since this is an Easter-oriented spirituality, the spiritual path is imaged as a Passover, a movement through death to new life. This is often reflected in the way that mystery-oriented spirituality takes very seriously the church year and the celebration of the mysteries of Christ's life, such as his ascension, the descent of the spirit, the period of Advent, and so forth.

The movement of the spiritual life is a symbolic one. There is no place in this form of spirituality for a nostalgic looking back at the Jesus of the Gospels. This is a courageous religious commitment to live the life of Christ, who transcends space and time. The passageway is life in Christ as it has been promised by the great prophets, as it is fulfilled in the Easter experiences during Holy Week and the period until Pentecost, as it is lived out during the course of the year, and as it is promised again in the future Christ brought to expression in that eschatological period of Advent, Christmas, and Epiphany.

The Sacramental Model

The sacramental model of spirituality is a spirituality of the church. It has a strong ecclesiological base in which one's relationship with God is experienced within the recognizable Christian community. This is the spirituality that many church members would easily recognize. This is especially true of Roman Catholics after the Second Vatican Council. One's union with God is not only facilitated by the church, but the individual Christian contributes to the larger spiritual life of the church itself. The major image around which the spiritual life is mobilized is that of the grace-filled community.

It would be a mistake to understand sacramental spirituality as one in which the church as an institution is prominent. Rather, it is the church as the body of Christ and the sacrament of God, which is foremost in the mind and heart of the one at prayer. The Holy Spirit is preeminent in this spirituality because it is experienced as the source and power of the inner unity that binds together Christians in the pursuit of holiness.

Those who see their relationship with God through the prism of the Incarnate Christ, for whom spirit and matter are inextricably bound together in that Incarnation, and in whom the symbols of the Christian tradition find their roots would be characterized as having a sacramental spirituality.

The Proclamation Model

This is a spirituality of listening and deciding. People who follow this path tend to be very sensitive to the presence of God, certainly as found explicitly in the Word of God, but also in all areas of life. They are listening for what God is saying, or better, proclaiming. Prayer and spiritual discernment is deciding how to respond to these calls from God. Thus, this spirituality has a certain ecumenical openness because of its evangelical character. It is a spirituality of dialogue, God and the person being in a conversation.

But it is also a spirituality of judgment in that persons see themselves as bound to the critical nature of the Word of God. The Scripture as two-edged is the criterion whereby they make decisions regarding the spiritual moving of their spirits. For although these people are in conversation with God, it is God who speaks first and so they are ever on the alert to hear that voice more clearly and respond more generously.

It is obvious then that this is a kind of relationship with God that is based on presence. The quality of the spiritual life is often measured by the quality (not quantity) of the mutual presence between the person and God. This is more than mere physical presence or some kind of comforting presence, although it may be that. Spiritual moments here are ones of new encounters, shocking deepening of the transcendent, divine surprises, and further bonding. Out of this dialogue with the divine presence, persons are created anew and life takes on meaning in terms of the various challenges that this divine reality presents to them.

The Process Model

A person of the process model would be very uncomfortable in any kind of otherworldly spirituality or an approach to the self and God that is dualistic. This perspective is more creation centered, where one works out one's spiritual life by being in harmony with the universe and open to whatever novelty life may present. Even for those who are committed members of some institutional church, the parameters of church life move far beyond what is usually recognized as Christian. To be in relationship with God means to be in relationship with the world. World and God go together and a person cannot have one without the other.

The goal of the spiritual life, that is, union with God, is ever present in the sense that being on the way is all important. It is not as if there is some ideal state in the future and the person is always trying to obtain it. Rather, full relationality and openness now indicate spiritual perfection. Being connected is being spiritual. And the process-oriented person is reluctant to define the limits of those connections too carefully.

In no other spirituality is the involvement of the individual with God so salient. What an individual does in his or her prayers and actions affects God. God is less than what God could be if the individual has not prayed and has not walked the spiritual road. God is there, ever offering new challenges along that path. God is the great seducer. And to the degree that the individual responds, God's own life is enriched. Leading the spiritual life is all about making a contribution to the life of God.

The Therapeutic Model

Self-transcendence is the word here. The moving beyond all those obstacles that prevent the full humanization of the person is the intent of this model of spirituality. Personal freedom is the goal of one's prayer life, spiritual direction, meditation, and various spiritual exercises. It is at the juncture of this model that Christian spirituality meets the modern twelve-step programs and those which have taken their inspiration from humanistic psychology. Thus, the language of the therapeutic model has the flavor of the process of self-making. Those who operate from this model would not be happy about making a clear-cut distinction between therapy and spiritual direction.

As with the sacramental model, this model uses the language of body, but the meaning is quite different. In the former, body is a theological metaphor referring to the assembly of Christians, whereas here body means individual embodiment, especially the aspect of flesh and sexuality. Salvation is making deep contact with those carnal aspects of one's life. It is not that carnality is absolutized, but one cannot dispense with it in the spiritual journey.

Spiritual direction will often follow the lines of personal autobiography since it will be their story telling that will have a healing effect on the directee. The language may be that of the psychiatrist's office, and the content may be about hurt, anger, and sexual orientation, but the larger story will be that of Jesus Christ. It is that story of God in the flesh that brings comfort, heals woundedness, and bestows significance on the one who relates to God therapeutically.

The Liberation Model

To build the spiritual life is to build the kingdom of God. In that sense, the liberation, like the process model, is a very this-worldly model. However, the liberation approach has an eschatological stress not found in the process model. The kingdom of God can only be anticipated, and the spiritual life is lived in the midst of that prophetic experience. Unlike the process-oriented people, liberation-oriented people are more comfortable with biblical imagery and language. For it is here that they get their inspiration for the betterment of the world, the tearing down of sinful social structures, and the envisioning of a new age of freedom.

Those who pray in a liberation-model fashion never pray along. They are ever in solidarity with their brothers and sisters, especially those who live on the margins. They have made a covenant with the poor and oppressed and are anxious to include them in their imaging of God and of a redeemed humanity. To be spiritual is to be responsible. It means to be committed to change, to newness of life, and to societal conversion. This means that often their spiritual journeys will bring them into conflict with the status quo, with the established powers of the day, and with vested interests in the church. Prayer and meditation are not exercises that one does before the protest and after the public challenge; instead prophecy and bold confrontation are themselves spiritual practices.

Union with God is synonymous with raised consciousness. Growing in piety means distancing oneself from sinful structures and the ensconced oppressiveness of daily life. Spiritual discernment is translated into the ability to be sensitive to areas of injustice in the world as one conducts one's ordinary life. But this sensitivity flows from an inner spiritual life where the person tries to experience what the kingdom of God will be like when it comes. These liberation-oriented people's love of humankind is founded on an inner drama of playing at the kingdom.

Of course, no number of models can capture the mystery of the spiritual life. Nor is God required to deal with any individual in terms of a set of models. But these models can serve as tools of understanding that most important relationship we shall ever have.

James Empereur

226 • Theological Dimensions of Worship and Spirituality

The following are twelve succinct theses regarding the theological bases of worship and spirituality. Offered here as a catalyst for thinking and dialogue, these statements highlight the importance of lay spirituality.

(1) The vocation to life in Christ through God's Spirit, i.e., holiness, is rooted in the priesthood of the baptized. Baptism is the act of initiation into the body of Christ, and through baptism one dies to self and rises with Christ through the power of the Holy Spirit.

(2) Participation of the body of Christ in his mission of salvation is incumbent upon the baptized, and therefore Christian faith is always corporate or communal, rather than private or individual.

(3) The mission of Christ (and therefore the church) is to reconcile all humanity with God and with each other. Spirituality is always characterized by the work of peacemaking, division-healing, and unifying.

(4) The Eucharist, celebrated together by all the baptized, identifies and effects the church into the one body of Christ. It is therefore the "source and the summit" (*S.C.*, 7) of spirituality for laity, clergy, and religious. Furthermore, this eucharistic center presents an appropriate Christological focus for believers, rather than excessive devotion to Mary and the saints as has sometimes characterized lay spiritualities of past eras.

(5) The mission of the body of Christ is to and within the broken world. Lay spirituality finds its fruitfulness not from moving the believer out of contact with the world, but rather into contact with the heart of world affairs in order to transform the world by bringing life, hope, peace, and justice.

(6) Spirituality finds nourishment in prayer that is rooted in sound scriptural knowledge and contemplation. The work of reading, studying, and pondering Scripture is central to the believer's prayer time, whether that time be brief or extended.

(7) Spirituality is rooted in a scriptural value-base that demands emphasis on a lifestyle that is characterized by simplicity and human dignity in a world sharply divided between the powerful rich and the oppressed poor. Lay spirituality calls not for radical impoverishment or nonownership of property as much as for responsible and respectful stewardship of the world's resources. Real holiness often emerges in the struggle to live and support a family in the world and not be swallowed up or possessed by a worldly value system.

(8) Spirituality is rooted in a healthy knowledge of self as a loved sinner before God. Today's holiness is identified in respect for one's own dignity and appreciation of one's talents, while possessing true knowledge of one's weakness and sinfulness. This provides a solid basis for love and respect for one's neighbors in a way that is nonpossessive and noncontrolling.

(9) Spirituality celebrates God's presence and loving mercy in a balance between the sacramental life of the church and the familial rituals of the domestic church.

(10) Spirituality is both affective and intellectual. A healthy human response to love is with the whole self. All dimensions of the human psyche are shaped by and shape one's relationship to God, which in turn shapes the relationship with all persons. Characteristically lay spirituality among married couples is enriched by a healthy appreciation of God's gift of sexual expression as a means for growing in love.

(11) Contemporary spirituality is not threatened by scientific advances, but is rather enriched by the search for truth on all frontiers.

(12) Spirituality is not confined or defined by denominational boundaries. Truly spiritual men and women see the call to unity among Christians at the heart of the mission of reconciliation and see the division and self-righteousness of denominationalism as destructive to the gospel message. Ecumenical and interfaith relationships are as rich and life-giving in faith as those within one's own tradition.

The growth of lay spirituality is one of the great gifts of the Spirit of God at a time in history when being Christian is so much more than wearing a denominational label and attending the church of one's choice on Sunday. The demands of the so-called post-Christian era of the waning years of the twentieth century upon all believing Christians are no less than those placed by Christ upon the first apostles. For any Christian to respond with less generosity is to deprive our broken world of the healing message that could be the only force between us and total self-annihilation. For the institutional churches to be anything less than utterly committed to the reawakening of the fervor of the church described in the Acts of the Apostles is to be untrue to the command of the gospel.

Eileen C. Burke-Sullivan[45]

227 • A Call to a Spiritually Based Ministry

The following article, written by an American Baptist, is a call for members of that tradition and all Christian traditions to place a vibrant spiritual life at the root of all Christian ministry.

Dostoyevsky said, "It is impossible to be human and not bow down; if God is rejected, before an idol we bow." Perhaps we bow because we have not learned to be still. Did God enjoin us to observe a Sabbath so we might remember to be still, to become holy and whole? In stillness, we best learn to worship and adore God with our whole heart, soul, mind, and strength. Out of the stillness, we can then make the journey because we know the One who goes before us and with us, in Ignacio Larranaga's words, "this God, the friend of life and of freedom, the One who accompanied Israel on the long pilgrimage through the desert."

Our Jewish spiritual ancestors well understood humanity's tendency to forget God and God's benefits. They knew that mortals often choose something other than abundant life. We forget to "give heed to the statutes and ordinances . . . so that [we] may live to enter and occupy the land the Lord is giving [us]." We forget to "keep the commandments . . . observe the statutes diligently," which shows our "wisdom and discernment." We are enjoined "neither forget the things your eyes have seen . . . nor let them slip from your mind all the days of your life . . . that you not make an idol for yourselves, in the form of any figure" (Deut. 4).

John Landgraf, former president of Central Baptist Seminary in Kansas City, citing his experience as a counselor for American Baptist ministers, says that "typical" American Baptist pastors understand their calling in terms of an active, "doing," extroverted life. This kind of understanding, he says, tends to produce a guilt-driven, need-based ministry, based on secularly defined success models of activism. The most common signs of such models are external and numerical: increased attendance, more programs, better statistics, and bigger budgets. These signs are looked upon (idolized) as producers of increased satisfaction and well-being. Yet people around us with the best statistics and greatest success are among the least satisfied and most insecure people we know. Landgraf says, "Instead of going with the flow of who God made when God made them, much of their action is reaction. They spin their wheels, spending energy ineffectively."

Such reaction-action success models pose dangers to any person's well-being. Those in activist denominations (such as American Baptists) and those in professional ministry are in gravest danger of growing out of touch with the inner life, which gets overshadowed by the demands of their lives. Pastoral counselors and spiritual directors, who observe this discontinuity between the inner and outer self—this draining away of vital energy from the center to the periphery—advocate disciplines that call counselees and directees to remember who they are and whose they are, an echo of the Deuteronomic injunction cited above. They also advocate a "detoxification" from "success addictions" and numbers games, replacing the "toxins" with sound spiritual disciplines.

Spiritual disciplines that emphasize reflection as opposed to action; being as opposed to doing; relationships as opposed to programs; worship focused upon God ("Grace to you and peace, from God and from our Lord Jesus Christ") as opposed to worship focused upon the worshiper ("Good morning. My, what a fine, large group we have here today!"); cooperation as opposed to competition; and so on are viewed suspiciously and approached cautiously by many activist, program-oriented Christians. Protestants—Baptists in particular—see these emphases as mystical more suited to Orthodox (Eastern) Christianity and out of place in a rationalist, post-Enlightenment, utilitarian (or "evangelical," free church), growth-oriented, Protestant (Western) theology.

Part of the struggle for activists is allowing themselves to lose control enough even to reflect on whether or not the models they work under are actually the sources of their burnout, guilt, and unease with themselves, their ministries, and their lives in general. Too often, it is not until *after* being broken and burned out that they turn to a lifestyle that accommodates and encourages reflection and relationship.

Among the growing number of Protestant spiritual directors, advocacy is gathering for a spiritual redirection within the denomination. This redirection has several major facets:

(1) a radical change in focus, from program-based to vocation-based ministries, practices, and theology;

(2) a radical change in perspective, from viewing ourselves as individualistic, autonomous congregations, composed of autonomous individualists, to viewing ourselves as autonomous but interdependent communities of cooperative individuals;

(3) a radical change from advocating activist goals, structures, and models that, not evil in themselves, have often led our churches and leaders to set these goals up as idols—as false gods—as ends in themselves, to advocating goals balanced between the countable and the uncountable goals (How do you quantify the reduction in misery of an abused child who finds help and safety?);

(4) a radical change in behavior, from an almost total doing orientation, to an orientation that advocates and rewards a healthy balance between doing and being.

Karl Rahner has said, "The Christian of tomorrow will be a mystic, one who has experienced something, or he will be nothing." More Christians, disillusioned by the hollow promises of the New Age or various cults and counterfeits, worn down and burned out by modern society and dead-end careerism are beginning to rediscover the One who said, "Be still, and know that I am God" (Ps. 46:10). American Baptists of this generation are beginning to rediscover the spiritual depth of their denominational forebearers. Indeed, they are reclaiming spirituality and spiritual disciplines as part of their rightful heritage, as Protestants and as authentic Christians in union with the communion of saints.

Inga T. Freyer Nicholas

228 ◆ BIBLIOGRAPHY ON WORSHIP AND SPIRITUAL FORMATION

The following is a selection of reference works that contain information on spirituality in a variety of Christian traditions. It also lists some works of liturgical and ecumenical interest that bear upon the subject of worship and spiritual formation.

Austin, Gerard. _Called to Prayer: Liturgical Spirituality Today._ Collegeville, Minn.: Liturgical Press, 1986.

Baptism, Eucharist and Ministry. Faith and Order Paper 111. Geneva: World Council of Churches, 1982. One of the most important ecumenical theological documents of the century; it articulates an ecumenical convergence of thought. A text from which further theological dialogue can continue.

Bernstein, Eleanor, ed. _Liturgy and Spirituality in Context: Perspectives on Prayer and Culture._ Collegeville, Minn.: Liturgical Press, 1990. A series of essays that explore how cultural context shapes the relationship between worship and spirituality.

Bondi, Roberta. _To Pray and to Love: Conversations on Prayer with the Early Church._ Philadelphia: Fortress Press, 1991. A good treatment of early Christian writers on prayer.

Bonhoeffer, Dietrich. _Life Together._ Trans. John W. Doberstein. New York: Harper and Row, 1954. A classic exploration of Bonhoeffer's experience of religious community in a German Lutheran seminary; Bonhoeffer's observations transcend the particularities of the situation that provoked them.

Brock, Sebastian. _The Harp of the Spirit: Eighteen Poems of Saint Ephrem._ Studies Supplementary to Sobornost No. 4. Fellowship of St. Alban and St. Sergius, 1983.

———. _The Luminous Eye: The Spiritual World Vision of St. Ephrem._ Kalamazoo, Mich.: Cistercian Publications, 1989.

Broyles, Anne. _Meeting God through Worship._ Nashville: Abingdon Press, 1992.

Burgess, Stanley M., and Gary B. McGee, eds. _Dictionary of Pentecostal and Charismatic Movements._ Grand Rapids: Zondervan, 1988. An essential reference work for anyone who wishes to understand Pentecostal and charismatic traditions of worship and spirituality.

Cunningham, Lawrence. _Catholic Prayer._ New York: Crossroad, 1989. A primer to spirituality in the variety of traditions found in the Roman Catholic church, with special reference to the liturgical life of the church.

Foster, Richard J. _Celebration of Discipline._ Rev. ed. San Francisco: Harper, 1988. A description of the classical spiritual disciplines of the Christian life, including a chapter on worship.

Hardy, Daniel W., and David F. Ford. *Praising and Knowing God.* Philadelphia: Westminster, 1985. An ecumenical systematic theology from the perspective of praise. Includes material on Pentecostal worship and has an excellent annotated bibliography.

Irwin, Kevin W. *Liturgy, Prayer, and Spirituality.* New York: Paulist Press, 1984. A book on the relationship of personal and communal prayer, with evidence for how common worship is a proper root of all Christian spirituality.

Jones, Cheslyn, Geoffrey Wainwright, and Edward Yarnold, eds. *The Study of Spirituality.* New York: Oxford University Press, 1986. Contains articles on a broad spectrum of subjects from all periods of Christian history. To be noted especially for the articles (with bibliography) by Sebastian Brock on Syriac Christian spirituality, by Gordon Wakefield on Quaker spirituality, and by James Cone on black worship.

Kannengiesser, Charles, ed. *Early Christian Spirituality.* Trans. Pamela Bright. Philadelphia: Fortress, 1986. A valuable collection of early Christian texts on spirituality by an eminent scholar of early Christian writings.

Maas, Robin, and Gabriel O'Donnell. *Spiritual Traditions for the Contemporary Church.* Nashville: Abingdon, 1993. An extended series of essays that examine many of the Catholic and Protestant traditions in spirituality that persist to this day, including black and feminist spirituality. Many of the essays relate spirituality to common worship.

Macquarrie, John. *Paths in Spirituality.* Rev. ed. Harrisburg, Pa.: Morehouse Publishing, 1992. A discussion of the various spiritual traditions in the Christian church, with special reference to the role of worship and the sacraments in each.

Madigan, Shawn. *Spirituality Rooted in Liturgy.* Washington, D.C.: Pastoral Press, 1988. Two-hundred-page book with index and sources at the end of each chapter. A historical perspective on liturgical spirituality, beginning with a chapter on Jewish spirituality, tracing the development and unfolding of Christian spirituality from the early Christian era through the Second Vatican Council and beyond. Develops two models of Christian worship and looks at the influence of Western culture on spirituality. The books return time and again to "the living of the Christian memory, to care for all people, [which] was linked to the celebration of universal love that the Lord's Supper clearly focuses."

McVey, Kathleen E., trans. *Ephrem the Syrian: Hymns.* The Classics of Western Spirituality. New York: Paulist Press, 1989.

Merton, Thomas. *Contemplative Prayer.* New York: Herder and Herder, 1969. While not directly concerned with liturgical prayer, the book provides a good introduction to the role of prayer in the inner life.

Porter, H. Boone. *The Day of Light.* Greenwich, Conn.: Seabury, 1960. A brief, yet comprehensive treatment of some of the major theological themes surrounding the observance of Sunday as a day of rest and worship.

Roccasalvo, Joan L. *The Eastern Catholic Churches: An Introduction to Their Worship and Spirituality.* Collegeville, Minn.: Liturgical Press, 1992. A fine introduction to the Eastern Christian tradition that observes how common liturgy is the central act of the church and root of all spirituality.

Brother Roger of Taizé. *Parable of Community: The Rule and Other Basic Texts of Taize.* New York: Seabury, 1981. A good edition of foundational texts from one of the most influential ecumenical communities of the post–World War II era.

Saliers, Don. *Worship and Spirituality.* Philadelphia: Westminster Press, 1984. A brief and stimulating treatment from an ecumenical perspective by a United Methodist theologian.

———. *The Soul in Paraphrase: Prayer and the Religious Affections.* New York: Seabury, 1980. Discusses the significance of liturgical prayer for shaping personal spirituality.

Senn, Frank, ed. *Protestant Spiritual Traditions.* Mahwah, N.J.: Paulist Press, 1986. Contains chapters on Lutheran, Reformed, Anabaptist, Anglican, Puritan, Pietist, and Methodist spirituality.

Tozer, A. W. *The Knowledge of the Holy.* San Francisco: HarperCollins, 1978. A famous treatise by an evangelical theologian, who contends that worship is an integral part of the Christian's response to God.

Underhill, Evelyn. *Worship.* London: Nisbet and Co., 1936. A historical and theological examination of Christian worship, with frequent mention of their relevance to living the spiritual life.

Wainwright, Geoffrey. *Doxology: The Praise of God in Worship, Doctrine and Life.* New York:

Oxford University Press, 1980. Wainwright's book has already become a classic exploration (from an ecumenical perspective) of the interplay of worship, theology, and Christian life.

Wakefield, Gordon, ed. *The Westminster Dictionary of Spirituality.* Philadelphia: Westminster, 1983. A valuable collection of short articles on a wide variety of topics.

Westerhoff III, John H., and William H. Willimon. *Liturgy and Learning Through the Life Cycle.* New York: Seabury, 1980. With several chapters dealing specifically with how liturgy shapes personal spirituality.

Zimmerman, Joyce Ann. *Liturgy as Living Faith: A Liturgical Spirituality.* Scranton, Pa.: University of Scranton Press, 1993. A discussion of the relationship of Christian worship and the spirituality of the worshiping community.

ELEVEN

Worship and Spiritual Formation in the Home

One beneficial way of integrating personal and family worship with the corporate worship of the church is to pattern worship in the home after the structures of corporate worship. This is especially important in the nurturing of children in the Christian faith. This chapter introduces readers to aspects of worship in the home and provides several sample liturgies for use there.

229 • AN INTRODUCTION TO WORSHIP IN THE HOME

Family worship serves an important role in shaping both children and adults in their Christian formation. More specifically, every family is continuously exerting influence on its members by the ways they order and live out their lives. This echoes the adage that Christianity is more often caught than taught. Therefore, the underlying question is not "Are we shaping our children for Christ?" Rather, it becomes, "Are we forming them to receive or reject Christ?"

Scripture reminds us:

Impress them (the commandments) on your children. Talk about them when you sit at home and when you walk along the road, when you lie down and when you get up. Tie them as symbols on your hands and bind them on your foreheads. Write them on the door frames of your houses and on your gates. (Deut. 6:7-9)

Barry Liesch observes that this worship is situational, affective, and based on the modeling of parents (Barry Liesch, *People in the Presence of God* [Grand Rapids: Zondervan, 1988], 54–56). The Puritans, like earlier Jewish families, understood the great forming importance of the family. They perceived the home as the church in miniature and therefore a place to pray, worship, and focus on God.

This approach to family worship assumes first of all that the adult members of the household have taken seriously their relationship with the triune God. How do they perceive and understand God in their own lives? What are they doing to draw nearer to God so as to more effectively model that to others? In this generation of change family structures have not been spared. No longer is the average home comprised of a husband and wife and a couple of children. Single parent homes, blended families, or even households headed by a grandparent can experience worship that is biblical, healthy, and positive when the adults are actively pursuing their own Christian growth.

Therefore, one of the central spiritual tasks of the family is the cultivation of awareness and celebration. Sara Shenk defines it this way, "Celebration is the honoring of that which we hold most dear. Celebration is delighting in that which tells us who we are. Celebration is taking the time to cherish each other. Celebration is returning with open arms and thankful hearts to our Maker" (Sara Shenk, *Why Not Celebrate!* [Intercourse, Pa.: Good Books, 1987], 3). Celebration is built on the symbolic repetitive acts of ritual, play, feasting, fasting, and acknowledging both joys and sorrows.

While celebration comes easy to children, that is not always true for adults. The cultural barriers of rationalism and materialism have done much to reduce the ability to celebrate. Rationalism has the tendency to strip the wonder, mystery, and imagination from life. At its basic core, rationalism converts everything into an object to be analyzed, controlled, and tragically exploited. The unfortunate derivative of materialism is that we, humans, have accumulated so much that large quantities of our time is spent in caring, guarding, or paying for our possessions. This gluttonous tendency further reduces the potential for celebration and gratitude.

Jesus Christ, the grand celebrator, can rescue us from these cultural obstacles and teach us how to worship with meaning. The Scripture captures Jesus in various settings, which exhibit his appreciation of and gratitude for life. He shared the joy of a newly married couple and provided wine when their supply was depleted (John 2:1-11). He dined with Pharisees, tax collectors, friends, and potential disciples (Luke 7:36; 10:38; 19:7; Matt. 9:10). He welcomed little children into his arms and blessed them with his love (Mark 10:16). When his dear friend Lazarus died, Jesus sought to console the grief-stricken Martha and Mary (John 11:17-37). As a Jew, Jesus continued to participate in the Jewish feasts and gave specific directions to his disciples so they could celebrate the Passover together (Matt. 26:18). The upper room gathering formed the foundation for the later celebration of the Lord's Supper (Luke 22:19; 1 Cor. 11:24-25).

The example of Jesus Christ encourages us to take seriously the realities of life. That is to say, celebration is not an escape or temporary reprieve from the difficult rigors of life. Rather, celebrations intensify reality and dynamically point us beyond ourselves linking us to God. Gertrude Nelson reinforces this concept, "All good ceremony asks us to engage and make real the problem at hand and to feel and express fully both the dark and light sides of reality, its joy and its fear or pain" (Gertrude Nelson, *To Dance with God* [Mahwah, N.J.: Paulist, 1986], 41). Further, Christian families do not celebrate in a vacuum. Their gathering in the name of Jesus Christ reminds them that Christ is present with them in both their joys and sorrows. Children and parents alike often find symbols helpful to reinforce and remind them of this presence. In our media age, we realize that today's images become tomorrow's memories. Creative expressions of pictures and symbolic objects that encourage children to offer their own examples can be a valuable means of connecting them with Christ and solidifying their worship experience.

Nor should we view our family celebrations as an idle waste of time or energy for they "give us perspective" and "save us from taking ourselves too seriously" (Richard Foster, *Celebration of Discipline* [San Francisco: Harper and Row, 1978], 168). Even amidst the dark seasons of life, worship and prayer can return our focus to God.

Yet another enriching result of family worship is the ability to create a growing sense of family identity and belonging (see Arlen Roy, "Use Family Rituals to Strengthen Church Families and Congregations," *Action Information* [Alban Institute] 17:6 [Nov./Dec. 1991]: 6–9). The world can often be cruel and unjust, seeking to tear us down. The home, however, inspired by the living presence of Jesus Christ, can communicate the necessary message of acceptance and affirmation. Family rituals, which include our observance of birthdays, anniversaries, deaths, special events and achievements, Christmas, Easter, and other dates of the church year, reinforce our relationship with God and to one another. The actual expressions and worship practices will vary greatly from family to family. That does not matter. The key principle is that families realize that they are not alone in the world and can draw upon the presence and strength of God to find both guidance in time of need and joy in times of gratitude.

The Cross Flamant. This unusual cross is distinguished by its flamelike edges, a symbol of religious zeal.

Before using the following liturgies for family worship, one additional comment should be made. Especially when young children are present, let us not fall into the trap of seeing worship as something we do "to" or "for" our children or family. A healthier and more balanced approach is to engage in these practices "with" our children and all who may be visiting within our home. That may necessitate altering certain words or forms, but sensitivity that provides opportunities for all increases the overall participation. Involving all our household will instill rich memories and assist in the dynamic process of Christ's formation within each person's life.

Robert Webber

230 ✦ LITURGY ON THE OCCASION OF THE BIRTH, BAPTISM, OR DEDICATION OF A CHILD

The following liturgies may be used in small or large family celebrations or in gatherings of the larger worshiping community. Adapt to local needs and customs.

——— **On the Occasion of a Birth** ———

Gathering

LEADER: We gather today in the spirit of rejoicing to celebrate the birth of [Name]. Let us bless the name of God who has brought this child into our home. Hear the word of the Lord from Matthew: "Let the little children come to me, and do not forbid them; for of such is the kingdom of heaven" (19:14).

Let us pray.

Father, we thank you for the life of this little one. May your blessing be upon her/him. Cause this child to grow in wisdom, and grant that we may provide a home of love and warmth, through Jesus Christ our Lord. Amen.

The Scripture Reading

READER 1: A reading from the book of Psalms:
"I will praise you with my whole heart;
Before the gods I will sing praises to you.

I will worship toward your holy temple,
And praise your name
For your lovingkindness and your truth;
For you have magnified your word above all your name.
In the day when I cried out, you answered me,
And made me bold with strength in my soul.
All the kings of the earth shall praise you, O Lord,
When they hear the words of your mouth.
Yes, they shall sing of the ways of the Lord,
For great is the glory of the Lord" (138:1-5).
This is the word of the Lord.

RESPONSE: **Thanks be to God.**

READER 2: A reading from the Gospel according to Luke:
"Now there were in the same country shepherds living in the fields, keeping watch over their flock by night. And behold, an angel of the Lord stood before them, and the glory of the Lord shone around them, and they were greatly afraid. Then the angel said to them, 'Do not be afraid, for behold, I bring you good tidings of great joy which will be to all people. For there is born to you this day in the city of David a Savior, who is Christ the Lord. And this will be a sign to you: You will find a babe wrapped in swaddling clothes, lying in a manger.' And suddenly there was with the angel a multitude of the heavenly host praising God and saying: 'Glory to God in the highest, and on earth peace, good will toward men!'" (2:8-14).
This is the word of the Lord.

RESPONSE: **Thanks be to God.**

The Prayer of Dedication

LEADER: Let us dedicate this child to the Lord. Gracious Father, you have taught us, through Jesus your Son, that those who receive a child in your name receive Christ Himself. We give thanks to you for the blessing you have granted through the birth of this child. May this child be brought up in the nurture of the faith, and may all that is good and true, especially lively faith in Jesus Christ, be this child's portion. We pray this in the name of Jesus Christ our Lord. Amen.

(Here the feast of joy may commence.)

─────── **On the Occasion of a Baptism** ───────

Gathering

LEADER: Dear family and friends, baptism is the glorious symbol of God's love for us and our response to Him. We gather under the sign of baptism today to celebrate the baptism of [Name]. Let us rejoice in the God who saves us and in the faith here affirmed.

Let us pray.

Lord, You have given us water as a sign of the new creation. Grant that this sign of your grace may be met by the soul's desire and bring us all to your glory, through Christ our Lord. Amen.

The Scripture Readings

READER 1: A reading from Romans:
"Or do you not know that as many of us as were baptized into Christ Jesus were baptized into his death? Therefore we were buried with him through baptism into death, that just as Christ was raised from the dead by the glory of the Father, even so we also should walk in newness of life. For if we have been united together in the likeness of his death, certainly we also shall be in the likeness of his resurrection, knowing this, that our old man was crucified with Him, that the body of sin might be done away with, that we should no longer be slaves of sin" (6:3-6).
This is the word of the Lord.

RESPONSE: **Thanks be to God.**

READER 2: A reading from Colossians:
"If then you were raised with Christ, seek those things which are above, where Christ is sitting at the right hand of God. Set your mind on things above, not on things on the earth. For you died, and your life is hidden with Christ in God. . . . Therefore, as the elect of God, holy and beloved, put on tender mercies, kindness, humbleness of mind, meekness, long-suffering; bearing with one another, and forgiving one another, if anyone has a compliant against another; even as Christ forgave you, so you must also do. But above all these things put on love, which is the bond of perfection. And let the peace of God rule in your hearts, to which also you were called in one body; and be thankful. Let the word of Christ dwell in you richly in all wisdom, teaching and admonishing one another in psalms, and hymns, and spiritual songs, singing with grace in your hearts to the Lord. And whatever you do in word or deed, do all in the name of the Lord Jesus, giving thanks to God the Father through Him" (3:1-3, 12-17).
This is the word of the Lord.

RESPONSE: **Thanks be to God.**

Affirming the Covenant

LEADER: In the early church it was the custom for all people to reaffirm their covenant at every baptism. Therefore, in the following words, we will reaffirm our faith and our commitment:
Do you believe in God the Father?

RESPONSE: **I believe in God, the Father almighty, creator of heaven and earth.**

LEADER: Do you believe in Jesus Christ, the Son of God?

RESPONSE: **I believe in Jesus Christ, his only Son, our Lord. He was conceived by the power of the Holy Spirit and born of the Virgin Mary. He suffered under Pontius Pilate, was crucified, died, and was buried. He descended to the dead. On the third day He rose again. He ascended into heaven,** and is seated at the right hand of the Father. He will come again to judge the living and the dead.

LEADER: Do you believe in God the Holy Spirit?

RESPONSE: **I believe in the Holy Spirit, the holy catholic church, the communion of saints, the forgiveness of sins, the resurrection of the body, and life everlasting.**

LEADER: Will you continue in the apostle's teaching and fellowship, in the breaking of the bread, and in the prayers? If so, answer, "I will, with God's help."

RESPONSE: **I will, with God's help.**

LEADER: Will you persevere in resisting evil, and, whenever you fall into sin, repent and return to the Lord?

RESPONSE: **I will, with God's help.**

LEADER: Will you proclaim by word and example the Good News of God in Christ?

RESPONSE: **I will, with God's help.**

LEADER: Will you seek and serve Christ in all persons, loving your neighbor as yourself?

RESPONSE: **I will, with God's help.**

LEADER: Will you strive for justice and peace among all people, and respect the dignity of every human being?

RESPONSE: **I will, with God's help.**

The Prayer of Commitment

LEADER: Father, we who are gathered here today rejoice in the baptism of [Name], and with him/her we reaffirm our baptismal vows. Deliver us, O Lord, from the way of death. Open our hearts to your faith. Fill us with your life-giving spirit. Keep us in your holy church, and grant us the power to live in our vows, through Jesus our Lord and Savior. Amen.

The Dismissal

LEADER: Let us greet the baptized with the kiss of peace.

(Here each may greet the baptized with a handshake or an appropriate hug, saying, "The Peace of the Lord be with you." In the case of an infant the greeting may be extended to the parents.)

On the Occasion of Infant Dedication

Gathering

LEADER: Dear family and friends, God has seen fit to bring the infant [Name] into the world. Let us rejoice together in the dedication of this child to the Lord, and let us pray together for his/her spiritual health and growth.

Let us pray.

Father, your Son, the Lord Jesus, welcomed the children into his kingdom. Protect, we pray, this child and bring him/her into a saving relationship with your Son, and into fellowship with your church, the body of Christ. We pray through Jesus our Lord. Amen.

The Scripture Readings

READER 1: A reading from Luke:

"And behold, there was a man in Jerusalem whose name was Simeon, and this man was just and devout, waiting for the consolation of Israel, and the Holy Spirit was upon him. And it had been revealed to him by the Holy Spirit that he would not see death before he had seen the Lord's Christ. So he came by the Spirit into the temple. And when the parents brought in the child Jesus, to do for him according to the custom of the law, he took him up in his arms and blessed God and said:

Lord, now you are letting your servant depart in peace,
According to your word;
For my eyes have seen your salvation
Which you have prepared before the face of all peoples,
A light to bring revelation to the Gentiles,
And the glory of your people Israel.

And Joseph and his mother marveled at those things which were spoken of him" (2:25-33).

This is the word of the Lord.

RESPONSE: **Thanks be to God.**

READER 2: A reading from 2 Timothy:

"I thank God, whom I serve with a

pure conscience, as my forefathers did, as without ceasing I remember you in my prayers night and day, greatly desiring to see you, being mindful of your tears, that I may be filled with joy, when I call to remembrance the genuine faith that is in you, which dwelt first in your grandmother Lois and your mother Eunice, and I am persuaded is in you also. Therefore I remind you to stir up the gift of God which is in you through the laying on of my hands. For God has not given us a spirit of fear, but of power and of love and of a sound mind" (1:3-7).

This is the word of the Lord.

RESPONSE: **Thanks be to God.**

The Prayer of Commitment

LEADER: Let us commit the life of [Name] to the Lord. Lord Jesus, we bring [Name] to you. For you alone are Lord of the universe. We confess that you are the Lord of [Name]'s life. We commit his/her life into your hands, and we pray you grant the will and wisdom needed to bring this child up in the fear and admonition of the Lord and in the fellowship of the church, your body.

RESPONSE: **Amen.**

(Here the festivities may commence.)

231 ◆ Liturgy on the Occasion of a Baptism, Confirmation, or Renewed Commitment of Faith of an Adult

The following liturgy may be used in family celebrations at the occasion of confirmation, profession of faith, baptism of adults, or any other occasion of renewed commitment. Adapt to local needs and customs.

Gathering

LEADER: Dear family and friends, today is a very special day in the life of [Name]; for on this day he/she has made a public commitment to the intent of baptism. [Name] has affirmed his/her personal faith in Jesus Christ as Lord

and Savior. Together with the angels we gather to celebrate this glorious occasion.

Let us pray.

Lord God, we bless you for your continued presence in the life of [Name]. Grant that the work that you have begun in his/her life will be maintained until that day when we shall all gather at the feet of Jesus your Son, in whose name we pray.

RESPONSE: **Amen.**

The Scripture Reading

READER 1: A reading from Paul's letter to the Ephesians:

"Blessed be the God and Father of our Lord Jesus Christ, who has blessed us with every spiritual blessing in the heavenly places in Christ, just as he chose us in him before the foundation of the world, that we should be holy and without blame before him in love, having predestined us to adoption as sons by Jesus Christ to himself, according to the good pleasure of his will, to the praise of the glory of his grace, by which he has made us accepted in the beloved. In him we have redemption through his blood, the forgiveness of sins, according to the riches of his grace which he made to abound toward us in all wisdom and prudence, having made known to us the mystery of his will, according to his good pleasure which he purposed in himself, that in the dispensation of the fullness of the times he might gather together in one all things in Christ, both which are in heaven and which are on earth—in him, in whom also we have obtained an inheritance, being predestined according to the purpose of him who works all things according to the counsel of his will, that we who first trusted in Christ should be to the praise of his glory. In him you also trusted, after you heard the word of truth, the gospel of your salvation; in whom also, having believed, you were

sealed with the Holy Spirit of prom-
ise" (1:3-13).
This is the word of the Lord.
RESPONSE: **Thanks be to God.**

The Words of Admonition
LEADER: I invite all who are here present to
offer a brief word of wisdom to
[Name].

(One or more may speak.)
At the conclusions of each speech, all shall say:
Amen!

The Prayer of Commitment
LEADER: Let us give thanks for the confirmation of [Name].

Almighty God, by the glorious
death and resurrection of your Son,
you have put to flight the power of
evil. Bless now [Name], who has been
sealed in your Spirit. Send him/her
and us forth in the power of your
Spirit to perform your service, to
lighten the paths of others, to glorify
your name, through Jesus our Lord.
RESPONSE: **Amen.**

(Here the festivities may commence.)

232 ◆ LITURGY ON THE OCCASION OF A BIRTHDAY

*The following liturgy may be used in small or large fam-
ily celebrations or in gatherings of the larger worshiping community. Adapt to local needs and customs.*

Gathering
LEADER: My dear friends, today is a special day
in the life of our family, for on this
day we celebrate the birth of [Name].
Let us begin by giving thanks to God
Almighty.
Let us pray.
Father, we praise you for every perfect gift that comes from above. You
have gifted us with [Name]. Now we
bless you for his/her presence in our
family. Grant, we pray you, that your
blessing may rests upon him/her all
the days of his/her life. Amen.

The Scripture Readings
READER 1: A reading from Ecclesiastes:
"To everything there is a season.
A time for every purpose under
heaven:
A time to be born,
And a time to die;
A time to plant,
And a time to pluck what is planted;
A time to kill,
And a time to heal;
A time to break down,
And a time to build up;
A time to weep,
And a time to laugh;
A time to mourn,
And a time to dance;
A time to cast away stones,
And a time to gather stones;
A time to embrace,
And a time to refrain from embrac-
ing;
A time to gain,
And a time to lose;
A time to keep,
And a time to throw away;
A time to tear,
And a time to sew;
A time to keep silence,
And a time to speak;
A time to love,
And a time to hate;
A time of war,
And a time of peace" (3:1-8).
This is the word of the Lord.
RESPONSE: **Thanks be to God.**

READER 2: A reading from the Gospel according
to John:
"There was a man of the Pharisees
named Nicodemus, a ruler of the
Jews. This man came to Jesus by night
and said to him, 'Rabbi, we know that
you are a teacher come from God; for
no one can do these signs that you
do unless God is with him.' Jesus answered and said to him, 'Most assuredly, I say to you, unless one is born
again, he cannot see the kingdom of
God.' Nicodemus said to him, 'How
can a man be born when he is old?

Can he enter a second time into his mother's womb and be born?' Jesus answered, 'Most assuredly, I say to you, unless one is born of water and the Spirit, he cannot enter the kingdom of God. That which is born of the flesh is flesh, and that which is born of the Spirit is spirit. Do not marvel that I said to you, 'You must be born again.' The wind blows where it wishes, and you hear the sound of it, but cannot tell where it comes from and where it goes. So is everyone who is born of the Spirit" (3:1-8).

This is the word of the Lord.

RESPONSE: **Thanks be to God.**

The Presentation of Gifts

(The gifts may now be brought.)

LEADER: [Name], these gifts are tokens of the love and esteem we have for you. Before you open them, we wish to express our love to you in words. Each of us has thought of something about you that we appreciate. We want to acknowledge you in this way.

(Each person may now state a positive characteristic of the person whose birth is being celebrated by saying: I like _____ or I appreciate _____.)

The Prayer of Dedication

LEADER: Let us dedicate [Name] to the Lord. Father, we dedicate [Name] to your service.

We ask that his/her life may bring glory to your name, through Jesus Christ our Lord.

RESPONSE: **Amen.**

(The gifts may now be opened and the cake shared by all.)

233 ✦ LITURGY ON THE OCCASION OF AN ENGAGEMENT OR BETROTHAL

The following liturgy may be used in small or large family celebrations or in gatherings of the larger worshiping community, serving as a means of both celebration and of challenge to the couple preparing for marriage. Adapt to local needs and customs.

Gathering

LEADER: Dear family and friends, we have gathered on this occasion to honor [Name] and [Name], who have announced their intention to unite in holy marriage. This is a festive and wonderful moment in their lives and ours; so let us be festive and rejoice.

Let us pray.

Lord God, you bring to pass all things under your providence. In your holy wisdom you have seen fit to bring [Name] and [Name] into a loving relationship. In this celebration of their intent, we praise you for your hand in their lives. As you have been present to them in the past, be with them now and throughout their life together, in Jesus' name we pray. Amen.

The Scripture Readings

READER 1: A reading from Genesis:

"And the Lord God said, 'It is not good that man should be alone; I will make him a helper comparable to him.' Out of the ground the Lord God formed every beast of the field and every bird of the air, and brought them to Adam to see what he would call them. And whatever Adam called each living creature, that was its name. So Adam gave names to all cattle, to the birds of the air, and to every beast of the field. But for Adam there was not found a helper comparable to him. And the Lord God caused a deep sleep to fall on Adam, and he slept; and he took one of his ribs, and closed up the flesh in its place. Then the rib which the Lord God had taken from man he made into a woman, and he brought her to the man. And Adam said:
'This is now bone of my bones
And flesh of my flesh;
She shall be called Woman,
Because she was taken out of Man.'

Therefore a man shall leave his father and mother
and be joined to his wife, and they shall become one flesh'" (2:18-24).
This is the word of the Lord.

RESPONSE: **Thanks be to God.**

READER 2: A reading from the First Epistle of John:
"Beloved, let us love one another, for love is of God; and everyone who loves is born of God and knows God. He who does not love does not know God, for God is love. In this the love of God was manifested toward us, that God has sent his only begotten Son into the world, that we might live through him. In this is love, not that we loved God, but that he loved us and sent his Son to be the propitiation for our sins. Beloved, if God so loved us, we also ought to love one another. No one has seen God at any time. If we love one another, God abides in us, and his love has been perfected in us. By this we know that we abide in him, and he in us, because he has given us of his Spirit. And we have seen and testify that the Father has sent the Son as savior of the world. Whoever confesses that Jesus is the Son of God, God abides in him, and he in God. And we have known and believed the love that God has for us. God is love, and he who abides in love abides in God, and God in him" (4:7-16).
This is the word of the Lord.

RESPONSE: **Thanks be to God.**

Words of Advice and Admonition

LEADER: [Name] and [Name], we wish to congratulate you and offer words of wisdom and advice from our experience. I invite those who have a word for your direction in life to speak now.

(Here as many as wish may make appropriate comments.)

Prayer of Commitment

LEADER: Let us pray for [Name] and [Name].

Lord, from you love originates. Father, Son, and Holy Spirit have been bound together in love. You bestowed love upon your creation. You poured out your love in Jesus Christ. Now, O source of love, grant that [Name] and [Name] shall love you and each other more and more, through Christ our Lord.

RESPONSE: **Amen.**

(Here may follow the opening of gifts and festive celebration of the engagement.)

234 ◆ LITURGY ON THE OCCASION OF A WEDDING

The following liturgy may be used at the time of celebration that accompanies the marriage service, perhaps as a devotional act at a wedding reception. Adapt to local needs and customs.

Gathering

LEADER: Dear friends, today is a most happy occasion; for on this day we celebrate the marriage of [Name] and [Name]. We believe God has called them to live together in holy matrimony, so we gather to give them our support and to wish them well.

Let us pray.

Lord God, you who adorn the sky with clouds and stars, you who beautify the earth with shrubs and flowers, grant that the marriage of [Name] and [Name] may be sanctified by your grace, to your glory and their enjoyment, we pray. Amen.

The Scripture Readings

READER 1: A reading from the Song of Solomon:
"My beloved spoke, and said to me;
'Rise up, my love, my fair one,
And come away.
For lo, the winter is past,
The rain is over and gone.
The flowers appear on the earth;
The time of singing has come,
And the voice of the turtledove
Is heard in our land.
The fig tree puts forth her green figs,
And the vines with the tender grapes

Give a good smell.
Rise up, my love, my fair one,
And come away!
O my dove, in the clefts of the rock,
In the secret places of the cliff,
Let me see your countenance,
Let me hear your voice;
For your voice is sweet,
And your countenance is lovely.'
Many waters cannot quench love,
Nor can the floods drown it.
If a man would give for love
All the wealth of his house,
It would be utterly despised" (2:10-
14; 8:7).
This is the word of the Lord.

RESPONSE: **Thanks be to God.**

READER 2: A reading from the First Epistle of John:
"Beloved, let us love one another, for love is of God; and everyone who loves is born of God and knows God. He who does not love does not know God, for God is love. In this the love of God was manifested toward us, that God has sent his only begotten Son into the world, that we might live through him. In this is love, not that we loved God, but that he loved us and sent his Son to be the propitiation for our sins. Beloved, if God so loved us, we also ought to love one another. No one has seen God at any time. If we love one another, God abides in us, and his love has been perfected in us. By this we know that we abide in him, and he in us, because he has given us of his Spirit. And we have seen and testify that the Father has sent the Son as savior of the world. Whoever confesses that Jesus is the Son of God, God abides in him, and he in God. And we have known and believed the love that God has for us. God is love, and he who abides in love abides in God, and God in him" (4:7-16).
This is the word of the Lord.

RESPONSE: **Thanks be to God.**

The Feast

(If a feast is part of the celebration, it may take place here after the prayer.)

LEADER: Let us give thanks to God for this food. Lord God, we acknowledge you as the giver of all good things. Bless this food to our enjoyment. May we feast together, celebrating your presence with us and with this marriage, through Christ our Lord. Amen.

The Final Prayers

(After the meal or reception, the leader may say:)

LEADER: Let us send [Name] and [Name] forth in prayer: Lord of heaven and earth, grant your servants [Name] and [Name] journeying mercies on their honeymoon. Bestow upon them love for each other and you, and bring them and us to your eternal kingdom, through Jesus Christ our Lord.

RESPONSE: **Amen.**

235 ✦ LITURGY ON THE OCCASION OF A WEDDING ANNIVERSARY

The following liturgy may be used in small or large family celebrations or in gatherings of the larger worshiping community. Adapt to local needs and customs.

Gathering

LEADER: We have gathered this day to celebrate the anniversary of [Name] and [Name]. We give thanks to God that they were brought together in holy matrimony [number] years ago, and we offer special thanks to the Father who has granted grace to them over the years.

Let us pray.

Father in heaven, we praise you for the marriage of [Name] and [Name], and we bless you for the witness of their life and love. Grant, O heavenly one, that they may be blessed with continued love and happiness together, through Jesus Christ our Lord. Amen.

The Scripture Readings

READER 1: A reading from Genesis:

"And the Lord God said, 'It is not good that man should be alone; I will make him a helper comparable to him.' . . . And the Lord God caused a deep sleep to fall on Adam, and he slept; and he took one of his ribs, and closed up the flesh in its place. Then the rib which the Lord God had taken from man he made into a woman, and he brought her to the man. And Adam said:

'This is now bone of my bones
And flesh of my flesh;
She shall be called Woman,
Because she was taken out of Man.'

Therefore a man shall leave his father and mother and be joined to his wife, and they shall become one flesh" (2:18, 21-24).

This is the word of the Lord.

RESPONSE: **Thanks be to God.**

READER 2: A reading from the Gospel according to John:

"On the third day there was a wedding in Cana of Galilee, and the mother of Jesus was there. Now both Jesus and his disciples were invited to the wedding. And when they ran out of wine, the mother of Jesus said to him, 'They have no wine.' Jesus said to her, 'Woman, what does your concern have to do with me? My hour has not yet come.' His mother said to the servants, 'Whatever he says to you, do it.' Now there were set there six waterpots of stone, according to the manner of purification of the Jews, containing twenty or thirty gallons apiece. Jesus said to them, 'Fill the waterpots with water.' And they filled them up to the brim. And he said to them, 'Draw some out now, and take it to the master of the feast.' And they took it. When the master of the feast had tasted the water that was made wine, and did not know where it came from (but the servants who had drawn the water knew), the master of the feast called to the bridegroom. And he said to him, 'Every man at the beginning sets out the good wine, and when the guests have well drunk, then that which is inferior; but you have kept the good wine until now.' This beginning of signs Jesus did in Cana of Galilee, and manifested his glory; and his disciples believed in him" (2:1-11).

This is the word of the Lord.

RESPONSE: **Thanks be to God.**

The Renewal of the Vows

LEADER: [Name] and [Name] will now repeat their vows as a sign of their continuing love and fidelity to each other.

HUSBAND: It is my will to continue to have you as my wife, and to live with you in the covenant of marriage. I will continue to love you, comfort you, honor and keep you, in sickness and in health; and continuing to forsake all others, I pledge you my faithfulness as long as we live.

WIFE: It is my will to continue to have you as my husband and to live with you in the covenant of marriage. I will continue to love you, comfort you, honor and keep you, in sickness and health; and continuing to forsake all others, to be faithful to you as long as we both live.

The Prayer of Dedication

LEADER: Let us rededicate [Name] and [Name] in marriage.

Father Almighty, in your divine providence you have willed to bring [Name] and [Name] together in holy matrimony. In this day when marriage is beset by stress, we pray for your special grace. Keep their love strong, their commitment steadfast; and may their joy increase more and more, through Jesus Christ our Lord. Amen.

Celebrating the Marriage

LEADER: Having witnessed the reenactment of these vows, let us now toast [Name] and [Name] with words of encouragement. I ask each of you to speak a word of encouragement or make reference to something from their life that has been of special help to you.

(Those who wish may make appropriate comments.)

The peace of the Lord be with you.
RESPONSE: **And also with you.**

(Greet each other with a handshake or an appropriate hug, saying, "The Peace of the Lord be with you.")

236 ✦ LITURGY ON THE OCCASION OF A RETIREMENT

The following liturgy may be used in small or large family celebrations or in gatherings of the larger worshiping community. Notice how the liturgy views retirement not as time to abstain from kingdom work, but as a time of a change in vocation. Adapt to local needs and customs.

Gathering

LEADER: My dear friends, today we have gathered to celebrate the work of our dear friend [Name] and to welcome his/her deserved rest from the daily demands of his/her work. Let us rejoice in God who has given us work to do, and let us be reminded of the promise of Sabbath rest.

Let us pray.

Father Almighty, in six days you created the world, and on the seventh you rested. You, who are known by your works, are the Lord of life and work. We bless you for the work of [Name]. Now grant him/her rest in the activities of retirement, through Jesus Christ our Lord. Amen.

The Scripture Readings

READER 1: A reading from Genesis:
"The Lord God planted a garden eastward in Eden, and there he put the man whom he had formed. And out of the ground the Lord God made every tree grow that is pleasant to the sight and good for food. The tree of life was also in the midst of the garden, and the tree of knowledge of good and evil. Now a river went out of Eden to water the garden, and from there it parted and became four riverheads. The name of the first is Pishon; it is the one which encompasses the whole land of Havilah, where there is gold. And the gold of that land is good. Bdellium and onyx stone are there. The name of the second river is Gihon; it is the one which encompasses the whole land of Cush. The name of the third river is Hiddekel; it is the one which goes toward the east of Assyria. The fourth river is the Euphrates. Then the Lord God took the man and put him in the garden of Eden to tend and keep it" (2:8-15).

This is the word of the Lord.
RESPONSE: **Thanks be to God.**

READER 2: A reading from Hebrews:
"Therefore, since a promise remains of entering his rest, let us fear lest any of you seem to have come short of it. For indeed the gospel was preached to us as well as to them; but the word which they heard did not profit them, not being mixed with faith in those who heard it. For we who have believed do enter that rest, as he has said: 'So I swore in my wrath,/They shall not enter my rest,' although the works were finished from the foundation of the world. For he has spoken in a certain place of the seventh day in this way; 'And God rested on the seventh day from all his works'; and again in this place: 'They shall not enter my rest.' Since therefore it remains that some must enter it, and those to whom it was first preached did not enter because of disobedience, again he designates a certain day, saying in David, 'Today,' after such a long time, as it has been said: 'Today, if you will hear his voice, do not harden your hearts.' For if Joshua had given them rest, then he would not afterward have spoken of another day. There remains therefore a rest

for the people of God. For he who has entered his rest has himself also ceased from his works as God did from his" (4:1-10).

This is the word of the Lord.

RESPONSE: **Thanks be to God.**

Testimonials

LEADER: We now wish to express our appreciation to [Name] for his/her work and to wish him/her well in the future.

(Those who have asked to make speeches may do so at this time.)

The Prayer of Dedication

LEADER: Let us dedicate [Name] to the Lord. Father, as there is a time to work and labor and a time to rest, grant that the rest into which [Name] enters may be filled with the joy of life. Protect his/her coming and going, fill his/her life with friendships, bless him/her with health, and grant him/her peace, through Jesus Christ our Lord we pray. Amen.

(Friends may now gather to congratulate and offer best wishes to the retiree.)

237 ◆ LITURGY ON THE OCCASION OF AN ILLNESS

The following liturgy may be used in small or large family celebrations or in gatherings of the larger worshiping community. Adapt to local needs and customs.

Gathering

LEADER: Dear friends, we have gathered together to pray for [Name], who is ill. We are reminded that Jesus demonstrated great compassion toward the sick. Let us now hear the instruction given by James regarding prayer for the sick:

"Is anyone among you sick? Let him call for the elders of the church, and let them pray over him, anointing him with oil in the name of the Lord. And the prayer of faith will save the sick, and the Lord will raise him up" (5:14-15).

Let us pray.

Lord Jesus, we acknowledge your power over sickness and all disease, which you demonstrated when you were among us. Give us hearts that are open to your power. We pray in your name. Amen.

The Scripture Readings

READER 1: A reading from the Old Testament: "Now Naaman, commander of the army of the king of Syria, was a great and honorable man in the eyes of his master, because by him the Lord had given victory to Syria. He was also a mighty man of valor, but he was a leper. And the Syrians had gone out on raids, and had brought back captive a young girl from the land of Israel. She waited on Naaman's wife. . . . Then Naaman went with his horses and chariot, and he stood at the door of the house of Elisha. And Elisha sent a messenger to him, saying 'Go and wash in the Jordan seven times, and your flesh shall be restored to you, and you shall be clean.' . . . So he went down and dipped seven times in the Jordan, according to the saying of the man of God; and his flesh was restored like the flesh of a little child, and he was clean. The he returned to the man of God, he and all his aides, and came and stood before him; and he said, 'Indeed, now I know that there is no God in all the earth, except in Israel'" (2 Kings 5:1-2, 9-10, 14-15).

This is the word of the Lord.

RESPONSE: **Thanks be to God.**

READER 2: A reading from the Gospel according to Mark:

"Then he came to Bethsaida; and they brought a blind man to him, and begged him to touch him. So he took the blind man by the hand and led him out of town. And when he had spit on his eyes and put his hands on him, he asked him if he saw anything. And he looked up and said, 'I see men like trees, walking,' Then he put his hands upon his eyes again and made him look up. And he was restored and saw everyone clearly" (8:22-25).

This is the word of the Lord.

RESPONSE: **Thanks be to God.**

The Anointing and Prayer of Healing

(The elders of the church and/or members of the family may gather around the sick person. After placing oil on the forehead of the person in the name of the Father, the Son, and the Holy Spirit, place hands on the head, saying the following prayer:)

LEADER: Let us pray.

O Lord, it is through your power that your Son Jesus healed the sick and gave new hope. Although we cannot presume upon your will, we do offer our prayer in faith for the healing of [Name]. In your will, grant wholeness of mind, body, and soul. Give peace and comfort to both the sick and the well, that we all may give glory to your name, through Jesus Christ our Lord. Amen.

(As the people depart, they may greet the sick person with a Christian greeting, saying, "The Lord be with you.")

238 ✦ LITURGY ON THE OCCASION OF DYING

The following liturgy may be used in the absence of a pastor to comfort a person who is dying. Relatives and friends of the dying may gather around the bed and read one or all of the following Scriptures.

Psalm 23

"The Lord is my shepherd;
I shall not want.
He makes me to lie down in green pastures;
He leads me beside the still waters.
He restores my soul;
He leads me in the paths of righteousness
For his name's sake.
Yea, though I walk through the valley of the shadow
of death,
I will fear no evil;
For you are with me;
Your rod and your staff, they comfort me.

You prepare a table before me in the presence of
my enemies;
You anoint my head with oil;
My cup runs over,
Surely goodness and mercy shall follow me
All the days of my life;
And I will dwell in the house of the Lord forever."

John 14:1-3

"Let not your heart be troubled; you believe in God, believe also in me. In my Father's house are many mansions, if it were not so, I would have told you; I go to prepare a place for you. And if I go and prepare a place for you, I will come again and receive you to myself; that where I am, there you may be also."

Revelation 22:1-5

"And he showed me a pure river of water of life, clear as crystal, proceeding from the throne of God and of the Lamb. In the middle of its street, and on either side of the river, was the tree of life, which bore twelve fruits, each tree yielding its fruit every month. And the leaves of the tree were for the healing of the nations. And there shall be no more curse, but the throne of God and of the Lamb shall be in it, and his servants shall serve him. They shall see his face, and his name shall be on their foreheads. And there shall be no night there: They need no lamp nor light of the sun, for the Lord God gives them light. And they shall reign forever and ever."

LEADER: Let us pray.

"Lord, we commend your servant, [Name], into your tender love and care. Grant him/her the joy of your kingdom and fill his/her life with everlasting peace; and bring us at that last day into the fellowship of our loved one. And may we live and reign together with you forever and ever.

RESPONSE: **Amen.**

239 ✦ LITURGY ON THE OCCASION OF A DEATH

The following liturgy may be used in times of family gathering at the occasion of a death, especially when a pastor is not able to be present.

Gathering

LEADER: Dear friends, we gather to mourn the death of [Name] who has gone home to be with the Lord. Let us not mourn as those who have no hope; let us remember the word of the Lord: "Death is swallowed up in victory./O Death, where is your sting?/O Hades, where is your victory?" (1 Cor. 15:54-55).

Let us pray.

Lord, God of life and death, we give you thanks for the life of [Name], and for the joy we have had in knowing him/her. Receive him/her into your kingdom. Grant him/her rest and peace in you. Be present, O Lord, to those who remain. Grant us consolation and hope, and may we live for that day when we will be united with our loved ones and with you forever. Amen.

Scripture Reading

READER: A reading from the Gospel of John: "Then Jesus said to them plainly, 'Lazarus is dead.' . . . So when Jesus came, he found that he had already been in the tomb four days. Now Bethany was near Jerusalem, about two miles away. And many of the Jews had joined the women around Martha and Mary, to comfort them concerning their brother. Then Martha, as soon as she heard that Jesus was coming, went and met him, but Mary was sitting in the house. Then Martha said to Jesus, 'Lord, if you had been here, my brother would not have died. But even now I know that whatever you ask of God, God will give you.' Jesus said to her, 'Your brother will rise again.' Martha said to him, 'I know that he will rise again in the resurrection at the last day.' Jesus said to her, 'I am the resurrection and the life. He who believes in me, though he may die, he shall life. And whoever lives and believes in me shall never die. Do you believe this?' She said to him, 'Yes, Lord, I believe that you are the

Christ, the Son of God, who is come into the world'" (11:14, 17-27).

This is the word of the Lord.

RESPONSE: **Thanks be to God.**

The Prayer of Commitment

LEADER: Let us commit our dear loved one to the Lord. Lord Jesus, you who suffered death on the cross, you who destroyed the power of death by your wounds, you who rose victorious from the grave, you who ascended into the heavens, you who are seated at the right hand of the Father, receive [Name] into the fellowship of your kingdom. Grant that he/she may join with the cherubim and seraphim to sing the new song and bless your holy name. In that place where there are no tears, nor death, nor sorrow, nor crying, nor pain, grant the joy of a new body and a new life for our loved one. And in that place where there is no more night, give to [Name] the light of your countenance. In the name of the Father and of the Son and of the Holy Spirit.

RESPONSE: **Amen.**

LEADER: Our loved one lives. Be at peace!

240 ◆ LITURGY ON THE OCCASION OF A HOUSE BLESSING

The following liturgy may be used in small or large family celebrations or in gatherings of the larger worshiping community. Adapt to local needs and customs.

Gathering

LEADER: Dear friends, we gather in his name to give thanks for this house, to dedicate it and the people who live here to the service of Almighty God.

Hear the word of the Lord from the Gospel of Matthew:

"And when you go into a household, greet it. If the household is worthy, let your peace come upon it. But if it is not worthy, let your peace return to you" (10:12-13).

Let us pray.

Lord, we give thanks for this house

and those who make it a home. May this be a place in which your presence is known in thought, word, and deed. May the lives of those who live here be rich in joy, and may those who come under this roof be filled with gladness and peace, through Jesus Christ our Lord.

RESPONSE: **Amen.**

Scripture Readings

READER 1: A reading from the Old Testament:
"Lord, who may abide in your tabernacle?
Who may dwell in your holy hill?
He who walks uprightly,
And works righteousness,
And speaks the truth in his heart;
He who does not backbite with his tongue,
Nor does evil to his neighbor,
Nor does he take up a reproach against his friend;
In whose eyes a vile person is despised,
But honors those who fear the Lord;
He who swears to his own hurt and does not change;
He who does not put out his money at usury,
Nor does he take a bribe against the innocent.
He who does these things shall never be moved" (Ps. 15)
This is the word of the Lord.

RESPONSE: **Thanks be to God.**

READER 2: A reading from the Gospel according to John:
"In my Father's house are many mansions; if it were not so, I would have told you. I go to prepare a place for you. And if I go and prepare a place for you, I will come again and receive you to myself; that where I am, there you may be also. And where I go you know, and the way you know. Thomas said to him, 'Lord, we do not know where you are going, and how can we know the way?' Jesus said to him, 'I am the way, the truth, and the life. No one comes to the Father except

through me.'" (14:2-6).
This is the word of the Lord.

RESPONSE: **Thanks be to God.**

(The following prayer may be said in each room or in one room representing the whole house.)

LEADER: Let us pray.
Father, you who are the giver of every good and perfect gift, we acknowledge your blessing in giving us/them this place to reside. Send your Spirit into this house that it may be a place of good and not of evil, a place of peace and not of chaos. Grant that those who live here may be filled with your Spirit. Cause that in this house the ministry of love and compassion may be experienced by all who come and go from this place. And grant us all your eternal joy, through Jesus Christ our Lord. Amen.

241 • LITURGY FOR THANKSGIVING DAY

The following liturgy may be used in small or large family celebrations, especially when the worshiping community itself does not gather on Thanksgiving Day.

Gathering

LEADER: Today is a special day in the life of our nation and in the life of our home. We gather together to give thanks to the Almighty for the blessings he has granted us and those whom we love.

HYMN: "Come, Ye Thankful People, Come"

LEADER: Let us pray.
Father, we acknowledge your goodness to us and to all humankind. Receive our words of praise to your glory, and bless this food. May it strengthen our bodies and nourish our spirits. Keep us, Lord, mindful of the needs of others, through Jesus our Lord.

RESPONSE: **Amen.**

(Here the meal may be eaten.)

Readings and Prayers after the Meal

READER 1: A reading from the Old Testament:

"I will extol you, my God, O king;
And I will bless your name forever
and ever.
Every day I will bless you,
And I will praise your name forever
and ever.
Great is the Lord, and greatly to be
praised;
And his greatness is unsearchable.
One generation shall praise your
works to another,
And shall declare your mighty acts.
I will meditate on the glorious splen-
dor of your majesty,
And on your wondrous works.
Men shall speak of the might of your
awesome acts,
And I will declare your greatness.
They shall utter the memory of your
great goodness,
And shall sing of your righteous-
ness . . .
My mouth shall speak the praise of
the Lord,
And all flesh shall bless his holy name
Forever and ever" (Ps. 145:1-7, 21).
This is the word of the Lord.

RESPONSE: **Thanks be to God.**

READER 2: A reading from Paul's letter to the
Romans:
"Oh, the depth of the riches both of
the wisdom and knowledge of
God! How unsearchable are his
judgments and his ways past find-
ing out!
For who has known the mind of the
Lord?
Or who has become his counselor?
Or who has first given to him
And it shall be repaid to him?
For of him and through him and to
him are
all things, to whom be glory forever.
Amen." (11:33-36).
This is the word of the Lord.

RESPONSE: **Thanks be to God.**

The Prayer of Thanksgiving

LEADER: Let us offer a prayer of thanksgiving
to God for his blessings on us this
past year. In the prayer I will pause

so that you may be able to offer sentence prayers of thanksgiving from
your own experience.

Let us pray.

Almighty God and Father, we most
humbly offer you our prayers of
praise and thanksgiving. We most especially thank you for the gifts and
benefits of this past year. (*Here may
be added personal prayers of the
people.*) Help us, Lord, to be ever
mindful of the needs of others,
through Jesus Christ our Lord. Amen.

242 ◆ LITURGY FOR MOTHER'S DAY

*The following liturgy may be used in small or large fam-
ily celebrations or in gatherings of the larger worshiping community. Adapt to local needs and customs.*

Gathering

LEADER: Dear family, this day is a very special
day for us all, for on this day we
honor Mother. Hear the word of the
Lord: "Honor your father and your
mother, as the Lord your God has
commanded you, that your days may
be long, and that it may be well with
you in the land which the Lord your
God is giving you" (Deut. 5:16).

Let us pray.

Lord God of the universe, you who
created and brought forth all things,
you have given us mothers who like
yourself bring forth life. Like you, our
mother has nursed, nurtured, and
tenderly cared over us. Feeding and
clothing us, our mother has drawn us
to her side, giving us her very life.
Grant that we should honor her and
love her, to her benefit and your
glory, through Christ. Amen.

The Scripture Readings

READER 1: A reading from Proverbs:
(HUSBAND) "Who can find a virtuous wife?
For her worth is far above rubies.
The heart of her husband safely trusts
her;
So he will have no lack of gain.
She does him good and not evil

All the days of her life. . . .
She extends her hand to the poor,
Yes, she reaches out her hands to the
  needy. . . .
Strength and honor are her clothing;
She shall rejoice in time to come.
She opens her mouth with wisdom,
And on her tongue is the law of kind-
  ness.
She watches over the ways of her
  household,
And does not eat the bread of idle-
  ness.
Her children rise up and call her
  blessed;
Her husband also, and he praises her:
'Many daughters have done well,
But you excel them all.'
Charm is deceitful and beauty is vain,
But a woman who fears the Lord, she
  shall be praised.
Give her of the fruit of her hands,
And let her own works praise her in
  the gates" (Prov. 31:10-12, 20, 25-31).
This is the word of the Lord.

RESPONSE: **Thanks be to God.**

READER 2: A reading from Proverbs:
"My son, hear the instruction of your
  father,
And do no forsake the law of your
  mother;
For they will be graceful ornaments
  on your head,
And chains about your neck. . . .
Bind them continually upon your
  heart;
Tie them around your neck.
When you roam, they will lead you;
When you sleep, they will keep you;
And when you awake, they will speak
  with you.
For the commandment is a lamp,
And the law is light;
Reproofs of instruction are the way
  of life" (1:8-9; 6:21-23).
This is the word of the Lord.

RESPONSE: **Thanks be to God.**

The Blessing

LEADER: Each of us will now bless Mother saying:

"What I like about you is _____"
or "I appreciate and acknowledge you
for _____."
Let us bless our mother in prayer.
Lord God, you have given mothers to
the world and blessed the fruit of their
womb. You, Lord, are the mother of
Elizabeth, the mother of John, and of
Mary, the mother of Jesus. Hear, O
Lord, our prayer and bless the mother
of this home. Grant her strength to
fulfill her calling. May she be filled
with joy and laughter. May she experience peace of mind and heart, and
may her children rise up to bless her,
through Jesus Christ our Lord.

ALL: **Amen.**

243 ♦ LITURGY FOR FATHER'S DAY

*The following liturgy may be used in small or large fam-
ily celebrations or in gatherings of the larger worshiping community. Adapt to local needs and customs.*

Gathering

LEADER: Dear family, this day is a very special
day for us all, for on this day we
honor Father. Hear the word of the
Lord: "Honor your father and your
mother, as the Lord your God has
commanded you, that your days may
be long, and that it may be well with
you in the land which the Lord your
God is giving you" (Deut. 5:16).
Let us pray.
Lord God, we gather in your name
to honor our father. Like you, our father provides for us, directs our paths
into truth, and leads us into the way
that is right. Grant that we should
love him to his benefit and your glory,
through Christ our Lord. Amen.

The Scripture Readings

READER 1: A reading from Proverbs:
(WIFE) "Hear, my children, the instruction of
  a father,
And give attention to know under-
  standing;
For I give you good doctrine:
Do not forsake my law.

When I was my father's [*son, daughter*],
Tender and the only one in the sight
   of my mother,
He also taught me, and said to me:
'Let your heart retain my words;
Keep my commands, and live.
Get wisdom! Get understanding!
Do not forget, nor turn away from the
   words of my mouth.
do not forsake her, and she will pre-
   serve you;
Love her, and she will keep you.
Wisdom is the principal thing;
Therefore get wisdom.
And in all your getting, get under-
   standing.
Exalt her, and she will promote you;
She will bring you honor, when you
   embrace her.
She will place on your head an orna-
   ment of grace;
A crown of glory she will deliver to
   you'" (Prov. 4:1-9).
This is the word of the Lord.

RESPONSE: **Thanks be to God.**

READER 2: A reading from Proverbs:
"My son, do not forget my law,
But let your heart keep my com-
   mands;
For length of days and long life
And peace they will add to you.
Let not mercy and truth forsake you;
Bind them around your neck,
Write them on the tablet of your
   heart,
And so find favor and high esteem
In the sight of God and man.
Trust in the Lord with all your heart,
And lean not on your own under-
   standing;
In all your ways acknowledge him,
And he shall direct your paths.
Do not be wise in your own eyes;
Fear the Lord and depart from evil.

It will be health to your flesh,
And strength to your bones.
Honor the Lord with your posses-
   sions,
And with the firstfruits of all your in-
   crease;
So your barns will be filled with
   plenty,
And your vats will overflow with new
   wine.
My son, do not despise the chasten-
   ing of the Lord,
Nor detest his correction;
For whom the Lord loves he corrects,
Just as a father the son in whom he
   delights" (3:1-12)
This is the word of the Lord.

RESPONSE: **Thanks be to God.**

The Blessing

LEADER: I invite you to join with me in blessing Father by saying: "What I like
about you is _____," or "I appreciate and acknowledge you for
_____," or "I give thanks to God
that _____."
   Let us bless our Father in prayer.
   Father in heaven, we bless you for
our father on earth. For you have
given him to us to be a mirror of your
fatherly goodness. From him we have
learned of your love, through him we
have experienced your covenantal
faithfulness, by his life we have a
model of your law, and from his sacrificial self-giving we have learned of
your sacrifice for us. Grant him fullness of life. May he enjoy strength
and health. May he experience joy
and laughter; and may his children
rise up to make him glad. We pray this
for his benefit and to the glory of God
the Father in whose name we pray.

ALL: **Amen.**

Robert E. Webber

✦ TWELVE ✦

Worship and Education

Faith in Jesus Christ and participation in the life of the church allow the Christian to share in the profound gift of God's Word as revealed in the Scriptures and to inherit a tradition passed down through many centuries. Yet a mature understanding of the Scriptures and an appreciation of the rich tradition and varied expression of the church is only possible through instruction in the faith. Thus, the church has for centuries schooled its members in all aspects of the faith. This ministry of education is also important for teaching worshipers how to worship more meaningfully. Worship, likewise, is an important means of education. More is taught through the actions of worship than through sophisticated church education curriculum. This chapter explores the relationship of worship and church education, noting how each is a vital component of the other.

244 ✦ THE FIVE-TASK MODEL OF WORSHIP AND EDUCATION

As the central task of the church, worship is directly related to the process of Christian education. True education will have worship as its end product. This article suggests one conceptualization of the ministries of the church, where liturgy is center of a web that also connects fellowship, challenge, proclamation, and service.

The central task of the church, which marks its distinctive role now and through eternity, is worship (*leitourgia*), the celebration and the expression of creativity that gives glory to God. This task can be placed at the center or hub of the circle in any model for ministry to designate its priority and the potentially integrative function that worship can have in the church. It is in relation to worship that people can experience the joy that God intends for all of creation through the redemption made possible in Jesus Christ and the presence of the Holy Spirit. Such an experience, though heightened in corporate worship, is not limited to that occasion. A sense of worship and of God's presence can encompass all of life and may be evident, whenever two or three are gathered in the name of Jesus. The central task of worship is directly related to the task of educating in the Christian faith. Christian educators must be able to link theory and practice to the primary tasks of the church with a priority placed upon worship. Without such a linkage, any discussion of ministry can remain just an intellectual exercise.

The Task of Christian Education

Christian education can be defined as the process of sharing or gaining the distinctives of the Christian story and truth (information), together with Christian values, attitudes and lifestyle (formation), and of fostering the renewal of individuals, communities, societies, and structures (transformation) by the power of the Holy Spirit in order to express more fully God's reign in Jesus Christ. This process involves a partnership between God and those persons who are called and gifted to teach; it also requires the openness of people to the possibility of renewal or transformation. This definition incorporates the three generally accepted elements of education, which are: content or information, persons or formation, and community/society or transformation.

A comprehensive vision of Christian education seeks to elaborate upon this "educational trinity" of content, persons, and community or society, by recognizing that people are taught content in the context of their community and society. Content, especially as it is encountered in worship, includes cognitive, affective, and lifestyle or behavioral dimensions. An exclusive emphasis on one or even two of the three elements (content, persons, or context) does not foster a comprehensive vision and can result in truncated practice or inappropriate reductionism in ministry and life. The quality of education resulting from a limited vision can impact the life of a community and society for generations, as evidenced by the history of Christian education.

A similar danger is present when teaching and learning are not related to the five principal tasks of the Christian church and the forms of ministry that relate to these tasks. It is possible to envision the five principal tasks of the church in terms of a web or network. This web can be visualized as a circle with four points or tasks on its exterior, with the fifth task as the hub or center. The four tasks on the circle include (1) proclamation (*kerygma*), (2) community (*koinonia*), (3) service (*diakonia*), and (4) challenge (*propheteia*); the hub is celebration or worship (*leitourgia*). The metaphor of a web suggests that these five tasks must be intimately connected if all are to be nurtured in the educational work of the church.

Much of life in this world forces people to preoccupy themselves with all that is created, holding sacred little or no time for an interest in the Creator. This preoccupation is broken only when a person chooses to come apart from these created things in order to worship God. The act of coming apart does not presume a relocation from the midst of everyday activities, demands, and contexts. It does require a willingness to encounter God in the ordinary affairs and interactions of life. People also need a place for Sabbath in their lives, where the designation of sacred time and space provides the opportunity to be recreated and refreshed by God's grace. This also affirms that people are created by God, and as such are themselves creative. In worship there is the possibility that people will be empowered by God to use their diverse creative abilities and energies for the glory of God in all of life.

Worship and *Didache* (Education)

The two-fold educational task in relation to *leitourgia* is (1) to foster a sense of worship that encompasses all of life, and (2) to explore avenues for integration through creative expression. When all participants in an educational program are given the opportunity for creative expression, the sense of celebration is heightened and occasions for worship are provided. In addition, both personal and corporate worship experiences enable individuals to put into perspective the demands of their personal and corporate lives.

The centrality of worship for ministries of Christian education or formation can be seen in relation to the three elements of education: content, persons, and context. Worship provides the opportunity for the Christian community to corporately center upon the essential content of faith; that is God, God's revelation, and humans' response. The human response calls for an openness of the total person to the wonder and majesty of God and an honesty before one's very Creator, Redeemer, and Sustainer. Second, worship engages people at the point of their humanity, with all of the joys, sorrows, longings, and dreams it entails. Third, worship in its corporate expression implements community by transcending differences of age, gender, race, culture, or ability. In so doing, it reflects the diversity of creation and the unity made possible in Christ. This coming together of the entire congregation in corporate worship must be balanced with the division into diverse groups for purposes of education.

Historically, the integration of worship and education is most effective at times when the environment is hostile to the faith. An example is the Jewish synagogue, which effectively combined worship and education during the period of the exile. Another example is provided by the Christian church, both Orthodox and Protestant, in the Soviet Union during times of often intense pressure from atheistic philosophy. Since the church could not conduct schools of its own, education in Christian traditions had to occur in the worship setting or through the liturgy. Worship provides the occasion, in which people can come before God as Teacher, with a spirit open to learn and to live in new ways as a result of the encounter.

Worship, Education, and Kerygma (Proclamation). One major task of Christian education is to share the Christian story and enable others to appropriate it to their lives. Included in the proclamation of truth about God must be an emphasis on choice, commitment, and a personal response to God's call. Knowing God in a biblical sense engaged head, heart, and hands in response to the Good News. In this knowing, people were willing to stake their lives on the new life offered to them in Jesus Christ.

From this perspective, Christian education is a matter of choice and commitment where people are confronted with God's view of the human situation and the clear and definite call to repent and be converted (Mark 1:15; Acts 2:38-39). This call to conversion is issued on the basis of the work of Jesus Christ and the gift of salvation offered to those who respond in faith. Although the gift is based upon the grace of God, it demands a new life lived in allegiance to God's will. The educational task in relation to _kerygma_ is to share information about God, Jesus Christ, and the human dilemma through worship. This information is necessary if people are to grasp what is offered to them and demanded of them.

Worship, Education, and Koinonia (Fellowship).

The task of _koinonia_ is embodied in turning from a life centered upon self, family, or group to a life centered in a community that breaks down all of the barriers normally associated with humanity. As the apostle Paul declares in Galatians 3:28, "There is neither Jew nor Greek, slave nor free, male nor female, for you are all one in Christ Jesus." With Christ there is no longer any place for the religious, cultural, linguistic, gender, and social distinctions that have served to alienate and divide individuals, communities, and societies. This new definition of community, which affirms the worth and dignity of every person, is modeled in corporate worship. All believers can be joined to the new community of God as it gathers for the fellowship of the Table.

The educational task related to _koinonia_ is to foster a sense of community, which produces lives of interdependence with God, other Christians, and the entire creation. Such a perspective as modeled in worship involves an awareness and appreciation of the universal Christian community.

Worship, Education, and Diakonia (Service).

Diakonia embodies the answer to the question, for what are people converted. In an ultimate sense, that question is answered in terms of glorifying and enjoying God forever. But in a penultimate sense, it is answered in terms of the care and concern of the whole people of God for the needs of individuals, societies, and the world.

This requires that all Christians identify with a pastoral calling that is not limited to the professional clergy, but includes the laity in various expressions of mission and ministry.

The educational task in relation to _diakonia_ is to foster the connection of a person's faith to faithful acts of service. Christians must understand that knowing Christ implies a willingness to serve in whatever capacity is needed in response to overwhelming needs that exist at every level of society. Corporate worship provides the occasion in which to celebrate service completed, to uphold in prayer the service currently being undertaken, and to challenge participants for future mission opportunities.

Worship, Education, and Propheteia (Challenge).

The prophetic task of the church is one that has not been readily owned or nurtured in recent history. This suggests that the Christian church has too readily accommodated the faith to the dominant culture and that Christians have assimilated to a highly materialistic and individualized lifestyle. But an emphasis upon prophecy and challenge is the task explicitly named for the church in relation to _propheteia_.

The prophetic task involves enabling Christians to understand the full implications of a commitment to God's reign in the community or society. Points of convergence between gospel virtues and those of one's culture are to be celebrated and conserved. But points of divergence and conflict require of Christians a stance of protest and a willingness to struggle for transformation or conversion. A Christian's first allegiance is to a Christian culture; believers must be willing to invest their lives in bringing society under the dominion of God. Societal changes require the work of the Holy Spirit at all levels of personal and corporate life and the willingness of Christians to accept their responsibilities as being in, but not of the world.

The challenge inherent in this prophetic task of the church calls for risk and vulnerability as modeled by the prophets of the Hebrew Scriptures. To avoid this risk is to neglect the ministry of reconciliation, which is given to the church (2 Cor. 5:16-21). The prophets of old assumed this task of calling peoples and nations to account before God. Christians today must not shrink from such a demand. This requires that prophetic words be honored in corporate worship and that believers demonstrate a willingness to respond to the demands of the gospel of Christ.

It is essential that the connections between worship and education be maintained in the interests of effective ministry and the continued renewal of the Christian church. The ultimate end of such efforts is that God may be glorified and enjoyed forever. The penultimate end of such efforts is that Christians may be formed as faithful disciples of Jesus Christ, as they actively participate in Christian worship throughout their lives.

Robert W. Pazmiño

245 ♦ WORSHIP AND LEARNING

Although liturgy and learning have been linked since the birth of the Christian era, this link has not always been maintained throughout the church's history. It is essential to restore the historical connection between liturgy and catechesis, as the entire congregation, including young and old, participates in worship.

Regretfully, religious educators and liturgists have gone their separate ways. Attempts to reunite their various concerns have tended to confuse the issue and distort important distinctions between them. Some religious educators have made the serious mistake of speaking of teaching *by* or *with* the liturgy, thereby reducing the liturgy to a didactic act. To *use* the liturgy is to do it violence. Of course, we learn through the liturgy; our rituals shape and form us in fundamental ways. But our liturgies should be understood properly as ends and not as means.

Nevertheless, both liturgy and catechesis are pastoral activities through which divine revelation is made known, mature faith is enhanced and enlivened, and people are prepared and stimulated for their vocation in the world. Perhaps the best way to differentiate between the two is by understanding that liturgy embraces the *actions* and catechesis the *reflections* of the community of faith. Together they form the *praxis* (reflective action) by which the community is made aware of who and whose it is; learns that for which and by which it is called to live and die; and comes to understand why life is as it is, as well as what it is to become. Liturgy nurtures the community of faith through celebrative symbolic acts of faith. Catechesis nurtures the community of faith through mindful attempts to communicate and reflect upon the story which underlies and informs these acts of faith. One is not the other. But the life of faith and the community of faith cannot exist without both. And faithful life implies their integration.

Catechesis and Ritual

Catechesis is essentially a pastoral activity intended to enable the people of God to meet the twofold responsibility which Christian faith requires of them, the responsibility for community with God and neighbor. It is the process by which people come to know, internalize, and apply God's Word in their individual and corporate lives.

Catechesis includes knowing, loving, and obeying God's Word. Social service and action are the church addressing the individual and corporate needs of those denied the benefits of God's intentions. Evangelism is the church witnessing in word and deed its faith in God's Good News. Stewardship is the church expressing God's will for individual and corporate life in the world. Pastoral care is the church ministering to the material and spiritual needs of all people. Fellowship is the church providing a sign of God's kingdom. Administration is the church ordering and organizing its common life of mission and ministry. Worship is the church providing a context for confrontation with, commitment to, and empowerment by the Word of God.

Catechesis is the means by which the community becomes aware of God's revelation, comes to faith, and acquires mature knowledge, understanding, and commitment so as to judge and evaluate its life of social action, evangelism, stewardship, pastoral care, administration, worship, and fellowship. It prepares and stimulates individuals and the community for faithful mission and ministry through every aspect of its corporate life. Catechesis is the means by which the church seeks to understand faith's requirements for its liturgical life, to evaluate and reform its liturgies from the perspective of this faith, and to prepare the community for faithful participation in its liturgies.

Perhaps no aspect of community life is more important than its rites and rituals. We humans are made for ritual; and, in turn, our rituals make us. No culture is complete without common beliefs and ceremonial practices. A community's understandings and ways are invariably objectified in ceremonial observances. No people group has ever been discovered, which fails to share some articulated set of beliefs about the world and their place in it, expressed in community myths. And nowhere is there a people who fail to engage in symbolic acts to sustain and transmit their myths. Faith and ritual cannot be separated.

Worship is at the center of the church's life. Orthodoxy implies right ritual. The rites and rituals of a Christian faith community are central to the church's life. Perhaps that is why our rituals are so difficult to change. We, Christians, all know that it is easier and more acceptable to preach a radical sermon, than it is to change the order of worship. The structures of our rituals provide us with a means for ordering and reordering our lives. Our rituals telescope our understandings and ways, unite us in community, give meaning and purpose to our lives, and provide us with purposes, guides, and goals for living. That explains why, when our understandings and ways of life change, we will very likely cease to participate in the rituals that once inspired and sustained us. It is also why, after casting aside old rituals, we seek to form new ones.

Without the support of meaningful rituals (symbolic actions), there is no meaningful personal life or political social action. Liturgy, the activity of the community, unites symbolic and social actions. Each needs and supports the other. To deny either one is to deny the whole. Because we have failed to understand the important unity between our rituals and our lives, we have improperly prepared people for meaningful participation in the faith community's ceremonial life.

Liturgy: The Work of God's Visionary People

Ritual (symbolic action) is an essential aspect of all life. Indeed, it is our orderly, predictable, repetitive, symbolic actions, which give life shape and form, meaning, and purpose. Without ritual, we lack a means for building and establishing community, identity, and at-one-ness in the world. Without ritual, we are without a means for making the changes in our lives meaningful and integrating. And without ritual, we are devoid of our most significant means for sustaining and trans-

mitting our understandings and ways. Indeed, there is no choice between ritual and no ritual, but only what our rituals will be. Ritual is foundational to life. In those historic moments when the church had lost its soul, it had also neglected its ritual. Correspondingly, every reform in the history of the church has been at its core a reformation of ritual. When our rituals change, our lives change. Furthermore when we change our understandings and ways, we change our rituals.

The chief problem for life in a pluralistic, secular, technological, urban world is attaining, owning, and maintaining one's identity as a follower of Jesus Christ. The claims for loyalty are legion; and the diverse communities which ask our allegiance are many. Only an identity-conscious, tradition-bearing community, rich in meaningful ritual, can help us to know and remember who we are. Life is fragmented and compartmentalized. We search for wholeness and at-one-ness in what is often an alienating world. Vital community rituals alone can prevent us from spiritual dislocation and lostness.

The church cannot live with rituals that divide the generations as if they had nothing in common. We cannot afford to accept the separation of children, youth, and adults for distinctive rituals. Community is the gift of shared rituals. The needs of various individuals may differ, but we grow only when we share our differences in community. Peer group isolation prevents growth. When we permit our rites of community to address the needs of some particular age group alone, everyone suffers. The norm for the church's community rite is the Lord's Supper or Eucharist, which by its very nature is inclusive of all.

The current trend, in which people are encouraged to create separate rituals for various age groups, can be divisive. The function of community rites is to form unity, not division. Besides, each generation needs the insights, experiences, and contributions of the others if any are to grow. We need to conserve a memory and maintain a tradition, just as we need to nurture visions and the incarnation of futuristic expressions. Without both continuity and change, we cannot maintain security and identity in the present. If our community rituals have ignored the needs of any generation or have been dominated by any particular generation, they need to be reformed and reshaped until all feel at home in them and all are stretched to newness of faith and life. We do not need special rites of community for children or youth, but we do need a place within our regular community rituals that speaks to children, youth, and adults.

——— A Liturgical Catechesis ———

One challenge confronting the church is that of integrating education, worship, fellowship, and service. At the core of this unified understanding of ministry is worship. And at the center of worship is God's Word. What follows, however, is not a program, but images of the corporate life of children, youth, and adults in the church, which speaks to this integration.

But first, we must reconsider the Eucharist. The norm for Christian life is the celebration of the Eucharist. This celebration is best understood as a joyful gathering of God's storytelling people to proclaim their faith and share a common meal with their risen Lord so as to be united in community and be refreshed and empowered for ministry in the world. This festive gathering is not so much a private, passive, individualistic occasion as it is a public, active, corporate activity. It is not a subjective act, in which we do something either for or to ourselves. Neither is it an objective act, through which we do something either for or to God. Rather, it is an occasion for the community to gratefully encounter God in Jesus Christ and act *with* God in the transformation of life and of our lives.

In the most recent past, we have tended to think of this Holy Communion in terms of our extreme unworthiness, depravity, and sin, a memorial for a dead friend or a solemn wake to mourn our condition. Is it not also necessary to understand Holy Communion in terms of our having been made worthy by Christ's passion and resurrection to stand joyfully before God—a cheerful thanksgiving, a victory party to celebrate God's Good News?

Imagine a congregation in which such a festive Eucharist is at the heart of its common life. Within such a congregation, children, youth, and adults, along with their minister, might gather regularly to reflect upon and plan for its weekly celebration. Imagine a congregation gathering for an hour of catechesis before the morning family Eucharist. The Eucharist is then followed by a family fellowship meal, at which reports and intentions for ministry in the world could be made and celebrated. Only our imaginations hinder the development of creative, corporate life in a learning and witnessing community of Christian faith. The challenge we face is clear. We need to integrate our lives of ministry and mission within a Spirit-filled body of committed, baptized Christians, who weekly gather to prepare and celebrate the Eucharist meaningfully and then scatter refreshed to live the Eucharist in the world. That is what it means to unite catechesis and liturgy within a faithful community of Christian faith.

John H. Westerhoff[46]

246 • WORSHIP AND THE CATECHESIS OF PRAYER

Although it may be understood in many ways, prayer remains a basic expression of human beings. Learning how to pray requires a recovery of the intuitive, life-changing aspects of religious experience, which are often neglected in favor of cognitive and analytical expressions of faith.

The twentieth century is not likely to be known as the age of spirituality. More reasonably, it may be remembered as the era of retarded consciousness. Many have lost or forgotten the experience of God, which lies at the heart of Christian faith. Still, we long and search for some sense of the divine: witness the renewed interest in the occult, Eastern religions, meditation, and personal religious experience. It is as if we humans knew we were more than rational beings; and that truth was more than reason could prove. Even we moderns are *homo religiosus*. Prayer and ritual are still the most basic expressions of our humanness.

Thomas Aquinas wrote, "Prayer is the peculiar proof of religion." Faith, in Luther's judgment, was "prayer, nothing but prayer." Baron von Hügel concluded that "prayer is the essential element of all life." And Schleiermacher observed, "to be religious and to pray are really the same thing." Still the word *prayer* lacks clarity. Some think of prayer as distressed cries to the heavens; others as a formality before meals and meetings or an experience on mountain tops. Prayer for some is a spontaneous emotional discharge; and for others a fixed rational formula to be recited. However, prayer, as the word is used here, is a generic term to describe every aspect of our conscious relationship with God. Prayer represents the spiritual life—daily existence lived in relationship with God—or piety, the daily activity of living in the presence of God through adoration, confession, praise, oblation, thanksgiving, and petition/intercession.

To live in _adoration_ is to focus our life upon the heart and mind of God, asking nothing but to enjoy God's presence. It is the life of the lover, the dreamer, and visionary, which makes possible viewing every aspect of life as a miracle. _Confession_ is life lived under the judgment and grace of God. It is the life of those striving to bring their individual, interior experience and belief into harmony with their social exterior practice and action. The life of _praise_ is a life alive with the memory of the mighty acts of God. It is a life of ecstasy, lived dancing, singing, and praising God even in evil days. _Thanksgiving_ is our celebrative awareness of God's continuing actions in our historical midst. It is the life that can still spy burning bushes, hear the voice of God, and grasp the presence of Christ in contemporary culture. _Oblation_ is an offering of ourselves, our lives and labors, for the purposes of God. _Petition/intercession_ is the continuous striving to bring our wills in line with God's will. It is life lived in conscious loyalty to the conviction that Jesus is the Lord, who passes moral judgments on what it means to be faithful.

The Christian life focuses upon the Spirit of God in us and in the world; its quest is for an active unity with the God of history. The climax of the Christian life is not enlightenment, but unification with the will and activity of God. Christian prayer assumes both an historical awareness and the integration of the receptive and active modes of consciousness.

Numerous examples of prayer in the Bible support this understanding. The Scriptures assume a historicist perspective. Operating from that perspective, the prophets used their intuitive abilities to hear the voice of God; they used their intellects to proclaim judgment on the people for their lack of righteousness and on the nations for their lack of justice. Moses' experience with the burning bush led him to bring to his people a vision and message of liberation. Jesus' struggle at Gethsemane led him to make a conscious decision to choose the foolishness of the Cross. The awareness of the presence of Christ in the breaking of bread at Emmaus led the disciples to lives of apostleship. Paul's experience on the road to Damascus led him to change from persecutor to defender of the faith. None of these experiences or their resulting actions were purely rational or intuitional. Each represents a worldly intuitive experience which, through the complementary use of the intellect, led to new sorts of moral behavior. Each represents finally a new worldly consciousness of God and praxis according to God's will. Each is an example of prayer.

Let me, therefore, suggest that catechesis for prayer requires first that we help people to regain their God-given ability to wonder and create; to dream, fantasize, imagine, and envision; to sing, paint, dance, and act. It requires that we help them to recover their natural capacity for ecstasy, for appreciating the new, the marvelous, and the mysterious; for sensual and kinesthetic awareness; and for expressing themselves emotionally and nonverbally.

Technological knowledge plays a dominant influence in our culture. Mostly analytical, verbal, linear, and rational, it has tended to deemphasize and devalue other modes of consciousness. Its concern for verbal, intellectual knowledge and its focus upon planning, organizing, and doing have served to screen out other sorts of knowledge and life.

Each of us arrives in the natural world as an unfinished product. Within the limits of nature, we collectively build a human world in which we can live and grow. Through largely unconscious means, we are socialized into valuing particular modes of consciousness, thereby determining our understanding of the world. Our culture has tended to place a greater value on one mode of consciousness—the intellectual. Our educational programs in both church and society have focused, therefore, upon verbal, analytical, logical, thinking skills.

The emphasis on the signative, conceptual, and analytical aspects of human life and the benign neglect of the symbolic, mythical, imaginative, and emotive aspects have limited our spiritual development and crippled us as a people. A whole person living the spiritual life should fully develop both the receptive and active modes of consciousness. However, a new awareness of the visual, artistic, imaginative, associative, and relational activities of the brain cannot be permitted to dull or limit our concern for speech, logic, cognitive reasoning, analysis, and linear activities. The religious life of activity and the interior life of experience must be united.

JohnH. Westerhoff[47]

247 ✦ EXPERIENCING THE FAITH-STORY IN WORSHIP

The worship environment is uniquely equipped to transmit the historical perspective that is foundational to biblical faith. Through the drama of rite and ritual, worshipers learn to experience and retell the faith-story, which embodies the Christian community's sense of identity.

Sustained observation of the work of people engaged in religious education reveals a primary concern with cognitive, rather than creative, learning tasks. The majority of teachers are faithful, caring, committed persons; some are exceptional teachers; a few are engaged in truly creative learning experiences with children. In most cases, however, learning tasks have been controlled by teachers, who are primarily concerned with the mastery of cognitive skills and the direct transmission of information, facts, or concepts. Creative activities, if used at all, have been supplementary.

It is true that a good deal of significant change has taken place in religious education in recent years. Nevertheless, while many creative teaching methods are being employed, religious education is primarily focused on the discovery of the general, the universal, and the abstract, rather than on the idiosyncratic, the concrete, and the experiential. Learning in religious education, in spite of many exciting innovations, is still dominantly verbal, conceptual, and analytic. The development of the intellect is primary. Little attention is given to intuition and the affections. The price to be paid for this educational imbalance is great: it may be making learning to pray difficult.

Participation in the arts as well as more structured opportunities for effective learning will be necessary. No longer can we, Christians, permit people to neglect the touch, smell, or taste of life; to escape the expressing of feelings; or to avoid creative expression through the use of the arts.

However, a rebirth of concern for the affections and the nurture of the intuitive mode of consciousness is not enough. As long as we continue our present educational practices, which neglect the development of a historicist perspective, true Christian prayer will avoid us. Therefore, we need to focus on the development of historical awareness.

The Judeo-Christian faith is founded upon a historicist perspective. Within the cumulative tradition of the faith, God is understood as one who acts—to create the world and all creatures, to sustain the world through interaction with those creatures according to the purposes of God, and to bring the world and all God has made to the ends for which God created them. God is an incarnate agent, who acts on and in the world. History is, therefore, intentional and directional. Through God's revelatory historical actions, we understand the past, gain hope for the present, and receive a vision of the future. Our lives, and indeed life itself, takes on meaning and purpose in the light of that story.

The significance of the biblical understanding of God as the one who acts is founded upon an understanding of the whole course of history; that is, history which is ordered toward God's ultimate goal—the kingdom of God. With the ultimate goal of history as our vision, we can understand the present and interpret the past. Religious education, therefore, ought to focus on helping people to live in and for God's kingdom, to live in the light of a hoped-for future, and to understand their place in life as essentially historical agents committed to fulfilling themselves through the exercise of their wills in reflective action.

To accomplish these goals, we will need to consider how people acquire their perspective or view of the world. Gordon Kaufman suggests that we as humans relate to the world in one or more ways: through thinking, feeling, and acting. Each approach to experience results in a particular way of viewing the world. A dominance of thinking tends to issue forth in a *secular* worldview, a view which ignores the depth of reality and our desire for insight about the future. Kaufman also suggests that when feeling is given a dominant place in shaping our understanding of life, a *religious* worldview results. Such a view of the world, while affirming the importance of the affections, neglects the moral dimensions of our volitional life.

Only when we make action the dominant mode of our world viewing do we establish what Kaufman describes as a *theistic* worldview, a perspective that speaks of a reality other than humanity and the world. "Theism takes the world to be ordered from beyond itself by intentional and purposeful activity rooted in the will of God" (Gordon Kaufman, *God the Problem* [Cambridge, Mass.: Harvard University Press, 1972], 219). Life according to this latter worldview is understood as derivative from God and God's purposes as revealed in God's historical action. Each of us is a thinking, feeling, willing self. For too long, we have emphasized either our thinking or feeling natures in religious education. We need to reemphasize our lives as praxis—willing, passionate, reflective action.

In the English language, faith is a noun, a word that refers or points to something else—a person, place, or thing. If we think of faith as a thing, we can easily say that we have "found it" or "lost it." From this point of view, faith is a possession understood as personal salvation, spirit (joy in the Lord), a resource for personal living, or knowledge. But it is more hopeful to think of faith as a centered integrated action, as a verb. We should speak of "being faithful" rather than of "having faith." Speaking of being faithful rightly emphasizes the integration of thinking, feeling, and willing. Faith is a matter of who we are, of how we think, and of what we do in response to what God does for us and how God acts in history. For this understanding of faith to take shape in our lives, we need also to develop a historical consciousness.

Such a historicist perspective is encouraged by participation in the life of a history-bearing community of faith, whose past is made present and personal. Too often, if we have told our story at all, we have told it as if it were a series of separate past events with a minimum of personal significance. For example, we recall how God once upon a time freed some Israelites from bondage in Egypt. How much more significant to relate this to God's action in our own lives, in which God freed us in our bondage once, continues to free us, and will free us ultimately.

If we continue to place our emphasis in religious education on doctrine (what persons ought to believe) or on the Bible (sacred literature to be learned), we will continue to make that historicist perspective, which is necessary for prayer, difficult to acquire. Instead, we need to consider directing our educational efforts toward storytelling. We need to transmit in meaningful ways the story of our faith, the story of God's historical acts in the lives of the people of God. From the earliest years, in the context of a celebrating faith community, children, youth, and adults need to experience the faith-story through song, dance, drama, and the visual arts.

It will be necessary for us to learn "our story" in ways that make the past part of the present and future. We need to seek ways to communicate *the* story as *our* story. When we have become involved in that sort of religious education, we will have begun to lay the foundations for the Christian life of prayer. Only when daily prayer (our conscious awareness of God's presence in our personal and social history) is a natural part of our lives will ritual prayer be purposeful. We do not proceed from ritual prayer to prayer; it is the other way around. Good rituals express and telescope our experience. Without experience, rituals remain dead forms.

Revelation and Response

Faith is a response to revelation. Revelation and faith belong together, just as theology and religion do. To speak of religion is to speak of institutions, documents, artifacts, customs, ceremonies, credal statements, and codes of conduct. Faith, on the other hand, is deeply personal and dynamic. Faith is not a result of a purely rational process. It is affectional, a relationship with God, which embraces the whole person and about which it is difficult to be objective. To be sure, faith always expresses itself in religion; and, as such, religion provides us with the means by which we grow in faith. There is a difference between learning about the doctrine of salvation and being saved. There is a difference between understanding justification by faith and being justified by it. There is a difference between understanding religion and religious experience and having an experience of God's presence. Faith is not knowledge about, or even intellectual assent to, truth or ideas. It is a response to a person.

Our ideas about God are important. Indeed, they can influence the sort of experiences of God we have and do not have. In one sense then, our revelation of God is made possible through the ideas of God, which are passed on through the tradition. But that is only a partial truth. Our experiences frame and form our ideas. People in the first century experienced the resurrected Christ and his presence at the breaking of the bread. Their ideas about God and God's new community were framed by that relational experience, which, metaphorically, we communicate each time we celebrate the Lord's Supper. To become aware of God's continuing revelation is to nurture the intuitional mode of consciousness.

Our faith experiences are always translated (and need to be) into religious beliefs. This process of institutionalization involves the symbolic transformation of the experience of God into less than ultimate forms. While this bringing of the sacred into profane structures is necessary, it provides a dilemma for the church. Since the faith experience of revelation is spontaneous and creative, the necessary institutionalization of revelation reduces such experience.

Ritual and Re-presentation

Ritual is a social drama, which embodies the memories and visions of a community. It is through the repetition of these symbolic actions that we evoke the feeling of the primordial event, which initially called the community into being with such power that it affects a present presence at that event. In other words, through the intuitional mode of consciousness, ritual re-presents revelation. An example would be the Christian rituals of baptism or the Lord's Supper, both of which re-present the event of Jesus' death and resurrection.

Through the power of symbolic actions, we order our experience; through the use of symbolic narrative, we explain our lives. Ritual operates on those levels of existential reality that undergird the conceptual. More importantly, ritual points to and participates in that primordial truth, which is located at the expanding edge of our horizon of knowing, in feeling and intuition, not in common sense or thinking. Without ritual, life becomes mundane and profane. For it is through ritual expression of the symbolic and through the foundational intuitive mode of consciousness that the sacramental and the sacred are best known and expressed.

When we participate in a ritual, we experience community. We reconcile and identify ourselves with our foreparents from whom the ritual has descended. And we reestablish continuity with the past and a vision for the future.

Ritual is drama; it is life in the world of the receptive mode of consciousness. When our intuition atrophies, our rituals lose their power. Correspondingly, meaningful ritual can enhance and enliven our intuitional mode of consciousness. Therefore unless ritual is raised to its proper significance, our spiritual lives will remain impotent.

John H. Westerhoff[48]

248 • WORSHIP AND PERSONAL CONVERSION

Because Christian faith runs counter to other understandings of life, rites of conversion and incorporation are important. The reorientation of values that occurs with the emergence of Christian commitment cannot be totally incorporated within the paradigm of nurture. Even those brought up within the church need to be "converted" in some significant way.

Initiation rites, as studied by anthropologists, comprise ritual actions and oral teachings which result in decisive changes in a person's religious and social status and role. Typically, through a series of ordeals, people learn the ways and the understandings of the adult community, encounter the sacred, experience death and rebirth, and emerge as new persons whose existence in the community is significantly transformed.

Historically, initiation plays an essential role in practically every known religion. Indeed, it appears that we only fully understand and are committed to religious truth insofar as we are initiated into it by acts of personal faith or conversion symbolically dramatized through ritual. Elaborate incorporation rites, by which Christians became full members of the church, were characteristic of the first four centuries of the Christian era. Wrapped in secrecy, after weeks of intense preparation, these rites were calculated to inspire religious experience and celebrate the occasion of a profound conversion. Initiation lies at the core of all genuine life, but in the modern Western world significant initiation rites are practically nonexistent. However, to understand those incorporation rites which have survived in contemporary Christian churches, it is necessary to differentiate between (1) faith commitment incorporation rites, through which people witness to personal faith, and (2) institutional incorporation initiation rites, through which persons join the church.

Faith commitment initiation rites are most typical of those reported upon in the historical and comparative study of religion. The Christian church during the first three centuries is a good example. Vestiges of this understanding still persist in some churches, but institutional incorporation rites appear most typically in contemporary churches of the mainline denominational tradition.

Conversion and Initiation

Few concepts are more vague and confusing to liberal mainline Protestants than conversion. Rarely have we used the word _conversion;_ and all too frequently we have limited our concerns to membership campaigns. However, until we find a place for conversion within our educational ministry, the church's mission will remain impotent. Indeed, without converts, the church will have difficulty being a community of Christian nurture.

Evangelism, as the word is used here, refers to the process by which the Christian community of faith, through the proclamation of the gospel in word and deed, leads people inside and outside the church to a radical reorientation of life—that is, conversion.

Evangelism is not indoctrination. It is testifying through transformed lives to the acts of God both within and without the community of faith. When we evangelize, we witness through word-in-deed to the acts of God in Jesus Christ. Without this witness to the lordship of Christ, to the Good News of God's new possibility, and to the gospel's prophetic protest against all false religiousness, the church loses its soul. It becomes an institution of cultural continuity maintaining the status quo, rather than an institution of cultural change living in and for God's new community. Evangelism is best understood, therefore, as the means by which the church continually transforms its life and the lives of its people into a body of committed believers, willing to give anything and everything to the cause of historically mediating God's reconciling love in the world.

Christian faith goes counter to many ordinary understandings and ways of life. It is hardly possible for anything less than a converted, disciplined body to be the historical agent of God's work in the world. Christians are not born. Neither are they simply made, formed, or nurtured. Conversion—a reorientation of life, a change of heart, mind, and behavior—is a necessary aspect of mature Christian faith whether or not one grows up in the church.

The church can no longer surrender to the illusion that child nurture, in and of itself, can or will kindle the fire of Christian faith either in persons or in the church. We have expected too much of nurture. We can nurture individuals into institutional religion, but not into mature Christian faith. The Christian faith, by its very nature, demands conversion. We do not gradually educate persons to be Christian. To be Christian is to be baptized into the community of the faithful, but to be a mature Christian is to be converted.

Conversion implies the reordering of our perceptions, a radical change without which no further growth or learning is possible. Conversion, therefore, is not an end, but a new beginning. It is a reorientation of a person's life, a deliberate turning from indifference, indecision, doubt, or earlier forms of piety to enthusiasm, conviction, illumination, and new understandings and ways. Conversion is not solely a shift from no faith or another faith to Christian faith; it is also an essential dimension in the life of all baptized, faithful Christians.

Those who have been baptized as children and reared in the church also need to be converted. At some point, all Christians must fully internalize the faith of the church and affirm their own faith by being confronted with the choice of whether or not they will accept or reject the authority of the gospel. Incorporation into the Christian church requires that persons be brought to a personal life-transforming commitment to Christ. However, since Christian maturity and conversion never exist apart from human maturity, we ought not to impose the demands of adult faith and conversion on those who lack the prerequisites of human maturity.

Children and youth are Christians and members of the community of Christian faith by their baptisms. They are to be nurtured in this community's understandings and ways. They are also to be evangelized by God's transforming Word until in their maturity (adulthood) they experience a moment or period of conversion.

Commitment is neither a single occasion nor a singular kind. In baptism, our parents and the church make a commitment on our behalf. When we celebrate our first Communion, we make a first commitment of faith and we declare our desire to participate in the life of a nurturing, tradition-bearing family. Later that commitment takes the strange and unsettling shape of personal doubt and struggle with the community of our nurture. Finally, in adulthood, following the experience of conversion, a new sense of personal commitment is realized. While not final, this commitment has the quality of a significant new start. Conversion, then, is best understood as a significant aspect of a long process in the growth and maturation of faith by Christians within the Christian family.

Thus, conversions experienced by Christians nurtured within the community of faith do not characteristically happen in a moment. They are not always sudden, dramatic, or emotional, though they may be all or any of these. Conversions are best understood as a radical turning from "faith given" (through nurture) to "faith lived" (through conversion). Conversions are radical because they imply internalization and the corresponding transformation of our lives. Conversions are the result of the witness of the faithful and imply a turning from one style of faith, typical of children and adolescents, to another style of faith, possible for adults.

Once again, we need to understand that both conversion and nurture have a place in the church's educational ministry if it is to be Christian. Our sole concern with nurture has contributed to our losing both an evangelical power and a social dynamic. While rejecting a sterile revivalism, we constructed a false evangelism through nurture. True evangelism and conversion mean helping people to see that they are called, not only to believe the church's affirmation that Jesus is the Christ but to commit their lives to him and to live as his witnesses in the world.

What the church's education ministry needs is a catechesis that evangelizes and an evangelism that catechizes. Nurture and conversion, conversion and nurture, belong together, taking different shapes and forms at various moments in a person's faith pilgrimage within the faith community. The gift of faith is something we are always learning. Conversions understood as process and multiple conversions throughout a person's life are basic to a living faith. Healthy rituals must both convert and nurture us.

Learning and Change

Our rituals effectively influence human emotion and thought toward some behavioral purpose. Dead rituals are those which have lost their power to stimulate or evoke such experience. Initiation rituals are aimed primarily at the transformation of an individual's psychological orientation—a conversion—a process of moving him or her from one place in the community to another. The ritual process of initiation needs to provide a significant detachment of the individuals from their present position or state in the community; an experience of liminality or in-between-ness; a psychic peak experience or conversion; and a reincorporation into the community as a new, "reborn" person.

Conversion brings forth a new perspective—be it a matter of many years or a few seconds, a single or multiple experience—and as such is essential to faith. Our belief, disbelief, and re-belief are related to what we expect from experience. Or to put it another way, we all filter the data of experience and identity, what we see, in terms of acculturated presuppositions and assumptions. If a person does not believe in God, it is because any data that might be interpreted to indicate the presence of God is either ignored (filtered out) or labeled with malicious intent to point to something else. Inevitably, our reflection upon our experience has, as a precondition, certain primordial symbols, learned from birth, which dictate in a real way the possibilities of what we perceive in our experience. Those symbols are continued most significantly in our rituals.

Milton Rokeach, a sociologist, has discovered in his work on values that it is possible to bring about a dramatic and lasting change in values by bringing out the conflicts in the values people hold. It is possible to suppress the conflict by professing opposing values. However when the awareness of these conflicts is made painfully unavoidable, it is our nature to make a choice between them. It is then that persons become disciples.

Christian initiation, the incorporation of persons into Christian faith and life, necessitates this movement from orientation to disorientation to reorientation. The possibility of the integrated spiritual life of religious experience and prophetic action necessitates this reorientation or conversion. Ritual is the primary context for this process. Catechesis, therefore, needs to focus its attention on the transformation of human lives.

Christian Initiation in Historic Perspective

The genesis of a faith community is marked by the shared religious experience of its members—the resurrection of Jesus experienced by the disciples. But the passing of this founding generation means that the community of faith contains people, who have not had this original conversion. Indeed, in our culture, many are born within the community and never sense the power of a transformed existence. How are we moderns to become "live" members of a "living church"? More significant initiation rites could provide a context and stimulant for the transformation of consciousness and life.

In the first few centuries of the Christian era when an adult was converted to the Christian faith, he or she was brought before the congregation by a sponsor, who testified to the candidate's sincerity of desire to embrace the faith. The moral life of the catechumen was then examined. If found worthy, the person was pronounced a Christian through the laying on of hands and the signing with the cross.

For the next two to three years, the catechumen entered a preparation period intended to shape his or her life according to the Christian way. Besides participation in moral instruction, converts were expected to attend the weekly ritual of the community, but only for the first half of the ritual. Following the reading of Scripture, the sermon, and prayers, the converts exchanged the kiss of peace and were dismissed so as not to witness or participate in the celebration of the Lord's Supper.

Periodically during these probationary years, the converts were brought before the congregation and examined. When a person was considered ready on the first Sunday of Lent, he or she signed the church register and the date of baptism was set, namely the forthcoming Easter. During this period, a more intense form of learning was conducted emphasizing the spiritual life and church dogma.

Participation in the Holy Week rituals marked the incorporation of the catechumen into the community of the faithful. Maundy Thursday was celebrated with exorcisms; Good Friday with prayers and fasting. Then, on Easter's eve, the final ritual began. The catechumen was once again exorcised; eyes, ears, and nose were anointed with oil. He or she renounced the devil and made a profession of faith. The salvation story was told. The candidate was stripped naked and was submerged in the coffin-like baptismal font to be baptized in the name of the Father, Son, and Holy Spirit. Coming out on the other side, he or she was anointed with oil and put on a white garment. Upon processing to the altar, the baptism was confirmed by the laying on of the bishop's hands. For the first time, the convert participated in the Lord's Supper. Baptismal garments were worn until Pentecost. The catechumen came to church each day for the celebration of the Lord's Supper and to learn the meaning of the rites, in which he or she had participated. Thus ended the initiation ritual.

Today the church often lacks such significant transforming rituals. In fact, it appears as if many parts of the church have abandoned rituals and left them in the hands of secular society. A challenge faces us. Can we evolve a meaningful rite of

**The Cross Saltire.** St. Andrew is believed to have died on this form of the cross. It is also used to symbolize the beginning and end of the Christian year and is the national cross of Scotland.

Christian maturity? Baptism is *the* rite of Christian initiation. At our baptism, we are made Christian and incorporated into Christ's church. Baptism needs to be given much greater importance and needs to be treated with greater seriousness. It would be well for us to celebrate our baptism day. It is essential for each of us to renew our baptismal vows at every new baptism.

We have a great deal to learn about ritual in the lives of individuals and communities. We have a number of important theological issues to address. And we have a host of educational possibilities to imagine and explore. Liturgy and catechesis belong together. The future of the church's educational ministry and the church's mission are challenged by an awareness of their contemporary estrangement and their historic union.

John H. Westerhoff[49]

249 ✦ WORSHIP AND PERSONAL GROWTH IN CHRIST

Personal growth in Christ may involve passage through a series of stages of faith, as the worshiper moves from a faith transmitted by his or her worship community, through a faith forged in the crucible of personal questioning and struggle, to a mature faith which is constantly expanding in the integration of profession and life. Along the pilgrimage of faith, appropriate rites can mark the passage from one stage to another. It is important to note, however, that these stages are also styles of faith, which may characterize the life of the worshiper throughout his or her lifetime.

For the Christian, baptism establishes Christian identity. Further, baptism is understood as a sacrament; that is, an initiation ritual in which God acts. People can oppose or resist God's action, but God's activity does not depend upon our doing. The Christian believes that at baptism inward and spiritual grace is given by Christ through the outward and visible sign of water; and people are thereby adopted into a family. Baptism celebrates a new birth, a new life, and the giving of a new name—Christian. This insertion into "Christ's body," the church, creates a change intrinsic to the person's life. The individual can reject or deny the adoption and its inheritance, but that does not change the fact of who and whose that person is.

Baptism is the means by which one becomes a Christian and a member of Christ's church. The Eucharist, the Lord's Supper or Holy Communion, is the sustaining rite of the Christian, the sacrament of continuing grace, the family thanksgiving meal of God and God's people. Baptism—and baptism alone—grants a person the right and privilege of participation in the Eucharist, an outward and visible sign in bread and wine of inward and spiritual grace. This Holy Communion sustains individual believers and the community in Christian faith and life.

Confirmation is a sacramental act (necessary, but not essential), whereby to those who recognize and affirm who and whose they are, God grants God's Spirit to assume and perform the ministry to which all those who have been baptized are called.

Faith, as understood in this context, represents the centered behaviors of persons, embodying their minds (beliefs), hearts (affections), and wills (actions) expressed through their lives in accordance with their growth or development. Faith, as such, is a verb. The activity of "faithing" has no age bounds, but appears to express itself in characteristic, identifiable ways at differing points in a person's faith pilgrimage.

Styles and Stages of Faith

Faith is a verb, a way of behaving that involves knowing, being, and willing. It is a deeply personal and dynamic act, a centered act of personality encompassing our hearts, minds, and wills, according to our growth and development. While each person's faith has its own unique characteristics, generalizations concerning the pilgrimage of faith can be described in terms of style.

We do not give a child faith. A child has faith at birth. While the content of our faith is acquired through our interactions with other "faithing" people, a person's faith can expand, that is, become more complex. Expanded faith is not greater faith; and, therefore, one's style of faith is not to be judged. The style of our faith is not directly related to our age. That is, faith expands only if a proper environment exists. If this environment does not exist, faith ceases to expand until the proper environment is established.

Faith's expansion is slow and gradual, moving

systematically over time to acquire additional characteristics. It cannot be speeded up beyond its normal rate of growth nor can characteristics of its various styles be avoided or passed over. The expansion of faith into new styles does not eliminate the faith needs of previous styles of faith. Rather, as it expands, it only becomes more complex. If, therefore, the needs of early styles of faith are denied or neglected, a person will strive to meet those needs until all are satisfied.

From a Christian perspective, God's grace is freely given to all. Though it is our potential to expand in faith, we do not earn anything by so doing. Indeed, the desire to expand in faith is, for Christians, only an act of gratitude for the gift given. We cannot manipulate or determine another's faith. At best, we can encourage and support it and its expansion. At worst, we can make that expansion more difficult. What is important is our own witness to faith and to the interaction of "faithing" persons in community.

With these considerations in mind, we may describe four basic styles or stages of faith.

Experienced Faith. An experienced faith identifies the faith of early childhood; perhaps it is better termed a pre-faith stage. In his or her early childhood development, a child observes and copies the behavior of parents or other role models. These role models become the foundation for a growing child's integrity of belief and action. The child acts and reacts, in relation to other significant persons; and in so doing ideally forms a basic trust which continues throughout life. The child explores and tests the limits of behavior in relationship to parents or other authorities. In these actions, we observe the roots of an openness or closed stance, which characterizes later life.

Affiliative Faith. Affiliative faith is typical of childhood, though it is not restricted to those years. Indeed, vast numbers of adults express their faith essentially through this style, either because its needs have not been satisfactorily met or because they have not been provided the necessary encouragement and environment to move beyond it. Still, even as our faith expands, we never seem to outgrow the characteristic needs of this or any other style of faith. That is, the needs of every evolving developmental style remains with us for life. If we cease to meet these needs, no matter

how far our faith has expanded, we will return to this style of faith until its needs are once again met.

Affiliative faith has three distinctive characteristics. First and foremost, it is faith centered in the affections. It is expressed as a religion of the heart, more than of the head or will. Individuals with affiliative faith seek their identity in the authority of a community's understandings and ways. Similarly, they long for belonging participation and service in the community's life. People are dependent upon the community for the content and shape of their faith. They need to experience and image through nurture and ritual the community's understandings and ways. Through memories told and lived, roots are established; through creative expression, the affections are nurtured and visions of a purposeful future emerge; through trusting, caring, affirming, accepting interactions, self-worth and identity are framed and the present is made meaningful. These needs cannot be neglected or denied.

In this stage or style of faith, a person identifies with "our story," "our way." The development of affiliative faith is the result of a search for conviction, the establishment of a firm set of beliefs, attitudes, and values. This is the stage of learning who, and whose, we are. The best way to understand youth's interest today in the variety of cults is that they provide a sense of community, intense religious experience, and, in a world of pluralism, a set of beliefs which claim ultimate truth.

There is no specific time span, identical for all persons, to satisfy these foundational needs of faith; nor do we ever outgrow their requirements. Perhaps more than half of all those going through the social condition of adolescence live within the limited perimeters of this faith style, as do many adults. Therefore, our ritual life needs to be expressive of this style of faith and speak to its needs, not only for the sake of those persons whose faith is affiliative, but for us all, including those who have moved beyond its bounds.

Providing that the needs of affiliative faith have been met satisfactorily, some time during the adolescent years a person can begin to acquire a new style of faith, that is, can begin to expand his or her faith to include new characteristics. This new faith style can be characterized as "searching faith."

Searching Faith. Searching faith is marked as a time when the religion of the head begins to predominate over the religion of the heart. The mind begins to search for intellectual justifications of faith. Critical judgment of the community's understandings and ways, as well as short-term multiple commitments to ideologies and actions, emerge as people strive to discover convictions worth living and dying for. That is, they learn what it means to give their lives away and live according to their convictions.

Having been "given" an identity during the childhood years, adolescents, in searching faith, struggle to find their own identity; and in so doing, they typically experience the "dark night of the soul." Often unverbalized questions—"What is truth? Who am I? What communities are worth belonging to? What causes are worth living for?"—dominate life's joyous, troubling, liberating, confusing days and nights. Still, persons in searching faith long to belong, especially to a community which shares their concerns for passionate action, critical thought, and experimentation. While they struggle with and condemn the structural authority of the community, they long for moral, intellectual, charismatic, or personal authority.

For many, these are the betwixt-and-between years, when the social conditions of adolescence that throw the individual into a state of limbo between childhood and adulthood (a period that can extend from thirteen to thirty) unite with the ordeal of searching faith with its sense of being on the periphery of the community. These are the years, when it may appear that faith is lost and the community's nurturing has failed. And these are the years, when a person appears to have matured into adulthood one day and the next to have regressed to early childhood. Difficult for both the individual and the community, these years of anxiety and storm must come before faith can assume its fullest dimensions.

Mature Faith. The faith of adulthood can be called "mature faith." It is not necessarily characteristic of all adults, for it appears that only those who have moved through searching faith can acquire its characteristics of centeredness and personal identity. People with mature faith are secure enough in their convictions to stand against their community of nurture when conscience dictates. Having begun as a heteronomous self and moved to autonomy, the theonomous self—the self in conscious, willed obedience to God—emerges. Still in need of community, individuals with mature faith reveal themselves to be inner-directed, open to others, but clear and secure in their own faith identity. Individuals with mature faith are concerned to eliminate the dissonances between rhetoric and life. Thus, the religion of the will, with its witness to faith in deed and word, predominates over the religion of heart or mind, although the mature faith encompasses both. Integrity of belief and action are realized.

Of course, mature faith is always expanding; it is not to be understood as a state of arrival or conclusion. New depth and breadth emerge. Importantly, the needs and characteristics of earlier styles of faith continue. Doubt and the intellectual quest never end. Nor does the need to belong, the need to have the affections nurtured, or the need for a sense of authority disappear, though these needs do express themselves somewhat differently. Indeed, if these various faith needs are not met, a person who has reached mature faith will return to an earlier style of faith until its needs are once again satisfied. Thus, faith is never static.

For example, to grow into searching faith, individuals need to have been given a sense of self-esteem and worth. They need to have learned to accept their strengths and weaknesses, to live in the hope that they will continue to grow, and to possess self-confidence. They need to have learned that they can meet the future. During the childhood years, people will, it is hoped, have experienced the grace of God in a sacramental community, where the authority of the Word and the conviction that Jesus is Lord is lived in the intimacy of a belonging, caring fellowship. To have a sense of oneness with God, to feel loved for nothing, to know that you are understood and valued are the gifts of a Christian community expressed through its common life and rituals.

However, for many adolescents, even those brought up in the church, the experience of loneliness, self-hatred, family conflict, estrangement, insecurity, closed-mindedness, dogmatic authority, and an affection-depraved environment have made searching faith difficult to attain. In spite of their adolescent social condition, they need a community which nurtures affiliative faith.

Those, however, who have begun to move into

searching faith need a community of social concern and action; a community whose rituals unite head and heart with a concern for justice; a community in which critical intellectual judgment is encouraged, doubt affirmed, and experimentation permitted. In some cases, people have been forced out of the church in order to meet these needs. This is especially unfortunate, for these persons still need belonging participation in a passionate community to be secure in its story and ways.

Each style of faith has its own character, but builds on characteristics of earlier styles. Thus as growth occurs, faith becomes more complex. The process is slow, gradual, and related to the presence of environments, which nurture development and growth. Life is not static. Each of us needs to be prepared for new conditions; and the communities of which we are a part need to have ways to reestablish equilibrium following each change in the life of one of its members. Further, a new generation needs to be prepared for and given an understanding of the changes that are part of individual and community life. A community's rites and rituals serve these important functions.

Faith Stages and Conversion. The development of affiliative faith can be a significant religious experience, especially in the North American milieu with its heritage of conversion. Such faith may be an often intense and dramatic response—whether of older children or of adults—to the call into a new life and incorporation into a community conscious of what it believes and how it should live.

Conversion in the stage of searching faith emerges in the context of questioning and doubt. Such conversions are often experienced as illuminations, resulting from new ways of "seeing and hearing." These illuminations may appear dramatically, but more typically involve a gradual process of multiple experiences, both intellectual and emotional, in the supportive context of the witness of faithful worshipers.

Some persons who have grown into mature faith have had the conversion experiences related to affiliative or searching faith, and some have not. All persons with mature faith have experienced one or more of the conversions characterized by the growth from searching faith to mature faith.

Transition Rites

There is a category of rites which is known by some as the rites of passage, transition, or life crisis. Instead of following the calendar as rites of the community do, these rites address the changes of our lives. Some correspond to biological changes, such as birth, puberty, and death; others correspond to social changes such as marriage, graduation, and retirement. Such moments of changed role or status are traumatic to both individuals and the community. Ritual aids us to make these changes purposeful; they reestablish order in the community and help others to understand the possibility and the meaning of change.

Rites of transition are comprised of three states: separation, transition, and reincorporation. The rite properly begins and ends with a ceremonial or ritual. The intermediate ritual telescopes these three stages into a single ceremony. For example, the rite of marriage begins with a ceremonial, the engagement, and ends after the honeymoon. The ritual of marriage (incorporating these three stages) is the wedding ceremony, which begins with the couple separated, and continues with their coming together to announce their intentions, making a series of promises, and being pronounced husband and wife. The ritual ends as they are blessed and depart together to be integrated into the community as a married couple.

In a life-crisis rite, once the separation from one's status or role is realized and before one is reincorporated into the community with a new status or role, an important period of transition occurs. It is, first of all, a period of limbo in which a person experiences a state of being betwixt-and-between, in this case, neither married nor single. Once a person's engagement is announced, old friends proceed with caution, checking out the appropriateness of old behaviors. During this period, the engaged couple experiences being set apart; that is, they are not typically invited either to the parties of married couples or to those of their old single friends. Normal interaction has been reduced and all the appropriate behaviors of the past have been suspended, while future appropriate behaviors are inappropriate. If this period of transition is too short or lacks the dynamic of an ordeal, the marriage and the role-status of wife and husband are apt to be less secure.

The gift of this ordeal is an experience of community, but the most important aspect of this transition period is "education." It is the time to acquire the understandings and ways of behavior (thinking, feeling, acting) appropriate to the person's new state or role. Typically, this education is informal, as in an engagement party. In the past, a woman's mother would hold a party for her daughter and other women. They would bring gifts, such as kitchen utensils, and exchange recipes. Today women sometimes get mixed signals and a confused education. That is, their friends also may hold a coed party and give an apron and recipes to the fiancée.

To give one further example of a life-crisis rite, at one time the "last rites" functioned as a ceremony of separation. During the ordeal and liminal period between that ceremony and the funeral, the person's relatives and friends were prepared for death. The funeral, then, ritualized the person's rebirth into that new state the church believes exists for persons among the community of saints.

I first became aware of these dynamics when I served a parish in New England. We could not bury people in the winter months. A tragic, unexpected death in the winter, with its winter funeral and spring burial ceremony, seemed to result in better family adjustment than was the case for those who suffered the same sort of tragic death in the spring months, when both funeral and burial were celebrated at the same time. It was then that I realized how important this liminal state could be if informal education or preparation was provided.

Education is always a central aspect of transition rites. People need to be prepared for their new status and role. Such informal learning properly includes only that basic knowledge, attitudes, and skills required by their new condition. This does not mean they need to rehearse all past learning or need to learn everything they will ever need to know. Only foundational learning for life in their new state is necessary or proper.

Typically informal learning during initiation takes place away from the initiate's home. It lasts as long as necessary to insure that the initiate is fully prepared for his or her new role or status. Most importantly, the educational methods used for learning are "symbolic" in nature. For example, through dance, boys and girls perform symbolic sexual acts. Indeed, girls and boys rehearse adult roles through games. Youth are tested on their knowledge of the community's understandings through puzzles and riddles. Through corporate living in simulated settings, songs, dances, and sacred stories, young people learn the meaning of community life.

Transition rights, thus, embody an educational component, which operates best through informal, natural interactions of persons, in contrast to formal instructional programs. Each will also have its unique characteristic consistent with the cultural ways and needs of the people involved. There is a mystery to the pilgrimage of faith and life in the Christian community. It cannot be programmed or organized as to age or any other particular. And especially important is the acknowledgment that transition rites are dependent upon the faith and life of the church's confirmed members.

Rites of Christian Identity

Christians are made, not born. Identity and transition during faith's pilgrimage are a central issue for the church. Just as membership in the old Israel was never a matter of nature or birth (Israel was adopted by God to be God's people), membership in the new Israel is by an act of God. Baptism celebrated that fact in the early church. That is, baptism was understood as a symbolic, sacramental act, whereby God adds persons to God's eschatological community. Baptism—the same initiation rite for men and women unique in the history of religions—is the means by which a person is adopted into an existing community.

Parenthetically, we would observe that in most societies there is a different initiation rite for men and women and that the male rite is considered the most significant. Within the Christian community, the picture is radically different. Both men and women share the same initiation rite—baptism. Thus, the Christian faith makes the revolutionary statement that men and women are equal and that in the eyes of God there is no male or female, Jew or Greek, adult or child, for in the church, they are all one in Christ. Regretfully, this is an essential affirmation of the Christian faith that has yet to be fully actualized in our corporate life.

Baptism. Baptism is, in and of itself, the central rite of Christian initiation. It is a sacrament in which God is the chief actor. In baptism, the Christian church celebrates its conviction that God loves us for nothing (grace). Before we can make any response to God, God acts for our good through physical objects and actions. Later we can oppose or resist, but God's action does not depend on either our acceptance or worthiness. By God's action, we are incorporated into that tradition-bearing community, which proclaims its faith through word and deed. Still for this radical action of God to be realized, we need to make some response. That is why the norm for the church's initiation rite is adult baptism. However, the church historically has been concerned about the children of the faithful, nurtured within a faith community. This concern has resulted in child baptism.

Communion. The Lord's Supper, the Eucharist or Holy Communion, is the sustaining rite of the Christian community. It makes real the continuing gift of God's grace celebrated at baptism. Baptism makes a person a full member of the church and is the only necessary condition for acceptance at the Lord's Table. However, it appears wise to wait until a person desires to commune and participate in this family meal. Therefore, first Communion is a decision of the child, granted after preparation by the child's parents.

Confirmation. Only if the adolescent pilgrimage has been affirmed and encouraged can individuals in early adulthood be prepared for confirmation. Confirmation is perhaps best understood as a rite of Christian maturity characterized by a "conversion" or transformation, which is understood as enlightenment or illumination. At confirmation, people celebrate their coming to mature faith and commit themselves to Christian ministry. While the pilgrimage of faith continues, a new start has begun.

For those who did not begin their pilgrimage at birth, the rites of baptism, first Communion, and confirmation can be united into a single rite of initiation following serious and lengthy (two or more years) preparation.

These are just a few images of the relationship between liturgy and catechesis. Numerous problems remain, but perhaps new insight and stimulus have been provided for the church's educational ministry.

John H. Westerhoff[50]

250 ✦ BIBLIOGRAPHY ON WORSHIP AND EDUCATION

Brown, Kathy, and Frank C. Sokol. _Issues in the Christian Initiation of Children: Catechesis and Liturgy._ Chicago: Liturgy Training Publications, 1989.

Browning, Robert L. _The Sacraments in Religious Education and Liturgy: An Ecumenical Model._ Birmingham, Ala.: Religious Education Press, 1985.

Buono, Anthony M. _Liturgy: Our School of Faith._ New York: Alba House, 1982.

Neville, Gwen Kennedy, and John H. Westerhoff. _Learning Through Liturgy._ New York: Seabury Press, 1978.

Ostdiek, Gilbert. _Catechesis for Liturgy: A Program for Parish Involvement._ Washington, D.C.: Pastoral Press, 1986.

Westerhoff, John H. _Learning and Liturgy Through the Life Cycle._ New York: Seabury Press, 1980.

———. _A Pilgrim People: Learning Through the Church Year._ New York: Seabury Press, 1984.

Wilde, James A., ed., _Before and After Baptism: The Work of Teachers and Catechists._ Chicago: Liturgy Training Publications, 1989.

⊛ THIRTEEN ⊛

Worship and Education: The Rite of Christian Initiation for Adults

The Rite of Christian Initiation for Adults, developed for use in Roman Catholic parishes and now widely emulated in many worship traditions, presents a fine model of how ministries of education can enrich and be supported by the worship of the church. The RCIA is a program for personal and communal spiritual growth that leads to baptism and then explores the meaning and significance of baptism for a life of Christian discipleship. It is much more than a program consisting of a series of truths to be understood; it is rather a model of a life to be lived. Christian teaching is woven together with worship, prayer, and spiritual direction, so that the new Christian, whether young or old, senses the wonder of being baptized in Christ and made a part of the Christ's body. The following chapter describes the RCIA in its history and present practice.

251 ✦ A HISTORY OF LITURGICAL CATECHESIS

The Rite of Christian Initiation for Adults is based on a long tradition of uniting the church's ministry of teaching (catechesis) with its ministry of worship (liturgy). This tradition has been recovered in the past two centuries in what has come to be called the "liturgical movement."

The word *catechesis* literally means a "sounding down," a "re-echoing down to another" (from the Greek *katechein: kata* [down] and *echein* [to sound]). Early Christians adopted the word in their follow-up work of teaching the gospel and used it to mean "instruction given by word of mouth" (e.g., Luke 1:4; Acts 18:25; 1 Cor. 14:19; Gal. 6:6). The word *liturgy* literally means "work of/for the people" (from the Greek *leitourgia: laitos/leitos* [of the people] and *ergon* [work]). In general usage, the word stood for "an act of the public service." Early Christians adopted the word to mean acts of service to others, donations, etc., on behalf of the gospel (e.g., Phil. 2:30; Rom. 15:27; 2 Cor. 9:12), the offering of Christian life as a sacrifice (e.g., Rom. 15:16), and acts of public worship (e.g., Acts 13:2; Heb. 8:2, 6). For the early community, there was an obvious continu-

ity and flow from preaching the gospel to catechesis, from catechesis to liturgy, from liturgy to further catechesis and to gospel service. The common goal of this combined pastoral ministry was to nurture the disciples on their journey of conversion, their faith, their Christian living, and their witness.

By the nineteenth century, the relationship between catechesis and liturgy had been severed for the most part; they occupied separate pastoral niches. Catechesis had been narrowed down to question-and-answer instruction in the truths of the faith, which were set down in a catechism and presented, primarily to children, for intellectual assent and understanding. Liturgy had been narrowed both in pastoral practice and in theory. Pastorally, liturgy was understood as the "ceremony" performed publicly by the priest before a passive congregation for the honor and glory of God; theologically, liturgy was reduced to the essential minimum (matter and form) required to "confect" a sacrament.

In the past century, both catechesis and liturgy have gone through an extended process of renewal. New questions now arise about how they are related and what shape liturgical catechesis might take. This article will survey the parallel renewal movements, will suggest a vision of a holistic pastoral ministry which draws catechesis and liturgy into close relationship, and will reflect on the nature and key qualities of liturgical catechesis.

Two Renewal Movements

The liturgical and catechetical movements have common roots in the mid- and late-nineteenth century. In church life, as in society in general, a movement of a "return to the origins" was underway. The past was to be retrieved, however, not in a static form, but in an organic process. The unfolding character of human history was increasingly accepted. The same sense of historicity and process was at work in the study of human life, with attention to human growth and development. During this period, historical research in the writings of the fathers and in the Bible spawned the patristic and biblical movements. A new ecclesiology elaborated a more active and organic sense of community and community life and action. It was in this context that the liturgical and catechetical movements took shape.

Liturgical Movement. The liturgical movement unfolded in a series of four phases. The first phase, in the latter part of the nineteenth century and through the turn of this century, has been called the monastic phase. At the Abbey of Solesmes in France, Dom Gueranger spearheaded a study of the liturgy and particularly a revival of the Gregorian chant. In this phase, the liturgical movement was more intent on restoring a liturgy to be celebrated in a monastic setting than on adapting it to the pastoral needs of the church at large.

The second phase, the pastoral phase, was inaugurated by Pius X's *motu proprio* on church music, *Tra le Sollecitudini* (1903), and by Dom Beauduin, under whose leadership a conference held in Malines, Belgium, in 1909, called for an extension and a more pastoral orientation of the liturgical movement. In this period, the liturgy came to be seen as the center of Christian life and spirituality. A priority was given to the "active participation" of the people, a phrase first used officially by Pius X. Early and frequent Communion was promoted; community singing was restored; the Roman missal was translated to provide a de-

votional manual for the people; and the liturgy's power to instruct people in Christian faith and life was rediscovered. These pastoral concerns, fostered first in Belgium and Austria (especially, by Josef Jungmann and Pius Parsch) and later in America (especially, by Dom Virgil Michel, who was equally devoted to issues of justice), found support in a renewal of liturgical and sacramental theology. In Germany, Dom Odo Casel inspired a theological discussion on the active presence of Christ in the liturgical assembly, which was to influence the teachings of both Pius XII and Vatican II and contribute to the "encounter model" of sacrament later developed by Schillebeeckx and others.

The third phase began with Pius XII's encyclical on the liturgy, *Mediator Dei* (1947), and continued throughout the *Constitution on the Sacred Liturgy* promulgated in 1963 by Vatican II. During this period, the central agenda of the pastoral phase of the liturgical movement received full ecclesiastical approval. In his encyclical, Pius XII officially set aside the purely ceremonial understanding of liturgy and spoke of it as the public worship of the entire mystical body, head, and members. The Easter Vigil was restored (1951); and Holy Week was reformed (1955), returning the paschal mystery to its central liturgical position. Guidelines were given for increased participation (*De Musica Sacra*, 1955); and the ceremonies of the liturgy were simplified (1955). During the 1950s, there was also a series of national and international conferences on liturgy, which brought together pastoral and theological concerns and prepared the way for the discussions of Vatican II. *S.C.* 7 contains the heart of the council's teaching on the liturgy. The teaching states that Christ is present in the liturgy in many ways and that the liturgy is the action not just of the priest, but of Christ and his body, the church. Several things follow: full conscious and active participation is the baptismal right and duty of every Christian (*S.C.* 14); appropriate liturgical instruction is to be provided of the faithful so that they can participate both internally and externally (*S.C.* 14, 19); and the rites are to be celebrated with the assembly present and actively participating (*S.C.* 27).

The fourth phase, the time since the council, has been one of implementation and renewal. The Roman rites have been revised under the direction of the *Consillium* established to oversee implementation of the liturgical reforms of Vatican II; and they have been translated into English by the International Commission on English in the Liturgy (ICEL). Extensive programs of instruction and catechesis have been an integral part of the liturgical renewal project. Throughout the postconciliar work of reform and renewal, the full, conscious, and active participation of the faithful has remained the most fundamental pastoral goal and principle.

Catechetical Movement. The nineteenth century themes of return to origins, of historicity, of process and human growth, themes that influenced the development of the liturgical movement helped to shape the catechetical movement as well. Dissatisfied with the catechism approach, forged as it was in counter-Reformation polemic and speculative theology, religious educators turned to human psychology, particularly to theories of learning and later to developmental psychology for help in renewing catechesis. This led to the concern for effective catechetical methods,

The Celtic Cross. Also known as the Irish cross and the cross of Iona, this cross originated in the earliest centuries of Christianity in Great Britain. In addition to being found on church buildings, these crosses are found by the wayside and in cemeteries. The circles connected with such crosses represent eternity.

which characterized the first phase of the catechetical movement early in this century. The "Munich method," devised in Germany in the early 1900s and imported into the United States in the 1920s, later inspired parallel attempts in Italy, France, and Spain. Attention to how humans learn and to the value of action and of learning by doing are common motifs that have lasted beyond the "methods" phase into present catechesis.

In the 1930s, the catechetical movement entered a second phase, usually designated the "kerygmatic" phase. Josef Jungmann's _The Good News and Our Own Preaching of the Faith_, published in 1936, triggered a shot of attention from method to content. The message handed on in catechesis is the "kerygma," the history of salvation centered in the person of Jesus of Nazareth. The goal of catechesis is a living faith, which responds to God's call to us in Jesus. Subsequent catechetical theory and documents have retained both the Christocentrism and the centrality of the Word espoused in the "kerygmatic" phase. Another leader during this phase, Johannes Hofinger, stressed that catechesis is a form of pastoral ministry, specifically a form of ministry of the Word. This theme was to become a staple of the catechetical movement as well; and it was incorporated into the Vatican II decrees on missionary activity (_A.G._) and the pastoral office of bishops (_C.D._). Method is not neglected; however, it is refocused on the four languages—biblical, liturgical, existential, and doctrinal—in which the "kerygma" is addressed to us. This "pedagogy of signs" was developed in the 1940s and 1950s, particularly at the Lumen Vitae center in Brussels, and has left its mark on the _National Catechetical Directory_ (_N.C.D._) of the United States' National Conference of Catholic Bishops (NCCB). During these decades, there was a convergence between the catechetical and liturgical movements not only thematically, but also in major figures involved in both movements, e.g., Joseph Jungmann and Virgil Michel.

The third phase of the catechetical movement, still underway, is often characterized as the "missionary" or "political" phase. Earlier stress on saving history during the kerygmatic phase quickly led to a complementary concern for contemporary human experience. A series of international study weeks, especially those from Eichstatt (1960) through Medellin (1968), provided a natural transition from the emerging anthropological concerns. These study weeks, all held in third world countries except for Eichstatt, set the theme of catechesis in the context of mission. The understanding that catechesis is a form of ministry of the Word, elaborated in the second phase and sanctioned at Vatican II, was expanded and nuanced in these study weeks. Catechesis is seen as the continuation of the proclamation of the kerygma first accomplished in evangelization, just as evangelization is the continuation of pre-evangelization. For this total ministry of the Word to be effective, it must address people in their own context. As the third world experience readily illustrates, that context is a complex web of political, cultural, socio-economic, and environmental factors. Themes of justice and liberation become part and parcel of the catechetical message. And the experiential catechesis, which had long been a part of the catechetical movement and an area of significant United States' contribution, can no longer be content to focus on isolated individual experience. It must attend to the larger issues woven into human interdependence on local, national, and global scales.

Convergence and Divergence. There are many points of convergence in the two renewal movements. Common themes and motifs run through both: the centrality of Christ; the preeminence of the Word; the need for actively engaging the people not only as recipients, but also as primary agents of catechesis and liturgy; the dynamics of process and address-response common to both activities; and the need for a more symbolic, holistic approach to the process of learning and celebrating.

The seeds of a potential divergence of interests and energy are also latent in the rhythms of the two movements. As noted in its third phase, the maturing liturgical movement won ecclesiastical approval, which culminated in the *Constitution on the Sacred Liturgy* of Vatican II. The current phase has been one of consolidation and implementation. The signals being given in liturgical documents on the relation between catechesis and liturgy are somewhat mixed. In the constitution itself (*S.C.* 14, 19), as in much subsequent documentation implementing the liturgical reform, the vision of liturgical catechesis seems to be limited to an immediate program of "liturgical instruction" on the revised rites and their meaning. Nevertheless, the restoration of the catechumenate has laid the foundations for a much broader vision of a pre-baptismal and post-baptismal catechesis integrated into a process of pastoral care and ritual celebrations (RCIA 75, 244-247)

By contrast, in the current "political" or "missionary" phase, the maturation and ecclesiastical approval of the catechetical movement have taken place in obvious interdependence; and the vision of catechesis is generally much larger. The themes of Christocentrism and the placing of catechesis within an unfolding ministry of the Word so prominent in the second and third phases of the movement had a strong impact on various conciliar decrees, especially those on the pastoral office of the bishops (1965), which affirmed the primacy of ministry of the Word (*C.D.* 12-13, 44) and on missionary activity (1965), which set the catechumenate within the pastoral task of evangelization (*A.G.* 13-15).

Three particular lines of mutual influence between the catechetical movement and official documents can be traced. First, the decree on the pastoral office of the bishops mandated the preparation of the *General Catechetical Directory* for the instruction of the Christian people (*C.D.* 44). That *General Catechetical Directory* (*G.C.D.*) appeared in 1971 and influenced both the First International Catechetical Congress in Rome (1971) and the preparation of national statements and directories such as the NCCB's *Basic Teachings for Catholic Religious Education* (1973) and *Sharing the Light of Faith: National Catechetical Directory* (1977; *N.C.D.*). Second, the degrees on missionary activity helped set the agenda and the theological vision for subsequent international catechetical study weeks, which explored the relationship between missionary activity and catechesis in the third world context. That linking of themes extended through the First International Catechetical Congress held in Rome (1971) to the General Synod on in the modern world (1974) and the General Synod on catechesis in the modern world (1977). These synods led to the apostolic exhortations of Paul VI, *Evangeli Nuntiandi* (*E.N.*) in 1975, and of John Paul II, *Catechesii Tradendae* (*C.T.*) in 1979. In these two strands of mutual influence there is a consistent stress on seeing catechesis as form of ministry of the Word within the pastoral office of the church. The third line of influence reaches from the conciliar decree on Christian education (1965) to the NCCB's pastoral message on Catholic education, *To Teach as Jesus Did* (1972). In these documents, as in the NCCB's *Basic Teachings*, concern for the integral content of catechesis becomes prominent.

Catechesis and Liturgy

The above survey suggests that there is a close relation between catechesis and liturgy (*C.T.* 234; *N.C.D.* 36, 113) and that there should be collaboration between them (*N.C.D.* 139). In both pastoral practice and theological discussion, however, catechesis and liturgy sometimes seem to co-exist or even to go off in different directions, making the link between them tenuous at best. Closer reflection on the relationship is needed.

The first and most important task may be able to recover a vision of a more integral pastoral care, which embraces both catechesis and liturgy. Three memories preserved in our tradition offer such a vision.

Emmaus. The first is the story of the two disciples on the way to Emmaus, the story of the "first Eucharist" in the Christian community. In that story, we find two disciples journeying *away from* the band in Jerusalem, their world in disarray, their inchoate faith in Jesus as the Messiah shattered. Their words to the stranger, "we were hoping that he would be the one . . ." (Luke 24:21), reveal the depth of their disillusionment. The stranger, with the care of a host, draws out their experience in all its hurt and bewilderment. And when their story is finished, he retells it from another point of view, that of its victory. "Did not the Messiah have to undergo all this so as to enter in to his glory?" (24:26). Their hearts captivated by his recasting of their experience, they invite him to stay with them. In return, he once again hosts them, this time in the breaking of the bread. "With that their eyes were opened and they recognized him" (24:31). Now they are able to name the burning in their hearts. Newly born in the Easter faith of the disciples, they immediately rise to return to those from whom they had fled, with a mission to tell them "what had happened on the road and how they had come to know him in the breaking of the bread" (24:35).

Several comments are in order. The journey of the two is a journey from a shattered first faith to a full Easter faith. To use contemporary terms, it is a journey from pastoral encounter to catechesis, from catechesis to liturgy, and from liturgy to mystagogy and mission. The catechesis was effective only because the stranger first listened to their story and only then retold it in familiar biblical words. Its effect was to set their hearts burning and to prepare them for the ritual moment that followed. It was only because the catechesis had thus readied them that they were able to recognize him in the breaking of the bread, to know him as the risen Lord and themselves as believing disciples. And it was only because that moment of recognition was so powerful that they were compelled into a mission of witness and service to the others. The connection between catechesis and liturgy is unbroken; and the stranger is the model host-catechist-liturgist.

Pentecost. The second memory is enshrined in the story of the "first imitation" in the early community, the sequel to the Pentecost story. In that story, two questions, two moments, and two thresholds frame the experience of the first converts to the new way. After witnessing the Pentecostal event, they are filled with amazement and even a little cynicism about new wine. Their initial question is one of idle curiosity, "What does this mean?" (Acts 2:12). This question triggers a kerygmatic moment, in which Peter cites prophet and Psalm to cast a different light on what they have experienced. Their question now becomes deeply personal, "What are we to do, brothers?" (2:37). In asking this new question, they have crossed a threshold, from a curiosity of the mind to the searching of a heart now open to conversion and faith. Their question invites a catechetical moment, in which Peter instructs them and urges them to "save yourselves from this generation" (2:40). The account ends with an idealized description of the life in common of "those who accepted his message" (2:41-47).

Again, a few words are in order. The account reveals a nuanced connection between evangelization and catechesis staged to address the developing quest of the converts. As in the Emmaus story, their human experience provides the starting point; and their questions mark new stages along the way. And as in the Emmaus story, catechesis leads to a profession of faith set in a context of ritual action. This moment is prolonged into mystagogy, liturgical celebration, and mutual service.

The Catechumenate. The third illustration is not only a memory, for the ancient catechumenate has now been restored in the Rite of Christian Initiation of Adults (RCIA). In the RCIA, catechesis and ritual celebration are brought back together, especially in the periods of the catechumenate proper (RCIA 75) and of mystagogy (RCIA 244-247). Together catechesis and liturgy are set in an unfolding process, a spiritual journey (RCIA 4.5). Christ in his paschal mystery stands at the center of the process (RCIA 8); and the entire community is charged with active responsibility for the initiation of new members (RCIA 9). The RCIA brings to realization what both the catechetical and the liturgical movements have sought to recover.

Catechesis and Liturgy. Gathering some motifs from the longer tradition's vision, it can be said that catechesis and liturgy are linked intrinsically to each other. Liturgy without catechesis can easily become an impoverished, hollow ritualism; and catechesis, which does not issue into liturgy, can become too intellectualized (*C.T.* 23). Both are rooted in faith. In its own way, each expresses, nurtures, and strengthens that faith as it enables people to reflect on its meaning in their lives. The goals of both are the same: to enable people to live the gospel, to be a prophetic voice in their world, and to share their faith and way of life with the next generation.

There is also a certain overlapping of the two that resists too radical a separation. Liturgy itself has a formative power (*N.C.D.* 36), exercised through proclamation of the Word and symbolic ritual gesture. As a ministry of the Word, catechesis also has a formative power to shape faith through reflection on what the Word proclaimed and celebrated means for daily Christian life. In a sense, catechesis itself is celebrative.

Catechesis and liturgy are not identical, however. In the larger sweep of pastoral care, catechesis first prepares people for full, conscious, and active participation in the liturgy and then helps them reflect back on the worship experience to relate it to daily life (*N.C.D.* 113). Thus, catechesis and liturgy are caught up in a recurring cycle, in which each reinforces the other.

To clarify the relationship between catechesis and liturgy further, catechesis can be described as a systematic, sustained effort to reflect on God's Word made known to us in the Scriptures, in liturgical proclamation and sacramental celebration, and in our experience of Christian life and service to God. This understanding, central to kerygmatic catechesis and the pedagogy of signs, points to an important aspect of the relation between catechesis and liturgy. In catechesis, the immediacy of God's call experienced in proclamation, celebration, and living service gives way to reflective appropriation of that experience. The classical theological dictum that liturgy is "first theology" and that what the theologians do is "second theology" offers us a parallel. Liturgy with its formative power is a "first catechesis," while the systematic reflection on that experience done under the guidance of a catechist is "second catechesis."

Liturgical Catechesis

What, then, is liturgical catechesis and what qualities are to be sought in shaping an effective liturgical catechesis?

Scope and Range. One functional description of catechesis reads: "Within the scope of pastoral activity, catechesis is the term to be used for that form of ecclesial action which leads both communities and individual members of the faithful to maturity of faith" (*G.C.D.* 21). In this view, the task of catechesis is "to foster mature faith" (*N.C.D.* 33), to "put people not only in touch, but in communion, in intimacy with Jesus Christ" (*C.T.* 5). Similarly, the function of liturgical catechesis is to enable people to participate actively, both internally and externally (*S.C.* 19), in the liturgy which celebrates that faith.

As the name itself suggests, liturgical catechesis is only one part of that larger catechetical ministry. Naming it *liturgical* catechesis implies a narrowing of the catechetical focus in some way. One such focus is to make liturgy the object, the content of the catechesis. If this is the only focus, liturgical catechesis risks making people self-conscious worshipers and turning their symbols into didactic signs. Another way to narrow the focus is to give the catechetical process a liturgical framework and orientation. Various forms of prayer and celebration are incorporated into the catechetical process, so that participants experience a movement from prayer to reflection to celebration. For example, catechumens gather not only for instruction, but also around the Word and for blessings, anointings, and scrutinies. A third way to focus on the liturgy is to use liturgical experience as a source for catechetical reflection, not just on the liturgy itself, but on the relationship between God and God's people celebrated in the liturgy. Though it is the most difficult of the three, this way of focusing liturgical catechesis is most central to its task.

In keeping with the model established for initiation, two kinds of liturgical catechesis should be distinguished. The RCIA calls for pre-baptismal catechesis and post-baptismal catechesis (mystagogia). The norm for every sacrament would then be both pre-sacramental and post-sacramental catechesis. The first prepares recipients for a sacramental rite, takes place in a specific period, and is of a more general, elementary kind. The second is life-long and leads people to reflect on their sacramental experience and its meaning for their lives (_N.C.D._ 6). In pre-sacramental catechesis, rehearsal of the rites and detailed interpretation of the symbols are far less important than a spiritual readying of the recipients to live in the liturgical moment when their growing relationship with the Lord is marked with a distinctive sacramental sign. Invitation into that relationship and formation in the symbolic ways, both human and religious, in which it is expressed, take pastoral priority for this catechesis. In post-sacramental catechesis, the liturgical experience of God's presence and action provides the starting point and focus for the catechetical reflection. In broad strokes, this mystagogy might simply be described as the reflective continuation of the "opening up of symbols" begun in the liturgy itself (NCCB, _Environment and Art in Catholic Worship_, 15).

Desired Qualities. Liturgical catechesis should be Christ-centered, formative-transformative, communal, and experientially-based.

Christ-centered. The first concern of liturgical catechesis is to help people develop the individual and communal relationship the crucified and risen Christ first nurtured and sacramentalized in the experience of Christian initiation (RCIA 8). Christ is the center of Christian life, liturgy, and catechesis; and his paschal mystery is the focal point for all Christian spirituality. The ultimate concern of liturgical catechesis is not liturgical history, the rites, symbolic objects, or the truth "taught" by the liturgy, but the person of Jesus and how the assembled people meet God in him. The key sources for liturgical catechesis are to be found where that Jesus is revealed to his disciples: in the proclaimed Word, in sacramental gesture, and in the living witness of those who live as his disciples.

Formative-transformative. Liturgical catechesis, like all catechesis and like the liturgy itself, is a formative experience. Formation in faith and in conversion would thus seem to be the appropriate goal for both. But entering into and growing in a relationship with Christ is ultimately a transformative experience accomplished only through the work of the Spirit. The appropriate goal of both liturgy and catechesis is to form people in a way that invites them into transformation; neither can be so programmed as to transform people automatically. The same holds true of liturgical catechesis; it forms for the sake of transformation. And since transformation is a journey of faith and conversion that takes a lifetime, liturgical catechesis is needed by disciples of every age according to their level of development (_S.C._ 19; _N.C.D._ 177-189), with a certain primacy accorded to adult catechesis as the "chief form of catechesis" (_N.C.D._ 188).

Communal. By its very nature, liturgy is a communal action. The assembly itself is the most important of the liturgical signs (NCCB, _Environment and Art in Catholic Worship_, 28). The very act of gathering , the constant use of the first person plural in public prayer, the common hearing of the Word of God, and the one sacramental action in which all participate shape the liturgical experience as a communal one in which the people meet Christ together. Liturgical catechesis needs a setting and a format, in which the reflection on the meaning of the liturgical experience can be done in common since the meaning is a public, shared meaning. Liturgical catechesis should also be communal in the sense that it is the common work of all in the community. All are to accept the formative role their witness has for others (RCIA 9). Adults in particular are to play a central role in their own catechesis (_N.C.D._ 185).

Experientially based. If catechesis in general should be concerned with making people attentive to their more significant experiences (*G.C.D.* 74), this holds especially true for liturgical catechesis. And if it is crucial for any learning method to take account, not only the goals and the learners, but also the subject to be studied, liturgical catechesis needs to devise methodologies that are attentive to what is most characteristic of the liturgical experience. Four such characteristics stand out.

First, liturgical celebration is *repetitious.* General structural patterns of gathering and sending, word and action, prescribed ritual dialogue, and patterned action repeat themselves in almost every rite. Within a given liturgical rite, most words are prescribed, even prescripted; and the ritual interactions are stylized and predictable. Like all ritual, liturgy is a "known language" in which people dwell and which they use, not to create a totally new story, but tell of and mark a journey of discipleship already underway.

Second, liturgical celebration is *symbolic* in expression. This is true not only of ritual actions, but to a great extent of the words as well. Liturgy conveys its meaning not in an explanatory, didactic fashion, but in a metaphoric, evocative way. Symbols speak to the whole persons in whole ways, not just to the mind for the sake of information sharing. Space, time, action, and speech form a highly nonverbal array of interlocking liturgical languages. In addition, the symbols used in the liturgy have roots not only in religious tradition, but also in human usage. For example, bathing and anointing someone or sharing food together serve as both human and religious symbols. Religious symbolism typically incorporates and builds on human symbolism.

Third, liturgical celebration is at its core symbolic *ritual action.* Ritual has its own way of valuing and knowing, prior to and often without words. Liturgical rites enact meaning rather than talk about it. In liturgy, God and people literally keep covenant in Christ, in the remembrance of his dying and rising. Liturgy is a saying-doing of the complete God-human *Amen* uttered in Christ (2 Cor. 1:20).

Fourth, liturgical celebration is repeated symbolic ritual action *which the people do together.* Though each one in the assembly can find personal meaning in the rites, the meaning symbolically enacted is a shared, public meaning, which goes beyond personal meanings. In the moment of ritual, individual stories and journeys are transposed and become part of the larger story told and enacted in memory of what God has done in Christ.

These four characteristics together urge that liturgical catechesis follow a procedure which does several things. From the perspective of human experience, liturgical catechesis first evokes the experience beneath liturgical symbols, such as bathing with water and anointing with oil, not just in its individual expression, but also in its cultural, political, and socioeconomic context. It attends to the dark side of the symbols as well as the bright side, e.g., that we both bond and fight with food. Second, it enables people to interpret that experience in its fullness and in the light of God's Word revealed in Jesus and handed on to us in the community, such as the memory of the breaking of the bread. Third, it entrusts to people the tasks of living out that human experience in the world in full consonance with faith, so they may spread the story of how they came to know him.

What does this mean from the religious point of view? First, liturgical catechesis will start with the people's experience of the liturgy itself. It will pay careful attention to the ways in which symbol and ritual help them to see and mark the place of God's presence and action in their lives and to hear the call to further conversion. Second, the larger liturgical tradition will be presented as a living history of a people at prayer to the God, who walks as a companion on the journey so that we as Christians can more easily relate to that story. Third, the meaning of liturgy for people today and tomorrow should not be imposed, but should be called forth in the creative meeting of contemporary human experience and received tradition.

The twin renewal movements in liturgy and catechesis have opened the way to a closer collaboration between these two ministries. A more holistic vision of pastoral ministry, in which liturgy and catechesis support and complement each other, can now be recovered. Out of that vision, a liturgical catechesis that is Christ-centered, formative-transformative, communal, and experientially based can take shape.

Gilbert Ostdiek[51]

252 ✦ AN INTRODUCTION TO THE RITE OF CHRISTIAN INITIATION OF ADULTS (RCIA)

This article describes the whole process by which the Roman Catholic church brings new adult members into its communal life. The process culminates with baptism at Easter Vigil, which is both preceded and followed by periods of instruction and spiritual formation.

Once upon a time, in the not too distant past, adults who wanted to join the Catholic church went through six weeks of "convert instructions" and were baptized quietly on a Sunday afternoon in a dark church with a few relatives present, two of whom probably also served as godparents. A short time later, perhaps the following Sunday, the new converts received their first Communion, but probably with little attention to the fact that they were joining the community at the Table of the Lord. Confirmation was left until the next visit by the bishop. Since 1972, that approach to adult baptism has changed radically, thanks to the revised Rite of Christian Initiation of Adults (RCIA).

"New" Aspects of the RCIA Process

The RCIA makes four essential changes to the scenario described above. First, it restores the original order of the sacraments of initiation, which is baptism, confirmation, and the Eucharist. The three sacraments are celebrated as one sacrament of Christian initiation at the Easter Vigil.

Second, the RCIA stresses the need for a *living* experience of the church and not just *knowledge* about the Eucharist. Although the RCIA includes instruction in the facts of faith, instruction is but one part of a much larger experience of *living the faith* with members of the church. As Thomas Merton said about his own conversion to Catholicism in *The Seven Storey Mountain*, "Six weeks of instruction, after all, were not much, and I certainly had nothing but the barest rudiments of knowledge about the actual practice of Catholic life."

Third, the RCIA puts an end to the quiet, dark, almost secretive baptism of adults and makes the welcoming of new Christians a public community event. In the former approach, the priest was often the only member of the parish community with whom the converts came in contact. This inevitably gave converts a very limited experience of church members. It could also cause them to feel very much alone when they joined the community on the Sunday after their baptism, simply because they never had the chance to get introduced to members of the parish.

Fourth, the RCIA stresses that conversion is begun by the Holy Spirit and is an extended process. The desire that a person exhibits for becoming a Christian is a response to what the Spirit has already begun and is seen in the context of a journey to faith that is most often much longer than six weeks of "convert instructions."

In many ways, the new Rite of Christian Initiation of Adults, promulgated in 1972, is the most radical and revolutionary document to have come from the renewal of Vatican II. It is radical because it thrusts us back to our roots and challenges us to relearn what it means to be the church. It is revolutionary because it also thrusts us forward, calling us to become the church of tomorrow.

A Brief History of Adult Initiation

While the RCIA is radical and revolutionary, it is not really new. In the earliest centuries of the church, adult baptism was the norm. Infants were baptized only when they were children of adults, who had converted to Christianity.

The early church invited people, who were interested in Christianity, to join the community on a journey of faith. Those who accepted the invitation became the candidates for the sacraments of initiation (baptism, confirmation, and the Eucharist). The candidates were called catechumens and entered in to a step-by-step process toward full membership in the church. This process, called the catechumenate, included a lengthy period of formation, instruction, and testing, lasting one to three years or more. It was time of serious discernment regarding whether or not the catechumens could break with their pagan background and accept and live the Christian faith. It was also a time for newcomers to explore with the Christian community their responsibilities in carrying out the church's mission and ministry. Joining the church in the early centuries was no easy matter. In an age of persecution, such a commitment was not to be taken lightly.

The entire church would pray for and with the catechumens, instructing them in gospel values, sharing with them the faith-life of the church, and celebrating the stages of their faith journey with special rituals of welcoming and belonging. A person's coming to faith—or conversion to Christianity—was looked upon as a community responsibility and demanded total community involvement.

The final Lent before their initiation was a special time for catechumens. It was like a forty-day retreat, which included prayer, fasting, and other self-scrutiny as they prepared to accept the faith and be received into the church that Easter.

Initially, the purpose of Lent was totally related to baptism. It was a time of final formation for those catechumens preparing to be initiated into the Christian community and a time for the faithful (the already initiated) to remember and renew their baptismal commitment.

The early church joyfully recognized the culmination of the catechumens' journey to faith and welcomed them into the saving reality of the paschal mystery by celebrating the sacraments of initiation at the solemn Vigil of Easter, the great paschal feast that celebrates the life, death, and resurrection of Christ. The sacraments of initiation were celebrated only once a year, and only at the Easter Vigil. After their baptism, there was another period of instruction for the new Christians; namely, one that led them into the deeper mysteries of faith.

Unfortunately, this beautiful, community-supported journey to faith was short-lived. With the conversion of the Emperor Constantine in 313, Christianity became a fashionable, rather than a persecuted religion. Some people even entered the catechumenate for political reasons—to get jobs or special positions in the empire, for example—with little intention of ever being baptized. The standards of the catechumenate were relaxed, as people eventually stopped joining the catechumenate altogether and were simply baptized on request.

By the beginning of the fifth century, the catechumenate process itself had virtually disappeared. The sacraments of initiation became three separate sacraments celebrated at separate times. Soon adult baptism declined; infant baptism became the norm; and the Rite of Christian Initiation of Adults as practiced in the early church became a lost art.

In the period following World War II, the church began to experience a need for a fresh approach to the welcoming of new members. New ideas were put forth. In some dioceses in Africa, for example, church leaders reached into the church's rich heritage and began to apply the ancient catechumenate process to modern situations.

This return to former practice was motivated by a desire to assure greater stability among the converts coming into the church. The more lengthy instruction and formation provided by the catechumenate allowed greater time for the faith of converts to mature. Such good results were reported that when the bishops assembled for the Second Vatican Council, they called for a study and restoration of the process of Christian Initiation of Adults.

In 1972, after nearly ten years of study and research, the official text (in Latin) for this new/old process of initiating Christians, the revised Rite of Christian Initiation of Adults, was published. The rite once again became an integral part of the church's sacramental system. The English version came out in 1974.

What is the RCIA?

It is important to realize that the revised RCIA is much more than an updated or expanded program of "convert instruction" like that experienced by Thomas Merton. The RCIA is a process of conversion. As we shall see later, it is divided into four continuous phases that correspond to a candidate's progress in Christian formation. But, before discussing the specific structure and phases of the rite, let's look at the underlying principles of the RCIA.

(1) The RCIA is first and foremost a process. To see it as anything else, particularly to see it as a static program, does violence to the dynamic nature of the rite. This is true because the RCIA is for and about people: people on the move, people being remade in the image of Christ, people being reborn in the Spirit, people on a journey toward faith—and people whose faith journey cannot be programmed because programs as such do not cause conversion, only God brings about conversion.

(2) The RCIA is a community event. The initiation of adults is about the Christian community initiating new members into itself; and therefore it must take place in community. In no way can it be a private celebration or process. The RCIA sees the church as community, as *us,* and also sees

us as the primary ministers of the RCIA.

(3) The RCIA ministry is basically one of witness and hospitality. Although the RCIA involves many parishioners in various ministries, such as sponsors, catechists, prayers, spiritual advisers, and social justice ministers, everyone in the community is responsible for ministering to prospective converts by the witness of their lives and the openness of their attitudes. The document is particularly strong in this respect when it says, "the initiation of adults is the concern and business of all the baptized" (RCIA 41).

Each member of the Christian community must be equally attentive to and involved in the whole conversion process, because the total community is responsible for welcoming new members and showing them what it means to live the Christian life. When we initiate newcomers, we welcome them into the flesh-and-blood body of believers and establish a living bond between the new Christians and ourselves as the church.

(4) The RCIA is ongoing and multidimensional. Christians are made, not born. That means that there is nothing automatic or instantaneous in the initiation of adults. Conversion takes time. Committing oneself to gospel values and perspectives on every level of life requires a change of heart that cannot be accomplished by an educational program alone.

While doctrinal instruction is a part of the process, the initiation of adults aims at changing the heart and transforming the spirit, not just supplying a bank of knowledge. Therefore, the RCIA includes all aspects of parish life: worship, pastoral care, counseling, spiritual direction, social justice and apostolic involvement, and education.

(5) The RCIA restores the baptismal focus of Lent and reinstates the Easter Vigil as the honored time for initiation. The document points out that only for serious pastoral reasons should the initiation of adults take place outside the Easter Vigil.

The focus and primacy of the Easter mystery are also restored by the RCIA. This means that the whole initiation process centers on the candidates' gradual incorporation into the paschal mystery—the mystery of Christ's life, death, and resurrection. Baptism, confirmation, and the Eucharist are the sacraments, which celebrate in one symbolic action, a person's initiation into that mystery.

(6) The RCIA is a step-by-step journey punctuated by corresponding rituals. The document sees the process of initiation divided into four basic steps. Between each of the steps, the community celebrates a special ritual, which brings closure to the preceding period and moves the candidates into the next.

A Walk through the Process

Journeys have beginnings, middles, and ends. They also have certain thresholds or signposts that signal the steps or stages along the way, which help us get from one point to another in our travels. The four-step journey to faith embarked upon by candidates for Christian initiation has such a structure.

The First Step: The Precatechumenate. The RCIA journey begins with the precatechumenate—a term, like the other terms used in the document, that is borrowed from the church's ancient rites of initiation. The precatechumenate is a preliminary step in the journey of faith. It is a time for inquirers to hear the Word. But more importantly, it is a time for community members to listen to the inquirers and answer their questions. The questions most inquirers have are questions like, "Why are you Catholic?" "How do you pray?" "What are those little saucers at the doors of your church for?" "Why is Mary so important to you?" "How do you say the rosary?" These questions are answered not with theological dissertations, but honestly from the heart and faith of each person.

The precatechumenate period could be compared to our inquiring about a new job. While we might be sincerely welcomed to the company, we want to take a long hard look at what the job entails and offers before accepting it. The inquirer takes that long hard look at the church during this preliminary stage in the journey. How the community lives and shares its faith speaks volumes to inquirers during this time.

Then, just as our warm heart and inviting spirit need some accompanying physical gestures—such as a handshake or hug—when we welcome someone into our home, so the welcoming community called the church needs some rituals to welcome new members to itself during this process of initiation.

The RCIA provides such a ritual for the inquirers when they are ready to proceed to the next phase of the conversion process. This ritual is called the "Rite of Entrance to the Catechumenate." It is celebrated in the presence of the Christian assembly, preferably at Sunday Mass, so that the community can welcome the inquirers to the second step of their journey to faith.

The Second Step: The Catechumenate. With their welcome to the catechumenate phase of the RCIA, the inquirers are referred to as "catechumens." The ritual and the new title signal a difference in the life of the aspiring Christians. They move from being inquirers to being people who have already begun to live as Christians, even though they are not yet full members of the church.

At this point, the catechumens are joined by sponsors from the community who serve as guides, companions, and models of faith for them. The ministry of sponsor is an extremely important one. Sponsors provide personal support for the catechumens, share the Christian life with them, and help to make them feel at home. Sponsors commit themselves to being a vital link between the catechumens and the community. They present the candidates to the church and also represent the church to the candidate throughout the RCIA process.

The catechumenate is often the lengthiest period in the RCIA process. The length is determined by the personality and the needs of the catechumen and by the community, but it can last from several months to three years. During this time, catechumens are instructed in the faith, participate in community activities, join with the community in prayer and worship, and work actively with the community in the apostolic life of the church.

Although the catechumens are invited to worship with the community, they are dismissed from the eucharistic celebration after the Liturgy of the Word. Since they are not fully initiated and cannot receive Eucharist with the assembly, they leave with their catechists (and sometimes with their sponsors) to ponder the Scripture readings they have just heard. It was because of this aspect of the catechumenate in the early church that the parts of the Mass, before Vatican II, were referred to as the "Mass of the Catechumens" and the "Mass of the Faithful."

When the catechumens are ready to respond totally to God's call to faith through the sacra-ments of initiation, the RCIA once again provides a ritual to mark this step in the conversion process. This ritual is called the "Rite of Election." It is designed to take place on the first Sunday of Lent and is the church's way of confirming God's call in the life of the catechumens. The ritual provides an opportunity for the catechumens officially to request entrance to the church through the Easter sacraments of initiation and for the community to respond to that request by saying, in effect, "We confirm God's call to faith in your life, and will welcome you into the church this Easter."

The Third Step: The Lenten Period before Initiation. The "rite of election" introduces this third step of the journey and also marks the final Lent before the catechumens receive the sacraments of initiation. Beginning with the first Sunday of Lent, the catechumens enter into their forty-day retreat of focus on deepening their awareness of God's grace through prayer.

To emphasize the importance of this last Lent before initiation and to help express the penitential and reconciling aspects of the season, the church also celebrates other rituals with the catechumens, called *scrutinies.* These are prayers of healing prayed by the community (on the third, fourth, and fifth Sundays of Lent) that the catechumens will have the strength to withstand evil and remain pure and free from sin as they journey toward initiation, continued conversion, and maturing faith.

The scrutinies are powerful rituals that also remind us, the faithful who are already baptized of our need for the penance, healing, conversion, and reconciliation that are part of Lent for all of us. Once the RCIA is implemented in a parish, Lent just isn't Lent without catechumens. While we minister to them, they provide a visible reminder to us of the meaning and purpose of Lent and minister to us through their presence.

Then, finally, the great night arrives—the night of Easter Vigil at which the sacraments of initiation are celebrated and the catechumens are made one with the body of Christ called the church. This is the community's final ritual gesture, which says, "Now you belong, for you have been born again of water and Spirit. Come, you are welcome at the Table of the Lord." It is the climax of the conversion journey, but not the end of the journey.

The Fourth Step: The Post-Initiation Phase. This concluding part of the journey to faith is called the *mystagogia* (from the word *mystery*). In the early church, it was the time when the community explained the mystery of the sacraments that the catechumens had experienced. Today since the sacraments are usually explained before the Easter Vigil, this step is seen more as a time for the newly initiated and the community to move forward together toward a closer relationship with each other and toward a deeper understanding of God's Word, of the sacraments, and of the lived Christian life. The RCIA places this phase in the Easter season (the fifty days between Easter and Pentecost), but in reality this step in the journey continues for the rest of a Christian's life. We are all constantly growing toward closer relationships and deeper understandings of the mysteries of our faith.

Not for Converts Only

The RCIA brings us full circle. It compels all of us, who have been Christians since our baptisms, to look critically at our roots as a church and to renew ourselves in light of our tradition. The RCIA really gives us, who were baptized as infants, the opportunity to reassess, reexamine, and renew our faith and God's part in that faith.

Once the RCIA is begun in a parish, it is a continuous process that begins and climaxes only for individuals, but never really ends as far as the *parish community* is concerned.

The initiation of adults is for the life of the whole church, not just for converts. The presence of catechumens journeying toward initial conversion in our parishes models for us the deeper conversion to which we are all called. Conversion, after all, is not a once-in-a-lifetime thing. We all experience God's call to turn around or change our lives and improve our relationship with the Lord—especially during Lent.

Flannery O'Connor, the American novelist and short story writer, said it well when she wrote a friend who was considering converting to Catholicism:

> I don't think of conversion as being once and for all and that's that. I think once the process has begun and continues that you are continually turning inward, toward God and away from your own egocentricity and that you have to see this selfish side of yourself in order to turn away from

it. I measure God by everything that I am not. I begin with that. (*The Habit of Being: The Letters of Flannery O'Connor* [New York: Farrar, Straus, Giroux, 1979].)

And so does the RCIA.

Sandra DeGidio[52]

253 • THE PRECATECHUMENATE

The RCIA process begins with a season of prayer and preparation that is known as the precatechumenate. During this stage, the gospel is proclaimed and every potential catechumen is welcomed and embraced by the community, all in preparation for the more formal structure of the catechumenate that will follow.

Each stage of the Rite of Christian Initiation of Adults has a distinct character. Although the rites invite creativity and adaptation according to the local needs, the process is not wide open to random bright ideas. It has a definite framework suited to the unfolding of this layered experience. The rites delineate four unique stages, identify specific areas to be confronted, and set guidelines for demonstrable progress in those areas before advancing to the next stage. From a human point of view, the effectiveness of the whole process hinges upon a sensitivity to that structure—allowing the journey to unfold smoothly. If one stage is not easily distinguishable from another in the real situation, then violence is being done to the process.

If you liken the RCIA to any good ritual that embodies gathering, listening, sharing, and sending forth, then the precatechumenate represents the gathering.

Dialogue of Stories

This first stage is described as a time of inquiry and evangelization—a time for "hearing the first preaching of the Gospel" (RCIA 8-9). The context here is the apostolic kerygma, the first encounter: "Master, where do you dwell?" "Come and see." It is a matter of gathering in order to hear the story.

Everyone has a personal story, a memory of where I have come from, my uneasy truce with the present, and my hope or fear of where I may be going. I *must* have a story—it is my identity.

Without it I am amnesiac, cut off, and alone in a world of relationships. We all have stories like we all have dreams; but like dreams, we may or may not be aware of them. And of those aware of their stories, some interpret them and some do not. The first goal in story-telling is to heighten that awareness, to get in touch with personal experience. The ultimate goal is to sensitively interpret that experience in the light of the gospel. This is, in fact, the dynamic of evangelization: a dialogue between a personal history and the gospel story. Great care must be taken to see that personal faith-sharing provides the catalyst, by which the inquirers can *identify this dialogue in their own lives*. This is the business of the precatechumenate.

If the question of encounter and relationship with Christ becomes a vital business in the precatechumenate, then doctrinal questions should be secondary or nonexistent at this point. If, on the other hand, "egghead" questions abound, it may be a good indication that the heart of the human/divine encounter, the evangelizing dialogue, has not been reached. Should these questions dominate, it is important that the RCIA team respond, not so much to answer them, but to discover why such surface concerns have usurped the primary task of discerning the dwelling place of the master. These questions should not be ignored, but put in perspective. This is a time of inquiry, not into the bylaws of an organization, but into the eternal question, *Quo vadis?* ("Where are you going?"). It is not the time to assume that the Catholic church is the cut-and-dried answer to that question. Therefore, defer "churchy" questions, as much as possible, until after the basic questions of identity and orientation, conversion and faith, have been confronted—preferably until the catechumenate. On the other hand, the time will never be more vital than in the precatechumenate to discover that Christ (and therefore his church) is indeed a reality and that to seek Christian faith is to choose that real, living Christ—not a domesticated, boxed, and possessed commodity.

The subject matter of the precatechumenate is clearly laid out in paragraph 15 of the RCIA. "The candidates are required to be grounded in the basic fundamentals of the spiritual life and Christian teaching." These basics are first faith, initial conversion, a sense of repentance, the practice of prayer, and the first experience of the society and spirit of Christians! Faith, conversion, repentance, prayer, Christian society—these are not items to be taught, but experiences to be shared. The presumption is that the inquirers are put into contact with real Christian community, in which these experiences are the "givens."

Precatechumenate in Practice

How is all of this to be implemented? If Christian community is the context of these experiences, then hospitality is of the essence in the precatechumenate. God forbid that this be limited to the cold and unwelcoming walls of the church classroom. It seems imperative to me that if the inquirers are to experience the "society and spirit of Christians," then a much more nurturing, affirming, and private environment must be provided, at least in the early stages. A Christian home environment is much more creative. And its advantages are well suited to the work of the precatechumenate:

(1) The groups are limited to an intimate size conducive to personal sharing and honest questioning.

(2) In a small, intimate group, it is much easier for the *inquirers* to set the agenda; whereas in the classroom the agenda is almost always that of the team leaders.

(3) Small core groups learn how to listen to each other, care for one another, and support one another, thus becoming authentic communities.

(4) They learn to pray together.

(5) The sponsors become "soul-friends"—not by appointment, but by real bonding.

(6) The RCIA team does not appear as the "experts" who have the final say, but as representative members of the engendering community *whose Christian authenticity is held in common.*

(7) This small, family-style community sets aright a common and pernicious inclination to initiate people into an "RCIA reception committee," instead of into the parish community.

(8) Finally, it requires of the RCIA team a good deal of trust in the sponsoring individuals or families and, more importantly, in the Spirit of God at work within the church. This means that a great deal of care and prayer should go into the selection and training of sponsors. The sponsors themselves need to be people of prayer, open to the divine encounter. The team leaders must then

relinquish proprietorship with the healthy realization that conversion and faith are not the work of humans, but of the divine initiator.

I do not suggest that the entire precatechumenate experience be limited to small group meetings. On the contrary, I would insist that the entire group get together in a festive manner a number of times during the course of the precatechumenate. At these times, socializing, sharing individual group experiences—their progress, fears, joys, funny stories, whatever is part of who they have become—is all proper subject matter. As the time of the rite of the catechumenate approaches, this kind of gathering should be more frequent so that the candidates become comfortable with the larger community.

The core community structure does not eliminate the need for initial private interviews with the candidates either. The purpose of the interview is to discover what led the candidates to the point of inquiry, to discern individual needs and attitudes, and to uncover any special situations requiring timely attention. Likewise, follow-up interviews throughout the process assure the candidate a sense of guidance and aid in the process of discernment at the time of entry into the catechumenate.

As I perceive the sense of the documents, although the precatechumenate is the time for the "first hearing" of the gospel, _it is not a time to gather the candidates at the Sunday Liturgy of the Word._ After all, they have not yet decided to commit themselves to this household of faith. According to paragraph 11 of the RCIA, any explanation of the gospel given to the candidates at this time is in order that "they receive the help they are looking for." In other words, the gospel story selected within the core groups is in direct response to wherever each individual is in his or her life. That means that telling the story is only half the agenda; the other half is that we must listen to a life story. We are far too anxious to teach and tell, as if the candidates had nothing of value.

Faith-Filled Discernment

As the inquirers progress toward decision, an important responsibility of discernment rests on the catechumenal team and the pastor. The guidelines are clearly laid out in paragraph 15 as mentioned above: the candidates must be grounded in the preliminary aspects of faith, conversion,

prayer, and an experience of the Christian spirit. Such discernment cannot be approached with a proselytic attitude. In the past, it seems that the only thing of importance was that people be baptized. I think we still err in that direction. The rites make stringent requirements of the candidates before they complete the precatechumenate. Lack of courage on the part of the catechumenal team to discern unreadiness as well as readiness depreciates the Christian commitment, encourages shallow motivation, dilutes and perhaps disrupts the catechumenal process, and ultimately runs the risk of making the whole process a membership drive. The person, who understands that conversion is God's doing, will not try to force the Lord's timeline to fit the RCIA's calendar nor fear to challenge the candidate with the realities of Christianity. But through mutual prayer and careful listening, the pastor and the pastor's representatives will discern _with_ the candidate when the proper time arrives to commit to the life of a catechumen.

Bobbie Hixon[53]

254 ✦ THE CATECHUMENATE

The second stage of the RCIA process is a time of structured prayer and study. In this stage, the catechumens work together to learn the basic teachings and actions of the Christian faith, under the guidance of mentors from the larger Christian community.

The catechumenate is a period of formation of undetermined length during which an individual desiring incorporation into the Christian community prays, studies, and discerns, in conjunction both with others who seek the faith and with members of the faith community who are chosen to assist these individuals.

Incorporation into the Christian community demands a conversion of life, a transformation of the individual in Christ. Erik Erikson demonstrates the significance of stages in development of the human person within the human community. Ritual plays a significant role in Erikson's process of becoming an adult member of a given society. Generally, initiation into any society places a balance between the needs of the individual and those of the community. The individual needs to be accepted and needs to experience a sense of belonging, in order to accept as one's own the philosophy of the group. The community, on the other hand, needs assurance that the new member will be one who will live the life professed by the group and will support the members of the group in their pursuit of the life within the community.

The Christian community lives the life of Christ. Conversion to this life in Christ implies acceptance of the challenge offered by Christ to his followers to bring about the kingdom through the proclamation of the gospel. Thus one who desires incorporation into this body, the church, evidences a passion for this mission of Christ. Membership in the church is not limited to an adherence to rules and teachings. It is a way of life. It is a life lived in relationship with Christ, particularly through prayer. It is a life lived in relationship with the Christian community, particularly through the proclamation of the gospel as evidenced in an approach to life and in the expression of the unity which exists within the church in the liturgy.

Historical evidence points to the presence of a catechumenate in the ante-Nicene communities. During the period of the catechumenate (which lasted from several months to years), the individual experienced growth in the acceptance of the Christian way of life. Members of the community worked with the individual to enter into a change of lifestyle. During the period of the catechumenate, the candidates led a life of prayer and fasting. Various rituals were used to mark transition moments during the course of these years of discernment on the part of the individual and of the community.

Included among the decrees of the Second Vatican Council is the call for the restoration of the catechumenate:

> The catechumenate for adults, comprising several distinct steps, is to be restored and brought into use at the discretion of the local ordinary. By this means the time of the catechumenate, which is intended as a period of suitable instruction, may be sanctified by sacred rites to be celebrated at successive intervals of time. (*S.C.* 64.)

The challenge set forth in the Liturgy Constitution was met with the promulgation of the Rite of the Christian Initiation of Adults in January 1972. Included in the decree from the Congregation for Divine Worship is the reception of the council's call for the restoration of the catechumenate.

The catechumenate is preceded by a period of evangelization often referred to as the precatechumenate. During this period, the Good News of salvation is heard for the first time by the individual who begins to inquire into the faith. Those who are not yet members of the Christian community are introduced to gospel values, as they meet informally with Christians and begin to hear of the love of God for them.

The catechumenate is a period of formation in the Christian way of life. It is a time for discernment and prayer. While the various dogmas and precepts of the church are introduced by priest or catechist, primary emphasis is placed on hearing the Word of God within the context of the assembled faithful and then discussing how that Word might transform the lives of all, in particular, the lives of the catechumens. The catechumens are formed by their participation in the communal life of the assembly, including its apostolic works by instruction and through participation in the various liturgical rites.

The individual seeking incorporation into the Christian community generally participates in the order of catechumens, a group of individuals who participate in the formation process together, sharing faith with members of the community and participating in the various apostolic works of the community. While responsibility for the formation of the catechumens is given to the entire community, some members are chosen to minister directly to the process. It is with these individuals that the catechumens meet to listen to the Word and share faith within the context of the Liturgy of the Word.

Catechists and other ministers encourage the catechumens to enter into reflections on the Word in dialogue with their life experiences. This lectionary-based catechesis is based on readings from the Bible, which yield the church's self-identity. Rather than being didactic, this liturgical catechesis breaks open the Word of God for the catechumen. Catechesis is not simply education, but conversion; and conversion takes time.

Catechesis takes place within the context of prayer. Liturgical rites during this period are designed to assist in the formation of the catechumens. The public nature of these rites underscores the fact that not only the catechumen, but the entire Christian community, is in the process of entering into a new relationship.

The first of the rituals of the catechumenate is the "rite of acceptance into the order of catechumens." In the presence of the assembly, the priest or deacon greets the catechumens and their sponsors. During the liturgy, the catechumens are marked with the sign of the cross and are given the book of Gospels during the Liturgy of the Word. The names of the catechumens are written in the registry; and after the community prays over them, they are dismissed. They will not participate in the Liturgy of the Eucharist until the Easter Vigil. While these are the general signs of acceptance suggested by the ritual, other optional rites are permitted where a particular culture might have a distinct ritual act associated with such an acceptance.

Once accepted into the order of catechumens, the individual now enjoys a particular relationship with the Christian community. Each catechumen will hear the Word weekly proclaimed within the context of the assembled body. In the event of death during this period, the catechumen will be buried as a member of the community.

The length of time spent by any individual in the catechumenate will depend on the particular needs of that person and of the community. While catechumens enter into the conversion process with others seeking incorporation, the group is not a class, but rather individuals sharing faith as they hear the Word in common. Therefore, some members of the group might be ready to enter the next period of formation before others.

In addition to participation in the weekly gatherings for the celebration of the Word, various liturgical rituals are suggested during the period of the catechumenate. Great flexibility is suggested in the use of the various minor exorcisms, blessings, and rites of anointing offered for use during this time in the life of the individual undergoing conversion. Catechists, priests, deacons, or other ministers lead the catechumens in prayer and offer the various rituals when deemed appropriate.

Of great significance to the entire catechumenate is the season of Lent, often called the great retreat of preparation for the celebration of the sacraments at the Easter Vigil. On the first Sunday of Lent, catechumens appear before the assembled community where testimony is given of those involved in their formation. The church then accepts this testimony and chooses the catechumens for entry into the church. Generally, the election is followed by the enrollment of names of the catechumens in the book of those seeking initiation.

Now, the "elect" participate in the Lenten celebrations as the final stage of their preparation. During this period of purification and enlightenment, their spiritual formation is more intense. Godparents play a more direct role in the process as they assist the catechumens to achieve an ever deeper awareness of the presence of Christ working in their lives.

Particular ritual components assist the process. Within the liturgy during the Sundays of Lent, scrutinies with their accompanying exorcisms are included in the Liturgy of the Word to assist the catechumen in the conversion process. During the final days of Lent, after the completion of scrutinies, the creed and the Lord's Prayer are formally presented to the candidates.

Mary Alice Piil[54]

255 ✦ THE POSTCATECHUMENATE

Following baptism at Easter Vigil, the RCIA concludes with a period of reflection on the purpose and significance of Christian baptism. Following the practice of the early church, this is known as a period of mystagogy, a time of instruction into the meaning of what is now part of lived experience.

In the published editions of the Rite of Christian Initiation of Adults, the section dealing with the period of postbaptismal catechesis or mystagogy occupies a scant two pages. The terse prose of the ritual book is striking. The text gives only the briefest glimpse at how this fourth major period of formation in the Christian way is to be carried out.

In the early days of the implementation of the RCIA, little attention was given to this period. Most parish RCIA teams arrived at Easter Sunday morning so exhausted that little energy was left for the "how" and "what" of mystagogy.

Eventually, a popular wisdom emerged that claimed this was the time to teach about sacraments and to introduce neophytes to various parish organizations and ministries. The RCIA folks would maintain a regular weekly schedule of meetings, but now the focus would be on presentations of sacramental theology and visits by parish leaders, who saw the occasion as an ideal opportunity to recruit new workers for their particular area of concern.

Today there seems to be a new maturity developing regarding mystagogy. Many are realizing that those attempts were well-meaning but misplaced. RCIA teams are returning to the ritual book to read again numbers 244-251; and more careful reflection is being given to just what this period of formation is supposed to be about.

A better understanding of initiation has helped us see the period of the catechumenate—not the period of mystagogy—as the proper time to "introduce" candidates and catechumens to the understanding of sacrament and to the ministerial life of the community. If a community has waited until mystagogy to present the notions of sacrament, mission, and ministry, then formation of the catechumen has been incomplete.

We no longer live in the fifth century, when mystagogy is the time we tell new members the "secrets" of our faith, either about sacraments or the Christian mission. However, mystagogy in our day still needs to be very much a time of learning about sacrament and mission in new ways. The challenge faced by RCIA teams, then, is how best to accomplish the mystagogical task, i.e., how best to do postbaptismal catechesis in a way that will help neophytes to appreciate in new and vital ways the meaning of belonging to a sacramental community, whose focus is the Christian mission.

It is interesting how easily we can overlook things that are obvious. Many who are returning to the rite for direction with the period of mystagogy are struck by how clearly it says that the *primary* focus of our pastoral energies during this period should be what happens in the Sunday assembly, not on gatherings during the week or on efforts to "connect" neophytes to parish organizations. For those who must make the practical decisions regarding "how to do it" during mystagogy, it is obvious that their attention needs to be, first and foremost, on what happens in the Sunday assembly.

Reflection on the historical roots of mystagogical catechesis confirms that this insight is on target. The classic examples of mystagogy be-

queathed to us by the ancient church can all be found in the midst of the liturgical gathering. Mystagogy was what the bishop-homilist did, in the presence of the neophytes and the rest of the community, as they gathered to celebrate the new life that had been poured out during the night of the Great Vigil.

The homilies were recognized as important statement for the entire community; they were recorded and circulated widely from the very beginning. Their aim was not just to comment on the immediate experience of those gathered. Rather, the bishop's mystagogical homilies were major statements, which attempted to articulate the foundational meanings of Christian belonging in a way that would shape and direct the community's life all year long.

RCIA strategists on the eve of the twenty-first century need to develop ways to recapture something of that significance for their own local communities. In this regard, the intuitions of our early efforts to implement RCIA were correct: understanding sacrament, and mission are crucial to the success of the mystagogical task. Or, to express it more accurately, a proper understanding of the linkage between sacrament and mission is the key to the success of the period of mystagogy.

The rite gives several cues that signal the importance of the Sunday gathering. It suggests that the neophytes sit together as a group, preferably with godparents and sponsors, and that general intercessions and homily be keyed to their presence. The involvement of the entire community is called for, and cycle A readings of the lectionary are recommended for use. In fact, a careful reading of those texts seems foundational to any elaboration of the meaning of mystagogy.

In those readings, the themes of new life, belonging to community, sacramental participation, and Christian mission are intimately intertwined. Those responsible for the period of mystagogy will want to call for careful reflection on those texts by all who are involved in setting the direction of parish life. Practically speaking, that means an invitation to the homilists to dialogue with selected parish leadership (or RCIA catechists or others) regarding the vision of Christian life offered to the neophytes in those texts.

Long before the immediate task of homily preparation, the homilist needs to be involved reflecting on these texts as foundational for the life of the parish community. In particular, those who are part of this reflection must wrestle with the connection between sacramental participation and commitment to the Christian mission.

What better time in a parish's life to reexamine policies regarding sacramental preparation and the call to conversion that must be clearly part of a parish's way of celebrating the sacrament? What better context in which to discuss stewardship in a parish?

The readings will see to it that the focus is not just on money gathering. Instead, they make it clear that we are all gifted by the Spirit for the upbuilding of the community and the spread of the gospel. Christian mission, in the vision of these readings, is set in its proper context as a consequence of a community's encounter with the risen one in sacramental celebration. In this sacramental encounter, we are gifted in an incredibly rich fashion as the Spirit is poured forth upon us and we are nourished at the Lord's Table.

If the RCIA team is able to convoke gatherings to reflect on the meaning of the mystagogical texts for the life of the parish community, then it will be a logical next step to use the homily time to expand the dialogue to the wider community. Some homilists may be willing to engage in actual dialogue with the assembly regarding the foundational meanings that have been identified in the earlier reflections. Imagine asking long-time parishioners to stand up and tell neophytes what it is that is expected of them by way of Christian mission, now that they have "completed" their initiation! Or, imagine inviting the neophytes to give witness to how they hear the Scripture readings calling them to Christian mission! However it is accomplished, what seems essential in order for authentic mystagogical catechesis to occur, is that the neophytes and the community together engage in serious reflection on how our encounter with the risen Lord in the sacraments calls us to Christian mission in the world.

The bulk of our remarks have been devoted to how the RCIA team should focus its energies on the Sunday celebration during the time of mystagogy. This has been a deliberate choice, and one which in many communities will require a significant rethinking of "job descriptions" and priorities. It may even be distressing to those whose practical bent wants only a list of how-to's. The decision to focus on the Sunday gathering—and

especially preparation for the proclamation of a mystagogical homily—is, however, an eminently "practical" choice.

Yet, we do not wish to suggest that our efforts at mystagogy stop with the Sunday gathering. In fact, other efforts do need to be put forth that will help neophytes assimilate and integrate their new experiences. This means that there will have to be gatherings outside of the Sunday assembly, when leaders will help them unpack the meanings implicit in the powerful rituals which they have experienced at the Vigil. They need also to be helped to articulate how their new experience of eucharistic participation and their new sense of belonging to the community will shape and define their Christian faith in the future. Certainly, there will to some extent be a place for helping them sort out new ministerial involvements and new ways of living Christian mission. But that should come as a consequence of the meanings which are unfolded, rather than being presented as a recruitment event to fill out committee membership rolls. In planning for the period of mystagogy, emphasis must always be on sharing the meaning of our _being_ in Christ, not just on our _doing_.

Robert D. Duggan[55]

256 ◆ BIBLIOGRAPHY ON THE RITE OF CHRISTIAN INITIATION OF ADULTS

Albertus, Karen. _Come and See: An RCIA Process Based on the Lectionary Using Catholic Updates._ Cincinnati, Ohio: St. Anthony Messenger Press, 1987.

Anderson, William Angor. _RCIA: A Total Parish Process: How to Implement the RCIA in Your Parish._ Dubuque, Ia.: Wm. C. Brown, 1986.

———. _Journeying through the RCIA._ Dubuque, Ia.: Wm. C. Brown, 1984.

Barbernitz, Patricia. _RCIA: The Rite of Christian Initiation of Adults: What it Is, How It Works._ Liguori, Mo.: Liguori Publications, 1983.

DeGidio, Sandra. _RCIA: The Rites Revisited._ Minneapolis: Winston Press, 1984.

Duggan, Robert D., ed. _Conversion and the Catechumenate._ New York: Paulist Press, 1984.

Dunning, James B. _New Wine, New Wineskins: Exploring the RCIA._ New York: W. H. Sadler, 1981.

Ellebracht, Mary Pierre. *The Easter Passage: The RCIA Experience.* Minneapolis: Winston Press, 1984.

Hixon, Barbara. *RCIA Ministry: An Adventure into Mayhem and Mystery.* San Jose, Calif.: Resource Publications, 1989.

Jackson, Pamela E. J. *Journeybread for the Shadowlands: The Readings for the Rites of the Catechumenate, RCIA.* Collegeville, Minn.: Liturgical Press, 1993.

Mick, Lawrence E. *RCIA: Renewing the Church as an Initiating Assembly.* Collegeville, Minn.: Liturgical Press, 1989.

Morris, Thomas H. *The RCIA: Transforming the Church: A Resource for Pastoral Implementation.* New York: Paulist Press, 1989.

Parker, James V. *Food for the Journey: Exploring Scripture for Catechesis in the RCIA.* Notre Dame, Ind.: Ave Maria Press, 1989.

Powell, Karen Hinman, and Joseph P. Sinwell. *Breaking Open the Word of God: Resources for Using the Lectionary for Catechesis in the RCIA Cycle B.* New York: Paulist Press, 1987.

Rite of Christian Initiation of Adults: Complete Text of the Rite Together with Additional Rites Approved for Use in the Dioceses of the United States of America. Chicago: Liturgy Training Publications, 1988.

Timmons, Gary. *Welcome: An Adult Education Program Based on the RCIA.* New York: Paulist Press, 1982.

Wilde, James A. *Commentaries: Rite of Christian Initiation of Adults.* Chicago: Liturgy Training Publications, 1985.

PART FOUR

Worship and the Church's Mission to the World

As the church gathers for worship, its attention is directed not only toward God and the needs of the worshiping community, but also toward the world that God has made and is redeeming. The church at worship is constantly reminding itself of the needs of the world so that it may pray for them. It is sensing the presence of those estranged from the community so that it may welcome them. It is searching for seekers so that it may proclaim the gospel to them. Through the church, God ministers to the needs of a broken world. In worship, the church offers those needs to God in prayer and seeks to meet them through hospitality, proclamation, and celebration.

This link between the worship of the church and life of the world is perhaps the least explored and most often misunderstood dimension of worship. Neglect of this link turns the church in on itself and aborts the very purpose for which the church exists. Simplistic conceptions of this link reduce worship to nothing more than a form of evangelization. This reduces the church's prayer, praise, proclamation, and celebration of God's work in Christ to nothing more than a means to the end of having a numerically large assembly. The following chapters intend to challenge readers to avoid these errors in favor of a grand, Spirit-filled vision for the role of the church in the world. Not every question can be exhaustively answered in the selections that follow. But the questions that are raised provide a rich and challenging agenda for any denomination, congregation, or group of worshipers who seek to invigorate their ministry to the part of the world in which they live.

❧ FOURTEEN ❧

Worship and Hospitality

An important, if neglected, symbol of Christian worship is the simple act of gathering for worship. In the act of coming together, the church testifies that it is a community that has come together in Jesus' name. Significantly, the worshiping community is not a closed community. Strangers are always welcome. Seekers are always sought. In receiving and welcoming strangers, the worshiping community both ministers to them and further testifies to the nature of Christ's love for the world. This suggests that the ministry of hospitality offered as the church gathers for worship is no mere formality, but an essential action for all God's people. This chapter explores some of the many ways in which worshipers offer hospitality to all who have gathered.

257 ◆ A THEOLOGY OF WORSHIP AND HOSPITALITY

Worship is the symbolic expression of the Christian faith. As the church gathers for worship it provides a picture of the body of Christ. The ministry of hospitality offered as the church gathers for worship communicates the reality of fellowship in Christ and welcomes the stranger into the body.

What we as Christians practice on Sunday, we live on Monday. And one thing we practice on Sunday is hospitality. In order to understand liturgical hospitality more clearly, we must first understand what hospitality itself is and then review what exactly liturgy does.

Hospitality is a set of formal, public behaviors designed to advance the common good by making the others around us feel comfortable and welcome. These behaviors do not seek long-term or lasting friendships in the first instance. They make demands upon us and others only for the duration of the event in question and not beyond. Yet it may be that through these behaviors, we may experience God's presence.

That, of course, is exactly why people come to church in the first place—to gain an experience of God. They are on a quest to discover what it is that seems to be missing from their lives. Ultimately, what they are looking for is God. Their

experience of God may be expressed in words like *community, prayer, fellowship, devotion,* or even *obligation.* But by whatever name, the divine One is the object of their search. It is through the practice of hospitable behaviors that we help each other and the strangers among us to experience God.

What happens to those who are unsuccessful in their search? They look somewhere else. They look to false gods. Money, drugs, alcohol, or sex might all, for a time, fill the gap the searchers long to bridge. For a short time, the searchers feel better. They find temporary fulfillment and even peace. But soon the contentment wears thin and the search begins again, often leading to despair and hopelessness.

What is our role as Christians in the face of this reality? First, of course, we must recognize it. We must make ourselves aware that every Sunday there is a searcher in our midst. There is someone who has come to our assembly to see what gives us strength and spurs us on. For some, this may be the last effort, the final attempt to make sense of it all and find meaning in life—a last-ditch effort to reach out and connect with God. There is somebody like that in your parish and mine every week.

In order to reach out to that person, we must be fully conscious of our own faith experience. Is our faith something we take for granted, or is it a living expression of our belief and being? How do we name and express our faith? How can we "show" our faith to the searchers and hand it on?

The fullest and clearest expression of faith for Christians is the gathered body, celebrating on the Lord's Day. At least it should be. The worship can and should be a solid bridge. It is a bridge to God. It is a bridge that spans the gap we all feel. It is a bridge to the promised land, the heavenly banquet, the Father's house.

What Does Worship Do?

Worship is made up of a complex set of symbols that interact to provide a metaphorical picture of an indescribable God. St. Paul says that it is like seeing through a dark glass. The whole liturgy depends upon the use of symbols.

A symbol is a thing that points to reality that is larger than itself. For example, our wedding rings are a symbol of our love for each other. Our love is not contained in the rings; and yet they are somehow a real part of the complex reality we refer to as our marriage. They give evidence to our love and point to it.

The more complex the reality that is to be symbolized, the more complex the symbol must be. It does not have one, clear meaning, but several competing and even contradictory meanings. Think of water as a symbol for baptism. How many different experiences of water could be named by those gathered for the initiation?

By contrast, a stop sign is not a symbol. It is flat and literal. It has one clear meaning. It is efficient because there is never any doubt about the intent of a stop sign.

Symbols are inefficient. We have to take time to wrestle with them and sort them out. We get into trouble when we try to make our worship symbols efficient because the result is to flatten out the meaning. This is exactly what we have done with the bread, we use for Communion. Real bread produces crumbs; and it can't be stored in the tabernacle for long. It takes too much time to tear; and some people don't like the taste of it. It does not lend itself to being placed on another person's tongue. So we settle for a flattened out wafer that is not at all complex and therefore masks the complexity of the feast.

We need strong symbols to describe God because of who God is. We will never be able to say fully who God is. But by using good symbols, with their ambiguous, intriguing qualities, we will come as close as human hands and hearts can come to describing the indescribable One.

In the liturgy, we take a number of symbols and orchestrate them into a ritual form (the form itself being symbolic) that is our fullest and most real expression of God. We should be able to answer the searchers who ask, "What do you believe and why do you believe it?" by taking them to church with us on Sunday. Sunday should be our greatest evangelistic tool. It should be our most complete expression of who we are as Christians. It should, in other words, be a model of hospitality.

That is because Christ is hospitality. Christ welcomes the stranger. Christ feeds the hungry and clothes the naked. Christ visits the sick and those in prison. Christ is the great reconciler. Christ is the great unifier. And on Sunday, we become and we are the body of Christ.

Hospitality in the Local Parish

The critical question each community must constantly ask itself is, "Are we doing all we can to be a hospitable parish? Are we doing all we can to be the body of Christ?

There are three basic things a church community must do to be able to answer yes to that question. The first two, we have discussed. First, our worship must focus on strong, rich symbols that express the complexity of our faith. We must stop minimizing and flattening the central symbols of the Eucharist. Secondly, we must understand and respect the liturgical structure that governs the use of these symbols. That is because the structure itself is symbolic and reveals the Holy One.

Third, we must understand the formal role of hospitality in the liturgy. There is a trend afoot to identify particular members of the assembly as hospitality ministers. Sometimes they are referred to as greeters. While this is a positive development, there is a negative side. To the extent that a community shirks its collective responsibility to be a community of justice while placing greeters at its doors on Sunday, hospitality ministry is a farce. It does no good to greet at the doors on Sunday, if it has no effect on our lives on Monday. Our Sunday hospitality is both real and symbolic (as is everything in liturgy). We give a sincere hello to those who come through the door. But our greeting is also a commitment to greet other strangers throughout the week. Our handshake is a commitment to reach out to the fringes of society to lend a helping hand. In finding a seat for our neighbor, we commit to finding room at our tables and in our hearts for those who have been shut out by the larger society.

The burden, then, that we lay upon the hospitality minister is the same burden Christ lays upon us. We are to love the Lord our God with all our heart, mind, and soul; and we are to love our neighbor as ourselves. The greeters at the doors and the ushers handing out the bulletins are none other than ourselves. And we are none other than the body of Christ, sent by the Spirit to bring about God's hospitable reign of justice and peace.

Nick Wagner and Peggy Lovrien[56]

258 ✦ WORSHIP SPACE AND HOSPITALITY

Written from a Protestant perspective with the evangelistic church in mind, the following article provides some challenging insights regarding how the very space we use for worship can aid the church's ministry of hospitality.

Winston Churchill once said that first we shape our buildings and then our buildings shape us. His observation may have been made with a view to the magnificent and ancient British parliamentary buildings, but it also applies to the church and its buildings. Once we build a building, we surrender a certain amount of leadership to it.

For centuries church building concentrated on worship space. Many of the buildings we worship in each Sunday reflect this emphasis: a rectangular sanctuary with row upon row of pews facing the front, which holds the pulpit. The entire building models the concept of worship as dialogue between God and the people. The pastor and the pulpit represent God; the pews and the worshipers represent the people. But often even the notion of dialogue is muted; and the sole emphasis is on teaching in a monologue format. The sanctuary looks like an old-fashioned classroom, with the pews arranged in straight rows in front of the teacher's lectern.

Planning for Hospitality

How does a congregation plan a building that offers hospitality?

The architecture of hospitality begins in the parking lot. Visitors won't feel welcome at a church that has barely enough parking places for its own members. So a church that wants to grow should offer plenty of parking and reserve five or six of its best spaces for visitors.

At the church entrance, prominent signs should direct worshipers to the nursery, restrooms, pastor's office, and sanctuary. The narthex should be roomy, perhaps featuring an attractive visitors' center where people can find out more about the church and denomination.

The nursery should be planned carefully, reflecting the church's awareness that today's parents are fussy about where they leave their children. The room or rooms should be clean, well lit, and very well-staffed. If possible, the nursery should have its own washroom facilities and changing area; it should be compartmentalized into two or three age groups. It's a good idea to have someone register the children each Sunday, paying special attention to visitors.

The worship place itself should be bright—

The Cross of Triumph. This small Latin cross resting upon a banded globe is also known as the cross of victory, the cross of conquest, and the cross triumphant.

pews or chairs arranged so people can see one another. Worship, after all, is a double dialogue; the people not only talk to God, but also to each other. The pews or rows of chairs should be relatively short; few people like to sit in the middle of a long row. Well-trained ushers should make sure worshipers are evenly distributed throughout the seating area.

It's also important that the space between the front row and the pulpit doesn't look like the Grand Canyon and that the platform is roomy enough to permit a variety of activities. Newer churches have begun using plexiglas pulpits in order to avoid making the pulpit a barrier between the minister and the people.

A church will want to ensure that everyone can hear the sung and spoken Word and that the leader can be heard from any place on the platform. Where the acoustics are inadequate, a congregation should consider, if possible, investing in a sophisticated sound system. A blank surface or screen is also a good investment—something that will enable the church to show films, display overhead transparencies, and project the words of hymns on transparencies or slides.

Choosing the Right Design

It's obvious from all the discussion and changing trends that church architecture is no longer a matter of drawing a rectangle and deciding whether classrooms should go on the main floor or in the basement. Churches often go through a lengthy process of deciding who they are and what God wants them to do. Building committees travel to various locations to see what other churches are doing.

Any committee that spends time examining newer trends in church architecture will discover some interesting and helpful information. For example, seating arrangements in newer churches are helped by the trend to fan-shaped sanctuaries. Each of these designs is said to promote intimacy, provide expandability, and contain cost.

Another surprising trend a building committee might uncover is the move away from traditional church buildings. Many newer churches are designed to resemble commercial buildings. Some congregations who don't own a building now choose to meet in leased warehouse space, instead of in the traditional school auditorium or gymnasium. Why? Because the warehouse meet-

ing space is more likely to attract the unchurched.

Anyone who is planning to build or remodel a church building should carefully consider not only these recent trends, but also the basic nature of their congregation. A church building should fit a congregation's concept of ministry. With a little imagination and foresight a building can be a powerful tool to inspire communal worship and a welcoming atmosphere.

Dirk Hart[57]

259 • THE WORSHIP USHER AND HOSPITALITY

Often overlooked, but of immense importance, are the contributions of ushers to the worshiping assembly. The ministry of ushers includes not only the supervision of the congregation's gathering and dispersing but also the modeling of a spirit of prayer.

Every art requires a special skill that gives it particular form and beauty, including the artistry called forth in the ministry of hospitality. All who come together in liturgy are invited to enhance the sense of belonging, but ushers have the unique ministry of creating a sense of a caring people who gather to pray. Ushers are usually the first liturgical ministers that the people meet as they enter into the sacred space to celebrate Eucharist. "When did we welcome you away from home? . . . I assure you, as often as you did it for one of these you did it for me" (Matt. 25:37-40).

From the beginning of a celebration to its closing, the usher extends a caring presence among the assembly. Ushers, as an integral part of the assembly, should always be in the main body of the church building unless needed elsewhere. They are models of participation through their attention to the readings, their sung responses, and their attitude of prayer and reverence throughout the liturgical experience.

For many years, our parishes have affirmed ushers as service ministers. Service continues to be an important characteristic of every minister of hospitality, but even more important is the quality of "being present" to the assembly. Indeed ushers are special "signs," not only of doing for people, but of taking time with those who gather. An important quality of ministers of hospitality is a sense of liturgical prayer that allows the minister to enter into the communal prayer and encourages others to do the same.

The second essential quality of this ministry is the gift of graciousness. Some personalities have a spontaneous outgoing sense of hosting, while in others this gift is sometimes latent and needs to be encouraged. Many who have been ushers for several years simply need to know what is expected of them. Their response will be generous and cordial.

Ushers may be men and women, parent and child, families, teenagers, disabled and able-bodied, and representatives of different ethnic cultures. Anyone who is gifted with a smile and a caring presence has the tremendous potential to be a minister of hospitality. Children, too, find the role of welcoming the assembly an excellent experience in hospitality.

Training programs, as well as renewal times, are as important for ministers of hospitality as for any of the liturgical ministries. Such a training session has the following segments. First, a basic understanding of the theology of worship as well as a deep appreciation of the Sunday Scriptures is essential.

Secondly, some historical perspective is very beneficial. In the Old Testament, we read of doorkeepers in the temple. Second Kings 22 speaks of these persons being sent to the high priest with the offerings. Second Chronicles 9 holds such persons as responsible members of the tribes and highly esteemed. In the New Testament, Paul urges the Corinthians to "let things be done decently and in order" (1 Cor. 14:40). Ushers could certainly resonate with this as they aid the particular movement of the assembly. In Acts 6, the community set aside certain people to give collected goods to the poor. With the influx of many people into Christian faith during the first centuries, several new ministries were established.

Beyond the theological-scriptural and the historic dimensions, ministers of hospitality appreciate knowing what expectations or responsibilities are theirs. They are to be at the church in plenty of time to have matters in order and thus be able to truly greet both regular and new people, assisting the handicapped and seating people in front.

Collecting the monetary offerings and enabling smooth flowing processions are among their many other practical responsibilities. At the close of a liturgy, the bulletins are given to the assembly (unless the order of worship is included in the bulletin) with a gracious smile or a word of sending forth. Just as an usher's responsibility begins well in advance of the liturgy, so it concludes only after the church building is cleaned after the celebration.

The artistry of hospitality does indeed shape the life of a church. Ushers, as ministers of hospitality, are men and women of faith whose attitudes will set the tone for prayer-filled worship. Ushers, who find their ministry to be an art, have the magnificent opportunity of welcoming the people gathered in Christ's name.

Jean Ackerman[58]

260 ✦ The Passing of the Peace and Hospitality

The simple gesture of greeting one's fellow worshiper in the name of Jesus paints a profound picture of the love of Christ and his church. It signals the commitment of each worshiper to each other and embodies reconciliation in the body of Christ. This article elaborates on the meaning of this simple ritual gesture and provides an example of how the thoughtful worshiper can approach every action in Christian liturgy.

Before the liturgy was reformed by the Second Vatican Council, Roman Catholic Christians used to kiss just about everything during a solemn Mass except each other. During a Mass at which the bishop presided (in preconciliar days), vestments were kissed as they were put on; the altar was kissed; the censer was kissed; the book was kissed; the cruets were kissed; the paten was kissed; and at Communion time, the prelate's ring was kissed as he delivered the bread to each communicant. But when it came to human beings, the so-called "kiss of peace" in the old liturgy was a push-away, at-arms-length gesture that resembled rather a ritual of rejection, than one of reconciliation.

Today, happily, the greeting of peace has been restored in a recognizably human form. People look one another in the eye, smile, embrace or shake hands, exchange a kiss on the cheek or a word of warmth and welcome. Sure, that moment in the liturgy gets a bit untidy sometimes; and there are always a few unruly worshipers who want to work the crowd by greeting everyone in the assembly. But by and large the greeting of peace has become a treasured part of Sunday's human face in our parishes.

If we as Christians pass for a moment from the level of simple observation to the level of meaning, we may find it a little more difficult to say exactly what the greeting of peace signifies. Is it simply a bit of "huggy-bear-kissy-face" that is tolerated in the liturgy because it promotes neighborliness? Is it (as some critics charge) a ritualization of middle-class values of "togetherness" and "membership in approved groups"? Has it been restored to the liturgy simply because it is an ancient and traditional gesture that responds to the gospel mandate to "go first and be reconciled" before laying gifts at the altar (Matt. 5:23-24)?

Before we suggest answers to questions about what the greeting of peace means, we need to remember a few things about liturgical ritual. Ritual, as Gabe Huck has written recently, "is the rehearsal of life," the embodiment in sound and gesture and all our arts of who we mean to be. Because they are rehearsals, rituals have more to do with "training for a way of life" than with fleeting moods or surface feelings.

As a ritual gesture, the greeting of peace is not so much about "how I (or you) feel," but about what we mean to and for each other in the assembly of faith. The greeting of peace does not invite us to engage in shallow conviviality—still less does it try to manipulate us into "feeling good" about being at worship or being in one another's presence. The sign of peace is a ritual sign that points to our shared meaning as God's agents of reconciliation in the world (2 Cor. 5:18). For Doris Donnelley states in these moving words:

> Reconciliation is God's dream for the world. It involves restoring broken relationships, healing our deepest wounds, and transforming hearts in the peace of Christ. Reconciliation cannot happen unless we come to terms with the alienation we experience with our divided selves, with each other, and even with God.

God's Dream for the World

Whenever we exchange the greeting of peace, therefore, we rehearse God's dream for the world. This dream of God's links each human to all others around a table where all are equally nourished and the presence of the "greatest" does not diminish the importance of the "least." This is the dream that dominated Jesus' religious experience, fueled his preaching, and prompted his scandalously "irregular" vision of a new human community. This community would be one in which mutual acceptance and shared values override competitive categories that divide people into haves and have-nots and so lead to rivalry, repression, hatred, and violence. Jesus' vision radically redefined the way humans relate to one another and to God. He torpedoed the notion that God has an ego that somehow competes (with whom?) for loyalty and attention—for strokes. In its place, Jesus proposed a God who is known and loved only in and as one's neighbor.

The consequences of such a view are revolutionary. Since God has no ego to be massaged, humans need no longer base their relationship with the divine and with one another on a basis of shame and guilt. Since God's love for the human family is absolute, and absolutely unconditional, we are free to experience and celebrate our lives as pure forgiveness. Here, forgiveness does not mean canceling a debt, or absolving a sin, but rather God's "giving forth," that is, God's self-bestowal, God's blessed arrival in the present moment of our lives. To experience life as forgiveness is to experience nothing less than God's own vitality and energy poured lavishly and passionately into our waiting hearts.

When we exchange the greeting of peace, we welcome one another into this world of unconditional acceptance and forgiveness. We invite one another to share God's dream of a world healed and reconciled.

The world dreamed by God is a world without weapons, walls, or wedges that drive us apart. In such a world, the call to love God becomes a call to enact justice, mercy, and charity for those "least ones" whom it is easy to despise or ignore. In such a world, God's power is experienced as empowerment for the down-and-out; and God's will becomes our willing good, our willing peace, to all who feel broken, bored, or burdened by life's arbitrariness.

Once again, our ritual act of greeting one another with the sign of peace is not a statement about how we feel, but a rehearsal of what we mean to be for each other.

Love That Is Vulnerable

There is yet a further dimension to the sign of peace we exchange in the liturgy. In welcoming one another to the world of God's dream, we also make ourselves vulnerable to others' needs. Our ritual sign is not an empty, idle gesture. It is our pledge to keep faith with one another, to _care_—actively and prayerfully—about one another. This is especially important in an era when the needs and concerns of other people are routinely dismissed as "not my problem." While it is true that each of us must accept responsibility for personal issues and choices, it is also true that in the Christian perspective, our hearts and our destinies are deeply interconnected in the being of God. As Quaker theologian Douglas Steere has noted, there is a "metaphysic of vulnerable love" that challenges us to take the risk of truly caring for another, of believing that "when we love someone in the presence of God, our prayer does make a difference and does lower that person's threshold to awareness of God's love and infinite caring."

Our exchanges of the greeting of peace means that we commit ourselves to "being there" for each other. The "willingness to assume the spiritual costs of entering into a measureless involvement in the caring for another," writes Steere, is a part of that costly grace to which we commit ourselves in the community of faith. "If someone wants your coat, give your cloak as well; if anyone forces you to go one mile, go two" (Matt. 5:40-41). In the Christian dispensation, our caring cannot be limited to words, even the holy words of liturgical prayer; it has to take flesh, blood, and bone in acts of service. For Steere notes:

> Apart from the psychical cost of this vulnerable involvement for others . . . [our caring] almost inevitably involves us in physical responsibilities for them, whether we meant to do that or not . . . this may consist of time for visits, gifts of food, books, letters, and often many forms of physical support. These simply go with the ticket. If you care enough, nothing will be held back.

So our exchange of the greeting of peace opens us to the demands of vulnerable love, renews our covenant of service for one another, and welcomes all into the world of God's dream for a reconciled humanity. When we open our arms and hearts to one another, holding nothing back, we rediscover the paradoxical truth that lies at the center of the Christian message: we can only keep what we are willing to give away; we can find ourselves only when we abandon ourselves for another's sake.

Nathan Mitchell[59]

Worship and Evangelism

The relationship between worship and evangelism is increasingly being rethought by American church leaders. Attempts to strengthen the church's witness to the world have led to new approaches in both evangelistic outreach and in worship. Through the Spirit's power, such developments may undoubtedly strengthen the life of the church, especially when they are rooted in careful study of the Scriptures. This chapter attempts to outline the scriptural and theological foundations of the important relationship between worship and evangelism. This provides an indispensable context for discussing the important relationship of these two vital ministries.

261 ♦ WORSHIP AND THE MISSION OF THE CHURCH

The act of Christian worship is itself a witness to the world. Particularly important is the Eucharist, or Lord's Supper, which proclaims the coming kingdom of God. This argument resists two extremes: the denial of the relationship between worship and mission on the one hand and the promotion of worship as merely an evangelistic service on the other. The following article is a detailed but persuasive presentation of this theological argument.

"The church has missionary power in direct proportion to its liturgical integrity." In this thesis Stanley Hauerwas proposes that liturgy and mission have a necessary and essential relationship. The mission of the church in its most comprehensive sense is explicit witness to the kingdom of God, to Jesus, the Christ, as its ultimate grounding and final consummation.

Such an understanding of mission includes calling persons to conversion, initiating them into the church. But calling, converting, initiating is not in itself the mission. Rather it serves the larger mission of the church, that is, to be witness to the kingdom of God.

Liturgy originally meant citizens exercising their responsibility for the corporate life of a Greek city-state. Translated into an ecclesial context, *liturgy* means the baptized people of God engaging in the repeated action through which the community receives and expresses its identity. The Eucharist alone is the appropriate Sunday liturgy of the community that believes Jesus is the Christ because the Eucharist is the celebration and foretaste of the kingdom of God. The absence of the Eucharist means that the community is functioning as the pre-eschatological people of God, as if the Christ had not yet come. To be the church is to confess that Jesus of Nazareth is the Christ. If the gathered community does not celebrate the Eucharist, it cannot be identified as the church, and therefore it cannot give the witness it is called to give.

The Eschatological Event of Jesus as the Christ

The fundamental confession of the apostolic Scriptures is deceptively simple: Jesus has been raised from the dead. Jesus is the Christ, the Messiah. These two statements are two ways of saying the same thing. The resurrection of Jesus from the dead is the starting point of Christian confession. "Jesus is the Christ, the Messiah," is its substance. Both are "eschatological" in character.

When the disciples encountered Jesus raised as the eschatological Messiah, ascended to the final future of the kingdom of God, present as the power of the future, they were required to re-envision the future and re-appropriate the past. The resurrection of Jesus meant that his claim to embody and inaugurate the kingdom of God was indeed valid. His death by execution on the cross was not repudiation of his ministry. It was rather a central expression of his ministry. His mission to renewal Israel, to gather its "lost sheep," and to open it to the Gentiles was, in fact, God's mission. His teaching was not blasphemy. It was rather the Word that effected what it announced. His signs pointed to the presence here and now of the kingdom of God. Taking up the cross was to be both the way and the consequence of discipleship. Hence the past was to be re-appropriated as the disciple communities retold the stories of Jesus with the "a-ha" of post-resurrection insight.

But even more radically, they were required to re-envision the future. The resurrection meant that Jesus has death behind him. "Death no longer has dominion over him" (Rom. 6:9, NRSV). The future belongs to him. He can make promises not conditioned by death. The kingdom of God, not the reign of death, will have the last word. This is what lead the church to the eventual confession that Jesus is God. For if "God" means whatever has the last word in history, then Jesus now defines and determines what the church means by God. He and the "Abba" (whose mission he embodied) and the Spirit (their "down payment" on the eschatolog-ical future [Eph. 1:14]), are now the "name" by which God is finally known.

Something decisive has happened to the world. The power of death and the power of sin, which depends upon the power of death, have been broken. The world is no longer the same. When it acts as if death still has the last word, it is acting in bad faith. All the powers of the "old age" operate on the basis of death. They measure power in terms of their ability to deal in and threaten death. We share in the reign of death, live under the "old age" and its bondage to sin, whenever we engage in self-defense, self-aggrandizement, or self-hatred.

We trust the kingdom of God whenever we live as if there were more to do with our lives than preserve them. To believe the resurrection of Jesus is to see through the powers of death, to recognize that they are passé, and therefore to be free of their domination. Hence the ultimate *martyria*, the ultimate witness, is the freedom to suffer death because one knows that death does not have the last word.

Jesus' mission was the renewal of Israel so that it could fulfill its function in the eschatological triumph of the kingdom of God. Israel was to be the focus for the gathering of the Gentiles. Jesus suffered the cross because of his mission to Israel and to its future for the Gentiles. Hence he died for, on behalf of, the world. But he did not die in order to found a new religious community. His death was not the repudiation of Israel. It was rather God's final total commitment to Israel.

The earliest disciples of Jesus simply announced to Israel that Jesus was and is the eschatological Messiah. The words of the prophet Joel interpret the Pentecost experience. But whereas Joel 2:28 simply says, "It shall come to pass *afterwards,*" Luke pointedly uses an eschatological formula:

> And in the last days it shall be, God declares, that I will pour out my Spirit upon all flesh, and your sons and your daughters shall prophesy, and your young men shall see visions, and your old men shall dream dreams; yea, and on my menservants and my maidservants in those days I will pour out my Spirit; and they shall prophesy. (Acts 2:17-18)

The gift of the Spirit to all flesh, and not just to chosen individuals, is a mark of the messianic age.

Paul, among others, drew the conclusion that if Jesus was and is the Messiah, if the messianic age has truly come, then Gentiles are to be gathered to the people of God. If Jesus is now "the Way," the Torah, then to be baptized into Jesus replaces both Torah (see Galatians) and the "old age" powers of death (see Colossians). Jews and Gentiles together witness by their being one people that the messianic age has begun (see Romans, Ephesians).

The significance of this for the assemblies of the apostolic communities now becomes clear. The development of the communal rituals can be reconstructed. The Jewish disciples of Jesus continued to participate in the life of the synagogue and in the rituals of the temple. Paul also goes first to the synagogue when he comes to a new city, and he continues his devotion to the temple in Jerusalem.

Simultaneously, however, the disciples of Jesus assembled in homes for that ritual which identified them uniquely: the messianic meal. We find both features in the same passage (Acts 2:42): "And day by day, attending the temple together and *breaking bread in their homes,* they partook of food with glad and generous hearts, praising God and having favor with all the people." Obviously, the majority of Jews did not believe that

Jesus was the Christ. But those who did were identified by the ritual Luke calls "the breaking of bread," a phrase which became a technical term for the Eucharist. This is significant because the meal was understood to be a characteristic of the messianic age. If Jesus was indeed the Messiah, and if the messianic age had begun, they would witness to and participate in this messianic event by being at the messianic banquet table.

Initially, then, the worship of Jesus' disciples was participation in the Scriptures, exposition, and prayers of the synagogue in common with all Jews; and participation in the messianic age inaugurated by Jesus through the common meal for those baptized into Jesus in private homes. By the end of the first century, the break between Jesus' disciples and other Jews became complete. Jesus' disciples were no longer admitted to the synagogue. The place once occupied by the regular meal in the assemblies of the disciples of Jesus was not filled by a synagogue-type ritual of Scripture and prayer. Justin Martyr describes the ritual in the mid-second century (Apology I, 67):

> On the day which is called Sun-day, all, whether they live in the town or in the country, gather in the same place. Then the Memoirs of the Apostles or the Writings of the Prophets are read for as long as time allows. When the reader has finished, the president speaks, exhorting us to live by these noble teachings. Then we rise all together and pray. Then, as we said earlier, when the prayer is finished, bread, wine and water are brought. The president then prays and gives thanks as well as he can. And all the people reply with the acclamation: Amen! After this the eucharists are distributed and shared out to everyone, and the deacons are sent to take them to those who are absent.

Behind this simple ritual structure and action lies a consistent self-understanding: Jesus is the eschatological Messiah. The messianic age has begun and will be consummated. Here and now the mission of the community is to bear witness both to what has happened and to what it anticipates. The messianic community is identified by the messianic banquet.

The Eucharist as Messianic (Eschatological) Banquet

Such an understanding of the Eucharist as the ritual which uniquely identifies the communities of Jesus' disciples has its roots deep in the Scriptures of Israel. The basic work on this has been done by Geoffrey Wainwright in _Eucharist and Eschatology_ (London: Epworth Press, 1971). After tracing the role of the meal in cultic life of Israel, Wainwright explores the linking of the meal and God's future salvation in the prophets of the Exile, Deutero-Isaiah, and Ezekiel. According to Isaiah the Lord will feed his people on their homeward journey through the desert (49:9ff) as he fed the people of old in the wilderness (48:21). The nations will come to Israel to share in the blessings of the everlasting covenant (55:1-13). Wainwright calls special attention to the passage in the late Isaianic apocalypse "which is of particular significance for the Eucharist; it speaks of a future feast for all peoples, in a context of the abolition of death and a day of salvation and rejoicing."

> On this mountain the Lord of hosts will make for all peoples a feast of fat things, a feast of wine on the lees, of fat things full of marrow, of wine on the lees well refined. And he will destroy on this mountain the covering that is cast over all peoples, the veil that is spread over all nations. He will swallow up death forever, and the Lord God will wipe away tears from all faces, and the reproach of his people he will take away from all the earth; for the lord has spoken. (Isa. 25:6-8)

Following the Exile, the meal motif in relation to messianic expectation intensifies. The age to come will be an age of plenty. The God who fed the people with manna in the wilderness will feed his people again (2 Baruch 29:8). Wainwright quotes the Midrash Rabbah: "Just as the former deliverer (Moses) made manna descend, so also the latter deliverer (the Messiah) will make manna descend." Strong eschatological and messianic expectations came to be attached to the Passover by the time of Jesus. According to the Ethiopian Enoch (62:13-16), "The righteous and elect shall be saved on that day, and with that Son of Man shall they eat and lie down and rise up for ever and ever."

It is evident why and how the meal plays such an important role in the teaching and activity of Jesus. The feeding of the multitude is the only incident besides Jesus' baptism and the Passion week narrative that is present in all four Gospels (Matt. 14:13-21; Mark 6:32-44; Luke 9:10-17; John

6:1-15; additional feedings of multitudes are found in Matt. 15:32-39 and Mark 8:1-10). In John the feeding is the occasion for explicit messianic reflection (John 6:15-59). Central to Jesus' activity is his table collegiality with sinners and outcasts (Luke 15:1-2), and the parables that follow conclude with feasting when the lost is found or restored to the family. Jesus' parables of the kingdom of God include meal settings (Matt. 22:1-14; Luke 14:16-24). Jesus' sayings pick up the eschatological expectations of Gentiles at the messianic banquet table (e.g., Matt. 8:11). In the last meal with his disciples before his execution, Jesus interprets the bread and cup in terms of his imminent death. But of equal importance, Jesus looks beyond his execution to the eschatological consummation. "I tell you I shall not drink again of this fruit of the vine until that day when I drink it new with you in my Father's kingdom" (Matt. 26:29 and parallels).

In Acts the apostolic communities assembled on the first day of the week (to which they gave an eschatological name, the "eighth day") and when they assembled, it was for the "breaking of bread." In the resurrection of Jesus the eschaton had begun. They were at the messianic banquet table. Through their participation in the meal they were identified by the Messiah as the messianic community, the eschatological people of God.

Paul addresses the Christian community at Corinth on the subject of the Lord's Supper with a noteworthy preface, "when you assemble *as church*" (1 Cor. 11:18). Groups could assemble to be many things, but the ritual of a group's assembly as church was the eschatological meal. The apostolic scolding that follows involves the way in which some Corinthian Christians were violating their identity as church, as an eschatological community, by what they were doing (or not doing) at the eschatological meal. The more affluent members of the community had refused to share the food and wine they brought for both the regular and eschatological meal with the poor. Their self-protective refusal meant that their meal was no longer "the Lord's Supper," and they could not be the church when they came together for such a distorted meal. They could just as well stay home and eat. By their action they were oppressing and humiliating others, and thus they denied their identity as eschatological community. By their inability to engage in self-offering they demonstrated that they were still in the grasp of the power of death. Hence Paul rehearses the tradition once again, that the kingdom of God is characterized by Jesus' self-offering, not by his self-protection. When they participate in the messianic meal they proclaim the Lord's *death* until he comes. They participate in Christ's self-offering by offering themselves to be his body for the world.

The Eucharist and the Mission of the Church

The church eventually lost the apostolic understanding of itself as eschatological community. Whenever the church does not understand itself as eschatological community it has historically assumed a consumer orientation. The Eucharist is then no longer eschatological meal but becomes consumer goods, couched in terms of the minimum required for maximum benefit. In the competitive denominational climate of the USA, the consumer orientation reached its zenith. The Lord's Supper was offered on the basis of the presumed need of the congregation. The result was that in both Protestantism and pre–Vatican II Catholicism the connection between church and Eschaton, Sunday and Eschaton, Eucharist and Eschaton was no longer understood. The insight of J. J. von Allmen is that Protestants falsify Sunday by not having the Eucharist every Sunday; Catholics falsify Sunday by having the Eucharist every day. When the eschatological character of church and day and liturgy were lost, the church lost the connection between liturgy and mission, and with it lost authentic understanding of its mission.

Recovery of the church's liturgical integrity means recovery of the church's identity as eschatological community. Recovery of the church's liturgical integrity means recovery of the church's authentic mission. That mission is witness to the kingdom of God as it is grounded in Jesus and as it will be consummated in the outcome of history.

The church witnesses to the kingdom of God by its being, by the way it is constituted at the eschatological table, by the way it takes responsibility for the liturgy. Because the coming of the reign of God is the breaking down of the "dividing wall of hostility" between Jew and non-Jew (Eph. 2:11-22), the community which gathers for the Eucharist pre-figures the eschatological unity of all humanity. Every evidence of discrimination against and/or oppression of those who are "one in Christ Jesus" (Gal. 3:28) compromises the church's witness. Concern for the visible unity of the church is a necessary dimension of the church's life (1 Cor. 1:10ff; 1 Cor. 12:12ff; Eph. 4:1-6; John 17:20-26, etc.)

Because this witness is the function of the community's very being in the world, the liturgy is fundamentally the celebration of the people. It is what the people come together to do because they are and understand themselves to be the eschatological people of God. They come together to rehearse the stories of God by which their communal identity is created and shaped. They come together to offer themselves (and time and possessions) into the service of the kingdom of God. They come together to participate in the eschatological meal that anticipates the final banquet of the Messiah and that therefore shapes their witness in the world. One of the functions of common responsories and public books for liturgy is to facilitate the people's ownership of the Sunday liturgy.

This understanding of the church as the eschatological people of God gathered to anticipate the eschatological banquets helps explain why the documents of the New Testament are utterly unconcerned about the identity of those who preside over the eucharistic celebrations. Although priests are among the disciples of Jesus (Acts 6:7), they do not function as priests in the liturgical gathering. There is evidence from the second century c.e. (_Didache_ 10:7) that itinerant prophets functioned as liturgical presidents along with presbyter-bishops.

That eucharistic presidency is now assigned to ordained clergy must not preempt the responsibility of the people of God for the celebration of the liturgy and therefore for the mission of the church. Thus it is significant that the leader is designated _president_. At the time of Justyn Martyr the president of the liturgical assembly is responsible for just two features of the rite: the sermon and the Great Thanksgiving.

If the being of the church is its witness, it is important that ordained leadership be open to all, specifically to men. The basis for this is most profoundly the church's identity as eschatological community. For in the eschatological community authority comes from the future, from the eschatological promise of the kingdom of God. As eschatological community the church offers hope and possibility to those who receive neither from the precedents of the past. That is central to the meaning of the Holy Spirit as eschatological gift. The Spirit is the "down payment" on the future (Eph. 1:14; 2 Cor. 1:22). The full participation of women in every dimension of the church's life is in our time one of the most eloquent signs of the church's witness to the kingdom of God.

The most important function assigned to the laity is prayer. Prayer in the Christian community does not mean finding the right words or fulfilling the condition through which we have a chance of getting whatever we request from a manipulated deity. Rather prayer in the name of Jesus identifies us as the messianic community and becomes the place where we work at the concrete implications of that identity for our life and mission.

The people of God have the responsibility of identifying their agenda. Prayers for the sick, the bereaved, those about to be married, and others seeking pastoral services emphasize that these are ministries of the community, not chaplaincy services of the clergy. Prayers for the whole church, the nations, and those in need will expand the vision beyond the parochial. Attention to the specific needs of other Christian communities, of synagogues, and of adherents of other religions will enable us to struggle with the ecumenical (universal) character of God's mission in the world.

Two aspects of Christian prayer must never be neglected. First, the eschatological gospel of the kingdom of God shapes and even changes our asking, our petitions, our struggle to discern the will of God as revealed in Jesus. Second, we become the agents and ministers of the kingdom of God individually and corporately in our vocations.

As a matter of course, the community's "business" will come to expression in the prayers of the people. Everything that the community does—stewardship, evangelization, ministries of care, social ministry, ecumenism, education— should and can originate in and be shaped by the Sunday liturgy. Of special significance for the relationship of liturgy and mission is the offertory prayer. The laity should set the table with the offertory prayer because they are placing _themselves_ on the table. Through baptism they are initiated into the community of the Messiah, the community which anticipates the final consummation of the kingdom of God.

The Eucharist is not a private tête à tête with God. To be part of the eschatological community at the banquet table of the present and future kingdom of God frees us for witness to the universal vision of peace with justice when every tongue confesses "that Jesus Christ is Lord, to the glory of God the Father (Phil.2:11)." We can receive our sending with the acclamation, "Thanks be to God." Whatever we ask, believing, in the name of Jesus, will be given. For what we ask in that name is nothing less than to participate in his mission.

"The church has missionary power in direct proportion to its liturgical integrity." If identity and mission are determined by the eucharistic liturgy of the gathered people of God, then time spent in teaching about, planning for, and doing the eucharistic liturgy is not time taken from other ministries that serve the mission of the church. It is rather time devoted to and determinative of all ministry and mission of the church.

Walter R. Bouman

262 ◆ THE RELATIONSHIP BETWEEN WORSHIP AND EVANGELISM

Worship and evangelism are vitally linked ministries; without one the other cannot thrive. This article describes the theological basis for this relationship, identifies issues which the church currently faces that relate to this problem, and then provides several suggestions for how this relationship can be cultivated in the local parish.

Evangelism in Protestantism has invariably been connected with worship and has taken place through the combination of preaching by ministers together with the people's invitation to others to experience God through participation in worship. Evangelism is integrally linked with the proclamation of the Word of God in preaching.

The originating setting of the proclamation may be a street corner, a schoolhouse, a tavern, or a home. But evangelists have as their aim and goal incorporating persons within worshiping congregations and bringing them to full participation in services of worship. Only in such a context and setting can the sermon have its fullest effect among hearers.

Theological Considerations

The Nature of God. The corporate worship of the church and the witness/outreach of the church have a common theological basis. Each derives from the nature of God as a sending God. God is a God who is always reaching out. God is never content to remain self-contained. Creation itself is an example of God's reaching out. The history of Israel sounds the constant theme of God's desire that all creation should acknowledge and give glory to the Creator. The life and teachings of Christ who is sent from God stress that those who hear and keep the gospel in turn are sent in to the world. The concept of a vocation to servanthood unites the Old and New Testaments on this theme.

The prophets saw the majesty of God propelling our witness to the very ends of the earth, that all nations might acclaim salvation (Isa. 52:10; 55:5). This outreach is a constant, especially with the later prophets.

This divine intent is clearly stated in Christ's high-priestly prayer. Jesus prays, "as you have sent me into the world, so I have sent them into the world . . . that the world may believe that you have sent me" (John 17:18, 21). This mutual sending is repeated again two verses later. It is repeated a third time in one of the resurrection appearances when Jesus breathed on the disciples and said, "Peace be with you. As the Father has sent me, so I send you" (John 20:21).

God's awesome majesty, so eloquently expressed in the Old Testament, is inextricably joined to Christ the Son, whom God sent. Linked in Christ's resurrection and glorification, the majesty of God and the exalted Christ are united. The result of this exaltation is the explosive witness of the gospel as it is recorded in Acts. The nature of a sending God is that every person in every nation should worship and adore the risen Christ, "so that at the name of Jesus, every knee should bend, in heaven and on earth and under the earth, and every tongue should confess that Jesus Christ is Lord, to the glory of God the Father" (Phil. 2:10-11, NRSV).

Paul said, "for to me, living is Christ." (Phil.

The Eastern Cross. *The upper arm of the Eastern cross represents the inscription placed over the head of Jesus. The lower, slanting arm represents the foot-rest. In contrast to most Catholic and Protestant churches, the Eastern church believes that Jesus was crucified with his feet side by side and not on top of each other.*

1:21, NRSV). To live in Christ is to participate in the very nature of God who is always reaching out and sending. The triune, sending God revealed in Jesus Christ is the source of all witness and mission, as well as the focus of worship. Both worship and witness derive from the nature of God and of Christ. A church that is not a sending church has not adequately seen God, and the worship of such a church is incomplete.

God sent Jesus Christ; then God sent the Spirit, and now God sends the church and every Christian out into the world. Through our worship every Sunday, God sends us into the world. In that way God continues to send Christ and to send the Spirit.

The Old Testament prophets stressed that the vocation of Israel was to servanthood and not to privilege. The suffering servant of Isaiah stressed this vocation. In that same vein, Jesus emphasized that he came to serve (i.e., to reach out to others and to draw them to himself). As it was in the Old

Testament and with Jesus in the New, so it is the vocation of the church to reach out to serve and by holding forth Christ, to draw the world to itself.

Our Chief End. A primary theological affirmation of Protestantism is signaled in the answer to the first question in the Westminster Shorter Catechism. Our chief end, it notes, is to glorify God and enjoy God forever. This is the chief end not only of the church. Rather, the glorification of God is the chief end of all humankind.

We seek to glorify God in worship and through our worship we are called to extend the glorification of God to all of life and to bring others to this same worshipful glorification of God. This is our witness and mission. Evangelism arises from worship and worship is the end result of evangelism. Each is maimed without the other. Each expresses itself and is fulfilled by the other.

Worship is always a prelude to witness, whether that witness be through evangelism or service in the social sphere. Conversely, such witness is, biblically speaking, a preparation, a new prelude, to the formal and corporate glorification of God that takes place in worship. The church moves from worship to witness, in order that through that witness, the world might be brought to glorify God and be brought to worship.

—— Issues in Evangelism and Worship ——

The Individual and the Corporate. The Scriptures convey a remarkable balance between the individual and the corporate. The "people of Israel" and the New Testament "church" provide the context within which individual commitment and faith are balanced within a corporate setting. The place where these two meet the most intensely is in corporate worship. It is in the worship of the body that the individual most frequently experiences God. God can also be experienced in a one-to-one relationship, but to assume that the one-to-one is the norm or rule would seem to misread Scripture.

There is a strain of Christianity arising out of Protestant pietism that defines worship as something that happens primarily or even solely between an individual and God. Thus viewed, worship is individual and inward. Within this view, conversion is most often viewed as individual and inward. In both worship and evangelism, God's action is equated with my individual conscious apprehension of it.

There is another strain within Protestantism that has defined worship as corporate, an action of the church in which we participate. Within this view evangelism and conversion are seen as taking place within the body, the community of Christ. Invitation is to Christ, into the body of Christ, that the body might be more complete and whole, both in its worship and its evangelism

Worship is the place where the body ordinarily tells its story, shares its experience and expresses its life. There God can best be experienced, and there one can best be led to join with the gathered throng in giving glory to God. It is there that the individual makes commitments which are according to the will of God.

Worship as Converting and Nurturing Center. Worship is the "intergenerational" activity of the church, where new Christians find their entry point into the body of Christ and where maturing Christians are nurtured in the faith. Worship is the context for long-term discipleship. Worship is the setting where the majority of Christians hear new calls from God, embark on new commitments, and enter more deeply into the Christian life. In worship the evangelizers are evangelized. In worship the invited guest (or the outsider) sees the vitality of the caring Christian community and accepts the invitation to enter into it.

Witness (evangelism), understood as the vocation of the church, is primarily concerned with the formation and establishment of the body of Christ within which God's will, both for worship and witness, is fulfilled. There conversion and individual salvation will be experienced as by-products of incorporation into Christ.

The goal of worship and preaching is to lead people so that they will find themselves as participants in the divine story of salvation, that they will come face to face, so to speak, with the God whom no one can face and remain the same. The goal of preaching is encounter. Preaching is only secondarily to convince, to present cogent arguments, to bring people to give their assent to Christian doctrine, and to solve exegetical problems.

Worship is to focus on God, and give glory to God. Evangelism too must focus on God and not point to ourselves or even to our church.

The Altar Call and the Table Call. The "altar call" is a part of the American vocabulary, a Protestant Christian phenomenon which originated in the revival movement(s) of the free churches. People raised in a portion of American Protestant religious culture assume that every evangelistic sermon ends with an altar call.

Some have suggested that an alternative to the altar call might be called the Table call. In worship we invite people to join us at the family table where we relate with one another and where we find our common nurture.

The concept of a Table call is integrally built into the regular Sunday worship of the church when both Word and sacrament are celebrated. The Word is read and proclaimed, and then in response, both by mature and by new persons within the assembly, an invitation to commitment is given, an invitation to come to the Table and to partake of the bread and the cup as a part of the body of believers.

The Table call is radically communal. It is ecclesial, set within the context of the family of believers. The call to the Table of the Lord is communal even if only two or three gather at the Table. It is a call to Christian discipleship, a call to total involvement in the worship and sacramental life of the church, and through such worship, to total life involvement in the world.

The altar call is radically individualistic. It focuses on the individual "getting right with God," repenting of sin, and consciously receiving salvation. Even if there is a congregation present, or even if there are thousands present at an evangelistic crusade, the altar call is a call to the person in his or her own individuality. It is often without integral reference to a congregation, though many crusade leaders seek to link a convert with a local congregation. It is often isolated from awareness of the social dimension of church life and of the ethical demands that extend beyond the personal.

The Table call is a call into fellowship as well as into ethical responsibility. Within the body of believers one has mutual duties of love, both within and beyond the fellowship of the church. As my sister or brother becomes a bearer of Christ to me, so the gospel imperative lays upon me the duty to be a bearer of Christ's reconciling love to every neighbor.

High Educational Standards and a Shortage of Ministers. From the earliest days of American Protestantism, congregations struggled with the problem of too few ministers and the lack of ministers to send to the frontier. At first, qualified ministers were "few" from parent denominations in Europe. Even after seminaries were established in this country, there were often shortages of pastors for existing churches, not to mention for service as evangelists. Churches that emphasized high educational standards for ministers were often the ones that failed to send evangelists into the frontier. Those denominations were not prepared to modify a dominantly cognitive criterion for the ministry of preaching and evangelizing.

Tension over the issue of educational standards remains in the church today. Some of the older Protestant denominations continue to believe that there should be more emphasis upon the classical theological disciplines, while others prefer to focus on a closer obedience to the call of the Holy Spirit and stress that more attention should be devoted to the development of the practical skills needed by pastors and evangelists.

The Future of Evangelism and Worship

Thus far we have focused on the relationship of evangelism and worship, and we have reviewed some related history and theology. In the light of these, we now look at possible future directions or emphases which would strengthen the church's worship and its evangelism.

First, of all, there is a remarkable similarity of emphasis and concern among those who are responsible for liturgical change in our denominations and those who are concerned about evangelistic outreach. There is agreement that a liturgical renewal in the congregation highlights and emphasizes evangelism. One of the steps for the future is to embrace and become fully familiar with the new worship and liturgical resources of the several denominations. Such a focus will unify the life and worship of the local congregation and the church's witness activity in reaching out to individuals, to society, and to the world.

Life and Worship of the Congregation. The life of the congregation itself has great significance, not only for the witness that occurs beyond its bounds, but for the conveying of faith from generation to generation within that congregation and for the nurturing of the faith of all members of the particular congregation. The following questions highlight the concerns which must be addressed in worship if that worship is to be an effective base for a local congregation's evangelism.

(1) Does our worship communicate and embody the presence of God? How might we more adequately express the awesomeness of the Almighty? the holiness? And how do we effectively draw people into the glorification of God?

Music is the vehicle of transcendence for most of our congregations. Are we a singing church? Does our music lead us beyond words, into what might be called ecstatic utterance? Are we using the hymnal to its best advantage?

Does our worship carry a mood of expectation? Do we come expecting to meet the eternal God, to be in the very presence of Jesus Christ? Does this anticipation of "meeting God" permeate the life of the congregation? Do our members understand that when they invite friends to church, they are inviting them to join them in such a meeting?

(2) Do we provide for the identification of our body of believers gathered for worship with believers throughout the whole world as well as with the hosts of heaven? Is there that dimension of "beyond time and beyond history" in our worship? Do we talk about the world? Do we utilize the materials available that link us in mission with the whole world? Do we open options to our people such as volunteering in mission programs? Are the eyes of the people always being lifted to farther and farther horizons, both in the church and in the world?

(3) Does our worship share the biblical witness in the most effective way possible? Is the Scripture lavishly read (or do we use small snippets) and are readers well prepared for the proclamation of the Word of God? Is the Scripture put into new parables, using contemporary terms and events?

There is a need for the cultivation and exercise of liberated imagination in bringing scriptural truth to the twentieth century mind. Above all, there is a need for increased biblical literacy among our people.

(4) Does our worship call for a real and tangible, acted-out response on the part of worshipers? (Or, does it only aim for assent and mental agreement with ideas, positions, and interpretations?) Does our worship allow for, or even encourage a variety of responses on the part of the people, as they survey their talents and gifts?

(5) Does our worship send people out as a continuation of Jesus' prayer and of his command to his disciples? Are worshipers made aware that the gospel, through Word and sacrament, is for them, so that through them it may be for others as well?

(6) Do we highlight and emphasize those portions of worship that have specific outreach implications?

For example, the Lord's Prayer includes at least three sections that refer to the outreach of the church. "Hallowed by your name" asks that God's name might be acknowledged by all, both within and outside the church. "Your kingdom come, your will be done, on earth as in heaven" is a prayer for the whole earth and for all that is in it. It assumes that the person praying is committed to the furtherance of that kingdom. "Give us today our daily bread" acknowledges that the bread is for all, and not only for those of us in this church or in our denomination.

In the act of praise, our adoration is caught up with the praise of all people, past, present, and future; and not only with all people, but with all creation. We need to be reminded that just as we are invited to join in this adoration, we too should continue to extend that invitation to others.

In our confession of sin we confess our failure to be a welcoming and accepting body, and pray that we may not judge, but that we might witness and converse in the name and for the sake of Christ.

At the time of the offering we should acknowledge that the gift of generosity is to be exercised for others, not only for ourselves. We give that we might be a blessing. We give as an indication of a commitment to keep on giving throughout the week.

The announcements about the life of the church should go beyond the life of the local congregation. While it is important to emphasize the fellowship of our congregation, it is important to announce also our linkage with the wider church and the world.

The charge and benediction should carry their weight in sending the people forth as ambassadors for Christ. The people are blessed as they depart in order that they, in turn, might be a blessing to others. They are sent in the name of a sending God who promises to be with us in our going out and our coming in, both now and forever.

Outreach to Society and to the World. There is a mounting awareness of the unity between out-reach in mission and evangelism and outreach through social services. There is a mounting concern for the witness of the church beyond its congregational domain. The church and its individual members must reach out in witness, in ministries of compassion, advocacy, peacemaking, reconciliation, and care for creation. It is the worship life (and program) of the congregation that must motivate and give impetus to this witness activity as the congregation reaches out to individuals, society, and the world.

The local congregation reaches out to individuals either directly or through representatives. Each Christian is sent and has the responsibility of inviting others to consider the claims and to accept the promises of Christ. "Come, see, go tell," is the mission of the Christian church. When two of John's disciples saw Jesus and asked where Jesus was staying, Jesus answered, "Come and see." The Samaritan woman at Jacob's well used the same admonition. The gentle Johannine interpretation of Jesus' invitation, "Follow me," has about it an air of simple friendliness, of mundane hospitality.

For us, "come and see" must be more than an invitation to come and see the machinery working, with leaders "doing their thing." Rather, the worshiping congregation must be marked by Spirit-filled living and must reach out and accept others.

Outreach to individuals may be delegated. We formerly called the delegates missionaries. In some cases they were called evangelists, those sent out to establish other congregations so that another part of God's creation might be brought to worship, hear the Word, receive the sacraments, and in turn be sent out to others.

The apostle Paul, writing to the Ephesians, intimates that not all have the gift of being an evangelist (Eph. 4:11). It is appropriate for delegation to take place, even within the local congregation as it reaches out to its surrounding community. It is most important, however, that the task of witness and outreach is being done in order that the purpose of the gospel might be fulfilled.

In conclusion, we return to the basic theological affirmation with which we began. Evangelism is more appropriately defined by its source and origin than by its objective. The nature of God, or Jesus Christ the Son, and of the Holy Spirit defines both worship and evangelism. And, evangelism and worship both have their proper place within the community of shared faith, the congregation. Both worship and evangelism are Christocentric, taking their shape and expression from God's self-revelation, Jesus Christ as a sending God. Evangelism and worship are both primarily concerned with a new heaven and a new earth, with the reign of God over all things and over all people and social orders. Evangelism is the outreach of God's love to all people, that drawn into Christ's body, they might acknowledge and worship the one from whom they come. Evangelism is the work of God, through Christ, in the power of the Holy Spirit, in bringing all things to their true purpose, which is to give God glory.

Arlo Duba

263 ✦ Worship and Evangelism in Nineteenth-Century Revivalism

In America, nineteenth-century revival movements forged a relationship between worship and evangelism that continues to be widely influential today, even in worship traditions not traditionally associated with revivalism. Understanding the history of this relationship provides a context in which its current influence can be appreciated and critiqued.

Throughout the early history of American Protestantism the Lord's Supper has been very much a part of revival movements. The emphasis upon experiential religion and conversion has gone through several stages, included in the Great Awakening of the eighteenth century and the Western Revivals of the nineteenth, climaxed by the Cane Ridge Meeting in 1801.

A Presbyterian Approach to Evangelism

Until midway through the nineteenth century American revivalism took place in the framework of the Presbyterianism brought to this country from Scotland and Ireland. From early in the Reformation Scottish churches developed a pattern of annual celebrations of the Lord's Supper in each congregation. These day-long events were preceded by several days of preparation in which people were instructed about the meaning of the sacrament and brought back into a reconciled re-

lationship with the church. Large numbers of people from both the immediate and surrounding communities were active participants. In the background of these sacramental seasons was the immensely popular but not prohibited feast of Corpus Christi, also a public festival honoring the Eucharist (see Leigh Eric Schmidt, _Holy Fairs: Scottish Communions and American Revivals in the Early Modern Period_ [Princeton: Princeton University Press, 1989]).

It was Presbyterian practice to seat people at tables for the Lord's Supper, during which time the Communion liturgy would take place. When large crowds attended, the tables would be set up in the church building so that the central sacramental act could take place there successively until all communicants had participated, with the celebration often extending into the evening hours. The entire congregation, communicant and otherwise, often several thousand strong, would remain outside where preaching services would continue throughout the day. It was advantageous to schedule the service on a Sunday near the full moon. Or they would break off the service at a convenient time and resume the following Sunday.

Moving to America

The tradition of annual sacramental seasons came to this country, spreading from the eastern settlements across the mountains into the Ohio Valley. Joseph Smith gives a romanticized account of Presbyterian beginnings west of the Alleghenies. The normal custom was for a minister to conduct the Eucharist annually in each of his two or three congregations. People from one church would go to neighboring congregations on Communion Sundays, thus enlarging the crowd and increasing their frequency of communicating. Thursday served as the day of preparation, with much preaching and an active process of reconciliation.

The Sunday celebration itself usually took place outside in a grove near the church, where large trees provided shade. A wooden covered platform called a tent was constructed, six or eight feet wide, ten or twelve feet long, and about four feet high. The space in front of this tent was reserved for the Communion tables, rough hewn logs at table height, with plank or log seats around them. At the central point of these tables, a table of more finished character held the Communion elements and was the place from which the Communion ceremony itself was conducted. On Communion Sundays the tables were "covered with snowy linen, all radiating from the large Communion table, containing the vessels of the sacred symbols, and all this covered with white napkins" (Joseph Smith, *Old Redstone: Historical Sketches of Western Presbyterianism* [Philadelphia, 1854], 154).

Smith describes seating for the full congregation, with a large block of log benches spread in front of the tent, and smaller sections on either side, also facing toward the tent. The drawing that he includes is evenly balanced, suggesting that these occasions were highly ritualized. We know from later studies that this tightly controlled environment and a tightly controlled set of activities were characteristic of the camp meetings throughout the rest of their history (see Dickson Bruce, *They All Cried Hallelujah: Plain-Folk Camp-Meeting Religion, 1800–1845* [Knoxville: University of Tennessee Press, 1974]).

The service began as the presiding minister in the tent offered prayer, the congregation all standing. They sang a psalm; another prayer was offered, and another psalm sung. Then came the sermon. Following these preparatory parts of the service, the Communion itself was administered to successive tables of worshipers.

Earlier revivals along the Atlantic seaboard, such as those led by the Tennent family, followed a similar pattern, and sermons from at least one of their sacramental seasons are extant. What makes the Kentucky Revival exceptional is that for a brief period of time these sacramental occasions became climaxes for the outpouring of the Holy Spirit. Even this phenomenon was not new, however, for earlier in Scotland a similar development had taken place. The greatest revival in Scottish history took place at Cambuslang in 1642. Here, as would later be at Cane Ridge, some 30,000 people were reported to have participated, and remarkable spiritual exercises took place.

James McGready and the Camp Meetings

This Kentucky version of this charismatic phenomenon began in churches pastored by Presbyterian James McGready in southern Kentucky and northern Tennessee. The major steps in traditional sacramental seasons took place in much

their usual way and the behavior of the people was serious and ordinary until the sacrament had been concluded. Then would come the thanksgiving service in the evening after a very long day. By now the emotional energies generated by several days of strong teaching and exhorting would be compressed to the highest pressure that the crowd could contain. All that was needed was for someone to pull the cork so that the power could explode. In the first of McGready's camp meetings, a visiting Methodist preacher did what none of the Presbyterians knew how to do. Sensing the power present in the crowd, he sprang to his feet, shouting out his message; and the night broke open with the cries of terror and exclamations of joy. From this point on until dismissal the next day, the Eucharist itself was forgotten as large numbers of people experienced directly and dramatically the very salvation which the Lord's Supper had portrayed.

Thus the spiritual exercises were God's way of applying to specific people the redemption that the Eucharist presented in a more general way. Or so one of those communicants concluded, young Barton W. Stone, who went back to his own Presbyterian churches in northern Kentucky. That August he presided over the Cane Ridge sacramental season. The more explosive the post-eucharistic awakenings, the more authentic the sacramental celebration was seen to be. Seeing God's Spirit at work convulsing sinners, who could doubt that in the bread and wine God had powerfully communicated Christ-crucified for the sins of the world?

Our knowledge of what was preached during these revivalistic celebrations of the Lord's Supper is limited; nor do we know what was prayed in the eucharistic prayers. A few sermons are extant, especially a group prepared by McGready himself. The central term in his eucharistic theology, as offered in these sermons, is meeting Christ. McGready states unequivocally that at the sacramental table Christians meet Christ. By this language he means that in the Eucharist there is a direct, sensible encounter with the fullness of Deity. In an "action sermon" he says" "every place where God and the believing soul hold communion . . . is solemn and dreadful; but as the sacrament of the supper is one of the most affecting institutions of heaven, and one of the nearest approaches to God that can be made on this side of eternity, and in which believers are permitted told intimate conversation with our blessed Jesus, we will particularly accommodate the subject to that occasion" (McGready, _Posthumous Works_, ed. James Smith [Louisville: W. Worsley, 1831], 175).

McGready stand in the center of the Anglo-American tradition in which covenant and discipline are the formative images. The Eucharist functions as the occasion for the exercise of the church's moral discipline in personal life and as the vehicle for the most intense awareness of union with the Holy. The heightened sense of discipline in McGready's system seems to have been the catalyst for the more intense experience of union with Christ.

In McGready, and also in Barton W. Stone, we look in vain for traditional catholic and Anglican ideas about eucharistic presence. The leading themes of Calvin's doctrine of union with Christ in heaven are also missing, but in their place is a vivid phenomenology of eucharistic life that makes these other theologies of the Eucharist seem lifeless and pale.

The Separation of Sacrament and Revival

It was not long, however, before this union of sacramental and revivalistic religion dissolved. A similar separation had already begun in Scotland near the end of the eighteenth century under the leadership of James Alexander Haldane, Robert Haldane, and Greville Ewing. Their "new measures" evangelism included itinerant preaching, done by laity rather than by ordained clergy alone, and the establishment of large tabernacles in cities where crowds of people would come to hear this stream of evangelical preaching.

These preachers were committed to reproducing biblical Christianity, which included baptism by immersion and frequent celebrations of the Lord's Supper. There was quite a variety, however, in the pace of development and the enthusiasm of their adoption of these new sacramental practices.

Although several generations of Presbyterian immigrants to the United States had been formed by the earlier Scottish practice, a new wave of immigrants were influenced by the new measures movement. Particularly interesting among this group of newcomers is the young Alexander Campbell, who soon took charge of the movement

which his father had initiated. Within two decades after the beginning of the Campbell movement, it had also absorbed much of the earlier movement initiated by Barton W. Stone. Although there is no evidence that Alexander Campbell had deliberately abandoned the earlier Scottish practice, with its emphasis upon sacramental seasons, it is clear that before immigration he had been greatly influenced by the new measures leaders. In its early years the Stone movement had sought to retain the older pattern; but around 1830 most Stone preachers and congregations gave in. The price they paid for amalgamation with the Campbell movement was the abandonment of the connection of Eucharist and revival.

Alexander Campbell and the New Formation that he led were eucharistic, but they emphasized the "every Lord's Day Lord's Supper" rather than the annual sacramental season. Thus they regularized the Eucharist, pulling it away from the explicitly revivalistic setting that had been so common in the Presbyterianism they had known.

Regular Presbyterians, who had been central figures in the sacramental seasons, soon recognized the tension between eucharistic piety and camp meeting spiritual exercises. Most of them decided that the two were contradictory and sought to redo their eucharistic patterns in order to rule out the kind of religious exercises that had emerged in the camp meeting.

The other side of this same development is the participation of Methodists. Not only did Methodists take the lead in turning sacramental seasons into camp meetings, but they also became the major preservers of the camp meeting format. Often the quarterly or annual conference was set up in the camp meeting format, which meant that the Lord's Supper would be administered. Yet Methodists were less interested in the sacramental aspect of the weekend and more interested in the revivalistic experience.

The Significance of the Relationship Between Eucharist and Conversion

The basic question to be considered is the significance of the relationship between Eucharist and conversion. Was the revival the result of the fact that great crowds of people came together to listen to preaching? Or was the revival the direct outcome of the fact that the crowd had come together to celebrate the Lord's Supper?

One support for an argument that Eucharist led to conversion is the fact that for a long time in the history of American Christianity, the Eucharist had been looked upon as a converting ordinance. The long and intense debate in eighteenth century New England between Solomon Stoddard and Increase Mather revolved around this very question. Mather represented orthodox Puritan doctrine when he insisted that only those who discerned the Lord's body, which meant that they had already experienced salvation, could come to the table without risking damnation. In contrast, Stoddard argued that the very nature of the Eucharist is evangelical and that it is given for the purpose of leading to conversion. He believed that everyone who was orthodox in theology and obedient to churchly canons of behavior could properly come to Communion. Then it would be God's own doing if these persons were to be converted and from time to time in Stoddard's ministry this converting experience took place.

My conclusion is that the sacramental setting was a strong contributor to the probability of conversion. Preachers in the Reformed tradition had regularly emphasized the importance of means in the conversion of sinners. Foremost among these means had been preaching that emphasized the terror of the law and the sure resolution that came from the gospel. Preaching during the sacramental seasons focused with special clarity upon the center of the Christian gospel, the death and saving work of Jesus.

This preaching would have been especially poignant and forceful since it emphasized sacrifice and the shedding of blood, the awesomeness of God, and the divine mercy, and provided a way of insisting upon the importance and the possibility of being saved. Then would come the eucharistic celebration itself in which this sermonic message was graphically expressed in strong and powerful symbolism. The combination of very clear exposition and strongly emotive liturgical form provided a strong intensification of the possibility of conversion.

This combination of Eucharist and conversion led to the relocation of the outward signs of divine presence. One of the religious questions that persists through the generations is: *How can we experience the direct presence of the Holy Spirit?* The traditional answer is that the Eucharist exists for the very purpose, the bread and wine being tangible signs of the presence of God. By contemplating these physical things, we come again into the presence of the Crucifixion and the other events surrounding the passion of Christ. By eating and drinking, we share in the very life of Christ that was given for the life of the world. Although our senses continue to experience bread and wine, the various theologies have asserted, our spirits experience the direct and true union with God revealed in Jesus Christ.

According to McGready's description of the revival, the question of tangible experience was important among his parishioners in Kentucky. They were formed by Calvinist theology, which insisted that God saved those whom God desires to save. Thus the long standing question remained: how do I know if I am one of the saved? Among people who believed in the objective power of sacraments, the answer had always been that baptism and reception of Eucharist in a worthy manner were the proofs that God had saved them. After the revivals were over, representatives of the Stone movement could argue that they did not need the spiritual exercises because they had already been baptized. Here is a clear indication of the mentality of the sacramentalists.

Yet the effect of the camp meetings was to shift the outward signs of divine presence away from the objectivity of baptism and Eucharist to the objectivity of physical and psychological experience. The people would know that they were saved when some power other than themselves took control and drove them to do things which could not be explained in any other way. I am not sure if McGready had intended this to happen, but finally the answer that he gave to his parishioners was: if the Spirit seizes you, drives you to do the remarkable things, totally transforms your emotional life, then you will know that you have been saved. This answer is clearly a precursor to later developments in American Protestantism in which the spiritual exercises are the decisive evidence of regeneration.

Another aspect of the significance that comes from this episode in American religious history is that it represents a shifting of the Godward focus from Christ to the Spirit. Classical Christian theology argues that God is revealed most fully in Jesus, whose life and teaching depict God's will and God's presence in a full and complete way.

By yielding ourselves to Christ, we enter into a full and complete relationship with God. Jesus promised the Spirit as a down payment for that inheritance in heaven that would someday come to all of us and as a comforter during the time when Jesus is physically absent. Thus, the Spirit would continue to make present the reality of God's self-revelation in Jesus. Clearly, the Eucharist in its classical texts maintains this point of view. It becomes the continuing power of the Christian life because of the full and complete identification of worshipers with Jesus. The Holy Spirit is an instrumentality that helps maintain the completeness of this union of Christian and Christ.

What seems to have happened in the camp meetings is that the union with Christ became the subsidiary element and possession by the Spirit became the dominant one. From that time on, at least in the churches shaped by the revival, the chief means whereby God is revealed to people today is the Spirit that transforms the psychological makeup of those who encounter the word.

Keith Watkins

264 ◆ Three Models for Evangelism through Worship

Manifest-presence evangelism, seeker-service evangelism, and liturgical evangelism are three ways in which those outside the church encounter, experience, and believe in God and are drawn into a vibrant community. These models are explained in the following article.

There is a story in the _Russian Primary Chronicle_ that tells how Christianity came to Russia. According to this true story, Vladimir, Prince of Kiev, sent several of his followers in search of "true religion."

First they went to the Moslem Bulgars of the Volga but returned with the report that they found "no joy" but only "a mournfulness and a great smell."

Next they went to Germany and Rome, where they found the worship more satisfactory but still lacking in power.

Finally they made a trip to Constantinople, where they visited the Church of the Holy Wisdom, and here they found what they were looking for.

They went home and reported to Vladimir,

We knew not whether we were in heaven or earth, for surely there is no such splendor or beauty anywhere upon earth. We cannot describe it to you: only this we know, that God dwells there among men, and that their service surpasses the worship of all other places. For we cannot forget that beauty. (Timothy Ware, The Orthodox Church [Harmondsworth, U.K.: Penguin, 1964], 269)

Evangelism through Worship

What these seekers experienced in Constantinople was _evangelism through worship._ In other words, the worship service they took part in allowed them to truly encounter, experience, and believe in God.

Many of us expect such evangelism to occur through our worship services. But does it? Do visitors to our worship services "know that God dwells there among" us? As we prepare for worship, we should keep before us four characteristics of worship that will evangelize those who gather with us.

First, we should recognize that _worship itself arises out of the gospel._ Worship is not primarily a classroom in which the Scripture is taught, an evangelistic service that preaches for decision, or a psychiatric couch that reaches to the needy. While true worship may accomplish all of this, real, authentic biblical worship is at its fundamental core a celebration of the living, dying, and rising of Christ in recognition that through this historical action the powers of evil have been dethroned and will ultimately be destroyed.

Second, we should understand that _worship that would evangelize must grow out of community._ The public celebration of the Christ event was never meant to be individualistic. God, through Christ, brought into being an _ekklesia,_ a fellowship of people who are the "people of the event." As people of the event, we now share a common experience that results in a new fabric of social relations. We embody the reality of the new creation as we live our lives out in authentic relationships of love, compassion, friendship, giving, and the like. Such a community has the magnetic power to draw people into faith in a subliminal way.

Third, we should know *worship that evangelizes needs to be aware that evangelism is a process.* Instant conversions do occur. But more often, conversion and subsequent growth in Christ is a journey that includes various stages of development and growth. Worship that truly celebrates God's saving deed in Jesus Christ in authentic community provides both the impetus and context in which the whole community is continually evangelized.

Finally, we should understand that *worship that brings people to Jesus recognizes the complexity of evangelism.* Because the gospel speaks to us as whole people, evangelism touches different aspects of the person. Ultimately, evangelism has to do with faith in Jesus as Lord, but people may need to come to that faith in different ways. Some may need their morals or values evangelized; others may need to experience the church as a Christian community; still others may need to encounter the reality of God. All these needs are addressed in a worship that celebrates the Christ event and applies the meaning of that event to the lives of the people.

Fortunately for those of us who wish to evangelize through worship, there are models worth examining. I will refer to three, and develop the third one in particular.

Manifest-Presence Evangelism

Manifest presence, our first model, may be described as the experience of being grasped by the overpowering presence of God in worship. Karen Howe writes of her experience of manifest presence in an Episcopal church:

> I became a Christian sitting in a pew, experiencing worship. It wasn't the sermon that did it. No one presented me with the plan of salvation or led me in a prayer of commitment (though that did come later). I simply basked in the presence of God as the worship service progressed around me, and when I left the church, I knew that God had entered my life. He was alive. I had encountered him. That day I was born again in my spirit.

Being "grasped by God" in worship may occur in many different ways. It may "happen" through the hospitality of the community, through the proclamation of the Word, through singing (God inhabiting the praises of the people), or through the presence of Christ in the bread and wine.

Seeker-Service Evangelism

A second model of evangelism through worship (or a kind of worship) is the seekers' service. This approach, pioneered by Willow Creek Community Church in South Barrington, Illinois (the second largest church in the U.S.), separates the seekers' service (designed for non-Christians) from believers' worship (designed for Christians). The seekers' service is held on Saturday night and Sunday morning, while believers' worship takes place midweek.

The seekers' service fits into an overall sevenfold strategy of mission at Willow Creek. In summary, the steps are as follows:

Every member should:
(1) take part in evangelism.
(2) be able to give a verbal witness.
(3) bring the person he/she is witnessing to the seekers' service.
(4) bring converts (after their conversion and baptism) to believers' worship.

Converts will then:
(5) attend a small group in which they can be discipled.
(6) discover their personal gifts and put them to work in the church.
(7) learn stewardship of money and life.

The seekers' service is designed as a nonthreatening service for secular people who, because a member of the church has entered into relationship with them, wish to be exposed more fully to the faith. It is not like a church service, although it contains elements of Christian worship.

The Willow Creek auditorium, where seekers' services are held, is more like a theater than a church. It contains no Christian symbols and provides a neutral context in which an unchurched person can feel comfortable and unassailed. Also, both the music and the message at seekers' services are subtle and deal generally rather than specifically with spiritual themes.

In a seekers' service I attended recently, for example, the theme was parenting: How do you raise children in a world full of turmoil and temptation? One of four points was, "Don't neglect the spiritual side of the child," but nothing specific was said about Jesus Christ. Witnessing about Christ and his work is rather the responsibility of the friend who brought the seeker.

Liturgical Evangelism

The third model of evangelism through worship is a third-century model that has been resurrected by the Roman Catholic church. Among Catholics it is called the Rites for the Christian Initiation of Adults (RCIA). I like to call it liturgical evangelism.

This kind of evangelism may be defined as follows: Liturgical evangelism calls a person into Christ and the church through a conversion regulated and ordered by worship. Services that span the church year order the inner experience of repentance from sin, faith in Christ, conversion of life, and entrance into the Christian community.

In the third-century church, evangelism was based on seven progressive steps that took place over a period of three years:

(1) Inquiry
(2) The Rite of Welcome
(3) The Catechumenate
(4) The Rite of Election
(5) The Period of Purification and Enlightenment
(6) The Rite of Initiation
(7) Mystagogue

Note that of the seven steps, four are periods or times for growth and development (inquiry, the catechumenate, the period of purification and enlightenment, mystagogue), while three are rites of passage (the rite of welcome, the rite of election, the rite of initiation). Each of these steps can be tied to a place in the church year in a very meaningful way—by Protestants as well as Catholics.

Inquiry. The point of beginning is Pentecost Sunday. On that day you may celebrate a special commissioning service for those in your community of faith who are called to the work of evangelism. These persons will now seek to fulfill their calling in a special way in the months of the season after Pentecost. They will invite friends and neighbors to church and will engage with them and possibly other members of the church or elders in discussions about the gospel and its meaning for their lives. During these months, some of these people will consider a deeper commitment. We can speak of them as "converting persons."

The Rite of Welcome. The next step, the first passage rite, is the rite of welcome, a ritual that is celebrated today on the first Sunday of Advent.

As part of this rite in the early church, the converting person renounced false gods, received the sign of the cross on the forehead, and was received into the church as a catechumen.

Similar symbols may be used today. Each church may develop symbols that express a renunciation of the old way of life and the embracing of the new life in Christ.

The Catechumenate. The catechumenate is the longest stage. In the early church it spanned two or three years, depending on how certain the church leaders were of the spiritual formation of the converting person.

During this stage the converting person is instructed in the Scripture, in prayer, and in holy living. Today this period of learning stretches from the first Sunday of Advent through the Epiphany season. Some churches extend it for another full year, but that is not typical.

The Rite of Election. Once the instruction of the catechetical period is complete, the converting persons gather in public worship for the second passage rite, the rite of election. This ritual takes place on the first Sunday of Lent.

In the ancient church and again today the primary symbol of this ritual is the dramatic moment in which the converting person, in response to a question such as "Do you choose the one who has chosen you?" will step forward, say yes, and then write his or her name in a book placed in front of the pulpit.

The Period of Purification and Enlightenment. This fifth stage, which occurs during Lent, is a time for intense spiritual preparation for baptism. It is a time to wrestle with the principalities and powers' that seek to control life.

In the ancient church the converting person came to the church for daily exorcisms during this stage. Today, a church may instead lay hands on the catechumens and pray for them in the struggles they have with the powers of evil that continue to knock on their door and bring temptation into their lives. In this way catechumens may learn that the Christian life is a life of struggle, a life that demands constant attention to the ways in which the church offers God's help in times of temptation or distress.

The Rite of Initiation. The sixth state is then the act of baptism itself. In the early church and again today, converting persons are baptized on Easter Sunday morning in the context of the great Paschal Vigil.

As part of the early church rite, those to be baptized renounced the powers of evil, received the baptism of water in the name of the triune God, were washed with oil, exchanged the kiss of peace, and for the first time celebrated the Lord's Supper with the faithful. Today the adaptation of these rites for the converting persons places special emphasis on the completion of one phase of the journey of faith and the beginning of another.

Mystagogue. The continuation of the converting person's lifelong experience of faith is expressed in the final stage, the period of *mystagogue,* an odd term that means "learning the mysteries." Today, as in the early church, the stage of mystagogue occurs during the fifty days of the Easter season.

In the early church's mystagogue, new converts were instructed in the meaning of the Eucharist and were incorporated into the full life of the church. Today, churches use this time to discern the new convert's gifts and to enroll the fully converted person into an active membership wherein his or her gifts are used in the life of the church.

While you may not have heard of liturgical evangelism, let me assure you that it is a form of evangelism used quite effectively by renewing Catholic churches around the world and by an increasing number of Protestant liturgical churches (especially the Episcopal church).

But a congregation does not have to be strictly liturgical to use this form of evangelism. Any church that celebrates the pilgrimage of the Christian year can use this form of evangelism effectively both for converting persons and for bringing new life into the present congregation. In this approach the whole church is aware of the process and can even be involved in a continual process of conversion ordered by the meaning of Advent, Christmas, Epiphany, Lent, Holy Week, Easter, and Pentecost.

——————— **Three Steps to Change** ———————

These three approaches to evangelism through worship demonstrate that there is no one way to do evangelism through worship. If your congregation is not engaged in any form of evangelism through worship, I suggest you take three steps.

First, discuss these three approaches to evangelism and decide which one is most suitable for your congregation.

Second, having chosen one or the other, study it. Read books. Attend a conference. Bring someone in who can present the approach to the entire congregation.

Finally, do it. You may find yourself faltering at first, but as you continue to experiment and perhaps fail, pick yourself up and try again. The approach will take shape in your congregation and will stimulate you to be an evangelizing community of worship.

Robert Webber[60]

265 • A Theological Critique of Church Growth Worship

Especially influential in the last generation of American church life has been the school of evangelistic strategies sometimes known by the term church growth strategies. In recent years, such strategies have increasingly shaped the worship of churches in many worship traditions. This article examines church growth worship from a theological perspective, evaluating both its strengths and weaknesses in light of both the history of Christian worship and present trends.

In the beginning of *Understanding Church Growth,* marketed as the "foundational church growth text," Donald McGavran says, "Those interested in liturgy find that church growth may say very little about their concerns" (*Understanding Church Growth,* 3d ed. [Grand Rapids: Eerdmans, 1990], 8). Indeed, McGavran, the father of the church growth movement, seems to show a liturgical conservatism in this book whenever he speaks of certain Christian ways of worshiping, which converts increasingly adopt. But these are only passing references. For the most part this book confirms McGavran's suggestion that church growth theory has little to say about liturgical concerns.

How wrong McGavran has proved to be! In the twenty plus years since church growth practitioners began to apply their theory to American churches, an explosion of interest in worship has occurred. Today an avalanche of books, seminars, newsletters, and video tapes greet the inquirer who wishes to explore how church growth evangelism relates to liturgy. Readily available are materials to explain how to increase the number of worship services, how to customize these services to meet the needs of a target audience, and even how to develop a new kind of service, the seekers' service, which is aimed specifically at the unchurched. In fact, church growth material has grown increasingly aggressive in talking about proper worship forms. Existing worship forms are frequently portrayed as being the main obstacle to evangelism and church growth. In light of the increasing influence that church growth theory is having on American worship, a closer look is appropriate. After defining the phenomenon, this article will investigate its benefits while raising appropriate questions. The goal is to provide a reappraisal of church growth worship which can distill its contributions yet avoid its pitfalls.

A Definition of Church Growth Worship

Although the term *church growth worship* is not used in the literature of the movement, such a phenomenon does exist. Church growth worship is made up of two discernable elements—one old and one new—that define this approach to worship.

The "old" aspect of this worship is a spirit of pragmatism that sees worship as a tool to achieve some explicit human end, usually moving people to some action or experience. Commonly this pragmatism includes considering all external elements of worship as open to change in order to achieve the desired goal. In this approach, "the test for worship is its effectiveness" (James F. White, *Protestant Worship: Traditions in Transition* [Westminster/John Knox Press, 1989], 177). This "old" aspect is not really that old: it was created in the American frontier early in the nineteenth century. It continues in the church growth approach to worship.

Specifically, the church growth approach to worship continues pragmatism's disdain for tradition. To do things the old way just because they are traditional is anathema for liturgical pragmatists. The desired goal is the all-important thing and to this greater concern everything is subservient. Sometimes this pragmatism will even call into question a liturgical biblicism, a common Protestant approach which tries to conform worship practices to biblical models. And so church growth worship has little need for liturgical tradition and liturgical biblicism. Instead a freedom is promoted to do whatever it takes to achieve the desired goal.

The "new" aspect to church growth worship is to define the desired goal of worship in numerical terms. Quantitative results have become the goal for the liturgical pragmatist. Often great emphasis is given to this standard. As one book notes, "authorities on church growth suggest that worship attendance is the most realistic evaluation of spiritual health for a church" (Joe A. Hardin and Ralph W. Mohney, *Vision 2000: Planning for Ministry into the Next Century* [Nashville: Discipleship Resources, 1991], 60). With this conviction, material on church growth worship characteristically will describe different things that can be done in order to stimulate attendance.

Church growth worship is characterized therefore by these two basic elements: (1) an underlying sense of pragmatism that sees liturgical particulars as having to contribute to the desired goal for worship and (2) a defining of this goal as increased numbers in attendance. Frequently, combining these two can lead to new images for the church, for instance, portraying the church as a business. In this new conceptual framework, explicit marketing terms explain how churches should approach worship. Prospective attendees are worship "shoppers." The church must tap into their consumer mentality and offer a variety of choices in worship. And the church must "package" its message appropriately in order for the gospel to be heard (cf. Timothy Wright, *A Community of Joy: How to Create Contemporary Worship* [Nashville: Abingdon Press, 1994].) While this business terminology is not necessarily found in all discussions of church growth worship, this language does reveal the two main characteristics of this approach. These characteristics, a pragmatic framework and a concern for increased numbers, define the phenomenon which can be called church sgrowth worship.

Helpful Contributions

The most important of church growth's contributions is to recognize a connection between worship and evangelism. This connection has been too easily lost in other concerns. For example, worship was often relegated to aesthetics.

Worship was an art form to be grouped together with other art forms. Liturgists were to discuss matters with musicians and other artists. The goal for worship was beauty. Too often the standard was whether the worship was as inspiring as a Mozart aria might be.

In contrast the church growth movement calls the church back to a fundamental work, proclaiming the salvation of God in Christ. And in this call the movement correctly reminds the church that worship and evangelism are interrelated aspects of this central task. Thus the movement helpfully suggests that the goals in worship and evangelism not be divorced.

In this way the movement provides its second contribution: reconsidering whether current worship properly fits contemporary culture or is out of step with the new ways in which American culture expresses itself. This concern is not foreign to liturgical specialists, who call the process through which worship becomes an unique expression of a particular culture by the name of *inculturation*. The church growth movement thus serves to remind the contemporary church not to become too complacent but to reconsider, for example, whether nineteenth-century gospel songs can still serve to express adequately twentieth-century faith. In particular, some church growth churches have made significant inroads in understanding what it means to attend a public, communal meeting today. Surely people's experiences of going to a public place like a mall do affect what they experience when they go to a church to attend worship. Other church growth advocates have helpful insights into the diversity of subcultures that exist within a larger racial or ethnic group. Rightly do they caution when they warn about worship where one size fits all. To remind the church of the goal and obligation of inculturation is the second contribution of the movement.

This concern for proper inculturation can create another benefit: providing a different set of criteria, other than the personal tastes of the worship planners, to make worship decisions. Even the best-intentioned planners can lapse into designing worship services which actually reflect their faith more than the congregation's. Often the result is worship designed to benefit the congregation by offering them something of substance but which is so foreign to the congrega-

Easter Cross. A white Latin cross with Easter lilies entwined around it is a symbol of the risen Lord and of Easter day.

tion that it cannot legitimately be called the common worship act of the church community. A church growth emphasis in worship would seem to be able to avoid this error by emphasizing culturally appropriate worship.

Questions and Shortcomings

Despite these positive contributions, church growth worship can have some negative consequences for American churches. Most of these problems come from its one-dimensional understanding of the church.

Ecclesiological Confusion. The specific theological difficulty is a confusion between the goal *for* the church and the goal *of* the church. The goal for the church in this world, evangelism, is made synonymous with the eschatological goal of the church as the community of redeemed humanity. Much church growth material seems to imply that the church fulfills itself as God's eschatological people when it is evangelizing with numerical success. A vision of a people redeemed by God, reconciled to God and to each other, pursuing justice, mercy, and other concerns of the kingdom (that is, a vision of the goal *of* the church) is often forgotten in the desire to achieve evangelism as the present goal for the church.

And since worship, in the biblical vision, is the

primary "work" of God's people in the eschaton, a second confusion then occurs between evangelism and worship. At best worship is considered the same thing as evangelism; at worst, worship is made subject to evangelism. What is not allowed is to recognize worship as a distinctive eschatological activity in which the church reveals its unique relationship to the kingdom of God. Thus the lack of reflection about worship's deeper nature is a symptom of a more fundamental flaw in the church growth material, a failure to define adequately the relationship of the church to the kingdom of God.

Because the centrality of the church is so important in the church growth material, this lack of clarity is surprising. On the one hand the material is specific about the importance of the church. Responsible membership in the church is considered a mark of conversion and salvation. The numerical increase of the church is a desirable goal to which limited resources should be shifted. Increased worship attendance is seen as an indication of a congregation's spiritual health. But the question not answered with respect to these goals is: _Why are these things desirable goals in themselves?_ The question would seem to cry out for some deep connection of the church to the kingdom, specifically, an understanding of the church as a manifestation of the kingdom of God. Outside of some positive connection between the two, this ecclesiocentrism is dangerous because it can make advancement of the church an end in itself. The danger is to incorrectly promote pragmatic success itself as the sole mark of the church.

Unrestrained Pragmatism. Indeed this danger is perceived by those within the movement. For example, a recent study of church growth ecclesiology notes the narrow—but common—connection made between the church and the kingdom: the church is an instrument for proclamation of the kingdom (Charles van Engen, _The Growth of the True Church_ [Amsterdam: Rodopi, 1981], 344). While this dimension of the relationship is true, it does not adequately describe the full relationship between the church and the kingdom. Without a more adequate description, as this same study notes, a "vicious circle" can be created in which "the true Church exists, apparently, to grow the Church which exists to grow more Church"

(Van Engen 479). The danger is in seeing numerical success as validating any means used to achieve growth.

Without the balance of a vision of the church as the eschatological community, this self-justifying pragmatism seems to recognize no limits. Even those things are negotiable which would seem fundamental to expressing the eschatological nature of the church, including certain traditional aspects of worship. For example, one book suggests decreasing or increasing the frequency of Communion depending upon what will increase attendance (Lyle Schaller, _44 Ways to Increase Church Attendance_ [Nashville: Abingdon Press, 1988], 75). Theoretically, one presumes, Communion should be eliminated entirely if doing so achieved greater numbers. And, theoretically, other traditional aspects of worship, like reading the Scripture and preaching, could be evaluated by the same criteria. In fact, one church in New Jersey has already developed a service which has eliminated sermons and sacraments in order to develop a popular, twenty-two-minute service (Associated Press article, February 12, 1994). However, if there is no preaching and no sacraments, should such meetings even be considered worship? Without theological criteria, how can one decide ultimately what is worship or, indeed, the church?

Thus pragmatic criteria, emphasizing numerical success, are not by themselves adequate guidelines for thinking about worship but must be balanced by some theological reflection about worship. The first step is to admit that the church is more than just an instrument to proclaim the kingdom but also is a manifestation of the kingdom in some way. The second step is to recognize worship's unique role in this relationship, specifically, to see worship as how the kingdom is most fully revealed in the church. This theology is consistent with the Bible, which portrays heavenly life by emphasizing worship. Thus worship has eschatological priority among the church's activities because it most uniquely expresses what it means to be a community of redeemed humanity. Simply put, to worship means to achieve something of the goal of the church, to become the community redeemed by God's grace and responding in love to God.

This understanding of worship's eschatological character points to certain defining elements for worship which is truly Christian and biblical. Worship that is true to the eschatological vision is God-centered and full of praise. Likewise worship should be full of remembrance of all that God has achieved in Christ. Worship that is biblical and eschatological is also communal, the common activity of the assembled church and not just of some who perform for the entertainment of others. And worship that is biblical emphasizes baptism and the Lord's Supper as key moments when the power of the kingdom most clearly intrudes into the present age.

Specific Problems. This fundamental flaw in church growth ecclesiology, the inability to define adequately the relationship of the church to the kingdom, leads to several specific problems. The first of these problems is that church growth worship often is not "catholic." When overly concerned with being attractive, worship may not properly represent the universal nature of the church. If a local church becomes mesmerized by making everything in its worship easily accessible, its worship may become too inculturated. This sort of worship never challenges or reminds the local church that it is called to be a local expression of the universal ("catholic") church. (Compare 1 Corinthians 1:2 where the local church is seen as a manifestation of the one church of God.) When this biblical approach is lost, the danger is for the local church to become too comfortable with merely expressing its own cultural distinctiveness, as some have noted with respect to church growth worship specifically (Frank C. Senn, *The Witness of the Worshiping Community* [New York: Paulist Press, 1993]) and with respect to church growth theory as a whole (Harvie M. Conn, "Looking for a Method: Backgrounds and Suggestions," in *Exploring Church Growth* [Grand Rapids: Eerdmans, 1983]).

Another specific charge against church growth worship is that sometimes its witness has ceased to be apostolic. An apostolic witness is, first of all, firmly rooted in the remembrance of the historical activity of God, particularly as accomplished in Christ's life, death, and resurrection. An apostolic witness is to proclaim that God's historical acts have both cosmic and individual implications. In contrast, because church growth worship is so focused on making its message relevant, it can tend toward packaging the gospel in

such a way as to focus only on individual struggles and needs. The worship shopper must become convinced that the gospel is instantly gratifying and relevant in order to want to return. Unfortunately, to pursue this approach can easily diminish the gospel into individualistic, ahistorical psychodrama.

Church growth worship advocates would respond that what is being changed is only the form for presenting the gospel and not the content itself (see Walter P. Kallestad, "Entertainment Evangelism," *The Lutheran* 3 (May 23, 1990): 17). Thus church growth worship is only using communication methods that are entertaining, making the gospel directly relevant to solving the needs and concerns of contemporary listeners.

However the response that only the form is being changed is incorrect. Form and content cannot be divorced from each other. To change form is to change content. To receive a beautiful card with handwritten expressions of love on a wedding anniversary is much different than walking by and seeing a note taped on the refrigerator which says, "Another year, feelings still the same." Similarly, the gospel's call to repentance and confession of sin will be heard much differently if it is given in a "fun" way. The gospel will effectively lose its content if always forced into an entertaining package.

Thus church growth worship has already changed the content by changing the form. Worship which seeks to be attractive as one of its basic characteristics is likely to become controlled by a desire to be of immediate service to the worship attendee. The danger is for worship to become human-centered rather than centered on God, thus leading to a subtle reimaging of God. Worship packaged to meet needs is likely to create a picture of God as a heavenly waiter, always eager to be of service when humans call. Such worship turns the traditional idea of who is being served in worship on its head. No longer does the church assemble to serve God in praise and thanksgiving; rather, the church assembles to be served by God.

Such worship appears untrue to the biblical vision if it is too concerned with immediate effects—particularly emotional or psychological effects—on the worshipers. In the Bible the church praises God not so much because the worshipers find it beneficial but precisely because God is worthy of the worship. For example, the songs of the heavenly host proclaim "You are worthy, our Lord and God" and "Worthy is the Lamb, who was slain" to receive praise (Rev. 4:11; 5:12). This heavenly host does not sing, "It makes us happy to praise you." The praise of God may indeed have that effect, along with others, on the individual worshiper. But that should not be the expressed aim of the worship service. The appropriate reason for the church to worship is the worthiness of God to receive praise for the mighty acts achieved in Jesus Christ. A worship service is sub-Christian and unbiblical if it devalues the praise of God and the declaration of God's acts of salvation as ends in themselves. Because church growth worship has another corner, convincing the worshiper that the worship is of benefit to them, church growth worship must be cautious to avoid being untrue to a biblical vision of worship.

Two unrelated concerns finish this critique of church growth worship. The first confronts the presumption that lies behind how some present the necessity for church growth practices. Often the message is that anyone who wants to be considered evangelical should be adopting these methods wholeheartedly. This approach is false, as history shows. Prior to the development of nineteenth-century liturgical pragmatism, evangelicals always approached worship with additional factors that modified any desire for "results." For example, John Wesley, one of the premier evangelists of the eighteenth century, always tempered his desire for vital worship with insights he gained from worship history. Wesley typically saw the tradition as providing the basic ideas and boundaries for recovering dynamic worship. Thus Wesley shows that a concern for worship tradition does not have to be at odds with successful evangelism.

A final note concerns whether church growth churches will be able to maintain the same degree of change in worship that is presently advocated. Can the present high level of change be maintained as time passes? To believe that it can indicates a ritual naiveté. Any one way of Christian worship, like other forms of ritual behavior, is soon endowed with meaning beyond surface appearance. As this generation experiences God's grace in church growth worship and begin to associate this form of worship with an experience of God, a new tradition will be formed, which itself will resist change. This process is what happened to the Salvation Army in the previous century. Experiencing tremendous growth in evangelism, the Salvation Army created many new forms of worship to achieve these ends. Today, however, the Army no longer seeks the same level of adaptation that characterized its first generation. Indeed it cannot, for its group identity is closely tied to its own distinct rituals. Will the same thing occur with the radical changes advocated by the church growth movement? Will present innovations be considered quaint in a hundred years? Given that possibility, a faithful church best chooses its worship not by immediate success, but by what enables it to reveal itself as God's redeemed people, humbly acknowledging the God who is worthy of praise.

Suggestions

Several suggestions can be made for future direction to both church growth and liturgical "types."

Church growth advocates should learn to distinguish between worship and evangelism. Reducing worship to evangelism actually distorts the nature of worship and perverts its formative power on the church, one of its most important functions.

Worship planners need to go beyond pragmatism and gain a touch of "cosmic" thinking. What must be revealed in worship is not merely our own small world but the presence of the kingdom of God in our world. The truths revealed must be cosmic ones, aiming at the heart of what it means to be human, to be creation, to be saved, to be the Savior, and to be the transcendent God. To reveal these deep truths will mean risking a worship that may be opaque to the unchurched, but that is a necessary risk. Otherwise worship cannot form the church by a vision of its eschatological goal and nature.

Thus worship planners should pay special attention to certain elements that are key witnesses to the kingdom. For example, sacraments should be performed in such a way as to bring the focus on the deep mysteries of Christ's death and resurrection instead of on merely individualistic or sentimental dimensions. Calendars are another good area for witnessing to the kingdom. Paying attention to the traditional Christian feasts, instead of marking secular and cultural holidays, can be a way of proclaiming with Christ that "the time has come—the kingdom of God is near" (Mark 1:15). Similarly churches should not be afraid to have key symbols adorn its worship space. The worshiping church should be a distinctive people with beliefs and rituals that define and form the community.

To distinguish between worship and evangelism should also mean a tightening of language concerning services designed for the unchurched and those for the churched. If a church has developed a seekers' service whose main aim is to evangelize, it should be honest enough not to call it worship. And this church should be intentional in trying to prepare people, once evangelized, to participate in a true worship service. (For an example, see Barbara Steward, ed. *Willow Creek Community Church: Church Leader's Handbook* [South Barrington, Ill., 1991].) The church's ministry to new converts should include training them to worship. Let evangelism lead to worship.

Perhaps the contribution of the church growth material is in providing innovate ways of evangelizing, whether it is in becoming aware of simple ways to make a church setting more hospitable or in developing brand new types of services.

Those interested in liturgy might do well to pay attention to these new forms of services, for they might help in avoiding a liturgical danger. As one liturgist has noted, a danger lurks in having a monolithic, ideal form for worship in that this one form may be unable to include appropriately the variety of people who gather for worship (Joseph Gelineau, *The Liturgy Today and Tomorrow* [New York: Paulist Press, 1978], 34ff). To accommodate this variety, perhaps more types of liturgical entrances and exits need to be provided. Some of the church growth ideas may be useful entrances and exits to provide the unchurched and the quasi-churched an appropriate place in the church. This possibility should not be overlooked since each week brings to the church people wanting to hear the gospel. It would be a shame, or worse, to miss the opportunity.

Lester Ruth

266 ✦ HOSPITALITY, WORSHIP, AND EVANGELISM

Many churches give little thought to including the visitor and the stranger in their worship services. Familiar habits and stale worship forms can unintentially leave the outsider feeling unwelcome. This article attempts to correct this oversight by pointing out the sociological necessity of making the worship service accessible to all who attend.

The way most congregations of the mainline churches treat strangers in public worship reminds me of the liberal couple in the Hepburn and Tracy movie, *Guess Who's Coming to Dinner?* They profess a commitment to welcome strangers but are shocked when strangers actually show up expecting hospitality.

In the movie, Tracy plays the editor of a newspaper that under his guidance has taken very liberal stands on racism. He and his wife, played by Hepburn, have identified themselves with the civil rights movement. They are in all respects the ideal liberal couple. All this is fine until their daughter brings home to dinner a young, black man, played by Sidney Poitier, whom she wants to marry. They are shocked. What they thought they supported became quite a different matter when the cause came home to dinner.

Like the liberal editor and his wife, many congregations of mainline churches profess that they welcome strangers but are inhospitable when the stranger comes to worship. They know that worship is the single most important ingredient for drawing people to join and remain active members in a congregation. They realize that they need to welcome strangers, so they try to be a warm, open family. Some of them believe they have achieved this model, but few do achieve it.

Many congregations' service folders often have a word of welcome; their ministers reiterate that welcome sometime during the service. They may even ask guests to wear special identification tags and introduce themselves in the service. Despite this warm and open familial self-image and their well-intended offers of welcome, the congregation remains inhospitable. They are both accidentally and intentionally inhospitable.

Precisely because they think of themselves as family, they do not focus on hospitality to the stranger. The same service bulletin that welcomes the stranger may give the stranger no indication when to sit or stand or who the worship leaders are. The bulletin is made with the family in mind and is as much a hindrance as a help in welcoming the stranger. Until the congregation understands itself in a more public sense, it will continue to exclude. Until it understands better the linkage between public worship and evangelism, it will continue to experience the persistent erosion of attendance at worship and smaller numbers of active members.

The key to turning this situation around lies in the congregation's attitude toward the stranger. This is especially true of the attitude of those who plan and lead worship. As long as the stranger is an anomaly in the imaginations of those who plan and participate in worship, such worship will continue to exclude and will diminish membership.

Realizing the essential importance of the stranger begins in the imagination. Those who plan and lead worship need to reserve a place for the stranger in their imaginations. The imagination is the human ability to connect the abstract with the concrete. This connection takes place through images. When worship planners and leaders include the stranger in their imaginations, the gospel has free course and the congregation is regenerated by Word and sacrament.

Why the Stranger Belongs

The stranger belongs in the planning and practice of public worship in every congregation for many good reasons. In this article I explore three.

The first reason is simply a matter of understanding the public character of public worship. If we understand what public worship is, then we will see that strangers belong in its planning and practice. Clarity about what constitutes a public also corrects attempts to turn Christian worship into private affairs.

The second reason follows directly from the biblical witness regarding the gospel and the status of the stranger in public worship. From this biblical witness certain basic theological principles follow. The God whom we worship created all things and is the host in our public worship; all are welcome in the house of this God. Furthermore, God is often present through the presence of a stranger. God both commands and attaches a promise to hospitality to the stranger.

The third reason follows from human need. In our society, most people seek to bridge the public and private dimensions of their lives. Through public worship these persons can participate through ritual in a shared, public expression of profound values. These rituals allow them to integrate their public and private lives without exposing themselves to a shaming situation.

Imagining Worship as Public

The first reason the stranger belongs in public worship follows from what a public is. According to social psychologist Richard Sennett, "the interaction of strangers through a common set of actions constitutes a public" (Richard Sennett, _The Fall of Public Man: On the Social Psychology of Capitalism_ [New York: Random House, 1978]). Where there is no space for strangers, there is no public. It follows that if worship is to be public, then strangers are characteristic of, not incidental to it (Sennett 48).

Sennett uses _stranger_ in two senses. One group of strangers, like Sidney Poitier in the movie, is clearly made up of outsiders. They may dress and speak differently; they may be of a different class or race. These strangers, the outsiders, are obviously marked as different.

Most people gathered in public worship in the church, however, are not such obvious outsiders. They remain, however, outside the intimate group that tends to make up the leadership in most congregations. This second group of strangers fits between the intimate and the outsider. They are the inside strangers who are the majority gathered on Sunday morning. If they desire to participate meaningfully in public worship, they face many, though not all, the obstacles the outside strangers face. These obstacles are the result of our deformed sense of public space, public psychology, and our public myth.

In contemporary America, public spaces, especially in urban setting, are thought to be cold, violent, and dangerous. As a result, we live in a society afraid of strangers. We rush through these spaces encased in bubbles of silence. When we stop someone on the street for directions, we say, "Excuse me," since we believe we have broken into their sacred, private bubble.

Both in overreaction to the sense of public space as cold and violent and in acquiescence to the intimate society, we imagine public worship in private categories. We sense how fearful we are of public space; however, instead of developing the skills and sense of public myth, space, and psychology that would allow us to enjoy the interaction of strangers, we deny and project (cf. Richard Palmer, _The Company of Strangers_ [New

York: Crossroad, 1985], 46–55; Sennet 222ff).

We deny that public worship is public space. We project upon it private imagery. We imagine worship to be a private, family affair. We believe that this private, warm, and open family feeling will welcome the stranger. However, it works only for a rare few who wish to make the effort to become part of the intimate group. Those who are willing to make this effort must find a door into the congregation. Since the dominant image is that of family, they must find a person in the family who will sponsor their membership. Often such "family" congregations have only one or two doors.

A primary door to membership in most family congregations is the pastor, who functions as a parental or sibling figure. The pastor visits the stranger and achieves an intimate relationship. The pastor then sponsors the stranger who becomes one of the family. The entire process is a private, one-on-one affair (for an alternative model of pastor as evangelist, read Richard Stoll Armstrong, *The Pastor-Evangelist in Worship* [Philadelphia: Westminster, 1986]).

The majority of strangers, both outside and inside strangers, opts out. Some may not like the personality of the doors. Some may believe that the pastor is too young to be a parental figure or has the wrong political opinions to function as a best friend or sibling.

In the end the image of the warm, open family excludes most of the strangers. At best it is a very inefficient method of sharing the gospel. It lessens the chance that we will readily be hospitable to the stranger or that we will exercise the skills to enjoy the interaction of strangers. It uncritically accepts the intimate society's sense of public space, psychology, and myth.

God as Host and Stranger

Christian worship is not a private matter. We gather publicly around Word and sacrament. Here God is the host and we, a company of strangers, depend upon God's hospitality.

This sense of public worship is not simply the result of Constantinian Christianity or the easy identification of Christ with culture. It follows from the biblical witness in which God commands hospitality to the stranger. God was often present through the presence of the stranger and in the interest of the stranger. God attached a promise to the presence of the stranger. (John Koenig, *New Testament Hospitality: Partnership with Strangers as Promise and Mission* [Philadelphia: Fortress, 1985] is my guide in this section of the article.)

The Lord appeared in the form of the three strangers to Sarah and Abraham by the oaks of Mamre (Gen. 18:1-15). We, the readers, are told by the narrator that the strangers are the Lord, but Abraham and Sarah do not know. Abraham greets the strangers, "My lord, if I have found favor in your sight, do not pass by your servant." He begs them to enjoy a meal and refresh themselves. During the meal, one of the strangers informs Abraham, "I will surely return to you in the spring, and Sarah your wife shall have a son." This promise began with hospitality to God who appeared in the guise of three strangers.

Hospitality to the stranger in Israel's witness went beyond the home to the temple. Solomon, in his prayer of dedication of the temple remembers the right of foreigners to enter the Lord's house and be heard (1 Kings 8:41-43). The temple was the Lord's house, and Israel, like the foreigner, was dependent upon the Lord's hospitality. Thus, Israel's worship was to be hospitable to the stranger because God commanded it.

According to Solomon's prayer, the openness to the foreigner has an underlying purpose: "in order that all the peoples of the earth may know thy name and fear thee, as do thy people Israel, and that they may know that this house which I have built is called by thy name." The temple is the Lord's house, not Solomon's. The place of the stranger is thereby guaranteed by the Lord's hospitality. The final purpose of the strangers' presence in worship is the revelation of God for all the peoples of the earth that they too might worship the Lord.

In the New Testament, Jesus and his disciples are often portrayed as strangers seeking hospitality. Furthermore, they need to be continuously hospitable, not only to those outside their group but also to each other, since they are so diverse. Often Jesus, as God present for and through the presence of the stranger, comes to a banquet as a guest but ends up being the host.

On the evening of the Resurrection, Jesus joins two disciples walking to a village named Emmaus. We are told, as in the Abraham and Sarah story, that the stranger is the Lord. The disciples do not recognize him. He asks them what's up, and they are astounded that he has not heard of the big events surrounding Jesus' death. In the ensuing conversation, Jesus explains the Scriptures to them. He shows why it was "necessary that the Christ should suffer these things and enter into his glory" (Luke 24:26). As they enter their home, and sit at their table, he blesses the bread and is revealed to them as the risen Lord.

This sense of hospitality to the stranger endured into the early church. Paul, along with other itinerant preachers of his time, depended upon the hospitality of people at synagogue services to share the gospel. When he saw inhospitality in the Corinthian congregation he vigorously attacked their Table fellowship habits.

Some members of the Corinthian community excluded others at the Lord's Table. They arrived early and partied hard before the others arrived after working until nightfall. According to New Testament scholar Gerd Theissen, 1 Corinthians suggests a liturgical structure that guaranteed hospitality to all who would participate in the Lord's Supper (Gerd Theissen, _The Social Setting of Pauline Christianity: Essays on Corinth_ [Philadelphia: Fortress, 1982]; see especially "Social Integration and Sacramental Activity: An Analysis of 1 Corinthians 11:17-34," 145–74). In short, the beginnings of Christian liturgy around the Lord's Table emphasized hospitality to the stranger.

Liturgy: Bridging the Public and Private

Some in the Corinthian congregation wanted to turn the eucharistic fellowship into a private affair, the Lord's Table into their table. They sought to domesticate what was and is essentially public. Paul's suggested liturgy prevented it—as should ours.

Whether intentional or not, Paul's suggested liturgical structure in 1 Corinthians guaranteed hospitality to those being marginalized and recognized an essential characteristic of ritual: it bridges the private and public dimensions of people's lives. This bridging is a common human need.

During my sabbatical we lived in a small farm village outside Tübingen in the Federal Republic of Germany. I sang in the church choir. The same people rehearsed every Monday night, and everyone greeted one another every time with handshakes all around. I was continually amazed at how

every encounter of this group brought about the same ritual. I noticed that this pattern was typical of most public interactions, although the younger generation of Germans were becoming more like Americans.

As an American, I at first experienced this handshaking all around as a silly formality, a quaint, stiff ritual. However, after a time I began to realize that, although I was a stranger in this very tightly knit community, this ritual demanded that I be included in the conversation. Through the handshaking I was ritually granted public space. (See also Raymond Firth, _Symbols: Public and Private_ [New York: Cornell University, 1973], esp. 176ff.)

When we turn our face to a stranger and extend a hand in welcome, we are through ritual—this physical repetition of a transgenerational sign—opening our private world to the public. The handshake is neither a sign of intimacy nor of belligerence; it is a public sign of good will.

The handshake structures our emotions at the encounter with the stranger, not on the basis of warm, open trust, but through a shared public interaction. It says, although I feel very ambivalent about this encounter—I am afraid and delighted, interested in conquering and worried about being conquered—I extend my hand and structure those ambivalent emotions in a sign of good will.

The effective use of ritual, then, can be an extremely effective way of bridging the private and public dimensions of our lives. It can also structure hospitality to the stranger into our worship. In short, ritual, which according to the intimate society is the enemy of healthy human interaction, is instead a key ingredient to good public worship. (For an excellent discussion of ritual in pastoral care, read Elaine Ramshaw, _Ritual and Pastoral Care_ [Philadelphia: Fortress, 1987].)

This is not to say that any ritual is appropriate. It is to say that, if we want effective public worship that leads to effective evangelism, the liturgy is potentially a key resource. It all depends on how we deploy our liturgical worship.

If our liturgical worship only heightens the sense of intimate, private space, it is very effective at excluding both inside and outside strangers. However, ritual deployed within a public sense of space, psychology, and myth, includes the stranger as an essential characteristic of worship.

It takes seriously the theological principles that follow from the biblical witness. It reaches out to the marginalized and includes them as fellow strangers in this company of strangers gathered around the Lord's Table in the Lord's house.

Finally, it is a matter of the imagination. Is it shaped by God's Word of command and promise regarding the stranger or by our denial of the possibility of a good and meaningful public life and our projection of the intimate and private onto our Christian worship?

Patrick Keifert[61]

267 ✦ BIBLIOGRAPHY ON WORSHIP AND EVANGELISM

Theological Perspective on Worship and Evangelism

Dale, Peter Ernest. *Send Us Out: A Study in Worship and Mission*. Bramcote, Nottingham, U.K.: Grove Books, 1974. An Anglican perspective on the relationship of liturgy and the mission of the church.

Davies, J. G. *Worship and Mission*. London: SCM Press, 1966. A classic text that describes how the church at worship both inspires and fulfills its mission in the world.

Keifert, Patrick R. *Welcoming the Stranger: A Public Theology of Worship and Evangelism*. Minneapolis: Fortress Press, 1992. An extended argument for revitalizing the church's ministry of hospitality that describes how the church's act of worship is inevitably a public act that demands attention of those outside the worshiping community.

Schmemann, Alexander. *For the Life of the World: Sacraments and Orthodoxy*. Crestwood, N.Y.: St. Vladimir's Seminary Press, 1973. An Eastern Orthodox approach to the relationship of sacramental life and the mission of the church that argues that sacramental integrity is one of the richest gifts that the church can offer the world.

Webber, Robert. *Liturgical Evangelism*. Harrisburg, Pa.: Morehouse Publishing, 1986, 1992. A work that describes a model for evangelism practiced in the early church that is being revived in many settings today.

——. *Celebrating Our Faith: Evangelism Through Worship*. San Francisco: Harper and Row, 1986. An essay on the growth of liturgical evangelism in the early church, with suggestions for how this model can be appropriated by churches today.

The Seeker Service and Contemporary Worship

Dobson, Ed. *Starting a Seeker Sensitive Service: How Traditional Churches Can Reach the Unchurched*. Grand Rapids: Zondervan, 1993. A description of how one church (Calvary Undenominational Church, Grand Rapids, Michigan) instituted a seekers' service ministry and how others can do the same.

Guinness, Os. *Dining with the Devil*. Grand Rapids: Baker, 1993. A critique of the church growth movement that calls into question the relationship of current worship and evangelism practices with patterns of thinking prevalent in secular, modern culture.

Pederson, Steve, ed. *Sunday Morning Live: A Collection of Drama Sketches*. 3 vols. Grand Rapids: Zondervan, 1992. Collections of drama sketches used in the seekers' service ministry of Willow Creek Community Church, South Barrington, Illinois.

Senn, Frank C. *The Witness of the Worshiping Community: Liturgy and the Practice of Evangelism*. New York: Paulist Press, 1993. A critique of church growth worship and seeker-sensitive approaches. Details many recent developments in contemporary worship that call the church to fulfill its mission in the world by offering worship that is faithful to the Scriptures and tradition of the church.

Willow Creek Community Church. *An Inside Look at the Willow Creek Worship Service: Show Me the Way* and *An Inside Look at the Willow Creek Worship Service: Building a New Community*. Grand Rapids: Zondervan, 1992. A description of the worship of one of the founding churches of the seeker-service evangelism paradigm.

Wright, Timothy. *A Community of Joy: How to Create Contemporary Worship*. Nashville: Abingdon Press, 1994. A practical handbook for developing a ministry of worship in the contemporary and seeker-sensitive worship tradition.

SIXTEEN

Worship and Evangelism: A Charismatic Approach

Bold witness to the person of Jesus Christ in the midst of the city is the type of evangelistic strategy that is the subject of this chapter. In recent years, charismatic Christians have reconsidered the role of corporate worship as a means to evangelism and have reintroduced marching and public demonstrations as a way to witness to the Christian faith. This chapter describes this strategy, observing the close connection between this strategy and worship.

268 ✦ WORSHIP EVANGELISM

The term worship evangelism *itself suggests that worship is one means of witnessing to Christ's love. This article describes a vision for Christian worship that has at its heart a love for the unbeliever and a deep desire to see them become a part of the body of Christ. By expressing worship in a cultural language that most unbelievers can understand, many may be brought into the church, while worship itself can be enriched.*

———— A New Paradigm for Worship ————

Take a look across the American worship landscape today. The variety of emphases, forms, and expressions is immediately apparent. From traditional, hymn-based worship to intensely personal expressions, the evangelical panorama is a study in contrast. Yet, even as we gaze, the picture is changing. As Robert Webber concludes, "a kind of cross-fertilization is occurring, and each tradition is borrowing from other traditions" (*Signs of Wonder: The Phenomenon of Convergence in Modern Liturgical and Charismatic Churches* [Nashville: Abbott Martyn, 1992], 55). Truly, these are landmark times for worship as our God-given creativity is being unleashed to bring God glory.

It is out of this creative ferment that a new paradigm of worship is being formed. As the walls separating worship traditions are now crumbling, the walls separating worship from life outside the sanctuary are falling as well. This is the principle of the new paradigm: that worship is, first and foremost, a life. It is a life that brings honor to God—a life fully given to God and God's purposes. And although it is a life weekly punctuated by the corporate events we typically call *worship,* true worship remains, predominantly, a life. As Paul states in Romans 12:1, "Therefore, I urge you, brothers, in view of God's mercy, to offer your bodies as living sacrifices, holy and pleasing to God—this is your spiritual act of worship."

Second, the new paradigm asserts that worship is a witness. Fully worshiping believers can not help but witness. If a Christian is truly functioning as a "living sacrifice" during the week in this narcissistic, disintegrating society, he or she will naturally be attracting positive curiosity from nonbelieving relatives, neighbors, co-workers, and acquaintances. This person's joy and readiness to meet needs will radiate the gospel. A New Testament passage describes this process:

> But thanks be to God, who always leads us in triumphant procession in Christ and through us spreads everywhere the fragrance of the knowledge of him. For we are to God the aroma of Christ among those who are being saved and those who are perishing. (2 Cor. 2:14-15)

Third, worship as witness applies also to the corporate event. In this environment, believers not only celebrate the saving work of Christ, they give a witness to the world of Christ's actual presence—the living Christ, inhabiting their praises. In Acts 16, we're given a picture of how God used Paul and Silas's worship to witness to criminals in a Philippian jail. "About midnight Paul and Silas were praying and singing hymns to God, and the other prisoners were listening to them" (v. 25).

Here were two innocent men, bleeding from beatings and chained to their cells. And they worshiped? No wonder the other prisoners were listening, instead of jeering. There was something amazing going on in that cell. These men worshiped with their lives and their lips; and the Christ they adored was present in their praise.

Today, when lost and dying people have turned a deaf ear to the church, what does it take to get them to listen? How can we recapture the interest of a cynical society? Some would say "a service just for seekers" or "more practical, up-to-date programs." Others might concentrate on a large, attractive facility as the solution. Worship itself would probably not even make the top ten. But consider the evangelistic potential of authentic, culturally relevant corporate worship, not revivals, not crusades (although God can and does use these special events in a mighty way). We're talking about week-to-week, Sunday-after-Sunday worship that witnesses.

Now, here's a taboo question, on what basis have we tacitly excluded the unbeliever from our corporate honor of Christ? Of course, we don't really slam doors in anyone's face! Yet, aside from perhaps a welcome and a perfunctory altar call at the end of the service, the unbeliever must usually endure fifty-five minutes of foreign language immersion. There are those five King James language praise choruses in the key of C. Or, how about that congregational prayer in Christian-ese, followed by special music titled, "I'm Clad in the Heavenly Garment"? We typically use 1 Corinthians 2:14 to justify subcultural ruts like these. "The man without the Spirit does not accept the things that come from the Spirit of God, for they are foolishness to him, and he cannot understand them, because they are spiritually discerned."

We reason that since an unbeliever can't understand what we're doing anyway, let's just do it like we've always done it. But, what do we do with Christ's own statement in John 6:44? "No one can come to me unless the Father who sent me draws him."

Surely this should lead us to concede that the Holy Spirit is at work in the unbeliever's heart before conversion takes place! If our argument is simply that an unbeliever cannot worship, Scripture would agree with us. In John 4:24, Jesus clearly defines the requirements of true worship— we must do so in Spirit and in truth. The seeker is still being drawn *to* the truth and, therefore, cannot worship *in* the truth. Nevertheless, by the Spirit of the God, who is drawing the unbeliever, the things of God are being revealed. The unbeliever in whom God is working is, therefore, capable of at least some spiritual understanding and discernment. Even Pharisee Nicodemus was able to discern, by the Holy Spirit, that Jesus had come from God (John 3:1-2). And this discernment preceded conversion!

We love to set the boundaries for God's plan. We are like the apostle Peter with the Gentiles in Acts 10—slow to get the message that God actually wants to extend God's work beyond ourselves. Isn't it just easier to solve this whole worship matter by establishing, once and for all, that the unbeliever simply does not have the capacity to appreciate worship? Such neat categories make it easier to maintain that status quo. Then we resemble Tom Sine's description of the church, driving "headlong into the future with our eyes fixed on our rearview mirrors" (*Wild Hope* [Dallas: Word Publishing, 1992], 4).

The seeker-service model, popularized by Willow Creek Community Church, has been a bold and innovative attempt to open church doors to the unbeliever. Yet, significantly, the doors that are opening are not doors to worship. Rather, they are doors to a presentation environment—an attractive, nonthreatening place in which unbelievers can investigate the claims of Christ, insulated from the religious activity called worship that they cannot understand or appreciate. This is a highly controlled atmosphere. No one in the theater seats will audibly participate or respond, except perhaps to join in one corporate song and offer applause. Gifted professionals and laypeople present the claims of Christ in multifaceted splendor. But worship is not one of those facets. Why? The customary explanation is that seekers and worship do not mix.

The new worship paradigm contends that unbelievers _can_ respond positively to a worship that has been made culturally accessible to them. It also proposes that unbelievers come to church, not primarily to investigate the "claims of Christ," but to investigate the "Christ in us." In our post-Christian, post-rationalistic society, the lost darken the church door because they are broken people, alerted by the Holy Spirit to their emptiness and helplessness. They are longing for the supernatural to break into their world and make them whole. As Webber says, "They are searching for an experience of mystery. They're asking, 'Will I experience God here? Do these people sitting around me have God in their lives?'" (Webber 23).

Apologetics and entertainment may work wonderfully to get the basic concept of the gospel across. But believers in heartfelt worship can present a three-dimensional model that entertainment and apologetics cannot: humans restored to their original purpose—glorifying and honoring God. Through the window of authentic worship, unbelievers can actually see believers responding to God's redemptive gift in Jesus Christ. They are moved by observing Christians in relationship to God and to each other. Most importantly, they experience God's presence as he "inhabits the praises of his people" (Ps. 22:3).

If it is difficult to imagine that worship could be this dynamic, perhaps it is because we've been predisposed by our own boundaries to accept subcultural, exclusive, and downright paltry worship as the norm. One of the many things the seeker model has done right is to raise the standards of what is an acceptable sacrifice to God. In fact, Bill Hybels' central plea to pastors, ministry leaders, and laypeople when they come to a Willow Creek conference is not "become like us." Rather, it is to give God their unmitigated best—to do "whatever it takes to reach the lost." Perhaps that is why this ministry has come the closest to "opening the doors" to unbelievers in our country. Its sheer commitment to excellence, service, and cultural relevance puts Willow Creek in a class by itself.

Yet, the question now surfacing in evangelical circles is this: _What would happen if local churches that are committed to evangelism applied this same intentional "elbow grease," this whatever-it-takes attitude, to worship?_ According to John Smith, Australian church leader and social analyst, "We've asked the unchurched to go through a painful cultural circumcision in order to become a Christian." Religion, he states, has traditionally been the "culture bearer" for society. He points out that, in most world communities, religion still contains the culture." ("Bringing the Gospel to a Secular World," Christian Artists Music Seminar taped lecture no. E43; 425 W. 115th Ave., Denver, CO 80234). That description was true of Christianity in the United States until roughly forty years ago. Now, American Christian culture is an anachronism in its own backyard. We simply won't admit it. Foreign missions would come to a screeching halt if we were to insist on the kind of ministry-without-translation we proliferate in our worship services.

Ephesians 3:20 tells us that God "is able to do immeasurably more than all we ask or imagine, according to God's power that is at work within us." An increasing number of Christians think it's time for us to let God out of the box. It's time to bring our worship to the marketplace of life. And it's time for whatever-it-takes worship celebrations that allow the living God to touch the lost. We've got some decisions to make if we're through with self-justification. It's time to get real.

A Blueprint for Change

How do you reach the unbeliever through corporate worship? The first step is to get clear about the principles governing worship that witnesses.

Principle 1: Worship that witnesses affirms the culture of unbelievers by speaking their artistic and verbal language and speaking it excellently. John Smith contends, "We must know where people are in order to meet them where they are." In other words, we need to make it our job to study the unbeliever's lifestyle and be informed about his or her reading, viewing, and listening habits. Smith draws upon Acts 17:16-34, where Paul witnessed to the Athenian philosophers. Smith stresses that Paul affirmed them culturally before sharing anything about Christ. "Paul was deeply wounded by their idolatry, but he said to them, 'Men of Athens, I see you are very religious.'" Then, after acknowledging what was right with their culture, Paul lovingly pointed out its deficits. When he did communicate the gospel, he did so, not in Hebrew jargon, but in straightforward Greek—phrased specifically for the philosophical mind.

Worship that witnesses dares to do what Paul

did, only in the context of worship. It dares to affirm unbelievers' culture by using their good "stuff"—their style of dress and music, their turn of a phrase, their distinctive pattern of celebration—and using it excellently to communicate the love of God in Christ. Whether we're in an urban African American, border-town Hispanic, middle-class Caucasian, or rural German environment, we can witness more effectively through worship if we first of all affirm the culture by using its unique "language" and, secondly, transcend it with the gospel. It's what Smith calls "enculturating the truth into the vernacular of a broken world."

Principle 2: Worship that witnesses is participative; it is the whole priesthood of believers, responding to God and giving a "living" testimony of their relationship with God. Some have argued that evangelism and worship can't mix because evangelism is directed toward people, while worship is directed toward God. If we were to follow this line of thinking, any worship that is evangelistically oriented could not be worship because it is not participative. Instead, evangelistic "worship" would have to be an essentially passive event, fixated on the unregenerate sinner and his or her need to accept Christ. It would be a revival or a crusade, not worship.

But isn't this picture of evangelism a bit narrow? According to such a definition, evangelism is mere verbal persuasion. But, in reality, evangelism happens any time believers live out their faith with specific honor to Christ! Worship that witnesses is worship, and it is definitely participative!

Principle 3: Worship that witnesses is worship whose substance is truth. True Christian worship is a "Romans 12:1-2 worship." It says to God, "God, I love you. I praise you for all that you are and for your great mercy to me through your Son. Cleanse me, transform me. Here I am, wholly available." In such a worship, the complete gospel of Christ—salvation, and the power of living a new life—is at the very center, not on the periphery somewhere or included simply as "atonement" in an altar call.

We often assume that, since believers have already accepted Christ, the gospel is irrelevant to worship. Of course, that assumption is dangerous, if for no other reason than it is probable there are some unbelievers in the crowd! But viewing the gospel as irrelevant to believers represents a

serious reduction of what the gospel actually is. Jesus "became obedient to death," not only to atone for our sins and reconcile us to God, but to *transform* our lives in the here and now. Look at the words of the apostle Paul, where he refers to Christians as "those *sanctified in Christ Jesus* and called to be holy" (1 Cor. 1:2). Look again at Hebrews, where the author tells us to "fix our eyes on Jesus, the author and *perfector* of our faith . . ." (Heb. 12:2). As Dallas Willard observes, "the message of Jesus himself and of the early disciples was not just one of forgiveness of sins, but rather was one of newness of life" (*The Spirit of the Disciplines* [San Francisco: Harper and Row, 1988], 36).

What does all this have to do with the "nuts and bolts" of worship evangelism? It has to do with everything—because religion itself never evangelized anybody. And, if Christ is not the focal point of our worship or our lives, that's all we have—religion. Lacking Christ, we most certainly lack a message. But, more tragically, we lack any authentic Christian witness. There is no power for newness of life without Christ. We have only our own meager little selves.

Think about the worship you're planning for this Sunday. Will Melinda's unsaved neighbor who's been dabbling in New Age practices be able to differentiate what your church believes from "one of many paths"? Will she know what to do with her sin after God's whole character is blessed, but God as the way, the truth, and the life is deleted? Or, think about young Joey, the crack addict. Will he be motivated to kick the habit by this week's riveting reiteration of pull-yourself-up-by-the-bootstraps morality, a sermon on "Developing Self-Control"? What about Don, the depressed co-worker Bill prayed about last week? Will he be encouraged by the anointed Communion with the Holy Spirit if there is not one mention of the loving, healing Redeemer by whom that Spirit was sent? Will he see any Christians doing a gut-level reality check with God, seeking forgiveness, cleansing, and renewal?

Romans 5:8 exclaims, "While we were sinners, Christ died for us." John 10:10 says, "I have come that they may have life, and that they may have it more abundantly." Love and life through Christ is the message that is going to make a difference in our lives and in the lives of unbelievers. This must be the substance of our worship if it is to be truly Christian. We must proclaim it but, more importantly, flesh it out by openly acknowledging that we can't give this love and life to ourselves—that we need God's forgiveness and supernatural, transforming power. Then we will be real, and unbelievers will want what we have. They will want Jesus Christ.

Some Guidelines for Worship Evangelism

Worship that is fluent in the vernacular of the people, participative, and Christ-infused—what in the world would it look like? New covenant substance would immediately give it a distinctive personality. But the remaining features of participation and cultural relevance would give it as many shapes and faces as there are worshiping communities. So, rather than dictate a specific format that could prove irrelevant in your situation, listed below are guidelines for establishing direction, flow, and cohesion within a variety of formats. Then, to demonstrate how the principles could work in a specific cultural context, there is a sample cultural profile of a baby boomer community, along with a "boomer music bank"—a listing of high-impact, complete gospel praise and worship songs, organized by the "MTC" formula, explained below.

(1) Think of worship as a "funnel" representing our picture of God moving from the general to the specific and our distance from God moving from great to small. Begin at the wide end with praise to God for the broad strokes of God's character (holiness, righteousness, omnipotence, etc.) and with responses that require the least amount of vulnerability.

(2) Start narrowing the funnel by shifting the praise and thanksgiving toward God's mercy in Christ. Then, narrow it even further into opportunities for personal, reflective response. The MTC formula makes this process easier to remember. It is:

M—Remember God's _Mercy_ given to us through Christ, by proclaiming the redemption message and by praising and thanking God for that gift.
T—Seek _Transformation_, by allowing ourselves to grieve about our sin and asking God to change us.
C—_Consecrate_ ourselves (set ourselves apart for God's use), by confessing our sin(s), repenting, receiving forgiveness, and committing to live obe-

dient lives. For the unbeliever, consecration begins at conversion.

The MTC pattern represents a natural progression of the convicted soul after encountering or reencountering God's unconditional love in Jesus Christ. Although this order is certainly not set in concrete, it helps to keep mercy near the front end so people know _why_ they need transformation and consecration. Also, remember that it's a long way from the church parking lot with five squabbling kids to vulnerability with God! In other words, prepare believers and unbelievers adequately for baring their souls to the Almighty!

You don't have to mention Christ or Jesus directly in every MTC element, nor should you leave God the Father and the Holy Spirit on the bench in your zeal to focus on the Son. However, since Christ is the "exact representation of his [God's] being . . . (Heb. 1:3)," Christ alone gives a complete picture of who God is. You just need to make sure you offer the 8-by-10 glossy instead of just the half-developed snapshot sometime before people move into personal consecration.

(3) Use both participative and presentational elements as you narrow the worship funnel. If you group songs or hymns together in medleys, plan their order so that there is a gradual narrowing of the funnel, even with medleys.

(4) Effective worship prepares worshipers to respond to what God has to say to them. Fuse the message to the rest of worship by preceding it with carefully chosen MTC elements that also focus, either directly or indirectly, on the message's theme. And since the message is really an extended call for transformation, it works well to place some expressions of personal consecration afterward.

Mercy, transformation, and consecration—these should be the very cornerstones of our daily relationship with God, but even more so, the foundations of how we worship when we're together. This is because something powerful happens when, with one voice, we agree about the truth of who God is, who we are, and how we are made whole. God diffuses the self-righteousness that separates us not only from God's self, but from the unbelievers around us. What a payoff!

Sally Morgenthaler[62]

269 ✦ EVANGELISM AND THE PRAISE MARCH

The March for Jesus has become a worldwide means of witnessing to the love of Christ. It intends to portray to the onlooking world the joy of offering praise to God. This article describes the March for Jesus and suggests how praise is essential to it.

The March for Jesus is not a protest, not a publicity stunt, not a program, not a public church service. It is the act of declaring Jesus Lord of all the earth under the wideness of the heavens and the perplexed glare of unbelievers. It is a way of seeing the city differently. The city is God's city. It is a way of welcoming the entire city to love God. It is a way that evangelism seems less a matter of selling fire insurance and much more an invitation to glory. It is a way of seeing whole cities filled with an increasing extravaganza of affectionate adoration, adorned by a sturdy obedience in all dimensions of life. And if whole cities are the scene of such a knowing of God, then why not whole peoples and nations? Ultimately, what can restrain at least some from *every* people and tongue from joining this kind of procession of obedient worship?

Palm Sunday

The event of Palm Sunday provides the best vantage point from which to understand the astounding phenomenon of God stirring his people all over the world to assemble by the thousands and proclaim his truth in praise along the streets of leading cities.

What happened on what we call Palm Sunday? Somehow it lies tucked away in the church calendar almost entirely eclipsed by what became for Christians the larger affair: the death and resurrection of Jesus. Admittedly, the dying and rising of Jesus is central to everything, but look again at this marvelous crowning event of Jesus' earthly ministry.

Jesus nearly fled from most other crowds, but the biblical writers find it important to show Jesus was the organizer of the event. He ordered the colt which had never been ridden. He had made his destination known for weeks ahead of time. His launching point was where he had done his most amazing miracle. He seemed to plan whatever could be planned. And whatever poured out spontaneously he refused to restrain. Leaders

wanted the crowd rebuked. Jesus' reply? "If these become silent, the stones will cry out!" (Luke 19:39-40). Priests and scholars demanded that the continuing praise of children be hushed. Jesus deferred saying that they were doing just what God had intended from of old (Matt. 21:15-16).

Without question, this is Jesus' most public act. What did he want people to see then? What does he want people to see now? The disciples who were there soon saw that it was a prophetic event, fulfilling previously given words by Zechariah and others But certainly Jesus didn't go through his life with along list of prophecies to "fulfill" in a perfunctory way. Can you imagine him thinking "I better get the donkey ride in here soon; I've only got a week to live. Might as well get it over now." What then was Jesus saying to his followers and to the world? Was the act itself a prophecy?

The praise procession that Jesus led abides as a presentation to the world of the welcome of which he is worthy, giving an early echo of the crescendo of worship that will someday soon fill the earth before he concludes his work in history.

If there is any warrant to believe that there will be explicit worship rendered to God from every tribe and tongue and people *within history* (and there is plenty of biblical basis for such a hope), then Jesus' own praise march is enormously important for us now.

Why? Among other things, we can see something of what the Spirit is moving us to do through the light of this event. We can get an instructive glimpse of God glorifying his church as the church glorifies Jesus, all before the watching worlds of nations and heavenly powers.

Praise, Proclamation, Prayer

Today's praise march, like the Palm Sunday praise march, is characterized by praise, proclamation, and prayer.

Praise: A Celebration before God. The praise march is above all praise directed *to* God. "The whole multitude of the disciples began to praise God joyfully with a loud voice." (Luke 19:37). It was a spontaneous party, but not a milling, aimless mob. They borrowed songs and symbols from a grab-bag of festivals from coronation ceremonies, from military parades, and the holy feasts of Israel.

The focus of praise was sheer thankfulness "for

all the miracles which they had seen." (Luke 19:37). The praise looked backward at what God had done, but in a greater way, the praise looked forward to what the people believed they would soon see.

They were shouting "Blessed is he who comes in the name of the Lord!" (Luke 19:39, Matt. 21:15-16). However mistaken or true their notions of the kingdom may have been, Jesus never once coerced or corrected the praising crowd. Jesus twice refused to shut down the audacious expectations of the crowd that he, in the name of God, was coming to their city, bringing the fullness of the kingdom. And he did indeed bring a kingdom victory surpassing their hopes. The praising crowd was wrong only in that they had not lifted their expectations highly enough.

The celebration was a vigorous, loud, extravagant affair. How many garments were ruined as they were trampled, taken up, only to be laid down again? It was an ordered gathering, but quite out of hand in many leaders' view. Jesus did not seem to mind that objecting Pharisees were amidst the crowd (Luke 19:39) or that curious onlookers who knew Jesus only by hearsay were suddenly acclaiming him as their Lord (John 12:9-12). It didn't trouble Jesus. He knew that at the core were his trusted and tested disciples.

He also knew that the praise they were offering him was prepared for them. Psalm 8 was on his mind: "From the mouth of infants and nursing babes you have established strength, because of your adversaries, to make the enemy and the revengeful cease." (Psalm 8:2, quoted by Jesus in Matthew 21:15-16). There was in this procession, a certain innocence, a core integrity which was protected by God. Of course their statements were radical, outrageous claims. Religiously offensive. Spiritually risky. Politically dangerous. But they were stepping into that which was ordained for them.

What can we learn from this? Our praise in public procession must be simple, celebrant, a thankful reception of Jesus, fully expectant that he is about to increase his kingdom in wondrous ways. The simplifying principle is to keep everything focused on the person of Jesus.

This powerful focus on Jesus is why the celebration had an incredible power that did not require any hype by the disciples. There is no report of the disciples pleading for the people to give it

more volume or to sit closer to the front. With Jesus in view, the people just "let it rip." The March for Jesus challenges the notion that the rank and file of God's people have little interest in loving God. Quite the reverse may be shown true if the spotlight is on Jesus. Acclaim him and love him. Jesus is lovely enough and certainly sufficient to draw to himself his own people without desperate, despotic manipulation.

Proclamation: A Statement through the Heavenlies. They offered praise that fundamentally declared truth. They weren't just being merely honest with their feelings, they were declaring truth, eternal and powerful. They were confessing the very name of God. They didn't think of the words as magic incantations that "worked" somehow. They were very much addressing their words to Jesus.

They were basically telling God who he was and what he was doing. Can this possibly be necessary? It may seem a bit silly from a distance, but to tell God what he already knows about himself is to "bless" the Lord, thus establishing our love for him. As we declare truth with joined voices, we can personally extend to him our creeds and well-crafted songs as a sort of "truth gift." Once again, the simplifying principle is to keep everything relationally focused on the person of Jesus.

Of course, proclamation of gospel truth, though directed to God on high, will be heard by onlooking unbelievers, and they will be moved to ask, as they did at Jesus' praise march, "Who is this?" (Matt. 21:10).

This is not the hour to persuade hecklers to accept our views. Truth declared before the living God, unadorned with defense or argument takes on an unassailable fiery force.

We can be sure that the declaration of truth is heard as well throughout the heavenlies. The act of following in a procession advises the powers of darkness that they have utterly failed in turning worship away from God.

From an earthly view this thing may look like some kind of nutty religious parade. The worldly-wise and self-promoted may lecture us. The outright wicked may scorn us. It doesn't look like we are going anywhere; maybe around the block. What sillies we are. The very fools of earth, yet in fact, the greatest wonder of heaven.

Take note of where Jesus took his procession:

The Cross and Thorny Crown. *A slender Latin cross upon which rests a crown of thorns is used as a symbol of the Passion.*

into the temple. And today, we are going to the house of God to meet him there and to give him the worship of which he is deserving and desirous. Such physical worship, unwalled by church buildings serves notice to the heavenlies that as it is in heaven, so it will be on earth. Let evil powers see their failure. Let them conclude, as some earthly agents of evil did as they watched Jesus go by, that they "aren't doing any good; look, the world has gone after him." (John 12:19).

Prayer: Appealing with his Feelings. People prayed at Jesus' praise march. There was the insistent shriek of the blind man named Bartimaeus (perhaps before the main festivity, but there was already a throng following Jesus [Mark 10:46-52]). This man saw the amazing opportunity of the moment and cried out for mercy. His basic prayer should help recalibrate our glib recitation of requests. Some prayer meetings are so earnest in their attempt to be specific that the whole thing devolves to checking items off a shopping list. That is not at all how Jesus approached Bartimaeus. The procession stopped and Jesus asked him, "What do you want me to do for you?"

The March for Jesus is a time to get loud in a general appeal for mercy. In stirring up our hope that Jesus is near to heal our families and cities and the nations, we might find Jesus probing us to discover what it is that we greatly desire. It's a time to request that for which we really deeply long.

It would appear that Jesus missed the mood of the event. This was a festive party, was it not? Why did he virtually halt the procession to voice his own grief (Luke 19:41-44)? He wasn't afraid of mixing what is authentic in the human spirit: the profound, surging grief and remorse of wasted hours and lives, together with the brilliant cheer of hope and comfort.

Jesus viewed the entire city and let his followers know how he saw it, and the grief he felt. As saints walk through their city with open eyes, is it too much to expect that Christ may open our hearts to sense his grief? What do people do who feel God's grief? It's called "godly sorrow." It can lead to the grand sustained miracle of repentance. Repentance is not merely saying "Sorry" for a few mistakes. It's a powerful act of turning. Whole cities can repent (Matt. 11:20). The March for Jesus is the best opportunity, while actually beholding a portion of a city, to see our city with Jesus' eyes, and to grasp the sadness he feels for us. And thus, we can pray with Jesus, not just to him. Once again, the key principle is to focus on the person of Jesus.

Our repentance emerges from Jesus' own anguish: first, sorrow that "the things which make for peace" in our families and cities have been rejected (Luke 19:41-42). Won't we find faith to petition him with the same breath that God would infuse us with wisdom, righteousness, and faithfulness for a bonafide outbreak of heaven's peace in our cities?

The agenda from Jesus' own heart continues with his word about visitation. If we at all sense Jesus' deep disappointment, we'll be moved to cry out that God would be merciful and avert the tragic blast of wrath awaiting our cities; that our cities would recognize the hour of their visitation. Saints might find faith to cry out for a greater visitation of God to come upon whole cities and peoples! The cry "Hosanna!" itself is a deep anguished cry for God to come and rescue. It was a recognition that Jesus had come. It can be for us an appeal for God to come all the more.

Two Areas of Activism: Evangelism and Spiritual War

God has stirred believers as never before to evangelism and spiritual war. It is only natural that we would take note of the praise march as a wondrous endeavor of both evangelism and spiritual war. But the praise march would not be viewed as if God were just now rolling out a secret weapon. The great mistake, easily made, is to regard the March for Jesus as a weapon; to somehow see worship as a method or an instrument in our hands to be used; to touch men in love, or take a whack at demons.

March for Jesus as Spiritual War. The war we fight has no scoreboard. We are not trying to merely depopulate hell or to beat up on some spiritual bad guys. The war is a fight for worship. Which way will the affections and loyalties of people be turned? Who will they love? These humans—created in the very image of God most high, for a short season made lesser than angelic hosts, yet destined to judge them—just who will these people serve and love?

See for a moment the stakes of both evangelism and warfare, not so much as who is saved or damned, but in terms of what happens unto God: does God get the worship which he wants, of which he is utterly worthy? Or were potential worshipers, so dear to his heart, turned to eternal waste? Worship is not an eternal time-filler. We are redeemed for one express purpose: "Let my people go, that they may worship me."

The battle is for worship. Worship is not, ultimately, a weapon. Satan is defeated as we do it, but it is not so much a stroke against him, as it is an abiding delight to God.

There are many intricate dimensions to spiritual war. This is not an attempt to be simplistic. Any March for Jesus is best preceded, surrounded, and followed by every kind of fight that we can put on against evil. But appropriate warfare for the rank and file of the gathered believers is to declare the truth of God boldly, exalting Jesus. As such, the praise march becomes entry-level spiritual war for everyone. Dread things happen in the underworld as we simply follow the captain of the host to the very throne of God, exalting him.

The March for Jesus as Evangelism. Some have been troubled that evangelistic opportunities are being squandered. The juices star to flow in a preacher who sees 10,000 people who appear to not have anyone to listen to. We must be careful at this point. The March for Jesus is not a mere gimmick to rally the town into the revival tent.

Perhaps some find it hard to value something without a direct, immediate impact on the people or communities. It's easy to see the value of getting people saved, or getting people served. But just what is the point of getting them sung to? Look up. The praise march is for God. The fundamental value is the joy of God's great heart. He is so very worthy.

Some have objected that the ordinary pew sitter won't be interested in something that doesn't have immediate impact on our world. Supposedly, the people will lose interest. I have another idea. God will succeed in getting a people who love him lavishly and earnestly, willing to be fools and spiritually minded, tethering their souls tightly to the hope of glory before the very throne of God. If he's going to get such a people, why not us? Why not now?

There are two ways the March for Jesus yields evangelistic fruit. The praise march prepares God's people for evangelism. A shame complex is broken. That beleaguered feeling of embarrassment of mentioning Jesus publicly is shaken up.

The praise march can prepare a big city for evangelism, changing the spiritual climate. Just following Jesus' own praise march, it says "all the city was stirred, saying, 'Who is this?'" (Matt. 21:10). Let's allow the event itself to give testimony to our love for Jesus and spend following months explaining why we would be so foolish as to love God right out in front of everyone.

There is prophetic significance to the quest of Greeks, out-and-out Gentiles, who sought out Jesus (John 12:21). Is this an important part of the nations coming to see and know and worship Jesus with his people?

The standout feature of the Palm Sunday praise march was that they marched _with_ Jesus, not just _for_ Jesus. And Jesus is an excellent teacher and leader. The Spirit of God will indeed get Jesus loved by millions of ordinary people who are now almost bored by the programmatic, antiseptic church life we have lived. Certainly a growing throng of God-lovers will soon become a global affair, involving the distinctive obedient worship of every nation, joined with one voice.

If we listen well as we march our streets, we

will hear the promised voice of the Son of God himself, singing amidst the nations, drawing every single one of them (Rom. 15:5-13) to hope in God. If we follow well, we'll find many of us serving as priests to the nations (Rom. 15:15-21), helping them bring their love to God as a gift.

Steve Hawthorne

270 • A History of the Praise March

Witnessing to Christ's love through public marches and demonstrations has a long and important history. This history teaches us how effective this public proclamation can be for both advancing important societal goals and for bringing people to Christ.

There is nothing new under the sun, as the world-weary writer of Ecclesiastes commented (Eccles. 1:9). Worship in the open air is not an exception; it has all been done before. The interesting thing is that where it has been done before it has very often been connected with religious revival.

The earliest record in England of Christian songs being used outdoors is in A.D. 675. Alfred the Great's handbook records show Aldhelm, the Abbott of Malmesbury, decided that if the people wouldn't come to the message then the message would have to come to them. Aldhelm had studied music in Rome. When he returned to Wessex, the people obviously liked his music, but had taken to leaving church before the sermon started. As they came out, Aldhelm would be there singing the popular songs of the day, progressing to songs with a Christian message and slipping in a crafty preach when he'd gathered a crowd!

The medieval monks were the evangelists of their day and many of them didn't hesitate to use new forms of music in their missions. St. Bernard of Clairvaux (1090–1152) founded his own monastery and was a great church reformer, but he also moved among the common people, preaching, singing, and performing signs and wonders in the open fields and town squares.

Perhaps this timeless hymn was first made popular among peasants in the French countryside:

Jesus, Thou joy of loving hearts,
Thou fount of life, Thou light of men,
From the best bliss which earth imparts,
We turn unfilled to Thee again.

John Huss, leader of a revival movement in the fifteenth century, composed folk hymns in his native Czech for his followers to sing as they met in market places, fields, and meadows.

The Catholic and Orthodox churches still continue the tradition of processions in many places today, particularly those associated with pilgrimage. The banners you often see hanging inside Anglican churches were not intended for that purpose, but for taking out around the parish. Whit Sunday has always been a time for Christian processions, especially in the Midlands and the North of England.

The Salvation Army took their brass bands onto the streets in the late nineteenth century. They were not always very popular. The *Worthing Gazette* of 1883 described them as "excitable young men and hysterical young women who mistake a quasi-religious revelry for Godliness." At about the same time *Punch* magazine wrote about "Booth-eration:"

A procession is a nuisance at any time, and should only be permitted on rare and exceptional occasions. As to the noisy Religious Services which disturb the peace and quiet of neighborhoods on the Day of Rest, they should all be confined within the four walls of their own Tabernacle, Camp, Church or Conventicle, whatever it may be, and those walls should be, by Act of Parliament, of sufficient thickness to prevent the escape of noise.

In one twelve-month period, 669 Salvationists were assaulted, 56 Army buildings were stoned and damaged, and 86 members of the Army were jailed by magistrates. But the Army grew. In under ten years it had expanded twenty times over. The Army became respected and revered, perhaps because it backed up its noise with a great deal of social concern and action.

One of the Salvation Army's greatest processions was in 1885. It marched to the Houses of Parliament with a petition two miles long, bearing 343,000 signatures demanding that the trade in child prostitution (which was rampant at the time) be stopped and the age of consent raised from thirteen to sixteen years old. They succeeded and lives were changed. Drunkards sobered up and started to care for their families; prostitutes gave up their ways and turned to respectable employment. Salvation had turned their lives around. A converted coal-cart driver summed it up. "Well," he said, "no smoking, no drinking, no swearing, and the 'orses know the difference." The world began to notice the difference too.

When the Spirit was poured out upon Wales in 1904, society could not escape its impact. For a time the courts had no new cases to try and the taverns emptied. A report read: "Perhaps the most prominent feature is the lessening of drunkenness, for the night marches (converts on their way home from meeting) of praying and singing converts seem to have induced a considerable number of converts to abandon their evil ways."

Another commentator wrote: "The revival of 1904 united denominations as one body, filled the chapels nightly, renewed family ties, changed life in mines and factories, often crowded streets with huge processions, abated social vices and diminished crime."

And now in recent years God has been moving inside the churches like an underground stream, brining new growth and vitality. This is beginning to burst out. The church is becoming visible again. It has a voice which needs to be heard. The time has come to take to the streets again!

Graham Kendrick[63]

271 ✦ PRAYERWALKING

Like the March for Jesus, prayerwalking is a public demonstration of Christ's love. Its unique contribution is the emphasis placed on prayers offered for the needs of community in which the walk takes place and for the needs of the whole world. It is a valuable complement to the March for Jesus and can be a strategy for daily prayer.

In hundreds of cities world over, ordinary believers are *prayerwalking* through the streets of their communities. They pray while walking, with eyes open for the spiritual awakening God is bringing.

We define prayerwalking as "praying on-site with insight." There is no set pattern or proven formula. Prayerwalkers have set out with every imaginable style. There's nothing magic at all in the footsteps. God's Spirit is simply helping us to pray with persistent spontaneity in the midst of the very settings in which we except him to answer our prayers. We instinctively draw near to those for whom we pray.

Getting close-up to the community focuses our prayer. We sharpen our prayers by concentrating on specific homes and families. But we enlarge our praying as well, crying out for entire communities to know God's healing presence.

Prayerwalking bears significant similarities to the March for Jesus: Worship and warfare blend with intercession that Christ would be welcomed as Lord by many throughout the entire city. Quiet prayerwalks have preceded some of the most exuberant praise marches.

Prayerwalks give us a simple way to continue the March for Jesus, filling our streets with prayer the other 364 days of the year. Many are praying city-size prayers in low-profile style, ranging through their towns in small bands of two or three with disciplined regularity. Prayerwalking helps keep us in close range of our neighbors in order to touch our cities with the gospel in transforming service. Quiet triumphs often follow as God changes the city day-by-day and house-by-house.

A March for Jesus often brings a sudden shower of God's blessing on a city. May such downpourings be met with a rising tide of on-site intercession, that the earth may be "filled with the knowledge of the glory of the Lord, as the waters cover the sea" (Hab. 2:14).

Beginning a Prayerwalking Ministry

Join with other believers. Join your faith with others to help prayer flow in an engaging conversational style. Large groups sometimes fail to give everyone a chance to participate. Pairs and triplets work best.

Set aside time. Allowing one or two full hours gives prayerwalkers a good chance to manage preliminaries and follow up discussions, although much can be done in less time.

Choose an area. Ask God to guide you. It's best by far to learn the joys of prayerwalking in unfamiliar neighborhoods. You'll return quickly to your neighborhood with fresh vision for those close by. Centers of commerce and religion are fascinating, but there's nothing like touching families, schools, and churches in residential areas. Use elevated points to pray over a panorama. Linger at specific sites which seem to be key.

Pray with insight. Pray for the people you see. As you do, you might find the Spirit of God recalibrating your heart with his sensitivities. Enhance your responsive insights with research done beforehand. Use knowledge of past events and current trends to enrich intercession. Above all, pray scripture. If you have no clear place to begin praying, select just about any of the biblical prayers and you will find that they almost pray themselves.

Focus on God. Make God's promises rather than Satan's schemes the highlight of your prayer. Your discernment of evil powers may at times exceed God's specific guidance to engage them in direct combat. Consider the simplicity of first making direct appeal to the throne of God before attempting to pick street fights with demonic powers. Seek a restraining order from heaven upon evil so that God's empowered people may bring forth God's intended blessings on the city.

Regather and report. Share what you have experienced and prayed. Expressing something of your insights and faith will encourage others—as well as yourself. Set plans for further prayerwalking.

—————— Suggestions for Prayer ——————

Attempt to keep every prayer pertinent to the specific community you pass through. As you do, you will find prayers naturally progress to the nation and to the world. Use a theme passage of scripture. Unless God guides you to use another, try 1 Timothy 2:1-6. Many have found it to be a useful launch-point for prayerwalking. Copy it down so that you can read it through aloud several times during your walk. Each of the following prayer points emerges from this passage.

Concerning Christ: Proclaim him afresh to be the one mediator and the ransom for all. Name him Lord of the neighborhood and the lives you see.

Concerning leaders: Pray for people responsible in any position of authority: for teachers, police, administrators, and parents.

Concerning peace: Cry out for the godliness and holiness of God's people to increase into substantial peace. Pray for new churches to be established.

Concerning truth: Declare openly the bedrock reality that there is one God. Celebrate the faithful revelation of his truth to all peoples through ordinary people (1 Tim. 2:7). Pray that the eyes of minds would cease to be blinded by Satan so that they could come to a knowledge of the truth.

Concerning the Gospel: Praise God for his heart's desire that all people be saved. Ask that heaven would designate this year as a "proper time" for the testimony of Christ to be given afresh with simple power. Name specific people.

Concerning the blessing of God: Thanksgivings are to be made on behalf of all people. Give God the explicit thanks he deserves for the goodness he constantly bestows on the homes you pass by. Ask to see the city with his eyes, that you might sense what is good and pleasing in his sight as well as what things grieve him deeply. Ask God to bring forth an enduring spiritual awakening.

Steve Hawthorne and Graham Kendrick[64]

SEVENTEEN

Worship and Social Justice

Christian teaching has always challenged believers both to offer worship to God and to demonstrate love for others. Yet at times the church has unnecessarily separated these two dimensions of the Christian life, limiting worship to Sunday morning and leaving acts of social justice for everyday activities. This chapter demonstrates how liturgy and social justice are, in fact, importantly related. In liturgy, we sense anew the importance of justice and peace in God's coming kingdom and we offer gifts and prayers in response to the needs of the world. In acts of justice, we bring to God the worship of our lives and point the world to the love, peace, and justice that ultimately are rooted in the person of Christ. Without acts of justice, worship is meaningless and repugnant in God's eyes. Without worship, justice is mere activism and self-promotion. Worship and justice are not two separate ministries, but are vitally linked dimensions of the lives of Christ's followers.

272 ◆ AN INTRODUCTION TO WORSHIP AND SOCIAL JUSTICE

The author of this article urges us to reconsider worship practices that often perpetuate injustices. Because corporate worship requires imposing rules and customs to enable people to celebrate and work together, it is important that such customs ascribe worth to every member in the body of Christ.

Christian public worship is an important form of social control—a way to influence people. That may sound paradoxical or even evil, but until we admit that worship involves control, we cannot easily discuss worship's relation to justice.

Social control does not necessarily apply to private worship or personal devotion, although it can, because such worship is often heavily shaped by community practice. Whether in spontaneous or structured prayer, an individual worships privately—in isolation from others—more or less at his or her own pace and convenience.

Public worship is different. Because it is a social act, certain constraints are necessary. Social control in worship is not intentional or deliberate; worship leaders do not have a sinister desire to manipulate people. It is simply that in order for people to celebrate and work together, certain conventions are necessary, even if they may frequently limit or restrain individual self-expression.

In this context of inevitable social control, its effectiveness and use must be examined in light of Christian concepts of social justice. Justice within the church's worshiping community ascribes full human worth to all members of the body of Christ. Or, defined in still older terms, justice accords to each member of the body that which is his or her due. Paul indicates that by baptism, all participate in one body with "no sense of division in the body, but that all its organs might feel the same concern for one another. If one organ suffers, they all suffer together. If one flourishes, they all rejoice together" (1 Cor. 12:25-26).

Worship enforces social control in several inevitable ways. First, the basis for most Christian worship is orderly repetition; Sunday morning services are highly predictable. Most churches' order of worship rarely changes: the lessons are familiar, people prefer hymns they know, and even the sermon is usually quite predictable.

Second, Christian worship is based on the rehearsal of familiar, common memories that the community cherishes. These memories are structured on weekly and yearly cycles perpetuating recurring commemorations. Part of worship's power is precisely this ability to reinforce familiar patterns of belief and activity. But herein lies a danger: when something unjust occurs, it is likewise reinforced by constant repetition. Injustices, then, are rarely single occurrences because worship's repetitive nature usually guarantees that perpetuation.

An important dimension of worship is its divine context. Worship is not an indifferently or casually performed activity such as going to a movie or concert; the worshiper attends a service in the presence of the Living God. Thus, what is done in church occurs in a different context from that of the rest of life—namely, in deliberate consciousness of God's presence.

This means that consciously or more often, unconsciously, what we experience in church gains a sanction unequaled in the other aspects of our lives. This can actually lead to social injustices. I am reminded of a wedding in a large Presbyterian church in Dallas where the minister, in the course of prayer, informed the Almighty that it was the duty of the bride to stay home and provide a comfortable environment for her husband, who in turn must provide "shelter and raiment" for his wife. This type of act (which Henry Sloane Coffin once called "bouncing it off the Almighty") involves sanctifying by context a social pattern that is, to say the least, highly questionable in terms of justice.

Social patterns from everyday life tend to be taken for granted in worship; i.e., what is normal in daily life becomes normal in worship. But what is normal in worship has a way of becoming, in the course of time, normative. Thus it is not surprising that until recently, it was simply assumed that ushers *had* to be middle-aged men just because they had always been. And this norm still has not been seriously challenged in many congregations.

Those marginalized by society are likely to be marginalized in worship. Until recently this situation included women, and it still includes children. Those whose full human worth is likely to be denied outside of worship are almost certain to be similarly marginalized within worship. Quite frequently, this happens despite the community's own rhetoric. It is common in most churches to baptize infants and children and then immediately to "excommunicate" them. The churches justify this practice by implying that one has to be able to think like an adult—i.e., conceptually—in order to commune. Even though children perceive relationships, especially inclusion and exclusion, at very early ages, this fact is disregarded. The refusal to mean what we say about baptism's inclusiveness is a reflection of a society that denies children full citizenship.

Many of the actions of worship both reflect and reinforce social values. Again, children provide an apt example. Frequently, with good intentions, we exploit children for their cuteness—witness the children's sermon, evoking chuckles from the adults but blushes of humiliation and confusion from the children. Also, what we wear in worship is an important form of conveying values. For example, by dressing clergy in robes with padded shoulders, we make athletic appearance important to ministry.

Roles are an equally important means of stressing control. Who does the important things in worship? A very good way to distinguish a minister who presides from one who dominates is to observe how often he or she sits down; sitting, in effect, delegates leadership to others. A minister who is on his or her feet for the entire service is probably dominating the entire service. Leadership style suggests how the minister relates to the community in general.

We have seen in recent years how seriously spoken words suggest whom we value in society. But there is much more to this tendency than critiques of gender-exclusive language. Those qualities and actions of God which we choose to praise are indicative of our attitudes. It is no accident that the most heated quarrel in editing the new *United Methodist Hymnal* revolved around the use or rejection of "Onward, Christian Soldiers," a hymn deemed too militaristic for some. Words said and sung week after week shape the ways in which we perceive reality, showing whether—and how—we try to create solutions for the world's problems.

As a human activity, worship is not, then, immune as a source of injustice, but it can also be a source for justice. What it cannot be is neutral. We cannot deal with these matters in abstraction, as if worship were practiced everywhere in exactly the same ways. Rather, we can look at what happens in any particular congregation and propose ways for working toward more just forms of worship. We might do this through a four-stage process involving observation, analysis, normative judgment and reform, which moves from practice to theology and back to practice dialogically.

The first step is _observation_. This is not as simple as it sounds; most worshipers and worship leaders are so anesthetized by familiarity that they perceive little of what others do during worship. To be a competent observer, one has to cast aside all assumptions and attend worship as if unfamiliar with its conventions. Assuming this attitude may be difficult even for a nonchurchgoer.

One soon learns that many different dynamics are going on in worship according to age, interest level and role. The ways people arrive, leave and interact with each other are important dynamics. The process of observation examines whether the community does what it means. However, the meaning of what it does is not always clear even to itself. Observation involves learning to see and hear the way the community is expressing its faith.

Observation leads to _analysis_. We must look at the actions, roles and words we have observed in terms of faith and ethics; i.e., search for the hidden message. This process involves checking for self-contradictory statements, because our actions often contradict our words. For example, if we proclaim that everyone is welcome to worship with us in a church approached by twenty-one steps, we are ignoring the disabled and the elderly.

There are other, more subtle messages in worship. The choice of Scripture readings, hymns, and prayers is important. Presbyterians found in a survey that the average minister has 65 favorite texts that are imposed on congregations year after year. No minister deliberately limits a congregation to his or her own grasp of Scripture, but most do so unintentionally. It is necessary to analyze every segment of the congregation to see if all are given full due.

Analysis gives way to formulating _normative judgments_. This is the stage at which we must ask, "Is it just?" Are we engaging in practices that marginalize some or elevate a few at the expense of others? If so, we need to look for just alternatives. It is one thing to flag an unjust practice; it is quite another to find a just alternative. (It is all too easy to substitute one injustice for another, such as changing all male pronouns for God to female forms.)

Bringing about change in worship patterns threatens many people. Some older people were offended by the latest effort at revision of _The Book of Common Prayer_, feeling that because they would not live to use the new prayer book, their opinions were likely to be discounted. Even in producing changes that lead to more just practices, there is a danger of unjust methods; ingrained patterns must be changed without discounting their adherents. This often involves careful consultation so that these people are heard and respected. One does not change his or her way of addressing God after 70 years without feeling threatened. Therefore, normative judgments have to take into account where people are, not where they should be or where we wish them to be.

Finally comes the stage of _reform_ of actual practice. Here we use what we have observed, analyzed and judged in order to shape a more just approach. In every case, there is a spiral of ongoing action and theory, for we shall discover tomorrow what we missed today. Thus there is no guarantee of finding completely just forms of worship; we can simply hope that reformed practices bring about more justice than those they replace.

Fundamentally, all change needs to follow teaching. Only when people see reasons for change are they likely to endorse and participate in it rather than yield to it as yet another form of coercion. This means that ministers have no right to surprise people, even if to correct obvious injustices, for worshipers have a right to understand why they are being asked to change and then to assimilate such reasons fully. This means that worship reform moves slowly, but if worship is for all the people, this reality is inevitable.

Because of its nature, worship cannot escape being a form of social control. But it can avoid promoting injustice in the community and help to move both church and society toward justice. This goal requires diligent effort and constant vigilance. By observation analysis, judgment and reform, worship can become a force for shaping a community based on justice.

James F. White[65]

273 ✦ THE MINISTRY OF JESUS AND THE RELATIONSHIP OF JUSTICE AND WORSHIP

Jesus' ministry portrays for us a radical vision of the kingdom of God, where God is known through forgive-

ness and the human community is united in love and peace. Christian liturgy points us to this vision and must be shaped according to it.

The most radical and distinctive thing about Jesus' ministry was, indeed, his vision of a universe where God alone is ruler. This was not the typically eschatological vision common to many preachers and prophets in first-century Palestine—an eschatology which predicted an impending apocalyptic catastrophe that would overturn both nature and the political order, and result in victory and vindication for God's chosen elect (the land and people of Israel). Like John the Baptist before him, Jesus had "existentialized" eschatology, shifting its focus away from cosmic cataclysms and military victories to concern for the individual's relation with God. But unlike John, Jesus saw this relation "not as the harsh judgment of a terrifying God but as the intimate presence of a loving parent" (Thomas Sheehan, *The First Coming* [New York: Vintage Books, 1988], 59).

For Jesus, what is arriving is neither a cosmic explosion nor a judge with fire in his eyes, but a lover whose only "cause" is the *human* cause, i.e., the peace, joy and freedom of the human community. God's own self is given over *completely* to the human world, Jesus claimed, and so a radically new order of things is emerging—an order in which traditional expectations, opinions, and values are subverted or reversed. The Beatitudes point to this new order by calling "blessed" precisely those people we would rather ignore—the poor, the hungry, the weeping, the "bleeding hearts" (peacemakers, seekers of justice). Try putting some of our contemporaries among these "blessed ones," and the radical danger of Jesus' vision become clearer: "Blessed are the homeless . . . Blessed are the addicted wandering city streets . . . Blessed are the battered women . . . Blessed are persons living with AIDS."

The Unleashed Revolution

In nutshell, Jesus unleashed a revolution that requires both a redefinition of God and an utterly new way of relating to one another. Four aspects of that revolution deserve particular attention:

Jesus proposed a radical redefinition of who God is and where God is: Jesus rejected the notion of a God with "an attitude," whose ego and agenda are opposed to the interest of the human family. Instead, Jesus proclaimed the astonishing and unfathomable mystery of God's disappearance into humankind (see Sheehan, *First Coming*, 61). From now on, Jesus announced, God's "self" can be defined only in and as one's neighbor, only in and as "the least of these little ones." Moreover, all creation—the whole world with its limitless history of death and sacrifice, grandeur and decay—has become the holy temple where God is revealed, bestowed, met, loved, embraced and worshiped. In short, the first and most fundamental liturgy we are called to celebrate is the "liturgy of the world"—the holy festival which Chilean poet Pablo Neruda saw arising from the "confusing impurity of the human condition," from "the mandates of touch, smell, taste, sight, hearing, the passion for justice, sexual desire, the sea sounding—willfully rejecting and accepting nothing." This "liturgy of the world" is an ecumenical event shared with all other creatures who experience this world as grace: For Jesus, who is God and where God is can be known only in and as the human world—its persons, its passions, its purposes, its destiny.

Jesus proclaimed forgiveness as the basic name for our experience of God: But this forgiveness is not primarily a "moral category"; it is neither a need arising from our shame and guilt nor a reward for our good behavior. Instead, forgiveness has to do with Jesus' radical—and non-chronological—sense of time (time defined by content, not duration). Rejecting the "salvation history" model of time (with its ineradicable past, its present to be endured, and its future to be endlessly awaited), Jesus proclaimed the present-future. The "eschatological future" is already arriving, is already breaking into the world—quite literally—as God's forgiveness, as God's own gift of self erupting everywhere, appearing "on the inside of everything and on the outside." For Jesus, forgiveness thus means God's presence, God's arrival in the present moment of our human life and history. That presence floods the universe, and waits only to be acknowledged, grasped, shared and celebrated.

In Jesus' view, we experience the arrival of God's reign as forgiveness, and we extend it through the praxis of human liberation: If God is known only in and as one's neighbor, then God arrives only in and as the enactment of justice and mercy in our world. As Jesus understood it, the reign of God is transformed into the practice of human liberation, of working to free ourselves and others from anything and everything which keeps us from experiencing this world as grace, as gift, as presence and self-bestowal of God. Whatever prevents us or others from affirming "this earth as honey for all creatures and all creatures as honey for this earth" is contrary to God's reign.

Here we are at the threshold of some very serious questions about the relation between our celebration of liturgy and the praxis of human liberation. How—and to what degree—do our liturgies enable us to experience the world as grace, as gift/presence/self-bestowal of God? Can a liturgy roaring with psychobabble, convulsed by graceless gestures, cramped by ugly furnishings, and divorced from the great bodily cycles of mating, birth and death that inspire awe and arouse fascination in our species—can such a liturgy enable the assembly to experience the world as grace or to work so that others may find that experience? Indeed, can the liturgy have any meaning at all in a world (and sometimes, a church) that marginalizes its "have-nots" (its woman and children; its ethnic, racial and secular minorities; its economically underprivileged) and rewards those who resist changing the *status quo*?

Jesus believed God's reign signals the end of religion and the beginning of what religion is supposed to be about. As our sources describe them, there is little in Jesus' message or ministry to suggest he was interested in reforming religious practices or initiating new ones. Instead, Jesus seems to have been completely preoccupied by the paradox of God's presence—the arrival of God's forgiveness which, simultaneously, signals God's disappearance into people, into the liberating practice of justice and mercy (see Sheehan, *The First Coming*, 222). God can be found only where these latter are found—or, as the footwashing rite of Holy Thursday reminds us, "Ubi caritas et amor, ibi Deus est."

Liturgy and Justice

Paradoxically, then, Christian worship (like the Ruler in whose name it is celebrated) rehearses the *end* of religion, announces the arrival of that "new and more cheerful order of things" which Jesus called "the reign of God." Worship in Jesus' name is thus not a journey's end, but a point of departure that launches the community on vast

waters of exploration. Several characteristics that shape the liturgy of the Christian assembly flow from these facts:

Christian liturgy is historical—and so is acutely aware that it is a way of doing things that has not always existed. Compared to the rites of many archaic peoples (rites believed to have originated by divine fiat in some mythic, immemorial time), the liturgy of the Christian assembly is a tent pitched at nightfall by pilgrims who know they will have to pull us stakes and move on in the morning. Further, the language of our liturgy is the language of historical communities. The words we use to praise and thank God are the same time-bound words we use to make love or make amends—the words of our wrinkles, vigils, and dreams, the words whispered when our hearts are numbed by grief or surprised by joy. So too our gestures—touches, kisses, hands raised in petition or praise, bowed heads, bent knees—all are worn by time's trades, each is marked by a tumultuous human history of use. Because it is historical, Christian liturgy is inextricably linked to the human search for peace and the human struggle for justice.

Christian worship is provisional—and so is aware of the painfully limited nature of all our attempts to know and name the Divine. Our liturgies are not final answers to all theological questions. Rather, every liturgy is a hermeneusis, a lived interpretation of what human existence is. Notice how the liturgy never lets us linger too long on any single aspect of the mystery of faith, but rather rotates that mystery—like a jewel bending sunlight—through the repeated cycles of human years and human lives. Christian liturgy refuses to become ideology. It unfolds its wisdom by hints and guesses, by offering many different versions of what existence is and means. A liturgy that can celebrate a "happy fault," a "necessary sin," and a "blessed passion" is clearly conscious of the fact that to live by faith means to live with the ultimate undecidability of what is human or divine, nature or grace, within the complex textures of a world into which God has "disappeared." Liturgy does not teach us the answers; it teaches us to love the questions.

Christian worship signals the reign of justice and mercy—and so is never an end in itself, is never "art for art's sake." The whole point of our assembling Sunday by Sunday is to discover ourselves as the place where the mystery of the present-future (as Jesus envisioned it) comes alive and is enacted as liberation. In our liturgy, as Karl Rahner once suggested, we erect a small but indispensable sign that points to the world and all it contains as ceaselessly possessed by grace from its innermost roots. That grace which saturates Creation is made visible, however, only when we become what we celebrate, bread broken in mercy for the world. Because it rehearses the advent of God's reign, worship calls us to self-surrender—to the offering of ourselves as the compassion that lets in another's pain, as the acceptance that embraces another's failure, as the love than ends another's fear, as the life that kills another's death.

Christian liturgy celebrates the holy violence of conversion. "The law and the prophets lasted until John, but from then on the reign of God is proclaimed, and anyone who enters does so with violence" (Luke 16:16). Although these enigmatic words of Jesus are open to a variety of interpretations, one thing is clear: if you hope to become part of God's reign, you must let yourself be overtaken, knocked breathless, by a Presence, a Reality you can neither invent nor control. In a word, you have to open your life to the holy violence of conversion—a tumultuous experience that is liable to leave you feeling drenched and exhausted, as through the sea had seized, swallowed, and spat you back alive on shore. Newborn and salted, you sense that nothing looks the same, nothing can ever be the same—for in conversion's crucible a new and terrible beauty is born.

Nathan Mitchell[66]

274 • HOLINESS IN LITURGY AND LIFE

A primary theme in Christian worship is the holiness of God, which is celebrated by hymns and prayers found in every worship tradition. This virtue of holiness has important implications for how we view God, how we celebrate Christian liturgy, and how we relate our worship to our everyday life, all of which are discussed in the following article.

The Theme of Holiness in Christian Liturgy

Back and forth in the Christian liturgy echoes the language of holiness. Already by the fourth century the Sanctus had been introduced into the eucharistic prayer. The people, in response to the recalling of God's nature and the narrative of God's actions, are invited to join their voices with those of the hosts of heaven in the words:

Holy, holy, holy is the Lord of Sabaoth;
heaven and earth are full of thy glory.

The acclamation derives, of course, from the ecstatic song of the hosts of heaven which Isaiah heard when standing in the Temple (Isa. 6:3).

Holy, holy, holy is the Lord of hosts;
the whole earth is full of his glory.

The song was heard again by John of Patmos in one of his visions:

Holy, holy, holy, is the Lord God Almighty,
who was and is and is to come.

In the Orthodox liturgy of John Chrysostom, the priest responds to the people's acclamation of Sanctus with the words: "Holy and most holy are thou, and excellent is thy glory, who so loved thy world that thou didst give thine only-begotten Son, that whosoever believeth in him should not perish, but have everlasting life." In the liturgy of Basil the Great, the liturgy used in the Orthodox

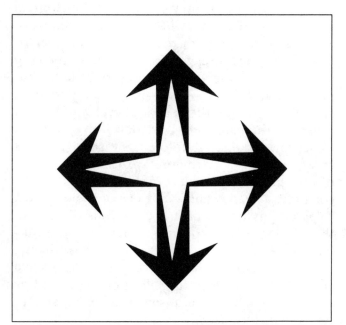

The Cross Barbée. The ends of this cross resemble the barbs of a fishhook or spear. It symbolizes the ΙΧΘΥΣ (Greek abbreviation for "Jesus Christ, God's Son, Our Savior") and the call of the disciples to be "fishers of men."

church on those few occasions in the year when the liturgy of John Chrysostom is not used, the response of the priest to the Sanctus similarly picks up the theme of holiness: "Holy indeed and most holy art thou, and no bounds are there to the majesty of thy holiness; and just art thou in all thy works, for in righteousness and true judgment hast thou ordered all things for us."

The theme of God's holiness is struck much earlier in the Orthodox liturgy, however, than at the singing of the Sanctus. Indeed, the theme pervades the Orthodox liturgy, more so than it does any other liturgy of Christendom. Before the reading of Scripture the priest says:

> For thou art Holy, our God,
> and to thee we ascribe glory,
> to the Father, and to the Son,
> and to the Holy Spirit,
> now and for ever for evermore.

To this the people respond with the so-called Trisagion Hymn, that is, the "thrice-holy" hymn. Three times they sing:

> Holy God,
> Holy and mighty,
> Holy and immortal one,
> have mercy on us.

Then they proceed with the words:

> Glory to the Father, and to the Son,
> and to the Holy Spirit;
> now and ever and for evermore. Amen.
> Holy immortal one, have mercy on us.
> Holy God,
> Holy and mighty,
> Holy and immortal one,
> have mercy on us.

The theme of holiness does not surface in liturgies only in the form of acclamations and ascriptions addressed to God. For example, in the liturgies of both John Chrysostom and Basil the Great we find the following dialogue between priest and people, occurring just before communion as the priest lifts up the sanctified bread:

> Holy things unto the holy.
> One only is holy, One only is Lord, Jesus Christ,
> to the glory
> of God the Father. Amen.

There is a variety of earlier versions of this same dialogue. For example, in the Liturgy of Saints Addai and Mari, coming to us from Syria, the dialogue takes this form:

> The holy thing to the holies is fitting in perfection.
>
> One holy Father, one holy Son, one holy Spirit. Glory to the
> Father and to the Son and to the Holy Spirit to the ages of ages. Amen.

"Holy God," "holy people," "holy things"—back and forth these phrases echo in the classic liturgies. The recognition and acknowledgment and hymning of holiness is a preoccupation of the Christian liturgy. Of course it is true that those who come from one and another free-church tradition will find a good deal of this liturgical language strange. But then in such traditions the Reginald Heber hymn, "Holy, Holy, Holy, Lord God Almighty," set to the familiar tune of John B. Dykes, occupies a prominent and much-loved place.

I think many of us feel that when it comes to holiness we have left behind such earthly, horizontal concerns as justice and entered a higher realm, the realm of the transcendent, of the divine. To cite the words of the Orthodox liturgy one more time.

> We, who mystically represent the cherubim
> and sing the thrice-holy hymn to the
> life-giving Trinity,
> let us lay aside the cares of life,
> that we may receive the King of all.

There is no such dichotomy between holiness and justice—not, at least, if we understand holiness aright. God's justice is a manifestation of his holiness; our justice is a reflection of God's holiness. When we deal with justice, we are dealing with the sacred. Injustice is desecration. The preoccupation of the liturgy with holiness does not separate liturgy from justice. On the contrary, holiness binds liturgy and justice together.

We can begin by noticing that the acknowledgment of *God's* holiness is inseparable from the recognition of an imperative for *our* holiness. This is suggested by the refrain, occurring several times in the Old Testament and picked up in the New, "You shall be holy, for I, the Lord your God, am holy" (Lev. 11:44-45; 1 Pet. 1:16). It is likewise suggested by the *epiklesis* in the eucharistic prayer of the classic Christian liturgies. Let me this time cite a contemporary example, from the Presbyterian Church USA:

Merciful God,
by your Holy Spirit bless and make holy
both us and these your gifts of bread and wine,
that the bread we break
may be the communion of the body of Christ,
and the cup we bless
may be the communion of the blood of Christ.
Here we offer ourselves to be a living sacrifice,
holy and acceptable to you. (Great Prayer of
Thanksgiving C)

In its *Constitution on the Sacred Liturgy*, Vatican II goes a step farther and says that the liturgy *as a whole* is for our sanctification, as well as for the glorification of God:

From the liturgy, and especially from the Eucharist, grace is poured forth upon us as from a fountain, and the sanctification of men in Christ and the glorification of God to which all other activities of the Church are directed, as toward their end, are achieved with maximum effectiveness. (Par. 10)

Members of other traditions of Christendom than the Catholic might disagree with, or hesitate over, one or another part of this sentence. What almost no one will dispute is that the liturgy is for making us holy.

However, to recognize that there is an imperative to holiness, and that the liturgy is not only for acknowledging God's holiness but also, in response to recognizing the imperative, for making us holy and for interceding with God that he make us holy, is not yet to see any particular connection between holiness and justice. That connection is what we must explore. We shall begin by asking what holiness is. For nothing in the language of liturgy and devotion is more alien to our contemporary secular mentality than speech about holiness. Once upon a time the concept of holiness was fundamental to the way in which human beings thought about reality and experience. That time—for us at least—is past.

Holiness in the Theology of Jonathan Edwards

A good way to set out is to consider what Jonathan Edwards, that great theologian of holiness, says on the matter. In his well-known *Religious Affections* (New Haven: Yale University Press, 1959), Edwards distinguishes between what he calls the *natural* attributes of God and the *moral* attributes. By "God's natural attributes" Edwards has in mind those attributes "of strength, knowledge, etc. that constitute the greatness of God . . ." (256). And then Edwards goes on to say that the

moral excellency of an intelligent being, when it is true and real, . . . is holiness. Therefore holiness comprehends all the true moral excellency of intelligent beings: there is no other true virtue, but real holiness. Holiness comprehends all the true virtue of a good man, his love to God, his gracious love to men, his justice, his charity, and bowels of mercies, his gracious meekness and gentleness, and all other true Christian virtues that he has, belong to his holiness. So the holiness of God in the more extensive sense of the word, and the sense in which the word is commonly, if not universally used concerning God in Scripture, is the same with the moral excellency of the divine nature, or his purity and beauty as a moral agent, comprehending all his moral perfections, his righteousness, faithfulness and goodness. (255–56)

Edwards goes on to say that it is the holiness of God which first, and above all, draws us to him. Again I cannot do better than quote Edwards' own lucid prose:

that kind of excellency of the nature of divine things, which is the first objective ground of all holy affections, is their moral excellency, or their holiness. Holy persons, in the exercise of holy affections, do love divine things primarily for their holiness: they love God, in the first place, for the beauty of his holiness or moral perfection, as being supremely amiable in itself. Not that the saints, in the exercise of gracious affections, do love God only for his holiness; all his attributes are amiable and glorious in their eyes; they delight in every divine perfection; the contemplation of the infinite greatness, power, and knowledge, and terrible majesty of God, is pleasant to them. But their love to God for his holiness is what is most fundamental and essential in their love. (256)

In support of this claim, that God's holiness is what fundamentally grounds our love of God, Edwards remarks that

natural qualifications are either excellent or otherwise, according as they are joined with moral excellency or not. Strength and knowledge don't render any being lovely, without holiness; but more hateful: though they render them more lovely, when joined with holiness. . , . And so it is in God, according to our way of conceiving of the divine Being: holiness is in a peculiar manner the beauty of the divine nature. Hence we often read of the beauty of holiness. (257)

Thus it is, says Edwards, that

> a true love to God must begin with a delight in his holiness, and not with a delight in any other attribute: for no other attribute is truly lovely without this, and no otherwise than as (according to our way of conceiving of God) it derives its loveliness from this; and therefore it is impossible that other attributes should appear lovely, in their true loveliness, till this is seen; and it is impossible that any perfection of the divine nature should be loved with true love, till this is loved. If the true loveliness of all God's perfections, arises from the loveliness of his holiness; then the true love of all his perfections, arises from the love of his holiness. (257–58)

On Edwards' account there is a very straightforward link between holiness and justice—or more precisely, between holiness and the virtue of justice. In both God and human beings the virtue of justice is one of the manifestations of holiness. For justice is one of those "moral excellencies" which go to make up the holiness of an "intelligent creature." To use Edwards' language, justice is a "holy affection." We may add that, on Edwards' view, "gracious and holy affections have their exercise and fruit in Christian practice. I mean, they have that influence and power upon him who is the subject of them, that they cause that a practice, which is universally conformed to, and directed by Christian rules, should be the practice and business of his life" (383). The practice of the virtue of justice yields justice.

Edward's account captures some, at least, of what goes into our concept of holiness. But it does not, I suggest, capture the whole of it. For on Edwards' account, we human beings find the holiness of God once we recognize it, altogether attractive. Edwards speaks repeatedly of the beauty and the sweetness of holiness. But recall once again the visionary experience of Isaiah in the temple. Isaiah's response on hearing the Sanctus hymn of the host of heaven was to recoil and to blurt out with the well-known words, "Woe is me! For I am lost; for I am a man of unclean lips, and

I dwell in the midst of a people of unclean lips, for my eyes have seen the King, the Lord of hosts!" (Isa. 6:5). We need not deny that Isaiah felt something of the attraction of which Edwards makes so much; but predominantly he felt fright, terror, awe. It is of course this peculiar paradoxical experience of *sweet terror*, of attraction to what frightens one, that Rudolf Otto placed at the center of his phenomenology of the holy in his famous book *The Idea of the Holy*. Edwards grants, of course, that we may be struck with terrifying awe before the face of God. But he suggests that it is our awareness of God's *natural* excellencies that produces this experience, when those natural excellencies are perceived without a similar perception of God's moral excellencies—that is, his holiness. Holiness, on Edwards' account, is all beauty—no terror.

Holiness in the Theology of Karl Barth

Karl Barth, in his discussion of God's holiness, enables us to take a necessary step beyond Edwards. Rather than seeing God's holiness as the totality of his moral excellence, Barth sees God's holiness as a facet of God's grace; and God's grace he sees, in turn, as one of the perfections of the divine loving. One of Barth's concerns is to avoid the picture, with which Edwards operates, of holiness as one-among-other excellencies of God. On Barth's view of grace is, as it were, an adverbial qualification of God's love—God loves in a gracious manner. And holiness is in turn an adjectival qualification of God's grace—the graciousness of God's love has a holy quality to it. "When God loves," says Barth,

> revealing His inmost being in the fact that He loves and therefore seeks and creates fellowship, this being and doing is divine and distinct from all other loving to the extent that the love of God is grace. Grace is the distinctive mode of God's being in so far as it seeks and creates fellowship by its own free inclination and favor, unconditioned by any merit or claim in the beloved, but also unhindered by any unworthiness or opposition in the latter—able, on the contrary, to overcome all unworthiness and opposition. (*Church Dogmatics* [Edinburgh: T. and T. Clark, 1975], CD, II/1, p. 353)

Wherein, then, is the *holiness* of God's gracious loving? In this, says Barth:

As holy, it is characterized by the fact that God as He seeks and creates fellowship, is always the Lord. He therefore distinguishes and maintains His own will as against every other will. He condemns, excludes and annihilates all contraction and resistance to. (359)

Though this is Barth's official explanation of holiness, the thought behind the words remains for us somewhat inarticulate. Better, I think, are these words:

> The bond between the concepts of grace and holiness consists . . . in the fact that both point to God's transcendence over the resistance which His being and action encounters form the opposite side. When we speak of grace, we think of the fact that His favorable inclination towards the creature does not allow itself to be soured and frustrated by the resistance of the latter. When we speak of holiness, we think, to the other hand, of the fact that His favorable inclination overcomes and destroys this resistance. To say grace is to say the forgiveness of sins; to say holiness, judgment upon sins. But since both reflect the love of God, how can there be the one without the other, forgiveness without judgment or judgment without forgiveness? (360)

Barth's first step, in comparison with Edwards, is to sharpen Edwards' reference to the moral excellencies of God. Those moral excellencies are all seen by Barth as located in God's love; they are the perfections of the divine loving. Barth's next step is to say that this loving has the quality of grace—that is, of forgiveness. But there cannot be forgiveness, he argues, without judgment. And it is this *judging* character of God's love, implicit in its forgiving character, that grounds his holiness.

> It is, then, only as God affirms His victorious good will, as the concept of grace implies, that what holiness specially denotes is true and actual—the aloofness with which God stands over against the resistance He encounters, His judgment upon sin. He exercises this judgment, His judgment, in such a way that it can be manifest and truly appreciated and experienced as divine judgment only in this way, the way of grace. But of course it must also be said that this way leads necessarily and unavoidably to the truth and reality of judgment, and therefore to the holiness of divine grace. . . . The holiness of God consists in the unity of His judgment with his grace. God is holy because His grace judges and His judgment is gracious (361, 363).

As Barth himself goes on to remark, this account explains at once the intimate connection in the Scriptures between the recognition of God's holiness and our feelings of awe—a connection which we found missing in Edward's account. "Woe is me," says Isaiah upon hearing God's holiness hymned by the hosts of heaven.

For our purposes, however, the gain we have made in proceeding from Edwards to Barth is tempered with a certain loss. Though we seem now to have a surer grasp on the concept of holiness, the connection of holiness to justice seems to have slipped away. So let us take yet a further step in our exploration of the nature of holiness. What Isaiah says, remember, upon hearing the Sanctus sung in heaven, is that "I am a man of unclean lips, and I dwell in the midst of a people of unclean lips." You and I are inclined to interpret this as Isaiah's confession that he has violated the moral law of God—that he has, in that way, sinned against God. That is also how Barth interprets it. Almost certainly that is not what Isaiah had in mind, however—or at least not the whole of what he had mind. A pursuit of what he might have meant by "uncleanness" will take us deeper into an understanding of holiness.

My guide here will be the remarkable discussion by the British anthropologist Mary Douglas in her book *Purity and Danger* (New York: Praeger, 1966). Her chapter on "The Abominations of Leviticus" succeeds in illuminating the cleanliness regulations of Leviticus and Deuteronomy to an extent which no one before her, to the best of my knowledge, had ever managed.

Every society, so Douglas argues, operates with certain distinctions between the clean and the unclean—though in our modern Western society these are less prominent than they are in most societies, and have furthermore been blurred, and obscured from view, by an overlay of hygienic distinctions. Fundamental to Douglas' argument is her contention that to understand the clean/unclean distinctions of any society, one must understand "the principles of patterning on which they constructed their universe," including their social universe (Douglas 7). Roughly speaking, a society judges as unclean those things which blur and threaten its pattering of society and reality. The challenge for an anthropologist, when confronted with a given society's regulations concerning defilement, is to discern the sense of cosmic and social pattern which lies behind these regulations.

Holiness in Leviticus and Deuteronomy

Within this general framework, Douglas offers a fascinating proposal concerning the clean/unclean distinctions to be found in Leviticus and Deuteronomy—this after she has first briefly canvassed the attempts at explaining these regulations which are to be found in literature. Some have argued that hygienic intuitions lay behind these regulations. As Douglas observes, however, there is no evidence for this hypothesis. Others have suggested that they are purely arbitrary regulations instituted by God so as to discipline God's people Israel. Douglas remarks that this explanation is the renunciation of any attempt at explanation. Yet others have argued that the clean and unclean animals were allegories of virtues and vices. For this hypothesis also no evidence is available. Lastly, some have argued that the point of regulations was to protect Israel from foreign influence. Douglas acknowledges that although some of the regulations probably did have this effect, there was nonetheless a great deal of foreign influence in Israel's life against which no regulations were instituted. Thus we are left wondering why these particular influences merited prohibition. As Douglas rather dryly remarks,

> it is no explanation to represent Israel as a sponge at one moment and as a repellent the next, without explaining why it soaked up this foreign element but repelled that one. . . . The Israelites absorbed freely from their neighbors, but not quite freely. Some elements of foreign culture were incompatible with the principles of patterning on which they were constructing their universe; others were compatible. (Douglas 43)

It is, then, the pattern of cosmic and social order reflected in Israel's regulations concerning defilement that Douglas tries to discern. Before she does so, however, she notes a remarkable feature of the way in which these regulations are represented in both Leviticus and Deuteronomy. In both cases they are the elements of a holiness code. God's declares himself to be holy. This holiness was connected with God's deliverance of Israel from Egypt—a confirmation, apparently, of Barth's understanding of holiness. And God then

calls Israel to be holy as God is holy. It is so as to reflect God's holiness that Israel is called to observe, among other things, the cleanliness regulations. In Leviticus 11:44-45, we read this:

> For I am the Lord your God; consecrate yourselves therefore and be holy, for I am holy. You shall not defile yourselves with any swarming thing that crawls upon the earth. For I am the Lord who brought you up out of the land of Egypt, to be your God; you shall therefore be holy, for I am holy.

Israel is called to an _imitatio dei_ throughout its daily existence: Be holy as I am holy. And to be holy one must avoid defilement. This remarkable connection between holiness and cleanness suggests that if we can discern the pattern of the cleanliness regulations of old Israel, we will also have discerned the lineaments of their understanding of holiness.

Before we set out on the attempt to discern this pattern, one more point must be introduced. Over and over it is said that blessing will come to Israel if it keeps itself clean; Israel will be cursed if it defiles itself. And this prompts Douglas to say about the regulations that

> observing them draws down prosperity, infringing them brings danger. We are thus entitled to treat them in the same way as we treat primitive ritual avoidances whose breach unleashes danger to men. The precepts and ceremonies alike are focused on the idea of the holiness of God which men must create in their lives. So this is a universe in which men prosper by conforming to holiness and perish when they deviate from it. (Douglas 50).

There can be no doubt, says Douglas, that _holiness_ means, for one thing, "set apart." This seems, in fact, to be its root sense. But this does not tell us much. Set apart with respect to what? "Granted," says Douglas, "that its root means separateness, the next idea that emerges is of the Holy as wholeness and completeness" (51). Correspondingly then, suggests Douglas, the clue to the holiness code is its concern with wholeness and completeness, these understood in both a physical and a social sense.

We can begin our uncovering of the pattern with some of those holiness regulations which, strictly speaking, do not involve defilement. "The culture of the Israelites," remarks Douglas, "was brought to the pitch of greatest intensity when they prayed and when they fought. The army could not win without the blessing and to keep the blessing in the camp the camp was to be preserved from defilement like the Temple" (53). Consider, then, these instructions which the officers were to issue to the men in camp:

> Then the officers shall speak to the people, saying, 'What man is there that has built a new house and has not dedicated it? Let him go back to his house, lest he die in the battle and another man dedicate it. And what man is there that has planted a vineyard and has not enjoyed its fruit? Let him go back to his house, lest he die in the battle and another man enjoy its fruit. And what man is there that has bethrothed a wife and has not taken her? Let him go back to his house, lest he die in the battle and another man take her." (Deut. 20:5-7)

The pattern seems clear. Those with significant projects which are incomplete, unfinished, are not to fight Israel's battles.

We can move next to the regulations concerning blemished and unblemished individuals. The animals offered in sacrifice must be perfect, unblemished specimens; and the priests offering the sacrifices must likewise be unblemished. We read that "no man of the descendants of Aaron the priest who has a blemish shall come near to offer the Lord's offerings by fire . . ." (Lev. 21:21). So also lepers were unclean, and priests might come into contact with death only when their close relatives died.

Next, if we think of the human body as a sort of container we can understand why bodily issues were regarded as making one unclean. "When any man has a discharge from his body his discharge is unclean, " we read in Leviticus (15:2). And likewise, "When a woman has a discharge of blood which is her regular discharge from her body, she shall be in her impurity for seven days, and whoever touches her shall be unclean until the evening" (15:19). The special importance of temple and army camp made it especially important that the regulations concerning bodily issues be honored in these precincts. In Deuteronomy we read that

> when you go forth against your enemies and are in camp, then you shall keep yourself from every evil thing. If there is among you any man who is not clean by reason for what chances to him by

night, then he shall go outside the camp; but when evening comes on, he shall bathe himself in water, and when the sun is down, he may come within the camp. (23:9-11)

The pattern which Douglas suggests—of wholeness, completeness, perfection, unity, integrity—does indeed seem clear in all these particulars. But what, finally, about the distinction between clean and unclean animals? Douglas' suggestion is that the Israelites saw a certain right and proper order as embedded in creation. Clean animals are those which exhibit this order; unclean ones, those which in some ways violate the order, mix it up. Though they may be perfect specimens of their kind, their very *kind* has a certain imperfection about it. Their very kind represents a violation of the proper boundaries. Their very kind is malformed. Specifically, Israel always worked with the distinction between the skies, the earth, and the water; and it had notions as to the proper form of locomotion in these. Those animals that violated the right form of locomotion for animals of their element were unclean. Thus worms and snakes are unclean because instead of walking or hoping on earth they crawl; eels are unclean because they move in water without fins; and birds with no wings, or inadequate wings, are unclean because they cannot fly.

Along the same lines we can now interpret the distinction between those animals which are clean to eat and those which, if eaten, will defile one. Douglas reminds us that the Israelites, as an agricultural people, would have given pride of place, in their thought about animals fit to eat, to their own domesticated animals. When they asked what it was that differentiated these from others, they noticed that these animals both chewed their cud and had cloven hooves This then defined for them the boundary between those animals fit for eating and those which would defile one. We can conclude, once again, "that holiness is exemplified by completeness. Holiness requires that different classes of things shall not be confused" (Douglas 53). And so, says Douglas,

> if the proposed interpretation of the forbidden animals is correct, the dietary laws would have been like signs which at very turn inspired meditation on the oneness, purity and completeness of God. By rules of avoidance holiness was given a physical expression in every encounter with the

animal kingdom and at every meal. Observance of the dietary rules would thus have been a meaningful par of the great liturgical act of recognition and worship which culminated in the sacrifice in the temple. (Douglas 57)

But where is justice in all this? Right at hand. Thrown right into the middle of the regulations concerning the clean and the unclean, the complete and the incomplete, the blemished and the unblemished, are regulations concerning justice. Where you and I would see a sharp distinction, no distinction is drawn. Near the beginning of Deuteronomy 4, for example, we read: "For you are a people holy to the Lord your God, and the Lord has chosen you to be a people for his own possession, out of all the peoples that are on the face of the earth." This is followed immediately by the instruction, "You shall not eat any abominable thing." What follows is a list of unclean animals. But shortly the list is broken off and some of the Jubilee regulations are introduced: for example, "At the end of every seven years you shall grant a release. And this is the manner of the release: every creditor shall release what he has lent to his neighbor; he shall not exact it of his neighbor, his brother, because the Lord's release has been proclaimed" (15:1-2). Then certain regulations are introduced concerning what we would regard as the cult proper. And those, in turn, are followed by an injunction to pursue justice, concluding thus: "Justice, and only justice, you shall follow, that you may live and inherit the land which the Lord your God gives you." In short, the pursuit of justice is treated as apart of the pursuit of holiness. If we are to be holy as God is holy, we must pursue justice. Injustice is a mode of desecration.

What is the connection? It's not explicitly said. But then not much here is said explicitly. We have to try to _spy_ the pattern. Part of the connection seems to be that a just judgment rendered in cases of conflict requires rectitude (Deut. 16:18-19); and as Douglas remarks about the list of actions found in Leviticus 19,

developing the idea of holiness as order, to confusion, this list upholds rectitude and straight-dealing as holy, and contradiction and double-dealing as against holiness. Theft, lying, false witness, cheating in weights and measures, all kinds of dissembling such as speaking ill of the deaf (and presumably smiling to their face), hating your brother in your heart (while presumably speaking kindly to him), these are clearly contradictions between what seems and what is. (Douglas 53–58)

I think it is plausible, however, to see justice and holiness as connected by more than rectitude. An important clue to the contour of justice as understood in the Bible is the repetitious reference to the three social classes of widows, orphans, and aliens. If society is to be just, such people as these must be rightly treated. The refrain is to be found not only in the prophets and Psalms but here in Deuteronomy. The Lord God, says Moses in his great farewell speech to his people, "executes justice for the fatherless and the widow, and loves the sojourner, giving him food and clothing" (Deut. 10:28). What, in particular, does the repetitious reference to widows, orphans, and aliens suggest as to the biblical understanding of the contours of justice? It seems quite clear: the widows, the orphans, and the aliens were the marginal ones in old Israelite society. They were the ones who had little or no voice in the society, and whose claim on the goods of society was, accordingly, fragile and precarious. If the society is to be a _just community_, there must be social arrangements and prices which assure to such people as these a voice in society and a fair share in its goods—whatever those goods may be. At the most fundamental level, those goods are the goods of sustenance. But as we learn from the Sabbath regulations, all the members of society also have a claim to a fair share in the Sabbath rest of the community—in its refreshment. We could cite other goods as well.

In short, what we find in Deuteronomy is that haunting biblical theme of God searching for the hundredth one, of leaving the ninety-and-nine to search for the one who is not yet incorporated into God's shalom, and asking us to accompany him on that search. A dimension of this is what nowadays is called "the preferential option for the poor."

With this understanding in mind of the contours of justice, it is not at all difficult to see why justice is treated as a manifestation of holiness. The unjust society is a society in which wholeness and integrity are lacking. For it is a society in which people exist on the margins, on the periphery, hanging on rather than being authentically incorporated into the life and welfare of the community. Such a society fails to mirror the wholeness of God. And when we as Christians recall that this God whose holiness we are called to reflect in our lives and our societies is himself a Trinitarian community, then it is obvious that the unjust society is an unholy society. It does not mirror God's communitarian wholeness.

One more important issue must be considered before we close our discussion. But before we explore that issue, let us stand back for a moment to reflect on what we have learned. Fundamental to the Old Testament understanding of holiness is the contrast between God's wholeness, on the one hand, and on the other, the brokenness of self and society and creation as a whole. The Torah throws up before us a tremendous variety of modes of brokenness. And what the Torah asked of old Israel is that it reflect the holiness of God by avoiding, in various ways, the broken things of our creaturely existence, and by pursuing wholeness. The conclusion is indeed compelling that God's holiness is his wholeness. Barth saw God's holiness as confronting us in our sin. Our own reflections lead to the conclusion that this is not the whole of the picture. God's holiness confronts us in the totality of our brokenness. And that confrontation will not always be in the form of judgment; sometimes it will be in the form of lament. Of course it's true that sin is also a form of brokenness. So the right way to make the point is this: God confronts us not only in our ethical brokenness but in our brokenness as a whole. It is in that confrontation that we discern God's holiness, God's wholeness. What Isaiah heard hymned by the hosts of heaven, as he stood in the temple, was the awesome wholeness of God. And what he so powerfully felt in himself by contrast with that holiness was brokenness, and the brokenness of the world with which he came into contact.

You and I, as modern Western men and women, have different notions of brokenness from those found in Leviticus and Deuteronomy. Though injustice is still for us a mode of brokenness, we do not see worms as examples of brokenness. For us it is quite all right if some of earth's animals crawl rather than walk or hop. The assumptions concerning defilement that underlay old Israel's holiness code have become alien to us. But for us who are Christians there is a second way in which we find ourselves distanced from the holiness

code of old Israel. The words and actions of Jesus mean for us that instead of avoiding, in one way or another, the broken people of this world, we are to embrace them.

Holiness and the Ministry of Jesus

Let us develop this final theme by calling attention to the central argument in a recent book by Marcus J. Borg, *Conflict, Holiness & Politics in the Teaching of Jesus* (New York: Edwin Mellon Press, 1984). Borg, I might add, is a participant in what some have begun to call the third quest for the historical Jesus. To read the New Testament after the Old is to be struck by the fact that the New Testament, and in particular the Gospels, speaks very little of holiness. In principle that might be an insignificant silence. Borg contends that it is significant.

Earlier I quoted the passage from Deuteronomy in which the leader of the army is told to dismiss from the camp all those who have significant incomplete projects. With that passage in mind, consider Jesus' parable of the Great Feast, found both in Matthew 22:1ff. and Luke 14:16ff. Let me quote the passage as it occurs in Luke:

> A man once gave a great banquet, and invited many; and at the time for the banquet he sent his servant to say to those who had been invited, "come; for all is now ready." But they all alike began to make excuses. The first said to him, "I have bought a field, and I most go out and see it; I pray you, have me excused." And another said, "I have bought five yoke of oxen, and I go to examine them; I pray you, have me excused." And another said, "I have married a wife, and therefore I cannot come." So the servant came and reported this to his master. Then the householder in anger said to his servant, "Go out quickly to the streets and lanes of the city, and bring in the poor and maimed and blind and lame. . . . For I tell you, none of those men who were invited shall taste my banquet."

Though the allusion to the Deuteronomy passage seems unmistakable, the point of Deuteronomy has been inverted. Where in Deuteronomy the army officer orders those with incomplete projects to leave the camp, here in Luke the host erupts in anger when those with incomplete projects beg off attending his dinner. And yet more remarkable, the host expresses his anger by inviting to the banquet those very ones whose blemishes would be seen by the writers of Deuteronomy as making them unsatisfactory for reflecting the holiness of God: the maimed and the blind and the lame.

Borg's thesis helps us to understand these astonishing reversals. The thesis goes like this: When Rome occupied Jerusalem and the temple in 63 B.C. and made Palestine part of the Roman empire, "Religious Jews were faced with the question, 'What did it mean in these circumstances to by loyal to Yahweh?' the answer provided by the postexilic development was clear: be holy." What arose in Israel was a cluster of movements dedicated to the pursuit of holiness. These movements were at one and the same time movements of renewal within Israel and movements of resistance to Rome.

As to how to be holy, different movements had different views. Common to all was the conviction that holiness entailed separation from those who were unclean and the careful observance of Torah, especially its Sabbath and cultic regulations and its regulations concerning defilement. The Essenes, so as to pursue a separated, Torah-faithful, holiness, withdrew to the desert and set up a separated community. The Pharisees, by contrast, tried to practice holiness within general society—and the holiness they tried to practice was not just the holiness Torah prescribed for Israelites in general but that which it prescribed for priests. "For the Pharisees, Israel was to be a Kingdom of priests and a holy nation, following the same laws of purity that normally applied only to priests in the Temple" (Borg 58). The project of the Pharisees was to make the home a little temple, with its paterfamilias a little priest.

The effect of those various holiness movements, dedicated both to internal renewal and resistance to Rome, was sharp internal divisions within the Jewish people. Not only were the various movements in conflict with each other; division was heightened between those within such movements and those on the outside. From their desert fastness the Essenes launched sharp attacks on the temple priesthood. And the Pharisees sharply separated themselves not only form Gentiles but from those called "sinners" in the New Testament—those engaged in unsavory and unacceptable occupations. These were counted by the Pharisees as Gentiles, no longer members of the holy people. To a greater or lesser extent the Pharisees also separated themselves from those of the common people who did not follow their own stringent purity regulations.

Within this maelstrom of holiness movements, aimed at renewal and resistance, Jesus initiated another renewal movement. But the essence of the Jesus movement, on Borg's interpretation, was a new and different vision of what Israel was to be—a new paradigm and not just a new strategy for attaining the old paradigm. Jesus, says Borg, "challenged the quest for holiness and replaced it with an alternative vision" (Borg 75). We are indeed to reflect God. But instead of trying to be holy as God is holy, we are to be merciful, as our Father in heaven is merciful (Luke 6:36). "Where Judaism spoke of holiness as the paradigm for the community's life, Jesus spoke of mercy," says Borg. And he adds that "this conclusion is supported by the near silence of the synoptic tradition in applying the term 'holy' to God or the community" (Borg 128). Whereas those engaged in the pursuit of holiness were concerned to separate themselves from external sources of defilement, Jesus says, by contrast, "There is nothing outside of a man which by going into him can defile him" (Borg 98).

What is it that Jesus meant by mercy? One of many clues is to be found in the passage immediately preceding Luke's report of Jesus' injunction, "Be merciful even as your Father is merciful." There we read that "God makes his sun rise on the evil and on the good, and sends rain on the just and the unjust." The thought is clear: The mercy of God is an *inclusive* mercy embracing the evil and unjust along with the good and just (Borg 128).

Borg proceeds, within this general perspective, to interpret a good many of the incidents in Jesus' life and to exegete a good many of the incidents in Jesus' life and experience that over and over his approach proves illuminating. We come to understand why Jesus had dinner with tax-collectors and sinners. And we come to understand the extreme annoyance of the Pharisees over this practice: These people were the very paradigm of the unclean, contact with whom defiled one. The angry accusations of the Pharisees evoked many responses from Jesus. His response, as recorded in Luke, included three great parables—the parable of searching for the lost sheep, the parable of searching for the lost coin, and the parable of receiving back the lost son who had defiled himself to the extent of herding swine for a Gentile. In each case the point was the same: Rejoice over the one brought in.

Borg summarizes his argument as follows:

> Jesus' understanding of God as merciful and of the norm for Israel's development as mercifulness account for his opposition to the quest for holiness. The shift in paradigm was directly responsible for . . . two highly specific yet centrally important applications . . . : table-fellowship with the outcasts, and love of enemies. the first was possible because God accepted such as these, God's children—Israel—were to do so as well. For Israel's internal life, this understanding pointed toward greater inclusiveness, toward an overcoming of the "intra-cultural segregation" which increasingly marked her life. The second was possible and necessary for the same reason, but with primary implications for Israel's "external" life, her relationship to Rome. To be merciful meant to eschew the path of violence. (Borg 137).

But is it true that we find in Jesus "opposition to the quest for holiness"? Granted that Jesus was opposed to the *Pharisees'* search for holiness. And granted that he speaks hardly at all of God's holiness, speaking instead of God's mercy and love and compassion. Nonetheless, it would be extraordinary if he who taught us to pray, "Our Father who are in heaven, hallowed be thy name," meant to repudiate all concern with holiness. Furthermore, what Jesus over and over insists on in his polemics with the Pharisees is not that we repudiate the Torah but that we rightly appropriate it. A right appropriation requires penetrating to its essence. But it would be remarkable if Jesus thought that the Torah, in its essence, had nothing to do with the holiness of God. "Woe to you, scribes and Pharisees, hypocrites!" Jesus is recorded in Matthew (23:23) as saying, "for you tithe mint and dill and cummin, and have neglected the weightier matters of the law, justice and mercy and faith . . ." (cf. Luke 11:42). Borg's comment on this passage seems to me entirely correct:

> To the extent that the imitation of God as holy led to this meticulous concern to the neglect of the weightier matters of Torah, holiness was inappropriate as the dominant model for Israel's self understanding and understanding of God. Instead such emphasis was subordinated to a concern pointing to the different dominant paradigm designated by the terms justice, mercy, and faithfulness. These, like holiness, were all characteristics of God and should on an *imitatio dei* model be characteristic of the community which would be faithful to Yahweh. (Borg 102).

What we find in Jesus, so it seems to me, is not the repudiation of holiness but a radically new understanding of how we are to reflect God's holiness. In Jesus we find, if you will, a new hermeneutic of Torah's concern with holiness. The holiness of the community is not to be located in which animals it eats and avoids eating, in whether it does or does not tolerate incomplete projects in its army camps, in how it handles those who have bodily issues, in how it classifies the plant and animal kingdoms. The holiness of a community resides centrally in how it treats human beings, both those who are members of the community and those outside, even those outside who are "enemies." And specifically, the holiness of a community consists not in its whole members avoiding contact with those who are blemished and diseased and broken and wayward. There are none who are truly whole. It consists in the members of the community embracing the broken ones, and working and praying for their healing. It consists in having dinner with prostitutes and traitors and paupers. It consists in healing the blind and lame and leprous. We learn from Jesus that the community which shuns the broken ones can never be a whole community—that is, can never be a *holy* community. The holy community is the merciful community, the just community.

The Pharisees understood their table fellowship as a little temple. But perhaps Jesus understood his own table fellowship in the same way. Of course it was a radically different kind of fellowship that he instituted—a radically inclusive one, an accepting fellowship instead of a rejecting one, a fellowship of justice and mercy. For Jesus understood differently how we are to become a holy community. At this table/temple fellowship of Jesus, "the poor and maimed and blind and lame" are present. In any case, Paul understood the new community which Jesus instituted as a new sort of temple—Paul of course being the former Saul the Pharisee. Twice over he uses the temple metaphor in speaking to his readers of the church—in 1 Corinthians 3:16-17 and in Ephesians 2:19-22. Especially the latter passage sounds the theme of inclusiveness:

So then you are no longer strangers and sojourners, but you are fellow citizens with the saints and members of the household of God, built upon the foundation of the apostles and prophets. Christ Jesus himself being the cornerstone, in whom the whole structure is joined together and grows into a holy temple in the Lord.

"Holy things for the holy," says the Orthodox priest as he raises the bread before the people. And the people answer, "One only is holy, one only is Lord, Jesus Christ, to the glory of God the Father." Jesus does not repudiate such language. Instead he offers us new understanding of how we are to respond to God's holiness and how we are to reflect it.

God's holiness is God's wholeness—God's awesome wholeness. Face to face with that wholeness, we feel acutely our own sinfulness and brokenness. "Woe is me! For I am lost; for I am a person of unclean lips; for my eyes have seen the King, the Lord of hosts!" In the tension of the contrast between God's awesome wholeness and our own tragic brokenness, we discern God's forgiving judgment and God's lament. And so, instead of cringing in terror, we in thankful confidence join in the heavenly hymn, "Holy, holy, holy, is the Lord God of hosts."

But God asks us for more than liturgical acknowledgment of God's holiness. God asks that we, in our communities, reflect God's holiness, God wholeness. Jesus, the Son of the Father, showed us what it is to do that. It is to befriend the broken ones and to work for their healing. To do that one must struggle for justice—for the day when all those on the margins have been given place and voice in the community, and when the enemy has been befriended.

Holiness joins liturgy and justice. In the liturgy we hymn God's holiness. In lives of justice and mercy we reflect God's holiness. In the liturgy we voice our acknowledgment of God's holiness. In the struggle for justice we embody that acknowledgment.

Nicholas Wolterstorff[67]

275 ◆ THE MORAL SIGNIFICANCE OF WORSHIP

Though we commonly think of worship as being for God's benefit, humans are also uplifted through the action of corporate worship. In this article, written from a sociological position, the author explains that the regularity of worship serves to maintain the individual in a continual state of moral tension. In worship the filter through which one views the world is regularly challenged, amended, and revitalized.

Worship is a subject which religious educators often ignore. Perhaps the reason for this is that worship seems disconnected from the realm of moral experience. Indeed, such works as Peter Berger's early book, _The Noise of Solemn Assemblies_, reflects this sense of the hiatus separating religious rite and ritual from everyday life. In the pages which follow, however, I wish to argue that in spite of a viable critique that may be issued against the linkage between worship and moral experience, there is an important case to be made that religious educators should not ignore the vital role which worship experience may play in shaping the moral life.

Worship: A Conservative Force?

Undoubtedly one place to locate the historic origins of the ambivalence which religious educators have felt towards worship is within the framework of Emile Durkheim's assertion that the object of worship is society: its values and collective sentiments (Emile Durkheim, _The Elementary Forms of the Religious Life,_ trans. Joseph Ward Swain [New York: Free Press, 1965]). Obviously such a functionalist perspective casts worship in a very conservative role (i.e., baptizing the values of the dominant culture). It is, of course, also from Durkheim that the notion of a "civil religion" comes, followed in recent times by a number of commentators seeing in such a development a nonheroic, nonprophetic expression of religion.

From another perspective worship has also been identified as conservative, and that is in the identification of worship with otherworldly mysticism. Although the mystics of the church have almost always denied the charge of narcissism (Cf. Evelyn Underhill, _The Essentials of Mysticism_ [New York: Dutton, 1960]), critics have often viewed mystics as inward, devoid of any redeeming social role (however glorious their private ecstatic experiences may be). Countering the mysticism-narcissism conjunction, however, is the witness of numerous powerful figures who have combined the inner with the outer life: not the least of whom in the contemporary period are such "saints" as Thomas Merton and Mother Theresa [cf. Thomas Merton, *Contemplative Prayer* (New York: Doubleday, 1971)].

Whatever negative perspective one may have on the moral significance of worship, one must acknowledge the widespread recognition by anthropologists and sociologists that rite and ritual are central to the unity and sustenance of communal experience, and therefore not to be lightly debunked (cf. Ronald Grimes, "Ritual Studies: A Comparative Review of Theodor Gaster and Victor Turner," *Religious Studies Review* 2:4 (October 1976): 13–25; Hans Mol, *Idenity and the Sacred* [New York: Free Press, 1976]; Sally F. Moore and Barbara G. Myerhoff, eds., *Secular Ritual* [The Netherlands: Van Gorcum, 1977]). Durkheim states that it is in the cult that one most clearly feels oneself to be a member of the collectivity. He likewise argues that every group has a need periodically to renew itself through collective rites and rituals (Durkheim, *Elementary Forms,* 240ff, 475). Without ritual assemblage, the autonomous individual lacks a feeling of union with the community. Hence, however cynical some commentators may be about worship experience, without rite and ritual religious institutions would not long sustain themselves.

Although I do not wish to counter the accuracy of such commentators as Herberg, Berger, and others who critique religious institutions for the nonprophetic role which they often assume (cf. Will Herberg, *Protestant-Catholic-Jew* [New York: Doubleday, 1955]), I do, on the other hand, wish to argue in this essay that worship—on four different levels—potentially plays a positive role in the development of the moral life. First, moral identity is crafted in community. To the extent that every community is a "moral community" (cf. Emile Durkheim, *The Division of Labor*, trans. George Simpson [New York: Free Press, 1964], 26; Ernest Wallwork, *Durkheim: Morality and Milieu* [Massachusetts: Harvard University Press, 1972], 75–119), and to the extent that worship functions as the central incorporative moment within the life of the religious community, worship and moral identity are closely linked. Second, the drama or worship and liturgy serves to image in a variety of ways an ideal moral order in which symbols, metaphors, pictures, and stories potentially exercise a

considerable role in providing an individual with a persuasive moral vision guiding lifestyle choices. Third, it is in worship that the individual potentially experiences the "otherness" that lends authority and legitimation to the moral vision thus proclaimed. Fourth, worship provides the structure, psychologically—through the rites of confession, absolution, and the announcement of "new hope"—for personal moral transformation.

The "mental picture" operant as a reference point in the discussion which follows is the liturgical form of worship practiced in the Anglican/ Episcopal tradition. By electing this particular style of worship as a point of reference, I do not wish to preclude from consideration more nonliturgical styles of worship—indeed, I believe there is as much ritual (if not more) in the worship service of a Southern Baptist congregation, or a Pentecostalist church, as there is in a Catholic, Lutheran, or Episcopal church (the former may be outwardly less "ritualistic," but the worship style itself conforms nevertheless to a highly structured "ritual form" as regards appropriate and inappropriate behavior, with drama being a not insignificant aspect of the entire experience), nor do I wish to imply that the position articulated applies only to the Christian context; I believe what I have to say holds equally true for the Jewish worship experience, as I have observed it and read about it.

One further qualification is in order. Just as various forms of worship are not homogeneous, likewise the *response* to worship is not uniform. The key term in assessing the moral significance of worship is "intentionality" (cf. Maurice Natanson, *Edmund Husserl* [Evanston, Ill.: Northwestern University Press, 1973], 84–104). The effect and importance of worship to the individual is dependent, first, upon the frame of reference which the individual brings to worship, and secondly, upon the meaning which the individual imputes to his or her experience of worship. Nevertheless, what occurs in the context of worship itself is not unimportant, for "reality" is always created in the dialectical exchange between what is external to consciousness and the filter of expectations which are brought to an experience (cf. Alfred Schultz, *The Phenomenology of the Social World,* trans. George Walsh and Frederick Lehnert ([Evanston, Ill.: Northwestern University Press, 1967]), 45–96).

The Incorporative Role of Worship

Moral identity is not structured in social isolation (cf. Herbert D. Saltzstein, "Social Influence and Moral Development: A Perspective on the Role of Parents and Peers," in Thomas Lickona, ed., _Moral Development and Behavior_ [New York: Rinehart and Winston, 1976], 253–265). It is through interaction with particular individuals and through group associations that moral identity is formed. Morality is necessitated because man exists in a _social_ world, and it is with other people that individuals negotiate their views of what constitutes appropriate social and personal relatedness. The significance of religious communities is that traditionally they have been the repositories and promulgators of specific value positions—membership in a religious institution implying one's commitment to an identifiable style of life and set of value commitments. In worship these values are announced and one is invited to join in their celebration and in the acknowledgment of the wellsprings from which they originate and by which they are sustained. Worship is certainly not the only context in which values are internalized, but for some individuals—for whom the religious community is a primary reference group—worship is the central moment in their lives for systematic moral challenge. And I would argue, that is as it should be.

Participation in corporate worship brings one under the symbolic frame which governs communal existence, thus potentially influencing personal attitudes, dispositions, and proclivities toward action. In any assemblage there is a considerable incorporative power in the very presence of a group of people who are united in a common act. Studies in mob psychology demonstrate repeatedly the power of a group to enclose in its ranks those who are on the fringe or periphery. An individual may be standing watching a demonstration or rally, and before long someone has stuck a picket sign in his or her hands and he or she is shouting and marching with the throng, a convert to the movement. Something not unlike this process potentially happens in worship, to a greater or lesser degree. There is an incorporative power in the liturgy: in group confessions of faith, the singing of songs, corporate recitations, and so on—each of which invites the individual to be part of the community. As one participates in these acts, one may indeed feel oneself become more a part of the collectivity. Internally this feeling may be expressed as the sense: "These are my people, my group, my tribe; this is where I belong."

As part of worship there may be rather specific incorporative rites and rituals which signal to the individual and to the community one's decision to affiliate with the group. Baptism and confirmation rites are, of course, the most common examples within Christendom, and bar mitzvah within Judaism, although every religious tradition has its equivalent rites of passage (cf. Arnold Van Gennep, _The Rites of Passage,_ trans. Monika B. Vizedom and Gabrielle L. Caffee [London: Routledge and Kegan Paul, 1990]). These ceremonies are milestones in that they symbolically "mark" one as a member of a particular community. This _stigmatizing_ act is important in that it provides one with a social identity. The collectivity into which one is initiated becomes a reference group to the individual, and individuals within the group function as "significant others" to the new member. In the act of membership the individual acquires specific reference points for personal behavior and development (cf. Robert K. Merton, _Social Theory and Social Structure_ [New York: Free Press, 1968], 279–440). In short, in facing specific moral quandaries, the group (and individuals within it) potentially functions in an "ideal observer" role a guides to what constitutes an appropriate moral response.

In addition to specific incorporative rituals, such as baptism and confirmation, there are other collective acts which serve to unify the individual with the community and with the tradition within which members of the community stand. One of these acts is the collective recitation of creeds. Within Christendom, to say the Apostles' or Nicene Creed is to affirm that there is a common symbolic core which all members of the community share. Even if this common symbolic is recognized as mythic, the impact of sharing a common story is unifying. In parallel fashion, Scriptures which are read—again regardless of whether or not they are interpreted as fact or fiction—elaborate the common ground of those who stand within the tradition.

The importance of labeling oneself as belonging to a specific tradition or religious community cannot be underestimated. Morality is not cultivated in the private sphere so much as it is arrived at through one's interaction with others, through identifying oneself as being "this" and not "that" (cf. Bryan Wilson, "Them Against Us," *Twentieth Century* 172:1017 [Spring 1963]: 6–17). The very act of typifying oneself as belonging to a particular group establishes an identity that carries with it certain expectations (cf. Alfred Schutz, *On Phenomenology and Social Relations,* edited and with an introduction by Helmut R. Wagner [Chicago: University of Chicago Press, 1970], 116–122). Every group is organized around specific shared sentiments, and thus group membership necessarily implies one possesses (at some level) a "moral identity" insofar as every group is (at some level) a "moral community."

Moral Vision in Worship

Theology and ethics, description and prescription, are almost always intertwined in worship (cf. Gene Outka and John P. Reeder, eds., *Religion and Morality* [New York: Anchor/Doubleday, 1978]). In everyday life, the so called "naturalistic fallacy" is regularly committed. Moral prescriptions flourish in great abundance in worship and most often times they are paired with statements about the nature of God, the nature of the human, what portends for the future, what has gone on in the past, and so on. One side of these prescriptions is inevitably stated negatively as prohibitions. But another, and perhaps more important dimension of the moral significance of worship is the range of positive images of what life *can* and *should* be. Worship services are often highly successful at conjuring affirmative images—of peace, love, justice and a host of other positive mental pictures of what social existence might be. Robert Bellah states: "There is a natural movement from liturgy, which is communion, to brotherhood, to caring and curing, to social concern" (Robert N. Bellah, "Liturgy and Experience," in James D. Shaughnessy, ed., *The Roots of Ritual* [Grand Rapids: Eerdmans, 1973], 217–234).

In the Christian community, Jesus is the symbolic form onto which moral virtues are projected and through which the Christian understands his ethical responsibilities (cf. H. Richard Niebuhr, *The Responsible Self* [New York: Harper and Row, 1963], 149–178). But Jesus is not the only symbolic form present in the context of worship. Not insignificant is the ambiance created through architectural forms: the beauty of symmetrical arches, the luminescence of stained glass windows, the smooth and worn feel of polished mahogany. Such architectural expressions share a congruence of spirit with the prodigious organ and choral works which fill these cavernous stone and wood forms. But perhaps central in many worship contexts is the focus on the verbal expressions present in the sermon. It is in the spoken word that "mental pictures" of specific moral ideals are imaged. Every religious tradition is filled with stories, parables, and biographies which admit to elaboration and revivification.

The function of images in worship is predicated upon the assumption that man is a symbolic animal, one who understands himself through images, stories, and myths (cf. Ernst Cassirer, *An Essay on Man* [New Haven, Conn.: Yale University Press, 1944]; Susanne K. Langer, *Philosophy in a New Key* [Cambridge: Harvard University Press, 1942]). Although man's symbolic capabilities permit him to think abstractly and propositionally, man reflects largely in pictures and images (as indicated by the rich repository of images latent within every religious tradition). These pictures have evocative power, as opposed to simply rational persuasiveness. For example, in Christendom, to talk about being "like Christ" clearly has meant to imitate the mental "picture" one has of the earthly Jesus. The idea of a Messiah, or of a coming Kingdom, have equally obvious evocative power as a result of the image which each conjures.

The importance of these images is that they potentially become the "guiding line" (what Alfred Adler called later in his career "fictional goals") (Alfred Adler, *The Individual Psychology of Alfred Adler,* edited and annotated by Heinz L. Ansbacher and Rowena R. Ansbacher [New York: Harper and Row, 1964], 76–100) by which individuals make life style decisions. They give direction to life. They provide ideals for which one may strive. They impact life style choices insofar as they picture holistic models of what it means to be truly human. There is a sense in which propositions about what is bad, wrong, or prohibited do not give the same overarching direction to life as do exemplary biographies or utopian social images (e.g., the "picture" of the faith of Abraham, or the "image" of the lion lying down with the lamb).

In the parables and stories of almost every religious tradition one finds dramatized the universal conflicts of life. One sees in picture form the battles between good and evil and the struggle of individuals to contend with themselves, God, and those around them. Such images permit personal identification in the present with these historic personages and their problems—and the resolutions they found to them—and hence such stories perform an important role in providing universal paradigms (known collectively by those in the community, and thus enabling a common moral discourse) upon which one may project one's personal struggle.

The achievement of the worship experience is contingent upon the degree to which it allows one to view the world differently as a result of participating in the drama of the liturgy. Within worship one is invited to look upon life with different eyes. One is invited to see "God's hand" in the events which greet one in reading the morning newspaper. One's personal existence is said to have meaning beyond the pragmatic problem of survival. A cosmic perspective is superimposed upon the everyday world and one is encouraged to respond to the world as the creation of God. To so perceive the social and physical world (as God's creation) is to imply a particular moral response, one in which the task of life is to live according to the divine will, rather than one's own.

A Legitimating Presence

On the level of purposeful intention, many individuals would state that the express reason for worship is to praise and glorify God. In the discussion heretofore our attention has focused primarily on the _latent_, as opposed to _express,_ functions of worship. It would be inappropriate, however, to lose sight of the expressly theological dimension of worship as experienced by those who engage regularly in worship. People come to worship, to praise God, to "sit" in his presence, to beseech him, to celebrate what he has done in the community and in their own lives. Furthermore, individuals report that they _feel_ God's presence while worshiping. The ways in which such experiences of the divine may be understood are, of course, subject to manifold interpretations, but I believe it is important to be both phenomenological as well as pragmatic at this point; if an individual feels that he or she experiences God, _then God is real to them,_ and his or her life is correspondingly affected.

The importance of the experience of the _mysterium tremendum_ in worship (cf. Rudolf Otto, _The Idea of the Holy_ [London: Oxford University Press, 1950]; Mircea Eliade, _The Sacred and the Profane_, trans. Willard R. Trask [New York: Harper and Row, 1957], 8–13ff) is that its "otherness" lends authority, or one might say a "legitimating presence," to the ethical vision which is presented in worship. The moral demands presented in the liturgy and the sermon are potentially subject to objectification: perceiving these pronouncements to be of nonhuman (godly) origin, and, therefore, possessing ultimate authority (cf. Peter L. Berger, _The Sacred Canopy_ [New York: Doubleday, 1967], 11ff). A behavioristically inclined psychologist might view this process as conditioning through "paired association," where because the individual's experience of "otherness" is associated in time and space with a particular moral vision and set of pronouncements, both become imbued with a sacred quality. In other words, the worshiping individual maybe likely to associate his entire experience within worship as participating in the realm of the sacred, thus also baptizing the moral pronouncements announced in worship with a certain otherworldly facticity.

It is outside the sociologist's or psychologist's purview as to whether or not what the individual experiences is to be identified as _real;_ subjectively it is real to the one who claims it to be, and consequently it affects his or her behavior in a corresponding manner. The moral significance of one's experience of the sacred within worship is that potentially one "sees" things differently (to the extent that one believes there is another reality beyond that of one's everyday consciousness). The altered vision in which one, for example, "sees through the eyes of Christ" is contingent upon affirming that there is another dimension (or perspective) which potentially transfigures the purely material conception of everyday activities. In his _Report to Greco,_ Nikos Kazantzakis tells of the words spoken to him by a monk at Sinai: "One morning you will rise and see that the world has changed. But you will have changed, my child, not the world. Salvation will have ripened in you." H. Patrick Sullivan states that the "fall" of man was the move into a divided consciousness in which he was no longer able to see the rootedness of all things in the sacred. In worship this dividedness is potentially transcended as the individual experiences a union between himself and what he perceives to be the very ground of his existence.

The Rites of Transformation

Within worship the potential for transformation of personal consciousness is related to three moments within the liturgy: *confession, absolution,* and various *affirmations* of "new life." Psychologically, these three occasions in worship form a perfect triumvirate as regards moral change: first, the individual admits to the moral transgressions and failures of the past; second, the individual is freed through absolution (or forgiveness) from the guilt of these failures; and finally, one is offered a vision of hope for a new direction in life. For worship to deal with any of these areas without the other two circumvents the complex unity of this psychological process. Moral transformation implies "death" to the *old ways* in order that "birth" may be given to a *new way* of life. Absolution, however it is experienced, is the central moment standing between confession and a vision of new possibilities in the future.

These three moments in worship, of course, have their parallel in the transformative process of psychotherapy. The patient (or client) "confesses" to the therapist or psychiatrist the failures of his past; the therapist "absolves" him or her by accepting these confessions in a nonjudgmental fashion; finally, the therapist works with the patient to build a new, hopefully less destructive, pattern for the future. In one sense, there is nothing novel about psychotherapy: the therapist is repeating the priestly function with few changes except for a modernized vocabulary, and a couch rather than a pew.

The power of worship lies in its regularity. Week after week one is confronted with the occasion to recognize both those things "which one has done" as well as "those things which were left undone." Week by week one is granted forgiveness. And week by week one is invited to a new wholeness of being. Although it is possible that such recitations are done unthinkingly, by rote, it is also possible, and for many individuals a reality, that the regularity of worship serves to maintain the individual in a continual state of moral tension. In worship the filter through which one views the world is regularly challenged, amended and revitalized. As the "real" and the "ideal" face each

other in worship, the occasion for symbolic reordering is provided. Old images are discarded in order to give way to new images; past ideals are replaced with new models.

Within this framework, perhaps the transformative power of the "Confession of Sin" (*The Book of Common Prayer*, 1979) can be appreciated.

Almighty and most merciful Father,
we have erred and strayed from thy ways like lost
sheep,
we have followed too much the devices and desires of our own hearts,
we have offended against thy holy laws,
we have left undone those things which we ought
to have done,
and we have done those things which we ought
not to have done.

These words are followed by a statement of absolution. The impact of making such a confession, however, is surely to place the recitator in a state of moral tension, reminding him or her of the disparity between what he or she affirms mentally and what he or she practices.

The various "Collects" likewise function to remind the individual that he does not live unto himself. Note, for example, the "Collect for Guidance" (*The Book of Common Prayer*, 1977).

O heavenly Father, in whom we live and move and have our being: We humbly pray thee so to guide and govern us by thy Holy Spirit, that in all the cares and occupations of our life we may not forget thee, but may remember that we are ever walking in thy sight; through Jesus Christ our Lord.

What is important in such a statement is the implication that life operates on more than one level. If one elects to be a part of this particular religious community, whatever it might be, then one does not live on the purely pragmatic plane; one lives "in God," and "through Christ"—however this experience may be symbolized in one's consciousness.

In conclusion, I have attempted to articulate—from a somewhat phenomenological perspective—the possible moral significance of worship. As related to religious education, my primary point has been to emphasize the central role which worship may play in shaping moral identity. The cognitive—teaching dimension—is important in the educative experience, but not to be ignored is the affective experience obtained in worship.

Donald E. Miller[68]

276 ❖ WORSHIP AND THE CROSS

Christian worship not only celebrates the resurrection of Jesus, but contemplates the cross. The following article, written from the charismatic worship tradition, reflects on how the meaning of the cross challenges some commonly held assumptions about the nature of worship.

In the last ten years, there has been a proliferation of praise and worship seminars, conferences, magazines, books and articles. "Praise and worship" is now recognized as the fastest growing segment of the Christian music industry. It's almost impossible to keep up with all the newly released worship songs and tapes that are being recorded by individuals, churches, small companies and large companies.

But more important than the broad growth of the worship movement is the _deep_ growth. I believe the renewal in worship is maturing.

At first we were mainly concerned with the _effects_ of worship, whereas we were not grappling with the _essence_ of worship. Now the _quality_ of worship is more our concern than just the _quantity_. Worship as the _event_ is making room for worship as the _lifestyle_. God is moving us beyond the song to the sacrifice—the laying down of our lives to do the will of God.

── Sacrifice: The Essence of Worship ──

I regularly notice recurring themes and phrases in the songs we review. Because these songs come from many different streams of the church from all over the world, these phrases serve as a very interesting indicator of what the Spirit is saying. One such theme is _sacrifice_. The phrases "sacrifice of praise," "living sacrifice," "a pleasing sacrifice," "our sacrifice," etc., are found in new songs almost to the point of overuse. At the time of this writing, Kirk Dearman's "We Bring the Sacrifice of Praise" is the most widely requested song tracked by Christian Copyright Licensing, Inc. Although it is a very good song, I am disturbed by the word _sacrifice_ because I don't think we know exactly where that word is leading us.

Paul appealed to the Romans to become the worshipers: "I urge you, brothers, in view of God's mercy, to offer your bodies as _living sacrifices_, holy and pleasing to God—_this is_ your spiritual act of worship" (Rom. 12:1). To paraphrase: "This is worship—to live sacrificially before God!"

Essentially, _worship is the act and attitude of wholeheartedly giving ourselves to God—spirit, soul, and body._ The central concept is self-giving. Singing is only worship if accompanied by yielded lives. And worship may not even involve singing.

── Mother Theresa on Worship ──

In 1988, I was involved with a pastors' seminars in India on worship. During that time, I had the privilege of interviewing Mother Theresa at her quarters in Calcutta. Someone who knew her suggested that I ask her about worship, which I did.

After introductions, I presented her with three Hosanna! tapes and told her about the worldwide revival of wholehearted worship. She was definitely "underwhelmed." I wondered if I had picked the wrong subject! At first, she refused the tapes saying that she and her mission had purposely decided not to have any tape players so as to not be distracted. Later, however, she said she would give the tapes to someone who would enjoy them.

Then I asked what worship meant to her. Without hesitation, she said that Jesus told us how to bless the Lord: "In as much as you have done it unto one of the least of my brethren, you have done it unto Me. Find the least," she said, "and treat them as you would treat the Lord." Where do you go from there? I asked her if she would pray that I would be a true worshiper, which she graciously did.

── Eagles and Ants ──

What Mother Theresa said had very little to do with smooth transitions between songs or the "flow of worship," but it had everything to do with the essence of worship.

In the letter to the Hebrews we learn that acceptable worship includes (1) lips that confess his name _and_ (2) doing good and sharing with others (Heb. 13:15, 16). This means vocal declaration _and_ deeds of kindness.

Today, if you use the term _worshiping church,_ what does it mean? Often the term refers to a church that sings enthusiastically. Should it not also mean a church that is serving the needs of others enthusiastically? Should not the term include churches that minister to the homeless or the addicted? Would the Good Samaritan qualify as a worshiper? Amos said that God didn't want to hear any more of our music until we became concerned with justice (Amos 5:23,24).

I am praying that the church of our generation will praise God vigorously *and* defend the helpless compassionately; that we will soar like eagles *and* work like ants . . . not just one or the other. This will require much more teaching on worship and the cross, by both precept and example.

The acts of worship—singing, clapping, shouting, dancing, and lifting hands—are simple *tokens* of our lives laid down to do the will of God. Yielding to God in the Sunday worship experience is like an enactment, or rehearsal, of the steps of obedience that are ahead of us in the week to come.

Corporate worship is a "transfiguration" of sorts, preceding the difficult choices that must be made by everyone who wants to live for God. It is a "prechoosing" of the daily death that comes to those who live by the cross.

Living the Cross

What exactly does it mean to take up our cross?

- It means releasing the privilege of self-determination. We are not our own. (2 Cor. 5:15)
- It means having crucified affections. God is over every treasure. (Matt. 10:37-38)
- It means embracing God-ordained suffering. (Rom. 8:18)
- It means humility and service. (Phil. 2:3-4)
- It means obedience. (Heb. 10:5-7)
- It means sacrifice. (Rom. 12:1)
- It means living out of Christ's life and not our own. (Gal. 2:20)
- It means the power of God. (1 Cor 1:18)

The message of the cross will probably never be a very popular message even in the church. However, God is deliberately drawing his people into his awesome presence; and he knows that once we get a little taste of his power and glory, we're hooked. Once we see the exalted Lord surrounded by the angels and hear their description of the whole earth filled with his glory, God knows we will be willing even to embrace the cross. We will say with Paul, "I consider that our present

sufferings are not worth comparing with the glory that will be revealed in us." (Rom. 8:18) The truth is: Worship is bringing glory to God, but the cross is the price of the glory. Even so Lord Jesus, be glorified in all the earth!

Gerrit Gustafson [69]

277 • PRACTICAL GUIDELINES FOR WORSHIP AND SOCIAL MINISTRY

Concern for social justice is properly reflected in the practice of Christian worship. The vision for the coming kingdom of God should shape not only the words of the Christian liturgies, songs, and prayers, but also the actions of the worship. This article briefly outlines ways in which very different congregations practice justice in worship and then reflects on their significance for the lives of worshipers.

The parishioners at St. Anskar's Episcopal church are gathering for the Sunday morning celebration of the Eucharist. Many of those who have gathered to worship are bringing food with them, canned goods and other nonperishable food items for contributions to the food pantry which this parish supports. As people enter the worship space they pass by a shopping cart. Here they deposit the food offerings they have brought for the food pantry.

As their worship progresses it will soon be time for the offertory. Here the monetary gifts of the congregation are collected, the tithes and offerings that support the ministries of this church. After the offerings have been collected they are taken to the front of the church to be blessed for their appointed work. At this same time, following Episcopal practice, the bread and wine are brought forward to the Table as a further expression of the people's self-offering to God of the most rudimentary elements of their lives: food and drink. What is unique about the offertory at St. Anskar's is that along with the offering of the collection and the eucharistic elements, the shopping cart is wheeled down the aisle, where it too is offered to God. In this very concrete and simple way, the ministry of the food pantry is placed front and center in the midst of the parishioners, creating a bridge between the meaning of their worship and the implications to their lives as Christ's disciples.

What allows this bridge between social ministry and worship to be built is the careful attention that is paid to its relationship to the three concentric circles which define a parish's worship. These three circles are, moving from the outer to the inner, (1) the universal theme of Christian worship which is the dying and rising of Christ, (2) the denominational or confessional context of the parish, and (3) the specific ministry of the local church.

The outermost, and all inclusive circle is that which makes Christian worship decidedly Christian—the cross and the empty tomb. All of Christian worship is not only a remembrance of what Christ had done, but a call for the church to pick up the cross and follow the example of our Lord. Just as Jesus fully embodied God's self-giving love, so too are we to strive to imitate Christ's life. Therefore our worship is not only a remembrance of what God has done for us through Christ, but is also an offering of our ministries to God, celebrating what God by the Spirit is doing through us in the world.

The second circle acknowledges that Christians do not have one single way of expressing the life, death, and resurrection of Christ in their worship. The worship at St. Anskar's is shaped according to _The Book of Common Prayer._ The support of a food pantry ministry would be celebrated differently in a Quaker service, where the worshipers might place the gifts of food in a place which could be seen that it may be a source of meditation while waiting on the Spirit. In a small, rural Baptist church with which I am familiar, the offering is collected by the worshipers coming forward and placing their gifts in a collection plate in front of the pulpit, which is mindful of the time they came forward in response to an evangelistic invitation. The offering of food for a pantry ministry could easily be incorporated into an offertory such as this, drawing a connection between one's acceptance of Christ as Savior and one's acceptance of Christ's command to feed the hungry.

The celebration of a church's ministry should fit naturally into the common worship practice of the church. It should not be an awkward intrusion. Likewise it must not reinterpret the worship service in a way which is unfaithful to that church's tradition. Wheeling a shopping cart to the Communion table in our small Baptist church would be just as untrue to the church's tradition

as having all the people at St. Anskar's bring their offerings forward. One's churchly heritage should be a guide to practice, not an obstacle to it.

The third and innermost circle is that of the worship and ministry of the local parish. The ministry of Christ was an expression of the universal and unchanging love of God, expressed in particular ways to meet the needs of specific situations. So, too, should the worship of God through Christ celebrate both the universal elements of Christian ministry (evangelism, care for the poor, support for the ill and grieving) and that parish's particular manifestation of that ministry or ministries. It is only appropriate to make our prayers to God somewhat concrete. So, too, our worship should make manifest those ministries which we offer to God in worship.

Care should be taken in the planning of this sort of worship that it is true to the ministry being offered to God. Some creativity must be used when celebrating such ministries as a homeless shelter, Alcoholics Anonymous (or other support groups), ministry to unwed mothers, and so on. One should be sensitive that those in the parish who may be participating in such a group, such as AA, would not be made to feel separate from the rest of the community. I would suggest that this required group discussion, involving those who are directly involve in the ministry and possibly even those benefiting from it within the parish.

Although not every church celebrates the service of the Table (Eucharist/Lord's Supper/Holy Communion) weekly, most churches celebrate it with some regularity, usually monthly or quarterly. It certainly is historically the central act of Christian worship, even if it is not the central mode of worship in each church currently. For this reason a brief description of the service of the Table as the universal theme of Christian worship is appropriate. In 1 Corinthians 10:14-17, when Paul writes of the cup and the bread, and asks if it is not a "sharing" in the blood and body of Christ, the word used for sharing is _koinonia_ , which has the same root as the word translated "fellowship." Celebration of the bread and cup is a joint sharing in the life of Christ, a participation in the life of Christ now. Paul concludes this argument by encouraging the people to imitate him, as he imitates Christ (11:1). Hence the worship of Christ is distinct from the worship of idols as Christian worship is that which draws the believers into a life of imitating Christ. Christian worship at its core is necessarily linked to the ministry of the Christian church. Therefore the universal nature of Christian worship, celebration of the dying and rising of Christ, calls us to die to ourselves and rise to new life in Christ. The fact that we are called to serve God in our baptism is reinforced in the regular life of Christian worship, particularly the service of the Table.

Todd E. Johnson

278 • A Bibliography on Worship and Social Justice

Avila, Rafael. *Worship and Politics*. Maryknoll, N.Y.: Orbis Books, 1981. Written from the perspective of liberation theology, this volume describes the unavoidable political ramifications of any act of gathering for worship as the church.

Egan, John J. *Liturgy and Justice: An Unfinished Agenda*. Collegeville, Minn.: The Liturgical Press, 1983.

Empereur, James L., and Christopher Kiesling, eds. *The Liturgy That Does Justice*. Collegeville, Minn.: The Liturgical Press, 1989. Essays on the role of liturgy in promoting justice, with particular attention to proclamation and the sacraments.

Grassi, Joseph. *Broken Bread and Broken Bodies: The Lord's Supper and World Hunger*. Maryknoll, N.Y.: Orbis Books, 1985. An essay on how the persistent problem of world hunger challenges unthinking participation in the Eucharist and reorients the symbolic significance of the act of eating. Participation in liturgy demands lives of servanthood and action on behalf of the poor and hungry.

Hebert, A. G. *Liturgy and Society: The Function of the Church in the Modern World*. London: Faber and Faber, 1935, 1961. An Anglican perspective on the relationship of the church as a worshiping community to the world.

Hellwig, Monika. *The Eucharist and the Hunger of the World*. New York: Paulist Press, 1976. Describes the significance of the symbol of taking bread in light of biblical and cultural studies.

Henderson, Frank, S. Larson, and K. Quinn. *Liturgy, Justice, and the Reign of God: Integrating Vision and Practice*. New York: Paulist Press, 1989. A book to challenge all worship traditions to integrate their understanding of worship and justice.

Hessel, Deiter T., ed., *Social Themes of the Christian Year: A Commentary of the Lectionary*. Philadelphia: Geneva Press, 1993. A week-by-week study of the Common Lectionary, with special attention to themes related to social justice, written by a variety of biblical scholars and preachers.

Hughes, Kathleen. *Living No Longer for Ourselves: Liturgy and Justice in the Nineties*. Collegeville, Minn.: The Liturgical Press, 1991. A series of essays written by both ethicists and liturgists.

Maxwell, John. *Worship in Action: A Parish Model of Creative Liturgy and Social Concern*. Mystic, Conn.: Twenty-Third Publications, 1980. A discussion of the sacraments, the Christian year, and the practice of worship from the point of view of social justice, including observations about the ethical implications of parish celebrations and suggestions for reform.

Reformed Liturgy and Music 19 (1985). A theme issue on worship and justice written from a Protestant perspective.

Searle, Mark. *Liturgy and Social Justice*. Collegeville, Minn.: The Liturgical Press, 1980. Four essays on how liturgy may be a vehicle for promoting justice.

Webber, Robert, and Rodney Clapp. *People of the Truth: The Power of the Worshiping Community in the Modern World*. San Francisco: Harper and Row, 1988. A discussion of how Christian worship can be an effective agent of social change, and this not by seeking to become a social and political gathering, but rather by the enactment of the Christian story through the proclamation of the Word and the celebration of the sacraments.

Willimon, William. *The Service of God: How Worship and Ethics Are Related*. Nashville: Abingdon, 1983. Calls for Christians to take seriously the role of worship in shaping their lives and calls ethicists and liturgists to work together to present a unified and integrated vision of Christian service, expressed in both worship and in lives of praise.

Wolterstorff, Nicholas. *Until Justice and Peace Embrace*. Grand Rapids: Eerdmans, 1983. A discussion of how Christian principles influence political theory and economic strategies. Includes a seminal chapter on the role of liturgy in the Christian's life.

To Do Justice and Right Upon Earth: Papers from the Virgil Michel Symposium on Liturgy and Social Justice. Collegeville, Minn.: Liturgical Press, 1993.

Works Cited

1. John Heagle, "When Israel Was a Child," *Liturgy* 3 (1981): 39–44.
2. Gail Ramshaw Schmidt, "Readiness for Liturgy: The Formation of Christian Children," *Assembly* 9:2 (Nov. 1992): 190–191. Notre Dame Center for Pastoral Liturgy. P.O. 81 Notre Dame, IN 46556.
3. Sue Wortham, "The Role of the Infant in the Christian Community," *Alert* (Nov. 1988).
4. C. Michael Hawn, "Guiding Children in Worship, Part 1," *Choristers Guild Letters* (Feb. 1986): 121–126.
5. C. Michael Hawn, "Guiding Children in Worship, Part 2," *Choristers Guild Letters* (Mar. 1986): 145–148.
6. Sonja M. Stewart and Jerome W. Berryman, *Young Children and Worship* (Louisville: Westminster/John Knox Press, 1989), 17–22.
7. David Ng, "Children in the Worshiping Community," *Liturgy* 3 (1981): 27–31.
8. C. Michael Hawn, "Hymnody and Christian Education: The Hymnal as a Teaching Resource for Children," *Review and Expositor* 87:1 (Winter 1990): 43–58.
9. C. Michael Hawn, "Hymnody for Children, Part 2: Teaching Hymns to Children—Procedures and Resources for the Church Musician," *The Hymn* 36:2 (Apr. 1985): 20–23.
10. Ronald A. Nelson, "The Ministry of Childrens' Choirs," *Liturgy* 3 (Nov. 1981): 51–58.
11. Marjorie Procter-Smith, "Women and Worship," *A New Dictionary of Liturgy and Worship*, J. G. Davies, ed. (London: SCM Press, 1986): 543–544.
12. Miriam D. Ukeritis, "Ministry, Women In," *New Dictionary of Sacramental Worship* (Collegeville, Minn.: The Liturgical Press, 1990), 848–851.
13. Rosemary R. Ruether, "Inclusive Language," *A New Dictionary of Liturgy and Worship*, 267–268.
14. Janet Walton, "Inclusive Language," *New Dictionary of Sacramental Worship*, 596–598.
15. From "Women in Worship," *Assembly* 17:1 (Nov. 1990): 501–502.
16. Ingram C. Parmley and Tresco Shannon, "Ministry and Persons with Developmental Disabilities," *Worship* 66 (Jan. 1992): 10–24.
17. Howard Rice, "Planning for Disabled People," *Reformed Liturgy and Music* 16:2 (Spring 1982): 76–80.
18. Thomas B. Hoeksema, "One in the Spirit: Involving Persons with Disabilities in Worship," *Reformed Worship* 18 (Winter 1991): 36–39.
19. M. Alverna Hollis, "Liturgies with Deaf Worshipers," *Liturgy* 4:4 (Spring 1985): 35–37.
20. Mark R. Francis, "Adaptation, Liturgical," *New Dictionary of Sacramental Worship*, 14–20.
21. Ibid., 20–25.
22. M. Francis Mannion, "Culture, Liturgy and," *New Dictionary of Sacramental Worship*, 310–313.
23. Peter Schineller, "Inculturation of the Liturgy," *New Dictionary of Sacramental Worship*, 598–601.
24. Terry MacArthur, "Towards Global Worship: Beyond the Headlines," *Reformed Liturgy and Music* 24:4 (Fall 1991): 164–167.
25. John S. Hascall, "Native American Ritual," *New Dictionary of Sacramental Worship*, 892–895.
26. Lucien J. Richard, "Sickness, Christian View Of," *New Dictionary of Sacramental Worship*, 1186–1189.
27. Lucien J. Richard, "Healing," *New Dictionary of Sacramental Worship*, 520–523.
28. James M. Schellman, "Sick, Ministry of the," *New Dictionary of Sacramental Worship*, 1165–1167.
29. Susan Jorgensen, "Pastoral Care: Heart of All Ministry," *Modern Liturgy* 19:6 (1992): 10–13.
30. Oliver J. Morgan, "Elements in a Spirituality of Pastoral Care," *Journal of Pastoral Care* 43:2 (Summer 1989): 99–109.
31. Kenneth R. Mitchell, "Ritual in Pastoral Care," *Journal of Pastoral Care* 43:1 (Spring 1989): 68-77.
32. Gilbert Ostdiek, "Human Situations in Need of Ritualization," *New Theological Review* 3:2 (May 1990): 36–48.
33. Marjorie Procter-Smith, "After Abuse is Liturgy Possible?" *Modern Liturgy* 18:1 (1991): 16–17.
34. *The Book of Blessings* (Collegeville, Minn.: The Liturgical Press, 1992), 141–145.
35. Paula Van Horn, "A Prayer for the Healing of Memories" (leaflet), 1973. Reprinted with permission of Dove Publications, P.O. Box 1080, Pecos, N.M. 87522.
36. Adapted by Richard Leonard from Frances MacNutt, *Healing* (Notre Dame, Ind.: Ave Maria, 1974), 161–169.
37. Ibid., 169–178.
38. Ibid., 178–192.
39. Ibid., 192–208.
40. Ibid., 208–232.
41. Robert E. Webber, "Worship and Spirituality,"

Reformed Liturgy and Music 20:2 (Spring 1986): 67–71.

42. Harold M. Daniels, "Spiritual Formation and the Liturgical Tradition," *Reformed Worship* 26:4 (Fall 1992): 209–212.

43. Gail Ramshaw, "Living the Eucharistic Prayer," *Weavings* 4:4 (July/Aug. 1989): 28–34.

44. S. Shawn Madigan, "Spirituality, Liturgical," *New Dictionary of Sacramental Worship*, 1225–1229.

45. Eileen C. Burke-Sullivan, "Lay Spirituality," *New Dictionary of Sacramental Worship*, 679–680.

46. Adapted by Richard Leonard from Gwen Kennedy Neville and John H. Westerhoff, *Learning Through Liturgy* (New York: Seabury, 1978), 91–106.

47. Ibid., 107–113.

48. Ibid., 115–132.

49. Ibid., 136–137, 145–159.

50. Ibid., 160–181.

51. Gilbert Ostdiek, "Catechesis, Liturgical," *New Dictionary of Sacramental Worship*, 163–172.

52. Sandra DeGidio, "The RCIA: The Art of Making New Catholics," *Catholic Update* C0186 (leaflet). St. Anthony Messenger Press, Cincinnati, Ohio.

53. Bobbie Hixon, "The Catechumenate Gathering for the Story," *Modern Liturgy* 16:15 (1989): 4–5.

54. Mary Alice Piil, "Catechumenate," *New Dictionary of Sacramental Worship*, 172–175.

55. Robert D. Duggan, "Sunday Meetings for Mystagogy," *Modern Liturgy* 18:3 (1991): 16–17.

56. Nick Wagner and Peggy Lovrien, "Doing Hospitality," *Modern Liturgy*, 17:8 (1990): 12–14.

57. Dirk Hart, "The Architecture of Hospitality," *Reformed Worship* 6 (Winter 1988): 34–36.

58. Jean Ackerman, "Ushering: Art of Hospitality," *Modern Liturgy* 9:6 (1982): 30.

59. Nathan Mitchell, "Greeting of Peace: Deep Welcome," *Modern Liturgy* 17:8 (1990): 15–16.

60. Robert Webber, "Bring Them In: Three Models for Evangelism through Worship," *Reformed Worship* 23 (Mar. 1992): 4–6.

61. Patrick Keifert, "Guess Who's Coming to Worship?: Worship and Evangelism," *Word and World* 9:1 (Winter 1989): 46–51.

62. Sally Morgenthaler, "Worship Evangelism: Bringing Down the Walls," *Worship Leader* 2 (Dec. 1992/Jan. 1993): 20–32.

63. Reproduced from the *Make Way Handbook* by permission of Make Way Music, Glyndley Manor, Stone Cross, Pevensey, East Sussex, BN23 5BS, UK.

64. Adapted from Graham Kendrick and Steve Hawthorne, *Prayerwalking: Praying on Site with Insight* (Altamonte Springs, Fla.: Creation House, 1993).

65. James F. White, "Moving Christian Worship Toward Social Justice," *Christian Century* 104 (June 17–24, 1987): 558–560.

66. Nathan Mitchell, "The Kingdom Journey," *Modern Liturgy* 18:8 (1991): 6–8.

67. Nicholas Wolterstorff, "Liturgy, Justice and Holiness," *The Reformed Journal* 39 (Dec. 1989): 12–20.

68. Donald E. Miller, "Moral Significance of Worship," *Religious Education* 75:2 (Mar./Apr. 1980): 193–203.

69. Gerrit Gustafson, "Worship and the Cross," *Psalmist* (Aug./Sept. 1990): 31–32.

Index

IN MEMORIAM

Larry J. Nyberg

1949–1993

Distinguished Project Editor
who suddenly entered into the kingdom
as his editorial work on
The Complete Library of Christian Worship
was nearing completion